VOICE AND DATA
COMMUNICATIONS
HANDBOOK

OTHER BOOKS BY REGIS J. "BUD" BATES

Bates *Voice and Data Communications Handbook 3/e*
   0-07-212276-5

Bates *Broadband Telecommunications Handbook*
   0-07-134648-1

Bates *Optical Switching and Networking Handbook*
   0-07-137356-X

Bates *Wireless Broadband Handbook*   0-07-137161-3

Bates *Hands On Client Server Internetworking*
   0-07-005442-8

Bates *Nortel Networks Layer Three Switching*
   0-07-212426-1

Bates *GPRS General Packet Radio Service*
   0-07-138188-0

Voice and Data Communications Handbook

Fourth Edition

Regis J. (Bud) Bates
Donald W. Gregory

McGraw-Hill
New York   Chicago   San Francisco
Lisbon   London   Madrid   Mexico City
Milan   New Delhi   San Juan   Seoul
Singapore   Sydney   Toronto

Osborne/**McGraw-Hill**
2600 Tenth Street
Berkeley, California 94710
U.S.A.

To arrange bulk purchase discounts for sales promotions, premiums, or fund-raisers, please contact Osborne/**McGraw-Hill** at the above address. For information on translations or book distributors outside the U.S.A., please see the International Contact Information page immediately following the index of this book.

Voice and Data Communications Handbook, Fourth Edition

4567890 DOC DOC 019876543

ISBN 0-07-213188-8

Publisher
Brandon A. Nordin

Vice President & Associate Publisher
Scott Rogers

Executive Editor
Steven Elliot

Project Manager
Jenn Tust

Acquisitions Coordinator
Alex Corona

Technical Editor
Roger Moore

Compositor and Indexer
MacAllister Publishing Services, LLC

ACKNOWLEDGMENTS

Well, here I am again, finalizing the latest book for McGraw-Hill. This one is special because it is the fourth edition of the *Voice and Data Communications Handbook*! The original book came out in 1995 but has blossomed quite a bit since then. It is hard to believe that so much has happened over these few years.

This book deals with the issues surrounding the telecommunications industry on voice and data topics as the two converge. As always, I chose to write the way I think, that is, in a non-technical fashion. I hope that this is consistent with you, the reader, because there is little published that is geared for the novice and business professional. Besides the new chapters, we added something new this time in response to many professors around the country. In the beginning of each chapter, we have an objectives section and at the end of the chapter we have added some questions. We hope this adds and rounds off the information based on this new information. We can thank the educators for their interest and requests.

To be fair about this production, we owe a lot of credit to many people. Some of the people interacted with us regularly, and others only occasionally. First, we must thank Steve Elliot, McGraw-Hill's executive editor on this book, who prodded me to keep going. In addition to Steve is Alex Corona who e-mailed us weekly, keeping the project on schedule.

Numerous other people aided in the editing and production of the book —far too many to name. They know who they are and can give themselves a pat on the back for their efforts. Special mention is warranted for Molly McHugh who had the misfortune of working with me on two books simultaneously, through the edits and rewrites, as well as the new materials I was creating at the same time. Keeping track of two books from the same author had to be a challenge in itself. Molly's tenacity is what got the final production together. Then there are the vendors and manufacturers we talk to daily regarding products, services, and opportunities. All add to the knowledge in this book.

Two people in my office deserve the lion's share of the credits for the ultimate graphical representation and production of this book. The first is Gabriele my wife and partner of more than three decades. She is the silent contributor of this production. Gabriele really deserves to have her name on the cover of this book. Second is a young lady whose energy and enthusiasm never seem to cease. Amber Hartmann and Gabriele worked dauntlessly to keep the graphics accurate and readable, while at the same time creating interesting renderings. Amber's age belies her maturity and ability to jump right in and get things done quickly, even though we change them constantly.

This team of people all pulled together to make this fourth edition of the *Voice and Data Communications Handbook* a reality. They deserve the credit.

Finally, I want to thank you the reader for giving up your time to read this book. I receive many calls and e-mails from readers who just want to let me know that they enjoyed my opinion or the way I present an idea. I hope I can continue to win your support. My best wishes to you all!

Thank you all,

Regis J. (Bud) Bates

CONTENTS

Acknowledgments   v
Introduction   xxiv
Format   xxv

Chapter 1   The History of Telecommunications   1

                 Who Really Invented the Telephone?   2
                 Evolution of the Telecommunications Industry   3
                 The First Telephone Companies Formed   5
                 The Regulatory Scene   5
                 Hush-a-Phone   7
                 The Introduction of Competition   8
                 The Divestiture Agreement   8
                 Tariffs   11
                 The Telecom Act of 1996   12
                 The Canadian Marketplace   16
                 Questions   17

Chapter 2   Voice Characteristics   19

                 The Medium   20
                 Sound   20
                 What Is Bandwidth?   24
                 Voices   27
                 Other Services   28
                 Questions   29

Chapter 3   The Telephone Network   31

                 A Topology of Connections Is Used   32
                 The Local Loop   34
                 The Network Hierarchy (Pre-1984)   36
                 The Network Hierarchy (Post-1984)   39
                 The Public-Switched Network   41
                 The North American Numbering Plan   41
                 The Area Code   42
                 The Exchange Code   43
                 The Subscriber Extension   43
                 Private Networks   44
                 Hybrid Networks   45
                 Local Access and Transport Areas (LATAs)   46
                 Wiring Connections: Hooking Things Up   47
                 Types of Communications   48

One-Way (Simplex)   48
Two-Way Alternating (Half Duplex)   48
Two-Way Simultaneous (Duplex or Full Duplex)   49
Equipment   49
Questions   50

Chapter 4   The Telephone Set   53

The Function of the Telephone Set   55
The Pieces   58
The Base   58
The Handset   59
The Transmitter   61
The Receiver   62
The Connector or the Handset Cord   63
The Inside of the Telephone   64
The Switchhook   65
The Dial Pad   66
The Ringer   70
Tip and Ring   71
Newer Sets   71
Speed Dialing   72
Call Hold   73
Call Transfer   73
Conference Call   73
Redial Last Number   74
Built-in Speakerphone   74
Hands-Free Dialing   74
Displays   75
Questions   75

Chapter 5   Analog Versus Digital Communications   77

Analog Transmission Systems   78
Analog-to-Digital Conversion   84
Digital Signaling   86
Digital Data in an Analog World   89
Questions   91

Chapter 6   Carriers   93

Incumbent Local Exchange Carriers   93
Local Dial Tone (Single-Line and Party Line) Service   96
Centrex Service   97
Business Service (Direct Inward Dial and Direct Outward
     Dial Lines and Trunks)   99
Residential Service   99
Local Calling Services   101

Pay Phone Service 101
Private Lines and TIE Lines 103
Foreign Exchange Service 105
WATS (Intrastate, Intra-LATA) 107
800/888/877/866 Service 111
Directory Services 112
Off-Premises Extensions 113
Access to Interexchange Carriers (Equal Access) 115
Competitive Local Exchange Carriers (CLECs) 115
Data Local Exchange Carriers (DLEC) 117
Interexchange Carriers (IEC/IXC) 118
Switched Long Distance (DDD) 118
Credit Card Service (Calling Card Service) 119
WATS Service 121
800/888/877/866 and 900 Service Offerings 124
International Access 125
Foreign Exchange Service 126
Off-Premises Extensions (OPXs) 127
Operator/Directory Assistance 128
Remote Call Forwarding (RCF) 129
Competitive Access Providers 129
Questions 131

Chapter 7   Lines and Trunks 135

Lines 136
Trunks 137
Comparisons 138
Common Configurations 139
DID 139
DOD 141
FX 141
OPX 143
TIE Lines 144
E&M 146
Signaling 148
WATS 149
Private Line 149
Questions 151

Chapter 8   Traffic Engineering Calculations 153

Traffic Engineering Studies 153
Where Can the Information Be Obtained? 156
Accomplishing the Mission 157
Using the Information 159
Gather the Data 159
Convert the Data to Daily or Hourly Usage 160

Choose the Appropriate Tool   163
Poisson Distribution   163
Determine the Grade of Service Desired   164
Erlang Distribution   166
Questions   172

Chapter 9   Equipment: Private Branch Exchanges   175

Private Branch Exchange (PBX)   175
Analog Systems   181
Digital PBX   182
Central Office Centrex   187
Centrex Service   188
Peripheral Devices   190
Questions   191

Chapter 10 Key Telephone Systems   193

Why Key Systems?   197
Features on Sets for Key System Vendor Interfaces   203
Innovations in the Key Telephone Systems — IP Telephones   204
The Vendor Proposal   207
Questions   208

Chapter 11 Voice Processing   213

Interactive Voice Response   214
Control Alternatives: Touch-Tone or Voice Recognition   214
Voice Dialing   215
Automated Attendant   216
A Few Important Points Not Directly Illustrated
   in the Dialogue   221
Automatic Call Distributor   222
Voice Mail   231
Interactive Voice Response   237
Questions   241

Chapter 12 Computer-to-Telephony Integration (CTI)   243

Other Applications   247
Why All the Hype?   251
Linking Computers and Communications   253
Unified Messaging Services   255
The Technology Advancement   256
The Final Bond   257
Technology Enhancements   259
Other Technologies   261
Automated Attendant   262
Integrated Voice Recognition and Response   263

Contents

Fax-Back and Fax Processing	263
Text to Speech and Speech to Text	264
Optical Character Recognition (OCR)	265
Questions	265

Chapter 13 Data Communications — 269

Concepts	270
Architectures	273
Protocols	274
Transmission Protocols (Synchronous Versus Asynchronous)	274
Error Detection	279
Parity Bit/Vertical Redundancy Checking (VRC)	280
Longitudinal Redundancy Checking (LRC)	282
Cyclic Redundancy Checking (CRC)	284
Plexes-Communications Channel Directions	286
One-Way (Simplex)	286
Two-Way Alternating (Half Duplex)	287
Two-Way Simultaneous (Duplex) or Full Duplex	288
Compression	289
Multiplexing	293
SDM	294
FDM	295
TDM	295
Codes	298
ASCII	299
Extended ASCII	301
EBCDIC	301
Unicode	303
Modulation	303
Amplitude Modulation (AM)	303
Frequency Modulation (FM)	304
Phase Modulation	305
QAM	306
V.90 Modems	307
Devices	308
DTE versus DCE	308
Categories and Examples of DTEs	309
Questions	309

Chapter 14 T1 and the T Carrier — 313

Evolution of the T-Carrier System	313
Analog Transmission Basics	314
The Evolution to Digital	317
Analog-to-Digital Conversion	320
The Movement to End Users	324
T1 Basics	325

Digital Capacities 335
Signaling 338
Clocking (Network Synchronization) 339
Bit Synchronization 340
Time Slot 340
Frame Synchronization 341
Potential Synchronization Problems 341
Performance Issues 342
D3/D4 Framing 343
Maintenance Issues 344
Error Detection 345
Errors of Omission/Commission 346
ESF — A Step to Correct the Problem 347
Framing 350
CRC-6 350
The Facility Data Link 351
Benefits of ESF 351
Problems with ESF 352
Questions 353

Chapter 15 The Open Systems Interconnect Model (OSI) 357

Other Network Architectures 381
SNA 382
SNA Components 383
The SSCP 384
The Physical Unit 385
The Logical Unit 386
Digital Network Architecture (DNA) 389
Internet Protocols (TCP/IP) 390
IP 391
TCP 393
Questions 394

Chapter 16 The Internet 399

A Little History 400
Structure (Who's at the Center — and Why) 404
Why the Hype? 405
Everybody as a Publisher 407
Commercial Opportunity? 409
Spam 410
Web Advertising 411
Web Site 412
Protocols 417
Naming Standards 420
Gaining Access 422
Internet Futures 425

	Voice over the Internet	426
	Voice over the Internet Protocol (VoIP)	428
	Quality of Service	430
	Questions	433
Chapter 17	Remote Access and Virtual Private Networks (VPNs)	437
	Components of the VPN	441
	Remote Access	443
	The Pressure Is On	444
	Remote Access Defined	445
	Security Issues	448
	PAP and CHAP as Part of the PPP	451
	L2TP Recommended by Microsoft and Others	451
	Questions	457
Chapter 18	Intranet	461
	Issues	464
	The Architecture	465
	Accessing the Network	468
	Intranet: The Logical Evolution	471
	Is It for Everyone?	473
	The Full-Service Intranet	474
	Applications	477
	Getting There from Here	478
	Other Issues	481
	Questions	482
Chapter 19	Packet Switching Technologies (X.25)	487
	Data Communications Problems	488
	The Data Communications Review	489
	Packet Switching Defined	490
	What Is Packet Switching?	490
	The Packet Switching Analogy	491
	The Packet Concept	496
	Overhead	496
	Summary of Packet Format	499
	The Packet Network	499
	The User Connection	499
	Benefits of Packets	507
	Other Benefits	507
	Advantages of Packet Switching	509
	Other Components of Packet Switching	511
	The X.25 Numbering Plan	514
	Applications for X.25 Services	514
	Other Forms of Packets	517
	Questions	519

Chapter 20 Local Area Networks (LANs)   523

What Are LANs?   523
  High Communications Speed   525
  Very Low Error Rate   526
  Geographic Boundaries   526
  Single Cable System or Medium for Multiple Attached Devices   527
A LAN by Another Name   528
What Do Users of LANs See When They Use the Network?   528
Why Are They Used?   529
  Performance   529
  Wiring   530
  Shared Resources   534
Distributed Systems   536
Client/Server Architecture   536
Scalability   537
How They Work   538
  Node Configuration Elements   539
  LAN Software for LAN Nodes   540
  LAN Network Interface Cards   541
Topologies   543
  Physical Topologies   544
  Logical Topologies   547
  Mixed Topologies — The Real World   549
Internetworking   551
  Repeaters   552
  Bridges   552
  Routers   553
  Gateways   553
LAN Switching versus Nonswitched   553
Questions   562

Chapter 21 Ethernet   567

Concepts   568
  Bus — CSMA/CD   568
  Half Duplex   571
  Bandwidth   572
  Destination Address   573
  Source Address   573
  Length   574
  Data   575
  CRC   575
Components   576
  10Base5   576
  10Base2   582
  10Base-T   587
  10Base-F (Fiber)   589

Contents

10Broad36   590
Fast Ethernet   592
Virtual LANs   602
IEEE 802.11 Wireless LANs   603
Questions   611

Chapter 22 Token Ring LANs   615

Token Rings   615
The IBM Token Concept   616
Initial Layout   617
Problems Encountered   618
    Lack of Power   618
    Lack of Connection   618
    Constant Changes   619
The Solution to Physical Problems   620
Cable Types Used   623
Speeds   626
Media Access Control Layer   627
The Types of Frame   628
    The Token   629
    The Abort Sequence   632
    The Data Frame   632
Case Example   636
Questions   642

Chapter 23 Baseband versus Broadband   645

Baseband and Broadband   646
Motivations Driving the LAN Decision   647
    Data Rates   648
    Interconnection   648
    Integrated Resources   649
    Compatibility Issues   651
    Cost Implications   651
The PBX   653
Baseband Cable Systems   654
    Baseband Is Cheaper Than Broadband and PBX Solutions   656
    Baseband Is a Very Scalable LAN Service   656
    Baseband Is Highly Efficient   656
Broadband Cable Systems   658
Baseband versus Broadband   666
Questions   667

Chapter 24 Fiber Distributed Data Interface (FDDI)   669

FDDI Design   670
FDDI Configuration   674

FDDI on the OSI Model	677
The FDDI Frame	680
Synchronization	683
FDDI Applications	683
Encapsulating Bridges	686
Translating Bridges	686
FDDI in the Metropolitan Area Network (MAN)	687
FDDI Recovery	688
FDDI-II	689
Questions	690

Chapter 25 Switched Multimegabit Data Services (SMDS) 693

What Is SMDS?	694
The Local Environment	697
Technology Used in SMDS	699
The SMDS Goal	699
Access Rates to SMDS	700
Accessing the MAN	701
The IEEE 802.6 Architecture	703
The DQDB Architecture	704
The MAN Access Unit	707
The Data Handling	709
Segmentation and Reassembly	709
The SMDS Data Unit	711
SMDS in a LAN Environment	714
Information Throughput	715
Questions	716

Chapter 26 Frame Relay 719

What Is Frame Relay?	720
Why Was Frame Relay Developed?	721
The Significance of Frame Relay	722
Comparing Frame Relay to Other Services	724
TDM Circuit Switching	724
X.25 Packet Switching	725
Frame Relay Speeds	728
Guaranteed Delivery	730
Advantages of Frame Relay Services	732
Increased Utilization and Efficiency	732
Savings Through Network Consolidations	732
Improved Network Up-Time	732
Improvements in Response Time	733
Easily Modifiable and Fast Growth	733
Standards-Based	733

Services Available   733
    TCP/IP and Novell IPX/SPX   734
    CCITT X.25 Protocol   734
    Facsimile (CCITT Group III or IV) Traffic   734
The Major Players   734
    Others   735
What the Standards State   737
    The Basic Data Flow   737
    Interface Signaling for Control   739
    Internal Networking   740
Voice over Frame Relay   740
International   742
Advantages   743
Disadvantages   743
Questions   744

Chapter 27   Integrated Services Digital Network (ISDN)   747

ISDN Defined   748
Who Is Making the Rules?   750
Why Do We Need ISDN?   751
The Overall ISDN Concept   753
    Telegraph   754
    Telephone   754
    Telex   754
    Data Communications   755
    Packet Switching   755
Integration   755
The ISDN Architecture   756
Physical View   756
Logical View   759
    Circuit Mode Services   760
    Packet Mode Services   761
    Application Services   763
    The Exchange Carrier Networks   764
    The Interexchange Network   765
    The Premises Network   767
Basic Operating Characteristics   768
Bearer Services   769
Questions   771

Chapter 28   Asynchronous Transfer Mode (ATM)   775

What Is ATM?   776
Broadband Communications   777
The Cell Concept   778

The Importance of Cells	778
Deriving Bandwidth	780
Cell Sizes and Formats	780
General Flow Control Identifier	780
Virtual Path Identifier	781
Virtual Channel Identifier	781
Payload Type	781
Cell-Loss Priority	782
Header Error Control	782
The Cell Format for User Data	782
The Adaptation Layer	782
ATM Standards Protocols	785
ITU	785
Rates	787
ANSI	788
ATM Forum	789
Switches	789
Public Switches	790
LAN to LAN via ATM	791
ATM and Frame Relay Compared	791
Network Interworking	792
Service Interworking Functions	794
Questions	795

Chapter 29	Digital Subscriber Line (DSL)	799

What Is xDSL?	800
Asymmetric Digital Subscriber Line (ADSL)	801
ADSL Capabilities	801
Modem Technologies	802
ISDN-Like Digital Subscriber Line (IDSL)	802
High-Bit-Rate Digital Subscriber Line (HDSL)	803
Symmetric or Single Digital Subscriber Line (SDSL)	806
Asymmetric Digital Subscriber Line (ADSL)	806
Rate-Adaptive Digital Subscriber Line (RADSL)	806
Consumer Digital Subscriber Line (CDSL)	807
Very High-Speed Digital Subscriber Line (VDSL)	807
Single-Pair High-Speed Digital Subscriber Line (SHDSL)	808
The Hype of DSL Technologies	809
xDSL Coding Techniques	809
Discreet Multitone (DMT) Modulation	810
Using DMT for the Universal ADSL Service (G.Lite)	810
Carrierless Amplitude Phase (CAP) Modulation	812
Comments on Deployment	813
Voice over DSL	813
VoATM over DSL	815
ATM Suitability for Voice Traffic	815
VoATM and DSL	817
Questions	818

Contents

Chapter 30   Cable Modem Systems and Technology   821

The Ethernet Cable   822
Cable TV Technology   824
The New Market   825
System Upgrades   826
Cable Modems   827
Standards   829
Return Path   830
Applications   831
The Combined Corporate and End-User Networking
    Strategies   831
Security on CATV   832
Questions   833

Chapter 31   Signaling System 7 (SS7)   837

Evolution of Signaling Systems   838
Pre-SS7   838
Introduction to SS7   839
Purpose of the SS7 Network   840
What Is Out-of-Band Signaling?   841
Why Out-of-Band Signaling?   842
The SS7 Network Architecture   843
SS7 Interconnection   844
Basic Functions of the SS7 Network   845
Signaling Links   845
   The Link Architecture   848
   Links and Linksets   849
   Combined Linksets   849
Routes and Routesets   850
SS7 Protocol Stack   851
Basic Call Setup with ISDN User Part (ISUP)   853
SS7 Applications   854
Questions   855

Chapter 32   Local Number Portability (LNP)   859

The Three Phases of LNP   860
LNP for Cellular and PCS Suppliers   861
   Cellular Providers   861
   Personal Communications Services (PCS) and Specialized
     Mobile Radio (SMR) Providers   862
LNP Differences   863
What's It All About, Anyway?   864
Where's the Money?   865
The Wireless Carriers' Decision   866
Basic LNP Networks   867
LNP Services Administration   868
Location Routing Number (LRN)   868

LNP Impact on Routing and Rating 870
Demand for LNP 870
LNP Operations, Administration, and Maintenance Impacts ... 871
Scenarios 872
Wireless and Wireline E-911 875
The Ultimate Goal — 2001 876
Benefits of Using LNP and Roaming Capabilities 877
   Incoming Calls to an Idle Mobile 877
   Calls to a Busy Set or a Set That Doesn't Answer 878
   No Answer with Call Forwarding 879
   Calls to a Busy Set with Message Waiting 879
Questions 880

Chapter 33 Cellular and Personal Communications Systems 883

Problems with the AMPS/IMTS 884
Cellular Communications 886
   Meeting the Demand 890
   The Telephone (Mobile) Set 891
Cellular's Success and Loss 892
Digital Transmission 897
   Digital 897
Voice Technology and Applications 898
Facsimile Technology 900
Data Transmission 902
Digital Cellular Evolution 904
Personal Communications Services 905
Technology 907
The Concept of PCS/PCN 908
Questions 912

Chapter 34 Wireless Application Protocol (WAP) 915

WAP Protocol Stack 918
   Wireless Application Environment 918
   Wireless Session Protocol 919
   Wireless Transaction Protocol 919
   Wireless Transport Layer Security 920
   Wireless Datagram Protocol 920
   Short Message Service 921
   Circuit-Switched Data 921
   Unstructured Supplementary Services Data 921
   General Packet Radio Service 922
WAP Clients and Gateways 923
Applications 925
The WAP Forum 926
   The WAP Forum Goals 927
   Standards Are Important 928
   Full Industry Participation 929

Bearer Independence   930
Device Independence   930
Interoperability   931
Why WAP?   932
Market Differentiation   932
Subtle Network Differences   933
Devices Are Definitely Different   934
Questions   935

Chapter 35 3G Wireless   937

Enter the Data   939
What to Call the Data Systems of the Future   940
What about the CDMA Folks?   942
IS-2000-A/cdma2000 3X   943
Third-Generation (3G) Wireless   944
Applications for 3G   947
What Does It All Mean?   950
Questions   950

Chapter 36 Light Systems   953

System Geometry   955
Atmospheric Conditions   957
    Absorption   958
    Scattering   958
    Shimmer   959
Site Selection   960
    Clear Line of Sight   960
    Adverse Mounting Conditions   961
Licensing Requirements   963
Bandwidth Capacities   963
Applications   964
    The Cable Decision   964
    The Radio Decision   965
    The Infrared Decision   965
Can the System Carry LAN Traffic Transparently?   969
Advantages of Infrared   970
Disadvantages of Infrared   971
Fiber-Optic-Compatible Systems   971
Questions   973

Chapter 37 SONET and SDH   975

Background Leading to SONET Development   976
The SONET Line Rates   977
    SONET Frame Format   980
SONET Topologies   982
    Point to Point   982

Point to Multipoint	983
Hub and Spoke	984
Ring	984
Synchronous Digital Hierarchy (SDH)	985
Synchronous Communications	986
Plesiochronous	987
SDH Frame	987
Waves of Light on the Fiber	990
The Benefits of a Combined Network	991
Questions	991

Chapter 38 Finances for Telecommunications | 993 |

Benefits	996
Hard Benefits	996
Soft Benefits	997
Costs	1000
Cost and Benefit Calculations	1000
Life Cycles	1000
Pricing Considerations	1003
The Decision-Making Process	1005
Justifying Costs	1005
Maintenance Issues	1006
Reduced Rates versus Improved Service	1007
Sample Calculations	1008
Initial Costs	1008
Add-On Costs	1010
Questions	1011

Chapter 39 Cabling Systems | 1013 |

Twisted Pair	1018
Coax	1025
Fiber Optics	1027
Applications of Fiber	1031
Fiber Differences	1032
Why Would One Not Use Fiber Wherever Possible?	1033
Questions	1034

Chapter 40 Planning the Communications Applications | 1037 |

Starting Point	1038
Make a Phone Call Anywhere in the World by Picking up Any Phone and Dialing It.	1038
Make a Data Connection.	1039
Make a Physical Inspection of the Wiring.	1041
Make a List of Features and Functions Added to the Phone and Data Network.	1042

Contents

Talk to the Users.	1042
Meet with the Appropriate Departments.	1043
Wrap up What You Learned	1046
Plan the Plan	1047
Implement the Plan	1048
Track the Results	1048
Report the Results	1049
Index	1051

INTRODUCTION

Welcome to the world of telephony and telecommunications! We are about to embark on a descriptive and narrative overview of the telecommunications industry. This book is designed to help "clear the air" for you. Because this is the fourth edition, it is possible that you have ventured down this trail before. Have no fear, we have expanded and updated this book beyond just a few pages. You will still get something out of this book.

One of the major problems with this technology and industry is the use of jargon, or "telephonese," which causes confusion and misunderstanding in the industry for users, purchasers, and vendors alike. Even professionals who have been in the industry for years can have difficulty communicating. The reason is simple: Too many acronyms are used, many with multiple meanings. An acronym will mean one thing to a voice telephony person and something completely different to an engineer who has 20 years of experience.

Your rule of thumb, therefore, should be to disallow the use of telecommunications acronyms in any discussions you have with any vendor, carrier, or end user. If the propensity exists for these people to use terms and acronyms, call a time-out. Have them explain all the alphabet soup they are using. You may still be surprised to find out that they can't explain the acronyms. This will obviously cause you some concern, but fear not; these folks will ultimately get to the point. Furthermore, because they won't be using all those buzzwords, communications should flow more smoothly.

Let's get into a basic discussion of telephony and telecommunications principles. No magic exists here, merely an understanding of what telecommunications is all about: the principles of a telephone, the line connections employed, the forms of communications used, and an understanding of the telephone company networks. We intend to make things as simple as possible as we cover the various techniques and terminology used throughout this book. Be aware, however, that no matter how simple we attempt to make this information and no matter how smoothly we attempt to steer you through the guides outlined, this is a technical subject. Therefore, from time to time, we may start sounding a little "techie." This is not done to impress or confuse you—we just cannot think of a way to make our explanation any more basic without destroying the flow. At any rate, this book is designed to give you a fundamental understanding of the overall concepts used in the telecommunications arena, both voice and data. Changes have been occurring at an escalating pace, so we must continue to look back at the history in order to see the future.

THE FORMAT

The format of this book is arranged to walk you right through the evolution of the industry as it has progressed. We approach the invention and the initial deployment of a network throughout the country on the basis of the original Bell System, and we look at the regulatory scene and the various legal issues that arose. A monopoly was created to curtail competition associated with the universal access to a telephony network, but also to be a wedge to recover the costs associated with the deployment of the capacities and services. In Chapter 1, we discuss the impact of the Telecommunications Act of 1996 and what has changed since the initial decisions. This one act opened the door to competition in the areas of telephony, long distance, cable services, and many other technologies. The past five years were exciting and confusing. Many skeletons lie on the side of the road to competition.

Next, we touch on the fundamentals of the voice evolution from the telephone company and end-user perspective. We look at the basic characteristics of the human voice and how the telephone network was developed. The discussion of network evolution encompasses the distinct dialing plans and how things have changed to accommodate phenomenal growth. We look at how the telephones have changed over the years. The discussion also shows how the telephone set converts a sound wave into an electrical wave and prepares the electricity for transmission across the network.

We next consider the changes following the introduction of digital standards. The old network was built as an analog system. It served us well. We hope that you will understand the differences between digital and analog after reading this.

Who are the players in the industry attempting to serve a user? We cover the different service providers, their offerings, and some of the financial considerations. This new edition also includes a discussion about rise and fall of the new players in the industry, called competitive local exchange carriers (CLECs). By comparing lines and trunks and explaining the real differences between them will explain why things happen the way they do when we order a pair of wires. We also have a mathematical discussion of how the carriers monitor the performance of their networks. All of these points should become crystal clear after this discussion.

We further compare the capabilities and features of the equipment that we can plug into our telephone network through some form of connecting arrangement such as the PBX. We also look at exposing you to Centrex, a service offering from the telephone companies that gives you PBX features and capabilities with the cost savings of building your own system. Stepping down to the lower-end equipment for the smaller organization, the key system comparisons of features, functions, and cost are explained. Voice-processing methods such as voice mail, automatic call distribution, and automatic attendants all constitute ways of serving customers. However, we caution you about the risks associated with these techniques.

We also look at computer-to-telephony integration and what that means to the consumer and businessperson alike. Linking the computer database to the telephone system means that information becomes a strategic weapon in building customer loyalty and confidence. See what we have to say about this.

We discuss a subject that normally causes even the strong of heart to shudder: the use of an analog telephone line to transmit critical data. How can we make digital data look like a voice call? What are the tools that will enable us to get the information in a usable and understandable form? This section gets quite lengthy and, from time to time, a bit technical; however, you need to understand this concept. The world will demand the use of data transmission techniques. Data is growing at an annualized rate of 30 percent, whereas voice is growing only 4 percent.

We explore the use of a digital network instead of an analog network, attempting to make this discussion simple, but again, there are some parts that get a bit complicated. Read this one in earnest; it is your future.

We enjoyed coming up with the best way to present certain models. The OSI section gets a little comical in the discussion of the standards that we use in just about all aspects of the industry. We think you'll really enjoy the way we present this very complex model, and how we can try to make all things simple if we take them one step at a time. So, draw your own conclusions and see whether this doesn't make more sense after you get through this chapter.

We discuss the explosion of the Internet around the world and how it works. This should be rewarding to read and will help you understand why things happen so slowly when you dial into the World Wide Wait! We also look at the demand rising for Voice over IP protocols and Voice over the Internet. Our intent is to get you talking and thinking about the services, then do more individualized research on your own.

Beyond the external networks, the discussion travels "in-house" to the Intranet. See what this technology can do for you and how the use of browsers can enhance the overall acceptance of technology.

We got a bit comical again as we attempted to describe the industry trend toward Virtual Private Networks (VPNs). This is one of those concepts that everyone talks about but few actually understand. Hopefully, you will stay awake through this section and see where the risks are.

The evolution of a packet networks using X.25 is one that we were very creative. We are not talking about some sci-fi robot or formula but a reliable delivery mechanism used across the network. It served us well and will be around for a while, so you will benefit from learning how this can also be taken into account. Our comparison and dialogue in this section is sure to amuse you and also to provide a very simple analogy on how X.25 works for you!

Many of our chapters look to moving data across a communications system called a local area network (LAN). The LAN evolves into a campus area network (CAN) and a metropolitan area network (MAN) and a wide area network (WAN) and a foreign area network (FAN). We cover the LAN, CAN, MAN, WAN, and FAN for you. Is your head spinning yet?

ISDN, (which does not mean "innovations subscribers don't need") means that we have several techniques to dial up a lot of voice and data on an all-digital network. ATM (not the automated teller machines) and Frame Relay are fast packet systems. They mimic packet switching on steroids. But if you read this section and don't scream, "I want it now," you missed something. You'll see!

Following the discussions of these networking concepts, we discuss the newer competitive way to access the high-speed communications services through xDSL and CATV Company services. Using this springboard, we will look at the speeds and capacities of these wired services.

Our discussion leads to some of the finer points of networks, such as the SS7 evolution for call setup and teardown. However, this is only one part of what SS7 brings to the networking strategies, because we can use SS7 for all the features and functions that bring new capabilities. Yet, with competition, we also need to look at the use of Local Number Portability (LNP) and the ability to move from carrier to carrier. However, we also discuss some of the other possibilities of using LNP, such as using E-911 to discover where a user is when in the wired or the wireless environment. Problems and pitfalls aside, we can see some of the benefits of using LNP from a wired and wireless integration plan.

After all this discussion of the wired network solutions, we then take a different approach. This is a discussion of connectivity without wires. We look at cellular communications and personal communications. The world is heading for an unconnected mode. Wireless voice and data are the rave of the industry (well almost!). Enjoy learning how the wired and wireless future will share the same trail. Discussions will also look at the third generation (3G) of wireless communications, including the steps through Bluetooth, WAP, and GPRS data protocols.

Then, with an eye to the costs of any communications method, we included discussion on rudimentary cost justification techniques that will help describe how to sell a system or network concept to management. This covers the basics of financial justifications. The speed of fiber brings us closer to the terabit throughput. With all the emphasis on SONET and Dense Wave Division Multiplexing (DWDM), we get the higher multiplexed rates and the benefits of different colors of light (so to speak). The capacities and compositions of these wiring systems are outlined to give the reader an understanding of what to look for and what to steer clear of.

We hope that you are intrigued and will read on. **Caution:** This is not a novel; it is not intended to be read from cover to cover. So, allot some time each day and take a chapter or a group of chapters together to gain an appreciation for the overall world of telecommunications. There is no reason this book cannot give you the tools necessary to deal with the novice or pro alike. Take some time to familiarize yourself with the ideas of the book; use the examples and analogies. Enjoy the stories and heed their message.

One closing thought: Many of our readers have sent us messages (e-mail, voice mail, letters) stating that we were technically incorrect with some of our concepts. Upon discussing this with them, we find that we are not incorrect, but we did not provide sufficient technical or engineering-specific detail for their needs or their liking. Wonderful! That is exactly what we were trying to do. Our philosophy with this book is the KISS method (keep it silly and simple). If you are looking for techno-babble as designed by propeller heads, there are many other books on the market. If you want to learn the basics without having a degree in engineering or in tech-speak, you came to the right place. Let's have some fun!

The History of Telecommunications

After reading this chapter and completing the questions, you will be able to:

- Explain how and why the telephone was invented
- Discuss the differences between the two inventors who were actively pursuing the development of the telephone
- Describe the basis of the monopoly established by the government
- Explain the reason the government wanted to break up the monopoly
- Converse with people in the industry regarding the changes that have taken place since the breakup of the telephone company

In 1876, an inventor named Alexander Graham Bell was awarded a patent for one of the most significant devices in our lives—the telephone set. Mr. Bell spent many years trying to develop a method of communicating with his wife. You see, Mrs. Bell was deaf. Alexander was looking for a way to convert sound into some other form of communication so that his wife could understand him. While she was in a hospital for the deaf in Boston, Massachusetts, he was busy at work trying to solve his basic problem of communications.

Having some experience with the workings of the telegraph, by which coded messages could be sent across a cable, Bell decided to mimic this means of communication. Using the basic principle that communications could be converted from sound into electricity, he would be able to speak into a communications device that, in turn, would convert the sound waves into electrical energy. Literally, what Bell wanted to achieve was the transmission of voice over the telegraph or, by today's standard, voice over a data network. This electrical energy could then be used to produce a coded message similar to a telegraph message. This all sounded good, but it led to long struggles during development. Many frustrations were experienced by Bell and his assistant, Dr. Watson. No matter how hard they tried, the success of the transmission of voice into an electrical current seemed to elude these two inventors.

Then one day, fate struck. While working in the lab by himself (Watson had been there, but left for a moment), Bell spilled some acid on his worktable. This acid acted as a catalyst to produce a battery effect. Without realizing what had occurred at the time, Bell called out for Watson. His call of "Watson, come here, I need you!" activated the experimental device they had set up for the communicator. His voice carried across a wire to a second room, where Watson was working. Hearing the call for help, Watson ran to the aid of his partner.

The two researchers discovered that if a battery is applied across the electrical circuit (the wires) while the user speaks, the sound wave produced by the human voice could be carried across this same pair of wires to a receiver set up to accept this electrical current and convert the electricity back into sound. Hence, on that fateful day, the birth of a new industry occurred. The telephone set was invented!

Bell and Watson were elated. They were the inventors of what we have grown dependent on, the basic voice communications telephone set. This was in light of similar activity taking place elsewhere.

Who Really Invented the Telephone?

A race was on from the outset between Dr. Bell and a German inventor named Dr. Elisha Gray, who had used a similar concept to Bell's, but he didn't complete the necessary documentation in time. Some say Gray actually invented the telephone before Bell, but he was too late in filing at the U.S. patent office. Gray filed suit against Bell for stealing his idea, but lost.

All this led to the birth of the telephony and telecommunications industry, which has proliferated to the point where we can't live without it. We've made the world smaller and have attached to the telephony network devices such as computers, fax machines, video conferencing equipment, and even interfaces to LANs. All these inventions make users feel they can't live, or do their jobs, without the use of a telephone.

Since the time Bell originally invented the telephone, many events have taken place. We examine these in closer detail to give you an appreciation of the industry in general. Incidentally, a theory even exists that Thomas A. Edison was the inventor of the telephone. With so many theories about the invention of such a remarkable piece of equipment, don't you wonder how the telephone proliferated as much as it did?

Evolution of the Telecommunications Industry

Historically, some of the important dates in the evolution of the telecommunications industry are shown in Table 1-1.

Table 1-1

Summary of Early Events in Telecommunications Industry

Year	Event
1872	Western Electric was formed; Bell worked for this company while developing the telephone.
1876	Bell was granted a patent for his invention (March 7, 1876).
1877	Bell offered to sell his invention to Western Union Telegraph for $100,000. Western Union rejected the offer.
1877	The Bell Telephone Company was formed.
1877–1878	Western Union formed a subsidiary company called the American Speaking Telephone Company to market its own telephone set (speaker developed by Tom Edison, receiver developed by Elisha Gray), the first competitor to the Bell system.
1878	The New England Telephone Company was formed as another of the first competitors to the Bell Telephone Company.
1878	Bell Telephone Company sued the American Speaking Telephone Company for patent infringement.
1879	Bell Telephone Company and New England Telephone Company merged and formed a new entity called National Bell Telephone Co.

(continued)

Table 1-1

Summary of Early
Events in
Telecommunications
Industry
(continued)

Year	Event
1879 —	The Bell and Western Union case was settled. Western Union agreed to stay out of the telephone business, and Bell agreed to stay out of the telegraph business in areas where Western Union operated.
1880 —	American Bell Telephone Company became the new name for the Bell System.
1882 —	American Bell entered into an agreement with Western Electric. WECO was the sole manufacturer of Bell equipment.
1884 —	The first long distance line was installed between Boston and New York.
1885 —	AT&T was formed as a subsidiary of American Bell to provide long-distance and telephone service for communities around the country and the world.
1887 —	The Interstate Commerce Commission was formed to regulate interstate carriers.
1893 —	Bell's first patent expired, opening the door for competition without patent infringements.
1899 —	AT&T acquired the assets of American Bell.
1910 —	AT&T aggressively fought the competition by acquiring controlling interest in Western Union.
1910 —	The Mann-Elkins Act was added to the Interstate Commerce Act to regulate the activities of the telecommunications industry.
1913 —	The Department of Justice (DOJ) considered antitrust actions against the Bell System. Woodrow Wilson made this commitment to break up private monopolies.
1913-1914 —	AT&T agreed to divest its Western Union stock and to stop buying up independent telephone companies, in a commitment by AT&T Vice President Kingsbury in return for dropping antitrust action.
1918 —	President Wilson placed the telephone and telegraph systems under control of the U.S. Post Office (until 1919).
1921 —	The Graham-Willis Act established the telephone company as a natural monopoly.
1934 —	The Federal Communications Commission (FCC) was created to regulate interstate, maritime, and international communications. Congress also established "universal service" as its goal. The FCC investigated Bell System operations and DOJ began to formulate a major antitrust action against Bell. However, World War II postponed action because Bell was considered critical to national defense.
1935 —	Public Utilities Commissions (PUCs) were formed to regulate intrastate communications and rate setting. Also, the PUCs were instrumental in formulating revenue sharing for calls using more than one carrier.

The First Telephone Companies Formed

Once the telephone was invented and proliferation started throughout the country, a group of telephone companies began to form independently to allow for interconnectivity. This technology started out with many saying the telephone was a frivolous toy and would only be used by the affluent. How wrong they were!

The first competitive telephone company to be formed was the American Speaking Telephone Company (ASTC), which was funded by the Western Union Telegraph Company, and used the pieces developed by both Gray and Edison. Edison had developed a transmitter that improved on the performance of the set, so this transmitter was used. The receiver was an invention of Elisha Gray. The combined transmitter and receiver (Edison/Gray) set was an enhancement over the Bell invention. Edison was also used to assist in the distribution of the wiring to local business and residential users. Edison's knowledge of electricity and the use of power distribution systems in the form of grids were applied to the telephone business. Of course, the Bell Telephone Company was actively challenging the ASTC's position on the basis that the company's use of telephony was an infringement on Bell's patents.

The New England Telephone Company followed the development of the two previously mentioned companies in building both telephones and network services. This was in direct competition with the Bell Telephone Company. A problem existed with this whole scenario: Any user who wanted to connect with a local telephone company, of which there were now three, couldn't communicate with another neighbor or business connected to either the other companies. Interconnectivity didn't exist. What this meant is, if I had needed to speak to three different businesses that used the services of the three different operating companies, I would have required three separate telephone lines and three different telephone sets on my desk. This is ludicrous to imagine, but true.

The Regulatory Scene

The telephone industry was rampant with suits and countersuits during the early stages of deploying the networks. Bell was active in trying to displace the "fake" companies on the basis of the patent infringements.

Many of the cases had a bearing on the future of the industry, in particular with the formation of the telephone companies as monopolies. Some of the key events are listed in Table 1-1.

This was quite a turn of events. American Telephone & Telegraph (AT&T) started out as a subsidiary of Bell and, ultimately, became the dominant force in the market. And all of this happened in the first 23 years of the industry.

Many smaller companies started up building either telephones or networks. By the 1920s, nearly 9,000 independent telephone companies were in operation. This number was reduced because AT&T (the long-distance monopoly at the time) wouldn't let the independents interconnect to the AT&T network. As a result, many were financially strapped and went bankrupt. AT&T began acquiring these failing operations, causing the number of independents to diminish (about 1,400 independent operating companies still exist in North America). AT&T had the single largest network in place and began to undercut prices, buying out competitors in an attempt to drive the smaller companies out of business. This left gaps in coverage for customers served by the independents, who couldn't connect to the major cities where AT&T had the market. One competitor AT&T was after was the ASTC. AT&T began to buy controlling interest in Western Union, the parent of ASTC in an attempt to control its operation and destiny.

AT&T began to cave in to public pressure. A statement from an AT&T vice president (Kingsbury) outlined new positions to the attorney general. Kingsbury agreed to

- Relinquish its holdings in Western Union
- Stop the practice of acquiring the independents, unless authorized by the Interstate Commerce Commission (ICC)
- Allow the independents to interconnect to the AT&T network

Still another major event in the industry was the Graham-Willis Act, which established the telephone system as a natural monopoly. For years, AT&T had dominated the industry, providing all telephone equipment and service through its normal distribution channels, the telephone companies. The network was a sacred cow, with only AT&T products and services allowed for interconnection to the networks. The philosophy was that any other product might harm the network, thereby keeping a monopoly over the products and services to be installed.

Hush-a-Phone

In 1947, the Federal Communications Commission (FCC) permitted the connection of customer-owned and provided recorders through special protective arrangements. These devices were used to record conversations, but were required to sound a beep when recording took place.

In the late 1940s, other manufactured devices could be attached to the telephone lines, so long as a protection device was used. This was an appeasement to the telephone companies, which stated the connection of a foreign piece of equipment on the network would disrupt the network and decrease its efficiency, as well as jeopardize national security.

In the 1950s, an innovation known as the *Hush-a-Phone,* an acoustically coupled device designed to eliminate noise and increase privacy, was tested before the FCC. The FCC agreed with AT&T's position and moved to prevent "foreign" devices from being connected to the telephone network. An appeals court later overturned this decision. Because the acoustic coupler was a nonelectrical device, the court ruled it would pose no threat to the integrity of the network. The U.S. Naval Department was one of the users who fought for the use of the Hush-a-Phone. After losing the battle in court, AT&T suggested if a recording device were to be allowed on the network, then a beep should be sounded on the line periodically (every 15 seconds). This beep would alert the user at the far end that the conversation was being recorded. The Bell system suggested if a beep were introduced to the line, then an electrical input was required. Bell fought for the right to install the equipment on the line that provided the beep. This was made possible because the Hush-a-Phone decision was made based on a nonelectrical input. The Bell system was then able to charge the U.S. Naval Department for the equipment that introduced the beep and all was settled.

In 1956, the Department of Justice filed an antitrust suit against the Bell System, which had been postponed because of World War II. In general, the suit was aimed at getting AT&T to divest itself of Western Electric. This was finally settled in what was known as the 1956 Consent Decree. The result was that AT&T could retain ownership of Western Electric if it only produced products for the Bell-operated companies. This decree went on to prevent the Bell System from offering commercial data processing services, limiting Bell to providing telecommunications services under regulation. This still left the Bell System a regulated monopoly with no competition for equipment and services in its operating areas.

Chapter 1

The Introduction of Competition

In 1968, however, the first true case was tested by a company called Carter Electronics of Texas. Carter made a device used to interconnect mobile radios to the telephone network via acoustic couplers. The FCC ruling was paramount in that direct electrical connection of devices to the network was allowed so long as a protective coupler arrangement was used. The decision had monumental impact because, prior to the Carterphone decision, manufacturers had a limited outlet for their products. They typically sold their products to the independent operating telephone companies. Now the floodgates were opened and these manufacturers had a whole new world of opportunity to market their products. Even the foreign manufacturers sped into the equipment market, offering end-user products that had previously been totally controlled by the Bell System. The European and Japanese marketeers were quick to enter the PBX and terminal equipment business. However, the use of a protective device was still an area of frustration with these equipment vendors. Rent for the Bell protective arrangements was a recurring cost that made the purchase of other equipment less attractive. The manufacturers continued to complain about this. These complaints resulted in the 1975 FCC registration program for all products that could be attached to the telephone network. As long as a manufacturer could pass the requirements of the FCC registration (Part 68), then its products could be attached to the network without the use of the protective devices. This began what was called the *interconnect business*.

Still, additional activity took place. In the 1960s, a small microwave carrier company called MCI began constructing a microwave network between Chicago and St. Louis. MCI's initial intent was to provide alternate private line services in a high-volume corridor. MCI took its interconnection request to the courts and won the capability to interconnect its network with the telephone company network. MCI further began to offer switched services, which was immediately reported to the FCC. The legal actions nearly put MCI into bankruptcy, but the little company prevailed and began the "other common carrier" industry—one more nail in the monopolistic coffin for AT&T.

The Divestiture Agreement

In 1982, the most monumental decision to be made since the inception of the monopoly in the telecommunications business was reached. In light of all the computer inquiries and consent decrees taking place, the Department of Justice was still after AT&T, Western Electric, and Bell Labs. This recent action started in early 1974 and was aimed at the complete breakup of the Bell System. In early 1981, the suit finally made it into the courts but, surprisingly, was brought to a halt on January 8, 1982, when an agreement was reached to drop the suit and submit a modification of the 1956 Consent Decree to the courts.

To achieve the goals targeted, AT&T would be relieved of the limitations keeping it from other unregulated markets. In return for this relief, however, the courts demanded the breakup of the Bell System. Because the Bell System operated as a monopoly and enjoyed the noncompetitive environment, it was to remain under a regulated status. The Modified Final Judgment (MFJ) considered the provisioning of local dial tone services as a monopoly and everything else as a competitive operating environment. Therefore, the local dial tone business provided by the local exchange carriers (LECs) would remain regulated. AT&T could pursue and operate in the competitive long-distance, equipment manufacturing, computer equipment/processing, and sales markets. The 23 Bell Operating Companies (BOCs) would be divested from AT&T (which retained its Western Electric Manufacturing, Bell Labs, and Long Lines divisions). Some of the salient points of the MFJ include the following:

- AT&T had to transfer sufficient personnel, assets, and access to technical information to the BOCs, or whatever new organization was owned by the BOCs, to enable exchange services or access to exchange services to be provided without any ties to AT&T.
- All long-distance services, links, personnel, and other facilities had to be relinquished by the BOCs and turned over to AT&T.
- All existing licensing agreements and contracts between AT&T or its subsidiaries and the BOCs had to be terminated.
- Equal access for all interexchange carriers into the BOCs' switching systems had to be provided. This broke down the special privilege AT&T enjoyed over its competition. The equal access for all carriers was to be provided within two years. The only exceptions were electromechanical systems, where it was cost-prohibitive to changes or smaller companies serving fewer than 10,000 users.
- After the breakup, the BOCs could provide, but couldn't manufacture, equipment.
- After the divestiture, the BOCs could produce and distribute directories to subscribers.

- Carrying calls between and among offices was defined as local exchange services and interexchange services. The LECs would hand off any interexchange call to an interexchange carrier (IEC). To define the boundaries of who carried the call and who shared in the revenue, a number of local access and transport areas (LATAs) were created. The calls inside a LATA were the responsibility of the LEC, and calls that left the LATA were the responsibility of the IEC.

- Joint ownership or participation in the network between AT&T and the BOCs was prohibited. Although this was a common practice before the breakup, it wasn't supported after the breakup.

The provisions of the MFJ were strictly aimed at the Bell System. This was a point of confusion for many people because they thought the whole network would fall apart, which it didn't. The greatest confusion arose when the MFJ was decided in early 1982 with an implementation date of January 1, 1984. Fear, uncertainty, and doubt reigned in the industry.

The business users were prepared for the breakup, but not much happened in the residential market. Although the BOCs and AT&T tried to communicate the message to end users, they were highly unsuccessful. Fifteen years after the breakup, many residential users still didn't know a difference existed between the suppliers. The small business and residential users were so accustomed to the "cradle-to-grave" services offered by their BOCs, they didn't grasp the significance of this breakup. No longer would one call do it all. Separate companies provided dial tone services and long-distance services.

The divestiture of the Bell system allowed advances in the industry that might not have occurred otherwise. With the introduction of competition and the capability of other suppliers to enter new markets, the evolution of the network and service offerings escalated dramatically. Digital architectures rolled out to customers at a rapid pace. Further, when divestiture took place, the costs associated with local dial tone increased by as much as 50 to 60 percent on a monthly, recurring basis. However, long-distance services and usage charges decreased by 60 percent or more. This might sound like a break-even analogy, but the ratio of local to long-distance service is a 20:80 rule. Twenty percent of a customer's actual monthly bill is for the fixed recurring charge, whereas 80 percent of the bill is for the variable usage-sensitive costs associated with long distance. From this, you could suggest we would gladly accept an increase of 50 to 60 percent on 20 percent of our bill, if the remaining 80 percent of our bill is reduced by 60 percent.

To add to the confusion, whenever a customer called a provider for a service that didn't fall within that provider's scope, the standard answer given was the judge didn't allow the vendor to provide such services. This reference to Judge Harold Greene of the Federal District Court, who presided over the suit and the MFJ rulings, was a standard escape clause used by LECs and IECs alike. Unfortunately, the MFJ was an agreement reached by the court and AT&T rather than an actual mandate. Thus, the burden of setting the rules in the telecommunications industry was placed on the shoulders of the courts.

Tariffs

Another escape clause used on a regular basis is "the tariffs don't allow this service," which is a clear misrepresentation. The BOCs and the AT&T organization write tariffs and submit them to their respective judicature, whether it's the FCC for interstate traffic for AT&T or the Public Utilities Commission for the BOCs. An easy way to avoid offering a service or to delay a customer request is to suggest the tariff doesn't allow something. But who writes the tariff? If a service or something out of the ordinary isn't covered in the tariff, then the logical solution is to write a new one. For a new tariff to be written is rare.

What is a tariff? A *tariff* is a description of a service that offers an appropriate rate of charge for that service and the rules under which the service is to be provided. A tariff is the basic agreement of terms for a service between the customer and the provider that must be submitted to the regulators for approval before any changes in service can be offered. In the United States, 50 different regulators rule on the tariffs—one for each state. We relegated the overseer function to the Public Utilities Commission and the FCC. In the rest of the world, rate settings and guidelines differ, depending on the country. Many of the telephone companies are under direct control of the local government. The telephone service is relegated to the post office agencies, called Post Telephone and Telegraph organizations (PTTs). The name stands for the services provided: postal, telephony, and telegraphy. Privatization is happening in several parts of the world. Telephone services are being removed from government control and passed on to private organizations. It stands to reason these organizations must face stiff competition for the services, much the same as has happened in the United States.

The Telecom Act of 1996

In February 1996, the Clinton Administration signed into law the Telecom Act of 1996. This act was the culmination of several years of trying to deregulate and provide a competitive marketplace in the telecommunications arena. This law, when enacted, opened the door to an open communications infrastructure. Essentially, what the administration put into play was the beginning of the concept of the information superhighway.

The Telecommunications Act of 1996 opened the way for myriad new players to compete for the local dial tone service. In the United States, dial tone amounts to a $115 billion per year industry. All the emerging players want a piece of that action. What this means, however, is a group of new players will emerge to provide dial tone services, while the local telephone companies are unshackled and allowed to penetrate new markets that were unavailable to them in the past.

During the beginning stages of this Telecom Act, elation and overwhelming support for the newly emerging marketplace from all players was the name of the game. As you would expect, however, things don't work as smoothly as they should initially. The Telecom Act of 1996 allows the long-distance companies (IECs) to enter into new business opportunities. These include dial tone, cable TV services, high-speed Internet access, and two-way video communications capabilities after the infrastructure is in place. The market is quickly becoming a data centric infrastructure—dial tone is the way the carriers get in the door.

The cable TV companies may enter into telephony and other forms of the communications business. These providers may offer voice communications, high-speed Internet access, two-way multimedia communications, and cable TV services, all on a single communications platform. As the cable companies look at their infrastructure, they already have a high-speed communications channel running either to or by everybody's door. They must recognize, however, that in the past, their primary service was to deliver one-way cable services. To provide high-speed Internet access, enhanced capabilities, and voice communications, these companies were forced to create a two-way communications cable system. This means they either had to add new cables or provide high-speed fiber in the backbone network to the curb, and then coax to the door. Although this sounds straightforward and easy, it does require significant investments on the part of the cable companies. This alternative proved effective with a hybrid fiber/coax arrangement that, by the end of 1999, the cable TV companies implemented in several cities in the United States and Canada to provide the high-speed access in a bundled pricing mechanism. Moreover, 1999 marked the year when AT&T (the now-streamlined carrier) acquired two of the largest CATV companies: TCI and Media One. Having invested over $100 billion in acquiring these cable companies gave AT&T access to many consumers' doors.

As the Telecommunications Act continues to be enforced, the original telephone companies (the BOCs) break out into new markets, such as offering long distance for less and providing cable TV services, Internet access, and videoconferencing capabilities on their local infrastructure. What the telcos must realize, however, is the local two-wire cable facility (called the local loop) wasn't designed to sustain the high-speed communications we're discussing here. Therefore, the telcos will continue to update their cable infrastructures. These companies are enamored with xDSL technologies that use high-speed digital subscriber links. Using various techniques such as asymmetrical digital subscriber link (ADSL) or very high-speed digital subscriber link (VDSL), the telephone companies can provide high-speed communications to the customer's door. In the ADSL marketplace, they envision delivering up to 9 Mbps to a customer's door, whereas outbound from the customer to the network the service will offer plain old telephone service (POTS) and up to 1.544 Mbps data transmission. Two occurrences have deviated from this scenario to start:

1. Rate-adaptive ADSL (RADSL) was introduced, allowing the telco to deliver less than the 9 Mbps downloadable to the door. Instead, they use a figure of 1.544 Mbps downloadable and adaptive rates of 256 to 1.024 Mbps uploadable. If the network is busy, then the consumer gets slower-speed access, but a contracted minimum comes into play. If the network is lightly loaded, however, the consumer can benefit from the higher throughputs.

2. One-meg modems were developed. The ADSL Forum looked at both the application and the need for the previously mentioned speeds. What this forum determined, in the short term, is the average consumer only really needs 1 Mbps downloadable and approximately 160 Kbps uploadable asymmetrical speeds. Therefore, they developed what was termed *ADSL Lite* or *G.lite specification*. Over time, this specification will allow higher-speed access but, for the short term, this is sufficient.

In the ADSL marketplace, the telcos deliberately dragged their feet implementing these services. Many reasons exist, but the most common is they didn't want to be forced to provide the xDSL service at a discounted rate, as they do the dial tone. In the VDSL marketplace, the telcos envision up to 51 Mbps to the customer's door with a much lower-speed communications channel outbound or a symmetrical 51 Mbps in each direction. Regardless of the technique used, the telephone companies are in a position to find technologies to support and sustain these speeds on their local, single twisted pair of wires to the customer's door. Experiments are underway in Phoenix, AZ by Qwest International (formerly US West); however, problems have been rampant because of inexperience and lack of skills. This is their challenge. Beyond the high-speed communications, the telephone companies can also enter into manufacturing, long distance, and cable TV service. The caveat of the Telecom Act of 1996, however, is these companies must first prove that an open competitive environment exists at the local loop. This was one of the contention points as the newer players emerged and attempted to get into either facilities-based or a non-facilities-based dial tone provision.

In the facilities-based environment, the carrier provides its own cables or wireless communications to the customer's door. At that point, all the communications will be carried right out to the wide area network (WAN), bypassing the local telephone companies.

In a non-facilities-based environment, the new players rent or lease facilities from the local telephone company at a discount from 17 to 28 percent off the local telephone company's tariffs. The telephone companies argue, by having to rent the services to competitors at a discounted rate, they are putting themselves in an unfair position. The resellers of dial tone merely turn around and rent services right back to the consumer at a rate less than what the telephone companies charge. The telephone companies contend this is a discount that shouldn't be provided and if competitors want to work in this market, they should build their own capabilities or rent from the telco at the same rates the telco charges other customers. Embroiled in all these battles are the other players, such as the long-distance and cable TV providers, who are equally distraught because they also have to pay for other access fees to provide services to their consumers. They argue that the telephone companies have been raising the rates for access because of the potential loss of revenue because of the Telecom Act of 1996.

An interesting event occurred in 1999 when AT&T acquired the local cable TV companies (TCI and Media One) to get access to the consumers' doors. Shortly after acquiring these giants, AT&T was challenged to offer the access to competitors at a reduced rate. AT&T immediately balked at that idea and appealed to the FCC because the local utilities commissions were ruling in favor of the competitors. AT&T is screaming about the unfairness of such a move, yet this worked just the opposite when they wanted access through the telco and were asked to pay the access fees.

Throughout all this maneuvering, the consumer may or may not win. Clearly, with competition, prices should fall to a more reasonable base and other discounts might exist. This will work in the major NFL cities.* The cost of dial tone and access to the long-distance network should drop. In rural communities where services and facilities have always been limited, however, no advantage or a slight disadvantage might exist. The consumers in the rural areas are going to be left in the lurch because few companies want to serve such regions. In the old days, the telephone companies had to serve it as a last resort. Under deregulation, all of this might well change. A couple of the Competitive Local Exchange Carriers (CLECs) have actually opened many third- and fourth-tier communities. Because they are the prime competitor in the town, users who are willing to take a chance will do so with the new provider. This has been a lucrative market for the new CLECs in this area, as opposed to the results in the major metropolitan areas.

As you might expect, several new providers entered the business. As of 1999, over 500 CLECs had jumped into the competitive local dial tone business, yet they have achieved only 3 to 5 percent penetration into the overall market. This penetration amounts to approximately $4 to $5 billion annually. Each of the competitors entering this market offers some form of discounts on cable services, dial tone, or long-distance access and services to pick up a few market points. Many providers are building out high-speed access on fiber-based networks bypassing the local telco. Newer providers are now offering the one-stop shopping method by offering a bundle of services, including dial tone, long distance, equipment, and internal wiring all on a single phone bill. AT&T, for example, began offering as much as a 26 percent discount overall for the bundled-service packages they now offer, including dial tone, CATV, and long-distance services. These new players used loss leaders to attempt to pick up their market shares. Through this loss leader market, they won't make any money. Consequently, the consumer may stand to gain for the short term, until these new emerging competitors realize they are making no money by offering heavily discounted services. At that point, the carriers will have to raise their rates or offer some other value-added services to gain new revenue.

---

*The reference to NFL cities is that any major city across North America with a professional football team has all the services and benefits, whereas the smaller communities that don't have a football team don't get the same level of service and accessibility.

In the year 2000, many of these competitors got in trouble financially and faced some serious loss of confidence from their investors. In fact, the companies began to run out of money. This forced a couple of the CLECs to fold; many others either merged with or were acquired by better-funded organizations. The stock prices for these organizations were soaring to heights never seen before, yet they all came tumbling to the ground. We can expect 2001 won't be kind to many of these providers. Expect that 25 percent of these CLECs will disappear in the near future.

The Canadian Marketplace

In 1994, the Canadian Regulatory Telecommunications Committee (CRTC) endeavored to do something similar to what happened in the United States. The goal was to deregulate or demonopolize the local dial tone provisioning service. On May 1, 1997, the CRTC provided its interpretation of how it would deregulate and open the market to dial tone to a competitive environment. You can expect that, one year after the Telecom Act of 1996 in the United States, the CRTC would likely model a good many services and provisions of the law after those accomplished by the FCC. The reason was to provide harmony throughout all of North America. While the CRTC endeavored to break up the dial tone monopoly, the cable companies, the long-distance providers, and a rash of emerging players, who are facilities based or non-facilities based, already filed and petitioned for the right to offer services. Once again, in the Canadian marketplace the influx of new providers and new opportunities overwhelmed the consumers, even though the implementation is ongoing.

In both the U.S. and Canadian marketplaces, all the dial tone and long-distance access services have traditionally been through the local dial tone loop. Now, with the cable TV companies trying to get into this business, the dial tone could be provided on either a cable or a local loop. More and more opportunities exist for a wireless connection to the consumer, however, whether residential or business. The wireless dial tone providers are constantly springing up around the country as they entertain the thought of the personal communications service (PCS). Through a combination of the dial tone, the TV services, the high-speed Internet access, and the multimedia communications capabilities to the local door, all these activities will come to culmination. No one service alone may warrant all the new emerging players but, as a whole, this marketplace is enormous.

Therefore, as the Telecommunications Act and the CRTC deregulation rolled out in the Canadian marketplace, you experienced dramatic changes in the way you do business. Through the convergence of wired and wireless communications, dial tone, and long distance, a variety of other services emerged to create a competitive potential for you. One-stop shopping is the way of the future.

Questions

1. Why do people still believe two different people might have invented the phone?

2. What role did Mr. Watson play in the development of the telephone sct?

3. What relationship did Elisha Gray and Thomas Edison share?

4. Who created the first telephone company?

5. What special status was afforded to the local telephone companies?

6. Why is providing interconnection between the different companies important?

7. When AT&T realized it was getting in trouble, who figured out how to stop the legal proceedings against the company?

8. What was Western Union Telegraph's involvement in the telephony business? Why was that significant?

9. What was the excuse AT&T and the Bell system used to prevent others from attaching equipment to the Telephone Company network? List the various reasons given.

10. How difficult do you think creating the telephone business again would be, under new rules?

11. What is the importance of the Carterphone decision?

12. The Navy was instrumental in forcing the acceptance of what device?

13. If a new supplier wants to get into the telephone business, what services do you think it would likely want to offer? List the services and the reasons for offering them.

14. What were the factors leading up to the breakup of the Bell System in 1982?

15. What agreement was reached, who were the players, and what is the agreement called?

16. The Telecommunications Act of 1996 allows the Telephone Companies to compete in the long distance market if they do what?

17. How many different phone companies were under the Bell umbrella?

18. How many independent telephone companies are in North America today?

19. What is the name for the new providers of dial tone?

20. What were the benefits AT&T received from the divestiture agreement?

Voice Characteristics

After reading this chapter and completing the questions, you will be able to:

- Discuss the characteristics of a voice
- Understand the concept of bandwidth
- Converse about the variations of a conversation (amplitude and frequency)
- Discuss the capacities of the various media used to carry information
- Listen for the changes and differences in a conversation

The telephone set transmits sound to the receiving party. If the telephone network and the telephone set were designed to carry voice signals from one point to another, then the characteristics of the voice signal had to be known. A great amount of time and effort went into studying the actual variables associated with sound created by our vocal chords. From these studies, you can derive the fundamental concepts of a telecommunications network. This implies the telephone set is designed to carry only voice. In reality, this is correct because all the effort was directed toward carrying the voice in its truest possible form from the sender to receiver. The word "telecommunications" involves this very basic concept. A definition is in order here because we cover the characteristics of the telephone network and its capability to carry the human voice.

Telecommunications is the transmission of information—in the form of voice, data, video, or images, across a distance, over a medium, from a sender to a receiver—in a usable and understandable manner.

This definition is complicated, but it can be simplified by breaking the two pieces apart and stating them differently.

Tele is a Greek root meaning from afar. This implies the information will be carried over some distance, from as little as a few inches to as much as thousands of miles.

Communicate comes from the Latin root meaning to make common. The implication here is, if we are to send any form of information across the medium, then it must be understandable or else it's wasted energy.

The Medium

A *medium* is any form of transmission capacity used to carry signals. In the telecommunications world, this can be in the form of copper wires, coaxial cables, optical fiber (glass or plastic), or air (radio signals). Other forms of media also exist; for example, this book uses paper as the medium to get the information to the reader. But we're dealing with a telephony concept, so we'll stick to these types of analogies. Depending on the medium used, the distances over which information is transmitted can vary greatly. However, strides have been made since the late 1870s, when the telephone set was first invented. Now we can transmit any information over thousands of miles as simply as we do over inches. The information takes on the form of electrical energy to re-create the sound waves generated by our voices in a representative form, so listeners at the distant end can understand the message.

Sound

Sound is nothing more than the banging of air molecules together at a rapid rate. As we generate sound with our vocal chords, we're banging these air molecules together to produce intelligible information that can be used and understood by others. This is in the form of air pressure changes. Hold your hand in front of your mouth as you speak. Do you feel the air pressure hit-ting your hand? This is the effect of sound as we generate the changes in air pressure. Our vocal chords, therefore, are moving back and forth and banging the molecules of air together. (You may look silly talking with your hand in front of your mouth, so do this in a private place.)

An old question asks, "If a tree falls in the forest and no one is there to hear it, does it create sound?" The answer must be an obvious yes. Although no one is there to hear it, the air pressure changes caused by the tree falling to the ground—regardless of where it falls—must still be producing sound. If we put a tape recorder in the forest and the tree falls, the sound will, most likely, be captured by the recorder. Even though no one is there, the recorder still captures the noises created by the air changes.

The telephone converts sound waves to their analog equivalent in the form of electrical pulses, which are then carried across the telephone network. *Analog* is the analogous form of the voice wave being created in a "look-alike" electrical wave. We can, therefore, assume that to communicate across the medium (wires), we must have some form of sound. The sound will be converted into electricity. The electricity is then sent across the telephone wires.

Sound is the banging together of air molecules at a rapid pace. This is called *compression* and *rarefaction*. The human voice produces sound at a constantly changing set of frequencies (pitch) and amplitudes (loudness). The human voice changes these variables of frequency and amplitude in cycles per second. The vocal chords compress the air molecules at a rate of between 100 and 5,000 times per second. To re-create the sound faithfully, the sound waves (or air pressure changes) are converted from sound into electricity. This is what the telephone set does. For a more detailed explanation of how this happens, refer to Chapter 4.

As the electrical equivalent of sound is created, compare the sound wave to an electrical wave. Electricity is typically generated in an analog form by rotating the electromagnetic energy around a center point. As the energy is on the rise, it increases the amplitude to a peak level in decibels, and then reverses direction and begins to fall. Because the wave is concurrent, its electrical field have both a positive and a negative side. Therefore, as the signal decreases from the peak of the positive energy, it moves back toward the zero line. As with a magnet, two poles exist: positive and negative. So, as the wave gets to the zero line, it continues to fall to the negative side of the voltage line until it hits some peak at the bottom of the energy field. From there, it, in turn, rises back up to the zero line (value) again. This, in effect, constitutes a 360 degree cycle around the baseline or one complete

Figure 2-1
The human sound
wave produces both
frequency and
amplitude changes.

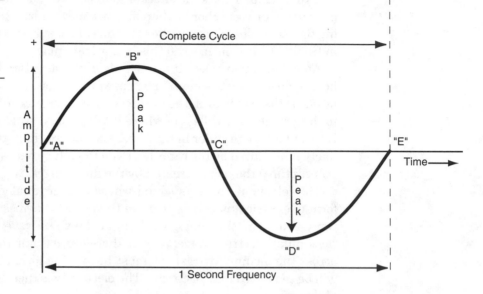

Figure 2-1
The human sound wave produces both frequency and amplitude changes.

rotation. This rotation is called a *sinusoidal wave.* This sinusoidal wave shown in Figure 2-1 is the analogous re-creation of the human sound wave in its electrical form. This single wave cycle over a specified period of time, usually one second, is called one *hertz,* named after the man who discovered this concept.* Hertz is normally abbreviated *Hz.*

The sound wave produced by a human voice has a constantly changing variable energy in both signal strength (the amplitude) and the number of rotations around the baseline over a period of time (the frequency). Voice characteristically creates 5,000 cycles of information per second. This is abbreviated into 5 kilohertz. *Kilo* means thousands and is represented by the *k* in kHz.

The human ear is responsive to variations in frequency and amplitude at rates from 25 to 22,000 Hz. This means the ear can receive and discern all the information contained in the human voice. This is important in telephony.

Differences exist in human responsiveness to sound. For example, older humans can discern sounds ranging only up to 7 to 8 kHz because of abuses and deterioration of the eardrums. People who have fired a weapon (rifle or

*Heinrich Hertz came up with this concept.

handgun) without proper ear protection can damage the upper and lower frequency responses, limiting the range of frequencies they can hear. A younger person, who hasn't had the chance to damage the ears, can receive and discern sound waves in the 16- to 18-kHz range. When we see these youngsters carrying those boom boxes on their shoulders, however, with the box blaring away and sitting directly next to the ear, we can only imagine how the ear is going to respond in a matter of time. The youngsters are inadvertently narrowing the range of frequency responses to which their ears can selectively respond.

The telephone company realized the majority of usable information in a human conversation can fit in a 3-kHz range, so it provides a pair of telephone wires—typically made of copper—that can carry all the usable information. The telephone networks were built to carry speech, and the most commonly carried signal on the network is the electrical equivalent of speech (voice). The telephone transmitter (mouthpiece) converts the acoustic signal (sound wave) generated in the human speaker's larynx into electrical waves.

Actually, the analog waves can be represented in frequency and analog changes over a broad spectrum (or band) from approximately 30 Hz to about 10 kHz. Most of the usable and understandable energy falls in the spectrum of 200 to 3,500 Hz, however. If we subtract the differences between the high end and the low end, the spectrum is 3,300 Hz, or 3.3 kHz, wide. It isn't necessary to re-create all the speech waveforms precisely to get an acceptable transmission of human speech across the telephone network. This is because the ear isn't highly sensitive to fine distinctions in the frequency changes, and the human brain can make up for any variations in the speech form by interpretation. Of course, if something doesn't come across the wire clearly enough, the human brain intervenes and causes the mouth to say, "What?" This, in turn, can cause the speaker at the transmitting end to generate the signal over again by repeating the words.

Because the cost of transmitting the signal across a telephone network is directly proportional to the range of frequencies carried, the telephone company uses a bandpass filter on the circuit. Commercially acceptable and usable information is transmitted in what is called a *band-limited channel*. This means all the usable information is allowed to pass onto the circuit, but the extraneous information that doesn't add significantly to the conversation is filtered off. If the extra energy is put onto the wire and carried from end to end, the costs go up at an equal rate; this is wasteful. So the telephone company limits the amount of information you can pass on the wire.

What Is Bandwidth?

One of the toughest concepts for anyone to understand is bandwidth. To the novice, bandwidth becomes even more perplexing when it's bandied about by telephone company personnel, engineers, and others. But bandwidth is the basis of most of what we do in the telecommunications and telephony world.

Think of bandwidth as a water pipe or a garden hose. The greater the size of the pipe, the larger the volume of water that can flow through the pipe. The smaller the pipe, the smaller the flow of water. Be careful not to confuse flow with pressure! We can constrain the pipe and cause the flow to gush out of the pipe, but did more water flow? Now, in telecommunications terms, think of bandwidth as a communications pipe. The bigger the pipe, the more information that flows through it. The smaller the pipe, the less information that can be carried through the pipe. Assume, for example, we have a lawn and we need to water the grass regularly to keep it green and moist. If we have an average-size lawn, the job can be done with the standard 5/8-inch garden hose, the type we can buy in any hardware store. When we turn on the spigot attached to our regular water pipes, a sufficient flow of water comes out of the hose. This is a regulated flow with several control mechanisms in place:

- The diameter of the water pipes is perhaps 3/4 inches, allowing a certain amount of flow through them to start.
- The garden hose is slightly smaller, so the flow from the larger pipe to the smaller-diameter garden hose is restricted, but pressure allows the flow to be constant.
- The spigot also can be used to regulate or to limit its flow to a specific level that's more to our liking.

This is a band-limited pipe that uses several constraints to control the flow of water through the pipe. Enough is allowed through to do the job; any more would probably cause flooding and over-saturation in certain areas. Therefore, the limitations meet our needs without being wasteful.

Now let's assume we want to handle the watering of the Super Dome, if its turf were real. This football field is much larger than the average home lawn, so if we use the tools we have in the home watering scheme, things would be tougher. Imagine trying to water this field with the average 5/8-inch garden hose! This would take forever. Not only would it take forever to get from one end to the other, by the time we got to the opposite end, we would have to start the job all over again. The first end would be parched dry because of the amount of time it takes to get from one end to the other.

This is ineffective. So, to do the job, we must purchase a garden hose with a diameter of six inches. Now we hook this six-inch hose to a spigot that also measures six inches and is connected to a water pipe at least six to eight inches in diameter. The flow of water through this pipe is significantly greater than that of the 5/8-inch garden hose. Thus, the job can be done in a reasonable amount of time.

Bandwidth is similar to this garden hose analogy, as shown in Figure 2-2. *Bandwidth* is the range of frequencies that can be carried across a given transmission channel. If more information is sent, more bandwidth is necessary. Therefore, this is a 3-kHz channel; it has 3 kHz of bandwidth. This is fine because, as we previously saw, all the usable information of a voice-grade conversation is contained in this amount of bandwidth. In actuality, the telephone companies break the available electromagnetic spectrum into slices, each about 4 kHz wide. Then, these 4-kHz slices (called *channels*) are

Figure 2-2
Bandwidth can be compared to a pipe or a hose.

limited with bandpass filters, as shown in Figure 2-3. Consider the spigot analogy, turning the water on faster or slower via the spigot valve. The result is we receive 3 kHz of the available 4-kHz slices.

Other forms of bandwidth requirements exist. For comparative purposes, we can see the differences in capacities used in various forms of bandwidth allocations, as shown in Table 2-1.

MHz (megahertz) is a new term here, which represents millions of frequency changes per second. You can imagine the amount of information carried in a TV signal, where sound, motion, and voice are all on the same channel. Think of how a video signal on a TV station would look if the channel were restricted to carrying only 3 kHz of information. By the time some moving picture was created on the set, the viewer would have lost interest.

Figure 2-3
Bandwidth of 4 kHz

Table 2-1

Summary of Channel Capacities to Carry Different Forms of Information

Service	Bandwidth Allotted
Voice channel	3 kHz
High-fidelity music	15 kHz
CD stereo player	22 kHz
FM radio station	200 kHz
TV channel on CATV	6 MHz
TV channel actually used	4.5 MHz

The frequency spectrum of a TV channel, as shown in Table 2-1, shows a community antenna television (CATV) channel is actually allocated 6 MHz of capacity. Yet, the amount actually used approximately 4.5 MHz. The difference is the band limitation on the channel, much the same as with the voice channel. In this case, the amount of flow is in the millions of cycles per second (a big pipe is needed here). The band-limited channel uses bandpass filters, so a guard band is between the TV channels. In other words, as you watch Channel 3 on your TV set, the filters are placed on the line to prevent frequencies and information from Channels 2 and 4 from overflowing onto Channel 3 (see Figure 2-4). These guard bands are placed on every channel, thereby restricting the 6-MHz channel to only 4.5 MHz of usable information.

The same concept holds true for nearly all the channel capacities used in the telecommunications industry. The available bandwidth is a function of need and cost. You get what you need, but any more is too expensive.

Voices

The human voice is a consolidation of the waves of electrical energy carried across the given channel capacity. Humans generate a combination of amplitude and frequency changes in a continuing flow. If the changes are held constant, then the conversation becomes monotone, highly unacceptable for the average conversation. Indeed, if everything were held constant, the recipient of the information would be lulled to sleep. We use the variations in our voices to reflect deviations in emotion, accentuation, or articulation and emphasis on certain points. Every voice generates a different

Figure 2-4
The bandpass filter separates the channels.

pattern of amplitude and frequency changes. This is what gives every individual a unique and recognizable speech tone.

Interesting to note is the female voice pattern typically generates more changes in frequency than in amplitude. This accounts for the squeaky sound in the female voice. Conversely, the male vocal pattern generates more frequency changes than amplitude shifts. This accounts for the low-pitched, more grainy tones of the male. These are averages; every human is different and the norm can be deviated from at any time. When someone is highly emotional, there are definite shifts from that person's normal voice patterns. The pitch might go up by varying degrees, showing the results of stress or anger.

The telephone links are designed to handle this widely varying pattern of shifts. From time to time, though, the voice pattern might exceed the differences in the allotted bandwidth. Then the frequencies in the voice go above or below the normal range. At this point, the bandpass filters start to remove the excesses. What can result is a pattern of tinny or flattened speech conversations. This can be also heard if someone uses the letters F and S where the frequency ranges on these two sounds might exceed the bandpass ranges; they get flattened.

Other Services

Because the telephone network was built to carry voice, the other services we want to communicate, such as data, facsimile, images, and video must be transmitted within the same constraints as voice calls. The network allows any telephone set to contact any other telephone set across a 3-kHz bandwidth. If you want to communicate anything else, such as data, it must be accommodated on this same 3-kHz bandwidth. This invokes a limitation on the speed of our data communications channel capacities. Although modems can transmit signals more quickly, they must be constrained into the size of the pipe. A video conference transmission also reflects non-real-time motion because of the channel capacities on a dial-up basis.

If you need to move more information across the channels, you have two choices. One option is to dedicate a high-speed line between the two or more ends. However, this approach eliminates the possibility of "any-to-any" connection and requires planning well in advance of communicating with the end points. Leased lines between the points might be underused and could be more expensive.

Another option is to have the bandpass filters moved out to (for example) 8 kHz between the end points. Unfortunately, similar limitations are here. If the switching network in the middle and the receiving end aren't equipped to handle the 8 kHz capacity, our call is then funneled down into the lowest common denominator. We would have to know every location we would be communicating with, losing the benefits of the any-to-any connection. Also, no guarantee exists that the switching systems will route the call over the same path on a switched dial-up connection every time. This would force us back into a 3-kHz channel along the route selected if it's different every time, eliminating the benefits of the wider channel capacity.

Questions

1. What two variables are constantly changing in a voice conversation?
2. How large does the telephone company create a channel? (What is the bandwidth of the actual channel?)
3. After the sounds enters the telephone set, it's converted into its electrical equivalent called what?
4. Female voices produce more of what type of shifts?
5. The telephone line uses how many pairs of wires?
6. The voice operates between what two ranges (high and low)?
7. The human ear, on the other hand, can differentiate subtle changes in sound ranging from what high and low ends?
8. The most common use of the network is built for what type of information?
9. What is the bandwidth of the voice channel?
10. Why is a modem limited to its speeds and throughput?
11. If you were to watch a television show, what bandwidth is being delivered across the cable or the airwaves?
12. What device is responsible for converting the sound into electricity?
13. How do we regulate the bandwidth on a pair of wires? (What are these devices called?)
14. Why can't we just dial up bigger pipe when we want to?
15. Why did the telephone companies limit the bandwidth on their net-

The Telephone Network

After reading this chapter and completing the exercises and questions, you will be able to:

- Explain how the telephone network is laid out
- Discuss the differences between the various office functions used in the hierarchy
- Describe the different names applied to the various carriers in the network
- Describe the basis of the local loop
- Explain the pieces used to connect to the customer location
- Openly recognize the problems associated with the local loop connections and the impairments that can occur
- Recognize the difference in the North American Numbering Plan and discuss the problems being posed now
- Understand why we're running out of numbers today

A *network* is a series of interconnections that form a cohesive and ubiquitous connectivity arrangement when tied together. Whew! That sounds ominous but, to make this a little simpler, let's look at the components of what constitutes the telephone network.

Generally, a network is a series of interconnection points. Over the years, the telephone companies developed the connections throughout the United States and the world so that a level of cost-effective service can be provided to their customers. To build out this connectivity, the telephone companies installed wires to the customer's door, whether the customer is business or residential. The spot where these wires terminate is called the *demarcation point* (demarc) or the minimum point of penetration (MPOP). The position of the demarcation point depends on the legal issues involved. In the early days of the telephone network, the telephone companies owned everything, so they ran the wires to an interface point, and then connected their telephone sets to the wires at the customer's end. This was the cradle-to-grave service that allowed the companies to expand the connections throughout their entire operating areas.

New regulations in North America changed this connection to a point at the entrance to the customer's building. From there, the customers hook up their own equipment, items they purchase from a myriad of other sources. Throughout many parts of the world, where full divestiture has yet to take place, the telephone companies (or PTTs) still own the equipment. Other areas of the world have a hybrid system under which customers might or might not own their equipment. The combinations of this arrangement are almost limitless, depending on the degree of privatization and deregulation. However, the one characteristic common in most of the world to date is the local provider owns the wires from the outside world to the entrance of the customer's building. This is called the *local loop*.

A Topology of Connections Is Used

In the local loop, the topological layout of the wires has traditionally been a single wire pair or multiple pairs of wires strung to the customer's location. This has always been an issue of money. Just how many pairs of wires are needed for the connection of a single line set to the network? The answer (one pair) is obvious. But, for some other types of service, such as digital circuits and connections, the answer is one or more (typically two) pairs. Depending on the customer, the number of wires run to the location has been contingent on the need versus the cost. As a result, the use of a single or dual pair of wires has been the norm. More recently, the local providers have been installing a four-pair (eight-wire) connection to the customer location. This is because the customer (both business and residential) has begun to use voice lines, separate fax lines, and separate data communication hookups. Each of these requires a two-wire interface, so the need for multiple pairs has grown. Installing multiple pairs the first time is far less expensive than installing a single pair of wires every time the customer asks for a new service. Many of the telephone companies are now adding sophistication to the local loop, however, by using a single pair of wires to the consumer's door (business or residential) and providing a xDSL service. For example, a customer can now use Voice over DSL, Data over DSL and Fax over DSL. The xDSL service only requires a single pair of telephone wires.

So, the topology is a dedicated local connection of one or more pairs from the telephone provider to the customer location, which is called a *star configuration*. The telephone company (whether ILEC or CLEC) connection to the customer originates from a centralized point called a *central office* (CO). In a star configuration, all wires home back to a centralized point, the CO.

Once the hundreds or thousands of wire pairs get to the CO, things change. The provider at that point might be using a different topology. Either a star configuration to a hierarchy of other locations in the network layout or a ring can be used. The ring is becoming a far more prevalent method of connection for the local telcos. A *ring* is a circular arrangement that the telco uses to protect the wiring and interconnections. If a cable cut occurs "backhoe fade," the ring is set up with intelligence to recognize that the path is no longer working. Then it will automatically reverse itself and provide the connection in the reverse direction. This redundancy is becoming the norm in the wide and metropolitan networks, but not as prevalent in the local loop (the last mile) because of the cost. Although we might also show the ring as a triangle, it's still a functional and logical ring. This star/ring combination constitutes the bulk of the networking topologies today.

At the local telephone company's (whether ILEC, PTT, or CLEC) office, the wires are terminated in what is called a wire center. The *wire center* is nothing more than a large extension of the customer's hookup. Thousands of hookups come together in this centralized point. From the wire center, a series of spokes is run out to the customer, to other central offices, to higher-level offices in the hierarchy, or to any location desired. The wire center is also called a *frame*; all the wires are connected to the frame.

At this frame, a series of cross-connections is made. These are either connected to other wires that go to other locations or to a switching center where the telephone company's central computer (in older offices around the world, this can be an electromechanical system) resides. This is called the *switch*. Most of the equipment today is a stored-program, common-controlled computer system that just happens to process cross-connections for telephone calls. Remember one fundamental fact: The telephone network was designed to carry analog electrical signals across a pair of wires to re-create a voice conversation at both ends. This network was built to carry voice. Only in the past 30 years have we been transmitting other forms of communication, such as facsimile, data, and video.

The switch makes routing decisions based on some parameter, such as the digits dialed by the customer. As these decisions are being made quickly, a cross-connection is made in logic. This means the switch sets up a logical and physical connection to another set of wires. The connection can be back to the frame, where the wires serve a neighboring pair of wires connected to our next-door neighbor or to another connection that links another central office. The possibilities are only limited by the physical arrangements in the office itself.

Between and among the offices built by the carriers (the local and the long-distance providers) is a set of connections usually laid out in a ring, but also possibly in a star configuration. These are the facilities that carry traffic and they're called *interoffice trunks*. In some COs, these are copper wires; in others, they are fiberoptic wires; and still in others, they may be on radio systems.

Throughout this network, more or fewer connections are installed, depending on the anticipated calling patterns of the user population. Sometimes there are many connections among many offices. At other times, it can be simple and single connections.

Tied all together, then, is a series of local links to the customer locations, through a central office where switching and routing decisions are made, then on out to a myriad of other connections from telephone companies, long-distance suppliers, and other providers. This is the basis of the telephone network.

The Local Loop

The basic model for our interface to the telephone company network is the single-line telephone set covered in Chapter 4. It stands to reason that we need to connect this set to the telephone company CO. The pair of twisted wires running from the telephone company's CO is called the *local loop*. Each subscriber, or customer, is delivered at least one pair of wires per telephone line. As a wireless world is rapidly approaching us, the equivalent of a single pair of wires will exist, even though only air is in between the CO and the customer. More telephone providers are looking at the use of wireless local loop configurations to satisfy growing demand and reduce the cost of provisioning the service. Installing a wireless connection to the consumer is less expensive than digging up the ground and laying wires and cables to the door.

Exceptions to this rule occur in rural areas where the telephone company might share multiple users on a single pair of wires. This is called a *party line,* and again, this is a financial decision. If the number of users demanding telephone service exceeds the number of pairs available, a telco might well offer the service on a party or shared set of wires. Rural parts of America still have some of these party lines. In other parts of the world, these may still be the more common way of conducting business.

The phone company distributes its outside plant, or distribution, to the customer by running large bundles of twisted pairs toward the customer location (Figure 3-1). This is done using feeders, which are composed of 50 to over 3,000 pairs of wires.

The feeders are run to splice points or breakout points called *manholes*[1] or *handholes.* At this point, the splicing of two reels of cable takes place, assuming the cable on a single reel wasn't sufficient. A lateral distribution can also take place here. *Lateral distribution* is the breakout of a number of pairs to run in a different direction. The lateral distribution or branch feeder is then strung to various customer locations. The end of the pair to the final customer location is called the *customer pair* or *station drop.*

In this outside plant—from the CO to the customer location—90 percent of all problems occur. This isn't to imply the telco is doing a lousy job of delivering service to the customer. These cables are exposed more to cable cuts because of construction (commonly called *backhoe fade*), flooding at the splice locations, rodent damage, and many other risks.

In the traditional analog dial-up telephone network, each pair of the local loop is designed to carry a single telephone call to service voice conversations. This is a proven technology that works for the most part and continues to get better as the technologies advance. The cables can be delivered via a telephone pole (aerial distribution), buried conduit (underground feed), or direct buried cables. Either way, the service is one with which we are familiar and feel comfortable. What was just described is the connection at the local portion of the network. From there, the local connectivity must

---

[1] The reference to a manhole is that a human can actually climb down into the hole where the telephone wires are located. They may have to pump out these manholes due to rain and water accumulation so that they can work in the hole and cross connect the wiring. Conversely, a hand hole only allows the individual to place the hands inside the hole. A whole body will not fit!

Figure 3-1
The local loop

be extended out to other locations in and around a metropolitan area or across the country. The connections to other types of offices are then required.

The Network Hierarchy (Pre-1984)

Prior to 1984, most of the network was owned by AT&T and its local Bell Operating Companies (BOCs). It evolved through a series of interconnections based on volumes of calls and growth. A layered hierarchy of office connections was designed around a five-level architecture. Each of these layers was designed around the concept of call completion. The offices are connected together with wires of various types, called *trunks*. These trunks can be twisted pairs of wire, coaxial cables (like the CATV wire), radio (such as microwave), or fiber optics. The trunks vary in their capacities, but generally high-usage trunks are used to connect between offices. Figure 3-2 shows the hierarchy prior to the divestiture of AT&T, with the five levels evident.

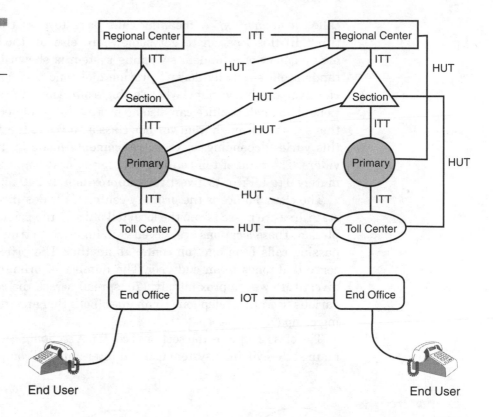

Figure 3-2
Network hierarchy
pre-1984

The class 5 office is the local exchange or end office. It delivers dial tone to the customer. The *end office*, also called a branch exchange, is the closest connection to the end user. Think of a tree: All the activity takes place at the ends of the branches and the customers are the leaves hanging off the branches. Calls between exchanges in a geographical area are connected by direct trunks between two end offices, which are called interoffice trunks. Over 19,000 end offices in the United States alone provide basic dial tone services.[2]

The class 4 office is the toll center. A call going between two end offices not connected together is routed to the class 4 office. The toll center is also used as the connection to the long-distance network for calls where added costs are incurred when a connection is made. This toll center may also be

---

[2]Prior to the 1984 divestiture, there were almost 66,000 end offices in the United States. The equipment is smaller and can handle more connections now, so the providers have been able to consolidate into fewer locations, giving them the opportunity to save money and real estate.

called a *tandem office,* meaning calls have to pass through (or tandem through) this location to get somewhere else on the network. A basic arrangement of a tandem switching system is shown in Figure 3-3. The tandem office usually doesn't provide dial tone services to the end user. However, this is a variable where a single office might provide various functions. The tandem office can also be just a *toll*—a connecting arrangement that's a pass-through from various class 5 offices to the toll centers. Again, this varies depending on the arrangements made by the telephone providers. The ratio of toll centers that serve local long distance is approximately 9 to 1. Prior to divestiture, approximately 940 toll centers existed.

The class 3 office is the primary center. Calls destined within the same state area are passed from the local toll office to the primary center for completion. These locations are served with high-usage trunks used strictly for passing calls from one toll center to another. The primary centers never serve dial tones to an end user. The number of primary centers prior to divestiture was approximately 170, spread across the country among the various operating telephone companies (both Bell and independent operating companies).

The class 2 office is the sectional center. A *sectional center* is typically the main state switching system used for interstate toll connections designated

Figure 3-3
A tandem (class 4)
office arrangement

for the processing of long-distance calls from section to section. Approximately 50+ sectional centers existed before the divestiture of the Bell System. These offices didn't serve any end users, but would serve between primary centers around the country. The class 1 office is the regional center and ten regional centers existed across the country. The task of each center was the final setup of calls on a region-by-region basis. However, the regional centers constituted one of the most sophisticated computer systems in the world. The regional centers continually updated each other regarding the status of every circuit in the network. These centers were required to reroute traffic around trouble spots (for example, failed equipment or circuits) and to keep each other informed at all times. As mentioned, this was all prior to the divestiture of the local BOC by AT&T.

The Network Hierarchy (Post-1984)

After 1984 the network took a dramatic turn, with the separation of the BOCs from AT&T. Many users screamed that things would fall apart and service would be affected, but none of this came true. This doesn't mean a lot of confusion didn't occur, because it did. Things kept humming along for the most part, though, and calls were completed through this series of interconnecting points called the *network*.

The hierarchy of the network shown in Figure 3-4 introduced a new set of terms and connections. The BOCs were classified the same way as independent telephone companies. They are all called local exchange carriers (LECs) and now Incumbent Local Exchange Carriers (ILECs). The seven spin-off companies formed because the divestiture became Regional Bell Holding Companies (RBHCs), which had regulated arms called the Regional Bell Operating Companies (RBOCs). Each RBOC had the Bell Operating Companies in its geographical area. Additionally, the RBHCs also had an unregulated side of the business, where they could enter into new ventures (such as equipment sales, finance, real estate, and so forth).

Equal access, or the capability of every interexchange carrier (IEC or IXC) to connect to the BOC for long-distance service, became a reality. Equal access was designed to allow the same access to other long-distance competitors that AT&T had always enjoyed prior to divestiture. Prior to divestiture, a customer attempting to use an alternative long-distance supplier would have to dial a seven- or ten-digit telephone number to get to this supplier's switch. Then, when this connection was completed, a computer

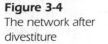

Figure 3-4
The network after
divestiture

would answer the call and place a tone on the line. From there, the caller would have to enter a seven- to eleven-digit authorization code. This code identified the caller by telephone number, caller name and address, and billing arrangements. Only after the computer (switch) verified this information, would it then send dial tone to the caller's ear. The caller would then have to dial the ten-digit telephone number of the requested party. This could involve lengthy and frustrating call set-up times—especially when the number called was busy.

Users chose not to use these alternative carriers because of the time and the number of digits required and the frustration of attempts to call busy numbers. That is, unless the organization forced the user to dial across the carriers' networks. The reason for all the digits was simple. The telephone company didn't pass on the caller information to the alternate carrier (MCI, Sprint, ITT, and so forth) that it passed to AT&T. Thus, the choice of many callers was AT&T because the process was simpler. Now the caller information is passed on in an equal basis, so the access is equal.

However, some of the independents and BOCs who haven't yet upgraded their offices don't connect to these IECs. These are called *nonconforming end offices*. The *point of presence* (POP) is the point where the IEC and the LEC are interconnected. This usually refers to the offices of AT&T, MCI,

Sprint, and other carriers. This name changed to point of interface (POI) as opposed to POP. The main reason is the acronym POP implies a switching system is at that location, which isn't always true. The *point of interface* is where the two parties—Bell or independent—and the interexchange carrier connect. This can be a closet in a basement or hotel, connected to a dedicated trunk to another part of the country. All of this, however, should be transparent to the end user.

The Public-Switched Network

The U.S. public-switched network has always been the largest and the best in the world.[3] Over the years, the network has penetrated to even the most remote locations around the country. Primary call-carrying capacity in the United States is through the public-switched network. Because this is the environment that AT&T and the BOCs built, we still hear people refer to it as the Bell System. However, as we've already seen, significant changes have taken place to change that environment.

The public network allows access to the end office, connects through the long-distance network, and delivers to the end point. This makes the cycle complete. Many companies use the switched network exclusively; others have created variations depending on need, finances, and size. The goal of the network hierarchies is to complete the call in the least amount of time and over the shortest route possible. The network is dynamic enough, however, to pass the call along longer routes through the hierarchy to complete the call in the first attempt wherever possible.

The North American Numbering Plan

The network numbering plan was designed to enable the quick and discreet connection to any phone in the country. The North American numbering plan (NANP), as it is called, works on a series of ten numbers as shown in Table 3-1.

---

[3] Roughly 95% of the US population has phone service implying that the penetration is ubiquitous.

Table 3-1

The North
American
Numbering Plan
as It Evolved

Timing	Area Code	Central Office Code	Station Subscriber Number
Original	N 0/1 X	N N X	X X X X
Pre-1995	N 0/1 X	N X X	X X X X
Post-1995	N X X	N X X	X X X X

The Area Code

Note, some changes have occurred in this numbering plan. When this plan was originally formulated, the telephone numbers were divided into three sets of digits. The first was a three-digit area code or numbering plan assignment (NPA). This started with a digit from 2 to 9 in the first slot of the sequence. In the second slot, the number was set as 0 or 1. In the third slot, it could be any digit from 1 to 0 (with 0 representing 10). The reasons behind this sequence were clever. For example, the first digit didn't use a 0 or 1 because these digits were used for access to operators (0) or operator services such as credit card calling, and so forth. The 1 was used to send a significant digit to the local switching office indicating the call was long distance; this enabled the switch to immediately start setting up a toll connection immediately to the toll center or tandem office. Thus, the exclusion of 0 and 1 in the first digit of the area code facilitated the quicker call setup. In the second slot, the digit was only a 1 or 0. This was used by the switching office equipment in a screening mode. As soon as the system sampled the second digit and saw a 0 or 1, it knew this three-digit sequence was an area code. The third slot was any digit; having no special significance, it was processed normally. Back in the early 1960s, we recognized we were running out of area codes, given that only 160 were available ($8 \times 2 \times 10 = 160$). In reality, only 152 were allowed for use by the various states because certain ones were allotted for special services (the N11 area codes, for example, 211, 311, 411, and so forth, were always reserved). Close administration of the area code assignments kept this scheme working until 1995, when the inevitable occurred. From the outset, the use of the entire numbering plan was limited, so it had to grow. In 1995, the area codes were expanded by allowing any digit in the center slot of the three-digit sequence. This expansion created 640 new area codes for the NANP. The use of these area codes has been so dramatic; there's speculation that even though we got a fourfold increase, these will be depleted by 2010 or sooner! (New estimates are we could be out of area codes again by 2005.) Our current rate of consumption of telephone numbers is alarming. When we think back to the beginning days of the networks, customers had a single number that sufficed. Now, the average household has three or more numbers (a second line for fax, a third line for modem, a fourth line for teens, separate number for cell phones, and so forth). We are facing a worldwide numbering shortage. Add to this number of lines, the use of cellular phones, pagers, and other numbers are quickly gobbling up all the numbers available to us.

The Exchange Code

Following the area code is another three-digit sequence called the *exchange code,* which is a central office designator that lists the possible number of central office codes that can be used in each area code. The exchange code originally was set up in the sequence NNX, meaning the first and second numbers used the digits 2 through 9, for the same reasons as in the area code. The digits 1 and 0 were reserved for operator and long-distance access, and the 0/1 exclusion in the exchange code prevented this three-digit number from being confused with an area code. In the third number slot of the exchange code, any digit could be used. Clearly the greatest limitation in the exchange codes was we would run out. With NNX, we have 640 possible exchange numbers to use ($8 \times 8 \times 10 = 640$), but these were used quickly.

In the late 1960s, we began planning the use of an exchange code-numbering plan that changed the sequence to NXX, expanding the number of exchange codes in each of the area codes to 800. This added some relief to the numbering plan. When using the NXX sequence, though, the need arose for a forced 1 in advance of the 10-digit telephone number, so the call screening and number interpretation in a switch wouldn't get confused. This met with some resistance, but ultimately, customers got used to the idea. The first two locations to use this revised numbering plan were Los Angeles and New York City early in 1971.

The Subscriber Extension

The last sequence in the numbering plan is the subscriber extension number. This is a four-digit sequence that can use any digit in all of the slots, allotting 10,000 customer telephone numbers in each of the exchange codes.

Because the four-digit sequence can be composed of any numbers, the intent is to give every subscriber his or her own unique telephone number. This hasn't changed yet, although the possibility that we can still run out of numbers always exists. Therefore, two ideas have been bandied around: add two, three, or four more digits to the end of the telephone number or add one or two more digits to the area code or exchange code.

In either method, users will be asked to dial more digits, an idea that's never popular, but might become a necessity. However, this is far more complicated than just adding a few more digits here and there. The whole world will be impacted by any such decision, and the length of time required to implement such a global change will be extraordinary.

Currently in North America, several new area and exchange codes have been installed where only one existed. This forces users in the area to dial 11 digits (1 plus the 10-digit telephone number) for local, as well as long-distance, calls. This plan has met quite a bit of resistance, because people don't like to dial that many digits and they have trouble remembering that many numbers. Regardless of their feelings on the subject, though, there aren't a lot of choices.

Private Networks

Many companies, depending on their size and need, create or build their own networks. These networks are usually justified on the basis of cost, availability of lines and facilities, and special need. Often these networks employ a mix of technologies, such as private microwave, satellite communications, fiber optics, and infrared transmission. The initial and ongoing costs of private ownership can be quite high (Figure 3-5). Because the costs for a private network must be borne by the end user, often the telecommunications department managers are under pressure to cross-subsidize the costs in other ways. Many companies with private networks are subjected to criticisms from end users that the costs are higher than those of the public-switched network. Individual sites or departments, therefore, begin reducing their own use of the private facilities. This increases the burden on remaining users, who then foot the bill for lightly used networks.

Still others who have built their own networks have stated they are amassing huge savings. When placed in a position of defending their networks, they can produce statistics of the savings reaped on a company-wide basis. If, however, they have a problem with underutilization, they can sell off some of their excess capacity.

Figure 3-5
The private network

This gives these organizations a little breathing room. Collections, maintenance, and administration costs tend to increase when reselling takes place. No single best answer exists here; each organization must look at its needs, availability, costs, and services before deciding which network to use.

Hybrid Networks

Some companies must wrestle with the decision of whether to use a private or a public-switched network. This decision isn't an easy one because often the numbers don't play out well. The return on the investment just won't be there.

As a result, these organizations use a mix of services based on both private and public networks (Figure 3-6). The high-end usage services (heavy volumes between two or more major company locations) are connected via private facilities; the lower-volume locations use the switched network. This usually works out better financially for the organization because the costs can be fully justified on a location-by-location basis. Pressure to install private-line facilities comes from the integration of voice, data, video,

Figure 3-6
The hybrid network

graphics, and facsimile transmissions. Only by combining these services across common circuitry can many organizations realize a true savings.

Local Access and Transport Areas (LATAs)

Local access and transport areas (LATAs) is a term introduced with the divestiture agreement in 1984. One of the problems facing the court system was dealing with the long-distance versus local calling areas. It was a revenue-sharing concern more than anything else. AT&T forced the issue by demanding some form of revenue sharing be put in place, so a single LEC wouldn't have the option of handling all calls and cutting out the IECs.

To solve this problem, an agreement was reached that stated the LECs would still maintain a monopoly on local dial tone and local calling. They would be restricted from carrying long-distance traffic, which would fall under the domain of the IECs. Many states cover large geographical areas, however, and calling from one end to another would be considered long distance. The country was broken down into 195 separate bounded areas for local calling (some local tolls are allowed) based on the density of population in each area. This again was financially motivated. The interconnection between two LATAs would be done by the IECs. A completely new set of acronyms emerged because of the divestiture agreement, of which LATA is only one. To complicate things even more, four types of calling are under the LATA concept:

- Intrastate-Intra-LATA belongs to the LECs
- Intrastate-Inter-LATA belongs to the IECs
- Interstate-Inter-LATA belongs to the IECs
- Interstate-Intra-LATA can be either/or, but was originally given to the LEC

The result of this is a confused public and, sometimes, confusing tariffs. For example, a call from Philadelphia to Los Angeles can be carried on the IEC network for as little as $0.10 per minute, yet a call from Philadelphia to Wilmington can cost as much as $0.40 per minute. The difference here is the 3,000-mile call is regulated on the long-distance basis and FCC jurisdiction. However, the 29-mile call between Philadelphia and Delaware is regulated by BOC tariff and the PUCs. These anomalies will change and are doing so now, but this is the confusion that can crop up when various players are trying to protect their interests.

After the Telecommunications Act of 1996 in the United States, this LATA boundary began to erode quickly. The local telephone companies and Competitive Local Exchange Carriers (CLECs) are all extending their reach in the local areas. At the same time, the IECs are offering services intrastate and intra-LATA. Many of the IECs are registered as CLECs now, offering a variety of services that, heretofore, were unavailable from the single source.

Wiring Connections: Hooking Things Up

The telco uses a variety of connections to bring the service to the customer locations. The typical connection is the two-wire service we keep discussing. This two-wire interface to the network is terminated in a demarcation point, as required by law. The *demarc* is the point of least penetration into the customer's premises, typically within 12 inches of where the telco cable comes up into the building. Normally, telco terminates in a block; this can be the standard modular block for a single-line telephone. If the customer has multiple lines, telco terminates in a 66 block or an RJ-21X. These are fancy names for their termination points. The typical modular connector uses an RJ-11C for telephones connected to a two-pair interface (not to be confused with the two wires) or an RJ-45X as a four-pair interface for both voice and data. Another version of connector for digital service is an eight-conductor (four-pair) called the RJ-48X.

When a telco brings in a digital circuit, it terminates the four-wire circuit into a newer RJ-68 or a smart jack. There's no major mystique in any of these connectors. The number is strictly a "uniform service order code (USOC)," so the telco can keep it all straight. When ordering a circuit, however, the telco asks how you want it terminated. The rule of thumb in a multiline environment is to use the RJ-21X (which is a 66 block with an amphenol connector on it). Sounds complex, doesn't it? A single line terminates in an RJ-11C or RJ-12.

Types of Communications

The next area is the directional nature of your communications channel. Three basic forms of communications channels can be selected. These are as follows:

One-Way (Simplex)

This is a one way and only one way service. You can use it either to transmit or to receive. This isn't a common channel for telephony (voice) because the occasions when we speak and everyone else only listens are rare. Feedback, one of the capabilities we prize in our communications, would be eliminated in a one-way conversation. Broadcast television is an example of simplex communications.

Two-Way Alternating (Half Duplex)

This is the normal channel we use in a conversation. We speak to a listener, and then we listen while someone else speaks. The telephone conversations we engage in are normally half duplex. Although the line is capable of handling a transmission in each direction, the human brain can't deal well with simultaneous transmit and receive.

Two-Way Simultaneous (Duplex or Full Duplex)

This is used in data communications, where a device can be sending to a computer and receiving from the computer at the same time. The direction of the information can be at differing speeds, such as 1,200 bits/s toward the computer from the keyboard (humans cannot type much faster than that) and 9,600 bits/s from the computer. This can also be done on a conversational path, when two people try to overtalk each other.

Equipment

Equipment in the telephony and telecommunications business is highly varied and complex. The mix of goods and services is as large as the human imagination, although the standard types are the ones that constitute the end points on the network. The computerization of our equipment over the years has led to significant variations and also to improvements. The devices that hook up to the network are covered in various other chapters, but a summary of some of these connections and their functions in the network gives the following list:

- The single line set
- The multiline set (called a key set)
- The PBX (private branch exchange)
- The modem (data communications device)
- The multiplexer (allows more users on a single line)
- ACD (automatic call distributor)
- VMS (voice mail system)
- AA (automated attendant)
- Radio systems
- Cellular telephones

- Facsimile machines
- Centrex (central office exchange)

This is a sampling of the types of equipment and services you encounter in dealing with vendors in this business.

Questions

1. How many levels were originally used in the network heirarchy?
2. What portions of the network remained with the Bell Operating Companies after the breakup of the telephone network?
3. How many regional offices were used across North America in the beginning?
4. What is the name given to the seven companies that were spun off from the AT&T organization?
5. What was the name given to the parent companies of the Bell telephone companies after the divestiture agreement?
6. What is the name of the wiring that the telco brings to the consumer's door?
7. What do we call the cable cuts that occur on the wiring running from the CO to the customer?
8. How many digits were used in the North American Numbering Plan? How are they broken down?
9. Name the places that are used to splice cables together when the telco is working toward the customer door.

   a.

   b.

10. How many telephone area codes do we now have?
11. When is it expected that we will run out of phone numbers?
12. What do they call the local point at the customer's door? When they refer to the least point of penetration, what do they call it?
13. How did the competitors gain access to the customer for long distance?
14. What were the factors leading up to the passage of Equal Access?

15. What is the name given to the local telephone companies after the breakup?

16. How many variations of LATA configurations exist? Name them.

17. When a company uses a combination of private and public networks, it is called what?

18. What are three ways we can connect a customer to the telco using the local loop?

19. What are the three ways we describe the way communications take place?

20. How many pairs of wires are typically being installed at the customer's door by the telcos today?

The Telephone Set

After reading this chapter and completing the questions, you will be able to:

- Explain how the telephone set works
- Name the different components inside the telephone set
- Describe how we initiate a call in the network
- Discuss the way a set creates the connection to the telephone company
- Explain why the Telephone Companies want to replace the older telephone sets
- Describe what is meant by Tip and Ring
- Describe why the telephone company wants to complete the call on the first attempt whenever possible

Most people take the telephone set for granted. How can this device that we have known and used since we were old enough to stand up be worth mentioning? Why should we even care? This attitude is not uncommon. Since the early days of the telephone network installation, users have accepted the device as the norm with no real concern. We had the device, and all we had to do was pick it up and use it. It always worked!

For the most part, this is true. However, from time to time telephones do break, and when they do, we feel lost. We do not have the foggiest idea of what went wrong or what to do to fix it. Yet the mystique is not just a carryover from the good old days when the telephone set was sturdy, dependable, and reliable. It seems that we were always told, prior to divestiture, that we were not allowed even to take this set apart. Because we did not own it, we were not allowed to tinker with it. The poor user who might have taken the set apart and not known how to reassemble the set would rue the day that he or she had to call the local telephone company and admit to committing the worst of all possible telephone crimes. Users would conjure up a vision of being put away for life, or, worse yet, losing one's privileges to use the telephone network. The telco would turn off our dial tone, take the set away, and leave us without a means of communicating. How awful!

This scenario might sound far-fetched to many novices in the industry, but surely the old-timers around can remember the stories well. The authors (not to imply that they are old-timers; that's a matter of mind) have heard of many similar cases. One story goes like this:

Several years ago, a farmer in St. Louis, Missouri wanted to know just what was inside the telephone set. So one night he decided to check it out for himself. Family members, realizing his plans, recognized that this was a major problem. They knew from the local telco that you were not allowed to open the cover of the set. To do so would violate all warranty and utility commission rules. They couldn't bear the thought of not having a telephone in their household. They begged and pleaded with the farmer to let it go, not to fall prey to the mystique of the set.

Unfortunately, the farmer would not be daunted by fear, uncertainty, and doubt. The decision was made. As a means of acquiescing to his family, he agreed to do his investigating after dark, when no one could see from outdoors. That night the farmer covered all of the windows of the farmhouse with blankets and proceeded to quench his thirst for knowledge about the telephone set. As he opened the set, he found a nest of wires running from here to there. There was no magic to be found in that. Not to be dissuaded, he quickly screwed the set back together and then proceeded to unscrew the mouthpiece from the handset. Alas, when he untwisted the mouthpiece, it came off the handset. When the set came apart, a number of small black particles fell out of the mouthpiece and rolled around on the floor. Before the farmer was able to catch these little black pellets, they rolled down between the floorboards. Back then the floorboards were installed with spacers in them, leaving large cracks between the boards. Well, as one might imagine, these pieces of whatever-they-were fell through the floorboards and were lost forever. Now the farmer was in a spot. What could they have been? Why were they inside the telephone set and why were they loose? Regardless of the answer, another thought loomed up in the farmer's mind. The dreaded thought of having to call the local telco and ask them to send someone out to fix the set wrought fear in the deepest crevices of the farmer's mind. How would he explain that he was merely inquisitive? What would they do? Would he lose his telephone privileges? Would they take away his dial tone and telephone set? For how long?

Being a quick study, the farmer recognized that the pellets, whatever they were, resembled something he had seen before. Aha! He remembered that this stuff looked just like gunpowder. The problem was solved. He would merely repack the mouthpiece of his set with the granules of gunpowder and be done with it. So he did. We heard that his next phone call was a real blast!

All kidding aside, this scenario is probably unfounded. However, certain issues were brought up here to make us stop and think. When AT&T and its Bell Operating Companies (BOCs) installed and controlled the original telephone network under its monopoly (the independents were not as severe in their treatment), we were left with the fear that if we tinkered with the telephone set and broke it, we would lose our phone privileges. Can you imagine that? Of course, since the breakup of the Bell System, things have changed considerably. The set now belongs to the end user. We can do anything we want with it or to it. If we break it, we buy a new one. Simple?

Despite this silly illustration, there must be some significance to just what this set is all about.

The Function of the Telephone Set

Chapter 2 covered the characteristics of voice. We stated that the voice can create sound wave changes at a rate ranging from 100 to 5,000 times per second, and those amplitudes and frequencies are constantly changing. From this understanding of how the human voice works, we then must understand that the network was built to carry voice. How then does the voice get put onto a telephone company network and carried to the other end of the line? The sound waves must travel down the one pair of wires that the telephone company has provided. The challenge is to take sound and convert it into something that the telephone network deals with: electricity. Yes, electricity is what runs across copper wires. The telephone company delivers a pair of copper wires to our door and then attaches a telephone set to those wires. So, the function of the telephone set is to con-

Figure 4-1
The telephone set
converts sound into
electricity.

vert sound into electricity. It will therefore act as a change agent (see Figure 4-1).

Conversely, when a voice is sent through the wires as electricity, the process must be reversed at the receiving end. Therefore, the telephone set must also function to convert this electricity back into sound. The change process must work in two ways. The "from" and "to" functions are what the set must accomplish. Figure 4-2 is a representation of the reverse process.

But wait, there's more. On the top of the telephone set, two little buttons are spring-loaded. They must have a function too. The *switch hook*, as these buttons are called, is a mechanism that originates and finalizes calls. When you press the springy-dingies on the top of the set, the dial tone goes away. If you lift the handset off the base of the telephone, you hear the dial tone (this is called going off hook). So, these buttons request and relinquish the dial tone from the telephone company.

Figure 4-2
The set also converts
electricity back into
sound.

By now, you will notice that the telephone is a complex piece of equipment. The invention of Alexander Graham Bell has come a long way from its founding. Nevertheless, functionally it still does the same thing. The first telephone sets had no dial pads; all calls were handled by a telephone company operator. In order to make a call, you would have to "flash" the operator and request the called party.

The next evolution was a crank phone. You lifted the handset and turned a mechanical crank, which sent a ringing voltage down to the telephone company operator (Figure 4-3). The operator still had to place the call, but the crank was a means of signaling the operator when you wanted service.

Other variations appeared as time went on. This was inefficient, so the manual call placement was eventually replaced with the rotary telephone set. Later came the Touch-Tone set, which was designed to improve efficiency and speed up the process. Still later, the digital telset created a whole new wave of interfaces to the network. Figure 4-4 shows a group of variations on the telephone set. The set's evolution has added features and functions, but the primary function is still the same after these 124 years.

So, let's back up a little and look at the pieces of a telephone set, at least generically. The telephone set consists of multiple pieces, each of which serves at least one function. Without one or more of the pieces, communication might not take place. They are all intertwined to work together so that we have constant service at any time.

Figure 4-3
The crank phone allowed the user to generate a signal to the operator by turning the crank.

Figure 4-4
A potpourri of
telephones has
evolved.

Figure 4-4
A potpourri of
telephones has
evolved.

The Pieces

The telephone set is made up of the following major components.

The Base

All of the components are either housed inside or attached to the base (see Figure 4-5). It is typically a plastic or space-age healed plastic case that will

Figure 4-5
The base of the set
houses a far more
complex system.

withstand many impacts, such as being dropped from a table or desk. This case protects the inner workings and other components from exposure to the most dangerous part of a telephone network: humans. We tend to spill things on the set. We also drop it or knock it over. When we are frustrated on the phone, we slam it down or beat it on the desk, taking out our anger and irritation on this device that is always supposed to work. Without the casing to protect the telephone, we would never have service. This casing also protects the inside of the phone from dust and other elements floating around in the air.

The Handset

The handset (see Figure 4-6) houses two separate components, the transmitter and the receiver. The handset is ergonomically designed to fit the distance from the mouth to the ear. The transmitter is located at the bottom portion of the handset, so that it is positioned in front of the mouth when we hold the handset to our face. The receiver is located at the top of the handset so that it rests against our outer ear when we hold the handset to our face. The first handsets consisted only of an ear mechanism; the transmitter was a stationary mount on the front of the base (see Figure 4-7).

Figure 4-6
The handset houses the transmitter and receiver.

Receiver

Transmitter

Now we move to the inner pieces of the handset. Figure 4-8 shows the handset with the transmitter and receiver indicated. Note that the wires also connect the pieces. Two wires run from the earpiece and two wires run from the mouthpiece. Remember that the telephone is going to convert sound into electricity. The wires carry the electricity created at the mouthpiece to the telephone set. The second set of wires carries electricity from the telephone set to the earpiece. So, the handset contains a four-wire circuit: two wires for the transmitter and two wires for the receiver. Each side of the function has its own two-wire electrical circuit at this point. Modern-day functions of the following parts are still the same. Although newer solid-state components have replaced the pieces, they perform the same functions as the pieces described in the following paragraphs.

The Transmitter

As mentioned in the discussion about the farmer wanting to see the inside of the telephone set, the transmitter houses some very sophisticated components. The first portion of the transmitter houses a diaphragm just under the outer casing of the mouthpiece. The diaphragm is a very sensitive membrane that will vibrate with air pressure changes. When we speak into the mouthpiece of the telephone set, we are really creating air pressure changes with our vocal cords. The sound pressure we create causes air pressure changes that move at the same frequency as the changes we produce by vibrating our vocal chords. The pressure changes cause the membrane on the diaphragm to move back and forth at the same frequency (see Figure 4-9).

Behind the diaphragm are loosely packed carbon particles (the black pellets the farmer dropped). When the diaphragm moves back and forth, it causes the carbon particles to move back and forth. This produces an electrical resistance to the charge that occurs at the same frequency and amplitude as the sound pressure changes created by the voice. The result is an analog sine wave that is directly (mostly) proportional to the frequency and amplitude of the voice, or the electrical equivalent of sound. This electrical energy is carried away from the transmitter across the wires behind the mouthpiece.

Figure 4-9
The transmitter has a diaphragm and loosely packed carbon particles that create the electricity.

Diaphragm

Carbon Particles

The resistance also protects us from creating a signal that is too strong for the rest of the components and network elements. If we did not restrict the flow of the energy, we could cause damage to equipment, not to mention what we could do to your eardrums. What? . . . What? . . . What?

The Receiver

The receiver is shown in Figure 4-10. When voice or other telecommunication in the form of electrical energy is being transmitted to us from the far end (the other party on the phone call), the network carries this electricity to the telephone set. The wires behind the receiver are run up to an electromagnet that is mounted inside the receiver portion of the handset. The electromagnet is attached to a diaphragm similar to that in the mouthpiece. The electricity comes through the wires to the magnet, and the magnet vibrates at the same frequency as the received energy. As the magnet vibrates, it causes the membrane on the diaphragm to move back and forth. This back-and-forth motion causes air pressure changes (vibrations) that are at the same frequency as the transmitted energy. As the air pressure changes occur, they cause the air waves to bounce off the inner eardrum, which is what produces sound to our ears. See Figure 4-11 for the eardrum comparison.

Figure 4-10
The receiver uses an electromagnet to change the electricity back into air pressure.

Figure 4-11
The eardrum receives air pressure and converts it into sound.

The transmitter and receiver complete the conversion of sound to electricity and electricity back to sound. We often refer to the handset functions as E&M, or the ear-and-mouth communications process. The *E* represents the direction of flow to the ear or to the receiver, and the *M* represents the direction of energy from the mouth or the transmitter.

The Connector or the Handset Cord

Coming from the handset and proceeding to the base of the telset is a coiled wire. It doesn't have to be coiled; that just makes it easier to manage. Inside the curly wire are four wires: two from the transmitter and the receiver, respectively. The modern sets use a connector that is called an RJ-11C. This is the four-wire connector that has a little spring-loaded clip on it to plug and unplug the connector into the female receptacle. The cord is double-ended with male RJ-11C connectors. This is also a matter of convenience. Because the cords and the connectors are the most likely pieces to wear out, it makes sense to use a plug-and-play module. Older versions of this cord used a screw-down version (called a spade lug), but this required that the telephone set be opened up to get at the screw mounts. Remember, this was an area into which we were not allowed.

A funny thing happens along this connector cord, however. When it gets to the base of the telephone set, it is plugged into the female version of the RJ-11. But inside this jack, a hybrid arrangement takes place. One of the transmitter and one of the receiver wires are connected to each other (see Figure 4-12). The other two wires that continue into the set are covered in the next section. The important thing here is to understand why the transmitter wire gets connected to the receiver wire. This creates a loopback arrangement of sorts. The transmitted sound is looped right back to the ear. We can hear everything we say in the conversation because the energy is transmitted back to the earpiece. You are probably asking yourself why this is done. The process produces what is called *side tone*. This side tone is a means of letting us know that an electrical connection across the network still exists. When you speak into a telephone during a conversation and you hear yourself, you recognize that there is still a connection to the distant end. You can also regulate your volume when you hear yourself speak. When you speak into the set and hear nothing or the sound is dead, you recognize that no one is out there—in other words, that you have been cut off. This is part of your basic training in telephone usage. Although no one ever explained this to you, it has been learned through experience.

Figure 4-12
As the four wires
enter the set, they
go into a hybrid
arrangement.

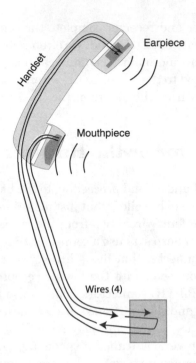

Earpiece

Handset

Mouthpiece

Wires (4)

The Inside of the Telephone

Once the wires are run from the handset to the base of the telephone, two wires go into the set. Actually, these wires meet up with a whole network of cross-connects (connections from place to place) inside the set, but we are concerned with the two wires. As shown in Figure 4-13, one of the wires, the transmitter wire, is connected inside the set to the dial pad (whether rotary or tone dial). This is used as an addressing mechanism. The telephone network uses a decimal numbering system in the form of a sequence of digits that we dial to the called party. The dial pad is used to send these digits out to the telephone company for delivery to the called party. This wire connected to the dial pad is also cross-connected to the switchhook (the spring-loaded buttons). The same wire is used to connect to another jack (RJ-11, RJ-12, or other), which is connected in turn to the outside world.

The second wire from the handset cord is connected through the network of wires to a ringer. The ringer can be in the form of a bell or a turkey warbler (electronic ringer), but the function is what is important here. The ringer is a receiver wire function. It is used to alert you that someone wants

Figure 4-13
The transmitter wire is connected to the dial pad and the switchhook. The receiver wire connects to the ringer.

to speak to you. If you do not have a ringer, you'd have to pick up the handset every now and then and listen to know whether someone is on the line. This would be inconvenient for you, not to mention for the caller, who would never know whether you would pick up the handset. Callers would be in limbo forever. So the ringer is a crucial component of the set and the process.

The Switchhook

Already mentioned and equally important is the *switchhook* function. This is the portion of the set that actually gets the dial tone from the telephone company or, when we are through with the call, gives the dial tone back. In reality, what happens is that an electrical wiring circuit is physically connected from the telephone company office to our telephone set. This circuit gives us access to the services offered by the telephone company, mainly the dial tone and the ability to make and receive calls. Under normal conditions, we do not have a dial tone at our set. This is a service that we must request.

To request the service, we lift the handset off the switchhook. When we do this, the little buttons pop up. At the same time, they "make" the circuit by adding a resistance across the wires. The telephone company equipment constantly monitors all of its connections to end users. When the central office computer (now they are computers) sees a change in the resistance across the wires, it recognizes this as a request for a dial tone. Actually, the telco installs a battery on the local loop. The battery current flows down the receive wire and gets stopped at the handset where the circuit is in the "break" mode. When we go off hook and "make," we have actually connected the transmit and receive wires together. This creates a continual loop as the battery current flows from the telco to the handset and then gets looped right back to the central office (CO). This is how the CO recognizes the change in the state of the telephone set. We call this a loop start circuit.

After we create the loop, the telco starts the process by returning the dial tone. If the dial tone is available, it will be provided immediately. In the time it takes us to go off hook and bring the handset up to our ear, the dial tone is there. Actually, it gets there much faster than that if everything is functioning properly.

As we use the line and make calls, we will use the other components in the telephone set, but the central office computer will monitor the line (wires) for the time when we are finished with our calls. When we disconnect, we place the handset back into the cradle. This pushes the spring-loaded buttons back down and breaks the circuit. The central office computer sees this change on the wires and recognizes that we are done. Therefore, the central office computer takes the dial tone away from us and provides it to other users who require it. Then the process starts all over again. The phone company uses a 10:1 ratio of users to dial tone. For every ten users, the company knows that statistically only one user requires service.

The Dial Pad

It really does not matter whether you have a newer set or an older one. The dial pad uses the set to address the network. When we have our dial tone, we then start a sequence of dialed digits indicating to the central office with whom we want to speak. As mentioned, the first telephone sets did not have a dial pad. Everything was manually performed through the telephone company operators. If you needed to speak to someone, you got the operator by going off hook. The off-hook process created the "make" on the circuit (looped the battery back to the operator) that lit a light or created a visual indication to the telephone company operator. The operator would answer and converse with you. At this point, you would pass on the name or number of the requested party and the operator would provide the connection. It was quite simple, but as things got busier, the human involvement became an issue. You could be on the line waiting for an operator forever if things were busy at the central office.

The rotary telephone set was the first attempt to automate the process (see Figure 4-14). Initially, it was well received; however, over time it became a nuisance. The rotary set is an electromechanical device. As you dialed the number, you would rotate the dial in a clockwise direction. When the dial was released, the counterclockwise return to the normal position created a series of electrical interrupts or pulses across the line to the telephone company office. The CO would interpret these pulses and make the necessary routing decisions. The main problem that led to frustrations was that statistically four attempts were necessary to make a call and speak to the intended party. Either the network was busy, the called party was busy, the phone at the receiving end went unanswered, or some other event got in the way. Thus, users felt frustration with this set, especially because it took so long to dial a number.

The pulses are generated at 10 per second (10 pps), which also created long call setup times because of the slowness of the dial pad. Additionally, because it was electromechanical, the system was prone to failures. The rotary set might stick or misdial the digits, or otherwise thwart the user. Users began to complain, and the manufacturers had to respond. The primary manufacturer at the time was Western Electric, a division of AT&T.

Why even bother to mention a set that is so old? At least 15 to 20 percent of U.S. telephones still use pulse dialing. We know of some folks in Illinois that are continually contacted by the telco with the offer to buy back the old

Figure 4-14
The rotary dial pad

phone. The telco doesn't want the phones; the idea is to get rid of them. There are many reasons for this, but some of the major ones are as follows:

- **Cost** The cost of Touch-Tone dialing is typically $1.00 more per month. Many people who make calls only infrequently don't want to pay for a service they seldom use.

- **Technology** Many independent (incumbent) local exchange carriers (ILECs) have old technology and have not yet planned to upgrade their equipment. Therefore, the service is only rotary.

- **Gimmes** A lot of folks who now own their own phones have subscribed to magazines and received free phones as a reward for signing up. These phones might have push buttons on the set. However, during dialing, the conversion from tone to pulse occurs inside the telephone set. The distinctive click-click in the ear identifies such phones as rotary sets.

The Touch-Tone phone was the second edition of the dial pad. This changed the look and feel of the dialing process. Instead of using the rotary dial to electromechanically produce the digits, this phone created by AT&T's Western Electric Division employed a tone dialing sequence. Using a group of tones that fall into the spectrum of voice frequency, the tone dialer has a set of buttons that send out frequency-based tones instead of electrical impulses.

The Touch-Tone telephone set was created to speed up dialing and call processing, reduce user frustration, increase productivity, and enable additional services through the dial pad. The touch tones are actually a dual-tone multifrequency (DTMF) system. Each of the numbers represented on the dial pad has both an X and Y matrix or cross-point. This was a decision that Western Electric made to create a number of tone generators that could be used at the set and tone receivers to be used at the central office. Western Electric did not want to have too many of these tone generators/receivers, because they are expensive. Therefore, under a dual-tone arrangement, they could get away with using only half of the generators needed to represent the same number of digits. See Figure 4-15 for the tone dial pad and note the frequencies as they appear on the chart.

When you press a number, two separate tones are generated and sent to the CO simultaneously. Each number on the dial pad has its own distinct set of dual tones, so the system recognizes each as a discrete number. The reasoning behind the dual tones is that the human voice could not generate a harmonic shift in frequency quickly enough to recreate these tones. Therefore, the telecommunications systems can recognize the tone shifts as dialed

Figure 4-15
The Touch-Tone
phone

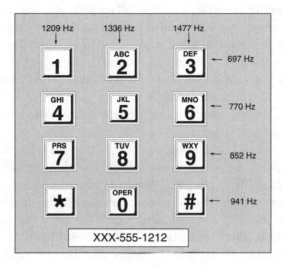

digits instead of conversational path information (voice). For the most part, this works; however, from time to time humans can generate these quick harmonics. It is rare, but it can be done.

In particular, a female voice generating more amplitude shifts will generate a quick shift in vocal pattern and create the digit 8, whereas the male voice will create the digit 7. This, of course, is rare, but it does happen and is called "talk off." This is important when we discuss later evolutions, such as voice messaging systems, where the digit 7 or the digit 8 means something to a computer system when a voice is being used.

An example would be the case where the male voice pattern generates the digit 7 to a voice messaging system and the digit 7 means delete. We must be aware that if we leave a message for someone on a voice messaging system and a reply never arrives, it may well have been that we deleted the message before sending it. This "talk off" arrangement can be controlled through the use of voice bandpass filters that can be acquired from the voice messaging system supplier.

Tone dialing is faster than rotary because the tones are generated at 23 pps, much quicker than the rotary set.

As the tone dial was introduced, a 12-button pad was created, adding two extra numbers to the telephone. The older rotary set only had ten numbers (decimal). The two new buttons enabled new features and capabilities to be introduced in the telephone world, using the pound (#) and star (*) keys as delimiters when dialing into computers, and so on. The extra keys enable feature activation in Centrex and private branch exchange (PBX)-type systems (for example, to put a call on hold, dial #4; to retrieve the call, dial *4). These extras also squared off the dial pad to make it easier to form.

Tone dialing also helps to get the call through the network more quickly because the tones are sent at a much faster rate than that of rotary pulsing. This improves network performance because the network processes the call setup and teardown faster, it creates happier users because they can dial their numbers much more quickly than with the tedious rotary dial sequence, and it promotes overall satisfaction.

One example of an improvement is the call setup time. Setup for a rotary call was 43 seconds, whereas with tone dialing the call can be set up in approximately six to ten seconds. Other improvements, such as improved signaling systems, have reduced this setup time further, but the tones were the first big thrust in gaining time back from the network. Is this important? Sure, it is! Think about the hundreds of millions of calls placed in any given month. If you had a system that took 43 seconds of call setup (the older system not only took that long, but tied up a line across the network for the same setup period) and you could reduce it to ten seconds, you have reclaimed 33 seconds of line utilization (which was not billable time) per call for other users. This is big bucks no matter how you look at it. There is a paradox in this situation, however.

Think about this for just a second: You as a user of the telephone network have a rotary dial set. You want to place a call from Boston to San Francisco (approximately 3,000 miles). You place the call and tie up 3,000 miles of wire for as much as 43 seconds. This is non-billable by the carrier. The clock only starts when the call is answered. So, now the carriers offer you the ability to speed up the process by using a tone dialer. You are obviously going to be happy with this arrangement because you can dial so much faster. The carrier stands to save 33 seconds (remember back then the cost per minute was $0.65) and get the call billing going that much faster. For this savings of approximately $0.30 to $0.35 per call that you make (which all rolls back into the carriers' profits), you have the privilege of paying $0.75 to $1.00 per month more on your phone bill for the convenience of tone dialing. Isn't this a wonderful industry?

The Ringer

As already discussed, the ringer serves the purpose of alerting the called party that someone wants to converse. The ringer has no mystique other than it must be "told" via an electrical current to ring. The current from the central equipment out at the telephone company office is sent to a ringing generator that produces the current across the line. A 48V direct current from a battery in the office produces an 80V alternating current at 20 Hz output across the telephone line to the customer location. This is as simple as can be. Occasionally, differences appear in the way these things are laid out or the voltages that are applied to the line, but we are using norms in our examples.

Tip and Ring

Tip and ring is a phrase that telco installers or repairers use all of the time. They love to talk about tip and ring. This is a description of the two wires that are connected to the telephone set from the outside world. You will recall that the four wires that left the handset went through a hybrid arrangement as they came into the telephone set. At this entrance point, only two wires were carried into the set to connect to the signaling systems inside the phone. The two wires, one from the transmitter and one from the receiver, now exit the set and proceed toward the telephone company connection. They call the transmit wire the "tip" and the receive wire the "ring."

Tip and ring are better described as the transmitter and receiver wires, but telephone company personnel held the words over from a bygone era. Tip and ring come from the use of the old operator cord boards. When the operator tested the line, the tip of an RCA jack was used. If a call was already in motion on a particular line, the operator would hear static on the line when tipping. If the line was not in use, the operator would not get any static from the tipping; the operator would then insert the jack on a cord board into the designated extension port on the board. This insertion would then cause a ringing voltage to be generated across the wires and your phone to ring. This system has all but disappeared here in the U.S., but in several other parts of the world, cord boards still exist. That's the main reason for the mention of where this all came from.

Newer Sets

The telephone is a remarkable piece of equipment that evolved over time. Conceptually, nothing has really changed, but the pieces continue to advance. Today's digital telephone sets provide far more than just a plain old analog telephone call. The older set functionally achieved interface to the network provided by the various carriers. This interface, with all of its electrical and mechanical components, got us to where we are today.

However, progress continues. Users wanted more features and functions from the devices placed on the desk or wall in offices and residences. Consequently, the migration to solid-state, microprocessor-controlled telephone sets became the wave of the future. The newer sets are digital. That means that they perform the same functions with less voltage, very discrete events are preprogrammed into them, and other characteristics of digital transmission will add to the quality of conversation. Digital transmission is covered in later chapters (Chapter 5 discusses the differences between analog and digital, and Chapter 14 discusses the T1 digital transport system).

The telephone set was a clear target for digital technology. The newer sets are varied by the number of manufacturers. Anyone can now manufacture a telephone set, or system for that matter, as long as they abide by certain registration techniques and parameters. A newer set is shown in Figure 4-16. On this set, several added features that enhance the call placement process are incorporated into the telephone set rather than being served by an external device. For example, some of the features that are now becoming the norm are as follows.

Speed Dialing

A user can preprogram from one to 100 numbers into the memory of the set. When you use a feature button or a preprogrammed button on the set, the

Figure 4-16
Newer digital sets are feature-rich but still perform the same functions.

telephone will dial a much longer string of digits (usually up to 33 digits) and connect you with the requested party.

Call Hold

A hold function will place the handset in the mute mode; both the transmitter and the receiver function are disengaged for a period of time. When you use this hold feature, a visual indicator will alert you that you have done something. In the case of a hold, a flashing light will let you know that the call is still there but on what is called a *hard hold*. This serves a mechanical function by keeping the link active but disengaging the set until the line button is pressed again to reconnect the parties.

Call Transfer

Assuming this feature is available at the central office or PBX equipment within your area, a call can be transferred to another line. This function is available in many central offices today. To activate it, you must press the hookswitch down and draw what is called a recall dial tone. Then you must dial the third-party number (the number transferred to) and wait for the line to ring. It's a good idea to wait for the new called party to answer and announce that the call is being transferred, and then hang up. However, many people don't provide this courtesy.

A problem exists with activating this feature; it requires that you press the hookswitch down for a short period (usually 100 to 200 milliseconds) to draw the recall dial tone. Most people fall into one of two categories: "fat fingers," who hold the hook switch down for one to two seconds and cut off the caller, or "skinny fingers," who press and release the buttons too fast and never get the recall dial tone. Consequently, a preprogrammed feature button on this newer set will perform these functions for the exact amount of time and prevent the problems associated with using a transfer.

Conference Call

This is similar to the transfer feature, but in this case, rather than transferring the call to a third party, the third party called will be added into the call. The conference feature enables the three parties to converse without the need to worry about cutting each other off.

Redial Last Number

Sets with this feature have their own internal memory, so they can automatically dial the last number called, even if it is not a speed number. This is great when you encounter a busy tone on the network. The problem with last-number redial comes into play when the call requires a string of digits longer than the normal 11 digits for a phone call. Pauses are required in some cases, but this feature will send the 11 digits plus the credit card number and any other digits dialed in the last sequence. This can cause some confusion, but it is a time saver.

Redial can also be a preprogrammed feature where some sets, on encountering a busy tone, will redial up to 99 times in a preset time period (over the next 60 to 90 minutes, for example). Not all sets will do this. The degree of sophistication is directly proportional to the dollars spent for the set.

Built-in Speakerphone

Many sets have the capability to turn on a speakerphone for hands-free, two-way communications. This can be *simplex*, which means that one must be careful not to overtalk the other end. If overtalk occurs, then the conversation becomes choppy because the set is bouncing between the transmitter and receiver, cutting off words or syllables. The other option some sets have is a *duplex* speakerphone. This means that simultaneous talk and receiving can occur without cutting in and out. This duplex circuitry has separate paths for the transmitter and receiver.

Hands-Free Dialing

Similar to speakerphone service, but not the same, hands-free dialing allows just that. Without picking up the handset to the face, a user can go off hook electronically by pressing the line button or an "on" button, and then dialing. This frees the users' hands for other tasks while the connection is being made. However, once the called party answers the phone, the caller must pick up the handset and converse. The speaker is only a receiving speaker, not a two-way. Many people get confused over this feature and cause a lot of grief or hangups when they attempt to use it improperly.

Displays

Where features are available in the central office, a display set can be used to show the incoming caller identification. This is not ubiquitous or even legal everywhere, but it is coming. Where the incoming caller display is not available or used, the display can still be used to display the number that the caller dials. Further, when the call is dialed, a timer can be used to keep the chronology of the length of call and so on. This can be used for client billing and chargeback or for reminders of what time it is in case you have a meeting.

Questions

1. How many wires are used in the telephone handset?
2. What is the purpose of the carbon particles inside the mouthpiece?
3. How does the telephone company CO know when you want to make a phone call?
4. What do they mean when they say make and break the circuit?
5. What is the purpose of the telephone set?
6. Name five of the various components that we typically come in contact with in the telephone sct?
7. What is the purpose of the ringer?
8. The dial pads can take on two forms. What are they?
9. The set converts human sound into what format?
10. How many pulses per second does the rotary dial create? How many does the Touch-Tone set create?
11. How long did it take to set up a phone call in the old days when we used a rotary phone?
12. How many seconds does the newer set save on the process?
13. What are some of the newer features you can get these days? Name four.
14. What do they call the process when the human voice creates problems by generating a harmonic that sounds like a Touch-Tone digit?
15. How would you describe the terms tip and ring?

Analog Versus Digital Communications

After reading this chapter and completing the questions, you will be able to:

- Explain what analog communications means
- Discuss the differences between analog and digital communications
- Describe the process of carrying the analog signal
- Explain impairments in the analog signal transmission
- Converse fluently about the use of digital transmission systems in the telephone hierarchy
- Describe the way we regenerate the digital signal on the link

In the data and voice communications field, one of the most common points of confusion is between the words analog and digital. Most people recognize that the term *digital* refers to the expression of information in terms of 1's and 0's. But few can easily make the mental connection between this fact and the real-world requirements of moving voice signals expressed in a 1's-and-0's format. In dealing with the term *analog*, everyone merely refers to voice communications. This chapter will help you to make and understand the connection between these two terms. Not that you will become an electrical engineer, but you will be able to converse with the best of them. If a single element must be understood, it is that analog and digital formats are means used to move information across any medium. Some media typically deal with analog, others deal with digital, and the rest deal with both. Thus, this understanding will help you to understand the reasons why the different transmission systems are used.

Analog Transmission Systems

As mentioned earlier, "the network" was originally developed solely to provide voice communications services. Initially, the communications circuits AT&T built through the Bell Systems and their own communications capabilities used strictly analog technology. Yes, it changed into a digital world, but it was built around analog communications for voice. What does this mean?

In an analog communications system, the initial signal (in this case, the spoken word) is directly translated into an electrical signal. Chapter 4 describes how the telephone set accomplishes this task in more detail. The characteristics of an analog signal deal with two constantly changing variables: the amplitude and the frequency of the signal. The strength (amplitude) of the electrical signal varies with the loudness of the voice, and the frequency of the electrical signal varies with the pitch or tone of the voice. Both variables (amplitude and frequency) change proportionately with the original sound waves.

If the signal were to be monitored with an oscilloscope, the displayed pattern would visibly and recognizably change as the sound changed. This is shown in Figure 5-1, where the signal characteristics can be seen on an

Figure 5-1
Using an oscilloscope, you can see the characteristics of an analog signal.

oscilloscope. For a more graphic example, think of the visual displays in some discos, where the music is fed into a light display that varies as the music changes. In an analog telephone communications system, the electrical signal, not light, changes. In Figure 5-2, an analogy to this concept using a musical beat is shown. The lights of the disc jockey's equipment will change and flash with the beat of the music. In this case, the lights are changing based on the electrical characteristics of the signal. What is actually happening? In telecommunications terms, you could say that the actual sound is produced by banging airwaves together. This banging of airwaves is really the movement of the air molecules. Technically, this is called compression and rarefaction. However, who wants to get technical?

The human voice is an interesting phenomenon. As we speak, we generate sound. We actually bang the air waves together quite a few times in a relatively short period. This was discussed in Chapter 3; but, to stick with this thought, we create an analogous sinusoidal wave. This wave is then converted into its electrical equivalent. Quite simply, if you were to take the sounds created by the voice and modify them based on the pitch and the strength of the sound, you could produce this sinusoidal wave (Figure 5-3). The wave is what would happen electrically if we were to use a magnetic field to change the sound into electricity. Working around a baseline of zero electrical voltage, we then would have a 360° rotation of electrical current. This 360° wave around the zero line is called a hertz, named after the

Figure 5-2

Comparing the analog wave to how the beat of the music changes lights in a DJ's equipment

Figure 5-3
The sinusoidal wave
rotates 360° of
electrical current
around a magnetic
force. This is one
wave or revolution,
called a hertz.

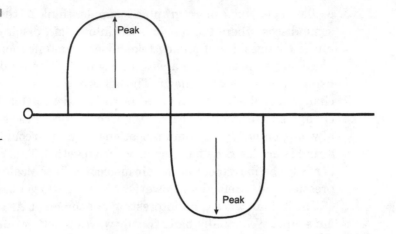

electrical engineer who documented this concept. The wave starts at the zero line and rises as the amount of energy increases. This will ultimately peak at some point and then begin its descent. The electrical energy will then proceed from the height on a downward slope to the zero line. From there, it will continue on its slope below the zero line to a peak (this is called the negative side of the wave). Continuing to a peak voltage on this side of the line, the energy will hit its peak value, and then begin an upward slope back to the zero line. The wave has made a complete 360° cycle. One complete cycle constitutes one hertz (1 Hz), used in a reference against one second in time. A 1 Hz signal produces one complete revolution in one second, whereas a 100 Hz signal completes 100 revolutions in one second.

The human vocal chords can bang the airwaves together between 100 and 5,000 times per second. Simply stated, the voice is producing up to 5,000 cycles of information per second. When this is converted into its electrical equivalent, up to 5,000 hertz exist. We do not like to state such big numbers; so we abbreviate this to 5 kilo (meaning thousand) hertz—5 kHz, for short. From this electrical equivalent, we now have an analogy or look-alike to our sound waves. This is a constantly changing variable of electrical energy. Both the amplitude and the frequency will change from 100 to 5,000 times per second. This is something that the telephone companies learned to deal with from the beginning of our communications industry. Over time, however, they found that the human voice actually generates from 300 to 3,300 cycle changes per second or 3 kHz of electrical cycles as a norm (Figure 5-4). As with any communications channel capacity, the telephone company did not want or need to give users any more than they needed to carry on a voice conversation. Over the years, as the network expanded, the telephone companies limited the bandwidth of a telephone

Figure 5-4
The human voice
produces usable
information in a
range of 300 to
3,300 Hz.

call to a 3 kHz channel capacity. This was a money issue. Given a limited amount of bandwidth, how can we enable a human conversation to take place across the network and produce reasonable representations of the original voice? And how can we do it cheaply? The range of frequencies generated spans from 300 to 3,300 Hz (Figure 5-5). The telephone company therefore limits our use of the channel to just that amount. In the radio frequency (RF) and electromagnetic spectrum, the telephone companies divided all of their capacities into 4-kHz slices. On each of these 4-kHz slices (wires or radio channels), they installed frequency bandpass filters at 300 and at 3,300 Hz. Anything that falls in the middle of this allocation of RF

Figure 5-5
The telephone
companies band-
limited their 4 kHz
channels to a usable
3 kHz with bandpass
filters.

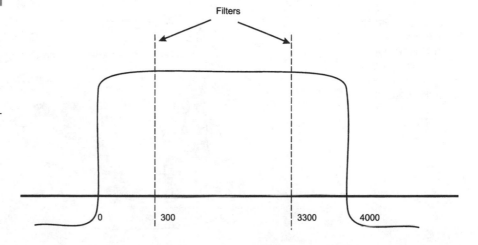

spectrum will be allowed to pass. Anything that falls outside of this range will be filtered out (thrown away). This is called a *band-limited channel*. Because the voice can go as high as 5 kHz, there will be cases where we hit the higher range of frequencies with our conversation (such as words with the *S* and the *F* sounds) and it will be flattened out through the filters. This might sound unreasonable, but what it really produces is a little fuzziness on the line. Neither the human ear nor the telephone equipment is sensitive enough to recognize any significant problems. Once the electrical equivalent of the sound is created (through the telephone set or another device), the electricity is sent down the wires.

When a call is proceeding down the wires, resistance in the wires to the electrical signal immediately begins to diminish its amplitude. The signal gets weaker and weaker. This weakening of the energy will eventually lead to the total absorption of the electrical energy, or the loss of the signal beyond recognition. This is called *attenuation* of the electrical signal. The signal can only travel so far before it runs out of strength and disappears. An analogy to this is a relay race runner who is trained to run around a quarter-mile track as fast as he or she can. By the time the runner gets to the end of the quarter-mile run, all strength and energy is expended. The runner is out of steam (Figure 5-6). If the runner did not have someone to pass the baton off to, but had to go around the track again, the second lap would take forever. That is, if the runner made it around the track at all before passing out and falling flat on the ground.

In order to keep the signal moving along the wires, amplifiers are used to boost the signal strength (Figure 5-7). These amplifiers are usually spaced about 15,000 to 18,000 feet apart. Typically, we only need one ampli-

Figure 5-6
The runner around the track is "out of energy," so he must hand the baton to a new runner.

Figure 5-7
Amplifiers are used
to boost the signal
strength along
the wires.

fier between the customer location and the telephone company central office—two, at most. The central office is usually located close to the customer, within five to seven miles on average. Only in remote locations will the central office be farther away. This may not be the case where the telephone companies have closed the CO. The consolidation of COs across the United States specifically has led to greater distances from the CO to the customer.

A second activity takes place on these wires concurrent with the transmission. Noise (introduced line loss, frayed wires, lightning, electrical inductance, heat, and so on) is ever present in the form of white noise or hiss. It also begins to cause a deterioration of the signal. Noise is always on the line, but its increased presence from cabling problems causes the degradation of the signal. Unfortunately, as the signal proceeds down the line, the noise and the signal begin to intertwine. Amplifiers cannot discern the noise from the actual conversation. Thus, the amplifier not only boosts the signal, it also boosts the noise. This creates a stronger but noisier signal, which leads to some extremely noisy circuits (Figure 5-8). The results of amplification are cumulative over distance. The more amplifiers that must be used, the worse the overall signal gets. Many of the longer-distance circuits were constantly being amplified. This again is not to imply that the telco doesn't want to do any better. It is a function of the equipment, the electrical characteristics, and the finances combined.

Figure 5-8
The amplifier is
amplifying both the
telephone signal and
the line noise.

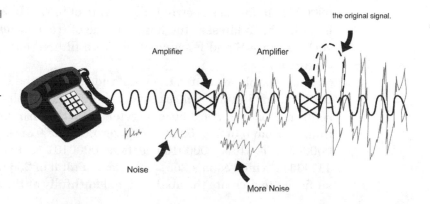

It is interesting to note here that some of the latest advances in digital signal processing (DSP) could now be used to clean up an amplified voice transmission somewhat if analog technology were still in wide use. However, a better approach to producing clean signals was developed many years ago.

Analog-to-Digital Conversion

Because the analog version of the network was a problem for the network suppliers and the telcos alike, both turned to a digital form of communicating. In order to convert the voice conversation from analog to digital, a device called an analog-to-digital (A/D) converter employs a sampling technique.

Sampling refers to the process of measuring (see how we are creeping up on quantifying a signal?) representative portions of a signal over time. We assume that chronologically adjacent portions will differ only slightly. If the samples are taken frequently enough, and played back faithfully at the other end, the ear will not be able to differentiate the playback from the original. A (nondigital) sampling technique is used in movies and other video applications. When a movie is made, no truly continuous record of the images exists; instead, a series of still images, sampling the reality at 30 samples (or "frames") per second, is recorded and later presented to the viewer. Normally, the viewer cannot distinguish between playback of the samples and the real thing.

As mentioned earlier, the bandwidth of the audio signal we wish to transmit is 3,000 Hz (3,300 minus 300). Based on the Nyquist theorem (which states that sampling should occur at a rate at least twice the maximum frequency of the line), the minimum sampling rate would be 6,600 Hz (2×3300 Hz). In fact, a somewhat higher rate of 8,000 Hz (samples per second) is used. This addresses the higher range of frequencies in a conversation, such as those S and F sounds that were filtered out in the analog world (Figure 5-9).

Each sample measures the amplitude level of the voice signal at a particular point in time. One sample comprises eight bits, where a bit represents a 1 or a 0. An 8-bit character or byte can represent any decimal number from 0 to 255 (00000000 is zero, 00000001 is one, 00000010 is two, 00000011 is three, 0000100 is four, 0000101 is five, and so on up to 11111111 which equals 255). Therefore, a total of 256 possible levels exist, sufficient to recreate the analog signal faithfully at the receiving end. More

Figure 5-9

During the analog-to-digital conversion, a sampling rate of 8,000 Hz is used.

samples would produce a higher-quality replication, but the ear is not sensitive enough to discern the differences.

Eight thousand samples per second, with each sample requiring eight bits, generates a digital stream of data at a rate of 64,000 bits per second. We know this as the *digital signal 0* (DS0), the digitized equivalent of one voice channel. The bits are each in the form of a square wave, in contrast to the familiar sinusoidal wave that is typically seen on an oscilloscope.

The square wave travels down the same pair of wires we are accustomed to, but in order to handle the digital signal, the amplifiers are removed. Additional equipment (such as loading coils) is also removed. In short, the entire circuit is reengineered from end to end. In place of the removed equipment, a digital regenerator (or regenerative repeater) is used. The strength of the digital signal is based on a 3 volt pulse of a very short duration; therefore, the repeaters must be placed closer together, typically every mile (Figure 5-10). This requires more equipment, which is an expense to

Figure 5-10

Repeaters are standard at approximately each mile of line between the telephone company and the end user.

the telcos and network suppliers alike. Nevertheless, when the samples are played back at the far end, customers receive the transmitted signal in a form indistinguishable from that sent from the original A/D converter at the sending location.

Digital Signaling

As mentioned earlier, digital signals consist of 1's and 0's. But even this statement can be a bit confusing; how does one insert a "1" or a "0" onto a wire? Unlike the varying levels used in analog transmission, signaling on a digital circuit is very simple; two different voltage levels are sent to represent 1's (that is, +3 V), while no voltage represents a 0. This is called a *unipolar signal*. The receiving equipment measures the voltage level once each bit time.

A *bit time* is the length of time that it takes to transmit one bit. For example, at 9,600 bits per second, one bit time equals 1/9600 of a second (about 104 microseconds). The measurement is taken in the middle of the bit time, when the likelihood of getting a precise level is maximized (Figure 5-11).

Actually two types of digital signaling exist. The previous description presents the type of signals used for local (that is, non-telco-based) digital signaling. A slightly more sophisticated scheme, called either alternate mark inversion (AMI) or bipolar signaling, is used for wide-area digital transmissions. A detailed discussion of AMI is covered in the chapter on T1. Because voice is inherently analog (that is, it varies continuously, rather than occurring in a discrete, numerically related pattern), an analog-to-digital (A/D) conversion must be performed if you want to transmit voice digitally. Later paragraphs cover how to change an analog signal into a

Figure 5-11
The measurement is taken in the middle of the bit time, when the likelihood of getting a precise level is maximized.

1 0 0 0 1 1 0 1 1 1 1 0 0 0 0 0

Sample Points

digital format. But first we must answer the important question, "Why bother to convert to digital?" The answer is quality.

Analog signal paths must use amplifiers if the paths cover any significant distance. Because amplifiers retain and even strengthen noise in a conversation, the more amplifiers used in a transmission path, the noisier the background. So, when you use an analog circuit to call your grandfather in the old country to wish him a happy birthday, you will be most fortunate if either of you can understand the other over the background noise. To compensate for this problem of a noisy overseas (or long-distance) call, we use an age-old philosophy: Yell!

By yelling into the phone to overcome the noise, we do little to help the situation. When we raise our voices to new heights, we increase the amplitude. This makes the signal very strong (stronger than what the telephone companies expect). The telephone companies have, however, installed equipment on the line that will hold the height somewhat to a level. These *pads*, as they are called, sense that the amplitude is much higher than normal, so they introduce loss to compensate and bring the amplitude down. This just serves to compound the problem, because the loss in decibels (dB) will steal away the amplitude but do nothing for the noise. So we have gained nothing (Figure 5-12).

The digital equivalent of an amplifier is a repeater. We commonly refer to this as a "schizophrenic cookie monster." Why? Well, let us explain.

As the digital pulse is placed onto the wires, only the 1's (+3 V) need to be of any concern. But as the pulse is placed onto the wire, it immediately begins to propagate down the wires. The wire will immediately begin to act on this pulse by diminishing its strength. The result will be a constantly decaying pulse of electricity (Figure 5-13). Because this decaying process begins immediately, the likelihood of the pulse falling into obscurity is very high. So this "cookie monster" is placed on the link at approximately every

Figure 5-12

When we yell into the set, the amplitude is increased, but equipment at the central office "pads" the signal to a norm. Therefore nothing is gained by yelling.

5,000 to 6,000 feet. As the pulse declines in strength, it must be kept at sufficient strength to be recognized as a pulse and not noise. This distance is used to keep the previous signal what is called the pulse detection threshold level. If the strength of the pulse falls below this detection threshold, the pulse will be mistaken for noise and ignored.

When the pulse arrives at the repeater, the repeater will act like the cookie monster. It will literally absorb the signal—eat it up and make it disappear. The cookie monster has done its job. However, the other side of this cookie monster is schizophrenic. Therefore, it will basically say, "There was a pulse there, so I'll be a sport and put a brand-new pulse on the line in the original's place." Thus, a brand new 3 V pulse will be introduced. The signal begins to propagate immediately down the next leg of the circuit, and the process starts all over again.

But whereas an amplifier simply strengthens the input signal, a repeater detects the 1's and 0's of the original signal and retransmits them out the other side as good as new. In particular, any noise introduced into the signal between the source and the repeater is completely ignored as long as it stays below a certain tolerance level. Amplitude decreases will still occur between repeaters, and noise will be introduced, but so long as a repeater can recognize the original pulses (1's), those are the only parts of the received signal that will be used to build the new output signal. Thus, if a communications path is built with digital technology, it is entirely possible to deliver to the ultimate receiver a signal that is identical to that sent from the first digital transmitter in the path (Figure 5-14). Because the pulse is short in duration and a discrete value of energy, rather than a constantly varying voltage level, more repeaters are required on the link. Telcos must use three to four times as much equipment on the same distance of wire with digital communications at the local loop.

Note the last part of the previous statement " . . . from the first digital transmitter in the path." Because voice is analog, there will be a conversion at some point. From the voice source to that first conversion point, noise can be introduced that will remain in the signal. Obviously, the closer to the voice source that the A/D conversion takes place, the better.

If you have a conversation with someone in another state or another country, and that conversation is as clear as it would be if the person to whom you are speaking were right in front of you, you can be sure that most if not all of the technology involved is digital rather than analog. Such quality results in happier customers, cleaner transmission, improved data communications, and happier carriers. This is why all the hype exists in the industry about the benefits of digital transmission.

Another benefit to using digital rather than analog transmission exists, although it directly benefits the service providers more than their customers: Digital technology facilitates combining and manipulation of signals, providing a carrier more flexibility in how it moves the signal from source to destination.

Digital Data in an Analog World

We have been focusing on voice transmission, a communications technology that starts and ends with an analog signal—a voice. But what about data communications? Because it starts out as digital, doesn't that simplify things? The answer is no, not so you'd notice.

Until the last few decades, digital service was not available to users. Because of this, an entire technology came into being that provided methods for carrying digital signals across the analog voice network. The critical component in this technology is the modem, a contraction of the terms modulator and demodulator. In a nutshell, a modem's function is to provide digital-to-analog conversion (and of course the reverse) for a digital device that needs to communicate with a remote digital device across the analog telephone network. Figure 5-15 shows this multiple conversion process.

Because, in fact, telephone companies' backbones are now mostly digital (with the local loop signals being digitized at the CO), a communications

Figure 5-15
Four analog-to-digital
or digital-to-analog
conversions.

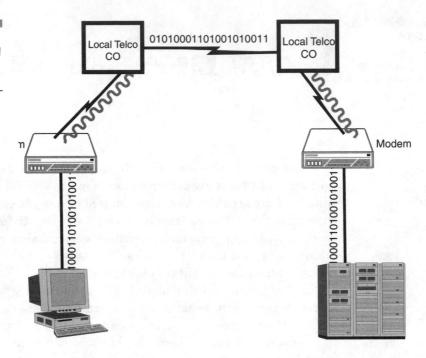

path using modems includes not one, or even two, but rather a minimum of four digital-to-analog or analog-to-digital conversions—and that's only one way!

Modems and other data communications equipment are addressed in more detail in Chapter 13.

Most voice and data transmission systems now use digital technology, with a few key exceptions. An exception that has particular impact is the telephone local loop. The local loop (sometimes called the "last mile" or other less printable terms) has been held back because of the vast installed base of analog telephones and amplifiers. However, even this last bastion of analog transmission is under assault.

A digital technology and telco service offering called integrated services for digital networks (ISDN) is slowly spreading. ISDN can provide digital voice transmission right up to and including the telephone. Chapter 27 covers ISDN in greater detail.

Digital transmission is the way the world is going. While in the past the cost of digital devices exceeded that of analog equivalents, the price curve for the analog devices has long since flattened, whereas the cost of digital components has steadily dropped and continues to do so. Until the local loop is fully digitized, we will operate in a world of mixed analog and digital components. But except for that local loop, expect virtually every other communications medium to employ digital technology.

Questions

1. When we say that the signal is analog we mean that the electrical equivalent of the signal is being carried down the wire.   T/F

2. The analog channel that the telephone company uses is how wide?

   a. 4,000 Hz

   b. 3,000 Hz

   c. 300 Hz

   d. 3,300 Hz

3. The telephone company offers us a _____ limited channel to transmit voice calls.

4. Certain sounds, like _____ and sounds are flattened by the analog limitations.

5. Analog _____ are placed on the line at approximately every 15–18 KFt.

6. Certain impairments like _____, _____, and _____ are always present on the line.

7. When using an amplifier, the device cannot tell the difference between the _____ and the _____.

8. Amplifiers boost up the signal back to its _____ strength.

9. If an amplifier increases the noise and the signal, the _____ effect of this amplification means that the signal and the noise become the same.

10. The amplifier increases the original voice to twice its original strength.   T/F

11. What is the term for losing the strength of the signal?

    a. Amplification

    b. Regeneration

    c. Attenuation

    d. Loss

12. To solve the problems with the original network, the telcos changed from an analog to a _____ transmission.

13. When the telcos wanted to change their architecture, they closed some of the _____ near the customer's door.

14. The distance typically from a CO to a consumer is _____ miles?

    a. three

    b. five

    c. one

    d. two

15. How far is the between a regenerator?

    a. 3,000 feet

    b. 18,000 feet

    c. 5,000 feet

    d. 15,000 feet

16. What is the term we use for a signal that has all positive voltages representing the signal?

17. What does AMI mean?

    a. alternate mean inversion

    b. alternative messaging index

    c. alternate mark invasion

    d. alternate mark inversion

18. What is the voltage level of a digital pulse represented in either positive or negative voltages?

19. What is the time that we use to represent a one or a zero?

    a. pulse

    b. width

    c. bit-time

    d. 104 microseconds

20. How many possible combinations of values do we get with the digital representation?

    a. 2

    b. 3

    c. 128

    d. 256

Carriers

After reading this chapter and completing the questions, you will be able to:

- Describe the different types of carriers
- Explain the difference between local and long-distance access
- Converse about the different types of services they offer
- Understand the new markets for these providers and the names we apply to the new providers
- Describe a CLEC, an ILEC, an IEC, and a DLEC

Incumbent Local Exchange Carriers

The incumbent local exchange carrier (ILEC) is the telephone company serving your area and providing you with dial tone services. The term local exchange carriers (LEC) came into existence after the breakoff of the Bell System from the AT&T network. The modified final judgment decree specified that the local telephone company, or dial tone provider, would be kept separate after divestiture. Prior to 1984, the carriers were called the Bell Operating Companies (BOCs), and they still are referred to this way. The names of the telephone companies attached to the older Bell System have changed a little, but some companies have tried to keep their identity as much as possible. Names that are still used in the industry today, such as Bell South are examples of this identity. However, the telephone companies were fighting to keep the Bell logo at the same time the parent organization (AT&T) was also trying to keep certain identities. The local carriers won this battle and managed to keep the logo and the Bell name. Surprisingly enough, even though the divestiture of the AT&T and Bell Systems occurred in 1984, many people still do not separate the two entities. For the public, this is the toughest part of the whole scenario. People still think of the system as one big entity rather than as organizations that were separated as a result of the court decisions.

In early 1999, 15 years after the breakup occurred, a number of users still did not recognize that the change ever occurred, although this number was fewer than ever. Of course, this leads to a lot of confusion because the problems that occur on a daily basis are always blamed on the telephone companies, regardless of where the problem actually resides. Additionally, the independent telephone companies, of which hundreds (1400+) exist, that were always referred to as independent, are also ILECs. Although they are not part of the Bell System, these organizations still provide the basic dial tone for many communities. Some of the larger of these independents include GTE Telephone (including their acquisition, CONTEL Telephone Systems), Commonwealth Telephone (which is now part of two different companies, RCN cable company and Frontier Communications), Standard Telephone Company, Centel, and so on. The numbers and the areas served by the various independents differ, but the function is the same. These companies provide local dial tone service as their primary charter. Now they are all considered ILECs because the term fits better with the service they provide.

The ILECs provide more than just the dial tone. Since the divestiture, when they were required by law to separate the customer premises equipment part of their service offering, the ILECs have a clearly defined demarcation point where the telephone company service stops and the customer takes over. This demarcation point, also referred to as the DEMARC, is the point where the rate and tariff process starts and stops. Figure 6-1 shows the termination of an ILEC circuit in a demarcation point. This will fall apart over time as the ILECs and CLECs enter every aspect of communications services in the future. All of the providers are trying to be the one-stop shopping provider of the future. In this particular reference, the demarcation point is a network interface unit (NIU), which is a smart ver-

Figure 6-1
The LEC terminates
the two wires at the
NIU (DEMARC),
where the LEC stops
and the customer
takes over. In this
case, the LEC may
provide a hard-wired
lug connector or an
RJ-11 jack. The
added RJ-11 jack
on top of the NIU is
for testing.

Line Tester

Standard RJ-11 Jack
(Possible)

sion of the RJ-11 jack. To have an idea of how this all evolved, remember that the telephone companies provided "everything from soup to nuts" in the early stages of the industry. They provided

■ The dial tone

■ The local loop of wire connecting to their equipment and the customer location

■ The telephone set to interface to the network

■ The interface to the local and long-distance portions of the networks and the access to the long-distance network

■ The billing and collection functions for all services

■ The installation of all related pieces and components to give the end user access to the network

■ The maintenance and repair functions

Because this was a single interface, the customer's only responsibility was to make a single call that did it all. The use of the network led to additional billings, so the only actual responsibility of the customer or user was paying the bill. This all changed in the 1984 divestiture of the network and telephone company interfaces. Consequently, the customer now must decide whom to talk to regarding services and equipment needs. However, with the

Telecommunications Deregulation and privatization occurring throughout North America and other parts of the world, the way we used to do this process is becoming the way we will do it again. What goes around comes around. Soon the ILECs will be able to compete and offer all of the services (and more) that they offered prior to 1984!

The following are some of the primary services that the incumbent local exchange providers or ILECs provide. This is a representative sampling of their services, not an all-inclusive or exhaustive list.

Local Dial Tone (Single-Line and Party Line) Service

This is the primary bread-and-butter service and the main service that the telephone companies are currently chartered to provide. The local dial tone can be in the form of a single-line service with one registered user per pair of telephone wires, or a party line service where multiple registered users share a single pair of wires. The use of a party line service was always a financial consideration, particularly in rural areas of the country. Many telephone suppliers did not have a financial justification for installing multitudes of wires outside of the major downtown areas. Therefore, as the rural users requested dial tone, the cost of running the wires to their locations was exorbitant. Consequently, the telephone companies enabled connection to multiple customers (two to four) on a single cable pair, with a distinctive telephone number and ringing tone for each user. This should not be confused with a multiplexing scheme. Only one of the users could use the dial tone line at a time. Others on the same physical pair of wires had to wait for the line to be available before they could either make or receive a call. If a local community was on party line service and user A (Figure 6-2) was on the phone, the wires were busy. When user B wanted to make a call, the process required B to pick up the handset and listen to ensure that the line was free and the dial tone was heard. Because A was already on the line, B would be able to hear the entire conversation on the wires, but would not be able to make a call until A was off the line. Additionally, if C was expecting a call, as long as A was on the line, an incoming call could not make it to C because the line was busy. This required the cooperation of the users sharing the service and a form of mutual respect. Because any one of these users could listen to the conversation, a good neighbor policy existed that stated that the user, on hearing a conversation on the line, would hang up and not eavesdrop on the other party. Also, a form of cooperation or scheduling was informally used so that when B wanted to make the call, he

Figure 6-2
With party line service, multiple users share the same pair of wires. This arrangement was used in many rural areas when the LEC did not have enough pairs to serve all subscribers.

or she would tell A, who was already on the line. Therefore, A would hurry the call to its conclusion so that B could have the use of the line.

This service worked well in rural America where neighbors were more dependent on each other and were far more cooperative in their communities. However, in the cities where this was also an offering at a reduced rate, the system could really become a major problem. Suppose that A had a teenager who liked to talk on the line for hours. B and C would be blocked out continually from the line. On the other hand, as they would continue to pick up the phone and hear a teen on the line, they would ask the teen to get off the line so that they could make a call. This could lead to significant hard feelings and even confrontations among the neighbors. Thus, the use of party line service was discontinued as much as possible. The rural parts of the country still have this service because no other option exists given the limited facilities in these areas. This variable depends on the local provider services and the geographical location.

Centrex Service

Central office exchange service (Centrex) is a technique that the ILECs offer as their flagship service for business users. The nature of Centrex is the subject of several discussions in the industry. When the Bell System was originally united with the AT&T organization, the rental of telephone service included the private branch exchanges (PBX). Because this service was rented or leased over longer periods of time, the Bell System always had the edge over competition. After all, the supplier of the telephone dial tone also provided the interface equipment at the customer's location. Therefore, the customer needed only to use the service and pay the bill. However, as competition was gaining ground over the existing installed equipment base provided by the Bell System, the telephone companies realized that their own limited product offerings were contributing somewhat to the move toward competitors' products. Many customers were locked into long-term equipment agreements and the AT&T systems were not advancing as fast as the competitors' products. This was the result of trying to keep pace with the market and at the same time, protect the embedded base of equipment without mass replacements that would be expensive and difficult to cope with. While this was happening, the central offices were moving ahead of the PBX marketplace by replacing the old electromechanical systems with the newer electronic switching systems (ESSs). Rather than replacing both ends—the customer hardware and the central office equipment—the logical selection of a central-office-based telephone system was offered. Therefore, the customer could rent a partition of the central office, both hardware and software, to act as the PBX surrogate. Further, the Centrex offering enabled the customer to get away from the hardware system roller coaster. Hardware changes can be very expensive, particularly with the constant upgrades that were being introduced by the vendors.

The use of Centrex service was therefore a stepping-stone for the Bell operating companies and the independent telephone operating companies, but once the breakup of the system occurred, the Centrex service became their flagship product to serve the large business customer. As it evolved, the offering became far more viable to the smaller customer with as few as two or three lines. The Centrex offering provides the features and functions of a PBX without the heavy investment requirements.

For some time after the divestiture of the Bell System, Centrex was the primary way the ILECs pushed services. However, as more business customers bought hardware (PBX and Key Systems), the use of Centrex started to wane. Initially, Centrex was only a North American service. A major drawback was that the ILECs originally offered Centrex to only the larger customers, usually with 100 lines or more. After the divestiture and the decrease in interest, this changed and it became available to any business, large or small. Companies with only one business line could now rent Centrex service. As the renewed flexibility was introduced, the ILECs saw new growth occur. Now over 34 countries offer Centrex services, and the growth rate is averaging 15 percent per year. Moreover, the competitive local exchange carriers (CLECs) began to appear after the Telecommunications Acts of 1996/97 in North America. Many of the CLECs began to offer Centrex-like services to compete with the ILEC in dealing with the business customer (ranging in size from 10-100 lines). Here the CLEC offered the dial tone and the equipment, and the internal wiring and long distance as a bundled package. The overall success of these programs is a mixed bag. Many of the CLECs dropped the offering because users were not interested in the analog dial tone and paying long-term contracts for all their services. The judge and jury are still out on this one.

Business Service (Direct Inward Dial and Direct Outward Dial Lines and Trunks)

Beyond the basic dial tone services for business and residential customers, the ILECs offer the rental of inward and outward dial services for the business user. The use of direct inward dial (DID) services enables the customer or outside caller to dial a user's telephone directly via an extension number. The call is passed into the telephone system (PBX) from the central office switching system and is redirected to the called party's extension telephone. Just as the caller can dial directly into the called party's extension on the telephone system, an added capability, called direct outward dial (DOD), exists on the telephone systems to enable the extension user to dial directly outside the system. This provides an access code for users to dial (the number 9, for example) that tells the telephone system to find a line or trunk to the outside world and return a dial tone. On receipt of this second dial tone, the station user then dials a seven- or ten-digit telephone number. No operator or manual assistance is required via this access method: hence, the term direct outward dialing.

Residential Service

Of course, the ILECs provide both business and residential services; the delivery of residential dial tone is a primary objective. Residential services include the single-line and party line services. However, the ILECs are always looking for newer sources of revenue. Therefore, they offer various features and functions in the residential package. The first and foremost choice that the residential user might have is the standard flat-rate residential service. In some cases, the ILECs also offer a measured usage service at a reduced rate. Flat-rate service can cost between $10.00 and $28.00 per month, depending on local regulatory rates. To help reduce the high monthly costs for the nontypical user (a user who does not make many calls per month), the ILECs offer the residential user the ability to rent a reduced-rate dial tone line for $8.50 to $10.00 per month, with a usage charge added for every call that is made (a message unit might be $0.05 to $0.07 per call) in excess of some predetermined number of calls. The third option is to use a further reduction of the monthly charge to a rate of $4.50 to $6.00 per month, with a usage charge for every call. Regardless of the selection made, the customer typically tries to match to his or her specific individual needs. Although this is attractive, some cases exist where the telephone company will offer the reduced-rate service as opposed to the flat-rate service, but with the stipulation that once a measured rate is selected the customer cannot go back to the flat rate. This would be a critical service decision if the caller has a variable usage pattern because the usage might be higher than the flat-rate service. In Table 6-1, the cost for service is compared at various usage levels.

In this table, it is assumed that the cost of the monthly flat-rate service is $15.00; measured service with the first 50 calls free is $10.00; and measured service with no free messages is $6.50. Each call above the allowance is set at $0.07. The rates for these services vary from state to state because the tariffs are all different. However, the rate per message is a new variable because the cost per call is now becoming distance and time sensitive. For example, a call might cost $0.07 for the first five minutes and an added $0.07 for each additional three minutes. Other variables exist, and the combinations are innumerable. Places where we still find these packages

Table 6-1

Comparison of the Various Residential Service Offerings with Measured versus Flat-Rate Service

Description	Flat Rate @ $15.00/mo.	Measured Rate @ $0.07/call	
		50 calls	No calls
10 calls per month	$15.00	$10.00	$ 6.50
50 calls per month	$15.00	$10.00	$10.00
100 calls per month	$15.00	$13.50	$17.00
200 calls per month	$15.00	$20.50	$20.50

include New York, Pennsylvania, Illinois, and Massachusetts. These are still tariffed services offered to residential and business services by the ILECs.

Local Calling Services

Direct distance dialing (DDD) is the ability to place a call at any distance within the ILEC's area of service. This includes the basic residential and business offerings at a monthly rate for the line and the usage. This is like a regular business line except that the business user can access the dial tone and dial wherever he or she wishes without the assistance of an operator. The acronym DDD characterizes the changes that have occurred over time. In the late 1960s, an operator was required to make some calls on a long distance or international basis. Evolution of the network beyond this point was a must because the manual intervention was expensive and labor intensive. In the earlier days of the telephone networks, this was not a major problem, but as the usage picked up and dependency on the telecommunications networks increased, the carriers realized that this access was a must.

Pay Phone Service

The existence of pay phones (coin telephones) is evident in the ILEC's service area, as shown in Figure 6-3. The LEC offers access to the local and long-distance networks via either a public telephone service, a semipublic telephone service, or a private telephone service. Each of these is handled differently on the basis of the access method chosen. The public pay phone is an obvious landmark on the streets of any city or town. These phones are the phone booths that are positioned in full view for use and access by anyone who wishes to make a call. The pay phone or coin-operated phone is designed to enable access to the network for the masses. If a user does not have a phone in his or her home or office, then the public phone is available for outgoing calls to the network on a pay-as-you-go basis. No monthly rental charge exists for this service because it is shared by the general public. However, the cost per call or per minute will be more expensive because operator or automated assistance is typically necessary to complete a call from a coin-operated phone. This is the most expensive type of call available on a dial-up basis. Along with this dial-up service, the caller can use a credit card to complete a call through the carrier of choice or can make a toll-free

Figure 6-3
A pay phone service
may be public,
semipublic, or
private.

(800, 888, 877 or 866) call without depositing a coin. The dial tone accessing the ILEC's network is present, so a call can be initiated without the use of a coin.

A new twist is occurring in the U.S. whereby the owners of the payphones are now starting to remove many of them. The mass market appeal of cell phones has dropped the dependency on pay phones and the revenues. Therefore, the owners of the pay phones are either removing them, or selling them off to a new third-party. This changes the telephony landscape. In many poor communities the local residents depend on the payphone, even though they may call collect or place toll free calls. This is no longer an option for these people.

The semipublic telephone service enables an organization or business to rent the set and line through the ILEC and place it within their offices or lobby, thereby denying access to the general public. The rental is normally based on a flat rate per month, which is less of a portion of the income that is generated by the pay phone. Normally, the renter of the pay phone guarantees a minimum amount of revenue to the ILEC. However, if the minimum is not met, the renter must pay the difference. The variables of the pricing arrangement are a complex aspect of the local tariffs.

A new twist to this part of the billing is the possibility that all customers using the pay phone may be initiating toll-free (800, 888, 877 and 866) calls. This obviously does not generate any revenue for the pay phone owner, so now the cost of the connection to the toll-free number is passed back to the holder of the toll-free number!

The final type of pay phone service is the use of a private coin telephone service. In this scenario, the pay phone can be rented from the ILEC or purchased by the customer from any third party. The customer also rents the access line to the ILEC's network for a fee (flat rates are still available in some areas) and then selects the long-distance carrier to carry any calls from this phone. The customer can allow selected users access to this phone, which is normally located well within the confines of the customer's building, perhaps in the cafeteria or lobby. Therefore, no one off the street can walk into the building to use the phone because it is not in a public place. From this phone, the customer can select the method and the price to be charged to the user on a cost-per-call or a cost-per-minute basis. The ILEC carries the local call and keeps track of the minutes of usage for billing and collection purposes. Under this arrangement, the ILEC might receive a percentage of the revenue for the administration and handling of the service. Another option is that the ILEC merely bills the customer for the basic service at the tariffed rate, with all revenues going to the owner of the pay phone. This has become a competitive tool for customers since the divestiture of the telephone system.

Private Lines and TIE Lines

Private and terminal interface equipment (TIE) lines are leased services that are rented from the ILEC on a flat-rate basis. A private line indicates that the service is dedicated to the user rather than accessible to others. This is a contrast to the public-switched telephone network, where many users compete for and share the lines and trunks from the ILEC. The private line is typically a flat-rate service connecting two locations of an organization. In the case of a TIE line, the ILEC installs a private line connection between two customer locations located in the same local access and transport area (LATA). The customer can use the TIE line to link two telephone systems (PBXs) together. The connection can be via a two-wire circuit with E&M signaling (which actually uses four wires) or a four-wire circuit with E&M signaling (which uses six or eight wires). The customer equipment used causes the variable nature. The four-wire E&M circuit will provide a higher-quality service because twice the bandwidth is available. Using six or eight wires enables two wires for transmitting, two wires for receiving, and the remaining wires for signaling outside the bandwidth of the circuit. After drawing internal dial tone from the PBX internal extension, a user dials some selected dial code (for example, 7 for TIE lines). Once the dial code is entered, the PBX draws a second dial tone from the remote PBX on the other end of the TIE line. From this second dial tone, the end user dials a three- or four-digit extension number to reach the called party at the other end. This access method enables the flat-rate connection between two company locations. No switching or routing of the call occurs across the network; it always takes the same path on the dedicated circuit. The ILEC only has to provide the dedicated pair of wires from location A through the wire center at the local central office and then right out the back end to another central office or directly to a cable pair to the second location. This is shown in Figure 6-4 for the connection between the two customer locations in different central offices. In Figure 6-5, the connection is the same, but is served by a single central office. In both cases, the central office only provides the service through the wire center rather than routing the connection through the switching center. The end user

Figure 6-4

A TIE line linking two customer locations in different COs in the LEC area—the wire centers are connected with physical connections rather than access switched services.

Two locations linked
together by a TIE line
in the same CO

gains access to the remote site without having to dial an outside line (the ninth level is typical in a PBX) and then a seven-digit direct inward dial extension number. This reduces the number of digits the user dials and eliminates the additional usage-sensitive costs of message units for local calls. Depending on the number of interoffice calls made between the two sites, the savings realized can be significant. A flat-rate service might prove advantageous over usage-sensitive rates. The ILEC charges for the service on a mileage basis for the dedicated pair of wires between the two locations.

Foreign Exchange Service

Foreign exchange (FX) service is a leased-line service that enables a customer to draw a dial tone from a remote central office in the ILEC's service area. The primary use of the foreign exchange is to provide a local telephone number for customers to call. The local seven-digit telephone number is connected to a leased line that goes to a central office in a remote location and is then passed along to the subscriber's location. This eliminates a long-distance call from a customer to a supplier, enabling the appearance of a local presence. The user pays the ILEC for a local dial tone line at the foreign central office and the mileage charges for the dedicated private line to the user's location. An example of this service is a customer located in Wilmington, Delaware calling a supplier in Philadelphia, Pennsylvania. Normally, this is a long-distance, intra-LATA call between the two cities served by the ILEC. The distance between these two cities is roughly 29 miles. At the current tariff rates, this call costs $0.40 per minute. Because the customer calls the supplier on a regular basis to place an order, it is advantageous from the supplier's perspective to allow the customer to call free of charge. Therefore, the supplier rents an FX from the ILEC. Normally, the customer calls (215) 555-1111, but using the FX service, the customer now calls a local seven-digit telephone number (302) XXX-1234. By calling this local number, the customer does not incur any local long-distance charges and will not hesitate to call the supplier on a regular basis. From the supplier's perspective, the leased line from Wilmington to Philadelphia will cost in the neighborhood of $200.00 per month. Given the cost for the toll call at $0.40 per minute, the break-even point is 500 minutes. Because the customer makes calls that can last up to 10 minutes each, 50 calls justify the circuit. Taking this to the next logical step, the supplier who is paying the cost of the monthly circuit charge can also use the FX when calling the customer back. The service can be set up on a one-way in, one-way out, or two-way basis. Therefore, the return calls help to justify the expense between the two sites and reduce the overall cost per minute for the usage fees. Other ways of handling this same service are available; this is only an example. Keep in mind that the service in this context is offered by the LEC and is a local toll replacement. If this capability is required between locations in other parts of the country, the ILEC will only provide the last mile on each end, whereas the interexchange carriers (IEC) provide the interstate, inter-LATA portion of the circuit. Table 6-2 provides a summary of the one- or two-way traffic, comparing it with local calling costs. This is calculated for a standard call of ten minutes in duration. Other variations of the pricing arrangements can be calculated on the basis of the ILEC's tariffs in the specific areas around the country. Each variation carries different pricing configurations and significantly different cost justifications.

Table 6-2 reflects a total number of ten-minute calls made between the two locations and only two parties. If the number of customers increases, the total number of calls and minutes used on a single line will be limited. Only one line exists between the two central offices and the supplier location. Therefore, only one conversation can be accommodated at a time. The number of calls and minutes will be limited because the total usage on a

Table 6-2

Summary of
Possible Savings
with FX Service

Number of Calls per Month at 10 Minutes per Call	Tariffed Toll Calls	FX Service Fixed Rate	Difference
50	$ 200.00	$200.00	$ 0
75	$ 300.00	$200.00	($ 100.00)
100	$ 400.00	$200.00	($ 200.00)
150	$ 600.00	$200.00	($ 400.00)
200	$ 800.00	$200.00	($ 600.00)
300	$1,200.00	$200.00	($1,000.00)
400	$1,600.00	$200.00	($1,400.00)

single circuit will not be equal to eight hours per day. This is because of the downtime when one caller hangs up and the other initiates a call. The circuit will only provide a certain percentage of availability to both ends. Typically, a single circuit will only result in 3 to 3 1/2 hours of total talk time availability. Therefore, if the number of calls exceeds those reflected, another FX line might be required. One can see, however, that the pricing differences and savings opportunities are substantial. The use of FX lines is a mainstay for the ILEC in providing cost-effective solutions for businesses.

WATS (Intrastate, Intra-LATA)

Wide area telecommunications services (WATS) are a special tariff that the Bell System created back in the 1970s. The original purpose of a WATS line was to enable large customers to access the local and long-distance network at a reduced rate. In effect, it is a volume discount offering that AT&T (the Bell System) created for the very large user or for the smaller business having large volumes of calls to specific geographical areas of the country. The way the WATS tariff originally worked varied depending on the volumes of calls that the customer had. This included the following types of service:

Bands The country, exclusive of the state the customer is located in, was originally broken down into concentric circles or areas of coverage depending on the user location. In Figure 6-6, the original banding is shown for

Figure 6-6
Original WATS bands
consisted of five
contiguous bands
emanating from the
originating point.
Band 1 lines cannot
be used to call areas
beyond that
contiguous band.

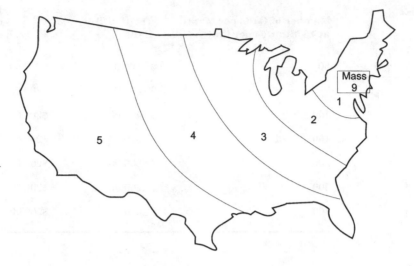

the East Coast, using Massachusetts as a reference point. In each case, the band selected by the customer allowed for calling into states by the area codes contained in the band. In the example of the East Coast, the band 1 line selected enabled calls into the eight New England states. Any call made into the area codes covered by this line was carried without any restrictions. However, if a caller attempted to place a call into a state that was not part of this band, a reorder (fast busy) tone sounded, meaning that service to that area was denied.

If the need to call a greater area of the country existed, then the next higher band was offered. The band 2 line enabled expanded calling coverage to the next concentric circle of states. The area covered in band 1 is included in the band 2 service area. Thus, the coverage remained inclusive as the concentric circles became larger. Using a band 5 WATS line enabled calls anywhere in the contiguous United States. The costs for the lines varied by banding, with band 1 bearing the least cost and band 5 bearing the highest cost. Companies using these services had to select the zones that they planned to call. The burden was on the users to configure the lines based on the communities of interest in their calling patterns.

Obviously, the selection of a mix of bands 1 through 5 was the preferred choice. A company did not want users to arbitrarily call a band 1 state (or area code) on a band 5 line because of the difference in cost for the service.

The carrier, in this case AT&T, created this configuration to appease the large customers without offering the same discounted rates to the smaller user. The FCC and the local public utilities commissions were very sensitive to the differentiation of pricing among groups of users. Therefore, AT&T developed a technique of offering WATS without the call detail that was associated with the standard long-distance direct distance dialing service. The customer was responsible for capturing the details of the calls for allocation purposes through extended call detail recording capabilities on the PBX or Centrex service, and the customer paid a flat rate for the service whether the line was used or not. Thus, the difference in the service justified the difference in price.

Full-time WATS   A full-time WATS service offering enabled the customer to pay a flat rate per line regardless of the number of calls or hours used. Actually, the cost was not truly a flat rate; up to 240 hours of usage per month (eight hours per day at 30 days per month) was allowed. When 240 hours of usage was reached, a premium was applied, but at an extremely low rate per additional hour. The flat-rate costs depended on the band selected. In Table 6-3, the original pricing is shown for the rates from the New England area. These prices differed depending on the location of the user.

Measured-Rate WATS   Measured-rate service became the option for either the smaller user who had certain volumes or the larger user who had a mix of flat and measured-rate lines. The measured rate enabled a customer to use the first ten hours at a fee. Each additional hour of usage bore an hourly rate at a cost that was higher, but still less than direct dial rates. Many customers used the measured-rate service as an entry level into

Table 6-3

Original WATS Flat-Rate Pricing for 240 Hours Usage per Month

WATS Band	Flat Rate Monthly Cost
1	$ 900
2	$1,100
3	$1,265
4	$1,440
5	$1,675

WATS service. On reaching a sustained volume at some break-even point, the customer converted to flat-rate services. This was more complex to manage and monitor on a regular basis. However, the typical break-even point ranged around 80 hours of usage. Once again, the onus rested with the customer to monitor and reconfigure the mix of services on the basis of sustained use.

ILEC Intrastate WATS   Where AT&T offered the interstate calling services, the local operating telephone companies offered the in-state service. Because the ILEC is constrained to offer services only in its LATA, distances covered by WATS line capability must be limited. The ILECs offer long-distance, intra-LATA WATS at a reduced rate over the toll call rates. As with the IEC version of WATS, when this was first introduced, the intrastate service had to be separated from the interstate service. The reason for this separation is obvious; the FCC controls the rates for the interstate, inter-LATA offerings, whereas the local Public Utility Commissions (PUCs) control the LATA and state rates. To offer some volume discount to their large business customers, the ILECs had to come up with a discount plan through a tariff filing that would be approved by the local PUC. WATS on an intrastate basis was the answer. The use of WATS on an intra-LATA, intrastate basis is founded on the basic line charge per month (typically $37.50 per month) plus usage charges based on hours of usage. The use of the line increases and therefore the cost per hour decreases. Many organizations have been able to reduce their costs per minute on WATS to a reasonable $0.10 to $0.15 per minute, as opposed to the direct dial rates of $0.20 to $0.25 per minute or more. Clearly, the benefits of volume discounts are the savings that can be achieved.

One Plus WATS   Once the costs for WATS service became a commodity, the carriers had to come up with a new offering to appease the smaller business. To do this, the One Plus WATS was offered. Using an access line to the long-distance network within the ILEC's domain, the user can place long-distance calls on a single access line to any point in the LATA. Therefore, separate lines are not required for the customer to use a discounted plan. As a matter of fact, the ILEC can provide the same service to route local calls alongside toll calls. Consequently, the business user can use the service even though the telephone system might not accommodate added lines for special purpose use. Discounts can be gained through a billing arrangement rather than through special circuits. This makes the service readily available to the masses and saves the customer a significant amount of time and money over the current mode of operation.

800/888/877/866 Service

Introduced over 25 years ago, the toll-free arrangement became the service to vie for. While businesses were reaping the benefits of reduced outbound calls through the WATS tariffs, the other side of the business dealt with the incoming traffic. As users recognized, the cost of telecommunications expenses was escalating dramatically. Customers located far from the supplier had some hesitation about calling long distance to place orders. Further, the supplier's salespeople out on the road were forced to carry pockets full of change or a telephone credit card. The credit card was kept as a perk for some; only senior executives were issued a credit card to place calls back to the office from the road. Consequently, many users of the telephone network set up a work-around procedure to overcome the cost of long-distance calling back to the office. A customer or an employee of the organization would dial an operator-assisted, collect person-to-person call. This was the most expensive way to make a call. However, the caller would ask for him- or herself or some fictitious individual. This would be used to indicate that the called party answering the incoming collect call should refuse the call by saying that the individual was not there. The operator would then suggest that when the asked-for party returned, he or she call "the caller" back at the number. The called organization would then hang up and grab an Out-WATS line and return the call immediately. This saved the user a good amount of money on the telephone bill because the call was sent out at a reduced rate. Further, the incoming collect call based on a person-to-person calling rate would not be billed to the recipient of the call because the call was not accepted. To overcome this use of the network for the incoming fictitious numbers, the carriers had to come up with a solution. They could not bill these calls, even though completing them tied up the network and human resources. This arrangement was also used by residential customers who had children in schools or who were traveling: The student could call home asking for himself, which became the signal that he or she had arrived all right.

Thus, the toll-free or 800 calling service was introduced. This is nothing more than a reverse-billing WATS service where the callers can enjoy the benefit of calling at any time without having to worry about the cost of the call. The owner of the 800 WATS service had to worry about the volume of calls and the origin of the calling party. The ILECs offer in-WATS, as part of the potpourri of services for the intrastate intra-LATA areas, to allow the reverse charges of the calls. This is a tariffed item that is similar to the outward service where a monthly access fee is charged for the line plus usage. When the 800 service was first introduced, the same flat- and measured-rate services were available. As the commodity business of WATS caught on, the same evolution took hold whereby a customer could use the same access line for incoming regular calls and for incoming 800 calls. The limitation is that only one call per line can be active at a time. If the customer calling a supplier uses the line for an 800 service call, then others trying to dial direct into the called party encounter a busy tone. With the possibility of having an 800 number, the supplier can accomplish the receipt of a call without inconveniencing customers through an expensive call to the location. This allows the customer to call toll free to the supplier regardless of the distance, feeling no remorse whatsoever about the long-distance call. The 800 area code numbers are rapidly depleting, so the carriers now offer 888, 877, and 866 as additional toll-free numbering schemes.

Directory Services

The ILEC also offers directory assistance for a fee. The typical arrangement offered by the ILEC is to look up called parties' numbers using operator assistance. Once the number is obtained, a voice response unit takes over, playing the number out loud to the interested party. The typical fee for this type of directory assistance ranges from $0.35 to $0.50 per call. Some companies offer an initial three, free operator assists for directory assistance. Newer versions of this service are emerging in which the operator still keys in the name of the requested number, and then the voice response unit offers to complete the call on delivery of the message. The fee for this connection and automatic dialing ranges from $0.35 to $0.85, depending on the location. These are newer methods of offering assistance while generating new revenue streams.

Although it might sound excessive or impractical to have a calling party agree to this arrangement, one need only think about trying to get a telephone number from a phone booth while on the road. The pen always runs out of ink at the time the number is being announced, or the rain starts to pour while you are trying to write on a piece of paper. Both scenarios are frustrating and normal. Trying to remember a number in your head compounds the problem all the more; therefore, this added service is not as far-fetched as it might sound.

Off-Premises Extensions

Another form of leased-line service offered by the ILEC is the use of off-premises extensions (OPX). Let's assume that an organization is in a large office building. This user has plenty of growth from a telephone system (a la PBX) perspective, but not as much square footage to sustain growth of human resources. In fact, if the organization runs out of space, it becomes necessary to move people off site for either short-term periods while reconstruction efforts can be accommodated or longer-term periods that could be months or years. In either case, moving people off site becomes a problem in terms of managing the telecommunications flow. A new phone system might be required as a purchase at the off-site location. Along with the new phone system, new lines will be brought into the building for the branch or department that is relocated. This means that customers might have to remember two different numbers when calling the organization. This can be inconvenient for the customer, and any such inconvenience could lead to an unhappy customer. By all means, telecommunications should be friendly, not inconvenient.

Beyond the problems caused for customers by this arrangement, one also must look at what it might do to the internal communications flow of the organization. When dialing between offices in the same primary building, one merely dials a four- or five-digit telephone extension number. However, when calling this remote group after getting an internal dial tone, the user must dial 9, followed by a seven-digit telephone number associated with the newer building. At this point, the call might go to a receptionist who screens all incoming calls because direct access to an individual is probably impractical. The receptionist will then either "buzz" the called party on an intercom or page through the building for the called party to pick up line 1 (or 2, 3, and so on). Frustrations might build with the inherent delay of this process. The process can also fail through constant cutoff conditions or through extended hold times while waiting for the intended party to come to the phone. Therefore, morale can be affected within the organization. Another issue is that the remote group will have to make long-distance and local calls from this new system, which might be more expensive. This gives these people the feeling of being orphaned children as far as the organization is concerned.

To overcome this problem, the use of off-premises extensions might fit the need better than the separate system as previously described. This means that every user that is relocated will maintain his or her extension number from the primary telephone system, but that the ILEC will run (or install) private lines between the two locations. Every extension will have a two-wire interface to the telecommunications system and a single-line set at a remote building. The ILEC merely provides the wires from the initial location to a demarcation point at the remote location (Figure 6-7). The ILEC bills this on a per-station mileage base per month, plus a one-time installation fee. Each provider handles mileage differently, so the pricing is deliberately avoided in this discussion. The customer then plugs into the outside lines from the ILEC with a piece of equipment (that is, a single-line set). The ILEC runs the wires through the wire center at the central office(s) involved, as it does with other private line services. The dial tone at the end unit is drawn from the customer's switch (PBX), not from the local central office. All features and functions available to the primary location, local and long-distance services, and extension users are accessible from this OPX. The only difference is that the buildings are separated and the single-line set might not give these remote users capabilities identical to those available in the office. This is an analog telephone set for the most part because digital display sets and feature buttons are not available on a single-line analog desk set. However, the users are still treated as part of

Figure 6-7
Using off-premises extension, the LEC provides a two-wire facility (leased line) between the two locations through the wire center. Dial tone at location B comes from the PBX location A.

the organization, and it is not apparent to the callers that this separation is in effect. This is the primary goal of the OPX, and it does work. Some suggest that the OPX is a better solution, whereas others suggest that separate systems work better. This is a matter of personal preference and should be analyzed depending on the actual circumstance.

Access to Interexchange Carriers (Equal Access)

The ILECs have also provided the access to the long-distance suppliers on an equal-access basis since 1984. Prior to 1984, the ILEC provided access to the IEC based on the interconnection arrangements that they had set up. Typically, this was through the AT&T network because that was the way things were done back then. But when equal access was mandated, the ILECs had to allow connections to any carrier of the customer's choosing. This is done according to user selection, not as a fee-based service. Any long-distance carrier marketing in a specific area is granted access to the customers on an equal basis, as was provided to AT&T. The IECs are charged for the access fees that they build into their rate structure and pass along to the user. The access is based on the type of connection available and the distances separating the carrier's point of presence (POP) and the ILEC's central offices involved. The customer is given a choice of primary (or presubscribed) interexchange carrier (PIC) for each line installed. The ILEC then sets a database on how to switch or hand off calls destined to the IEC from each customer. The connections are shown in Figure 6-8. The ILEC might hand the call up to the access tandem switch (class 4 office) or optionally have connections directly to the IEC in an equal access end office (class 5 office).

Competitive Local Exchange Carriers (CLECs)

Because of the deregulation and the Telecom Act of 1996 as discussed in Chapter 1, the competitive local exchange carriers (CLECs) can offer services very similar to those of the ILEC. As mentioned in Chapter 1, the CLEC may choose to offer both a facilities-based and a non-facilities-based

Figure 6-8
The LEC hands off calls to the IEC depending on the customer's selection of which IEC will carry the call. Various forms of media can be used to interconnect the LEC and IEC offices.

service. The competitive LECs initially offered dial tone as their primary vehicle to attract customers. This included newly emerging entrepreneurial organizations, the IECs, electric companies, local telephone equivalents, other utilities (gas, water, and so on), or cable TV companies. Regardless of who the player actually is, these providers emerged and appeared throughout the country. As they built their infrastructure or chose to use the telephone company facilities, they offered dial tone and a whole range of services as discussed above. Users must then decide whom to contract for the local access and dial tone services. Will the choice be a pricing arrangement? Or will the telephone companies have frustrated their end users sufficiently to warrant consideration of a new provider? In either case, the new providers will be in a position to provide services in a limited fashion to a localized audience.

These new audiences wanted one-stop shopping—the ability to use a single source for dial tone, long distance, cable services, equipment, internal wiring, desktop devices, LAN components, and any other new technology that comes along. These CLECs should have attacked the last bastion and the last mile. Many of these CLECs began offering Centrex service in their operating areas. With the Centrex service, they are offering local dial tone, long distance, equipment, and wiring all on a single bill. The equipment offerings are based on monthly or annualized rental agreements. This represents the first step toward the one-stop shopping mentioned throughout this book. As the CLECs began to spread out throughout the country, many users were exposed to four, five, or six providers within a community offering services. The authors mentioned the possibility that these CLECs vying for market share and market points offered some of these services at or below cost. At a cost or below-cost arrangement, the end user stands to gain significantly. One caveat we saw to this, however, is that it could not go on forever. The carriers were using money that was seed money from Venture Capitalists (VCs) or through IPOs on the market. This is a limited amount of funds, and as these carriers began to lose money, the well dried up. The years of late 1999 and 2000 were not kind to these providers. The money disappeared, the VCs withheld further investments and the shareholders were looking for returns on their investments. Of the 500 plus CLECs in the industry, few were making any form of profitability, and all of them were experiencing market losses of 75 to 90 percent of their capitalization. We even saw a few other things happen: Two major providers went under (bankruptcy) and many others merged. The year 2000 marked the beginning of the belt-tightening that we predicted in this book four years ago. Having regrouped, these new value-added providers began to go beyond the basic voice offerings and started offering xDSL and Internet access. Moreover, Voice over IP and Voice over DSL are in the making for many of these new providers. High-speed Internet access, two-way simultaneous conferencing, and video dial tone are now in the offering.

Many of the CLECs received much of their revenue from a reciprocal arrangement established by the FCC to handle traffic that passed between the CLEC and the ILEC. In some cases, this amounted to as much as 80 percent of the CLEC revenues. When this reciprocal arrangement ends in 2002 (possibly), the CLECs are in for another round of tough times, unless they can garner their forces and start selling for higher returns.

Data Local Exchange Carriers (DLEC)

The new players are also taking on the name of data local exchange carriers (DLECs), in which their specialty is strictly data offerings and not in a voice arena. Some of these providers also ran into hard times as they overextended their role or the budgetary constraints facing them. We shall see more of the DLECs in the coming years.

Interexchange Carriers (IEC/IXC)

The interexchange carrier (IEC or IXC) is the long-distance carrier. In general terms, this carrier connects to the ILEC or CLEC with circuits from its POP to the central office. Most of the major players in this arena are IECs such as Sprint, MCI/Worldcom, AT&T, Cable & Wireless, and so on.

The IECs can carry either long-distance switched and/or private line service. The major players provide both. Some of the IECs, however, primarily provide private line service, depending on their charter. Typical services provided by the IECs include interstate and inter-LATA capabilities as follows.

Switched Long Distance (DDD)

With DDD, the IECs enable the end user to pick up a phone and dial anywhere in the continental United States. As long as the end user has selected the IEC as the primary interexchange carrier of choice and the end user is served by an office that has equal access, the user merely has to dial 1 plus the desired ten-digit telephone number. The carrier then uses the capability of the switched public network to route the call to the appropriate end point. Many of the carriers have the ability to let the user access their network through the one plus network access or through a leased line into the carrier's POP. The POP can be either the access point into a switching system that will route the call to the appropriate state, or a closet in which the carrier has terminated equipment on a leased high-capacity circuit.

To better explain this concept, let's assume that a long-distance provider wishes to set up an operation in downtown Philadelphia. However, the closest points of access into the carrier's long-distance facilities (the microwave radio systems or the fiber-optic cabling system owned or leased by this particular carrier) are either in Washington, D.C. or New York City. To begin service in the Philadelphia area, the carrier could rent space, buy a switching system, and run cables or radio systems out into the area (Figure 6-9). A second option is to rent space and put some equipment (such as a multiplexer or a rack of dedicated wires) in a closet or a hotel room. As the carrier begins to add customers, the LEC connections from the customer

Figure 6-9
The IEC rents space, buys a switching system, and connects to POPs located in its area. This is a true switching center.

location to the IEC location will be on a two- or four-wire local loop. Rather than terminating into a switching system, the ILEC's or CLEC's* wires will be terminated onto a frame or backboard in the rental space defined previously. The IEC then takes the wires from the LEC demarcation point and cross-connect them to a different pair of wires running from Philadelphia to Washington or New York (Figure 6-10), where the carrier has a closet approach. At this point, the IEC will bring the customer's connection into the switching system located within the boundaries of the network connections.

Credit Card Service (Calling Card Service)

All of the IECs (and the LECs for that matter) offer the ability to take advantage of their network services using a credit card or calling card. This is a matter of convenience for the customer. When traveling, people need to

---

*For the sake of simplification, references to both CLEC and ILEC will be used as a generic LEC throughout the rest of the book.

Figure 6-10
To open a new area, IEC A may rent closet space only to provide a physical interface to the LEC wires. From there, the IEC can lease lines from a competitor or install its own lines to the city where a switch is located.

use hotel/motel phones, pay phones, and generally any other service that enables access to the long-distance networks. Rather than have a customer run around the country with a pocket full of quarters ($0.25 pieces), which would be difficult and would discourage the use of the network, the credit card enables the caller to access the network at will and use the service unhindered. This service carries a surcharge with it. For every call placed on the carrier's network, an initial surcharge of between $0.50 and $1.00 per call is tacked onto the first minute of the call. Given that the average length of a call on the network is five minutes, this adds a penalty of $0.20 per minute on the call. If a caller averages more than five minutes, the cost of the call becomes close to the direct distance dial rate. The benefits and discounts of using a single carrier help to offset this surcharge.

When the calls initially had to be handled by an operator-assisted arrangement, the surcharge was introduced to offset the cost of the personnel needed to process these credit card calls. However, this is a misnomer today because the automated process is now used where a customer dials 0 plus the ten-digit telephone number and waits for a tone (or bong). After receiving the tone, the customer continues by dialing the credit card number to be charged. From there, the call is processed across the network and completed. For billing purposes, this is straightforward. However, no operator was ever involved because the automation took care of the entire call. Why then do the carriers continue to charge the operator-assisted rates? To add insult to injury, if the need arises for an operator to complete the call for whatever reason (if a caller is not on a Touch-Tone phone, the dial pad is shunted out after the 0 and the ten digits are dialed), then the carrier bills a premium for the operator to assist in the completion of the call. This sounds like a double whammy in terms of the billing mechanism, and technically, it is. The carriers would have the user believe that the more expensive service of using a human in the call completion has been reduced under the automated process.

WATS Service

Like the LECs, all IECs have some form of WATS service as a volume-discounted offering. The more a customer uses this service, the less expensive the cost per minute will be. To use the WATS services of many of the carriers these days, customers have several options, which are listed in Table 6-4.

In each of the cases shown in the table, many options are available, indicating that the carriers are concerned with offering some form of discounted service to users, depending on the volume of calls and the distances that will be called. In every case, the user still benefits over the regular long-distance (DDD) rates, but the variables are really becoming commodity items again. When looking at the options, customers can easily become confused; yet with all of the changes going on in this industry, it cannot be assumed that the carrier's representative will be able or willing to point out added options or discounts. The best way to take advantage of this type of service is to consider no more than an annual contract period or a month-to-month contract with the carrier. This way, the user will not be locked into a pricing structure that prohibits on-the-fly changes and adjustments as usage changes. The carriers, however, will discourage this option by stating that the customer stands to benefit from longer-term contracts based on reductions offered over and above the standard offerings. Keep this straight and in perspective. The value of the end user is critical to the IEC because little or no price sensitivity occurs on the cost per minute. The differences

Table 6-4

A Summary of the
WATS Variations
and Pricing
Arrangements

WATS Service	Initial Cost	Variable Costs
Dedicated lines	$37.50	Based on usage by bands. The usage follows a rate structure: First 10 hours Next 25 hours All over 40 hours
Dial One WATS		Cost per minute based on distance and time of day.
Reach Out America	$10.00	Cost per minute based on distance and time of day. Minimal discounts applied.
Virtual WATS (SDN/VPN)	Access fee into VPN or SDN	Special billing based on distance, time of day, and volume used.
Special Tariff 12 service	Access fees at the T1 or T3 rates	Special pricing based on long-term WATS contracts of three to five years. Greatest discounts apply for WATS.
Pro WATS	$5.00	Plus cost per minute on distance and time of day.
Multilocation WATS	$2500	Flat rate to consolidate bills plus largest discounts possible on WATS.

between carriers can be as little as $0.002 (stated as two mills of a cent), but if the carrier sincerely wants the business, the differences can be far more significant. Let's assume that an IEC can deliver a cost per minute of $0.20 to a customer for long-distance calls. What is the carrier's actual cost, as opposed to the rate charged? Interestingly, the carriers (at least the major players) can deliver a call at their cost for $0.03 or less per minute. Now, in order to generate profits, they might mark this up to approximately $0.06 per minute (representing a 100 percent gross profit).

So, how can they sell service to the end user at $0.20? Well, first they have to pay access fees to the LECs to gain access on the LEC's wires to the customer's premises. The typical access fee charged on a call-by-call basis comes to $0.07 per minute per end. Looking at the total, the cost per minute is shown in Table 6-5. This table covers a call from San Jose, California to Philadelphia, Pennsylvania.

Obviously, the numbers reflected in this table are for the casual user of a WATS service, not the larger users who have thousands to hundreds of thousands of minutes of usage. The larger consumers (corporations) are

Table 6-5

The Total Cost Picture Charged at $0.20 per Minute to the End User

Description	Fees
Local access charges at the LEC end in San Jose	$0.07
Interexchange carrier cost	$0.03
Interexchange carrier profits	$0.03
LEC access fees in Philadelphia	$0.07
Total	$0.20

getting their long distance for $.03 a minute or less. However, to overcome these costs and to add some degree of new attractiveness to the end user community, the IECs are now offering bundled services on T1 access lines. This works out to mean that the IEC or the customer rents the T1 line as a dedicated link. The cost of the leased line is fixed, doing away with the usage sensitivity of the calls. At a cost of between $350 and $400 per month, the cost per minute is reduced. Table 6-6 shows the costs of the calls. This scenario compares the costs for 24 individual WATS lines and a T1.

This is just an aside from the authors: It is hard to believe that currently 80 percent of the consuming public is still so uneducated about the cost per minute. However, that same 80 percent of users still pays as much as $0.20 to $0.25 per minute for their long-distance calling. When they do try to get a special deal, they have to pay some minimum monthly fee or an up-front service fee ($4.95), and when they add their total minutes and divide them into these special service fees, they are nailed by the providers. This is a big

Table 6-6

Comparing Dedicated WATS (Analog) Lines to a T1 Service

Description	Using Dedicated WATS Lines	Using a T1 in Lieu of WATS Lines
Line rental	24 × $37.50 = $900	$400
Cost per minute on access	$0.07 × 24 = $16.80	0
Cost per minute for WATS	$0.15 × 24 = $3.60	$3.60
Cost of 100 hours usage	[60 × 100 × (3.60 + 16.80)] + 900	[60 × 100 × 3.60] + 400
Total	$123,300	$22,000

part of the $100 billion plus market for long distance in North America alone.

800/888/877/866 and 900 Service Offerings

As mentioned earlier, the 800/888/877/866 service is a derivative of WATS line service. When initially introduced in the AT&T network 25 years ago, the 800 service was called In-WATS. This was a mechanism to replace the inward collect calling services. As the name changed, the service was made more flexible. A call coming into the 800/888/877/866 number is billed at a usage-sensitive rate based on the band from which the call originates. Further, as a call is routed and delivered into an 800/888/877 service, the customer can specify that the network deliver the call to different locations or to specific agents in a call group on the basis of the call's origin. This inbound service can be called 800/888/877/866 service or 800/888/877/866 Megacom service, among other names. Further, small business services (such as Readyline or 800/888/877/866 Starter line) are available. In each of these cases, the service is priced according to the needs of the customer. For example, the 800/888/877/866 service will be used by a medium-size customer who selects dedicated lines for the inbound service. The 800/888/877/866 Megacom service will be chosen by larger customers who use a T1 line to bundle 24 In-WATS lines together. The Readyline service would be used by the small branch office that does not have line space on its existing telephone system and so it routes the calls into an existing incoming line that is shared with a regular incoming dial tone line. Finally, the Starter line would be used in a very small office or a home office where the customer uses the smallest volumes routed to a specific telephone number shared with a business or residential line. The prices vary with the choice

Table 6-7

A Summary of Various in WATS Offerings

Service Offering	Average Pricing
In-WATS 800 service lines	$37.50 per line per month plus usage at $0.15+ per minute
800 Megacom service	$400 plus usage at $0.10−0.12 per minute
Readyline service	$20 per month plus $0.20 per minute
Starter line service	$6 per month plus $0.26 per minute

selected, but the flexibility is what is being highlighted here. Table 6-7 shows the different uses as orders of magnitude pricing rather than specific pricing arrangements.

The 900 services are pay-per-use offerings that have drawn mixed emotions and reviews. When first introduced, the 900 offerings were the domain of pay-per-call providers, such as the lottery services, dial-a-porn, dial-a-joke, and so on. All callers willing to pay for the service charge associated with the call could access them. The owner of the 900 service offering establishes an account with the IEC. From there, the owner establishes a rate for the service ($2.00 per call, $25.00 per call, $0.50 per minute, or any other derivative of this pricing scheme). The IEC assigns a 900 area code number that the owner then advertises. The next step is that the IEC establishes a rate to be charged to the owner. The customers start to call the 900 number, based on the inducement to call, regardless of the offering. As the caller dials the number, the call is delivered to the advertised location of the owner. This is then billed to the caller based on the advertised rate. The IEC bills the call, collects the revenue, holds out a piece of the revenue based on the agreed-upon price (10 percent or more), and after collecting the revenue, sends a check for the difference to the customer (owner). Figure 6-11 illustrates the flow of this operation. This service has created many millionaires in the industry. Also, there are many scams that occur where you receive a voice message to call an 800 number to collect a prize. Of course, when you return the call and dial the 800 number, the call is forwarded to a 900 number. This gets expensive, but you can report it to the ILEC and they will remove the cost of this call ($2.00-$50.00 typically) from your bill.

However, to override these premium services, many organizations disallow the access to 900 area code numbers. Some schemes use the features of the telephone company to block this area code from access by individual users; others use the features of internal telephone systems to deny access to the area codes.

International Access

The IECs provide gateway access into international direct distance dialing (IDDD) through their service offerings. The call is carried across the IEC's network and delivered to the international carrier at a midpoint. In this arrangement, the IEC and the international carrier share the revenue. IDDD is a service that enables a user to pick up a phone anywhere and dial an international country code sequence, followed by a city code, and then

Figure 6-11
The flow of a 900 call
process

① Customer Dials 900#

Call is Routed to
② Appropriate Carrier

Carrier ③ Carrier Connects
Caller to 900 Service

900 ④ 900 Service Provides Info
Service or Service as Advertised

A: Who
B: How Long ⑤ Carrier Keeps Track
C: How Much of Billing Information

Bill ⑥ Carrier Bills Caller

⑦ Caller Pays Carrier

Carrier Receives Payment,
⑧ Takes % Out for Services
Rendered

⑨ Carrier Mails Remainder
to 900 Service

the variable-length telephone number of the called party. The IEC bills on
the basis of cost per minute, collects the revenue for the international call,
and disburses it according to a revenue-sharing arrangement with the
international carrier. This makes it simple for the user of the service;
because all the information is on one bill, the call can be logged and charged
appropriately without having to pull together different pieces from various
bills.

Foreign Exchange Service

From an IEC perspective, the foreign exchange (FX) service that spans
across LATA or state boundaries falls into the IEC's domain. An FX line
from Dallas to New York (or any other two points under the IEC domain) is

provided as a leased line with dial tone coming from the foreign central office. The IEC can bill this at a monthly rate for the mileage points between the two cities and will also be responsible for the end-to-end connection if the customer so desires. Many IECs and LECs make the long-haul portion of the circuit the responsibility of the IEC and the billing of the local dial tone service in the remote city the responsibility of the LEC. This is less desirable because the customer must then assemble various portions of bills to gather all of the facts and costs of an FX line. The service will be billed primarily at a flat rate; however, originating and terminating minutes might bear a cost from the LEC at the end of the circuit. One should verify all costs associated with the line as a means of cost justification. The use of an FX line between the two points mentioned might have applications other than the obvious benefit to a customer. Initially, the calls made by a customer to a supplier's location can be made on an FX. This allows the customer to place a local call that is connected to a long-distance line 1,000 miles away, avoiding the toll call for the customer. However, another application of the FX can be used for example for a Dallas-based company that is tentative about opening an office in New York. Rather than renting an office, buying or renting furniture, hiring a staff, and trying to break into a new market, this company can take a special group of agents to deal with future New York customers. Customers can call a local seven-digit telephone number. The local presence of the supplier is implied with this number. As some companies feel more comfortable dealing with organizations that are local, the supplier can present the image of local presence using the FX. Therefore, for a minor investment, the supplier can begin marketing in the New York area. If the volume of calls is sufficient to warrant a staff in the New York area, the Dallas-based organization can staff an office. However, if the volume and acceptance level do not warrant a full-time staff, the supplier can still service the customer base in New York without the investment in real estate and office furnishings. This is an effective use of telecommunications as a strategic corporate resource.

Off-Premises Extensions (OPXs)

When a customer of an IEC has many locations around the country or around many other LATAs, the IEC can provide private line service in the form of an off-premises extension (OPX). This has already been discussed in the LEC environment, so the IEC's involvement only includes the extension of this private line across boundaries that relegate the service offering to the IEC domain. Once again, the private line draws dial tone services from inside the customer-owned and -operated PBX or Centrex. The IEC merely provides a quality circuit to any point outside the originating LATA at a flat rate. Figure 6-12 is a representation of the use of an OPX in two different states. The cost depends on the mileage associated with the circuit. No magic occurs in this offering; the IECs provide many connections with this service.

Operator/Directory Assistance

Just as with the LECs, IECs also provide operator services to assist with call completion. A fee is charged for the intervention of the operator. More and more services are being displaced from the venue of human intervention to the use of interactive voice response and recognition services (IVR). In the systems of more than one carrier, operator and directory assistance are initially obtained through contact with a human, but then revert immediately to IVR. As more of these services are provided, IVR will provide the number, offer to complete the call automatically for an additional fee, and if a busy tone occurs, allow the caller to leave a voice message on the network and redial on a regular basis until the message gets through. This is also a fee-added service. Other systems are now using voice response so that callers on the IEC network can use voice-activated dialing to the ten most frequently called numbers in a preestablished database. The Fōncard2 offering enables a user to preestablish calls to "home," "office," "lawyer," and

Figure 6-12
IECs can provide OPX between two different states on a mileage (month-to-month) basis. This is a standard offering from the IECs.

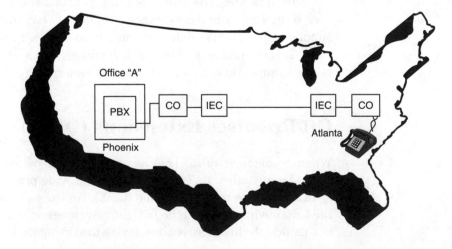

so on. When the caller simply speaks the word into the IVR, the call is automatically dialed. This is a convenience, but not a showstopper.

Newer operator and directory services emerged that will enable a customer to dial a special code (00) and have access to anywhere in the country. For a fee, the carriers are offering the ability to work with the caller to help find a number, even if the customer has limited information about the desired company. The operative words here are "for a fee." Nowadays, you can get almost anything you want from your carriers if a revenue stream is involved.

Remote Call Forwarding (RCF)

Remote call forwarding (RCF), as the name implies, is the ability to forward calls dialed into a number from the original location to a remote location across the IEC network. For a fee, the customer rents a dial tone line from the LEC and establishes an automatic call forwarding arrangement to a remote site in another city outside the LATA or in another state. The customer pays for the long-distance call from the original site to the forwarded site (typically about $0.25 per minute) on the basis of the distance and time of day. The situation is similar to that with the FX in that the caller is dialing a local seven-digit telephone number, but the call is routed to a remote site in another city (Figure 6-13). This is particularly useful in lieu of a private line service, where the private line can be an expensive proposition. If the calling volume is low, the use of call forwarding on a call-by-call basis might be less expensive. Thus, the option is straightforward regarding the outlay of money each month. If the volume stays low, the RCF remains in place. However, if the volume of calls increases and the price increases proportionately, a private line FX or other service can be used. Another option is the use of the 800 service, but this automatically implies that the called party is far away or long distance—even if this is not the case.

Competitive Access Providers

The local loop has been protected as a monopoly since early in this century. The LEC was the only carrier allowed to deliver dial tone. Regardless of the cost, service, or quality of the lines, users had no options except to bypass the LEC with their own equipment. This might include microwave, copper,

Figure 6-13
The remote call
forwarding process

The following steps are shown in the figure:

1. Customer Dials Local 7-Digit Phone Number
2. LEC Looks Up Table in Switch, Routes Call to IEC
3. IEC Table Looks Up Destination Address to Remote Customer
4. Call is Routed Across IEC Network, then Routed to Local LEC CO
5. LEC Central Office Delivers the Call to the Dialed Customer
6. IEC Bills Customer for Long-Distance Dialed Call on Cost per Minute

or satellite communications. However, a bypass only served to get access to the IEC or to another customer premise. The telephone company still provided dial tone and local-switched services. However, a group of entrepreneurs began to lay fiber optics in the ground, connecting multitenant buildings in major cities. The vendors began to offer all-digital, fiber-optic bypass solutions to the customers. Competitors offering reduced rates, volume discounts, and quick delivery times for the service invaded Bell's turf. These vendors are beginning to offer some attractive options to the end user. They might also offer some relief to the LECs, even though they are perceived as the enemy today.

The LECs might gain more from the presence of these carriers/vendors than they believe possible. Many of these competitive access providers (CAPs) are also CLECs, whereas others are strictly CAPs providing access and transport. The choice is up to the provider.

Questions

1. What do we call the telephone companies that used to be part of AT&T?

   a. ILEC

   b. RBOC

   c. DLEC

   d. CLEC

2. How many independent LECs are there?

3. What is the term used for the new providers of dial tone?

   a. ILEC

   b. LEC

   c. DLEC

   d. CLEC

4. What is the responsibility of the IEC?

   a. Dial tone

   b. Long distance

   c. Equipment

   d. None of the above

5. What area codes are used for In-WATS service?
   _____, _____ and _____

6. What service offers us the ability to have a phone in our home that appears to be in the office? _____

7. What service enables us to place and receive calls as though we were located in a different city?

   a. RCF

   b. In-WATS

   c. Out-WATS

   d. FX

   e. OPX

8. What is the name for the more than 500 competitors that have emerged since the Telecomm Act of 1996? _____

9. What are the newer data suppliers called? _____

10. How much can we expect to pay for long distance per minute if we are in a large corporation?

11. What percentage of the industry is still paying $0.20 to $0.25 per minute?

    a. 20 percent

    b. 50 percent

    c. 77.5 percent

    d. 80 percent

12. If a small business or consumer is lucky enough to get reduced long distance, they usually have to pay a(n) _____.

13. What is the name of the companies who are typically selling us long distance today?

    a. Aggregator

    b. Consolidator

    c. Reseller

    d. CLEC

14. What does Centrex stand for?

    a. Central Offices

    b. Central Office Exchange

    c. Corporate Exchange Service

    d. Central Exchange Service

15. When a long-distance provider handles the call, they usually have to pay the ILEC a(n)_____ fee for originating or terminating minutes.

16. The ability to use the dial-up telephone network is usually called:

    a. DID

    b. DOO

    c. AIOD

    d. DDD

17. What digit do we normally dial to get an outside line from a PBX?

    a. 6

    b. 0

    c. 9

    d. 8

18. When we link two PBX systems together in a local environment, we use a(n) _____ line.

19. What is the name of the service that will forward a call to another city at a fee?

    a. CFB

    b. RFC

    c. RCF

    d. CFN

20. When the independent telephone companies provide a service to their local community, they are called a(n) _____ .

    a. CLEC

    b. DLEC

    c. ILEC

    d. ITC

Lines and Trunks

I n this chapter we present a number of service offerings available from various carriers. Note that, with few exceptions, the offerings in this chapter are based on a set of identical technologies. They differ only in exactly where and how the connections are made, how they are billed, and what information is transmitted over the circuit in addition to the voice signal itself. The concepts of line and trunk underlie all of these offerings. We will use the term *circuit* to refer to a general point-to-point, voice-grade physical connection. We will also see that a line and a trunk might not have a physical difference because a two- or four-wire facility could be used for either. The real difference is the functional use of the wires that is applied to this linkage. The following section provides easy definitions of a line and trunk.

Lines

Unfortunately, the term *line* refers to more than one type of circuit. In most cases, it includes a connection configured to support a normal voice-calling load that is generated by one individual. In the case of a private branch exchange (PBX), the term line usually corresponds to one connection from the PBX to a desktop that is also a station. In the case of Centrex, a line is normally one physical connection from the customer site to the central office (CO). With a key system, it corresponds to one telephone number. However, a line might also be referred to as a trunk (Figure 7-1). Are you confused yet?

Figure 7-1
Places where lines
are defined

Trunks

The term *trunk* generally refers to a circuit configured to support the calling loads that are generated by a group of users, which could possibly contain many thousands of individuals. Thus, a general-use circuit from a PBX to a CO would usually be described and billed as a trunk. Connections between COs or offices higher in the network hierarchy would also be referred to as trunks. Note, however, that these trunks are physically identical to lines. Why use different terminology? This is shown in Figure 7-2 in reference to a trunk.

The ability of any given switching system, such as a CO or a PBX, to establish connections is limited. For example, although a PBX might be able to support 200 connections or ports, it might actually provide only 80 paths at any one time. In such a case, if 80 people were to connect to 80 other people (some of them possibly off site), it would account for 160 of the ports. If any of the remaining 40 telephones or ports attempted to access service, they would fail; that is, a user could pick up the telephone and not receive a dial tone. Some systems are configured so that such failures cannot happen. In the previous example, if only 160 physical connections were made to the PBX, it could provide simultaneous service to all of them. This type of

Figure 7-2
Trunks are used between intelligent switching systems.

Figure 7-3
Blocking in the PBX
arena

80 Lines   PBX   6 Trunks

CO

configuration is described as blocking (Figure 7-3). Figure 7-4 represents a non-blocking environment.

In most cases, a PBX's connections to the CO are configured so that a much higher utilization is achieved on those ports; a primary benefit of a PBX is the ability to buy fewer telco connections than one has telephones. The CO must be configured so that it can provide connection services to such trunks at this higher utilization rate, thus using more of the CO's overall switching and connection capacity. The telco naturally bills a PBX trunk at a higher rate than a single business line, even though the PBX trunk might be physically identical to that single line.

Comparisons

The following paragraph is a comparison of lines versus trunks.

A *line* is an end from a central switching service, such as a CO or a private automated branch exchange (PABX). It is represented as the end on the pair of wires regardless of where the intelligence resides. A line carries one single conversation at a time on the physical channel capacity. It is a billable location for the telephone companies. A *trunk,* on the other hand,

Figure 7-4
Non-blocking represents a one-to-one ratio.

80 Lines   PBX   80 Trunks

CO

connects two intelligent switching systems. The trunk might be a single circuit carrying a single call at a time, or it might be a bundled service that is multiplexed to carry multiple, simultaneous conversations. The difference is that a trunk is used for switching and routing decisions from the switching offices (CO or PABX). The trunk is used continually rather than occasionally. In the telephone company world, it is the connection between other offices in the hierarchy that we discussed in Chapter 3. In the private user (customer) world, it might be a single connection to the intelligent PABX from the CO. These distinctions offer some variations in billing and utilization.

With this in mind, here are some common configurations.

Common Configurations

DID

DID refers to direct inward dialing. From a caller's point of view, this service is in place if the caller can dial a ten-digit number from the outside of an organization and reach a specific individual without operator intervention.

Centrex inherently supports this capability without any additional configuration—everyone already has his or her own telephone number. A true key system (where telephone numbers are normally shared) can enable DID only if any given telephone number has a single appearance.

DID is usually referred to in the context of a PBX. It is a specific PBX feature that must be enabled and configured with elements set up within both the PBX and the telco. Consider as an example a new site intended to support 1,100 employees, each with his or her own telephone connected to a PBX.

The first step in arranging DID is to reserve the telephone numbers for all the employees. Let's say the main company's telephone number is 555-1234. The telecommunications manager requests a block of DID numbers from the telco, probably about 2,000 numbers. The telco might say, "Your DID numbers are 555-2200 through 555-4199." Notice that although the block (group of numbers) has a good chance of having the same exchange as the main number, it probably will not include (and we would not want it to include) the main number. The company pays for these numbers on a monthly basis, but they do not cost as much as actual telephone lines. So far, only the reservation of the block of numbers themselves has been arranged. The telco does not give these numbers to anyone else. Then, the telecommunications manager assigns each employee one of the numbers in the DID block.

Next, the telecommunications manager must determine how many trunks in the trunk group are required to support the calls from outside to the company's employees. These are inbound only, and are in addition to the normal in/out or inbound trunks that serve the main operator, so they must be engineered to a very low level of blocking. With DID, the telco passes the responsibility of handling answer supervision to the customer (for example, busy signals and ringing tones). The DID link is shown in Figure 7-5.

Figure 7-5
DID trunks link the PBX and CO together.

Therefore, if an external customer calls "Jane" at extension 2313, the customer dials (area code) 555-2313. The telco CO seizes the next available trunk in the DID group (if no trunk is available, the caller will receive a busy signal) and signals that extension 2313 has a call. At this point, if extension 2313 is busy, the PBX must handle it; the CO is merely passing along the signals. Possible PBX actions include forwarding to a message center, generating a busy signal, or forwarding the call to a specified alternate extension.

DID is most often used to reduce or eliminate the manpower required for a central answering position. The more calls customers can place directly, the fewer the calls that must be answered by the company operator. On the other hand, some companies prefer to have all incoming calls answered by someone trained in the way the company wants its telephones to be answered (for example, "Thank you for calling Kay's Deli! How can I help you?" versus "Hello?"). It would generally be a mistake for a telecommunications manager to make decisions about implementing DID without consulting company management.

DOD

DOD refers to direct outward dialing. If an employee can dial and reach an outside number without internal operator intervention, the company has implemented DOD. In the past, when less sophisticated telephone systems were available, it was not uncommon for a company to route all of its outbound calls through an internal operator. The operator's responsibility was both to screen calls ("no, you may not call Australia from that telephone") and to route the calls over the appropriate facilities (for example, the correct WATS line—see WATS section). With the advent of modern PBXs and Centrex, such limitations can be programmed on a telephone-by-telephone or even user-by-user basis, eliminating the need to involve an operator in outbound calls. The term DOD is not used often these days because most companies provide it.

FX

FX, not to be confused with FAX, refers to a foreign exchange circuit. In this case, "foreign" refers to a CO other than the local CO, not a location outside the country.

Consider the case of an airline that wishes to locate all of its reservation clerks in Atlanta. It cannot expect all of its customers to pay long-distance charges to make reservations. What are its alternatives? One possibility is a group of 800 circuits. Indeed, it will probably have a large number of those, but 800 trunks cover large areas (and are priced accordingly). What about service for customers calling from large, high-density metropolitan centers, such as Chicago? Perhaps a more focused service might be more cost effective. The FX grouping is shown in Figure 7-6.

Think of an FX line (or trunk) as two-thirds of a dedicated point-to-point (or TIE) connection. It starts at the customer's location, connects to the local CO, and extends from there to another foreign CO anywhere in the country. A fixed monthly charge is applied for all this mileage, but the miles have no usage-sensitive charges. At the foreign CO, the FX line is open. It has a telephone number associated with that foreign CO. Calls made to that number ring at the customer's location. Calls made from the customer's location over the FX line emanate from the foreign CO, incurring only local charges for the call from the foreign CO to the called location.

Companies often use FX lines to provide local numbers that customers can call in cities where the companies do not have offices. In the airline's

Figure 7-6
A foreign exchange (FX) connection between two major cities

case, it could arrange a group of FX lines from its Atlanta offices to a Chicago CO. All of the lines could share one Chicago local telephone number. People from anywhere could call the number, but mostly only Chicagoans would call because the number would be local and appear in their telephone book. If the airline wished to allow it, service representatives could also place calls from Atlanta to Chicago over the FX lines. The calls would be billed as though they were placed from within Chicago. Perhaps calls notifying customers of changed flight information might be placed this way.

OPX

OPX refers to off-premises extension. An OPX line permits a telephone that is not at a company's location to function to all intents and purposes as though it is located at the company's location. This capability becomes particularly interesting with the recent increase in telecommuting. Suppose an employee plans to work at home. One of the problems to overcome in such a case is the isolation that this worker might experience. Providing the employee with a telephone that looks like an internal line at the company might help to reduce the problem. Others calling the line within the company dial an internal extension, which rings at the employee's home; if the employee wishes to make a long-distance call, he or she usually dials 9 and the rest of number just as one would at a desk at the company's location. An OPX link is shown in Figure 7-7.

As with an FX line, an OPX connects from the company's location to the local CO, and continues via whatever intervening COs are necessary until it terminates directly on a telephone at another location. A key difference from an FX, however, is that an OPX is connected and configured as a telephone rather than a trunk on a PBX. This results in a limitation on the type of service provided; usually, only an analog telephone can be used at the end of an OPX because the digital signaling between a PBX and its proprietary telephones will probably not successfully make it through the various analog and digital circuits that make up the OPX. This limitation is not normally a showstopper; rather, it just imposes on the telecommunications manager the need to configure the PBX to support a certain number of analog telephones as well as digital telephones that might be used in house.

Figure 7-7
A typical off-premises
extension (OPX)

TIE Lines

In Chapter 3 we discussed the general categories of dial-up and private leased or dedicated point-to-point circuits. In the voice communications industry, a *TIE line* (also sometimes called a TIE trunk) refers to a private point-to-point circuit used to connect two voice facilities. TIE stands for terminal interface equipment (Figure 7-8). For example, a dedicated link between customer PBXs at two different locations would be referred to as a TIE line, as shown in Figure 7-9. Other examples of TIE lines might include a link between a PBX and a Centrex system, as shown in Figure 7-10, or a link between two Centrex systems. In all of these cases, it would be equally correct to refer to the circuits as private or leased lines. On the other hand, if one of the connected systems is not a voice system, the term TIE line would not normally be used.

Figure 7-8
A TIE line connecting
two PBXs over
distances (states)

One TIE line

Figure 7-9
A TIE line between a
Centrex and a PBX
arrangement

PBX

TIE Line

Centrex

CO

Figure 7-10
A TIE line connecting
two PBXs locally

E&M

When we refer to TIE lines (or trunks if they terminate in a switching system), we also refer to the types of wires and the signaling method used. We typically hear people talk about four-wire E&M TIE lines. What does this mean? First, let's try to clarify a few points.

Hey Don! Are you ready for this?

Oh yeah! But, before you start what does E&M stand for?

Good question. E&M stands for ear and mouth. When we signal on a TIE line, we use the *E* lead to signal from the CO to the customer, and as a call comes in, it is on the receive wire. When we want to place a call and grab dial tone, we signal the CO on our *M* lead (the transmit wire or where we send the signals from our mouth). So we use the E&M signaling to grab dial tone or make the circuit before proceeding. By the way Don, the term E&M was derived from the Latin words *Excipere* and *Mittere*, which mean "to receive" and "to send" respectively. Over time, it has more commonly been referred to as "ear" and "mouth" and even "earth" and "magneto," but the name generally refers to the E&M signaling leads that perform the supervisory function for the connection.

Is that clear?

Don, how many wires are there in a four-wire E&M circuit?

That is easy, four! Am I correct?

Well almost, let's first look at Table 7-1 to see how many wires are used for these circuits. This is an added confusion because we have no easy way to think it through.

Well, Don, did that clear it all up? Don? Don?

Let's take the next step in this process. Although E&M has many variations, it is found in four common forms—two of them are found more often than the others. The common forms are referred to as E&M Types I, II, III, and V. All use either two or four additional wires for supervisory signaling, making E&M a six- or eight- wire connection even though the term four-wire voice is often substituted for E&M.

E&M Type I is the most common interface found in North American PBXs and key systems whereas Type V is most common outside of North

Table 7-1

Comparison of the Number of Wires Used for TIE Lines

Designator	Number of wires	What this means	Why
2 wire E&M	4	2 wires for talking (tip and ring) plus 2 wires for signaling using E (ear) and M (mouth)	2 wires are used for the talk path and the other two wires are used for the signaling.
2 wire E&M	6	2 wires for talking, 2 wires for the E&M signaling, and sometimes telcos use another 2 wires called SG and SB	The Signal to Ground (SG) and Signal to Battery (SB) is another way they provide their signaling and control information. But they use an extra pair to do this.
4 wire E&M	6	2 wires for transmit, 2 wires for receive, and 2 wires for the E&M signaling	They added a pair of wires to create a better quality circuit connection by giving the user the full bandwidth in each direction.
4 Wire E&M	8	2 wires for transmit, 2 wires for receive, 2 wires for E&M signaling, and 2 wires for the SG and SB control	This is just a variation of the above scenarios.

Figure 7-11
E&M Signaling Type I

America. See Figure 7-11 for a diagram of the typical Type I connection. One advantage of using a Type I interface in channel banks and Voice over Packet devices is that it does not require the device connecting to the PBX to supply battery voltage, as is the case in the other E&M variations.

Signaling

Although discussions on signaling so far have focused on the signaling occurring between two ends of a T1 line, another set of signals is passed between the phones and switches involved in making a phone call. All telephony signaling can be categorized into one of three areas:

- **Supervisory** A mechanism that enables each end of the connection to advise the other end of its desire to seize the trunk and receive an acknowledgment. E&M signaling is a supervisory signaling mechanism.

- **Address** A way to pass the destination of the call to the other end

- **Informational** Status information that each end receives to understand where in the setup process a call is

WATS

WATS is an abbreviation for wide area telephone service. WATS lines come in two flavors: in-WATS and out-WATS. Another name for in-WATS is 800/888/877/866 service. When people refer to a WATS line, they usually mean an out-WATS facility. Both services are merely billing arrangements for reduced billing of long-distance calls based on a fixed monthly fee and discounts for larger calling volumes. The 800/888/877/866 service also has the characteristic of reversing the charges to the called party.

Historically, WATS lines have been separate facilities (physically identical to local PBX trunks or private lines). Their geographic coverage was also banded; thus, a user might have had a WATS line that only reached adjacent states (band 1), or all of the lower 48 states (band 5), or some intermediate variation. For out-WATS, either the PBX had to be smart enough to recognize the dialed area and choose the correct outgoing facility, or users had to dial special codes to select the correct WATS line. Any given band included all closer bands (but, of course, billed the calls at the higher rate for the wider band), and this caused a certain amount of difficulty in either configuration or training. Because different physical facilities went to different regions, this also resulted in a traffic-engineering nightmare. This complication was even more unreasonable because WATS calls (both in and out) are handled identically to all non-WATS calls; WATS is really only a bulk billing arrangement for calls that would otherwise be considered direct distance dialing (DDD or toll calls).

WATS service has never been free, although some of the older tariffs did specify certain (rather large) volumes above which all calls were free. Those tariffs are long gone; all calls are now charged on a per-minute basis. The only variable is the per-minute charge, which decreases as the calling volume increases.

One significant improvement is that WATS-type volume discount billing can now be set up on existing trunks; separate facilities into the local CO are no longer required for such an arrangement.

Private Line

Any circuit leased from a carrier from a point on one customer's premises to another point on a customer's premises (even the same premises) can be described as a private line or circuit. Of course, if an organization builds its own facilities (for example, a microwave link across a metropolitan area), these facilities would also be described as private circuits. In either case, the alternative is usually a dial-up link.

Many factors go into the decision of whether to set up a private facility (of either type). Some reasons why a company might set up a private link include:

- Private analog circuits can be tuned for higher performance (both in terms of speed and reliability) than dial-up facilities can.

- Many types of digital facilities are only available on a private basis.

- Management and troubleshooting of private facilities can be more tightly controlled than in a dial-up environment.

- High volumes of calls or data would generate higher charges on the public dial network than on a non-usage-sensitive private network.

Reasons to go with the public dial network include:

- Volumes of calls or data that are too low to justify a leased link

- Unwillingness or inability to coordinate and manage a private network (do you really want to be your own telephone company?)

- A large number of small locations that would be uneconomical to connect with private links

With few exceptions, this issue does not have a "right" decision; rather, any decision should be based on a set of trade-offs involving economic, management, and performance considerations. What might make the most sense today might be obviously uneconomical tomorrow.

A classic example of this kind of change is the decision of whether to build a private voice communications network of TIE-line-connected PBXs (called a tandem network—this is unrelated to Tandem computers). Many large companies built such networks for sound economic and functional reasons between the early 1970s and mid-1980s. However, the emergence of virtual networks, such as the Software Defined Network (SDN), made many of these private networks uneconomical by comparison. They continue to function, but many companies have retired them because in most cases, the virtual networks cost far less while delivering most of the characteristics that justified the construction of the original private networks.

Questions

1. The line is defined as a(n) _____ .
   a. Beginning point
   b. Telco CO circuit
   c. End point
   d. DID service

2. A line is installed to be used continuously.   T/F

3. A trunk connects between two _____ .

4. A trunk is designed to be used continuously.   T/F

5. DID stands for
   a. Direct in dialtone
   b. Dedicated in dial
   c. Direct inward dial
   d. Dial in dialing

6. DOD stands for
   a. Direct outward dialing
   b. Department of defenders
   c. Dial outward dedicated
   d. Dedicated outward dialing

7. A TIE line may also be a TIE _____ .

8. FX is a line that is typically installed and operates internationally.   T/F

9. FX stands for
   a. Foreign extension
   b. Far east exchange
   c. Foreign exchange
   d. Far exchange

10. An OPX is used when we want to set up a connection between two PBXs.   T/F

11. The alternative to having a collect call service is to install _____.

12. Out-WATs is the same as using a long-distance circuit for reduced costs.   T/F

13. WATS stands for
    a. Wide area telephone system
    b. Wide area telephone services
    c. Wide area telecommunications system
    d. Wide area telecommunications service

14. We usually relate to the in-WATS service as
    a. Toll paid
    b. Toll free
    c. Calling party pays
    d. Called party free

15. What four area codes are used for in-WATS?
    a.
    b.
    c.
    d.

16. How many types of E&M methods exist?

17. E&M now stands for
    a. Earth and magnetic
    b. Earpiece and magneto
    c. Ear and mouth
    d. Earth and motion

18. What is E&M signaling responsible for?
    a. Addressing
    b. Information
    c. Supervisory
    d. None of the above

19. We can link two systems together with a dedicated or _____ line.

20. A dedicated circuit can be used on the same customer's premises.   T/F

Traffic Engineering Calculations

After reading this chapter and completing the questions, you will be able to:

- Explain how and why the telephone companies engineer their circuits and Central Offices (COs)
- Discuss the differences between Poisson Distribution and Erlang Models
- Describe the use of the engineering formula for the busy hour
- Explain how to gather the information to model

Traffic Engineering Studies

The art of conducting true traffic engineering studies has all but died. In the early days of telecommunications systems, the telco planning and capacity engineers spent days and weeks designing their switching and trunking systems to provide optimal performance. Since the inception of computer technology, programs have been written that can perform all of the calculations and the various iterations necessary to fine-tune a network. What used to take the telco engineers weeks now can be accomplished in minutes of processing time. Beyond the telco engineers, telecommunications managers and designers were equally concerned, and they attempted to model their networks for the best accessibility and greatest utilization of their lines and trunks at the most reasonable price.

From the discussion in earlier chapters, we can see that options for usage-sensitive services do exist. Using the best mix of WATS lines, for example, could reap exceptional savings in the past. In all actuality, this is not an engineering case, but a mathematical computation of all probable events that can take place in a given time frame. No engineering takes place, but rather a modeling of the traffic needs of the organization and of the access lines necessary to support those traffic needs with a given level of service. It is the calculation of a random number of arrival events taking place over a specified period of time.

In the telecommunications arena, this is the number of possible first attempts to get an outside line, or possible times for an incoming line to ring into an organization on the first try. Because there is a finite number of time events, but an infinite number of possible attempts that can be made in a time period, we attempt to define the best possible level of service within a specified period of time. For the installation of lines and trunks, the goal is to serve the maximum number of callers at a single point in time (usually a one-hour period). Because the arrivals of calls are random, the design must equate to an hour's worth of possible arrivals, that number being 3,600. This is obtained by multiplying the number of one-second increments in a minute times the number of minutes in an hour (60 s × 60 min). From this possible random one-second arrival event, the concept of serving the worst-case scenario in a one-hour period (the busy hour) is calculated to arrive at the number of lines or trunks needed to serve the heaviest load in a one-hour period. For the rest of the day, there will be too many facilities, but for the busy hour, there will be an adequate number to deliver the level of service that has been decided upon.

An example of this would be similar to the work of road system traffic designers. These people are charged with the responsibility of creating road systems that will enable the maximum number of cars and trucks to traverse the roads in a city, town, or state. Because a good deal of money will be invested in building the road system, the engineers are requested to allow for the greatest number of vehicles to travel the road system within a reasonable cost estimate. From there, the engineers create a model for the traffic based on the hourly distribution of the vehicles on the road. They conduct counts at random times, clicking off the number of vehicles passing an area within a specified period. Then they allow for a certain amount of new traffic or growth as traffic patterns change. Armed with this information, they design a road system with the appropriate number of lanes to support the steady flow of traffic at a constant rate of speed (whatever is allowed by law in the area). Knowing pieces of the daily and hourly usage patterns, the engineers then design their roads to maximize the total throughput from end-to-end on the road that will be built.

Reality starts to set in when we perceive the actual daily conditions on our current roads. In the early morning and late afternoon rush hours, traffic is snarled and slowly stops for extended periods. The engineers have accomplished their mission: They have maximized the traffic on a road system; there is a car on every square inch of road. Unfortunately, during rush hour, one critical ingredient is forgotten. These cars were supposed to move across the road system at a constant rate of speed and then exit within a certain time frame. However, as we all know, they are all parked on the highway system. No one is moving, so congestion exists. Taking this one step beyond the rush hours, though, the engineers have designed a road system that enables users to get on the road and move at a steady rate of speed from an entrance point to an exit point. The level of service during nonrush hours is much better. Actually, the system is over-designed for these off-hours, when there is a somewhat inefficient use of the roads. However, you cannot add and delete lanes of highway for selected portions of the day.

This is exactly the same scenario that a telephone traffic study must follow. During an average hour of the day, all calls should be processed into or out of the organization with limited delays. The numbers of incoming and outgoing lines are crucial to ensure that the communication process works efficiently. However, the number of access lines is going to be fixed all day long because the copper or other medium brought into the building is not something that can be taken away or added on an hourly basis. For certain periods of the day, more calls might be required. This is called the *busy hour*. The telco or telecommunications analyst typically tries to design the number of lines to support the worst hour of the day. Yet, for the rest of the day, too many lines are available. The more lines that are sitting around at a fixed cost, the more expensive the organization's costs are. This is based on a mathematical probability, and the dynamics of the calling patterns of the users or customers must be looked at. Consider, though, the risks of a poorly designed network:

- If the customer attempts to dial into an organization to place an order and all the lines are busy, then that customer might hang up and place the order with a competitor.

■ If the outgoing traffic within an organization is severely blocked due to busy conditions, then the users might not be able to get mission-critical information as it is needed.

When busy conditions arise, users might find alternative ways of getting their jobs done. They might rent or lease their own lines, bypass the cost-effective facilities provided, or place calls via credit card or third-party arrangements through an operator-assisted call. In any case, all of these options will be far more costly to the organization.

Therefore, the services designer must consider the levels of service to be provided. This requires a thorough understanding of the traffic to be handled. From this perspective, a designer will have to consider the information that is available for study. This plays out in the paragraphs that follow. Information gathering is essential.

Where Can the Information Be Obtained?

Analyze the traffic that is coming into and going out of the organization. Access to this information might be a difficult portion of the desired study. To obtain the information, several points can be used:

■ The telephone bills for all incoming 800/888/877/866-service calls are good indicators of the total volume. But this bill will only show the completed calls, not the ones that encounter a busy tone when trying to call into the organization.

■ The telephone bills for all outgoing calls from an organization can be useful. These might be difficult statistics to obtain, depending on how the billing systems work. For example, if departments each receive their own bills and process them for payment, the information might be difficult to get. Or, as another situation arises, the billing cycle might be different for different types of lines and trunks. In many cases, the main billing for direct-dialed calls is received on the first of the month, whereas the long-distance portions of the bill might be received on the tenth of each month. This requires an inventory of all the line and trunk billings that are processed each month. Working with either the providers or the internal accounting department might well get this all started in the right direction.

The call-processing time must be considered when analyzing any requirement for access lines. Often, the novice telecommunications analyst ignores the amount of setup time for calls and therefore can miss a sizable chunk of time to be factored into a calculation. This figure can be obtained by dialing several calls and determining the average amount of time necessary until the call is completed to its destination point. Remember that the telco and long-distance carriers will bill on the duration of a call from the time it is answered until it is terminated, with some rounding (up to six seconds) possible. Therefore, the added time that a circuit is held up for call setup is important in calculating the total usage time, because the line or trunk is inaccessible to others during this time.

Many telephone systems, call distribution systems, and so on can provide management and statistical reports. These might not be generated on a regular basis, but they can be obtained when necessary.

Telco and long-distance suppliers alike can gather statistics through what is called a busy study and peg count. The *busy study* can usually be conducted for a week and can reflect all call attempts to the incoming line group of an organization, whether completed or not. Further, this study can indicate the hourly distribution of the incoming calls so that some hourly sensitivities are afforded in the design study.

The wrong mix of telephone lines will be frustrating for customers and users alike, yet the overkill situation might be too expensive. The charter of the telecommunications department within an organization has always been "to provide the proper mix of goods and services to accomplish the calling needs of the organization, increase productivity, and reduce the bottom-line expenses to the organization." All too often, we have made the mistake of trying to get to a bottom-line figure, forgetting the other portion of the mission statement.

Accomplishing the Mission

Armed with the calling information, the next step is to look at the role being accomplished. What will the design effort accomplish? You can create a design to improve customer service, to reduce costs, or to improve user connectivity. Another option is just to attempt to configure a new setup. Regardless of the choice, the basic elements are the same. Upon successfully garnering a mission, several steps can be taken to execute the design. This is the traffic engineering function at its best. The steps that should be taken are highlighted in Table 8-1. These are the basic steps that one would follow for just about any design of a configuration. Each of these is covered in greater detail later.

Table 8-1

Steps in Accomplishing the Traffic Engineering Function

Basic Steps	Action
1. Determine the traffic demand that will have to be satisfied.	Gather the data on incoming calls, peg counts, busy studies, and other sources of information.
2. Convert the information from a monthly basis to a distribution table based on daily and hourly statistics.	From the monthly information, plot the data into an hourly or daily distribution so that the design can be used.
3. Determine the appropriate traffic engineering tools to be used. The tools will include Poisson, Erlang, or extended Erlang.	Choose a tool that will assist in creating a rudimentary design, given the historical data that can be assimilated into a design tool.
4. Apply the information into the modeling tool.	Using the tools and tables, apply the data to the tool to obtain the desired format.
5. Select the grade of service to be delivered.	By establishing the grade of service, the percentage of calls blocked versus service within a specified period can be predicted.
6. Extract the information from the tools and tables, depending on the method chosen.	Actually, once the data is submitted and the grade of service is established, extracting the information is fairly simple.
7. Apply the information back to a monthly distribution.	From the hourly distribution, the monthly traffic that will be handled, as opposed to the blocked and overflow traffic, can be assessed.
8. Try various iterations of grade of service.	Since the data is known, the iterations will enable usage sensitivities and variable conditions that can be accommodated.
9. Select the right configuration based on the available information.	Using the information gathered in the iterations, select the design that best fits the need. From this design, costs can be estimated and equipment needs can be established.

Using the Information

From these steps, the information can now be set up for the calculation process. This entails following all of the steps in order to calculate the actual number of circuits needed to serve a purpose. There is no mystique here, just a formal mathematical computation of the data against a given set of rules.

Gather the Data

As already stated, the ability to gather the data will be contingent upon our ability to assimilate the various bills, reports, and studies that are available from the local telco and from the in-house hardware systems. From these reports, the amount of traffic to be served will be easier to determine. Differences will exist between the outgoing and the incoming traffic. In all cases, it might be preferable to give a better grade of service to incoming customer calls than to outgoing administrative calls. This all depends on the individual organization.

Assuming that all of the data is gathered, let's play out an example of an outgoing calling pattern for an organization. This example is based on a typical bill where the average usage is 500 hours per month. Note that this is the aggregated amount of calling in the one-month period. The data are then accumulated, and estimated averages are placed on the total number of calls. For the sake of this example, the average length of a call is estimated at four minutes. The total hours are then divided by four minutes per call to come up with the total number of calls.

$$\frac{\text{Total hours} \times 60 \text{ minutes per hour}}{4 \text{ minutes per call}} = \frac{500 \times 60}{4} = \frac{30000}{4}$$

$$= 7{,}500 \text{ calls per month} \qquad \text{[8.1]}$$

A certain amount of extra time must be added to the total calls per month. The 500-hours figure reflects what the telco will bill for calling time, not for processing time. As a matter of simplifying this, the average time allotted per call for setup and teardown, which consumes non-billed time on the circuit, will be 30 seconds per call. The 30-second figure is derived from

Table 8-2

Added Time to
Call Processing

Action	Time Allotted
1. Dialing an 11-digit telephone number from a Touch-Tone phone	8 s
2. Delay in telephone system (PBX) network processing	6 s
3. Delay in network processing and regenerating digits	7 s
4. Ringing, assuming three rings (1-s ring, 2-s pause)	9 s
Total time allowed	30 s

a tone-dialed call from its beginning until the call is answered and billing begins. This is broken down into the components shown in Table 8-2.

Thus, the added call-processing time must be accumulated with the hours of usage for the month. Therefore, these two numbers are added together. If this step is omitted, the engineer might design a system with a certain blockage level (grade of service) and not be able to deliver that level of service. Look at the amount of time added to the hours of usage.

$$\text{Total hours usage} + (\text{total calls} \times \text{added processing time})$$

$$= \text{Total time}$$

$$= 500 \text{ hours} + (7500 \times 30 \text{ seconds}/60 \text{ seconds})$$

$$= 500 \text{ hours} + (62.5 \text{ hours})$$

$$= \text{Total time of } 562.5 \text{ hours} \qquad [\mathbf{8.2}]$$

Note that if the extra 62.5 hours were not added into the total number, the design could be off by a factor of 12 percent in the overall traffic. This is a common mistake that people make when designing networks.

Convert the Data to Daily or Hourly Usage

Although the telephone billing records are possibly a source of the information, the calling patterns on a daily or hourly basis can become quite tedious. However, if a design is to be effective, this information must be converted into a usable and understandable format. The indication of traffic occurrences will assist in determining just how much traffic arrives within a given arrival time. The best way to achieve a good result is to look at hourly distribution. From the telephone bills, the total hourly distribution will likely vary from day to day and hour to hour. Consequently, scanning the bills into a computer database or receiving the information in some electronic format (such as on diskette, tape, CD, and so on) will allow a telecommunications manager or designer to read the information into a PC or computer system. From this read, a sorting of dates and hours can be achieved. This will give the best results. However, when the information is a combination of paper records and other forms of data, the choice is to draw some averages of the calling patterns.

Typically, a pattern of distribution will exist that can be used in assimilating the information into a calculable form. The call distribution for many organizations is shown in Table 8-3. This table reflects the hourly distribution averages for a typical example; it is not to be construed as applicable to any specific organization. Further, this distribution will be based on the services offered by the organization. Call centers might well experience an average hourly distribution, whereas a manufacturer might see a dual-mode distribution curve (see Figure 8-1). The example used in Table 8-3 is geared toward a manufacturing environment, with no traffic being carried during the lunch hour. This is usually a fair assumption.

The distribution would then be spread across a dual-mode distribution curve. This attempts to define the number of circuits required to satisfy the distribution of calls in the worst hour, as already stated.

These assumptions are made on the basis of various inputs and can be modified. Given that the information is now placed in an hourly percentage,

Table 8-3

Hourly Distribution of Calls for a Manufacturing Organization

Hourly Distribution	Percent of Calls per Hour
08:00-09:00	8
09:00-10:00	13
10:00-11:00	17
11:00-12:00	12
1:00-2:00	12
2:00-3:00	16
3:00-4:00	15
4:00-5:00	7
Total	100

Figure 8-1
The average usage reflects a dual-mode pattern.

the next step is to convert the data into hours of traffic in the hourly distribution. From there, the process can begin to take place.

Choose the Appropriate Tool

Several tools exist to model the data. The primary ones include Poisson, Erlang B, and extended Erlang B distributions. The best way to describe the tools is the way the iterations take place and why they do so. In Poisson distribution, a mathematical distribution of the loads placed on the number of circuits is not calculated. Rather, the numerical values assigned with the overall distribution as set in the tables are merely placed into a grade of service level and a number of circuits is selected. The load is assumed to be even over the number of circuits chosen. This is okay for some calculations, but if additional distribution is required, then the other tools will be used. For a comparative look at these tools, first look at how the Poisson distribution will work. Remember that the monthly traffic is 500 hours. From a daily perspective, some added criteria are needed. The added parameters are shown in the following list:

- The number of business days in the month is 22.
- The average day is eight hours long.
- The hourly distribution is shown in Table 8-3.
- The average length of a call is four minutes.
- The call processing time is 30 seconds.

Poisson Distribution

From all of these numbers, a set of parameters can be established. One added factor is that the Poisson distribution model uses a slightly different calculation. Remember in the earlier section of this chapter that the statement was to consider the random arrivals of calls (incoming or outgoing) based on a one-second arrival rate. Therefore, the number of possible arrival rates in an hourly distribution is 3,600 (60 min × 60 s). The Poisson distribution takes into account all 3,600 possible arrival rates and calculates these on the number of circuits necessary to support this traffic load. The telco engineers use a term called Centum (or hundred) call seconds (CCS). Rather than divide and multiply the hourly traffic by 3,600, the theory is that if we divide the 3,600 by 100, we arrive at a traffic load of 36 CCS per hour of traffic. Therefore, to use the Poisson distribution, all traffic is converted to CCS prior to submitting it into the model. Once the traffic is converted into CCS, the model will determine the number of CCS that can be carried within a specific design.

If you use these assumptions, the traffic load can be converted and then inserted. The resultant traffic load is therefore summarized in the following list. The traffic is based on a worst-case scenario in the busy hour. A grade of service level will be assigned to determine the number of circuits necessary.

1. Total traffic hours carried — 500
2. Added traffic for call setup — 62.5
3. Total hours divided by 22 business days (562.5/22) — 25.57 daily hours
4. Daily hours multiplied by busy hour percentage (25.57×0.17) — 4.3469 busy hour traffic
5. Busy hour traffic multiplied by 36 CCS (4.3469×36) — 156.48 CCS
6. Grade of service desired — P.05

Determine the Grade of Service Desired

As already mentioned, the grade of service (GOS) desired is the worst-case statement for the busiest hour of the day. The GOS is used to determine the number or percentage of calls that will experience a busy tone on the first attempt during the busy hour. A grade of service of P.05 (probability of five percent) means that five of 100 callers might encounter a busy tone on the first attempt. The service actually experienced might be much better than the P.05, but the worst case is five of 100. Using this information and the average busy hour load of 156.48 CCS that must be carried, the Poisson distribution model can be applied. A sample Poisson distribution table is shown in Table 8-4.

This table is read in the following way. Read across to the grade of service desired (P.05). At the column headed P.05, read down until the calculated load value is found. In many cases, the actual value of the load will not be even; therefore, round the number in the table up to the next value on the table. From the load number, read left until the column labeled Number of Circuits, where the numeral is the number of circuits that will be required

Table 8-4

An Excerpt of
a Poisson
Distribution Table

Number of Circuits Needed	Grade of Service					
	P.01	*P.02*	*P.03*	*P.05*	*P.07*	*P.10*
1	0.4	0.7	1.1	1.8	2.6	3.8
2	5.4	7.7	9.6	12.7	15.4	19.2
3	15.7	20.3	23.8	29.4	33.9	39.7
4	29.6	36.5	41.5	49.1	55.2	62.8
5	46.0	55.0	61.4	70.9	78.3	87.6
6	64.3	75.2	82.8	94	103	113
7	83.9	96.6	105	118	128	140
8	105.0	119	129	143	154	168
9	126.0	142	153	169	181	196
10	149	166	178	195	208	224
11	172	191	204	222	236	253
12	195	216	230	249	264	282
13	220	241	256	277	292	311
14	244	267	283	305	321	341
15	269	293	310	333	350	371
16	295	320	337	361	379	401
17	320	347	365	390	409	431

to carry the traffic. In this case, the number of circuits required to carry this traffic is 9.

Using the information in the highlighted area, reading across from left to right, then down, and back across from right to left, the answer is 9. This means that the number of circuits necessary to support the busy hour traffic is shown. However, during nonbusy hours, fewer circuits are used, which should mean the delivery of a far better grade of service. Rather than go into the details of the actual grades of service for each of the other hours, these are shown in Table 8-5. These grades of service are extrapolated from the information in the percent of calls in each of the hours and the number of CCS loads for each of these loads.

Table 8-5

Sensitivity of the Same Data with Differing Grades of Service Reflects Additional or Fewer Trunks Needed

Grade of Service	Number of Trunks @ 156CCS	Difference
P.01	11	+2
P.02	10	+1
P.03	9–10	0, +1
P.05	9	0
P.07	8–9	0, −1
P.10	8	−1

To conduct some sensitivities on this design, the number of CCSs can be kept constant and the grade of service can be either increased or decreased, with the results reflecting increased or decreased circuit requirements necessary to support this new service level. You can play this out in various sensitivities, which is why the excerpt from the Poisson distribution table includes P.01 to 0.05, 0.07, and 0.10. Bear in mind that the sensitivities still include the differences of the expected hourly load—worst case, this is the level of service. You might well expect that better grades can be achieved, because this is not a perfect science and the rounding effects of the calculations can become a factor.

Further, in arriving at the hourly percentages of the monthly calls, some estimates were used. If the organization has periods of fluctuation during certain months of the year, or days of the month, then these calculations could be off significantly, but the data supporting the way the calculations were performed did not reflect these monthly deviations. A true monthly detailed distribution would be more precise, but this would take much longer to analyze the actual call details.

Erlang Distribution

Mathematical computations of the traffic offered to a group of circuits can take different forms that use different assumptions. One such variation is the use of Erlang B techniques, as opposed to the Poisson distribution. Erlang B was developed in the early 1900s by K. Erlang of the Copenhagen Telephone Company. The assumption used is that if a caller encounters a denial or busy tone when attempting to place a call, the caller will be routed to a more expensive circuit (such as the long-distance network called DDD) or will give up trying to make the call. This last option would be devastating for a call center operation, if callers who experience a busy tone hang up and call the competition. However, the assumption is that some alternative facility would be available.

Erlang B is more effective in calculating call completion and attempts on an outward dialed basis, where callers can be routed through an automatic route selection process to a more expensive link. The network would not accommodate a queuing arrangement in the assumptions modeled with Erlang B computations.

Other models were created using Erlang assumptions; these introduced various options in the design of a circuit group. A summary of these variations is shown in Table 8-6, which compares the techniques and the basis for using each variation. The Erlang table comparisons assume that a queuing technique can be introduced and accepted.

For the purposes of describing a queuing technique, you can imagine a busy branch office of the local bank. During periods of heavy load, the bank might have two or three tellers available to service its customers. However, on paydays for many major corporations, the lunch hour becomes a very congested period for the banks. Even though three tellers are there to han-

Table 8-6

Variations of the Erlang Modeling Techniques

Model	Handling	Choice Considerations
Erlang B	No queuing	Use a route advancement technique automatically routing the traffic to the next available route, even if it is more expensive to service the call.
Extended Erlang B	No queuing	If all circuits are busy, the caller must hang up and try again later. No advancement of routes is used.
Erlang C	Queuing allowed	Calls are queued by a computer or an operator and wait until the next available circuit becomes available.
Equivalent Queue Extended Erlang B	Queuing allowed	Calls are queued for a specific time; in Erlang B, if a circuit is still not available, the system may then route the call to a more expensive route or give the caller a choice to try again later.

dle the customers, there will be more customers at any one time than there are tellers.

Thus, the bank installs the old cattle-car line arrangement. Using a series of weaves or redirection cords, the bank attempts to get the customers to line up one behind the other. This enables the bank employees to serve customers on a first-come, first-served basis. Because the arrival of the customers is serial, as they form (or queue) in the line, they should be serviced in the order in which they arrived. Of course, the length of time it will take to get service depends on the arrival rate and on what position the customer holds in the queue.

During busy conditions, the bank manager, seeing the queue building, might decide to assign more employees to servicing the queue. This might require that other employees with different functions be pulled into customer processing. Supervisors and managers of other departments might also be assigned until the queue is handled. All of these arrangements work based on creating additional resources for the handling of the traffic.

However, if the customers were to arrive during this rush hour, and the bank had taken a position that only one customer at a time would be allowed in the bank, the picture would change dramatically. Instead of receiving service, the customers would be told to go to a different branch office for service. This would infuriate the customers and could prove to be very costly. It would only take one occasion like this, and the customers would find a new bank to handle their accounts. So goes the Erlang technique — you can be queued for the same group of facilities, or you can be sent out across the network to a more expensive solution.

Each of the Erlang theories is a better gauge of the blockage and grade of service than the Poisson distribution theory listed earlier. Thus, the Erlang theories have been used in the most recent modeling techniques, since computers have been used in the modeling of traffic systems. An Erlang is equivalent to one hour's traffic in a one-hour period, or, stated against the Poisson model, an Erlang is 36 CCSs.

Using the same data as was applied to the Poisson distribution model, a computation can be made with the Erlang method. Therefore, the data to be used in the Erlang B formula is 500 hours of usage, with the average length of a call set at 4.5 minutes (this is the four-minute average plus the 30-second overhead). The application of the formula actually works out as shown in Equation [8.3]. This formula is used to calculate the number of circuits required to deliver a specified grade of service.

$$E(C, T) = \frac{\dfrac{T^c}{C!}}{\displaystyle\sum_{i=o}^{C} \dfrac{T^i}{i!}}$$

[8.3]

where T = traffic attempts
        C = circuits available

To make this a little simpler, the following shortcut can be applied using tables that have already been created, then applying a simpler format to the data, and deriving the number of circuits from Table 8-7. To create the scenario, look to the following formula:

Table 8-7

Erlang B Tables

Number of Circuits	Grade of Service				
	P.01	*P*.02	*P*.03	*P*.05	*P*.10
1					
2					
3					
4	0.87	1.09		1.52	22.05
5	1.36	1.66		2.23	2.87
6	1.91	2.28		2.96	3.76
7	2.50	2.94		3.74	4.66
8	3.13	3.62		4.54	5.60
9	3.78	4.34		5.37	6.54
10	4.46	5.08		6.22	7.50
11	5.16	5.84		7.08	8.49
12	5.88	6.62		7.95	9.47
13	6.61	7.40		8.83	10.46
14	7.35	8.21		9.72	11.47
15	8.11	9.02		10.64	12.48
16	8.87	9.83		11.54	13.51
17	9.65	10.66		12.46	14.52
18	10.44	11.49		13.37	15.55
19	11.23	12.33		14.31	16.58

$$\text{Erlangs} = \frac{N \times A}{3600}$$

[8.4]

where N = number of calls handled in the busy hour
        A = average length of calls, seconds

As stated, the Erlang result from the formula is then applied across a table in the same way as the Poisson distribution model to arrive at the appropriate number of circuits needed. Use Table 8-7.

You can see from these tables that some sensitivities exist, and that the difference between the number of circuits needed and the various blockages that could be experienced will produce differing results. An organization that is in the mode of trying various iterations can get between $P.01$ and $P.05$ with the possibility of minimal additions or deletions to the calculations. However, this is not just about the number of circuits needed. The obvious deduction that can be drawn revolves around the difference in "customer service" and the ensuing numbers of devices required to deliver that grade of service.

Another concern here is the possibility of staffing a call center operation. The number and cost of circuits are variables that are not necessarily that important anymore. Because the cost of renting additional circuits has all but become a commodity pricing arrangement, the number of circuits is irrelevant, other than with respect to the degree of blockage allowed. The cost of a WATS line, or an 800/888 service, these days is based on the monthly worst-case charge of $37.50. Thereafter, the usage cost is based on an average of hours used per circuit. However, as shown in Chapter 6 and Chapter 7, these costs are really based on the averages derived from the total number of hours used divided by the number of circuits. The costs are then applied to certain rate steps (0 to 15 hours, 15 to 40 hours, and over 40 hours). With this in mind, if each circuit will carry at least 40 hours of traffic, each added hour is a marginal increment, costwise. Nevertheless, the degree of frustration delivered to the caller will be the actual deciding factor. Now, applying this degree of frustration and the number of other ancillary devices is where the calculation of traffic demand will be used.

For example, if, after using the tables and drawing the conclusion that a five percent ($P.05$) blockage level will be delivered to the first-attempt callers, the telecommunications manager decides to see what the impact of a one-percent blockage will require, the calculation will take on new meaning. This can be extended to the following requirements:

- Ports required on the automatic call distribution system
- Agents required to service the calls
- Terminal devices required for the agent answering positions
- Floor space and desk space required for the agent to conduct business
- Benefits associated with hiring the agents
- Payroll costs associated with each agent
- Personal computers or mainframe terminal devices required for customer lookup and inquiry
- Wiring required

The costs associated with each of these devices and the human resource costs can amount to a significant number. The marginal cost to add one agent could be as much as $100,000 per annum (benefits and payroll taken into account) plus the capital costs associated with the equipment purchase and maintenance of the devices. This size number is not to be taken lightly, so a true analysis will be required to prove the benefits. The issues are not always related to costs, but a cost-to-benefit ratio could be applied that will either justify or prove that a better grade of service is warranted.

If the decision to improve levels from a $P.05$ to a $P.01$ grade of service is considered, then the additional costs can be compared to the expected increases in sales, revenues, or service benefits. For general discussion, many organizations use a 3:1 cost-benefit ratio before selecting a new system or a change to an existing one. If an organization meets or exceeds the 3:1 ratio, the decision is usually easily justified. The greater the ratio, the easier the sell to management. A representative cost-benefit ratio equation is as follows:

$$Cost\ benefit\ ratio = \frac{\text{Benefit}}{\text{Total cost}}$$

$$= \frac{450,000}{100,000}$$

$$= 4.5 \hspace{2cm} \textbf{[8.5]}$$

However, if the cost-benefit is below the 3:1 ratio, then one will have to struggle to gain management's acceptance or have some alternate plans ready in case the funding cannot be accommodated. The example used in

Equation 8.5 is for a new design that will cost a total of $100,000. However, the sales department is expecting to create $450,000 of new revenue from the installation of this system. Bear in mind that this is based on cost to benefit. If one were to create a profitability index on this installation, then the picture could change dramatically. What is the true benefit? What other choices would the organization have to implement a new program to generate $450,000 of new sales? If the differing projects pointed to the cost of implementing some other technique (such as a marketing campaign, promotions, and so on), then the cost comparisons could be used. For example, if sales would have to spend $600,000 in marketing campaigns and promotions, then the difference would be between the two choices ($100,000 versus $600,000 yields a 6:1 benefit-cost ratio). This enables a business decision to be made based on the facts, rather than strictly on some guesstimate or on emotional facts.

This is really all about what traffic engineering is. When this can be fully justified, then a business decision can be supported and defended before the senior management people who are charged with the custodianship of the organization's spending and the maximization of shareholder wealth. Therefore, the selling of communications lines and equipment is not for the benefit of the telecommunications department, but really is in support of the organization. Consequently, this is in support of the call center operation, whose personnel should have an input into the budgeting process, followed by the benefits expected from the installation of the new configuration or equipment. The use of traffic engineering is a means to get to an end, not the end in itself. Once this is clearly understood, the telecommunications department can proceed from there.

Questions

1. The art of conducting true _____ studies all but died in the past decade.
2. When we consider using a traffic study, we can use the road system analogy to come up with realistic goals.   T/F
3. What is a CCS?
    a. Core channel selector
    b. Century of call schedules
    c. Centum Call Seconds
    d. Call Completion Scenario

4. How many seconds is a CCS equal to?
   a. 1
   b. 1,000
   c. 10
   d. 100

5. What is the typical period for which we try to engineer?
   a. A business day
   b. Busy hour
   c. Monthly
   d. Per second

6. Information can be obtained from many places.   T/F

7. When calculating actual usage figures, you must consider an additional usage called
   a. Average length of call
   b. Number of calls usage per day
   c. Processing time
   d. Busy hour intervals

8. The telco and others gather statistics through studies by counting pegs and busy tones delivered.   T/F

9. On average, rounding can add up to _____ to a call process?
   a. 10 seconds
   b. 0 seconds
   c. 6 seconds
   d. 2 seconds

10. Traffic engineering used an age-old technique called Poisson.   T/F

11. The use of distribution tables considers that _____ seconds are in a normal hour:
    a. 60
    b. 36
    c. 600
    d. 3600

12. A dual mode distribution is the normal way we see traffic distributed throughout the day.   T/F

13. The GOS is called
    a. Geometric order of service
    b. Grade of serviceability
    c. Gauge of service
    d. Grade of service

14. The probability of having five calls per 100 arriving events blocked in the busiest hour means we have a $P.5$ service level.   T/F

15. Variations used in the mathematical modeling use forms of _____.

Equipment: Private Branch Exchanges

After reading this chapter and completing the questions, you will be able to:

- Explain what a PBX is
- Discuss the differences between the market providers
- Describe the basic features and functions of a PBX
- Explain the reasons why an organization chooses a PBX
- Converse fluently about the components of the PBX

Private Branch Exchange (PBX)

Let's start off with a quick definition of a private branch exchange.

Private—it belongs to an organization or individual; not a public service.

Branch exchange—remember the Telephone company hierarchy listed the Class 5 Office as the central office or the branch exchange. This is where the dial tone is provided. So the branch (think of it as the limbs of the network hierarchy tree) exchange offers dial tone to the end user.

A *private branch exchange* (PBX) is the typical telephone system for large organizations. It provides internal dial tone for a private organization. In this environment, an organization that is served by a central office dial tone from the local exchange company might need the capacity of high-volume calling and handling services. Clearly, a single-line telephone set with a dial-tone line for each user will work. But, it will only just work. It will not satisfy the needs of the organization.

Moreover, it will be expensive. Assume that a dial-tone line costs $20 per month. If the organization has a multitude of users, the cost per month will be significant. Table 9-1 highlights some of the typical costs associated with basic dial-tone service for various numbers of employees. These numbers are only representative, but they should get our point across. The table reflects the basic monthly cost and the annualized cost of renting a dial-tone line from the local carrier.

You can clearly see from these numbers that the use of a basic dial-tone service can get quite expensive. As a matter of fact, many organizations now say that telecommunications is the number-two expense item in their corporate expense registers, second only to personnel costs. This is both good and bad. It is good that organizations are depending on telecommunications more, as opposed to more expensive alternatives (such as travel, personnel, and other sales and marketing costs). Pound for pound, telecommunications still produce a greater return on every dollar spent.

But back to the point. The costs can be staggering to a financial or senior managerial person in an organization. But the dial-tone line costs listed in Table 9-1 give the user only dial-tone access. This is a full-time dedicated access line for two-way service for every single user. If you add just a single-line telephone set for each of these users, then some capital costs are associated with the ownership of these lines. Table 9-2 shows the costs of a single-line set for every user, at a base price of $60 per single-line telephone set. These are, again, basic assumptions on the purchase of these sets; one could do better.

Table 9-1

Summary of Dial-Tone Line Costs for the Organization

Number of Users	Monthly Cost at $20.00	Annualized Cost
100	$ 2,000	$ 24,000
500	$ 10,000	$ 120,000
1,000	$ 20,000	$ 240,000
2,500	$ 50,000	$ 600,000
10,000	$200,000	$2,400,000

Table 9-2

Summary of
Single-Line Set
Equipment Costs

Number of Users	Cost of Equipment
100	$6,000
500	$30,000
1,000	$60,000
2,500	$150,000
10,000	$600,000

Again, you can see that the equipment costs can mount quickly. But what is wrong with this picture? Well for starters, the single-line set limits what the user can do with the basic dial-tone service. Also, the single-line set does not allow for intercommunication between the users within the organization, unless they tie up their dial-tone lines as follows:

- Grab the dial tone by going off hook.
- When dial tone is received, dial the digits (seven or ten*) of the desired internal party.
- When the ring is generated and the party answers, conduct a conversation.

But this completely ties up two outside lines for the two parties to converse. If a customer tries to call either of these two parties, the customer will get a busy tone. That is, unless the call hunts to some other number. If the call does hunt, then a third outside line is occupied while a message is taken at the rollover line. Customers can be denied access, and can get frustrated. All of this can occur while the two parties could be talking to each other in the next office (see Figure 9-1). Note that however long the wires are that run back to the central office where the dial tone is provided, the call uses twice that to get the two conversationalists together. Clearly, this is not an optimized use of telecommunications services.

---

*Many parts of North America now must dial 10 digits for local calls because of the addition of new area codes in their operating area. This overlay of area codes may cause some concern for many of the PBX owners because they have to program the new area code without the use of 1+ dialing, whereas other area codes require the 1+.

Figure 9-1
The single line is busy
when A talks to B;
therefore, when the
customer calls in, a
busy tone is received.

It should be obvious from the preceding discussion that larger organizations require the larger capacity and capability of a PBX. These systems have names that come in many flavors, such as Private Automated Branch Exchange (PABX).

The generic term PBX is a private (customer owned and operated) branch exchange (like a central office, it switches and routes calls internally or externally and provides a dial tone to the internal users). The PBX marketplace is inundated with acronyms and features. However, they all do similar things: They primarily process voice calls for the organization. These devices are computer systems that just happen to do voice. Now they also do other things, such as provide data communications and data access.

On average, the all-digital PBX will cost approximately $750 to $1,000 per station. A station is the end-user device, and the figure includes the cost of all the associated hardware to support that telephone set. Included in this generic price is the card inside the computer that provides the dial tone and the logic, a portion of the common equipment that serves many users, and the telephone set, the wiring, and the installation.

The components of the PBX are shown in Figure 9-2.

■ The central processor unit (CPU) is the computer inside the system—the brains.

Figure 9-2
The components of a PBX

- The memory—any computer needs some amount of memory.
- The stations, or telephone sets, are also called lines.
- The trunks are the telco CO trunks that terminate into a PBX.
- The network switches calls inside the system.
- The cabinets house all the components.
- The information transfer, or bus carries the information to and from the computer.
- The console or switchboard allows the operator to control the flow of incoming calls, and so on.
- The common logic, power cards, and so on facilitate the system's operation.
- The battery back-up insures against power failures.
- The wiring infrastructure connects it all.

The PBX is a stored-program, common-controlled device. As a telephone system, it is a resource-sharing system that provides the ability to access a local dial tone and outside trunks to the end user. This stored-program controlled system today is an all-digital architecture. An actual picture of a PBX is shown in Figure 9-3.

Figure 9-3
A PBX

Figure 9-4
The Main Distribution
Frame

Further, all of the wires come to a central point at the Main Distribution Frame (MDF) where blocks are used to terminate the wires in a centralized location. The MDF is shown in Figure 9-4.

Additionally, the use of the main distribution frames internally may be in a telephone closet where patch panels are used to orchestrate the moves, adds, and changes to the telephone wires running out to the desktop user. The patch panel can be used for voice, data, or LAN connections, but it is best to keep them separate. Figure 9-5 is a sample of a patch panel in a closet.

Analog Systems

The analog system uses analog components to handle the call setup and tear-down for the entire system. A voice call is introduced into the system in much the same way that a business or residential user's input is introduced to the telephone company network. As the user generates a call, the telephone handset is picked up from the cradle. At this point, an input/output (I/O) request signal is sent to the main architecture of the PBX, which is usually a computer. Once the signal is sent to the common control, the system then returns a dial tone. The user then dials the digits for the party desired. This dialing sequence is done in-band on the wires in the talk path of the caller. The digits, either rotary (pulse) or tone (DTMF), are sent down the wires to the telephone system.

From there, the telephone system kicks in and generates a request through the architecture to a trunk card. The trunk card serves as the interface to the central office (CO) to request an outside dial tone. Then, the PBX, upon receiving dial tone at the trunk card interface, regenerates the pulses or the tones across the line to the central office. The CO processes these digits in the same manner that it processes individual line requests from a residential user. From the telephone company's perspective, this is the easiest way to process the information.

Digital PBX

All newer systems are basically digital. As a computer architecture, the system processes the information in its digital format. A digital coder/decoder (codec) in the telephone set converts the analog voice conversation into a digital format. The digital signals are then carried down the wires to the

PBX heart (the CPU) for processing. If a call must go outside to the world, the PBX has to determine the best route to process the call onto. In the case where the call will be traversing the telephone company's central office links on an analog circuit, the PBX must format the information for the outside link. In this case, a digital-to-analog conversion will take place. Even if the call is to traverse a digital link to the world, the PBX might have to go through a digital-to-digital conversion. This is because the digital signal at the PBX interface is a unipolar signal, whereas the signal to the telephone company is a bipolar signal (see Figure 9-6).

The PBX market has been plagued by soft sales. This is a function of the recession, the rightsizing and downsizing of corporate America, and the overall unsettled market from a technological standpoint. End users are uncertain of what to buy and when on the market curve they should buy. Therefore, the vendors resort to major markdowns, and they often throw in several other goodies. The buyer's market prevails in the PBX industry. As a result, significant discounts can be obtained if you work with the vendor and understand the product being offered. Many vendors will also compete severely with their distributors. Remember, this is a buyer's market. Table 9-3 is a summary of how the costs would look for the acquisition of a digital PBX, the basic telephone system for an organization. This table reflects three important pieces of the billing arrangements. It would not be unethical to see how the vendors price out their systems against this model. In Table 9-3, we use an average price per port of $1,000. The costs associated with a 1,000-user system, therefore, would be as they appear in Table 9-3.

Another item of note is the third line item, that being profit. We always want our vendors to survive for another day, no two ways about that. However, we do not want to pay a 30 percent total markup on a system for profit. In actuality, the margin is 37 percent, and we will see why later. This is unheard of. So, the discounts that might be passed along from the vendor might well be from the profit picture. Suppose that the vendor offers a discount of 20 percent off the top of the price. The total price is $1,000,000 and the discount is 20 percent, so you can expect to pay $800,000. That should make you feel pretty good, to get a $200,000 discount off the top of your system. But, wait! What if the vendor came back and said that the total discount is only $70,000? Where did we go wrong? Well, the issue is where the numbers are being calculated. The vendor discounted the 20 percent from the top of the system cost ($350,000 $\times$ 0.2 = $70,000). Now, you are paying around $930,000 total for the system, installed. That is not exactly what you thought you were getting a discount on. The vendor will explain that

Figure 9-6
The digital signal from the PBX is converted to analog to the telco.

Table 9-3

Summary of Costs
for a 1,000-Line
Digital PBX

Item	Price
Cost of hardware, software, training, all telephone sets, and interfaces with installation of the hardware	$ 350,000
Cost of wiring and installation for the building infrastructure	$ 350,000
Markup and profit	$ 300,000
Total	$1,000,000

the cost of the wiring cannot be discounted because they use a subcontractor and have to pay this third party for the installation. True, but the vendor also marks up the cost of the wiring and installation. That $350,000 fee to install and wire the system is probably only a $280,000 to $300,000 charge from the subcontractor. So, the manufacturer or distributor is getting a piece of the pie for the installation too.

Yes, this is true. Regardless of how we slice and dice the numbers, this is still a very lucrative sale for the vendor. With a $50,000 to $70,000 markup on the wiring (which is conservative), a $300,000 profit margin, and the remaining cost of the system ($280,000), you can imagine just how much the vendor is making on this system, can't you? Well, now look at the margins based on this new evidence (see Table 9-4).

Can you see anything wrong with this picture? Even though the vendor has given a 20 percent discount to you, and you feel so special for negotiating such a difficult deal for the vendor, and a great one for the organization,

Table 9-4

Summary of New
Profit Margins with
a 20 Percent
Discount on the
System Cost

Item	Original Cost	New Cost	Profit	Percent Margin
PBX system	$ 350,000	$280,000		
Wiring and installation	$ 350,000	$350,000	$ 70,000.00*	20
Margin and profit	$ 300,000	$300,000	$300,000.00	30
Total	$1,000,000	$930,000	$370,000.00	37

*Excludes the wiring contractor's profit margin for the installation and wiring

the overall margin of profit that the vendor has achieved is still 37 percent. This still leaves a lot of room for negotiation before the deal is done. If you consider that there is still room to cut the cost in the profit margin, the profits on the subcontracted piece of the wiring, and the overall system cost, then the dealing has only begun. In many cases, the ability to subcontract the wiring (for example) might produce more productive and competitive results. In this case, many organizations will act as the general contractor for the overall telephone system and then contract for the wiring separately from the telephones. An example of the wiring costs might look like the numbers shown in Table 9-5, where a separate contract is issued for the installation of a four-pair cable installed at 1,000 user locations, the horizontal wiring between the telephone closets and the main distribution frame, and any ancillary cabling needed to implement the system.

Keep in mind that these figures are generic and will require separate bids from various installation companies. If, however, you now consider this figure, and recognize that the wiring contractor has already built in the necessary profit margins to make money on the installation, then the PBX price now has a different perspective. The margin for the hardware, installation, and warrantee on the PBX is now subject to serious negotiation (see Table 9-6).

Table 9-5

Summary of
Wiring Costs

Cost per User Location	Extended Price
Cost of wiring a 1,000-user system at $250–280	$250,000–280,000
Cost for PBX manufacturer at $350	$350,000
Difference	$70,000–100,000

Table 9-6

Summary of New
Cost Structure and
Margins

Item	Cost	Percent Margin
PBX	$280,000	
Markup	$300,000	
Subtotal	$580,000	115
Wiring (as a separate contract and separate margins)	$280,000	15
Total	$860,000	

As you can now imagine, the cost for the telephone system is $280,000 with a profit margin of $300,000 (over 100 percent markup). No vendor will ever approach this structure; these are comparative pricing scenarios. However, if you consider that a 30 percent markup is what the vendor is entitled to, the following summary gives us a whole new structure to deal from. The intent is not to jeopardize the stability and profitability of the supplier, but to maximize the comfort between the two parties. This case will obviously consume a lot of time and effort. But, the overall results are significant (see Table 9-7).

Clearly the price has changed significantly. The system is now being considered at approximately $644 per user instead of $1,000. This accounts for a $356,000 discount overall. This is the way you can look at using the system pricing, rather than just accepting standard pricing. The pricing can vary quite a bit from the original proposal.

Central Office Centrex

An alternative to the purchase of a telephone system is called Centrex. Centrex is a service offering from the incumbent local exchange carrier (ILEC) and the CATV companies and CLECs. They bundle their services at a price that is very competitive with buying the pieces individually. In many cases, the CLECs have service offerings that add features not typically available from the ILEC. The consumer benefits from this one. Centrex stands for central exchange, or PBX services provided from the central office (exchange). The LECs, either the Bell Telephone Companies or the independent telephone companies, all have a service offering. The Centrex service

Table 9-7

Final Configuration of System Pricing

Item	Original Pricing	Revised Pricing	Difference
PBX	$350,000	$280,000	($70,000)
PBX markup at 30 percent of contract)	$300,000	$84,000	($216,000)
Wiring	$350,000	$280,000	($70,000)
Totals	$1,000,000	$644,000	($356,000)
Percentage			35.6 percent

is a partition inside the CO, which provides telephone service on a private basis to businesses (see Figure 9-7).

Centrex is usually rented on a line-by-line basis, month to month. Some companies have long-term agreements to hold down costs, but charging a monthly rate is more prevalent. Costs per line can range from $20 to $25 a month, depending on the company and the serving telco. However, with very large organizations, a long-term contract can be negotiated with the provider. This will result in costs that are in the range of $10 to $12 per month for a Centrex line. The overall result is a monthly savings of $10 to $15 per month per line. With a 1,000-line system, this can be a significant savings. An example is the 1,000-line system that we were using in the PBX comparison. Here, a system can cost approximately $12,000 per month on a long-term agreement. The $12,000 is for the dial tone and features; anything else is an extra. The user must still buy the station equipment (telephone sets).

The components of a Centrex are as follows:

- Central office, which is the serving office
- CPU or computer
- Station cards
- Switching network
- Line cards
- Memory
- Common logic and power cards
- Bus to carry information to and from the CPU

Centrex Service

The primary suppliers, as already stated, are the LECs. They provide the service as part of the central office function.

The list of Centrex providers includes

- **Bell Operating Companies** The four regional Bell Operating Companies (SBC, Qwest, Bell South, and Verizon) and their 23 operating telephone companies are the largest sellers of Centrex (ILECs).
- **Independent Operating Companies** These are such companies as Contel GTE, Centel, and Commonwealth (ILECs).

Figure 9-7
Central office Centrex components

- **Resellers of Centrex service**   Many arrangements have been made with resellers around the country.

- **Bell authorized agents**   These are authorized agents of the ILEC, but are not employees of the company.

- **CATV companies**

- **CLECs**

- **Electric companies**

Centrex service is typically found in North America. However, it is now available in 34 countries.

Peripheral Devices

The list of peripheral devices for the key systems, PBX, and Centrex markets is virtually unlimited. The devices range from items as simple as an external bell to very sophisticated management systems. The pieces are too numerous to list here (and change too frequently), but a lot of negotiating room still exists for any component you might need.

Some of the devices that might appear in the picture are as follows:

- Automatic call distribution
- Voice mail
- Automated attendant
- Call detail recording
- Modem pools
- Multiplexers
- Head sets
- Display sets (telephones)
- Paging systems
- Least cost call routing
- Network management systems
- Design tools
- Answering machines

Questions

1. What does PBX stand for?
   a. Private Branch Telephone
   b. Public Branch Exchange
   c. Private Branch Exchange
   d. Private Bell Exchange

2. What is the name for the Bell Branch Exchange or Central Office?
   a. Root and Branches
   b. End User System
   c. Central Exchange
   d. Class 5 Office

3. Who are the primary users of a PBX?
   a. Bell Systems
   b. CLECs
   c. End User
   d. Corporate Users

4. What is the motivation to use a PBX?
   a. Technical only.
   b. Financial only.
   c. Financial and technical.
   d. It is a nice thing to do.

5. Overall average, a PBX will cost between $_____ and $_____ per user.

6. The least cost method of installing a PBX is to use a _____ at every user's desk?
   a. Multi-line set
   b. Single line set
   c. Dial tone
   d. Hybrid set

7. When a user wants to acquire a PBX, the costs are fixed and non-negotiable.   T/F

8. A PBX can be either _____ or _____.

9. At the entrance to the building, all the wires are terminated on the _____ .

    a. SDF

    b. BDF

    c. MDF

    d. IDF

10. Another name for the MDF is the demarc.   T/F

11. PABX stands for:

    a. Private Analog Branch Exchange

    b. Public Analog Branch Exchange

    c. Public AutomaticBranch Exchange

    d. Private Automatic Branch Exchange

12. A PBX is usually installed with redundant critical components.   T/F

13. The main providers of the PBX are:

    a. ILECs

    b. Manufacturers

    c. CLECs

    d. CATV Companies

14. Centrex is an alternative to buying a PBX.   T/F

15. Centrex can be found in the US and Canada, but also in _____ countries.

16. Centrex offers a(n) _____ advantage to the end-user.

17. The *primary* suppliers of Centrex are:

    a. CLECs, cellular providers

    b. IECs and manufacturers

    c. ILECs and CLECs

    d. None of the above

18. Centrex can be rented on a month to month basis.   T/F

19. A Centrex dial tone can cost approximately $ _____ per month without any long term contracts.

20. With Centrex service the end-user must still acquire the _____ .

Key Telephone Systems

After reading this chapter and completing the questions, you will be able to:

- Explain where key telephone systems (KTS) may be used
- Discuss the differences between the key telephone systems and PBX
- Describe the components that comprise the KTS
- Explain why the movement to an IP telephone set has occurred
- Converse openly about the application and features of the key telephone systems

Another form of equipment is used in a smaller environment. If the user office is small or if a branch office is involved, a key telephone system is used. A key telephone system is another form of a resource-sharing device that is used to reduce the number of outside telephone lines and provide access to many end users.

The equipment selection depends on the size of the organization and the need for communications connectivity. Many small branch offices, small businesses, home businesses, and other such organizations require only a limited amount of telephone sets and can get by with a key telephone system. Figure 10-1 illustrates a key telephone system. This type of system usually consists of a predetermined number of telephone sets to outside

Figure 10-1
A key telephone
system
(Source: Nortel
Networks)

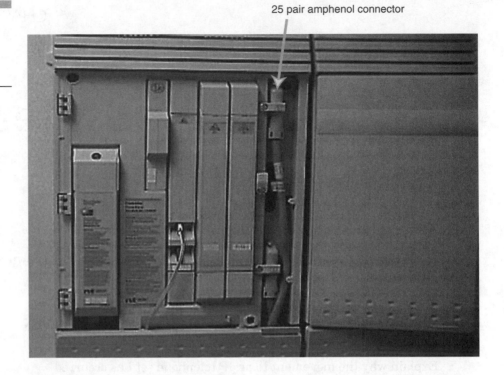

25 pair amphenol connector

lines. Note the reference to lines in this example; the telephone company sees the system as an end user connection in much the same way as a single-line telephone set. Therefore, the customer gets by with the use of lines instead of trunks. The nomenclature for a key system is normally outlined in the number of lines and the number of sets; for example, 1,648 equates to 16 outside telephone lines and 48 telephone sets that comprise the system. These are maximums on the systems; smaller amounts can be used where appropriate.

A key telephone system is composed of the following pieces:

- The *key service unit* (KSU) is the heart and brain of the telephone system.

- *Line cards* are the interfaces to the telephone company lines. They effectively provide the off-hook and on-hook signals to the central office in lieu of the individual telephone sets.

- *Station cards* are the cards that control the intelligence and interface to the end user's key system. The station card interfaces with the end user and the line cards for the access control of the system.

- *Intercom cards* are not always required. Some systems use an intercommunication card for internal connectivity, whereas others have this feature built into their functionality on the backplane of the system.

- *Telephone sets* are variable-user interfaces, whether they are single-line or digital multiline sets. The telephone set controls the intelligence that a user is allowed to access within the system.

- *Power supplies* and *logic cards*

- The *wiring infrastructure* that is used to connect the sets to the KSU central processor unit (CPU), the brains of the system.

Figure 10-2 represents several of these different pieces that might be included. For example, we see that the telephone company has brought in central office lines and terminated them in either an RJ-21X or an RJ-11. From there, the graphic shows a 66 block, sitting side by side with the RJ-21X, where a straight cross-connect arrangement is taking place. A fanned-out, 25-pair cable is punched down on the left side of the 66 block.

Figure 10-2

The key telephone system components

We can refer to this 66 block as the vendor block, whereas the RJ-21X is the telco block. The cable is run from the vendor block with the fanned-out, 25-pair cable into the key service unit, or the intelligence of the key telephone system. Here we might use an amphenol connector, a 25-pair pre-wired connector, for termination in the key service unit. The amphenol is also shown in Figure 10-1 inside the key systems on the right side of the picture. This merely simplifies the process of providing the connectivity. Looking at the other pieces, the system has central office (CO) line cards as opposed to the trunk cards that would appear on a PBX. Station cards are then installed, which provide the intelligence to the individual telsets that are installed within the system. Intercom cards enable intercommunication to prevent the problem that was mentioned earlier in the PBX section. One does not want to tie up all of the outside lines for two parties to be able to talk to each other internally. Therefore, the intercommunications device, or intercom, provides for the station-to-station talk path. Many key systems have an unlimited number of intercoms, whereas others have a very specific number of intercom paths available. This depends on the manufacturer. From the key service unit, we see two lines drawn over to another 66 block that would run in a separate telephone closet. We would call these lines horizontal runs. The *horizontal run* connects the key service unit to the telephone closet, where the 66 block is a termination point. The purpose of this horizontal run is to bundle cable pairs together using 25, 50, or 100 pairs of wire to the telephone closet. On termination on the 66 block, a separate station drop is run to the individual desktop device. At this particular point, the station drop is used on the basis of a two-, three-, or four-pair wiring system.

Each key system requires a different number of wires to the telephone set. For the key telephone systems available on the market today, a single-pair cable system can be used. However, it would be imprudent for the telecommunications personnel to install only one pair of wires to every desktop. The reason is probably obvious; it would leave the possibility of being cable limited, meaning that we would be short of wires in the future and have to reinstall more at a great cost. Once a telephone set is installed on that station drop using a single pair of wires, the inevitable would happen. The next day, users would complain that they needed additional wires for fax or modem connectivity. The telecommunications manager who has not installed enough wires to meet such needs is caught in a bind. Therefore, it is recommended that a four-pair cabling system is always installed regardless of the number of pairs a contractor requests. The four-pair cabling system allows flexibility for additional wires for fax, modem, or any other type of external communications connection. Moreover, the authors typically recommend the use of two, four-pair cables to every desktop. This allows enough future flexibility so that the expensive cost of labor to rewire the building can be avoided. Each of the four-pair cables should be terminated in what is known as an RJ-45 jack. The RJ-45 jack, an eight-pin interface, is the standard plug for the future. All four-cable pairs should be terminated into the eight-pin interface. All too often telecommunications personnel use jacks with less capacity than the RJ-45 and do not terminate all the wires. This means that extra wires are in the wall, but are unusable. It would require a lot of labor to reinforce the wires. Most key telephone systems today are computer-stored, programmed-controlled systems that are similar to the PBX discussed in Chapter 9. As a matter of fact, it is becoming far more difficult to differentiate the PBX and the key system. Key systems can be as large as 200+ ports, whereas PBXs now come with as few as 50+ ports. Functionally, these two types of systems provide the same services and features. The differences are so subtle that it is becoming almost a moot point to call them by different names. These systems are used extensively throughout the industry, so they are fairly perfected in terms of having simple connections, being rich in features, and having significant penetration in the business community.

The key systems are used by larger organizations too. In departments where groups of people require connectivity to each other or where a consolidation of features is required behind a Centrex or PBX, the key system offers some solutions. Although many organizations try to emulate the key system in a PBX with multiline sets, it is often more prudent to install the key service unit. Many dual systems provide the access to features of the PBX and the clustering of workers of a key system.

Why Key Systems?

It is not uncommon to hear business users question the need for a key system. The obvious choice is to go to the telephone company and rent a single line for each user in the organization, branch office, sales office, or home-based business. However, the same arguments that were discussed at the beginning of Chapter 9 hold equally true for the key system. It would be frivolous to rent a single line for every user in a sales or service office. The intent of the sales office is to provide a location where the sales force can schedule work and visit from time to time for meetings and report writing. However, the sales force might be road-based, with a primary emphasis on visiting the customer and meeting the customer's needs. According to this analysis, employees and outside lines should not have a one-to-one relationship. Of course, this assumes that the sales force is out of the office when calling on customers. If the charter is to telemarket, the entire scenario changes dramatically. When the office force drops in at varying intervals, it is unlikely that everyone will be around at one time. Therefore, a 3:1 ratio can usually be achieved, with three telephone sets being used for each outside line. This can save a significant amount of money in a small office and even more in the larger office environment. Table 10-1 shows a comparison of the use of outside lines on a 3:1 ratio. This does not include the costs for the key system; the costs will be shown in a later comparison. Suffice it to say that the comparison here is based on the recurring monthly telephone company costs.

The obvious reason an organization would choose a key system is the recurring monthly savings of $120 to $400, as shown in Table 10-1. However, the cost of the key system is not shown. The primary savings shown in this table are the cost of renting a telephone line for each user as opposed to sharing the number of lines with the resulting savings. Now we can add the cost of the capital equipment—the key telephone system. A typical key system with installation, hardware, software, and warrantee will cost an average of $500 per user. A comparative analysis of the costs associated with the acquisition of the system is shown in Table 10-2.

You can see from this table that the costs have been applied in a linear fashion. Better discounts might be available as the system gets larger. Fur-

Table 10-1

Comparison of Line Rentals With and Without a Key System

Number of Users	Without Key System	With Key System	Difference
10 @$20	$200	$ 80	$120 monthly
20 @$20	$400	$140	$260 monthly
30 @$20	$600	$200	$400 monthly

Table 10-2

Summary of Key Telephone System Costs for Various Numbers of Users

Number of Users	Key Equipment Costs
10	$ 5,000
20	$10,000
30	$15,000

ther, the system costs are associated with a basic telephone system. Other features that increase cost include:

- Voice mail
- Station message detail recording
- Automated attendant
- Least-cost routing
- Data and voice simultaneously
- Automatic call distribution

All of these features raise the cost of a telephone system. The wiring is typically sold to a user on the basis of the vendor's approach to installation. For example, many of these key systems use a two-wire (one-pair) connection to the desktop; others might use a four-wire (two-pair) connection and so on. In general, a good rule of thumb is to install a four-pair connection to every desk, whether you believe you need it or not. This will increase the cost of the wiring, but it is a good deal. The cost of the wire ranges approximately from $0.03 to $0.05 per foot for the added pairs. All things considered, the little add-on for the wires makes for an insignificant increase to the overall system. However, over the life of the system, the extra pairs of wires pay for themselves in no time. If a user needs a modem or fax machine, for example, then the extra wires are necessary. To have an installer come back and pull an entire new pair of wires will cost from $250 to $350, with most of the expense from labor. This can also be disruptive in the workplace. Table 10-3 compares the equipment costs and the monthly rental costs for the telephone lines to show the overall impact. Taking the comparative numbers from the original tables (Tables 10-1 and 10-2), we see the following cost structure.

Table 10-3

Summary of Costs for Key System versus Non-key System

| Number of Users | Without Key System | | Total 1-year Cost | With Key System | | Total 1-year Cost |
	Line Cost	Equipment Cost	Depreciation @ 3 Years	Line Cost	Equipment Cost	Depreciation @ 3 Years
10	$200	$ 600	$2,600	$ 80	$ 5,000	$2,660
20	$400	$1,200	$5,200	$140	$10,000	$4,980
30	$600	$1,800	$7,800	$200	$15,000	$7,400

Although Table 10-3 might look like it is a break-even outcome whether or not one uses a telephone system in lieu of the monthly rental of a line per user, some basic assumptions are being made here. The equipment cost for the non-key system is for the purchase of basic analog single-line sets. No multiline sets are involved in this scenario.

The monthly equipment costs are associated with a three-year depreciation cost on a straight-line basis. In reality, the finance department would likely write the capital off over five years. The finance department would also write the equipment off at an accelerated rate based on the IRS and financial policies accepted.

The one-year differences must be spread over the number of years the system is in place. After the payback period is achieved, the numbers change significantly.

Table 10-4 covers the same system costs over a five-year depreciation cycle, in which the system life is a ten-year period. In this case, after the fifth year, the equipment costs disappear and only the recurring monthly costs remain. These are simple calculations—any increases in the line costs are not included and factoring for maintenance is not built in. The assumption here is to look at the overall differences between having a system or not. The same assumptions from Table 10-3 are used: the number of users, the cost of equipment at $60 per single-line set (written off, in this case, over five years), the line costs held constant over the five- and 10-year life cycle, and so on.

Table 10-4

5- and 10-Year Comparative Costs

Users	Non-Key Costs	Line Costs Monthly	Total 5 Years	10 Years
10	$ 600	$200	$12,600	$24,600
20	$1,200	$400	$25,200	$49,200
30	$1,800	$600	$37,800	$73,800

	Key Costs	Line Costs	Total 5 Years	10 Years	Difference	
10	$ 5,000	$ 80	$ 9,800	$14,600	($2,800)	($10,000)
20	$10,000	$140	$18,400	$26,800	($6,800)	($22,400)
30	$15,000	$200	$27,000	$39,000	($10,800)	($34,800)

This table provides a much different picture of the financial impact of using the key telephone system. On the basis of an example of 30 users, the difference in raw costs over the five-year period is $10,800; over 10 years, the key equipment will save $34,800. These are significant savings over the life of the equipment when you consider that the entire organization might only be 30 people. The equipment will obviously pay for itself over the five- and 10-year period. Remember also that the key system includes the features and functions of a telephone system and includes multiline sets. The non-key system comparison includes only single-line sets and no added features. Each of these will change the equation and show a better payout for the key telephone system. Having drawn this to a conclusion, you can now see why an organization might consider the installation of a resource-sharing arrangement such as a key telephone system. However, a financial calculation is not the only factor involved in this choice.

As covered in Chapter 9, the systems approach has other advantages. For example, one advantage is the use of the intercommunications channel, called the intercom. The *intercom* frees the outside lines for incoming customer calls when two workers in the same office need to communicate. Using the intercom, party *A* calls party *B* on the internal communications paths in the system. Some systems have a fixed number of intercom paths, whereas others have an unlimited number. This is a function of the manufacturer equipment. When using the alternate system (the non-key telephones), the choices are far more restrictive. If party *A* wants to talk to party *B*, the two outside telephone lines associated with these two individuals are busy. The customer calls coming into the building for either party are blocked until they terminate their conversation. The customer might become frustrated and take his or her business elsewhere if this is a constant occurrence.

Moreover, it is far easier to add features and services in the key telephone system than in the single-line telephone set. Users will like the features that can be achieved in the key system, such as:

- Call transfer to another party
- Call hold by pressing a feature button
- Three-way or conference calling
- Consultation hold, where a call can be placed on hold while the user confers with another user in the system
- Speed dialing on an individual or system basis
- Speakerphones
- Hands-free dialing

Figure 10-3
Features on sets for
key system

Some of these features are displayed in Figure 10-3, where the buttons are allocated for the use of the specific features. No one telephone set or system offers everything the user wants, the way he or she wants it. However, strides have been taken in the past to accommodate to what users have asked for. Newer key telephone systems will use a soft key approach, where a visual display panel such as a light-emitting diode (LED) or liquid crystal display (LCD) is used on the telephone set. As features and functions are activated, instead of fixed keys on the telephone set, the display will have a series of buttons whose functions change as you move through the menus on the system. Although these are a little more expensive, they may add flexibility over time. In viewing the actual key telephone sets as shown in Figure 10-3, the feature keys are shown. Note the differences as they are shown on the drawing. When a user activates a feature, a new set of menu options appears for each of the soft keys. This provides a very flexible arrangement, but we must be aware that the end user's ability to grasp and use these features will make the sole decision of their effectiveness. Merely throwing features and functions at an end user does not assure ease of use or connectivity establishment. Users may feel intimidated by soft keys with LCD-driven menus and not use the capabilities of the system. We must be concerned with this risk. Therefore, it is highly recommended that the telecommunications manager select a few users to be pilots (guinea pigs) for testing this system before going to a state-of-the-art telephone system. This checks the ease of use and the users' ability to absorb the information and use the features. One should not select the super or power users, but take a mix of power users and novices alike to guarantee a good cross-representation of internal users. This will help ensure a win/win situation when installing a key telephone system. Without it, one may install a system that is not fully utilized and is expensive due to these limited features. We do not want to waste corporate monies on features and functions that people will not be able to use merely for the sake of having glitzy equipment.

Features on Sets for Key System Vendor Interfaces

The telephone interfaces in Figure 10-4 show different ways that a key system can be connected to the outside lines. Often, the telephone company brings in individual two-wire analog circuits (lines) and terminates these in an RJ-11C jack. This is the case for smaller systems of less than 10 lines. However, if the system is larger and more connections are required, the telephone company might be asked to terminate the lines in an RJ-21X. This is a call that can be made by the vendor who is requesting the service

Figure 10-4
Telco interfaces to a key system vary.

for its customers. Frankly, the connections have no major difference other than some not-so-obvious benefits.

For example, using the RJ-21X consolidates the RJ-11s into a single block that supports 25 two-wire connections. This is a little cleaner than having 25 individual RJ-11s installed on a wall. The convenience of testing and troubleshooting at one spot on the wall has some benefit.

However, the individual RJ-11s can be used in lieu of the larger block. Although these might take up more wall space, if the telephone system ever fails, a user can go into the telephone equipment room and unplug one of the circuit connections to the key system, plug in a single-line telephone set (2500 set), and make calls to obtain repairs from the telephone company or equipment vendors. Furthermore, if critical calls must be made, many users can take advantage of this special access method into the lines.

These systems have been around for a long time, so dealing with this connectivity has no mystique. For the most part, vendors have these systems down to a science. Users also have them under control. No major management issues appear in dealing with a key system, except when the system fails. The vendor or telephone company can usually rectify this situation quickly when problems arise. The interface is a two-wire analog connection that is similar to the residential connection. The main problems a user will have concern the power. We always recommend that a backup battery be provided with the installation so that a critical component of the system's performance can be preserved with the supplemental power. The backup battery adds some minor costs, possibly a few hundred dollars at the most, but it buys a lot of comfort and protection for the end user.

Innovations in the Key Telephone Systems—IP Telephones

Much ado is currently flooding the industry with the move toward Voice over IP. Consequently, many of the vendors now produce an IP telephone system and IP telephones. We are moving from a data-oriented Internet to one that also carries real-time voice traffic. It is relatively commonplace for computers to send messages via the Internet. Voice can be digitized and then transmitted just like any other type of data. Figure 10-5 shows an example of the IP telephone. This single-line Cisco phone also provides four dedicated feature buttons (line, hold, transfer, and settings), located promi-

Figure 10-5
The IP telephone
(Source: Cisco)

Figure 10-5
The IP telephone
(Source: Cisco)

nently under the display. A cluster of six feature access keys is located above the volume control rocker switch. The factory default configuration for messages (*msgs*), conference (*conf*), forward, speed dial (*speed 1, speed 2*), and redial can be programmed by a system administrator to perform other functions, such as Call Park, Call Pick-Up, and Night Service, as well as additional speed dials and other traditional telephone features. Another set shown in Figure 10-6 from VocalData is a top-of-the-line executive phone that offers 32 programmable buttons and five, fixed-function feature buttons (hold, transfer, redial, volume+, and volume−). The 40-character, two-line display provides detailed call information at a glance.

Figure 10-6
The executive set
using IP telephone
(Source: VocalData)

Now the vendors of IP telephony products are integrating software and application-based interfaces, as seen in Figure 10-7. The Voice Client Application is a Windows™ software program that lets users control their Vocal-Data IP-Ethernet telephone from their PC through an easy-to-use graphical user interface (GUI). The tabbed GUI enables Voice Client users to instantly access phone, directory, and voice mail features.

IP telephony uses the Internet to send audio between two or more computer users in real time to support real-time conversations. The first IP telephony product appeared in 1995; it used a software application designed to

Figure 10-7
The GUI interface
(Source: VocalData)

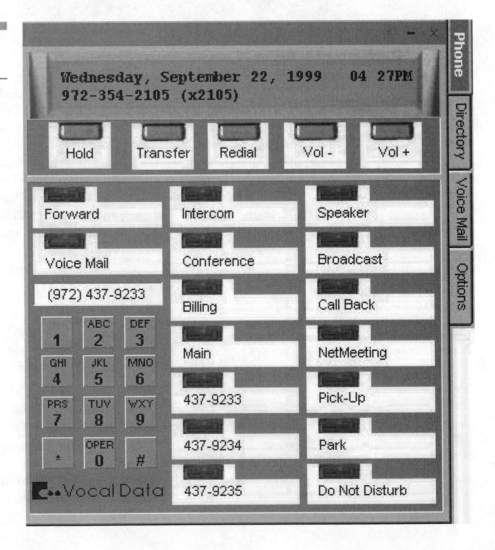

run on a multimedia PC. The quality was not the greatest, but people could place calls between PCs anywhere in the world (for free).

Improvements have made reasonable quality conversations possible. The original concept of combining voice and data on a single network was very innovative. Much of the work occurred since the Telecommunications Act of 1996 because the door was open for competition in the infrastructure.

IP gateways were introduced in 1996 and bring IP telephony to the general public. These gateways bridge circuit-switched phone systems, as well as telephone company central offices, from the traditional telephony world with the packet-switch world of the Internet. Gateways enable the use of standard telephones to talk over the Internet instead of computers. Several vendors have now introduced products that are known as IP telephones to satisfy the demand.

The Vendor Proposal

When dealing with the purchase of the key telephone system, you will be better equipped if all of the known benefits and features are discussed. The growth capacity of the system before a major upgrade is required is a beneficial piece of information. Never assume that the best deal is placed on the table on the first proposal. As a matter of fact, we prefer to do the following when considering a key system, a PBX, or any other piece of equipment:

- Conduct a needs assessment. Determine the needs of the organization —to meet the core business functions of the office or plant, or other objectives.

- Determine the buying motivations. Is the system being considered to allow growth, replace obsolete or broken equipment, or just deliver a needed feature?

- Conduct user surveys to see whether any hidden needs exist.

- Document the needs and the buying motivation.

- Send out a request for information (RFI) to gather information about the players in your area, the systems they offer, the average number of systems they have installed, and the typical sizes.

- Prequalify the bidders that you will use on the basis of the responses to the RFI.

- Determine future needs as they pertain to system growth.

- Develop a request for proposal (RFP) based on the consolidation of all the information gathered.

- Obtain budgetary approval in advance for some value of the system intended for purchase. Allow some discretionary funding for added features or growth that you didn't anticipate. Never buy a system that only satisfies today's needs; make sure that you have plenty of room to grow.

- Release the RFP and formulate a target due date for responses.

- Analyze the information and begin to select a short list of possible suppliers that you feel comfortable with. This includes checking references of other customers who are using a system similar to the one you are considering.

- Negotiate the contract. Be firm. Make sure all costs are shown and documented.

- Allow plenty of time for the whole process.

These steps are generic enough that the process can be used straightforwardly for any system or service that is being considered. You can never do too much homework to evaluate a system or a supplier. However, you can get caught into a "paralysis by analysis" syndrome, where the process takes too long. This whole process for a key system can be completed in a matter of weeks before getting to final negotiation. Nowhere is it written that such a study should take months to years. Technological advances and the product life cycles are such that you can only decide on the technology on the basis of the information that is available today. Things will change at a very fast rate.

Questions

1. Key telephone systems are used for smaller locations.   T/F

2. The following is not a prime candidate for using a key telephone system.

   a. Corporate headquarters
   b. One person shop
   c. Small office
   d. Home office

3. A KTS is used as a _____.
   a. Telephone company offering
   b. Regional telecommunications service
   c. Resource-sharing device
   d. Dedicated system for a user

4. A 1648 telephone system means that the system supports:
   a. 16 telephones and 48 lines
   b. 48 telephones and 16 sets
   c. 48 lines and 48 sets
   d. 48 telephones and 16 lines

5. The brain of the key systems is called:
   a. Brain
   b. KTS
   c. KSU
   d. Memory

6. All key systems use an unlimited number of intercom cards.   T/F

7. A pre-wired, 25-pair connector used on a key system is called:
   a. Multipair connector
   b. RJ-66
   c. RJ-45
   d. Amphenol

8. The connector used at the main distribution frame and throughout the building is called:
   a. 66 block
   b. RJ-45
   c. RJ-21X
   d. RJ-11

9. One advantage of a key telephone system is that all users have a single line set.   T/F

10. The ratio used to provide lines to telephones in a key system is:

    a. 10:1

    b. 5:1

    c. 2:1

    d. None of the above

11. Ideally, we can save a monthly amount of between $ _____ and $ _____ with a key system.

    a. 10–100

    b. 120–400

    c. 140–160

    d. 1,000–1,500

12. The average cost of a key system per user is $1,000.   T/F

13. The RJ-21x supports how many telephone lines?

    a. 25 four-wire connections

    b. 24 four-wire connections

    c. 25 two-wire connections

    d. 24 two-wire connections

14. How many wires are in an RJ-11?

    a. 4

    b. 25

    c. 2

    d. 8

15. How many wires are in an RJ-45

    a. 4

    b. 6

    c. 25

    d. 8

16. The single line set is called a 2500 set.   T/F

17. The IP telephone is used when we need to create an automatic call distribution center for our workforce.   T/F

18. The use of both voice and data on a single network caught on in the year _____.

    a. 2000

    b. 1998

    c. 1984

    d. 1996

19. What prompted the use of IP telephony?

    a. Cost

    b. Integration

    c. Ran out of voice networking strategies

    d. Management wanted more say

20. An IP telephone can integrate with a computer through a Windows™ based _____ .

    a. Telephone

    b. Computer network

    c. GUI

    d. Internet

Voice Processing

After reading this chapter and completing the questions, you will be able to:

- Explain what voice messaging does
- Discuss the differences between an answering machine and a voice mail system
- Describe the basics of an Automatic Call Distribution system
- Explain why an organization uses an Automated Attendant
- Converse freely about the benefits of automating the answering and voice processing functions

Voice processing encompasses a variety of technologies that can be categorized into two major areas: directing calls and message manipulation. As we will see, each application in this chapter focuses on one of these two major areas, yet also includes elements of the other area. Moreover, as time goes by and the vendors of these products enhance their offerings, the offerings become more and more alike. So bear in mind that these descriptions are of the essential functions present in each application; in fact, when you go out to buy, you might have a difficult time distinguishing one from another.

The technologies presented in this chapter include the following:

- Automated attendant
- Automated call distribution system
- Voice mail/messaging systems

Interactive Voice Response

Other technologies that are still evolving fall into the voice-processing category. These will include, for example, voice-to-text conversion and text-to-voice conversion.

Each of these technologies was designed to automate the processing of information, with one major limitation in mind: human beings. The major pitfall in the expansion of our telephony and telecommunications networks has been the inability of humans to keep pace with faster and more reliable communications. Organizations attempting to provide improved services with fewer people have implemented technologies to take up the slack. Many of these technologies have enhanced the price/performance ratios but have subsequently caused user frustrations. No technology is good if the implementation is for the wrong reasons, or if the acceptance isn't there.

Before getting into the details, however, let us discuss two methods that enable human beings to interact with some of these technologies.

Control Alternatives: Touch-Tone or Voice Recognition

Most voice processing technologies depend on Touch-Tone™ (AT&T) input from callers, if any input is collected at all. As described in Chapter 4, dual-tone multifrequency (or DTMF, the technical term for Touch-Tone signals) tones are specifically designed to be carried well by the analog telephone network. (Pulses, on the other hand, are generally not transmitted beyond a telephone's closest central office; it is impractical to use them for controlling voice processing.) Human beings can also press DTMF telephone buttons far more quickly than they can dial numbers on a rotary telephone.

An obvious alternative to any kind of finger control is voice recognition. After all, people generally prefer speech to pressing keys. And, in fact, some systems now do implement limited voice recognition. But voice recognition technology is not quite ready for prime time in the area of general fielding of calls from the public. The problem is vocabulary. Voice recognition systems generally can either recognize many words spoken by one user (or a limited set of users) or just a few words spoken by many users. Both approaches are being built into production voice processing systems. For example, the voice transcription systems now used by some medical examiners are ideal applications: a very small user population and a precisely definable vocabulary. Another example: Some telephone companies are replacing some operator functions with voice recognition. Again, a relatively small vocabulary is required. Have you heard this on the telephone lately?

- "If you are making a long-distance call, please say 'operator' for operator assistance, 'credit card' for calling card service, or 'collect' for collect calls now."

- "The number you called is not answering; please call back later."

- "The number you called is busy; to leave a message . . ."

These are forms of interactive limited vocabulary. They work well. If you mumble and do not say the word correctly, you will hear the response, "We did not understand your request; please say it again clearly."

Increasingly sophisticated algorithms and more powerful digital signal processors (DSP) and computers are driving up the meaning of many and expanding the definition of just a few in the first sentence of the previous paragraph. As time goes by, voice recognition will be seen on more and more systems. But to minimize the vocabulary that must be recognized, the inputs will initially be limited to little more than what callers could have entered on their keypads; that is, numbers, letters, and a small number of special characters. But today, most systems accept control from Touch-Tone only.

Voice Dialing

As technology continues to develop, the use of voice dialing finally caught on. Now with the ability to record a name in a system (that is, a PBX, key telephone system, cell phone), which enables a pre-programmed number to be called up in a computer routine and then automaically dialed. This enables us to save as many as 100 telephone numbers with the associated verbal command. The most common include

- Home
- Office
- Attorney
- Doctor
- Dentist
- Co-Worker
- Supervisor

This change also enables us to now dictate the number verbally into a set or into a carrier's network. Here the user dials into a network access number and then follows the prompts: If you are planning to make a call, please say or dial the number you wish to reach. This has also caught on at many of the frequent user locations (that is, dialing into an airline frequent flyer telephone line) where the prompts will ask the user to say or dial their account number. After catching the number and translating it, the system will then play it back for verification, "Is this correct? Please say yes to accept."

Automated Attendant

An *attendant*, in telephone lingo, is an operator for a private telephone system. At your organization, if you have Centrex or a PBX and dial 0, you will reach your attendant, if you have one. But if you have an automated attendant, there might no longer be a human in that role. Or if there is an operator there, the operator might be the last resort.

The use of automated attendants to supplement normal operators was intended to assist customers in cutting right through a telephone system if they knew to whom they wanted to speak. Furthermore, if customers didn't know to whom they wished to speak but knew the department, they could expedite their connections without human intervention. How often have you called an organization only to be greeted by a human with "Good afternoon, ABC Company. Please hold."? The operator had more calls to handle than time to do so. Thus, you were put on interminable hold.

Automated attendants were designed to take the rote or redundant answering function away from the operator, so that quality time could be spent with customers who legitimately needed assistance. Some examples of this might include items shown in Table 11-1.

However, too many organizations implemented the system incorrectly. Instead of giving their customers a choice (dial 555-1234 for the automated attendant, 555-1000 for the operator), these users installed the system without warning. Customers who called on Friday afternoon and spoke to a human (as they were accustomed to doing over the years) called in on Monday morning to be greeted by a machine. This shock to the customers' egos and psyches created frustration and a reluctance to deal with this company. Thus, a system designed to improve customer service and relations was instead destroying both. Good installations, coupled with an understanding and concern for the caller, would have prevented the problems.

Automated attendant systems fall into the "directing calls" category identified previously. Automated attendants usually perform some or all of the following functions:

- Answering the telephone (usually only calls coming in from the outside).

- Announcing options to the caller. These might include numbers of departments that can be selected, hours of business, and other information useful to callers.

- Accepting Touch-Tone input from the caller to direct the call either to other information provided by the automated attendant or to a human attendant.

- Forwarding the call to a human being if no Touch-Tone input is received.

Table 11-1

Applications for Automated Attendant

Organization	Application
TV station	Newsworthy items such as weather conditions, parade information, repetitive information regarding TV news and community interest
Radio station	Contest information, record requests
Mortgage companies	Current rates on mortgages, information on applications
Colleges/universities	Student activities, registration, class schedules, and fill rates
Movie theaters	Schedules, costs, and specials

Organizations typically use automated attendants to reduce payroll costs for live attendants. Some have eliminated live attendants entirely; others reduce staffing for the function but enable callers to escape the Touch-Tone system and reach a human attendant. A frequent application is as a night-answer attendant. In this mode, live attendants answer the telephone during business hours; after hours, callers can select an internal extension if they know one.

Another possible use is to provide the daytime functional equivalent of direct inward dialing (DID) without implementing this with the telephone company. With this approach, callers must dial an additional four digits—but no additional trunks, DID or otherwise, need be acquired. The use of DID might not be practical if the key system or PBX is not equipped with these cards, or if an older system is not upgradable. This is a supplement to using the DID trunks, which are more expensive. Depending on the calling population, this can be a very effective supplement to a live operator. Callers, who know the extension they want, simply enter it; others either select the live attendant from the prompts or time out and speak to the attendant.

Note that an automated attendant is not itself a PBX; it fits logically and architecturally into the same role as a live human attendant. Figure 11-1 illustrates an automated attendant configuration. Although from callers' points of view the automated attendant is in front of the PBX, in practice it might be integrated into or reside behind the PBX as shown in the figure. When the automated attendant is active, the PBX initially routes all calls that would normally go to the human attendant (usually all calls, unless DID is implemented or the automated attendant is present to handle overflow only) instead. The automated attendant attempts to determine the caller's real destination. It then uses the normal PBX call transfer capabilities to route the call to the correct extension, or to the operator if appropriate. The conversation with the automated attendant might go something like this:

AA: Thank you for calling XYZ Company. If you know the extension of your sales representative, please enter it on your Touch-Tone telephone at any time. For a list of department extensions, please press the pound sign. If you would rather speak to an operator, please press 0, or just stay on the line and someone will be with you momentarily.

Caller: (Presses pound)

Figure 11-1

An automated attendant configuration

AA: For sales, press 31. For accounting, press 32. For installation scheduling, press 33. For customer support, press 34. To hear this list again, press the pound sign. To go back to the first greeting message, press 39. If you would rather speak to an operator, please press 0, or just stay on the line and someone will be with you momentarily.

Caller: (Presses 32)

AA: Your call is being transferred.

Note that in this example, no internal extensions would begin with the digit 3. The sample dialogue illustrates some important design considerations:

- Unless it is impossible or you are certain that it is not necessary, always give callers an out to a human operator. If you do not, you risk angering two groups of callers: those whose telephones do not generate Touch-Tones (and many of these still exist) and those who refuse to interact with any kind of telephone answering machines.

- Be friendly—it costs you nothing and will please some callers while offending few or none.

- Keep it short. The longer any one message (or the entire set through which callers must proceed), the higher the percentage of callers that will hang up (also known as balking or reneging). We have encountered one system where the menuing function took us through 12 layers. (We only called that number once!)

- Keep it simple. Some calling populations are very technical (many of those calling technical support for a local area network vendor, for example). But more are not. A lowest-common-denominator approach, simple but not insulting, is usually justified.

- Give people information on how to repeat messages, and never leave them in a position where they will be stuck unless they remember the prompts.

- Do not use telecommunications jargon. You understand it; your callers do not. For example, do not refer to the attendant as such; he or she is the operator.

- When possible, use obvious codes. For example, try to use 0 for the operator. Also, try only to assign a single use to a single code. In the example, the pound sign (#) always provides the department list, no matter where in the dialogue it is pressed.

- When providing a list of alternatives, provide the more specific choices first, then the more general ones. Not unreasonably, people will often select the first choice that sounds as though it might fit. "Customer support" can cover a lot of ground. If the department list had started with customer support, many callers who might better have been routed to one of the other departments would select customer support instead.

- If your system permits it, allow callers to enter choices at any time; do not make them wait until a message finishes. People who listen to the end will not notice either way, but those who move more quickly and already know the choices from frequent use will appreciate the flexibility of the dialogue. Personally, this is a frustrating experience when we cannot enter the digits immediately, but instead have to wait for the prompts to finish. Normally this is a company we try not to call often because their systems are unfriendly.

A Few Important Points Not Directly Illustrated in the Dialogue

When a machine answers a call, callers often immediately drop into a fault-finding mode; many will be extremely easy to irritate. (Some will already be irritated, a price of using this technology. As evidence that this technology can be a two-edged sword, there is at least one mail-order hardware vendor that includes in its advertising the fact that a human always answers the phone—"no annoying machines!") So consider designing your dialogues to be as inoffensive as possible, even to the point of blandness.

If your system is to be operational both during the day and after business hours, use different dialogues for different conditions. One of the more frustrating things you can do to callers is to inform them that they can escape to an operator, and then prevent them from doing so because the operator(s) went home. Worse, if they dial the 0 for the operator and the calls ring into oblivion. It is truly amazing how lousy some recorded greetings sound, even those of billion-dollar companies, and what a bad impression such recordings make on callers. Use a professional studio, announcer, and recording equipment to produce your messages, or your announcements also can fall into the "lousy" category. Remember that this is the doorway to your organization. First impressions are long lasting.

Dialogues must be designed and programmed (written out) much like computer programs. A poor flow of either words or choices will also reflect badly on the called organization. Although it is important to list choices in an order that will cause the correct choice to be made, saving the most frequent choice for last is one of the surest ways to irritate people. If a large proportion of callers will correctly want a particular choice (such as, customer service), consider providing a different telephone number for those people to call in the first place.

Try to incorporate a bypass through the prompts if the system allows it. As callers get used to the system, they will not want to listen to every offering. Rather, they'll try to dial the sequence immediately, expecting to get the party they always call.

If you make a material change in the choices, and your system has been in use for some time, announce early in the first menu that the choices have changed. Otherwise, your experienced users will blithely key their way down incorrect paths.

By itself, an automated attendant normally does not take messages or, without direction from callers, route calls other than to a default live answering position. But, as mentioned previously, the lines between voice processing systems are somewhat blurred. Do not be surprised if you find a voice mail system or automatic call distributor that encompasses all of the previous functions.

Automatic Call Distributor

Automatic call distributors (ACDs) are the grandparents of voice processing systems. Although automated attendants are a newer development, ACDs have been around for several decades. When you call an airline, you will not immediately reach a human being. Instead you will reach an ACD. If you respond to a television advertisement that states, "operators are standing by," those operators will be reached via an ACD. ACDs are used extensively for high volumes of incoming calls. This is a load-balancing system to let the agents on the receiving end of the calls spread the workload evenly among the agents. Distributors used in the early days only used a hunt system. The hunt would always start at the first agent and proceed down the line until an available agent was found. Unfortunately, if you were in the lead group of numbers, you would be swamped all day long, whereas an agent at the end of the group might only get an occasional call. This was an uneven distribution and caused a lot of stress and frustration in the workforce. The ACD rectifies this by leveling the load by number of calls, amount of time on the line, or other parameters set by the administrator. Just about every company has an application for an ACD today. The purpose of the ACD is also to create a smooth and orderly flow of incoming calls into an organization—for example: by customer, by region, or by product line. Primary responsibilities are

- Prioritizing the calls
- Routing calls to the appropriate agent
- Delivering any announcements, queue
- Directing busy calls to announcements
- Handling messages for call backs

Because the machine is doing so much in terms of routing the calls to appropriate agents, or overflow to other groups of agents, companies can have far more incoming lines than they have people to answer them. This might or might not have some impact on the customer service function, because frustrations can arise. Think of how you feel when you get to an airline and are told: "All agents are busy. Your call will be handled in the order of receipt; please hold on." The ACD system can be configured in a stand-alone mode (see Figure 11-2) where all calls bypass the organization's PBX and go directly into the ACD for processing. This is similar to a PBX in that it has its own trunk cards, station (or agent) cards, CPU, printer, memory, and power supply. The system can be simplex or redundant, depending on the finances of the organization. These systems can be as simple or as sophisticated as the company is willing to buy. The ACD can also be a part of the company's PBX system, either integrated into or as an adjunct to the PBX manufacturer's product line. The integrated system uses the same architecture, CPU, memory, power supplies, and so on as the PBX. The agent's terminal is merely an extension of the PBX. There is some merit in having a single product for additional coverage, space considerations, and so on. Again, this depends on the customer's willingness to integrate into a sole source. However, the PBX manufacturers are in the business of making PBXs and the ACD is a spin-off of this product line. Therefore the system might not be as powerful or as fully featured as a stand-alone system designed strictly for the ACD function.

Another variation of the ACD function in PBXs is uniform call distribution (UCD), a basic system with less functionality than the normal ACD. Its

Figure 11-2

The ACD system configured in a stand-alone mode

function is to uniformly distribute calls to a group of agents, but without the high-end services of a full-fledged ACD.

ACDs can also be used with Centrex service (see Figure 11-3). The ILECs will offer a UCD function, as the ACD capability of a central office is somewhat limited, or, as shown in the figure, the customer can run Centrex lines, 800/888/877/866 lines, 900 lines, or the like directly through the Centrex into a customer premises system. The variations do not limit your ability to serve your customers.

Keep in mind the customer service side of the equation. Too few agents can create ill will toward your organization; too many will waste money. Thus, a traffic engineering calculation is required to come up with the right mix of agents and lines for the maximization of service (see Chapter 8). Like automated attendants, ACDs fall into the "directing calls" category. But although automated attendants typically are used to replace one to six live attendants and interact with callers, ACDs typically provide access to dozens or hundreds of live agents and do not give callers any choices (although the ACD might make choices itself). An ACD routes calls primarily on the basis of characteristics of the call other than input from the caller. These characteristics might include the line on which the call arrives, the time of day at the answering location, what agents (not "attendants" in this case) are busy, and so on. A typical call to an ACD can go something like this:

ACD: Thank you for calling SuperSoft customer support! All of our support people are serving other callers at the moment, but please don't hang up! Calls are answered in the order they arrive, and the average wait time at the moment is five and a half minutes. (music on hold for 30 seconds)

ACD: SuperSoft also operates a support bulletin board at area code 212-555-7654, with modem speeds up to 28,800 bps at settings No parity, 8 data bits, 1 stop bit. (music on hold for 30 seconds)

ACD: The probable wait time is now about four minutes. (more music on hold)

ACD: Your call is being transferred.

You get the idea. The previous monologue illustrates some key characteristics and capabilities of some ACDs.

Unless integrated with other systems such as voice response units, ACDs are not prepared to accept input from callers.

Figure 11-3

ACDs used with Centrex service

Because the main purpose of an ACD is to smooth calling loads to make the most efficient use of agents' time, a key purpose of an ACD script is to keep callers from hanging up. One way to do this is to provide useful information to the callers—for example, information on how soon they might speak to an agent (a recently developed capability of some of the more advanced ACDs on the market) or other information related to the company's services.

The preparation of an ACD's response sequences is called *scripting*. Scripting is every bit as critical to a successful implementation as the dialog in a television commercial. Usually the process begins with the construction of a flow diagram (see Figure 11-4). An automated attendant passes on a call and "forgets" about it. An ACD might also function as a PBX (or with one), and might track, retain, and report on numerous details about calls, including

- The originating numbers
- How long each caller had to wait before an agent was assigned (queue time)
- How many callers give up (balk or abandon) before being assigned to an agent
- The agent to whom each call was passed
- How long each agent took to answer each call
- How long the calls took to handle

As can be seen from the previous list, an ACD is a management tool as well as a sophisticated call director.

ACDs are now being used with the automatic number identification (ANI) feature that enables the caller's number to be displayed to the agent when the call arrives (see Figure 11-5).

Using the ANI feature, the caller's number can be routed to specific messages on the basis of who is calling, from where, and so on. Priority can be given to special clients using this service. Another slant on the use of ANI with an ACD is to create a computer to PBX/ACD interface, an example of computer-integrated telephony (CIT). Figure 11-6 shows a graphic on this integration. With the customer's number delivered (inband) with the call, the system can route the caller ID information to a computer via an X.25 or IP packet switching link. The computer reads the incoming telephone number, looks up a database of numbers, searches and retrieves a customer database file, and delivers the call and a screen of customer information to a computer terminal simultaneously. This enables the agent to get right to

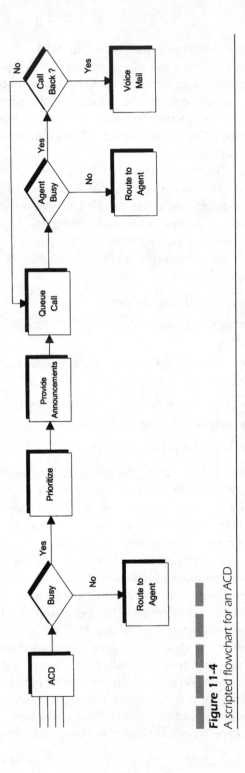

Figure 11-4
A scripted flowchart for an ACD

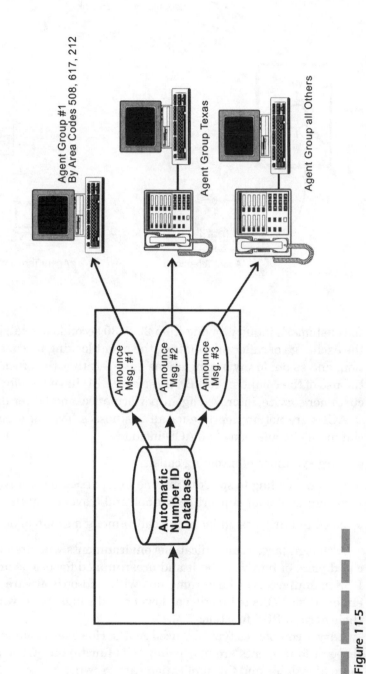

Figure 11-5
ACDs with an automatic number identification (ANI) database

Figure 11-6
A computer-to-
PBX/ACD interface

the customer's inquiry, saving from 20 to 30 seconds per call by eliminating the exchange of caller information, the agent looking up customer information, and so on. Many organizations have felt that the efficiency gained by the use of the computer-to-PBX interface (CPI) have paid for themselves in customer service, improved agent performance, and better morale.

ACDs are not appropriate for all businesses. Typical requirements that can justify acquisition of an ACD include

- Large volumes of incoming calls
- Callers needing to speak to anyone in a particular group (such as, order takers, customer support personnel, and travel agents)
- Need to fairly assign incoming calls among a group of agents

Although large communications environments will often acquire a dedicated piece of hardware built and programmed for use as an ACD, several PBX manufacturers have come out with add-on software packages that enable their PBXs to function as low- or mid-range ACDs while performing their normal PBX functions.

Larger companies typically used ACDs. However, companies as small as three or four agents are now using ACD functionality. The architecture is more affordable and the applications are growing.

Voice Mail

With fewer people in the office, organizations began to seek new technology to enhance their operations. Voice mail was originally designed to reduce the amount of busy tones in the office. Users were absent from their offices more frequently, and the old method of a secretary taking the name and number of the caller was not meeting the needs of the organization. Frequently, the called party diligently returned the call, only to find that the calling party was away from their desk. This game is called telephone tag. However, some of these messages were information only; they did not require an interactive conversation. Thus, voice mail could provide a means of leaving one-way information without the telephone tag. Further, the messages could be delivered at any time, at the convenience of the recipient. Figure 11-7 illustrates some of the ways voice mail can enhance productivity:

- It can be used as a remote dictation machine, although this is not its primary mission.
- It can be used to deliver a message to a recipient who is unavailable (or on the telephone) when the caller makes his or her initial call attempt.
- It can be used to remind oneself of important tasks; the reminders can be triggered at a specific time, as can other messages.
- It can be used to deliver identical messages to a target group with a single action.
- It can be used to dial out and deliver a message remotely to someone not even on the system.

Users have been somewhat reluctant to accept voice mail. From an internal perspective, the system can be effective. However, from an external standpoint, it can be a point of irritation. Users sometimes begin to hide behind the system, screening their calls before answering. Coupled with this problem is the response mode. If a caller has taken the time to leave a detailed message and expects a return, the called party owes them a return call. Human nature states that the called party will not return the call if he or she is busy or if the call is of an unpleasant nature. Thus, the frustrations begin. If one looks at the responses that are returned from voice mail, the percentage is constantly dropping. *Voice mail has become an excuse to never answer your phone again.* We have left messages at companies with very specific details about a problem. This assumed that we would receive a response. When none came, we called again, this time more irritated. The

Figure 11-7
Some of the ways that voice mail can enhance productivity

result of course was to receive voice mail again. (Author's note: I have one organization that I have been leaving a message every week for the past six months and still counting. I want to see how long this continues. Hmmmm. Maybe they don't like me!)

Voice mail does have benefits. It can gain additional hours of availability for your users, especially when dealing with callers from other time zones. Users can be satisfied that although they are not in the office, they can still receive information. Thus, the technology does have its positive side. As long as the users are properly trained in the use of the system and the administration provides a follow-up on the appropriate use of the system, it can work and save an organization both time and money.

Voice mail, like automated attendants, is based on separate equipment. But voice mail falls into the message manipulation category. Voice mail systems were originally designed to do for voice what electronic mail or messaging does for typed communications. That is, using Touch-Tone pads, users can

- Dictate messages to the system
- Specify to whom those messages will be delivered
- Listen to, forward, or delete messages directed to them
- Build and use distribution lists for messages
- Modify various characteristics of their "mailboxes"
- Provide a verbal buckslip (routing slip) attached to another voice mail, to be forwarded to another on the system for action and comment

To be most productive, voice mail systems require a fairly high degree of integration with their host PBX or Centrex. In particular, it is important that the voice mail system be able to indicate to users when they have new messages. For users with indicator lights on their telephones, the voice mail system must be able to tell the PBX to light the light. For other users, the PBX should provide a "stutter" (intermittent) dial tone to indicate new messages when the handset is raised.

Figure 11-8 illustrates a typical voice mail installation. Like OPXs, voice mail systems are normally connected on the line rather than the trunk side of a PBX (although they will also usually have some of their own external trunks to enable users direct access from off site).

As with other telecommunications configurations, the number of trunks serving a voice mail system is a critical success factor. More than with most systems, the usage pattern on voice mail systems is not a smooth one. Instead, users tend to check their voice mailboxes at similar times of the

Figure 11-8

A typical voice mail installation

day: on arrival at work, when returning from lunch, and shortly before departure at the end of the day. The first of these, because it is often the same for the entire user population, often generates a peak demand for circuits far above the expectations of the system designer. Consider the reaction of your user population if 30 percent of them try to reach the system at the same time and only 10 or 15 percent succeed.

Low-end PC-based voice mail systems (typically limited to one or two physical telephone lines) are also available. An additional circuit card, along with appropriate software, is required for the voice processing; however, such systems can be implemented for little more than $100 (on top of the cost of the PC, of course).

Large systems are configured similarly to a PBX or key system. To avoid the access problem described previously, a traffic study is conducted on the inbound and outbound traffic. Then, using the traffic engineering tables from the Poisson distribution, the number of lines and ports can be determined. Typical configurations are in increments of four trunks/lines. Systems come in configurations of 4, 8, 16, 32, or 64 lines, and so on.

An additional key factor is message retention capacity. High-end systems are normally configured by the number of users they will support. This drives assumptions as to the number of hours of messages that must be stored. Because these systems digitize voice and compress it on hard disks, large capacities are used for the storage of voice messages. These drives are usually described in hours of storage. Examples would be 8, 16, 32, or 64 hours of storage, and so on, although capacities can also be in hundreds of hours.

Because all of the voice messages are digitized (although usually at less than the 64,000 bps of "toll-quality" voice—the messages are compressed, sometimes down to as little as 8,000 bps), a key consideration is the amount of disk space. So, whoever is configuring the system must estimate an average message length, then decide how many messages the average user will retain (or will be allowed to retain) in his or her mailbox. Knowing the bits per second at which messages are stored on a particular system will then enable a calculation of required disk resources. For example, the figures in Table 11-2 represent a sample of the calculations used.

Table 11-2 The Typical Calculation for the Hours of Storage Required	200 users retaining 5 messages each, averaging 90 seconds, digitized at 8,000 bits per second requires 200 × 5 × 90 × 8,000 = 7 20,000,000 bits, divided by 8, divided by 1,000,000, gives 90 megabytes.

Doesn't sound like much, does it? But consider that at the standard 64,000 bps for toll quality, the total would instead be 720 megabytes. Compression helps. This calculation was much more important a few years ago, before the cost of disk storage dropped to its current levels. (A 60-gigabyte disk can easily be acquired for less than $500 on a PC). Proprietary systems charge more but the cost per byte is definitely dropping. Note also that when a vendor touts the number of hours its system stores, and justifies the cost on the basis of that storage, if you can discover the digitization rate, you can calculate how much disk storage you are actually getting for your money. Those could be very expensive disks.

Vendors, of course, will be happy to recommend a configuration to suit your requirements. But understanding that one of the key considerations is disk storage capacity should arm you in your discussions.

Watch for a few pitfalls in the implementation of voice mail systems. Some organizations have implemented voice mail systems as their primary answering positions. Like automated attendant systems, voice mail systems have the potential to irritate (or infuriate) callers who either do not ever want to talk with a machine or just take exception to the structure of menus on your system. Organizations have lost customers this way, so be careful. What is even worse than the structured messaging service is winding up in the voice mail loop. You have probably already been exposed to this one:

Caller dials called party number and gets, "Hi, this is Janet. I'm not available to take your message right now, but if you leave a name and number, I'll get back to you as soon as I can. If this is an emergency, please dial 0 and ask the operator to connect you to Bud, who is covering for me."

Caller dials 0 and asks for Bud.

Caller gets "Hi, this is Bud. I'm not available to take your call right now, but if you'll leave a name and number, I'll get back to you as soon as I can. If this is an emergency, please dial 0 and ask the operator to connect you with Don, who is covering for me."

Caller dials 0 and asks for Don.

Caller gets "Hi, this is Don. I'm not available to take your call. If this is an emergency, dial 0 and ask the operator to connect you with Janet, who is covering for me."

Caller hangs up!

Some organizations initially target these systems at selected individuals. Such implementations almost always are abysmal failures, because unless everyone has the facility, almost no one will use it. Few have the patience to ask themselves, "Does this particular employee have voice mail?" before every message. The problem is similar to what might happen if the office mail room only delivered to selected individuals; everyone would deliver his or her own mail to ensure it got there. So if you want to put in voice mail, give it to everyone.

If you do give it to everyone, watch out. With a good kickoff, good training, and a good implementation, voice mail might take off to the point where your original traffic estimates err on the low side. So be sure to get a system that is not near its maximum configuration, as you will likely need to add disk capacity or trunks to keep users from receiving busy signals.

Interactive Voice Response

Interactive voice response (IVR) refers to technology supporting the interaction of users with the system (similar to voice mail or automated attendant), but also implies that information will be provided to the caller by the system itself.

The line between IVR and the previously described voice processing technologies is a fuzzy one; after all, an automated attendant often can provide telephone numbers to a caller. But typically, an IVR system is used to provide callers with information unrelated to the system or the technology itself. The data is normally either accessed directly in another system or loaded into the IVR in advance from that other system.

For example, many mortgage companies have implemented IVR to enable clients access to their own mortgage records. A typical dialogue follows:

IVR: Thank you for calling Millie's Mortgage Machine. For current mortgage rates, press or say 1. To access information about your own account with us, press or say 2. To repeat these choices, press or say 9. To speak to an account representative, press or say 3, or just stay on the line.

Caller: (Presses 2)

IVR: Please enter your account number using the touchtone pad or speak your 15-digit account, followed by a pound sign.

Caller: (Enters account number and a pound)

IVR: Thank you. Please enter or speak your personal identification number, followed by a pound sign.

Caller: (Enters PIN and pound)

IVR: Thank you. Your account is current through October 31st. As of November 1, your remaining balance is $83,432.21. Your monthly payment is $997.92; at 9 percent, you have 132 payments remaining. To have a balance payout statement mailed to you, press or say 1. To hear your account information again, press or say 2. To return to the previous menu, press pound sign. To hang up, press 8 or say "bye." To repeat these choices, press or say 9.

Many of the points of voice processing systems also apply to IVR systems. The previous dialogue illustrates some additional key characteristics and capabilities of IVR systems.

Many systems require the entry of a PIN. Any system capable of providing confidential information to callers should have at least this level of security. Normally, PINs are a minimum of four digits. Some service providers enable users to set their own; other organizations assign PINs to authorized users. Either way, the system's organization must administer the PINs, a requirement sometimes initially overlooked when planning a new IVR system.

Whereas an automated attendant or an ACD is primarily dedicated to providing communications between a caller and another human being, an IVR system's main reason for existence is often to directly provide the caller with automated information. In fact, many organizations install IVR units to reduce the number of agents required on the phones. Even if the initial setup cost of the system is tens of thousands of dollars, the savings in salaries can easily result in a payback within one year. IVR systems always incorporate computers. Therefore, in addition to simple retrieval of data, they can also perform operations or calculations on that data. In the preceding example, most of the numbers were probably calculated during the call rather than retrieved from storage. In another popular application, computers at banks can trigger electronic funds transfers (in effect, pay bills with paperless automated checks) under control of a caller's telephone call. The computer, probably interacting with another computer, adjusts the caller's balance as part of each such transaction. You can bet that both account numbers and PINs are required for such calls. The integration of computers and telephones is sometimes referred to as computer-integrated telephony (CIT) or computer-to-telephony integration (CTI). Figure 11-9 illustrates a possible architecture for such an application. In the figure, the IVR units access the computer database as needed to satisfy caller

Figure 11-9

Computer-integrated telephony is becoming more prevalent. Newer applications include LAN-to-telephone integration.

inquiries. The IVR is separate from the computer, a configuration that might appear less and less frequently as computer manufacturers begin to offer voice interfaces and processing capabilities on their own machines.

IVRs can also be used in combination with ACDs. Figure 11-10 shows a representation of this arrangement. As an example, an IVR can be used in a customer support application to optionally provide callers access to a recorded database of common questions and answers. If the caller elects to inquire against the database (using his or her Touch-Tone telephone to specify the questions to be played), an agent might not be required at all. If the caller selects Speak to a customer support person from the automated IVR menu, then the call can be directed to an ACD for queuing and ultimate connection to an agent.

Some ACDs now have built-in IVR capabilities as an option. We expect an expansion of such combinations as ACD providers seek out new ways to be competitive.

Figure 11-10
Access to computer systems through ACD and IVR integration is now a possibility.

Questions

1. What is the purpose of an automated attendant?
   a. Get rid of the customer
   b. Answer the phone
   c. Take a message
   d. Route the call to the first available agent

2. When a company installs an automated attendant, they can immediately get rid of their operators.   T/F

3. When an automated attendant is planned, the best choice is to:
   a. Keep it simple
   b. Let everyone know in advance that it is coming
   c. Give people a different number to call if they want to use it
   d. All of the above

4. When using the automated attendant, the system is usually behind the PBX.   T/F

5. An ACD is a method of keeping track of the volume of calls coming into the building.   T/F

6. ACDs are positioned:
   a. In front of the PBX
   b. Beside the PBX
   c. Behind the PBX
   d. In a Centrex
   e. None of the above
   f. All of the above

7. ACDs are designed strictly for large companies with very large volumes of calls.   T/F

8. ACDs can be used to route calls to a voice mail systems as an option.   T/F

9. An ACD can also handle calling card functions for the organization.   T/F

10. An organization's wishing to use an ACD can place it in service with little concern.   T/F

11. What should be done first to plan the installation of the ACD?

    a. Conduct a needs assessment

    b. Be the first with one

    c. See if the competition has one

    d. Conduct a traffic study

12. The process of developing the verbiage on a ACD is called:

    a. Talking it out

    b. Scripting

    c. Authoring

    d. Verbiage selection

13. When the ACD is used, many reports are available to understand the volumes and time of handling a call.   T/F

14. The process used to identify the caller information and route accordingly is called:

    a. DNIS

    b. CLID

    c. ANI

    d. DNS

15. Voice mail can be used to satisfy a company's need for extending access to the employee.   T/F

16. When leaving a voice mail, the caller should leave the name and number only.   T/F

17. What is the big consideration that must be used before installing a voice mail system?

    a. Number of ports

    b. Amount of storage

    c. Number of users

    d. Number of menus that a person has to go through

    e. All of the above

    f. A, B, and C only

18. A voice mail system can be used to overcome time zone problems.   T/F

19. An IVR is the same as an automated attendant.   T/F

20. IVR can now understand Voice Prompts, Touch-Tone Prompts and Rotary Dialed Prompts.   T/F

Computer-to-Telephony Integration (CTI)

After reading this chapter and completing and questions, you will be able to:

- Explain what the integration of computer and telephony is doing today
- Discuss the differences between the components that were stand alone in the past and now integrated
- Describe the components of CTI
- Explain where CTI might fit within an organization's plan
- Look at the various components that constitute CTI and effectively select the pieces that fit your need

In the previous chapter, we mentioned the topic of computer-to-PBX interfaces in a cursory manner. In this chapter, we will look at the computer-to-telephony integration (CTI). Over the years, much time and effort has been spent in trying to develop interfaces that would tie the computer and the telephone network together. As technology has changed, many new interfaces and applications can be created through the integration of these two techniques. As a result, a whole new industry has emerged. The ability to link computer systems and voice systems together offers some new possibilities on how we approach the office. An example of this was mentioned in an earlier chapter. When one thinks of the automatic call distribution systems with the ability to link the automatic number identification (ANI) and a database to provide screen-popping capabilities, it becomes an exciting opportunity.

In Figure 12-1, a representation of the computer-to-telephony integration capability using a screen-popping service is shown. In this particular case, as a call comes into the building, it is initially delivered to an ACD. At this point, the ACD captures the automatic number identification of the calling party. When the called party's number is packaged into a small data packet, it is then sent to the computer as a structured query language (SQL) inquiry into a computer database. Assuming the database already exists for the established client, the SQL will open up the client file and respond to the query.

In this particular case, the telephone number of the calling party is being used to create the query from the database. Once the database entry is recognized on the basis of the telephone number, a computer screen will "pop" to the agent's desk. This occurs at the same time the telephone call is being delivered to the agent's desk. Now the agent taking a telephone call does not have to ask the caller for all of the associated and applicable information, such as

- Name
- Address
- Telephone number

Figure 12-1
The screen-popping capability of computer-to-telephony integration.

ACD

Computer

Agent Telephone

Agent Terminal

- City and state
- Account number
- Any other pertinent information

Of course, if the customer's name and address is not in the database, it can immediately be entered. As the agent answers the call, the absence of customer information attached to the telephone number (ANI) is a clue that this is a new caller. The agent can then ask the appropriate questions and build the entry into the database. By reducing the time spent gathering this information because it is already available in the database, a savings of 20 to 30 seconds of call-processing time can be achieved.

However, the 20 to 30 seconds is not the critical part. Instead, the ability to satisfy the customer and to provide better service levels is what is important. By saving the 20 to 30 seconds of call processing time, an organization will save significant amounts of money. When one thinks of other alternatives that might exist here, it can also initiate a couple of thought-provoking ideas.

For example, assume that an agent has received a call from an established customer and a screen-pop of information. In this regard, the established customer has saved all the time by not having to give his or her name, telephone number, and so on. The agent gets right to the task at hand— identifying and verifying the customer. Now that the agent has the information, historical files on such things as buying or usage patterns can be developed so that the agent can suggest products and services to the customer on the basis of past buying experiences. Moreover, if there is a problem with a particular customer, such as delinquent payment, the agent can readily obtain this information while talking to the customer.

Let's extend that thought a little further. Assume that the agent does encounter a delinquent customer who hasn't paid his or her bill for three months. While talking to this customer and trying to sell through suggestion, or taking an order, which is what the customer called for, the agent sees on the screen that the customer is delinquent and that collection action must be taken. Rather than placing him/herself in the position of being a collections manager, the agent can immediately suggest to the customer that the call must be transferred to the accounts receivable manager. When the agent switch hooks or transfers the call, not only does the call go to the accounts receivable department, but also the screen from the database follows.

Now, when the accounts receivable department receives the call, the manager there will have a full screen of information about why that call has been sent to him or her. Answering the call, the accounts receivable manager can then immediately and proactively get to the job at hand, *collecting the money*. Instead of picking up the phone and asking for the same information (name, address, telephone number, and so on), which would totally frustrate the customer, the accounts receivable manager can immediately introduce him/herself and suggest that payment terms can be worked out. The dialog may be along the lines of, "We really appreciate your business, and we would like to continue to ship you our products. So if you will Federal Express us a check for the past-due amount, we will immediately ship (after receiving the check) all of the goods and services you have just ordered." This is proactive as opposed to negative collections.

Now the accounts receivable manager, after obtaining an agreement from the customer to pay, can transfer the caller immediately back to the agent. The agent's record and the screen have been kept by the system. When the call goes back to the agent, the screen plus all of the documentation or notes that the accounts receivable manager has entered return as well. Once again, the agent sees who is on the phone and what has transpired. This prevents the replication of information gathering and keeps the entire conversation in a proactive mode. It is this positive handling of calls, particularly those of a negative nature, that helps to boost customer service and influence the continued buying relationship.

The previous scenario assumes that certain things have taken place. It must be assumed that the caller is calling from a pre-specified location and that the database already exists. If, in fact, the database does not exist, the initial data gathering can be accomplished at the receipt of the first call. Thereafter, any time the customer calls from the same telephone number (which is displayed at the agent's console), the database will be hooked and brought with the screen-pop. The first time is the most labor-intensive. Each successive contact between the customer and the organization selling the products and services will be much more simple.

Using this database and screen-pop arrangement, companies have successfully achieved several things, including

- Improved customer service
- Improved customer satisfaction
- A reduced number of incoming lines
- A reduction in the number of agents necessary to handle the same volume of calls

Through the combined savings of 20 to 30 seconds for each successive attempt, the average hold time (talk time) can be reduced significantly. In

Chapter 8, where we looked at traffic engineering, the discussion of how many agents are required to handle a particular volume of traffic is covered. When the average hold time is reduced, however, the amount of agents and the grade of service change dramatically. The number of agents declines, while the probability analysis for serving the customer quickly increases. This is a win/win situation.

Other Applications

Although the screen-pop capability of an ACD is one of the primary uses today, other applications can take advantage of the computer-to-telephony integration (CTI). The newer integrated PBX will become a voice server on the local area network (LAN). In Figure 12-2, the integrated PBX is shown as a voice server residing between two separate LANs.

Now that the various communications vendors have produced an open applications interface, the ability to use a PBX for several components exists. One of the primary applications would be to install a third-party bridge or router card inside the PBX. The PBX now serves as either the bridging or routing function between the two LANs, even if they are disparate in nature (token ring and Ethernet). Using the PBX also as a voice server enables an extension of PBX access to the local area network services such as printing or file serving applications. A remote user who is too far away from the LAN can be serviced through the PBX wiring.

All of the PBX manufacturers today are devising schemes to implement high-speed multimedia communications to the desktop. This way a computer user, as shown in Figure 12-2, can be remotely attached over the same cabling system as the telephone system. Inside the architecture of the PBX will be a high-speed communications infrastructure such as ATM, SONET, or FDDI (each of these are covered in later chapters). Each manufacturer has chosen a different route in providing this capability.

With a high-speed communications backbone residing inside the PBX, the remote PC is attached into the PBX and onto the high-speed backplane. Then the router card or bridge card acts as a bridging and routing function between the high-speed infrastructure (like FDDI) connecting to the installed LANs. The PBX manufacturers have devised means of running 10 Mbps or 100 Mbps and now 1000 Mbps to the desktop.

When dealing with the high-speed communications to the desktop, the user now has access to all of the voice features, LAN features, and

Voice Server

Ethernet

PBX

Local Exchange Netw

Figure 12-2

The PBX acts as the voice server on the LAN providing CTI.

multimedia applications that may be running inside or peripheral to the PBX. The cost of this PBX architecture is considerably greater than that of a normal LAN and a PBX environment, but as a combined investment, the differences are minor.

By virtue of the high-speed multimedia applications to the desktop, the user also has access to the PBX-type features. In this case, the user can use the PBX as a communications server. A modem pool can be attached to the PBX and bridged onto a user's connection on demand. This is shown in Figure 12-3. All of the features and functions of the modem pool now become available to the users on the PBX as well as the LAN.

As a true communications server, the PBX can also bring other services such as trunk queuing, automatic route selection, least-cost routing, and station message detail recording to the data communications environment. These added features could be available on a LAN, but they are easier to implement on a PBX, where the features and functions have been available

Figure 12-3
The modem pool can be added on as needed.

for decades. Now, with the convergence of communications and computers, the administrators within organizations have many choices.

Still other features can be included with this integration of CTI. Voice messaging, as integral or peripheral to the PBX, can now become available as a feature or a function hooked to the LAN. As an outside caller dials into an organization's PBX, the ability to capture the automatic number identification (ANI) and hook to the database server on the LAN enables the delivery of the caller ID to the desktop. This makes it possible for a user who has a screen (PC or other) on his or her desk to be able to see the voice messages in the queue. In reality, what the user sees is not the message, but information regarding the message. This helps to prioritize, or select from a queue, calls that are necessary or important. Moreover, the end user can print out a list of voice messages, a customer database of people who have called, ANI information to be included in a database not yet built, or many other useful and productive types of data.

Beyond the voice messaging capability, the capability to hook to an automated attendant can also be integrated into this CTI application. When an outside caller attempts to reach a particular extension or department, a database can be built regarding who the callers are and what extensions are typically used most frequently. This also extends the ANI right to the desktop of the called party so that the database can also link to some form of a screen-pop. By delivering the ANI to a database server on the LAN, the user can immediately run a structured query on the database to pull up the customer file. A simpler way would be to have the database automatically deliver all the information about the calling party to the LAN terminal device. This doesn't work in all applications, but it does offer some unique capabilities and opportunities that never before existed.

Each of the services that have been discussed, as well as many other opportunities that have not yet been thought about or produced, can all be tightly coupled in the combination of computer and telephony integration. CTI offers the capability to link multiple databases, multiple communications channel capabilities, and the LAN-to-PBX server functions. The PBX becomes the voice server, whereas the LAN server becomes the PBX's database. Corporate directories, departmental lists, product lines, and other types of usable information can all be made available to the desktop device when a called or calling party needs access. Although the cost is incremental, overall the increases in productivity and satisfaction from both employees and customers may well be worth the effort. This is one of those decisions that a user must make.

In the same manner, you take higher risks by putting all of your eggs in one basket: having a single-server environment. However, the distributed computing architectures that are emerging minimize the risks. Distributed computing architecture can also add to the depth of the PBX by using servers on a LAN that can be voice servers; the functions and the real estate required for a PBX architecture can now be combined and reduced. No longer will a very large room with special air conditioning be required. The servers can just be deployed wherever they are needed to serve a group of users.

We can see the excitement and the benefits of the computer-to-telephony integration when we look beyond the basic functionality of each individual box. Hence, the decision-making process becomes a little bit more complicated than the purchase of a PBX or a server when thinking about acquiring a combined infrastructure to support the communications needs of the organization. But isn't that what communications excitement is all about?

Why All the Hype?

Business has reached an intensity and a pace that is extraordinary. Competition and the changes in technology are driving the pace exponentially. Keeping pace with the industry and maintaining the competitive edge has become a crucial element in the survivability of an organization. Therefore, the demands on organizations have escalated dramatically to basically provide for

- The ability to deal with corporate decision-making processes at a very rapid pace
- The readiness to deal with issues regardless of the time of day, day of week, or availability of executives
- The continued restructuring and re-engineering of the organization, requiring fewer people to perform more functions
- The changing workforce, in which talent and skill sets are no longer as available as they were, making technology a necessary solution
- Preparing the administrative assistants who have supplanted the administrative and support staff of old (secretarial support) to deal with issues when the senior staff is not available

■ Ensuring the availability of the information that is needed to achieve these goals

Therefore, employees must have information readily available at their fingertips (a few keystrokes away). Using both computers and communications provides the edge to maintain the link between the employee and the customer. It is not necessarily a given that these technologies will always be the solutions, but the right implementation can have significant benefits if done correctly.

This book contains several examples that show how organizations have tied their computers and communications together through various network technologies to facilitate the timeliness and usability of information. Using a computer-to-telephony integration system, employees share information on the spot by using updated information on a call-by-call basis. Each of these tools and capabilities is an absolute must if a business is to remain competitive.

Many authors in the industry have written about the re-engineering of the organization, the rightsizing, downsizing, and capsizing of the organization, or just a restructuring in a target market where companies have focused more clearly on serving the niche needs of their customer. Examples of this are clearly demonstrated in both the financial community (credit card organizations, stock brokerage firms, the mortgage banking industry) and the airline industry. Customers can no longer be looked on as a nuisance; rather, they must be seen as the most valuable resource and asset that an organization has (excluding its own internal personnel).

Providing the necessary treatment and care of the customer becomes one of the primary goals of the organization. It should have been the goal all along, but the focus on driving costs down and increasing productivity began to erode the customer and organizational relationships. It is much more feasible to restructure and reaffirm the relationship between the two parties.

Customers expect to be treated as individuals who are special for the size and volume of the business that they do. Competition in any segment of industry is fierce. Therefore, if the necessary care and treatment is not provided, customer loyalty shifts dramatically. Changing market demands due to the rightsizing, downsizing, and capsizing in external organizations places more demand on your organization to meet the customer's needs.

In planning our technological innovations, we must therefore look to how we can better satisfy the customer's needs by

■ Giving our customers unlimited access to our employees to place orders, check on status, or make inquiries.

- Assuming that the employee/agent will have that information readily available and not put the customer on interminable hold.

- Anticipating the demand for products on the basis of sales projections and customer demands so that "out of stock" problems or back-ordering can be curtailed.

- Having technical support available to the agent so that a question can be easily answered either by the technical or the administrative/sales person.

- Considering that the customer's success in business and/or product lines can be matched to your ability to meet the customer's demands for products and services.

- Anticipating customers' needs and satisfying their demands, so they will not be exposed by the diminishing inventories and just-in-time manufacturing processes of today.

If the previous conditions can be satisfactorily met, the customer will feel better about placing orders or checking on the status and availability of products with your organization. This equates to better sales. Telecommunications and computer integration can therefore increase productivity and also assist in increasing sales. Using the right technology in the right mix at the right time can enhance a relationship that is ever so fragile in today's competitive marketplace.

Linking Computers and Communications

Today, more than ever, organizations are using distributed computing and what is known as client/server architecture. This architecture of using a three-computer technology is the result of many years of evolution and revolution within the computing platforms. The LAN emerged in the early 1980s as a means of moving away from control by a single entity known as the MIS department (a more detailed discussion of the LAN is contained in Chapter 20). As this evolution moved away from a controlled single computing platform, users were empowered to manipulate their own data, handle their own information, and share that information with others on a selective or exclusive basis. Because of this movement, a lot of pressure was placed on the communications side of the business to provide interconnections using a cabling infrastructure to the various desktop computers and departments that would interrelate. Management saw an opportunity to produce ad hoc reporting, allow flexible data manipulation, and provide more timely information to managers and departments alike.

As LANs emerged, they were primarily tied to a desktop and an individual server within a department. Later in its evolution, the client/server architecture started to emerge more strongly by allowing multiple departments within a single organization to fulfill their data communications and data access needs by accessing each other's databases or sharing the files that they had created on their customers. It is this sharing that created additional appliance affiliations within the different groups. The personal computer (PC) basically allowed users to store their applications and files on a single device. By linking these computing systems together with a communications medium, the user can best seek the information wherever it resides within the network. If a new application is needed, either a server can be adapted to fit that need or a new server can be added.

From a communications perspective, devices emerged that included such things as electronic mail within departments, fax servers for transmitting information directly from a desktop to a customer, and voice recognition and response systems that enabled customers to call in and literally talk to the server, as opposed to having to talk to a human. Furthermore, the linkage of all of these systems through a communications medium became the glue that bound everything together.

The PC of old, although structured as strictly a desktop device, has changed dramatically. Now, new features include

- Extensive processing power
- Sophisticated operating systems
- Integrated voice boards or sound cards
- Integrated video conferencing capabilities
- The client/server software that enables all of the pieces to be pulled together

With the use of CTI, an organization's needs can be easily met using the build-out of the desktop devices connected to the LAN. As already mentioned, the client/server architecture has the capability to bring together the computers that reside on the LAN and telephony services that can be built into either the PCs or these servers that reside on the LAN. This all becomes possible by bonding these two technologies that began in the mid-1980s and matured in the mid-1990s. The architecture within an organization has dramatically changed. In place of a single provider of information, such as an administrative assistant or a particular sales group, there now exists an integrated homogenous work group that can share information, transfer calls among members, or add other departments on calls as needed, which has already been shown in our examples.

Unified Messaging Services

While this information process was taking place, organizations began to connect to the outside world and to their customers through the use of their telephony services. In the early 1990s, a new explosion took place within the industry. The emergence of the World Wide Web (WWW) and the use of the Internet as a commercial resource added to computer telephony development. Attaching an organization to the outside world through the Internet enabled customers to use their telecommunications services to check inventories, catalogs, and other services that would otherwise not normally be available to them.

The ability to introduce fax-back servers also enabled customers to obtain catalog information or technical brochures immediately instead of having to wait for an agent to mail products or brochures through the postal service. This increased the availability of information by linking the communications infrastructure to the computing architecture. Moreover, as organizations started to use electronic document interchange (sometimes called EDI), they created the ability to place orders, perform functions as dynamic work groups, and facilitate the ordering and payment process. These services enhanced the true organizational abilities.

The mid-1990s also marked the innovation and growth of this computer and telephony integration through the use of intranets. The intranet is discussed in Chapter 16. For now, think of it as the internal Internet of an organization. Using the intranet and communications infrastructures within an organization's client/server architectures, internal organizations can access the same information that might be available to a customer. Furthermore, internal organizations can share files, technical notes, and client notes regarding their customers as well as other valuable information that would not be readily available to the masses. Specific files or bulletin boards can be set up within the organization to achieve that end result.

So, it is through the integration of our communications systems and the capabilities of the far more powerful and processor-intense desktop device that the pieces are coming together quickly. No distinction can be made anymore between computing and communications, because the two really draw on each other's resources to facilitate the organization's day-to-day mission—to serve the customer and maximize shareholder wealth. Serving the customer increases sales. Increased sales and, hopefully, decreased costs, raise profits. This maximizes the shareholder's wealth, which is the charter for all business organizations.

The unified messaging technologies enable the end user to have a fax, telephone, mobile phone, pager, voice mail, and home phone number all linked together. When a call arrives, the network or internal device forwards the call to the various devices or lines, and the first one to assume the call can take the message. This integration scheme makes it possible to be available any time and anywhere.

The Technology Advancement

Through the integration of computer and telephony-type services, the old philosophy of telephony being a necessary evil has passed. Advances in computing technology have enhanced the telephony world. The age of mass pools of telephone operators is gone. Newer technologies enable customers to call and proceed through an organization without ever communicating with an operator or a secretary. The customer can get directly to the person or information that is desired, especially in light of the unified messaging services.

In the key system marketplace, the old labor-intensive electromechanical system is now a computer-driven telephone system. However, these computer-driven systems are now rich in features and laden with capabilities undreamt of in the past. The integration of voice messaging, ACDs, and automated attendants in key systems is now commonplace. Key systems are also emerging as voice servers within the organization.

The PBX, serving hundreds if not thousands of employees within an organization, enables an internetwork of services and capabilities to spread throughout an organization. What was once just a stand-alone telephone system is now the high-end computer that just happens to handle voice. Today's technology enables full digital transmission systems or services and permits linkage to all devices that were exclusively used by the elite. PBXs now integrate tightly to our computing systems.

The PBX also acts as the high-end server on a digital trunk capability to the outside world. By linking to a high-speed digital communications trunk from the outside world (called a T1 and referred to in Chapter 14), users can now access ANI. Using inbound 800/888/877/866 services and a common channel-signaling arrangement enables the delivery of the caller ID directly to the called party. Moreover, with enhancements in software such as call forwarding, overflow arrangements when agents or other individuals are busy and other services can all be chartered into a single PBX architecture. Another service called directory number information service (DNIS) can be used on the 800/888/877/866 service to direct the call to a specific group, such as technical support or marketing.

The Final Bond

As the client/server architecture and the communications systems all were developing throughout the 1980s and into the 1990s, it was the software vendors who became the aggressors. Through the use of operating systems that could work on a LAN-based server, the software vendors were aggressive in finding the integration tools necessary for the organization. Microsoft Corporation developed a de facto protocol called the telephony application program interface (TAPI) in a Windows environment to bring the telephony services right to the desktop LAN-attached device. A TAPI interface on a Windows platform enables users to access information through what is called a graphical user interface (GUI, pronounced gooey). Throughout this whole architecture, a server application can handle the distribution of calls to members within work groups or departments. This includes such services as screening calls, rerouting calls to new agent groups if the primary agent group is busy, or routing calls to the voice messaging and voice response systems as necessary.

Similarly, Novell and AT&T developed what is known as the telephony services application programmers interface (TSAPI) as a means of providing the computer with telephony integration capabilities from a local area network. TSAPI basically works with Novell's NetWare telephony services.

The basis for using this particular product is to gain what is known as *third-party call control*. Third-party call control uses the CTI application on behalf of any clients in a work group or department. The application is running a shared environment, typically on a server, so no direct contact or connection takes place between the user's PC and the telephone interface.

What happens then is that a logical connection is produced where the PC applications talk to the server, which in turn controls the telephone switch.

The server then is the controller and sends the order to the PBX to make calls or connections on behalf of the end user. The shared-server environment can handle individual as well as dynamic work group applications, such as directories, individual personal information managers (PIMs), and other work group functions that would occur within a larger organization.

Therefore, the server provides all of the linkage for all calls being handled within a dynamic work group. This is a more powerful arrangement as regards call control. A central server can handle the distribution of calls to any member in a work group and provide such services as call screening, call answering groups, backing up agents, or routing calls to a supervisory position in the event of overflow. Many of the CTI vendors have seen this as the benefit and strength of the CTI applications.

Developers and manufacturers alike therefore have seen the application working like a telephone set. This is instrumental in designing the capabilities of a call-answering/call-processing environment, but more can be done through the use of the computer-based technology that is available on the market today. The applications that run in server or computing platforms can use call-monitoring features within the PBX and collect information of any type. Using the call monitoring features, a CTI can watch every keystroke that an agent group enters. This can include such things as dialed digits, when agents "busy out," answering a call, and how long the call is off hook. Additionally, by monitoring the trunk groups within the PBX, the CTI application can see all the incoming calls and collect the data associated with each call. This uses the service described earlier, called ANI, and DNIS to watch where the call was directed and when it was answered.

The selectivity available in a CIT application therefore enables the supervisor to monitor the activity of each agent within a work group and get a clear picture of what transpires during the course of a day. This helps in determining workload effort, staffing requirements to meet a specific demand, or any seasonal adjustments that must be made on the basis of time of year. About 65 to 70 management reports can be generated on an ad hoc basis. Supervisory personnel can monitor the work flow, the productivity of each agent in a group, abandoned calls that were not answered soon enough, or any other anomalies that might occur within a given day. Through these useful tools and reporting structures, the supervisors know whether they have enough, too few, or too many agents on board at any one time. This can aid in work flow scheduling as well as in determining the productivity of the individual agents or of the work group as a whole. In the event an agent is not performing satisfactorily, management can then take whatever corrective actions are necessary.

If abandoned calls are escalating because the agents are on the phone too long, several other activities might result. These could include such things as new training, analysis of the call type and the information requested, or simply determining the morale and productivity within the work group.

Beyond the call-processing and the call-monitoring capabilities, CTI can be implemented to integrate the facilities and capabilities of the PBX, as well as the computer systems, into one homogenous unit. The typical PBX today has features that are rarely used. There can be as many as 300 to 400 of these features, which are designed to either improve productivity or make the job simpler. Even though the average user typically activates only three or four of the normal features, many of the functions are available but never used. The CTI applications can customize features and functions for individual users within a work group and enable a more powerful interface using point-and-click GUIs. The screen on a PC through a CTI application can be used for dialing, activating features, conference calling, call transfer, or any other feature necessary. Using the mouse to click a feature resembling a telephone set on a PC screen removes the risk and the unfamiliarity of the PBX features from the end user. This would prevent cutoffs or lost calls and facilitate better utilization of the PBX features.

Taking this one step further, each individual user within a group supported by a CTI application can customize his or her own features and functions in personal folders on the PC. These can either be stored on the individual PCs or alternatively on the server. Therefore, using the CTI application, individuals may select different forms of call screening, call forwarding, or call answering according to the applications and the individualized services they most prefer.

Technology Enhancements

When CTI was first introduced in the industry, it was done through two very large computing platforms, either the mainframe or the high-end midrange computing systems. These included such things as the IBM mainframe, AS/400, DECVax, or HP-type systems. Although they worked, they were very expensive and very sophisticated, requiring extensive investment as well as application programming interfaces that made the service available only to very large organizations.

With the implementation of the server-based platforms, or LAN-based platforms, the technology has trickled down to the very small organizations.

No longer can one determine or assume that a company using CTI applications is very large. As a matter of fact, many of the CTI applications are now rolling out on PC-based platforms for the very small organization. Companies with three or five call-answering or telemarketing positions have implemented CTI very effectively. These lower-cost solutions have made CTI a reality within organizations around the world.

It was through LAN technology and not PBX technology that CTI actually got a foothold within organizations. Imagine if we had waited for the PBX manufacturers and the telephone companies/long-distance companies to roll out CTI integration for us. Unfortunately, we would probably still be waiting. In the past few years, the computer manufacturers have provided the push and the software developers the innovations to make CTI a reality. This relatively new yet rapidly accepted approach to using the server as the instrument to provide CTI has thrust CTI into the forefront of telecommunications technology.

As mentioned earlier, the voice server on a LAN is designed to connect directly to the public switch telephone network, handle calls coming into the group, and then process those calls directly to the desktop. Priority customers and special handling arrangements enable specific users to work around the high-end PBX and Centrex platforms and go directly to the individual department or customer service group without proceeding through the corporate platform. This in turn changes the architecture because of the CTI applications that can work on a server platform.

PBXs, once known for their large investments and proprietary nature, can now remain single-line telephony service providers. When higher-end features and functions are necessary, the end user merely has to buy computer-based software as opposed to high-end PBX architectural software. Of course, the PBX manufacturers have recognized this shift in the technology implementation and all of the PBX manufacturers are now developing the CTI interfaces or the software with third-party developers to reclaim customers.

Because the PBX need only be an uncomplicated telephone system for the masses within the organization, the technology can last significantly longer. In the old days of the PBX, the plan was to keep the system for a period of about ten years. However, reality said that the PBX was changed on a basis of about five to seven years. This involved major investment and changes within an architecture and caused a significant amount of corporate stress.

As a quick side note, whenever a new PBX was installed, it usually meant that the telecom manager within a corporation would be leaving soon. Regardless of how many technological advancements or enhancements were installed, users' expectations were never met. The frustrations of the users and the complaints made to management usually led to the telecom manager's demise. Now, with the features and functions having moved to a PC-based platform, the telecom manager can breathe easier. Without the need to upgrade the PBX or change an entire infrastructure, the telecom manager can implement on a department-by-department basis whatever features or functions are necessary and available. On a larger scale, all PBX features would have been available to all users. Using the CTI implementation on a server, features can be purchased on a department-by-department basis and subsequently be less expensive. This has been the boon of the 1990s.

Other Technologies

Because of the innovations and enhancements in the telecommunications environment, and the server marriage, many other applications and features can be made available by other producers. For example, through the use of the telecom server on a LAN, the automated attendant, voice messaging, ACD, and integrated voice recognition and response (IVR) functions can all be united in a single server-based platform.

The developers of voice messaging systems' automated attendants recognized this opportunity several years ago. They leapfrogged the market, bypassing the PBX manufacturers, and developed single-card processing systems that could use high-end digital trunking capabilities directly in the servers. Using microprocessor control devices, these companies were able to write the necessary software that would provide the capabilities of all of these features. No longer would an organization have to buy a room-sized voice messaging system; this function can now be performed on a PC-based platform.

When voice messaging was first introduced, the size, heat, and cost of systems were exorbitant. Now, using PC-based systems, just about every vendor offers the capability of enabling several hundred to several thousand active users on a voice messaging system or a call-processing system at a much lower cost.

Actually, it's becoming much more difficult to tell a PBX performing CTI applications from a CTI server performing PBX capabilities. This convergence and marriage is blurring the lines between the various departments.

Many of the organizations that now produce systems with these capabilities may have once been niche market providers but are now moving across the border that once separated these two technologies. Just about every feature, function, and capability can now be had using a very low-end server platform at a very reasonable price.

The integration includes such features and functions as

- Voice messaging
- Automated attendant
- IVR
- Text to speech
- Speech to text
- Directory services
- Fax services
- Fax-back services
- Mobile telephony
- Intranet access for catalogs

Taking these one at a time, we'll see how they can all work together and provide unified messaging and integration capabilities. The integrated messaging and unified messaging services enable the desktop user to functionally perform all day-to-day operations at a single interface device, now the desktop PC.

Automated Attendant

With the technology moving as quickly as it is, the use of single processing cards in a PC can deliver a combination of voice messaging and automated attendant functions directly to the CTI application. Literally, a digital signal-processing capability can compress voice calls so that they can be conveniently stored on a hard disk drive. The voice is already in a digital form when it arrives from a digital trunk or digital line card; therefore, storage is a relatively simple technique. The application software used in a voice mail system is basically a file service, where storage and retrieval can be easily accommodated.

Integrated Voice Recognition and Response

Integrated voice recognition and response systems are based primarily on the same type of technology as the auto attendant and voice mail. Using a single digital processing card, the capability now enables users to arrange for prescripted calling capabilities that will actually walk a caller through a menu. The IVR will play digitally stored messages and solicit a response from the caller at each step, usually in the form of a Touch-Tone from a telephone set. The response from that tone will then cause the next step of the message to be played in accordance with the script. This is useful when a user is trying to access information from a host-based system, for example, and a played-back message will enable the user to retrieve any form of information. This IVR capability has been used by several medical providers or insurance providers to enable a caller to dial in and access information regarding a payment or the processing of claims by merely using the Touch-Tone phone.

When dialing into the IVR, the user is prompted each step of the way by the system. As the user enters his or her ID number, a query is sent to a database in a host computing platform. This appropriate information is then retrieved and provided in a played-back message: "Payment to your provider was mailed on this date." Using this CTI application saves an immense amount of time for an organization, because this normally labor-intensive activity can now be achieved through technology. One can just imagine how much savings could be achieved if we no longer needed humans to answer these routine and repetitive types of normal questions.

Fax-Back and Fax Processing

The digital signal processor (DSP) card can also be programmed to function as a fax modem that can provide for the sharing of fax services within a single server environment. A fax image can be downloaded across a LAN, converted by a fax card, and transmitted out across the network over a digital trunking facility. In the reverse direction, if an incoming fax is received from the network, it is then converted back to a file format that is easily usable within the PC environment. This can then either be stored in a fax server file for later retrieval by the individual recipient of the message or redirected by a fax operator.

Some of these systems and services take more effort to implement and facilitate, but they may well be worth the effort in terms of the organization's needs. Fax-back capability means that when a user dials into an organization equipped with CTI applications, that user can be directed to a fax server that has a numerical listing of specific documents that the user can retrieve by keying in a telephone number. When the user enters the telephone number, the server retrieves the fax from the file and then automatically transmits it to the designated telephone number the user has just entered. Through this application, catalog information or specific customer information can be retrieved without the use of human intervention. One can see how much could be saved by using these types of services.

Text to Speech and Speech to Text

In speech-to-text applications, a pre-stored pattern of words can be used through the CTI application to enable a highly mobile workforce to dial into a server-based platform and literally speak to the machine, as opposed to using Touch-Tones. Speech from the callers, whose voice patterns are already stored in the computer, can then be converted into usable text using a server-based CTI application. This is instrumental when the user cannot access a Touch-Tone phone (yes, many places around the country do not yet have Touch-Tone services, such as hotels, pay phones, and public telephones). Without the Touch-Tone phone, the user would have to carry a portable Touch-Tone pad generator, which is very inconvenient. Inevitably, the batteries on these devices die at the very moment when the user needs access to information. Consequently, the use of voice patterns or speech patterns that have been pre-recorded with a series of words such as get, save, retrieve, file, and so on can be used to facilitate and walk through a computing system.

The text-to-speech applications are comparable in that when a user accesses a particular file, again without a terminal device, for example, the system can convert the text into a speech pattern. What this effectively means is that e-mail and files can literally be read back to us no matter where we are. This is exciting because an end user can dial into the CTI application while traveling on the road and learn that he or she has six voice messages and four e-mail messages waiting. Rather than that user being forced to log on with a different form of terminal device, these e-mail messages can be read right down the telephone line to the end user, facilitating the easy retrieval, storage, or redirection of messages. It is through these types of services that the CTI applications are drawing so much excitement.

Optical Character Recognition (OCR)

Another form of digital-signal-processor-based technology can convert scanned images into text. When used with fax machines or fax images, OCR can change an incoming fax into a document that can easily be edited or incorporated into other types of applications. This would include editing a fax and plugging it into a word processing document for easy edit capabilities. Then the additional storage capabilities convert that OCR, which usually would be a file of significant size, into a text-based document, which would be much smaller. Furthermore, using the OCR by scanning a pretyped document, for example, the application can then incorporate the scanned document into a text-to-speech application, where it can be read aloud. One can just imagine the uses and applications for some of these technologies as they start to come together.

Questions

1. The integration of the computer and telephone is called:
   a. CPI
   b. CIT
   c. CTI
   d. PCI

2. The technology that started the whole process of integration is the telephone.   T/F

3. ANI and computer integration schemes first delivered the information and features to:
   a. Voice messaging
   b. Automated attendants
   c. Automatic call distributors
   d. Fax servers

4. What is the main thrust of the information need?

   a. Saving time

   b. Saving money

   c. Improved customer relations

   d. Saving circuits

5. Using a screen pop, the agent can save approximately two minutes.   T/F

6. Another area of saving is the area of _____.

   a. Time outs

   b. Hold time

   c. Cost per minute

   d. Agent salaries

7. The features we expect to use in an integration plan include

   a. Fax services

   b. Voice mail services

   c. Fax back services

   d. E-mail applications

   e. All of the above

8. The PBX becomes the voice server on the LAN using these services.   T/F

9. Information must be no more than a few _____ away.

10. The capability to link mobile, telephone, fax, voice mail, and other services together is called:

    a. Super servers

    b. Uniform call distribution

    c. United services

    d. Unified messaging

11. Anticipating future demand for products and services is not a part of the computer-to-telephony integration.   T/F

12. The charter for the organization is to:

    a. Introduce as many new technologies as possible

    b. Satisfy the agent and management

    c. Minimize the involvement of the customer

    d. Maximize shareholder's wealth

13. When an organization wants to introduce an integration plan, they can do it without discussing it with the customer.   T/F

14. PCs today are much more powerful and have voice cards and fax cards built in them.   T/F

15. The technologies today can generate about how many management reports on an ad hoc basis?

    a. 10 to 12

    b. 50 to 55

    c. 90 to 100

    d. 65 to 70

16. Which interface on a Windows platform enables users to access information through what is called a graphical user interface?

    a. GUI

    b. API

    c. MAPI

    d. TAPI

17. Which systems are based primarily on the same type of technology as the auto attendant and voice mail?

    a. ACD

    b. TAPI

    c. IVR

    d. AA

18. Which technology can change an incoming fax into a document that can easily be edited or incorporated into other types of applications?

    a. A fax server

    b. A fax board

    c. An OCR

    d. An e-mail server

19. The _____ card can also be programmed to function as a fax modem that can provide for the sharing of fax services within a single server environment.

20. With the _____ of communications and computers, the administrators within organizations have many choices.

Data Communications

After reading this chapter and completing the questions, you will be able to:

- Define data communications
- Understand why everyone is excited about data transmission
- Define the components of a data transmission system
- Describe the steps in communications of data devices
- Discuss the means of getting more bang for our data-communications buck

Everyone who has ever had to deal with data communications has shuddered at least once. Telecommunications engineers, data processing personnel, and vendors alike all throw data communication terms around as though they were going out of style. The interesting point is that many of them really don't understand what they are talking about. Many people think, "If I learn the buzzwords, everyone will think I know what I'm talking about."

Nothing could be further from the truth. These folks make complete fools of themselves in front of knowledgeable professionals. However, there is really no mystique associated with the use of data communications. Although some complexities do exist in this technology, the basics are fairly straightforward. If you can surmount the initial hurdle of setting up a data transmission, the rest can be fairly well assimilated.

In 1997, for the first time in the history of the telecommunications industry, data was carried across the networks in an equal share as voice. This showed the heavy emphasis on the growth of data communications. Currently, the growth of voice on the networks is averaging between three and four percent per year. However, data is growing at a rate of 30 percent per year. It will take 12 years to double the amount of voice carried on the network today at the current growth rate, whereas the data is doubling approximately every 90 days.

It is important to understand that the data world grew out of the voice world. Voice traditionally paid for the data transmissions on the network, and still today, 90 percent of all the revenues generated across the wide area networks are the result of voice usage. But that will all change quickly as we see more emphasis on data. The use of the analog dial-up network is where it all started.

In order to communicate from a terminal, computer, or other piece of equipment, you merely have to put the pieces together in the proper order:

1. Select and deal with the transmission media.

2. Use communicating devices that will present the proper signal to the line (the communicating device is called the DCE).

3. Add a device called the data terminal equipment (DTE).

4. Set up or abide by accepted rules (protocols).

5. Use a pre-established alphabet that the devices understand.

6. Ensure the integrity of information before, during, and after transmission.

7. Deliver the information to the receiving device.

This chapter demystifies the elements involved in all data communications processes. Later chapters focus on specific technologies, using the concepts and terminology introduced here.

Concepts

Like learning computer programming, learning data communications technology is a nonlinear process. That is, whatever starting point one chooses, one almost has to use terms that will be defined elsewhere. The usual solution to this problem is *iterative teaching*: Teach a basic set of concepts and then go back and both use and expand on those concepts, refining them along the way. (I prefer to think it works like this: I am going to tell you what I am going to tell you. I am going to tell you. Then, I am going to tell you what I told you!)

Our basic set begins with a discussion of some important concepts that permeate the world of data communications. Those concepts include

- Standards
- Architectures
- Protocols
- Error detection
- Plexes
- Multiplexing
- Compression

A *standard* is a definition or description of a technology. The purpose of developing standards is to help vendors build components that will function together or that will facilitate use by providing consistency with other products. This section discusses what standards are, why they exist, and some of the ways they could affect you. Specific standards are mentioned in other sections where applicable.

Two kinds of standards exist: de facto and de jure.

De facto means "in fact." If more than one vendor "builds to" or complies with a particular technology, one can reasonably refer to that technology as a standard. An excellent example of such a standard in data communications is IBM's Systems Network Architecture (SNA). No independent standards organization has ever "blessed" SNA as an "official," or de jure, standard. But dozens, if not hundreds, of other vendors have built products that successfully interact with SNA devices and networks.

Note that de facto standards rarely become standards overnight. SNA was available for some time before vendors other than IBM could or would provide products that supported it.

Moreover, some technologies become standards because the creating vendors intend them to become standards (such as Ethernet), while others become standards despite the creating vendors (such as Lotus 1-2-3 menu structure).

De jure means *in law*, although standards do not generally have the force of law. In some parts of the world, when a standard is set, it in fact becomes law. If a user or vendor violates the rules, the penalties can be quite severe.

A user who installs a nonstandard piece of equipment on the links could be subject to steep fines and up to one year in prison. These countries take their standards seriously. In the United States, no such penalties exist; we are more relaxed in this area. But a standard is a de jure standard if an independent standards body (that is, one not solely sponsored by vendors) successfully carries it through a more or less public standards-making procedure and announces that it is now a standard.

You might well ask, "What's the difference? And who cares, anyway?" But understanding which technologies fall into which category, if either, can be a factor in deciding what to buy. Generally, de facto standards are controlled by the vendors that introduced them. For example, Microsoft Windows is a de facto standard; many vendors provide programs that comply with and operate in this environment. But if it decides to change the way a new version of Windows works, Microsoft in theory can obsolete all of those programs. (In practice, Microsoft is most unlikely to do this, at least intentionally, because much of its market power stems from the fact that all those other products are built to its standard. Were Microsoft to make such a change, it is likely that those other software providers would look elsewhere for a target operating system. Microsoft's stock would drop precipitously, to say the least! Or as we saw, the Department of Justice would alter the way Microsoft does business.)

One reason that vendors often build to de facto standards is that the standards-making process tends to be somewhat lengthy. A minimum of 4 to 12 years for a new or revised standard is not at all uncommon in the industry. With product cycles under one year in some areas of the communications industry, waiting for the finalization of a standard before introducing a product could result in corporate suicide. Ethernet is a good example of a standard that started as a de facto standard. Intel, Xerox, and Digital Equipment Corporation (DEC) introduced Ethernet with the intent of making it a de jure standard. But that process took years, and the final result was slightly different than the technology originally created by the three vendors. Nonetheless, many networks were created based on Ethernet before the 802.3 de jure standard was finalized, bringing profit to its creators and operating environments to their customers.

In the real world, the standards-making bodies rely in large part on vendors to develop the details of new and revised standards. In fact, most standards bodies have vendor representatives as full participants. It is a fascinating political process with much pushing and pulling to gain advantage in the market. The vendors participate for several reasons, not the least of which is to get the jump on competitors that are not as close to the process. Other reasons include the ability to state in marketing materials that they contributed to or were involved in the testing of a new standard, as well as the opportunity to influence the actual details of a standard to favor technology with which the vendors are most familiar.

To be fair, it should be stated that the primary goal of most of those involved in the standards process is to define a good and useful standard. But when the process produces a dual standard, as in the case of the Ethernet and Token Ring local area network standards, one can presume that the "best" was compromised somewhat in favor of what could be agreed on.

Even de jure standards (usually identifiable by virtue of their unintelligible alphanumeric designations, such as X.25, V.35, V.42 bis, and so on) change in ways that significantly affect the market—and you. One set of standards that affects thousands of users is the set of modem standards, discussed later. But beware a vendor that trumpets compliance with a "new standard!" The vendor's claim might be legitimate, but if no other vendors have products available in the same space, the company might simply be hyping its own product in hopes that it eventually will become a standard. Or there might be a standard under development but not yet approved. In the latter case, if that standard changes before final approval, the vendor's current products will instantly become nonstandard without changing in any way.

Architectures

As with constructing a building, an overall design is needed when planning a communications environment. For a building, that design is described by architectural drawings. A communications architecture is a coordinated set of design guidelines that together constitute a complete description of one approach to building a communications environment.

Several communications architectures have been developed. Some of the best-known include IBM's SNA and DEC's DNA. Architectures are covered in much greater detail in Chapter 15, but for those already familiar with the open systems interconnect (OSI) model described in Chapter 15, most of this chapter (excluding codes, which reside at the presentation layer) addresses the physical and link layers. The newest architecture to run away with the industry and the fancy of all developers is the Internet architecture using TCP and IP protocols. Every day new applications and protocols are being developed to run on the Internet architecture. This includes voice, data, streaming audio and video, and multimedia applications.

The data communications architectures were modeled after the voice architectures. This is understandable, because data is merely a logical extension of the dial-up voice network. Devices are therefore constructed to fit into the overall voice network operation. Data equipment is designed and built to mimic the characteristics of a human speech pattern. Now, however, we see that voice is data and data is too! This paradigm shift marks the true convergence of voice and data onto a single architecture. The world appears ready to embrace the technologies that will result from this convergence.

Protocols

Protocols are key components of communications architectures. Architectures are guidelines on how environments connecting two or more devices can be constructed, so most components of a given architecture in a network will be found on each communicating computer in that network. Protocols provide the rules for communications between counterpart components on different devices.

More detail, with examples, is provided in the discussion of the OSI model in Chapter 15. However, one aspect of protocols also applies to hardware: whether they are synchronous or asynchronous. These key characteristics are covered in the following section.

Transmission Protocols (Synchronous Versus Asynchronous)

All lower-level data communications protocols fall into one of the two following categories: synchronous or asynchronous. The words themselves are based on Greek roots indicating that they either are "in" or "with" time (SYNCHRONOUS) or "out of" or "separated from" time (ASYNCHRONOUS). The underlying meanings are quite accurate, so long as one understands to what they must be applied.

All data communications depend on precise timing, or *clocking*. The discussion of analog versus digital transmission in Chapter 5 covers how voltage levels are sampled in the middle of a bit time in order to maximize the odds that the sample value will be clearly distinguishable as a 1 or a 0. But how does the equipment determine precisely when the middle of a bit time occurs? The answer is clocking; equipment at both ends of a circuit must be synchronized during transmission so that the receiver and the sender agree regarding beginnings, middles, and ends of bits during transmissions. This clocking can be done in two fundamentally different ways: asynchronously and synchronously.

Simply put, asynchronous transmissions are clocked (or synchronized) one byte at a time. Synchronous transmissions are clocked in groups of bytes, but the differences in how these two approaches work go beyond the differences between individual bytes and groups of bytes.

Asynchronous communications is also called start/stop communications and has the following characteristics. Every byte has added to it one bit signaling the beginning of the byte (the start bit) and at least one bit (possibly two) added at the end of the byte (the stop bits). Bytes with seven data bits typically also include a parity bit (which is an error-checking bit), whereas eight-data-bit bytes usually do not. Thus, generally speaking, 10 or 11 total bits are actually transmitted for every asynchronous byte. To get seven usable data bits, we must transmit approximately 10 to 11; strictly speaking, we use a 30 to 35 percent overhead.

Figure 13-1 shows the layout of a data byte in an asynchronous form. This was a special concern when data communications were initially used in the late 1950s and early 1960s. Back then, the cost per minute of a dial-up line was $0.60 to $0.65. Using that value, 30 cents of every dollar was

Figure 13-1
To send seven usable bits of data, we must use one start, one parity, and one or two stop bits.

S T A R T   1 000 001 P   S T O P P   S T O P P

spent just to provide the timing for the line. This amount of waste concerned everyone.

This also makes nominal speed calculations for such connections easy. Dividing the rated speed of the circuit (such as 9,600 bits per second) by ten bits per byte gives a transmission speed in characters per second (960 cps). As a rule, we divide the bits per second by 10 to get the nominal speed of an asynchronous circuit. (Nominal here means best-case; in the real world, circuits rarely deliver 100 percent of their nominal capacity, but it's a starting point for capacity calculations.)

The bytes are sent out without regard to the timing of previous and succeeding bytes. That means that none of the components in a circuit ever assume that just because one byte went by, another will follow in any particular period of time. Think of a person banging away on a keyboard. The speed and number of characters sent in a given period do not indicate in any way how many or how quickly characters can be sent in the succeeding similar period.

Clocking is controlled by data terminal equipment (DTE). For example, when a personal computer is used to dial into CompuServe, clocking on bytes going toward the service is generated by the sending PC (see Figure 13-2). That first start bit reaching the modem begins the sequence, with all succeeding bits in the same byte arriving in lockstep at the agreed-on rate until the stop bit is received. Then clocking stops until the beginning of the next byte arrives. Any intervening devices (especially modems) between the communicating DTEs take the clocking from the data sent by the originating DTE for any given byte.

Figure 13-2
The data terminal equipment controls the timing to the data communications equipment (modem) as the bits are sent in an asynchronous protocol. A start bit and one or two stop bits help to set the timing.

Most PC and minicomputer terminal communications employ asynchronous techniques. The default communications ports on PCs (the "serial" or COM ports) only support asynchronous communications. To use synchronous communications on a PC, a special circuit board is required.

Synchronous communications have the following characteristics:

■ Blocks of data rather than individual bytes (characters) are transmitted.

■ Individual bytes do not have any additional bits added to them on a byte-by-byte basis, except for parity.

However, bytes are sent and clocked in contiguous groups of one or more bytes. Each group is immediately (with no intervening time) preceded by a minimum of two consecutive synchronization bytes (a special character defined by the specific synchronous protocol, of which there are many) that begin the clocking. All succeeding bits in the group are sent in lockstep until the last bit of the last byte is sent, followed (still in lockstep) by an end-of-block byte. This layout of the synchronous characters (SYN) is shown in Figure 13-3.

Clocking is controlled by data communications equipment (DCE).[1] Specifically, on any given circuit, one specific DCE component is optioned (that is, configured) at installation time as the master device. When the circuit is otherwise idle, the master generates the same synchronization character mentioned earlier on a periodic basis to all other DCE devices so that all DCE clocks on the circuit are maintained in continuous synchronization.

Except in cases where smaller numbers of bytes (fewer than about 20) are sent at a time, synchronous communication makes more efficient use of a circuit, as can be seen from Table 13-1.

Generally speaking, all circuits running at greater than 2,400 bits per second actually operate in synchronous mode over the wire. This is simply

Figure 13-3
The layout of data transmitted synchronously—in this case, the block size is 512 bytes.

S Y N	S Y N	S O T	S O T	Data up to 512 Bytes	E X T	E O T	S Y N
8	8	8	8	4096	8	8	8

---

[1] DCE also stands for data circuit terminating equipment.

Table 13-1

Comparison of the
Utilization of the
Circuit

Data Bytes	Asynchronous Bits	Synchronous Bits	Synchronous Savings
1	10	32	−220%
5	50	64	−28%
10	100	104	−4%
20	200	184	8%
30	300	264	12%
100	1,000	824	18%
1,000	10,000	8,024	20%
10,000	100,000	80,024	20%

because building modems to reliably operate asynchronously at higher speeds over analog circuits is much more difficult than taking this approach. Asynchronous modems that run faster than 2,400 bits per second actually incorporate asynchronous-to-synchronous converters; they communicate asynchronously to their respective DTEs but synchronously between the modems, as shown in Figure 13-4. This doesn't normally impact performance. When smaller groups of characters are sent, there is time to include the additional overhead for synchronous transmission. When larger groups are sent, the reduced overhead of synchronous transmission comes into play. In practice, these higher-speed modems actually

Figure 13-4
The data communications equipment (modem) sets up the communications synchronously. Blocks are used to create the synchronous transfer.

communicate with other modems at even higher rates than their rated speeds; the extra bandwidth is used for overhead functions between the modems.

Error Detection

We mentioned at the beginning of the chapter that ensuring the integrity of the information was one of the key responsibilities of a data communications environment. This does not mean that the data must be kept honest. Rather, it means that we must somehow guarantee with an extremely high degree of probability that the information is received in exactly the same form as it was sent.

More precisely, two tasks are required: detecting when transmission errors occur and triggering retransmissions in the event that an error is detected. It is the responsibility of protocols to trigger and manage retransmissions (see Chapter 15). Here we discuss some of the various approaches that have been developed to detect errors in the first place.

All of the code sets used in data communications (see the following) are designed to use all of their bits to represent characters (letters, numbers, other special characters). A not-so-obvious implication of this fact is that every byte received in such a code set is by definition a valid code. How can we detect whether the received code is the code that was sent?

The solution is to somehow send some additional information, some data about data (sometimes described as metadata), along with the primary data. All error-checking approaches depend on sending some additional data besides the original application-related data. The additional data is created during the communications process, it is used to check the underlying data when it is received, and it is then discarded before the information is passed to its final destination.

In order of increasing reliability, the major methods used to detect data communications errors include

- Parity bit, or vertical redundancy checking (VRC)
- Longitudinal redundancy checking (LRC)
- Cyclic redundancy checking (CRC)

Suppose you are my rich aunt and that I am living in Paris (to further my cultural education, of course) and have run out of money. I've called you (collect, of course) to request that you electronically transfer some money into my account at the Banque de Paris. In a fit of generosity, you have decided to send me $1,000.00. If the network used is not perfectly reliable and appropriate error detection methods are not applied by the transmitting financial service, a change in a single character—for example, changing the period after the first three 0's to another 0—could result in you sending me considerably more money than you intended: a total of $1,000,000.

What are the chances of my getting my inheritance early in this way? Not very high, given the odds that only the decimal point would change, and only to a 0 (out of either 126 or 254 other possibilities). But consider the probability of detecting the error, assuming that it has occurred. Using parity bits, the likelihood of detecting this kind of error (which requires several bits to be wrong at one time to change an entire character) is about 65 percent. A somewhat better method, longitudinal redundancy checking, would up the odds of detection to about 85 percent. But the cyclic redundancy checking method improves the odds of detecting and correcting such a multibit error to 99.99995 percent.

Because the networks used to send monetary amounts generally use CRC techniques, it doesn't look as though I'm going to get rich because of their errors. But let's examine these methods in more detail anyway.

Parity Bit/Vertical Redundancy Checking (VRC)

The parity bit approach to error detection simply adds a single "parity" bit to every character (or byte) sent. Whether the parity bit is set to 0 or 1 (the only two possibilities, of course) is calculated by the sending digital device and recalculated by the receiving device. If the calculations match, the associated character is considered good. Otherwise, an error is detected.

This is much simpler than it sounds. Two approaches are typically used: even and odd parity. Other forms of parity exist, such as mark or space parity. It makes no difference which is used; the only requirement is that the sending and receiving devices use the same approach.

To illustrate even parity, consider the ASCII bit sequence representing lowercase letter a: 1100001. Because we are using even parity, we require that the total number of 1 bits transmitted to the receiver to send this a, including the eighth parity bit, be equal to an even number. Their position in the underlying byte is irrelevant. If we count the ones in the seven-bit pattern, we get three, an odd number. Therefore, we set the parity bit to 1, resulting in 11100001, an eight-bit pattern with an even number of (four) 1's. (The parity bit is sent last. In our illustrations, the bits farthest to the right are sent first, so we show the parity bit being added at the left.)

Figure 13-5 shows an ASCII illustration of the word "hello," complete with even parity bits. As you can see from the illustration, the bytes are represented as vertical sets of numbers, thus vertical redundancy checking is used. If we orient the digits vertically, we add a vertical bit that is redundant to help check the correctness of the underlying byte. The vertical orientation is arbitrary, of course. However, when we illustrate longitudinal redundancy checking, you will see that there is a reason for this display approach.

Having gone to the trouble of describing parity bits, we must confess that they are of limited use in data communications. Parity checking will catch 100 percent of the errors when the number of bits in error is odd (1, 3, 5, and so on), but none of the errors when the number of bits in error is even. Put another way, if an error occurs (and communications errors rarely affect only a single bit), there is only about a 65 percent chance that parity

Figure 13-5
The vertical redundancy check shows the flow of data. The parity bit is added after each character is generated.

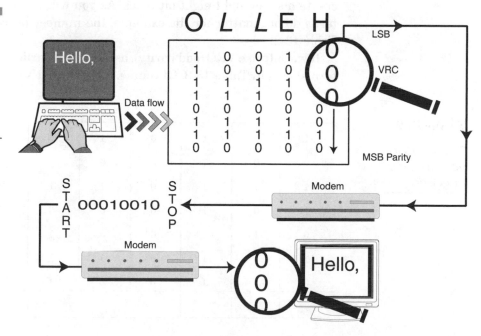

checking will detect it. (The probability is better than 50 percent because somewhat more one-bit errors occur than any one type of multibit error, whether the numbers of the latter are odd or even.)

Parity checking is used extensively inside computers. It makes sense there because it is entirely plausible that errors would occur one at a time (if they occur at all). Parity checking does well in this environment. Also, some networks (such as CompuServe) still have users set their communications software to use parity checking, but even CompuServe uses a more sophisticated protocol for file transfers. Some more sophisticated error-detection protocols are described in the following paragraphs.

Longitudinal Redundancy Checking (LRC)

The concept of LRC follows directly from VRC, taking VRC a step further. This example uses eight-bit rather than seven-bit bytes, but LRC checking needs to operate on a group of bytes, rather than on one byte at a time. For this example, it doesn't really matter what the bits represent, so let us create a set of eight eight-bit bytes. As you will see, although the bit patterns do not matter for the example, the number of bytes used does (see Table 13-2).

If we only use VRC (odd parity), as described earlier, we produce the pattern shown in Table 13-3. Of course, we said that VRC only catches about

Table 13-2

Setting Up for
Vertical Parity
Checking

1	0	1	0	1	0	1	0
0	0	1	0	0	0	1	0
1	1	1	0	1	1	1	0
1	0	1	0	0	0	1	0
0	1	1	0	0	1	1	0
1	1	1	0	1	1	1	0
0	1	1	0	0	1	1	0

Table 13-3

The Parity Bit Is
Inserted in VRC

1	0	1	0	1	0	1	0
0	0	1	0	0	0	1	0
1	1	1	0	1	1	1	0
1	0	1	0	0	0	1	0
0	1	1	0	0	1	1	0
1	1	1	0	1	1	1	0
0	1	1	0	0	1	1	0
1	**1**	**0**	**1**	**0**	**1**	**0**	**1**

Table 13-4

The Vertical and
Longitudinal
Redundancy
Checks Are
Inserted Here

1	0	1	0	1	0	1	0	1
0	0	1	0	0	0	1	0	1
1	1	1	0	1	1	1	0	1
1	0	1	0	0	0	1	0	0
0	1	1	0	0	1	1	0	1
1	1	1	0	1	1	1	0	1
0	1	1	0	0	1	1	0	1
1	**1**	**0**	**1**	**0**	**1**	**0**	**1**	**0**

65 percent of errors, which is hardly acceptable, but what if we apply odd parity checking across the bytes in addition to vertically? In that case, the completely filled-in Table 13-4 would be generated.

Adding both the horizontal and vertical checking, together referred to as longitudinal redundancy checking, improves the odds of detecting errors to about 85 percent. Not bad, although we wouldn't want to trust our money to such a transmission, but LRC has another disadvantage. Using eight-bit bytes for every eight data bytes, an additional two LRC bytes must be transmitted. That works out to 20 percent added overhead for error checking (two LRC bytes divided by the ten total bytes transmitted in the set), not counting any degradation due to the time required to compute the check bytes. This is not an efficient error-checking mechanism. In fact, considering that error checking is only one of several sources of transmission overhead, it is abysmal.

LRC does have one advantage over cyclic redundancy checking (CRC), the approach discussed next. Far fewer computational resources are required for calculating the LRC bytes than for calculating a CRC (unless the CRC is implemented with hardware). In fact, until recent generations of PCs became available, with their vastly more powerful CPUs, CRC checking for asynchronous data communications in the PC environment was not practical because of its computationally intensive nature. Now, however, it is routinely used. Read on to see why.

Cyclic Redundancy Checking (CRC)

Although no practical error-checking algorithm can guarantee detection of every possible error pattern, CRC comes close. A complete explanation with examples of how CRC works would (and does, in several data communications textbooks) require several pages of somewhat hairy binary algebra. Rather than put you through that, we'll describe some of the method's key characteristics and indicate how this method is used.

Like the previously described approaches to error detection, CRC relies on an on-the-fly calculation of an additional bit pattern (referred to as a frame check sequence, or FCS) that is sent immediately after the original block of data bits. The length of the FCS is chosen in advance by a software or hardware designer on the basis of how high a confidence level is required in the error-detection capability of the given transmission. All burst errors, or groups of bits randomized by transmission problems, with a length less than that of the FCS will be detected. Frequently used FCS lengths include 12, 16, and 32 bits. Obviously, the longer the FCS, the more errors will be detected.

The FCS is computed by first taking the original data block bit pattern (treated as a single huge binary number) and adding to its end (after the low-order bits) some additional binary 0's. The exact number of added 0's will be the same as the number of bits in the desired FCS. (The FCS, once calculated, will overlay those 0's.) Then, the resulting binary number, including the trailing 0's, is divided by a special previously selected divisor (often referred to in descriptions of the algorithm as P).

P has certain required characteristics:

- It is always one bit longer than the desired FCS.
- Its first and last bits are always 1.
- It is chosen to be "relatively prime" to the FCS; that is, P divided by the FCS would always give a non-0 remainder. In practice, that means P is normally a prime number.
- The division uses binary division, a much quicker and simpler process than decimal division. The remainder of the division becomes the FCS.

Specific implementations of CRC use specific divisors; thus, the CRC-32 error-checking protocol on one system should be able to cooperate with the CRC-32 protocol on another system. The CRC-CCITT protocol (which uses a 17-bit pattern, generating a 16-bit FCS) likewise should talk to other implementations of CRC-CCITT. Selection of a specific P can be tuned to the types of errors most likely to occur in a specific environment, but unless you are planning on engineering a new protocol, you needn't worry about the selection process. It already has been done for you by the designers of your hardware or your communications software. Figure 13-6 illustrates the CRC creation process.

Figure 13-6
The creation of a
CRC cycle

CRC is typically used on blocks or frames of data rather than on individual bytes. Depending on the protocol being used, the size of the blocks can be as high as several thousand bytes. Thus, in terms of bits of error-checking information required for a given number of bytes of data, CRC requires far less transmission overhead (for example, CRC-32 sends four eight-bit bytes' worth of error-checking bits to check thousands of data bytes) than any of the parity-based approaches.

Although binary division is very efficient, having to perform such a calculation on every block transmitted has the potential to add significantly to transmission times. Fortunately, CPUs developed in the last few years are up to the challenge. Also, unlike other check-digit types of error correction, the receiving device or software does not have to recalculate the FCS in order to check for an error. Instead, the original data plus the FCS are concatenated together to form a longer pattern and are then divided by the same P used as a divisor during the FCS creation process. If no remainder results from this last division, then the CRC algorithm assumes that no errors occurred, and, 99.99995 percent of the time, there aren't.

Plexes-Communications Channel Directions

The next area of discussion is the directional nature of your communications channel. Three basic forms of communications channels exist.

One-Way (Simplex)

This is a service that is one way and only one way. You can use it to either transmit or to receive. This is not a common channel for telephony (voice), because very few occasions arise where one person speaks and everyone else listens. Feedback, one of the capabilities that we prize in our communications, would be eliminated in a one-way conversation. Broadcast television is an example of simplex communications.

Designing an efficient data communications application using a simplex channel can require quite a bit of ingenuity. A good example is stock ticker tape radio signals. Bear in mind that in a true simplex system (such as this one) absolutely no feedback is possible from the receiver to the transmitter. How then does someone using such a signal get useful, timely information?

After all, unless one is simply gawking at the symbols as they go by, it is not practical to wait for, on average, half of the symbols to go by in order to find out that the particular stock in which you are interested just went up or down a bit.

The answer is a combination of communications and computer technology. The applications that implement this technique memorize locally (on a PC) the entire repeating communications stream once, and then accept each new symbol/price combination received as an update to the local "database." The user inquires against that local database, getting what appears to be instant information, even though it might have been received several minutes ago. Naturally, the computer must be set to continually receive; otherwise, the user will have no assurance that the data is even remotely current.

Another approach requires the user to specify in advance to the software a set of symbols to collect. As that stock information goes by, the program snags only the specified information for retention and local query. This is not any faster than the previous approach, but it does require less local storage capabilities.

Two-Way Alternating (Half Duplex)

This is the normal channel that is used in conversations. We speak to a listener and then we listen while someone else speaks. The telephone conversations we engage in are normally half duplex. Although the line or medium (air, in this case) is capable of handling a transmission in each direction, most human brains can't deal well with simultaneous transmission and reception.

Many computer and communications configurations use half duplex technology. Until a few years ago, most leased-line multidrop modems were half duplex. One of the key differentiators among such modems was their turnaround time, that is, how quickly a pair of such modems could reverse the channel direction. This was measured in milliseconds—the fewer, the better. Entire communications protocols were built around this technology (such as IBM's Bisynchronous Communications or BSC).

All-block mode terminals (such as IBM 3270s) still operate in half duplex mode only, even if full duplex facilities are available. This simply means that at any given time, the terminal is either sending to its associated computer or receiving from it, not both at once. This does not cause a problem because the entire system is designed around this behavior, and it works quite well. Of course, almost half of any given circuit's raw capacity (if the capacities of the two directions are added together) is wasted. (IBM's more recent SDLC-protocol-based front-end processors can talk to one terminal and receive from another at the same time, minimizing this waste, but the individual terminals are still functioning as half duplex devices.)

With some technologies, half duplex can be used so effectively that the one-way-at-a-time characteristic of the circuit is invisible; it appears to be full duplex (see the following section). An excellent example of such an approach would be local area network communications. Most actual LAN technologies, including both Ethernet and Token Ring, are actually half duplex on the wire, but the information moves so quickly, and the responses are so fast, that the path appears to an observer to be full duplex.

Two-Way Simultaneous (Duplex) or Full Duplex

True full duplex communications make maximum use of a circuit's capacity, if the nature of the communications on that circuit takes advantage of it. In data communications, a circuit is implemented and used in full duplex mode if a device can send to a computer and receive from the computer at the same time. Although we mentioned that human conversation is typically half duplex, there is an exception to this: conversation among teenagers, who seem to be able to speak and listen (somewhat) at exactly the same time.

A common example of full duplex communications is when one dials into an online information system such as CompuServe or Prodigy. Such systems enable users to continue typing at a keyboard even while the service is sending information to the user for display on the screen. Were the connection not a full duplex one, this simultaneous bidirectional communication would not be possible.

One point that confuses some people is that the terms simplex, half duplex, and full duplex can refer to varying levels of a communications architecture. If the three levels are considered to be three points on an increasing scale of capability, one can say that a given level of a communications architecture must rely on lower levels with at least the capability of that given level, as presented in Table 13-5.

What does this table mean? It means that a wide-area analog data circuit built to handle full duplex communications (requiring the telephone

Table 13-5	This Capability Level	Requires All Lower Levels to Have at Least the Following Capability	But Can Also Function Without Impairment on Top of Levels with the Following Capabilities
Comparing the Capability and Directionality of the Circuit	Simplex	Simplex	Half or full duplex
	Half duplex	Half duplex	Full duplex
	Full duplex	Full duplex	(No additional levels)

company to support simultaneous communications in both directions and use of full duplex modems) can fully support half duplex or simplex communications. But if a similar circuit is implemented with half duplex modems, then full duplex communications on that circuit will not work, although simplex will. A citizens band radio provides half duplex channel-two directions, but only one way at a time. Simplex would work—one sender could lock down a key and just keep sending—but full duplex would be impossible.

Air is a full duplex channel, but a simplex signal such as the output from a stereo speaker system has no trouble traveling this full duplex channel.

Compression

Although compression is not exactly a modulation technique, it does (usually) produce faster transmissions. To understand how compression works, consider first how human beings communicate. Most human communication is inherently redundant. This does not imply waste; rather, human beings use that redundancy as a continual cross-check on what information is really being sent and meant. For example, in face-to-face conversation much more information is being sent than just the words. Facial expressions, tones of voice, body language, and other less obvious cues all contribute to the information stream flowing between two people having a conversation. But much of the information is duplicated. For example, anger can be communicated by the words themselves, but it can also be conveyed by tone of voice, facial expression, involuntary changes in the color of one's complexion, the stress in the voice, arm movement, and other cues. If some of these items were removed, the message received might be just as clear, but the total amount of raw information might be reduced.

In data communications, compression is a technique applied either in advance to information to be transmitted or dynamically to an information stream being transmitted. The underlying technology is essentially the same in both cases. The removal of redundant information, or the expression of the information in a more compact form, is used to reduce the total number of bytes that must pass over the communications medium in order to reduce the time the medium is occupied by a given transmission to a minimum.

A detailed discussion of compression techniques is beyond the scope of this book, but in this section we describe two very basic approaches in order to elucidate the fundamentals of the technology. Later, during the discussion of modems, we will briefly identify and describe the power of some compression techniques that are often built into such devices.

The simplest form of compression is the identification and encoding of repeating characters into fewer characters. For example, consider the transmission of printed output across a network to a printer. A typical report contains a very high number of blank characters, often occurring consecutively. Suppose every such string of four or more consecutive blanks (which are, of course, themselves ASCII characters) is detected and replaced with a three-byte special character sequence encoded as follows:

- The first character is a special character (one of the nonprint characters in the ASCII code set, for example) indicating that this is a special sequence.

- The second character is one occurrence of the character that is to be repeated, in this case a blank.

- The third character is a one-byte binary number indicating how many times the character is to be repeated. With one byte (using binary format), we can count up to 255, high enough to get some real savings!

How much can we save? Look at Table 13-6. We'll assume that on average, blanks occur in ten-byte consecutive streams, a very pessimistic assumption.

As can be seen from the table, the savings depends on the number of occurrences of the character to be repeated. In practice, this is a reasonably powerful technique. In the example, we addressed only blanks. In practice, any character except the special character would be fair game.

Table 13-6

Quick Analysis of
Compression
Benefits

Total Characters in Print Stream Before Compression	Blanks in Print Before Compression	Total Characters in Streamprint Stream After Compression	Percentage Savings
000	10	993	1
1,000	100	930	7
1,000	500	650	35
50,000	2,000	48,600	3
50,000	5,000	46,500	7
50,000	20,000	36,000	28

But what if we actually want to send that special character? After all, unlike print jobs, many transmissions must be able to handle every possible code; none are left over that are "special." No problem—we add the following rules:

- We'll never try to compress multiple occurrences of the special character.

- Every time we encounter the special character as input during the encoding process, we'll simply send it twice. If the receiving hardware sees this character twice, it drops one of the occurrences.

With this approach, we only have to select a special character that is unlikely to occur frequently. If it then does occur frequently in a particular transmission, our compression algorithm doesn't break; it will just be very inefficient for that one transmission.

Note how the overall redundancy is squeezed out of a transmission using this approach. But, just as in human communications, eliminating redundancy increases the risk that some information will be misinterpreted. In human communication, if the reddening of an angry person's face and other visual cues were not visible (if the conversation were on the telephone) and the speaker was otherwise very self-controlled, the listener might misinterpret angry words as being a joke. After all, many American subcultures routinely use affectionate insults without anger. Unrecognized anger is a very serious loss of information. In data communications without compression, the omission of a single space in a series of spaces might cause a slight misalignment on a report, but it will most likely not seriously distort its meaning. If compression is used and the binary count field is damaged (that is, it is changed to another binary digit), dozens or even hundreds of spaces or other repetitive characters might be either deleted or added to the report, seriously compromising its appearance and perhaps distorting its meaning. Consider the havoc that could be wrought on a horizontal bar chart. The error-checking techniques discussed earlier become much more important in a system that uses compression.

Another more sophisticated method of compression requires pattern recognition analysis of the raw data rather than just detection of repeating characters. Again, some special character must be designated, but now it precedes a special short code that represents some repetitive pattern detected during the analysis. For example, in graphics displays capable of showing 64K (65,535) colors, every screen pixel has associated with it two eight-bit bytes (which together can represent 65K different values) indicating the color assigned to that pixel. If someone sets the screen to display white on a blue background, the two-byte code for blue is going to appear thousands of times in the data stream associated with that display. The repeating one-byte compression algorithm described earlier will not detect anything to compress. If analysis shows that a two-byte pattern occurs many times in succession, however, a more sophisticated approach might assign a specific character (preceded by the special character) to represent precisely 20 (or some other specific number of) consecutive occurrences of that two-byte sequence. The savings can be considerable, but they again depend on the characteristics of the data being transmitted.

A third, very computationally intensive approach to compression has been designed especially for the live transmission of digitized video signals. Unlike most other compression methods, this approach does not involve the movement of representations of the entire digitized data stream from one point to another. Video signals consist of a number of still frames composed each second (visualize 30 photographs per second, in the highest-quality case). Although the first picture must, of course, be sent in its entirety, special equipment and algorithms must then continuously examine succeeding video frames to be transmitted, identifying which pixels have changed since the last "picture" was taken. Thus, information addressing just the changed pixels is sent to the receiver, rather than the entire new frame. The receiving equipment uses this change information combined with its "memory" of the previous frame to continuously, locally build new versions of the picture for display. This approach is particularly fruitful for pictures that in large part remain static, such as video conferencing. In video conferencing, usually the only moving features of the picture are the human beings. The table(s), walls, and other room fixtures stay still, therefore requiring transmission only once. Frequently, only the lips move for long periods of time.

One other compression-related concept is worth mentioning: lossy versus lossless compression. "What?" I hear you ask. Does lossy mean what it sounds like? Would we ever tolerate transmission that loses information? The answer, for some applications, is yes. Moreover, you have probably settled for information loss when working daily with computers, and it caused you no hardship at all. If you use a personal computer with a video graphics adapter (VGA) screen but display any type of graphic that inherently has Super VGA (SVGA) level resolution, your VGA screen loses the additional definition in the image that is visible only when an SVGA controller card and monitor are used. In fact, this example, while not involving compression as such, demonstrates precisely the type of situation where lossy compression would be tolerated: in the transmission of video images. Some compression algorithms used for the transmission of video images lose some of the resolution of those images. However, if the received image is acceptably precise, the maintenance of the speed of the moving image might be more important.

Multiplexing

The paths available for moving electronic information vary considerably in their respective capacities or bandwidths. If a company requires many paths over the same route (for example, many terminals each requiring a connection to one distant computer), it often makes sense to configure one large-capacity circuit and bundle all the smaller requirements into that one big path. The process of combining two or more communications paths into one path is referred to as *multiplexing*. Three fundamental types of multiplexing exist, all of which have significant variations. These main types are

- Space-division multiplexing (SDM)
- Frequency-division multiplexing (FDM)
- Time-division multiplexing (TDM)

SDM

Space-division multiplexing (SDM) is the easiest multiplexing technology to understand. In fact, it is so simple it would hardly rate its own special term, except that it is the primary method by which literally millions of telephone signals reach private homes. With SDM, signals are placed on physically different media. Then those media are combined into larger groups and connected to the desired end points.

For example, telephone wire pairs, each of which can carry a voice conversation or be used for data communications, are aggregated into cables with hundreds or even thousands of pairs (see Figure 13-7). The bigger bundles of cables that are aggregated are run as units from telco COs out to wiring center locations, from there splitting out to individual customer buildings.

The biggest advantage of SDM is also its biggest disadvantage: the physical separation of the media carrying each signal. It is an advantage because of the simplicity of managing the bandwidth; one only must label each end point of the medium appropriately. No failures (other than a break in the medium) can affect the bandwidth allocation scheme, but because a direct physical correlation exists between the physical link and the individual communications channel, a provider has some difficulty in electronically manipulating the path to achieve efficiencies of technology or scale. For example, probably the largest single factor blocking the conversion of the overall telephone network to all-digital technology is the embedded base of copper wire (and analog amplifiers) supplying telephone service to millions of homes and businesses.

Figure 13-7
Individual pairs are bundled together into much larger cables on a one-to-one ratio.

Wiring Center Location

Cable

Telco

FDM

Frequency-division multiplexing (FDM) is inherently an analog technology. It achieves the combining of several signals onto (or into) one medium by sending signals in several distinct frequency ranges over that medium.

One of FDM's most common applications is cable television. Only one cable reaches a customer's home, but the service provider can nevertheless send multiple television channels or signals simultaneously over that cable to all subscribers. Receivers must tune to the appropriate frequency in order to access the desired signal. Figure 13-8 demonstrates the combining of signals on a cable television coaxial cable.

Certain modems have built-in FDM capabilities. Users can modify, with controls on the modem, how much bandwidth each connected digital device will be provided.

TDM

Time-division multiplexing (TDM) is a digital technology. It involves sequencing groups of a few bits or bytes from each individual input stream one after the other and in such a way that they can be associated with the appropriate receiver. If this is done sufficiently quickly, the receiving devices will not realize or care that some of the circuit time was used to serve another logical communication path. The really high-speed communications technologies covered in later chapters all, without exception, use some form of TDM, so it is worthwhile to try to understand it.

Figure 13-8
Frequency-division multiplexing breaks the whole bandwidth into separate full-time channels.

Consider an application requiring four terminals at an airport to reach a central computer. Each terminal communicates at 2,400 bits per second, so, rather than acquiring four individual circuits to carry such a low-speed transmission, the airline has installed a pair of multiplexers (see the following section), a pair of 9,600-bit-per-second modems, and a dedicated analog communications circuit from the airport ticket desk back to the airline data center, as illustrated in Figure 13-9.

The time-division multiplexers work together to merge the data streams onto the 9,600-bit-per-second circuit in such a way that each terminal appears to have a dedicated 2,400-bit-per-second circuit. The multiplexer has enough buffer (or storage) space so that, as any of the four clerks presses a key, the keystroke is stored locally (in the multiplexer or mux) until the time slot assigned to that clerk's terminal comes along. The flow of information for four hypothetical clerks named Ellen, Joe, Susan, and Allan is shown in Table 13-7.

As an example, we'll assume that Joe is inquiring as to the availability of space on XXXXX Airlines flight 243. As part of this inquiry, he types the letters XA243. At the same time, Susan is looking for a vacancy at the Compris hotel in Chicago, so she types Compris. The other two clerks are out to lunch; their terminals are inactive. Those letters will be interspersed among others typed by their colleagues. TDM assigns time slots to each configured device whether or not the slots are used. If the data stream is to be interleaved one byte at a time, the data stream toward the computer resulting from this typing might look as shown in Figure 13-10 (the information on the right goes toward the computer first).

This is not really a form of compression, because the same number of bytes is sent as is typed. In fact, as can be seen from the figure, there is a certain inefficiency here. Those four-byte blocks are being pumped out by

Figure 13-9
In time-division multiplexing, the entire channel is allocated for short periods of time.

Table 13-7

The Flow of
Information for
the Various Time
Slots Used

Byte	From
1	Ellen
2	Joe
3	Susan
4	Allan
5	Ellen
6	Joe
7	Susan
8	Allan

Figure 13-10
The use of TDM and
the data time slots for
two operators

the multiplexer no matter whether anyone types a character or not. The first position in each four-byte block is reserved for Ellen's characters, while the fourth position is reserved for Allan. Because Ellen and Allan are both at lunch, their blocks are empty and wasted. Joe is a slower typist than Susan, so even though he types fewer characters, his last character goes at the same time as Susan's last; some of his slots are empty. He "missed the train."

In real life, many more slots would be empty because the capacity of the line is 240 characters per second—per clerk! No one can type that quickly. Also, in real life, multiplexing is more commonly done at the bit level rather than at the byte level. This would be harder to illustrate understandably, so we use bytes in the example, but the principle is identical.

Next, we modify the example to assume that the characters typed (XA243 and Compris) are coming back from the computer instead of being typed. In such a case, they will be coming at "wire speed." The computer can pump them out far faster than the line can absorb them, so we are now talking about wasting some time (see Figure 13-11).

If the multiplexer was configured for only two clerks' terminals, the information from the computer could appear much more quickly (see Figure 13-12).

▬ ▬ ▬ ▬

Figure 13-11
The time wasted on the circuit can be compensated for using TDM techniques.

▬ ▬ ▬ ▬

Figure 13-12
The TDM is now configured for only two users, so the data will be less wasted.

This, in effect, is what a variation on a TDM, called a *statistical time-division multiplexer* (STDM), does. The sending STDM analyzes the data stream on the fly to determine which ports or "tail circuits" are active, that is, how much service they require. If they are inactive, or less active (slow typists?), they are provided fewer of the time slots (or bandwidth). This allocation changes dynamically depending on the traffic pattern. Again, this is not compression, because all the information is sent. Nonetheless, it seems like compression because extending this technique allows overcommitting the line. If 10 terminals are connected to a 9,600 circuit via an STDM, each terminal can be set to 2,400 bits per second. So long as not all terminals are busy at full speed at every moment, the STDM can make it look as though each terminal has its own 2,400-bit-per-second circuit, even though the aggregate bandwidth required to support these settings without using an STDM would be 24,000 bits per second.

Paradoxically, STDM techniques are used more at lower speeds than on the really fast multimegabit circuits. At very high speeds, the equipment is so busy just performing TDM functions that too much extra computer power would be required to do the on-the-fly analysis for STDM.

Codes

Chapter 5 covered digital transmission. The concept of a bit, an electronic expression of a 1 or 0, should now be clear. However, how do you get from 1's and 0's to transmitting your resume over wires?

The alphabet must be built up from sets of 1's and 0's. Specifically, we employ one or more sets of codes or alphabets, standard definitions of patterns of 1's and 0's that we will agree to use to represent letters, numbers, and other symbols that we want to transmit and receive.

The alphabets most frequently used are either American Standard Code for Information Interchange (ASCII), which is fairly universal, or Extended Binary Coded Decimal Interchange Code (EBCDIC), which is an IBM alphabet. These two code sets, or alphabets, are used to convert a series of 1's and 0's into an alphabetic or numeric character.

ASCII

One character (also known as a byte or octet) must be represented as a consistent bit pattern by both sender and receiver. As we use a keyboard, we create a stream of a combination of letters, numbers, and symbols (standard typewriter keyboards are known as QWERTY keyboards because of the sequence of the first row of alphabetic keys reading left to right).

When ASCII (usually pronounced ass-key with a mild accent on the first syllable) was originally defined for use by the U.S. government, the bit pattern was defined to be seven data bits long. With seven bits, it is possible to differentiate 128 different patterns. So, to recreate these typed characters with 1's and 0's, we can use a combination of up to 128 possible ASCII characters (see Figure 13-13).

Using the combinations in this table, we should be able to transmit just about everything we presently understand in our vocabulary. In fact, for many years, the seven-bit ASCII was used for most non-IBM mainframe communications, but two factors caused this form of ASCII to become less popular.

First, most computers handle data in eight-bit chunks (rather than seven) to represent characters. The terms *byte* and *octet* almost always refer to eight-bit, not seven-bit, patterns. Second, while seven-bit ASCII can indeed represent all the English letters and numbers, with some symbols left over for special characters and control information, many other characters used in written communication cannot easily be expressed in a 128-character code set. Accented characters in the Romance languages, character graphic drawing symbols, and typographical indications in word processors (bolding, underlining, and so on) are just a few examples of symbols difficult to handle with standard ASCII.

Bit 7	Bit 6	Bit 5	→ Col		0	0	0	0	1	1	1	1
					0	0	1	1	0	0	1	1
					0	1	0	1	0	1	0	1
Bit 4	**Bit 3**	**Bit 2**	**Bit 1**	**Row ↓ Col →**	**0**	**1**	**2**	**3**	**4**	**5**	**6**	**7**
0	0	0	0	0	NUL	DLE	SP	0	@	P	`	p
0	0	0	1	1	SOH	DC1	!	1	A	Q	a	q
0	0	1	0	2	STX	DC2	"	2	B	R	b	r
0	0	1	1	3	ETX	DC3	#	3	C	S	c	s
0	1	0	0	4	EOT	DC4	$	4	D	T	d	t
0	1	0	1	5	ENQ	NAK	%	5	E	U	e	u
0	1	1	0	6	ACK	SYN	&	6	F	V	f	v
0	1	1	1	7	BEL	ETB	'	7	G	W	g	w
1	0	0	0	8	BS	CAN	(	8	H	X	h	x
1	0	0	1	9	HT	EM	)	9	I	Y	i	y
1	0	1	0	A	LF	SUB	*	:	J	Z	j	z
1	0	1	1	B	VT	ESC	+	;	K	[	k	{
1	1	0	0	C	FF	FS	,	<	L	\	l		
1	1	0	1	D	CR	GS	-	=	M	]	m	}
1	1	1	0	E	SO	RS	.	>	N	^	n	~
1	1	1	1	F	SI	US	/	?	O	_	o	DEL

Figure 13-13
The ASCII code set

Extended ASCII

Extended ASCII is a superset of ASCII. Extended ASCII is the code used inside virtually all non-IBM computers, including personal computers. It is an eight-bit code set, doubling the possible distinguishable characters to 256. The seven-bit ASCII codes are present in extended ASCII in their original form with a 0 prefixed to the base seven bits. Another 128 characters are also available with the same base seven bits as the original ASCII, but with a 1 prefixed instead.

ASCII is a standard, whereas extended ASCII is . . . well, not quite standard. Although the original 128 characters communicate well from vendor to vendor, even in extended ASCII, every application defines its own use of the additional 128 characters. For example, you can easily write out ASCII text from most word processing programs, with the result being readable by most other word processors. If you attempt to read a document created by a word processor in its native form with another, different word processor, however, you will only be successful if the latter specifically contains a translation module for material created by the first.

Nonetheless, the lion's share of non-IBM communications is now conducted using extended ASCII. Virtually all personal computers use it, including IBM's. If you set your communications protocol to N,8,1 (no parity, eight data bits, one parity bit), those eight data bits are encoded using extended ASCII.

EBCDIC

IBM, not a company to follow the herd, realized early on that 128-code ASCII did not contain enough patterns for its requirements. So, IBM created an entirely different code set, one twice as large as the original ASCII code set. IBM's eight-bit, 256-character code set, used on all of its computers except personal computers, is called Extended Binary Coded Decimal Interchange Code or EBCDIC. (Most people pronounce it eb-suh-dick with a mild accent on the first syllable.) Actually, IBM had already created the EBCDIC code set before ASCII was created. ASCII was created to have a non-proprietary alphabet.

As with ASCII, certain of the characters are consistent wherever EBCDIC is used, but other characters vary depending on the specific communicating devices. In Figure 13-14, the white space can be used differently depending on the EBCDIC dialect in use.

The EBCDIC code set (Figure 13-14). Characters are located by the high-order bits (8 7 6 5) selecting the row and the low-order bits (4 3 2 1) selecting the column.

Bits 8 7 6 5 \ Bits 4 3 2 1	0000	0001	0010	0011	0100	0101	0110	0111	1000	1001	1010	1011	1100	1101	1110	1111
0000	NUL	SOH	STX	ETX	PF	HT	LC	DEL			SMM	VT	FF	CR	SO	SI
0001	DLE	DC1	DC2	DC3	RES	NL	BS	IL	CAN	EM	CC		IFS	IGS	IRS	IUS
0010	DS	SOS	FS		BYP	LF	EOB	PRE			SM			ENQ	ACK	BEL
0011			SYN		PN	RS	UC	EOT					DC4	NAK		SUB
0100	SP										¢	.	<	(	+	|
0101	&										!	$	*	)	;	¬
0110	-	/									|	,	%	_	>	?
0111										`	:	#	@	'	=	"
1000		a	b	c	d	e	f	g	h	i						
1001		j	k	l	m	n	o	p	q	r						
1010		~	s	t	u	v	w	x	y	z						
1011																
1100	{	A	B	C	D	E	F	G	H	I						
1101	}	J	K	L	M	N	O	P	Q	R						
1110	\		S	T	U	V	W	X	Y	Z						
1111	0	1	2	3	4	5	6	7	8	9						

Figure 13-14
The EBCDIC code set

Unicode

Two hundred fifty-six combinations of codes in EBCDIC might seem to be all anyone would need, but consider the requirements of Chinese, which has thousands of characters, or the Cyrillic alphabet, which, although it does not have a terribly large number of characters, does not overlap any of those defined in ASCII or EBCDIC. Another code set, called Unicode, is now being implemented in some products. Unlike the eight-bit extended ASCII and EBCDIC code sets, Unicode uses 16 bits, or two bytes, per character. Although only 1's and 0's are used, this enables up to 65,536 (2 to the 16th power) separate character definitions. Of course, each character takes up as much storage and transmission time as two eight-bit characters, but Unicode is a truly international code set, enabling all peoples to use their own alphabets if they want.

Modulation

How does the transmission process work? How does the data get onto the voice dial-up telephone line? We use a device to change the data. This device, known as a *modem*, changes the data from something a computer understands (numeric bits of information) into something the telephone network understands (analog sine waves or sound). A modem generates a continuous tone, or carrier, and then modifies or modulates it in ways that will be recognized by its partner modem at the other end of the telephone circuit. The modems available to do this come in variations, each one creating a change in a different way.

Remember that the word *modem* is a contraction for *modulation/demodulation*. In order for the communications process to work, we need the same types of modems at each end of the line operating at the same speeds. These modems can use the following types of modulation schemes (or change methods).

Amplitude Modulation (AM)

Amplitude modulation (AM) represents the bits of information (the 1's and 0's) by changing a continuous carrier tone. Figure 13-15 illustrates amplitude modulation. Because the data has only two stages, 1 or 0, you can

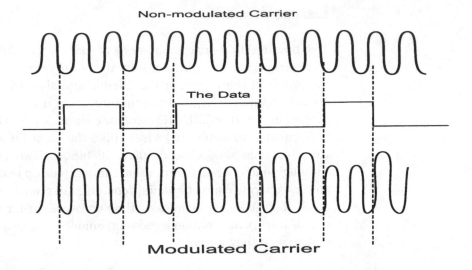

Non-modulated Carrier

The Data

Modulated Carrier

let the continuous carrier tone represent the 0 and the modulated tone represent the 1. This type of modem changes the amplitude (think of amplitude as the height or loudness of the signal). Each change represents a 1 or a 0.

Because this is a 3-kHz analog dial-up telephone line, the maximum amount of changes that can be represented and still be discrete enough to be recognizable to the line and the equipment is about 2,400 per second. This cycle of 2,400 changes per secondis called the *baud rate*. Therefore, the maximum amount of data bits that can be transmitted across the telephone line with AM modulation is 2,400 bits per second. Most amplitude modulation modems were designed to transmit 300 to 1,200 bits per second, although others have been made to go faster.

As we look at the different ways to change the 1's and 0's generated by the computer into their analog equivalents, we have another choice in the process. Voice communication (or human speech itself) is the continuous variation of amplitude and frequencies, so we could choose to use a modem that modulates the frequency instead of the amplitude. An explanation of this type of modem follows.

Frequency Modulation (FM)

Frequency modulation is provided by an FM modem. This modem represents the 1's and 0's as changes in the frequency of a continuous carrier tone. Because we only deal with two states, we can represent the normal

Figure 13-16
The concept of
frequency
modulation (FM) for
data modems

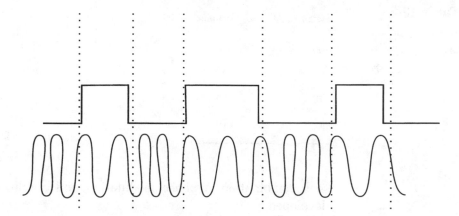

Figure 13-16
The concept of
frequency
modulation (FM) for
data modems

frequency as being a 0 and slow down the continuous carrier frequency when we want to represent a 1 to the telephone line (see Figure 13-16).

The modem uses the same baud rate on the telephone line as the amplitude modulation technique, that being 2,400 baud or discrete changes per second. These modems modulate one bit of information per cycle change per second, or a maximum of 2,400 bits per second. Note that the baud rate and the bits per second rate are somewhat symmetrical.

Although both AM and FM modems are designed around what was once considered pretty fast transmission rates, we have continually been unsatisfied with any rate of speed developed. We want more and more, faster and faster, and throughput is expensive under the old dial-up telephone network. Therefore, we asked for additional speed to get more throughput and less cost. The engineers came up with a new process that modulates on the basis of phases.

Phase Modulation

If we can change the phase of the sine wave as it is introduced to the line, at positions of 0, 90, 180, and 270 degrees, we can encode the data with more than one bit of information at a time. A phase modulation technique enables us to transmit a di-bit of information per signaling-state change. This gives us 4,800 bits per second of throughput. The di-bit represents the information as shown in Table 13-8.

As you can see, two bits of information at 2,400 baud gives us the 4,800 bits per second. This is a step in the right direction, but we wanted more,

Table 13-8

The Four Phases in
Phase Modulation
Cause a 90° Shift
When a Di-Bit
Is Received

Bits	Phase
00	0
01	90
10	180
11	270

so a combination of phase modulation and amplitude modulation was developed.

QAM

Called quadrature with amplitude modulation (QAM), this combination enables us to use up to 16 possible steps of phase and amplitude modulation. QAM is mostly used with four bits of information per baud rate, thereby producing 9,600 bits per second of throughput across an analog telephone line. Theoretically, the system should be able to produce 38,400 bits per second of information (four phases at four bits per phase at 2,400 baud equals 38,400 bits per second).

However, in practice, line rates can rarely support sustained throughput across the telephone network at this speed. Also, the telco limits the bandwidth to 3 kHz, and we use 2,400 baud. If we try to send more data at a higher baud rate, the band limitation (bandpass filters) will strip the frequencies that go beyond the filters. This is a function of the telco equipment on the line at the CO. Thus, we usually have to settle for an analog data transmission at slower speeds.

The driving force behind improving modulation techniques has always been to increase the speed possible over an analog circuit. Why? In addition to the obvious reason (accomplishing the task more quickly improves productivity), the cost of communications over dial circuits is directly proportional to the amount of time those circuits are in use; going faster saves money. When the absolute best available modulation technology is in use, however, one has not yet necessarily squeezed the absolute best transmission volumes out of a circuit. One can push it even further by using compression.

V.90 Modems

Practically all new PCs and laptop computers sold today have a new modem integral to them. The use of modem technology has become commonplace. However, as modems have dropped in price, the ability to go faster has increased. Today, the new modem technology is asymmetrical in that it transmits at one speed and receives data back at a different rate.

The world has been looking for better ways of moving data but had to deal with the limits of the wires in the local loop. Over the decades, the cost of modems has dropped, while the ability to move the data was going in an upward fashion. Something had to be done because the amount of data we were moving was escalating exponentially. Enter the 56 Kbps modem (V.90 standard), which operates at a 33.6-Kbps transmit rate and a 56-Kbps receive rate.

The rated speeds can be misnomers because in North America the FCC and the Canadian CRTC limit the speed that a telco can offer to a customer to no greater than 53 Kbps. The rate was selected years ago when we were still trying to drive modem communications at 9.6 Kbps. So, the arbitrary decision was something that no one ever thought would occur. Alas, here we are with a modem that can achieve 56 Kbps and the regulators have capped it.

Moreover, the asymmetrical rate of speed facilitates access to one of the most commonly used networks today, the Internet. The 56-Kbps modem works well because the user has little data to send (typing **www.tcic.com**, for example, requires very little data) but lots to receive (a Web page can be millions of bytes large). So, the different speeds enable dial-up communications on a telephone company circuit (a voice channel) in one direction and a digital-access method for the return path at a much higher rate of speed.

Typically, however, when a user accesses the network with these modems, they will transmit between 28.8 and 33.6 Kbps upline and receive approximately between 38 and 45 Kbps downstream. One can get a slightly better response from the 56-Kbps modem, but limitations still must be dealt with.

Let's put all this in perspective though. In the early 1980s, we were transmitting data between 4,800 and 7,200 bps, and the modems were expensive (hundreds to thousands of dollars at the time). Here, in a mere decade, we have achieved quantum leaps in technological advancements, and we have seen the cost drop exponentially to a few dollars. What we can expect is faster and better, but cheaper, through the new millennium.

Devices

DTE versus DCE

A basic of data communications is that every communicating device is either a terminal-type device (data terminal equipment, or DTE, also referred to as data circuit terminating equipment, or DCTE) or a communications-type device (data communications equipment, or DCE). DTEs use communications facilities; their primary functions lie elsewhere. DCEs provide access or even implement communications facilities. Their only role is moving information.

You might presume that some cosmic requirement is satisfied by this overall categorization, but in fact the nitty-gritty reality of cabled communications is the primary cause of this division. Although we will get into cabling standards later, consider the following situation.

Two devices, A and B, must be connected. The connection will be via two wires, numbered one and two. Let's assign wire number one to transmit the data, and number two to receive. But wait! If A transmits on number one, and B also transmits on number one, and if they both receive on number two, neither will listen to what the other is sending. It would be as though two people each spoke into opposite ends of the same tube at the same time, with neither putting the end to his or her ear.

The solution seems simple: Have A transmit on wire one, B listen on wire one, A listen on wire two, and B transmit on wire two. But now let us introduce device C. How should C be built? If it is configured as is A, it cannot communicate with A. If it is configured as is B, it cannot communicate with B.

Devices are not configured at random, however. For example, terminals do not usually connect directly to terminals, printers are never connected directly to printers, and so on. Perhaps if one broad category of devices usually connects not to another in that category, but rather to a device in another category, we could standardize on only two default configurations. This is what was done with DTEs and DCEs.

Categories and Examples of DTEs

The grouping is not perfect. Some devices routinely connect to both DTEs and DCEs (such as multiplexers). Such devices do not clearly fall into either category and must be configured depending on the specific installation requirements, but for the most part, any data-processing device that can communicate falls cleanly into one of these two categories. Most of the devices covered in this book are DCE devices.

Here are some examples of the DTE devices to which we provide data communications services:

- Computers (mainframe, mini, midi)
- Terminals (CRTs, VDT, teletype)
- Printers (laser, line, dot matrix)
- Specialized (bar code readers, optical character recognition)
- Transactional (point-of-sale equipment, automated tellers)
- Intelligent (personal computers)

The remainder of this section will focus on DCEs and ways of connecting components.

Questions

1. The use of data communications is growing at three to four percent per year.   T/F

2. The voice networks are actually paying the fare for the data networks.   T/F

3. Voice communications amount to approximately _____ percent of the revenue in 2001.

4. When we want to start the communications process, we follow these seven steps:

   a.

   b.

   c.

   d.

   e.

   f.

   g.

5. When we transmit, we can send the data either in time or out of time, which is called:

   a. Transmit and receive

   b. Synchronous and Asynchronous

   c. STDM

   d. Timing the data sequence

6. The main reason we check the data for errors is because we want to get $1,000,000.   T/F _____

7. Data transmission can be classified as either _____ or lossless.

8. The two most common alphabets we use today are _____ and _____.

9. Using the ASCII code set, we can get 256 combinations of 1's and 0's.   T/F

10. How many combinations will we get with the IBM code set?

   _____

11. The four main forms of multiplexing are _____, _____, _____ and _____.

12. The modem is called the DTE.   T/F

13. How many bits does it take to create a byte?

   a. 7

   b. 8

   c. 5

   d. Alphabet (codeset) dependent

14. What is the baud rate of a 33,600-bps modem?
    a. 33,600
    b. 56,000
    c. 24,000
    d. 2,400

15. When we use an FM modem, we typically transmit data at _____ bps.

16. The two ways to get more data on the circuit is to use:
    a. Compression and code sets
    b. Multiplexing and demultiplexing
    c. Compression and rarefaction
    d. Compression and multiplexing

17. The two different forms of standards used today are:
    a. IBM and DEC
    b. De jure and de facto
    c. Telco and computer manufacturers
    d. National and international

18. When transmitting at greater than 2,400 bps, all data transmissions are sent asynchronously.   T/F

19. The standard typewriter keyboard is called _____ because of the position of the keys on the keyboard.

20. Computers, printers, or cash registers are examples of types of:
    a. DCE
    b. Mux
    c. DTE
    d. Code sets

T1 and the T Carrier

After reading this chapter and completing the questions, you will be able to:

- Explain the implementation of the T Carrier system.
- Discuss the differences between the analog and digital systems to carry the voice and data.
- Describe the framing and formatting of a T1.
- Explain why the digital transmission protocols have differences.
- Converse about the use of ESF and SF protocols.

Evolution of the T-Carrier System

In the early 1960s, the Bell System began to introduce and use a new digital technology in the network. This was necessary because the older carrier and cabling systems were rapidly becoming strained for capacity. The demand for newer and higher-speed communications facilities was building among customers as well as within the systems themselves.

When this digital technology was being introduced, it was deployed in the public network as a means of increasing the traffic capacity within the telephone company on the existing wire-pair cable facilities as interoffice trunks. The older systems, including the N-carrier system, used a two- or four-wire connection through an analog multiplexing device to deliver either 12 or 24 analog channels. This was still an inefficient use of the line capacity; and the analog service was noisy and required expensive line-treatment equipment. Therefore, the telephone company introduced its newer technology to overcome the limitations of the existing plant and transmission services.

Some of the problems with the analog systems were also related to the circuit quality. Anyone who can remember the older analog network knows that a call placed across the country from East to West Coast was significantly different than such a call made today. The static and noise on the line made the call sound more like it went to the moon and back. Because that's all that was available, that's what the user became accustomed to.

The use of older analog systems was ending within the telephone company networks. The telcos had to find a way of improving the utilization of the cable plant on an interoffice basis to overcome problems with underutilized pairs of wires; and the continued installation of inefficient systems was expensive and bulky. The average length of the wires between the telcos' offices was approximately 6.5 miles. As calling requirements continued to grow, the telcos needed to increase the traffic-handling capacity on these interoffice routes. They were in a quandary, however. First, they didn't want to continue running bulky cables between offices because there simply wasn't enough space. Second, costs for maintaining the cable plant were escalating. Something had to be done quickly. Figure 14-1 shows the use of wires between the telco offices. These wires provide the interoffice communications from telco to telco. The end user or customer was kept on the old analog twisted pairs of wire. From a user's perspective the changes were invisible, except that some improvement in call quality was evident.

Analog Transmission Basics

Before going much further, it would be prudent to furnish a brief description of the dial-up telephone network to aid in understanding the need for the digital architecture that was introduced through the use of the T-carrier system. The telephone system was designed around providing analog dial-up voice telephony. Everything was based on voice communications services on a switched (non-dedicated) basis. A user could connect his or her own telephone to that of another user on the network through either an operator-connected or dial-up (a later evolution) addressing scheme.

Figure 14-1
Bell used high-
capacity services
between its offices.
Users were still kept
on twisted-pair
analog.

Because voice is the primary service provided, the telephone set (see Figure 14-2) has evolved into a device that takes the sound wave from the human vocal cords and converts that sound into an electrical current, represented by its analog equivalent. The human voice produces constantly changing variables of both amplitude (the height of the wave) and frequency (the number of cycle changes per second). As these constantly changing variables of amplitude and frequency are produced, the telephone set converts the sound pressure into an equivalent electrical wave. This electrical energy will be carried down a pair of wires. As the electrical energy is introduced into the wires (using twisted pairs of copper for this reference) certain characteristics begin to work on it. First, resistance occurs on the wire, impeding the flow of electricity and reducing the strength of the created signal. Second, the wires act as an antenna, drawing in noise (such as static, cross talk, or electricity from other conversations on wire pairs adjacent to yours, and so on). This loss of signal strength coupled with the introduced noise continues to distort the signal.

To overcome these problems, analog amplifiers are used to boost the signal strength back up to its original value. The amplifiers are normally

Figure 14-2
A representation of
the analog wave
being created

Figure 14-2
A representation of
the analog wave
being created

placed on circuits greater than 18,000 to 20,000 feet in length. Figure 14-3 shows how the electrical signal on the wires is attenuated or weakened. As the signal is boosted back to its original strength, the noise begins to accumulate, causing further distortion of the call. Figure 14-4 represents the analog amplifier on the line boosting up the signal. To overcome the loss on the line and to ensure that the signal gets to the other end, the telcos used analog amplifiers. These amplifiers were used on circuits to increase the strength of the analog transmission. However, they were prone to failures and had other qualities that were undesirable. Figure 14-5 is a representation of the problem encountered with the amplification process. As the sig-

Figure 14-3
As the electrical
signal is introduced,
attenuation begins
immediately. If the
signal must travel
great distances, it
could run out of
strength and
disappear.

Figure 14-4
As the signal gets weak, the telco uses analog amplifiers to boost the signal and keep going.

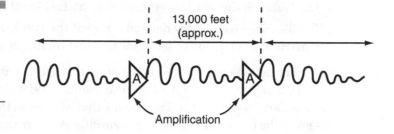

Figure 14-5
As the signal and noise are amplified, the noise takes on a cumulative effect until the transmission becomes virtually useless.

nal is amplified, the signal and all the noise on the wires are amplified together. This does enable the signal to travel further, but after each amplification process, noise also accumulates. A good deal of the problem stems from the fact that the amplifier can't distinguish the analog signal from the noise; therefore, it amplifies everything.

The Evolution to Digital

The T-carrier system was developed to cope with these amplification problems. The telcos were looking to enhance the quality of calls and better utilize the cable facilities. The T-carrier system allowed them to increase the call-carrying capacity while taking advantage of the unused transmission capacity of their existing wire pair facilities and to improve the quality of transmission by migrating away from the older analog techniques. The evolution to T-carrier was important for a number of reasons:

■ It was the first successful system designed to utilize digitized voice transmission.

■ It identified many of the standards that are employed today for digital switching and digital transmission, including a modulation technique.

- The transmission rate was established at 1,544,000 bits per second.
- The T-carrier technology defined many of the rules, or protocols, and constraints in use today for other types of communications.

As mentioned earlier, the analog transmission capabilities were inefficient. In many cases, the telephone companies used a single pair of twisted wires to carry a phone call. This meant that as uses of the interoffice facilities grew, the cable plant grew exponentially. As more central offices (or end offices) were added, the need for meshing these together grew. Interconnecting each office with enough pairs of wire to service user demands was becoming a nightmare. Figure 14-6 depicts the need for cabling or interoffice trunking to support the growing demand for services. As each new end office was added, the wiring systems had to grow to serve customer demands.

Remember that the telephone companies saw this carrier system as a telco service only. Even as the end user population grew, the telcos still held

Figure 14-6
As more central offices were added to the network, the need for wires grew exponentially.

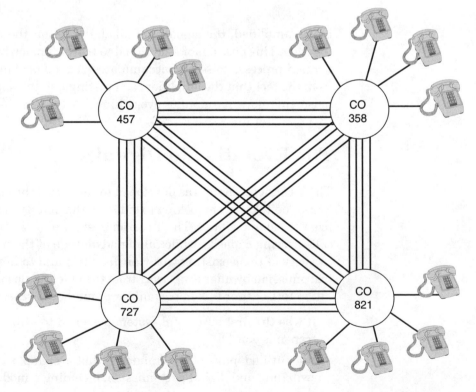

back on deploying this digital capability to the end user. The telcos used the higher efficiencies to support the end user digitally, from end office to end office or through the network. The user was still relegated to a single conversation on a twisted pair using analog transmission. Thus, this system operated in an analog format on the local loop, but digitally on the interoffice trunks (IOTs). In metropolitan areas, the telcos were reaping the benefits of the T-carrier system. Figure 14-7 is a representation of the telephone company deployment of analog/digital transmission capacities.

Some immediate benefits were achieved: The quality of transmission improved dramatically, and the utilization of existing wire facilities increased. A single four-wire facility on twisted wires could now carry 24 simultaneous conversations digitally at an aggregated rate of 1.544 Mbps.

As digital switching systems were introduced into the dial telephone network, they were designed around the same techniques employed in the T-carrier system. The digital switching matrices of the #4 and #5 electronic switching systems (ESSs) developed by Western Electric (now called Avaya) and the DMS systems (10, 100, and 250) developed by Northern Telecom, Inc. (now called Nortel Networks) utilize pulse code modulation (PCM)

Figure 14-7
The telephone companies reaped the benefits of interoffice trunking, using digital transmission.

internally, so that digital carrier systems and channels can be interfaced directly into the digital switching systems. By adhering to the standards set forth, the operating telephone companies and the long-haul carriers could build integrated digital switching and digital transmission systems that

- Eliminated the need to terminate the digital channels or equipment to provide analog interfaces to digital switching architectures.

- Avoided the addition of quantizing noise that would be introduced by another digital-to-analog conversion process. Whenever a conversion of the signal from analog to digital or from digital to analog is necessary, the risk of errors and noise increases.

These techniques were used to provide lower-cost, better-quality dial-up telephone services. However, this same technology underlies the idea of full end-to-end digital networking services that is the basis of integrated services digital networks (ISDN), the future and the higher-end broadband services that are emerging.

Analog-to-Digital Conversion

Prior to covering the T-carrier fundamentals, it would be appropriate to discuss the analog-to-digital conversion process. Digital architecture dictates the use of a digital bit stream; therefore, the analog wave must be converted into a useable format. Digital pulses are represented by a 0 or a 1. As the analog signal is being transmitted to the network, it must be converted from a wave of varying amplitudes and frequencies to a digital format of 1's and 0's (or presence and absence of voltage).

The analog wave must be sampled often enough and converted to create a stream of 1's and 0's that is precise enough to be re-created at the distant end, producing a signal that sounds like the original conversation. According to the Nyquist rule, a digital signal is created by sampling the analog wave at twice the highest frequency on the line. For an analog circuit, delivered by the local telephone company, the frequency range on a twisted pair of wires is represented in hertz (Hz). To maximize the utilization of the older carrier systems, the telcos delivered a usable bandwidth of 3,000 Hz (3 kHz), as compared to the 4,000 Hz (4 kHz) capable of being carried on the line. The difference between the 3-kHz and 4-kHz services is in how the line is filtered. The human voice produces understandable information in the range of 300 to 3,300 frequency changes per second. Therefore, the telcos knew that all they had to provide to the user was 3 kHz of usable bandwidth. But for separation between conversations and to minimize cross talk and other interference, they allocated 4 kHz per analog line. Using Nyquist's rule, the sampling of an analog wave at twice the maximum frequency of the line meant that a minimum of 6,600 samples per second should be sufficient to re-create the wave for the digital-to-analog and analog-to-digital conversion. However, to produce the quality of the higher range of frequencies of the human voice, the number of samples is rounded up to 8,000 per second.

The sample now had to be created into a bit stream of 1's and 0's, as already stated. To represent the true tone and inflection of the human voice, enough bits need to be used to create a digital word. Using an 8-bit word creates enough different points on a wave to do just that. The wave is divided into 256 possible amplitude combinations at the moment of the sample itself. Figure 14-8 shows how the sampling is accomplished using two states and 8 bits to create 2^8 or 256 points on the analog wave. As each sample is taken, the amplitude of the wave is sampled.

Once the sample has been taken and the digital equivalent created into an 8-bit word, the digital (or square) wave can be transmitted. The

Figure 14-8
With 256 possible points being samples, the quality of the digital transmission, when converted back to analog, should be exact.

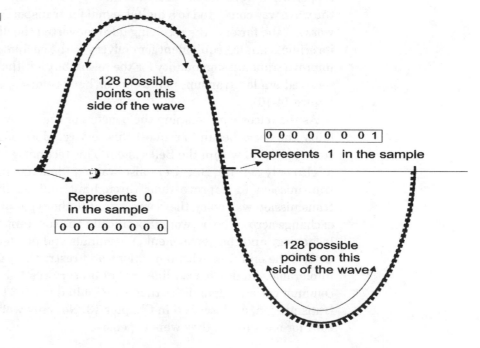

128 possible points on this side of the wave

0 0 0 0 0 0 0 1
Represents 1 in the sample

Represents 0 in the sample
0 0 0 0 0 0 0 0

128 possible points on this side of the wave

Figure 14-9
A sampling of the
analog wave yields a
transmission of 8 bits
in a stream. Two
pulses (voltages) are
required in this
sample in the sixth
and eighth positions.

Figure 14-9
A sampling of the
analog wave yields a
transmission of 8 bits
in a stream. Two
pulses (voltages) are
required in this
sample in the sixth
and eighth positions.

1 represents the presence of a voltage and the 0 represents the absence of a voltage (see Figure 14-9).

This conversion uses pulse code modulation (PCM) to create the sample. Using PCM and the rules established, the transmission of the digital equivalent of the analog wave results in 8,000 samples per second × 8 bits per sample = 64,000 bits per second as the basis for a voice transmission in PCM mode. Whether the end user transmitted voice, data, or facsimile, the copper wires were used to carry the analog wave to the central office, where the wave was converted to a digital signal for transport across the telco network. At the far end, the receiving telco converted the digital signal back to its original analog equivalent for delivery to the customer. All this served to improve transmission quality for the telcos, but left the customer, who still received analog transmission to his or her premises, out in the cold (see Figure 14-10).

As the telcos were reaping the benefits of their new transmission capability, the users began to request this service. More user demands created some upheaval within the Bell system. This technology was perceived to be a telco-only service. But users also wanted (demanded) end-to-end digital transmission to improve their throughput and quality. Because analog transmission was noisy, there was a limit to the types of signals users could exchange across the network. Specifically, the constant growth in computer technology and the deployment of terminals and printers around the country left the end user with limitations and restrictions that were becoming intolerable. Analog leased line or dial-up services left the user with data communications capabilities that were limited to a 9.6 to 19.2 Kbps (leased) transmission, as described in Chapter 13. Not only were these services too slow for most users, they were expensive.

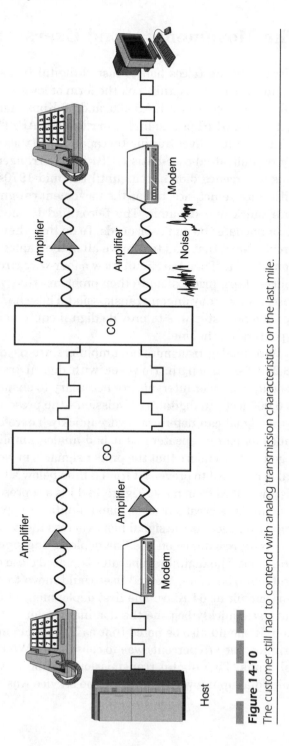

Figure 14-10

The customer still had to contend with analog transmission characteristics on the last mile.

The Movement to End Users

Ultimately, the telcos had to install digital transmission to the customer premises. Originally, this took the form of lower-speed digital data services (DDSs) at speeds of 2.4, 4.8, 9.6, and 56 Kbps digital. Newer introductions added 19.2-64 Kbps and high-capacity (HICAP) T1 services at 1.544 Mbps.

In order to deliver this digital capability to the customer, a special assembly or individual-case-basis (ICB) tariff arrangement was initially used. This emergence didn't occur until the mid-1970s. At first, this was done with some reluctance, but as the movement caught on, the deployment was both quick and dynamic. The telcos had to modify the outside plant to accommodate the end user needs. To do this, they first had to engineer the circuit. Next, they had to remove all of the analog transmission equipment from the line. Then the circuit (now a four-wire circuit) had to be checked for splices, taps, bridges, and other problems that would introduce loss and noise and thereby impair transmission. These had to be removed or cleaned up. The next step was to provide digital equipment, called regenerators or repeaters, on the line.

With analog transmission, amplifiers are used on circuits greater than 18,000 feet in length. However, with digital transmission, repeaters are used at whatever intervals are necessary to ensure quality (typically 2,000 to 6,000 feet). In digital transmission—the presence or absence of a voltage—the signal can deteriorate very quickly. Therefore, the telco needed four times as many repeaters as it had analog amplifiers. These repeaters or regenerators ensure that the proper signal is moved across the line. The signal is repeated to prevent it from falling below a threshold where it can't be distinguished from noise. Figure 14-11 is a representation of how the signal is actually re-created rather than amplified to produce the quality we have come to expect. As the signal moves across the wires, the same problems are inherent; resistance on the line depletes the signal strength, and noise is prevalent. The digital regenerator is placed close enough to get around this problem. Therefore, the end user could move to an effective use of a four-wire circuit at 64 Kbps. The first deployment of this service was for voice, but data quickly became the dominant rider of the new digital transmission. It should also be noted that as T1 became more readily available, the primary use (75 percent) was to consolidate WATS lines onto a single digital trunk. This digital transmission capability was designed around the voice dial-up network; therefore, the service was a natural fit.

Figure 14-11
A representation of
how the signal is
re-created.

T1 Basics

T1 is characterized by the following operating characteristics.

A Four-Wire Circuit Because this technology evolved from the old twisted-pair environment, four wires were used. Two wires are used to transmit and two are used to receive. Other facilities can be used, but for now, think of it this way.

Full Duplex Transmission and reception can take place simultaneously. Many customers derive other uses, such as one way only for remote printing, file transfer, and so on, or two way for alternate service such as voice communications.

Digital This is an all-digital service. Data, analog facsimile, and analog voice and the like are all converted to digital pulses (1's and 0's) for transmission on the line.

Time-Division Multiplexing The digital stream is capable of carrying a standard 64-Kbps channel; 24 channels are multiplexed to create an aggregate of 1.536 Mbps. Time division enables a channel to use a slot 1/24 of the time. These can be fixed time slots made available to the channel.

Pulse Code Modulation   Using the example, the analog voice or other signal is sampled 8,000 times per second; an 8-bit word is used to represent each sample, thus yielding the 64 Kbps channel capacity.

Framed Format   As the pulse code modulation scheme is used, the 24 channels are time-division multiplexed into a frame to be carried along the line. Each frame represents one sample of 8 bits from each of the 24 channels. Added to this is a framing bit. The net result is a frame of 193 bits. There are 8,000 frames per second; therefore, a frame is 125 microseconds long. Framing accounts for 8 Kbps overhead (1 bit × 8,000 frames). Adding this 8 Kbps to the 1.536 Mbps discussed in the paragraph on time-division multiplexing yields an aggregate of 1.544 Mbps.

Bipolar Format   T1 uses electrical voltage across the line to represent the pulses (1's). The bipolar format serves two purposes. It reduces the required bandwidth from 1.5 MHz to 772 kHz, which increases repeater spacing. And the signal voltage averages out to zero, allowing direct current (dc) power to be simplexed on the line to power intermediate regenerators. Think of it as an alternating current (ac) version of a dc line. Every other pulse will be represented by the negative equivalent of the pulse. For example: The first pulse will be represented by a positive 3 V (+3 V), the next pulse will be represented by a negative 3 V (−3 V), and so on. This effectively yields a 0 voltage on the line, because the+−+−equalizes the current. This bipolar format is also called *alternate mark inversion* (AMI). The mark is a digital 1. Alternate marks are inverted in polarity (+,−).

Byte-Synchronous Transmission   Each sample is made up of 8 bits from each channel. Timing for the channels is derived from the pulses that appear within the samples. This timing keeps everything in sequence. If the devices on both ends of the line do not see any pulses, they lose track of where they were (temporary amnesia). This means that the T1 will be synchronous unto itself, but not to others. When using the T1 as the basis of other higher multiplexing schemes (like T2 and T3), this is important to remember. The timing is derived from the pulses on the specific link, so the link is timed to itself. If one needs to multiplex into higher-speed services, additional stuffing bits may have to be added to get the individual T1s timed to each other.

Channelized or Nonchannelized   Generically, T1 is 24 channels of 64 Kbps each, plus 8 Kbps of overhead. This is considered channelized service.

However, the newer multiplexing equipment can be configured in a number of ways. For example, the T1 can be used as a single channel of 1.536 Mbps (such as for a router connection to the WAN); or two high-speed data channels at 384 Kbps each and a video channel at 768 Kbps. These examples can be mixed into a variety of offerings. The point is that the service does not have to be configured in 24 channels, but can be nonchannelized into any usable data stream needed (equipment allowing, of course).

Any other suitable medium (fiber, digital microwave, coax, and so on) can also be used. The T1 is still treated as a four-wire circuit. When the other media forms are used, the T1 will be suitably taken from the transmission mode and converted back to the appropriate interface. For a four-wire circuit, the carrier will normally terminate the four wires into a demarcation point (DEMARC) or network interface unit (NIU). Individual circuits can be terminated into a recommended jack—RJ-48 (sometimes called dumb jacks) or RJ-68 (called smart jacks). These jacks serve as the interface to the four wires. In a larger environment or where multiple circuits are involved, other methods of termination can be used.

For example, an RJ-2IX or a BIX block can be used for terminating a T1 on a main distribution frame in a customer location. From the RJ-48, a cable (using a subminiature 15-pin DIN connector) will be extended to the customer premises equipment (CPE). Usually, the CPE is a channel service unit (CSU). Figure 14-12 is a representation of the connection from central office to CPE.

The customer premises equipment uses time-division multiplexing to carry the multiple voice and data conversation across the line. Time-division multiplexing is somewhat efficient in that it allows time slots to be dedicated to each of the conversations to be carried on the line. Using this fixed time slot, a conversation will be in the same bucket (or slot) at each sample time.

Remember that the equipment using the Nyquist rule operates at twice the highest frequency of the line. Therefore each individual conversation is sampled 8,000 times per second. Twenty four (typical) paths are being simultaneously multiplexed onto the T1. Each of these paths therefore carries one sample (1/8,000 of a second) of voice, data, fax, video, and so on.

The time slot is always present, and if no traffic is being generated between points across the line, the time slot goes unused. The slot is empty. For this reason, time-division multiplexing is inefficient. Attempts to get the most amount of service from a T1 would be thwarted because of the fixed time slot problem. Figure 14-13 is a representation of this time-division multiplexing (TDM or Mux) scheme.

Figure 14-12
A representation of a four-wire circuit terminating into an RJ-48. This is probably the most common method of delivery. The RJ-48 is an eight-conductor modular jack.

Customer Premises Equipment

Figure 14-13
The time-division multiplexing scheme

Framed Format T1 uses some very specific conventions to transmit information between both ends. One of these is a framing sequence that formats the samples of voice or data transmission. It's easy to think of a frame in terms of the 8-bit samples of the 24 channels being strung together in a logical sequence. After the 192 bits of information are compiled, a framing bit is added, creating a frame of 193 bits of information.

The framing bit can be equated to a pointer or address. Because the line is moving bits of information at 1,544,000 per second, it would be very easy to skew left or right and get information out of sequence. Therefore, the extra 8,000 bits of information (1 bit per frame, 8,000 frames per second) create a locator for the equipment to lock in on. This pointer allows the devices to read a pattern of bits in order to know which frame is being received or transmitted, and the location of each channel thereafter.

Framing has undergone several evolutions over the years. The first use of T1 service was for voice, so the information was easier to use. The evolution of framing followed a sequence as outlined in Table 14-1.

The D4 superframe uses a framing pattern for voice and data. The framing pattern in the D4 superframe is a repeating 12-bit sequence (1000 1101 1100) that allows signaling bits to be "robbed" in the 6th and 12th frames of the superframe. The 8th bit from each sample in frames 6 and 12 is used to provide signaling. This pattern of the framing format is shown in Figure 14-14.

Table 14-1

Framing Evolution

Framing	Use	Pattern/Use
D1	Voice or analog data	Alternating 1's and 0's
D2	Voice or analog data	12-frame sequence Superframe
D1D	Voice or analog data	Upgrade compatibility for D1
D3	Voice or analog data	Superframe format and sequence bits
D4	Voice and data (digital)	Superframe
D5*	Voice and data (digital)	Superframe
ESF	Voice and data plus maintenance	Extended Superframe (ESF)

*D5 really doesn't exist as a standard. However, in the electronic switching systems, this framing was termed a software version of the D4 format.

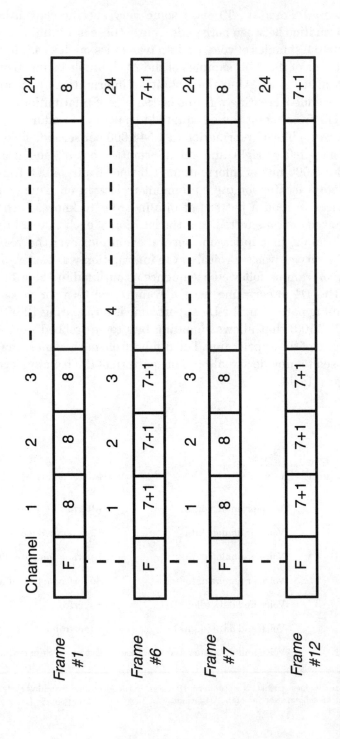

Figure 14-14
The robbed bit signaling framed format

Table 14-2

Superframe
Format, 6th and
12th Frames Used
to Denote the
Presence of
Signaling Bits

| Frame | Bit | Framing Bits | | Bit Use in Each Time Slot | | Signaling Bit Use Options | |
		Term Frame F1	Sig Frame F1	Traffic (All Channels)	Sig	T	Signaling Channel
1	0	1	—	1–8	—		
2	193	—	0	1–8	—		
3	386	0	—	1–8	—		
4	579	—	0	1–8	—		
5	772	1	—	1–8	—		
6	965	—	1	1–7	8	—	A
7	1158	0	—	1–8	—		
8	1351	—	1	1–8	—		
9	1544	1	—	1–8	—		
10	1737	—	1	1–8	—		
11	1930	0	—	1–8	—		
12	2123	—	0	1–7	8	—	B

Table 14-2 shows the actual framing of a data stream in the D4 framing format. The framing bit pattern repeats every 12 frames. Twelve frames make up a superframe.

Once again, this requires each of the 24 channels to be robbed of the least significant bit (LCB) in the 6th and 12th frames. This has an impact on the data capacity that always limits the user to 56 Kbps of effective throughput (resulting in a net overhead of 192 Kbps given up to provide signaling).

Bipolar When encoding the voice and data streams onto a digital circuit (the T1), as mentioned earlier, up to 1,544,000 bits of information can be transmitted. The 1's show the presence of a voltage, and are represented by 3 V per pulse.

As a result, the bipolar concept was introduced. The first pulse (a 1) is represented by 3 V positive, followed by the next pulse, which is represented by 3 V negative. This would serve to bring the overall line voltage down to zero. Figure 14-15 is a representation of the voltage/pulses on the line. Bipolar encoding does the following things:

- Reduces the bandwidth necessary for transmission from 1.5 to 0.772 MHz.

- Allows the use of isolation transformers for inexpensive connections.

- Allows simplexed dc voltage to power intermediate repeaters. This can be as much as + and − 130 volts.

Byte Synchronous   When transmitting on the T1, timing and synchronization come from the bits transmitted. Because each sample is made up of 8 bits, a byte is formed. The transmitters and receivers synchronize on the basis of the pulses in the byte format. If a string of 0's is transmitted in several frames, then synchronization is lost; the devices get amnesia as to where they were. Consequently, conventions on the transmission of the byte were established. These conventions are called the 1's density rule. What this means is that in order to maintain synchronization, a certain amount of 1's must be present.

For voice communication this doesn't pose a problem, because the voice generates a continuous change in amplitude voltages which, when encoded into an 8-bit word (byte), displays the presence of voltage (1's). However, in data transmission, strings of 0's are possible (even probable) when refreshing or painting screens of information. Hence the 1's density rule comes into play.

Simply put, the 1's density rule states that in every 24 bits of information to be transmitted, there must be at least three pulses (1's), and that no more than 15 0's can be transmitted consecutively. A more stringent requirement set by AT&T in the implementation of their digital transmission was that in every 8 bits of information, at least one pulse (1) must be present.

Think of how this affects data transmission. If your data must have at least one pulse per byte, you have to change the way you deliver data to the line. A technique known as pulse stuffing is used to meet these conventions. The 8th bit in every byte was stuffed with a 1. This limited the data transmission rate to 56 Kbps, because 7 usable bits plus a stuff bit had to be transmitted. The end receiving equipment will receive 00000001 and not be able to tell if we sent 00000001 or if we sent 00000000 and the last bit was forced to a 1 for timing purposes. Because of this rule, we cannot trust the eighth bit, so we relegate ourselves to using 7 bits for data and the eighth bit for timing, all the time. Figure 14-16 is a representation of the 1's density rule and pulse stuffing.

To overcome this bit stuffing, yet meet the 1's density requirement, a technique was developed. This is known as bipolar eight 0 substitution (B8ZS—pronounced bates). At the customer location, B8ZS is implemented in the channel service unit (CSU). As data bits are delivered to the CSU for transmission across the line, the CSU (a microprocessor-controlled device) reads the 8-bit format. Immediately recognizing that a string of 8/16/24 zeros will cause problems, it strips off the 8-bit byte and substitutes a fictitious byte.

- Eight 0's are stripped off the data stream and discarded.
- The CSU then inserts a substitute word (byte) of 00011011.

However, to let the receiving end know this is a substitute word and not real data, two violations to the bipolar or AMI convention are created. Remember that the bipolar convention states that alternating voltages will be used for the pulses.

Figure 14-16
When strings of 0's must be transmitted, a 1 is stuffed into the eighth position (LSB). This yields a 56-Kbps throughput on the line.

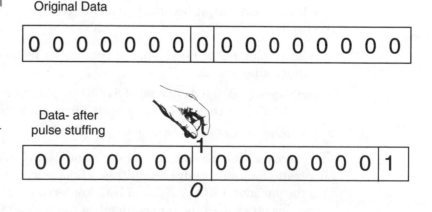

Original Data

| 0 0 0 0 0 0 0 | 0 0 0 0 0 0 0 0 |

Data- after pulse stuffing

| 0 0 0 0 0 0 0 | 0 0 0 0 0 0 0 1 |

In the fourth and seventh positions, violations will be created that act as flags to the receiver that something is wrong. See Figure 14-17 for a graphic representation of this substitution.

Channelized versus Nonchannelized   Up to now, discussions have focused on using the T1 for 24-channel capacity at 64 Kbps per channel. For the average user, this was the norm. However, as newer uses for the T1 service became evident, it became possible to configure the capacity to meet the need:

- A single channel of 1.536 Mbps is possible for point-to-point video conferencing.
- High-speed data on a channel of 512 Kbps, plus 16 channels of lower-speed data and voice at 64 Kbps each, are possible needs.
- Any other mix of services might be required.

To accommodate the mix of needs, the end user (CPE) equipment can be superrate or subrate multiplexed. This is fine, except that you must ensure that the provider (LEC, CLEC, and IEC) knows you are using the service for something other than the conventional 24 channels at 64 Kbps.

If confusion exists, the carrier or provider could do some reconfiguring in the network (at its end) that could literally disrupt service for the throughput being used. Consider what would happen if a 512-Kbps data channel were somehow rerouted through a telco office and then brought back and forced into a single 64-Kbps channel. This obviously would not work. Hence, all parties should know what uses are being made of the transmission capacity.

Digital Capacities

One of the by-products of the T-carrier system was that the transmission rate employed became the standard building block for a multiplexing hierarchy. In high-speed digital transmission systems, a carrier combines many lower-speed signals into an aggregate signal for transport. To simplify this process and to hold the line on the costs of equipment, standard rates were defined.

Each of the transmission rates was assigned a number that identified the rate and configuration for the signal. Each time a higher speed is created, the lower speeds are combined and extra bits (bit stuffing) are added to come up to the signaling rate. These extra bits allow the equipment (multiplexers) to compensate for distances, clocking, and so forth, which cause transmission delay cycles.

The designations for the digital transmission are called digital signal level X (DS-x). Many times people will transpose or intersperse these designators. For example, a T1 is often referred to as a DS1 in the industry. To clarify this point, T1 is the first level of the T-carrier system. It is physical components such as the wires, plugs and jacks, repeaters, and so forth. These physical devices combine to create the T1. DS1 is the multiplexed digital signal, first level, carried inside the T-carrier. The DS1 is the electrical signal (the pulses) running on the T1.

The digital hierarchy for North America includes the following:

DS0 Although originally not a formally defined rate, the DS0 is a 64-Kbps signal that makes up the basis for the DS1. Twenty four DS0s combined produce the DS1. The standard 64-Kbps pulse-coded modulation (PCM) signal is the basis for all of the future networks employing digital signaling. Included in this is the integrated service digital network (ISDN).

DS1 The digital signal level 1 is a time-division multiplexed (TDM) pulse-code modulation aggregate of 1.544 Mbps, regardless of the medium used to carry the signal. The physical side of this capacity is called the T1. Comparative costing for a T1 between the East and West Coasts is approximately $19–20,000 per month.

DS1C   This is a digital signal equivalent to two DS1s, with extra (stuff) bits to conform to a signaling standard of 3.152 Mbps. Few (if any) of these circuit capacities are still in use today. In the early days of digital and data transmission, the 3-Mbps data rate was used to link mainframes together. The physical side of this circuit is called T1C.

DS2   This is a composite of four DS1s multiplexed together yielding an aggregate rate of 6.312 Mbps. The Bell system used a DS2 capability to deliver subscriber loop carrier (SLC-96) to customers. A total of 96 DS0s could be carried across the DS2. This service was used more by the LECs in their outside plant world. However, the 6-Mbps data rate is now becoming re-popularized with the promise of ADSL technologies in the local loop. If we can get 6 to 8 Mbps downloads from the Internet on our local wires, the carriers (ILEC and CLEC) stand to gain from not having to replace their infrastructure. This is also called a T2 by the ILECs.

DS3   This 44.736-Mbps aggregate-multiplexed signal is equivalent to 28 DS1s or 672 DS0s. The T3 service is typically used by high-end data and voice customers who can afford the cost of this channel capacity. A price used for comparative purposes is from the East Coast to the West Coast, for which the T3 costs approximately $103,000 per month. One can see where smaller companies could not financially justify the use of the T3.

DS4/NA   This 139.264-Mbps aggregate-multiplexed signal is equivalent to 3 DS3s or 2,016 DS0s. The high-end and long-haul telecommunications carriers use this size of channel capacity. It is unlikely that a DS4 would ever be installed at a customer location.

DS4   This 274.176-Mbps aggregate-multiplexed signal is equivalent to 6 DS3s or 4,032 DS0s.

See Table 14-3 for a summary of these bandwidths. These rates are based on the ANSI T1.107 guidelines. From an international perspective, the ITU has set a hierarchy of rates that differs from the North American standard. A comparison of these rates is shown in Table 14-4. As can be seen, differences between the North American standards and the international standards exist.

Table 14-3

ANSI T1.107 Rates

Designator	Capacity (Kbps)	Equiv. DS1	Equiv. DS0	Stuff Bits
DS0	64	—	1	
DS1	1,544	1	24	8,000
DS1C	3,152	2	48	64,000
DS2	6,312	4	96	136,000
DS3	44,736	28	672	1,504,000
DS34/NA	139,264	84	2,016	5,056,000
DS4	274,176	168	4,032	14,784,000

Table 14-4

International CCITT
G.702

Designator	Capacity (bps)	Equiv. DS1	Equiv. DS0
E1	2,048,000	1	32
E2	8,448,000	4	128
E3	34,368,000	16	512
E4	139,264,000	64	2,048
DS0	64,000	—	1
DS1	1,544,000	1	24
DS2	6,312,000	4	96
J1*	32,064,000		
DS3	44,736,000	28	672
J3*	97,728,000		
DS4	139,264,000	84	2,016

*J designators are for Japan's network. These capacities also will be used for the BISDN rate H21.

However, other rates are evolving for transmission capacities. The standard 64 Kbps is derived from using pulse-code modulation. In several vendor products, 64 Kbps for the transmission of voice and/or analog data is considered too much bandwidth to carry traditional voice or analog data. Therefore, lower speed capacities are derived at 32 Kbps.

Signaling

Signaling comes into play when dealing with voice and dial-up data services. Traditionally, signaling is provided on a dial-up telephone line, across the talk path. This is referred to as in-band signaling. You might recall that the need to find bits to send between transmitter and receiver was accomplished in the 6th and 12th frames. Bit robbing, or stealing the eighth bit in each of the channels (1–24) in these two frames, allows for enough bits to signal between the transmit and receive ends. These ends can be customer premises equipment (CPE) to the central office for switched services, or CPE to CPE for PBX-PBX connections, and so on.

The most common form of signaling on a T1 line is four-wire E&M signaling of type I, II, or III. It would be safe to say that the easiest implementation, acceptable to all vendors and carriers alike, is four-wire E&M type I.

Signaling is used to tell the receiver where the call or route is destined. The signal is sent through switches along the route to a distant end.

The common types of signals are

- On hook
- Off hook
- Dial tone
- Dialed digits
- Ringing cycle
- Busy tone

Four-wire E&M is used for tie lines between switches. Occasionally, other services are bundled onto a T1 circuit. These could include

- Direct inward dialing (DID)
- Direct outward dialing (DOD)
- Two-way circuit
- Off-premises extension (OPX)
- Foreign exchange service (FX)

With these other services, the type of signaling might differ. DID/DOD on a PBX might use ground-start trunks, which requires a ground to be placed on the individual circuit to alert the central office that service is requested or some other change is on the line. Regardless of the type signaling or the services used, signaling requires bits of information. There is a way to overcome the robbed-bit signaling that limits data to 56 Kbps. *Common-channel signaling* (CCS) is a method to get the clear channel capability back.

Remember that constant demands are on the use of T1 for clear channel capacity. The use of bit stuffing to conform to the 1's density rule for timing was overcome by using B8ZS. Now, to overcome bit robbing for signaling, CCS can apply.

If the 24th channel in the digital signal is dedicated, 23 clear channels can pass 64,000 bits of information. The choice is how much to give up. Table 14-5 is a decision table to help decide this process.

This common-channel signaling technique is also called the transparent mode for signaling. A single 64-Kbps channel (#24) is given up rather than 8 Kbps per channel [[×]]24 (192 Kbps) for robbed bit. Carriers now use CCS7 (or SS7 as it is called in the United States) in their newer digital dial-up services under the auspices of Intelligent Networks and ISDN. In the T1 world, this means the primary rate interface (PRI) at 23B+D—simply stated, 23 bearer (B) channels at 64 Kbps clear channel, plus a data channel for signaling at 64 Kbps (D). The choices are not always obvious, but understanding the requirements helps to steer the decision better.

Clocking (Network Synchronization)

Any digital network synchronization between sender and receiver must be maintained. As the DS1 (the digital signal level 1 of 1.544 Mbps) is delivered to the network, it is likely that it will be multiplexed with other digital streams from many other users. All of these signals will then be

Table 14-5

Decision Matrix for Deciding on Robbed Bit or Common Channel Signaling

If (Switched)	Then	O/H Given Up (Kbps)
Voice only	Robbed bit	192
Voice and analog data	Robbed bit	192
Voice, analog data, and 56 Kbps digital data	Robbed bit	192
Digital voice or digital data at 64 Kbps	CCS	64
Digital data at 64 Kbps or greater	CCS	64

transported as a single signal over high-capacity digital links (DS3 and above). Further, if the line is directly interfaced to a digital switching device, then synchronization must be maintained between the customer's transmitter and the switch.

Synchronization is imperative in a digital transmission system. If the timing of arrival or transmission is off, then the information will be distorted. Regardless of whether voice, data, video, or image traffic is present, the presentation of a digital stream of 1's and 0's is contingent on a timed arrival between the two ends.

There are a number of ways to synchronize a digital network, but the issue must definitely be addressed. Some of the ways to address the synchronization deal with levels of synchronization.

The levels are

- Bit
- Time slots for time-division multiplexing
- Frame

Bit Synchronization

As a digital stream of 1's and 0's is delivered to the line, the timing (or clocking) of the bit is important. The transmitter should be sending bits at the same rate the receiver can take them in. Any difference—faster or slower—could result in lost bits. Therefore, the bits must occur at a fixed time interval. This is a bit technical, but the timing for the bits is set up in a window of 648 nanoseconds (that is, 648 billionths of a second) and the pulse must occur in 1/2 of that window. Therefore, the pulse is 324 nanoseconds in duration. When we only have a 3-volt pulse, and it occurs for only 324 ns, one can see why the timing is crucial—a slight delay and the timing is off by a lot. If the timing is off enough, the pulse can wind up in the wrong time slot. This is called "jitter."

Time Slot

Whenever several links are connected or routed through a network processor, switching system, or end mode, the potential for lost bits or degradation of the link increases exponentially. Using the pulse-coded modulation technique, 8 bits are encoded from each sample of information. These 8 bits are then assembled and placed into a time slot. As signals and links are processed through a network, it is the 8-bit pattern that is routed from time slot to time slot. Should a slippage or mismatch occur, multiple streams of information will be lost.

Frame Synchronization

After the data stream of 192 bits of information is assembled (8 bits $\times$ 24 channels), an extra overhead bit is added to let both transmitter and receiver know the boundaries of the frame (think of it as a start/stop bit sequence). When dealing with a T1, the bit sequencing is easier to derive. However, at multiplexing schemes above the T1 rate, additional bits are inserted in the data stream to maintain a constant clocking reference. The use of these overhead (or stuff) bits brings both transmitter and receiver up to a common signaling speed to maintain frame synchronization.

Potential Synchronization Problems

When a digital system is scheduled to receive a bit, it expects to do just that. However, clocking or timing differences between the transmitter and receiver can exist. Therefore, while the receiver is expecting a bit that the transmitter hasn't sent, a slip occurs. There will most likely be slips present because of multiple factors in any network. These can result from the two clocks at the ends being off or from problems that can occur along the link.

Along the link, problems can be accommodated. The use of pulse stuffing helps, but other methods also can help. Each device along the link has a buffer capability. This buffer creates a simple means of maintaining synchronization. Pulse stuffing is done independently for each multiplexer along the way, enhancing overall reliability of the network. However, pulse stuffing has its negatives too. The overhead at each multiplexer is basically a penalty. Further, at both ends, the location and timing of each stuff bit must be determined, then signaled to the receiver to enable it to locate and remove the stuff bits. When de-stuffing occurs, a timing problem known as jitter can cause degradation of the signal. When passing through multiple switching sites, the signal must be de-stuffed from a received signal, and then re-stuffed to a newly transmitted signal. This is expensive in both equipment and overhead.

Obviously, when slippage occurs or if a problem exists in the network buffers, the retransmission of a frame or frames of information will be required. For voice, this isn't too bad, but for data transmission it can result in errors that can render the data unusable. The result will be retransmission requests (NAKS) that will affect the throughput of the link and potentially increase the burden on other systems to detect and correct the errors.

Performance Issues

Once a decision is made to use digital transmission capabilities and to consolidate 24 or more voice, data, or video circuits on a single T1, the performance of the T1 becomes an issue. The placing of all the eggs in a single basket is an issue to be dealt with.

The first users of this technology were risk takers. If 24 analog voice and data lines are being used and one fails, 23 are still working. However, when 24 lines are digitally encoded on a single circuit and one fails, they all fail. This is a concern to many users. Further, it should be noted that failures do occur. A T1 is based on the four-wire circuit in an error-prone network. Equipment failures, cable cuts, flooded cable vaults and the like all contribute to circuit failures. If total circuit failures were the only problem, the risks would be minimized. But cases can occur that cause distortion, high bit-error rates, timing slips, and loss of framing sequence (to name a few), which can impair or disrupt transmission. The thought of all these situations can leave the potential user's knees weak.

A further statistic that causes concern is that 90 percent of all errors/failures will likely occur at the local loop (the last mile from central office to customer premises). This is not to imply that the local exchange carriers (LECs) are doing a poor job of provisioning these circuits. It is merely a statement of fact, because the local loop is exposed to more of the external problems mentioned previously.

Considering average performances, the use of T1 technology is based on seven days per week $\times$ 24 hours per day. Table 14-6 is a summary of total hours and percentage comparisons at availability times. With these statistics, you can see the impact of a few percentage points in terms of downtime and your exposure to lost time.

Although these numbers are dramatic, the actual performance is completely different on the basis of the problem, customer, location, and so on.

Table 14-6

Total Hours
Available
@24 × 30 = 720

Performance (Percent)	Hours Down/Month	Hours of Yearly Downtime
99.5	4	48
99.0	8	96
98.5	11	132
98.0	15	180
97.0	18	216
95.0	36	432
90.0	72	864

Situations have been recorded where services have been out for six to seven consecutive days because of variable circumstances. However, such extreme outages are rare.

To ensure availability of the circuit and the call-carrying capacity of the channels, carriers, equipment vendors, and the like have all adopted a new standard. This new standard is known as extended superframe format (ESF). Before delving into ESF, however, an understanding of the older format is appropriate.

D3/D4 Framing

First, the D3 and D4 framed formats were designed to format the channelized information of a T1. Because D3 was a voice-only (analog data input) and fixed format for input, the use of T1 was designed around tie lines, WATS lines, and dial-up analog data. The evolution to the D4 frame was to accommodate voice, data, and image. Both of these formats had their limitations. The superframe (SF) format used provisions to allow for signaling (robbed bit) and 1's density for timing (stuff bits). These two capabilities, combined with the framing bits, were constantly taking channel capacity from the T1. All of the user information was designed around a 56-Kbps data stream. The robbed or stuffed bits were designed around control. Yet, when looking at the potential for maintenance and diagnostic capabilities, no spare capacity exists for the data channels to do this, short of giving up additional overhead. Given the pricing structure and the other forms of overhead, this option was not acceptable.

Maintenance Issues

Whenever a user of T1 with D3/D4 framing experienced problems on the line, the sequence of events became elongated and disruptive. Things would occur in the following order:

1. *The user would experience some hits on the line (or downtime) that affected data throughput.* These hits would be in the form of loss of framing, loss of synchronization, bipolar violations, and such. Regardless of the problem, disruptions on the circuit for seconds or longer occurred. The user could see lights flashing on the channel service unit (CSU).

2. *The user would notify the appropriate carrier (either local exchange or interexchange carrier) of the problem.* Further discussions would evolve regarding the errors and so on.

3. *To test the line, the carrier would ask the customer to get all users off the circuit and give the line to the carrier for testing.* In many cases, this might be an immediate situation; in other cases, it was a scheduled event. Whether or not this was scheduled for a later time, the issue at hand was the need to give up 24 channels of voice, data, or image for a couple of hours for testing.

4. *The carrier would then test the line.* A loopback arrangement would be used in some cases. The carrier would loop the circuit from the exchange office to the CSU or demarcation point. A pattern of 1's and 0's was transmitted to the customer premises and immediately shipped back around to the originating office. As the data was shipped out, a comparison was made with what was received back. If any errors were evident, the necessary fixes could be either done on the spot or scheduled.

5. *However, often the carrier conducted the tests and detected no problems.* A technician might then be dispatched to the customer's premises to provide further testing. Equipment using test patterns (quasi-random signal source or QRSS) was used. Again, the possibility existed that no errors would be detected.

6. *The carrier would then give the circuit back to the customer.* When challenged as to the nature of the problem, the carrier's response was no trouble found (NTF). Obviously, the customer had problems accepting this answer. The feeling that the carrier was either hiding something or just didn't know what was going on prevailed.

7. *Once the circuit was placed back in service (two hours later), the customer might see errors again.* At this point, the cycle would start all over again, usually with the same end result—NTF. Consequently, the working relationships and confidence levels between the customer and provider would become very strained.

Error Detection

The easiest way to describe errors on a T1 is as the process by which any logical 1 is changed to a 0 or a logical 0 is changed to a 1. These logic errors are the source of the corrupted data on the line. The errors can be caused by noise from a spike of electrical energy on the line (such as lightning) or induced by electromechanical interference (such as a large motor in a building). Further types of errors can be caused by cable losses, flooded cables, rodent damage, or cross talk on the line, to name a few. Equipment can introduce errors from the digital repeaters, multiplexers, or DACS on the line. Unfortunately, the process of detecting these errors can be tenuous. Any pulse (a 1) or absence of a pulse (a 0) transmitted along the line is subject to noise that can change the actual data. When traveling through equipment such as multiplexers, repeaters, DACS, CSU, DSU, and the like, the pulses are accepted as valid. The equipment therefore cleans up the valid pulses, but because the electronic systems can't differentiate between valid and erroneous pulses, it cleans up the entire data stream. Consequently, the receiver at the distant end accepts the clean, well-timed input as correct information. Hence, errors are introduced and undetected.

You might think that an error on the line could be easily detected by the equipment because certain format problems might also be evident. For example, an error (an extra pulse on the line) might violate the bipolar format convention, or a dropped pulse might violate the 1's density rule. Clearly, these would be easy to detect. However, if the signal must pass through equipment along the way, that equipment might clean up the errors. The equipment does have the ability to log an error on the inbound side, then reformat the signal on the outbound side and make it appear to be valid.

To further understand this process, look at both errors—where a pulse is inserted and where a pulse is dropped.

Errors of Omission/Commission

The errors are either dropped pulses (omitted) or inserted pulses (committed). An error where a pulse is omitted should in turn create a bipolar violation. If the number of pulses omitted is even, the bipolar violation won't be created. Only an odd number of errors causes this violation. Figure 14-18 is an example of how this works with an even number of removed pulses.

An error occurring with an odd number of pulses being dropped would be detected. Figure 14-19 is a representation where three pulses are dropped, causing a bipolar error.

When pulses are introduced (committed), a similar problem occurs in detecting the errors. For example, when an odd number of pulses is introduced, a bipolar error will occur, but when an even number of errors occurs, a bipolar violation might be created. This is not guaranteed, however. Figure 14-20 shows the commission of an odd number of pulses, which will create a bipolar violation.

However, as mentioned earlier, when an erroneous signal passes through equipment along the link, the signal is cleared up and put into a correct format state. Figure 14-21 is a sample of how this would work.

The detection of errors, therefore, becomes more difficult in the transmitted data stream due to these problems. A format error (bipolar violation) implies that a logical error has occurred; thus, the data is erroneous.

Figure 14-18
An even number of pulses being dropped will not be detected from a bipolar convention.

Original data

Even number of pulses

Even pulses dropped

An even number of pulses dropped in a row will not be detected from a bipolar violation convention.

Figure 14-19
Because an odd
number of pulses
changes, a bipolar
error occurs. This
error can be
detected.

Original data

Since an odd number of pulses changes,
a bi-polar error occurs. This error can be detected.

Figure 14-20
When an odd
number of pulses is
inserted, a bipolar
violation will occur,
either with the first
pulse inserted or with
the first valid pulse
after the commission
of the pulse.

Original data

Odd pulses inserted

Violation

Violation

ESF—A Step to Correct the Problem

In the early 1980s, AT&T suggested the implementation of the extended
superframe format as a means to provide nondisruptive error detection and
perform nonservice affecting diagnostics on T1 circuits. This represented a
step toward correcting the problem of lost customer confidence and the
disruptive performance testing. As service providers, the interexchange
carriers write tariffs to provide service within certain guidelines of availability. ESF helps to address this problem.

Figure 14-21
As the data with errors and bipolar violations passes through the MUX, CSU, DACS, DSU, and so on, the electronics cleans up the signal so that it comes out properly formatted.

Original Data

Errored data

Errored data after MUX pass through is cleaned up

MUX

Essentially, because overhead on the circuit is at issue, customers are unwilling to give up more channel capacity for maintenance and diagnostics. ESF uses the 8 Kbps of overhead normally assigned for the framing format, and therefore does not affect the data bandwidth.

What Does ESF Do?   Extended superframe format, as its name implies, extends the superframe from 12 consecutive frames of information to 24 frames of information. The 8 Kbps of overhead, originally used strictly for framing, is now subdivided into three functions. Table 14-7 summarizes how the overhead is shared to support ESF.

ESF takes advantage of newer technologies to use the 8 Kbps of framing overhead and uses only 6 bits (2 Kbps) for framing synchronization. Six additional bits are used for error detection by means of a cyclic redundancy

Table 14-7

The Original 8 Kbps of Overhead in SF Format Is Now Subdivided to Provide Three Separate Functions

Original SF Format	Revised ESF Format
8 Kbps for framing only	2 Kbps for framing
	2 Kbps for error detection (CRC)
	4 Kbps for facility data link

check 6 (CRC-6). This leaves 12 of the framing bits for a facility data link communications channel (4 Kbps). Table 14-8 is a comparison framing bit use for SF and the newer ESF.

Table 14-8

Frame Bit
Definitions

Frame	Bit	FPS	FDL	CRC
1	0	—	m	—
2	193	—	—	C1
3	386	—	m	—
4	579	0	—	—
5	772	—	m	—
6	963	—	—	C2
7	1158	—	m	—
8	1351	0	—	—
9	1544	—	m	—
10	1737	—	—	C3
11	1930	—	m	—
12	2123	1	—	—
13	2316	—	m	—
14	2509	—	—	C4
15	2702	—	m	—
16	2895	0	—	—
17	3088	—	m	—
18	3281	—	—	C5
19	3474	—	m	—
20	3667	1	—	—
21	3860	—	m	—
22	4053	—	—	C6
23	4246	—	m	—
24	4439	1	—	—

Using this shared facility, the carrier has the option of performing the three functions necessary to support the customer needs:

■ Framing synchronization

■ Error detection

■ In-service monitoring and diagnostics

Framing

As already stated, the fundamental purpose of the bit pattern is framing synchronization. Framing is important because its loss can impact performance through incorrect synchronization. (Channel 1 could wind up connected to channel X [2−24] if the framing is incorrect.) Errors might cause a loss of frame and disrupt the circuit, and far-end and/or intermediate equipment could be thrown into a loss-of-frame condition and thereby a loss of data. While the devices along the circuit are reframing data, throughput is disrupted for a period of time. Depending on the equipment in use, this loss could be quite substantial (approximately 200 ms). Newer equipment performs a reframing operation in less time (approximately 10−20 ms). This helps to improve performance. With ESF using only 1 of 4 bits, the delay could increase significantly unless the proper equipment is purchased.

CRC-6

Cyclic redundancy checking is designed to detect errors that occur on the line. Because the network is error prone, it is a foregone conclusion that errors will occur. Using CRC-6, an entire ESF (24 frames of information or 4,608 bits) is checked for accuracy. This check is a fictitious number created by the CSU as it performs a mathematical computation on the 4,608 data bits. When the math is calculated using a prime number polynomial, a 6-bit pattern is the end result. In the next ESF (24 frames), the result of this mathematics is transmitted to the distant end.

At the distant end, the receiving CSU calculates exactly the same mathematical operations on the ESF data and then computes an answer. When the next ESF is received, the result of the first calculation is contained in the CRC bits (6 bits) of the overhead. When the two results are compared, the answers should be the same. If, however, they differ, an error has occurred. The use of CRC-6 allows for an error detection efficiency of 98.4

percent for a single bit error, or, simply stated, detection of 63 of 64 errors and 99.9995 percent of bursts of errors less than 16 bits.

The Facility Data Link

The 4 Kbps of overhead set aside for facility data link control is a synchronous communication channel. This channel can serve multiple purposes, one of which is the exchange of information between equipment devices along the circuit. AT&T publication 54016 specifies a set of standard message formats for communicating across the data link to the storage devices. The standard conforms to a basic X.25 (BX.25) link procedure and uses an AT&T standard known as telemetry asynchronous block serial protocol (TABS). The carrier or end user can communicate with the remote equipment (CSU) using a maintenance message format. Some of the maintenance messages allowed under the AT&T technical reference (54016) include

- *Send 1-hour performance data reports.* This includes the existing status of the link, time since the last check (up to 24 hours), errored seconds, and failed seconds in the present 15-minute cycle, the overall 24-hour cycle, and the past four 15-minute cycle performances.
- *Send 24-hour errored seconds (ES) performance data.* The CSU will send specific error events logged within the past 24 hours in 15-minute increments.
- *Send 24-hour failed seconds (FS) performance data.* The CSU sends the 24-hour historical information of errored events logged in 15-minute increments.
- *Reset registers.* Empty the buffers and start counting errors all over again.
- *Send errored ESF.* The CSU will send the current count of errors accumulated (up to a maximum of 65,535).
- *Reset ESF register.* Empty the buffer and start at zero.

Benefits of ESF

The reasons to use ESF are to increase circuit availability and improve performance. Once again, putting 24 channels (circuits) on one T1 puts the user at risk if performance is poor. Just about all of the major carriers (interexchange) have implemented ESF. Because all of the interexchange carriers internetwork—that is, they connect to each other—the use of the AT&T standard (54016) is the norm.

Vendors and carriers can see the improvements brought about by ESF. When a burst of errors occurs, the carrier need only access the CSU from the facility data link and query for status. The problem of old, the "no trouble found" situation, tends to fade into the background because the CSU has buffers to collect the errors for later retrieval. Further, with the facility data link, the carrier can monitor real customer data traveling across the line non-disruptively. Errors occurring on the line can be seen and diagnosed in real time. This all leads to a better track record. In fact, many of the carriers will contractually guarantee circuit availability between 98.4 and 99.5 percent because of the proactive capability gathered in ESF.

This seemed to solve the problem for users and carriers alike. Despite the passive collection capability and the on-line diagnostics, the parties all began to create a working, rather than an adversarial, role.

Problems with ESF

Unfortunately, one player that is not mentioned in this scenario and yet is an essential ingredient in the total circuit is the local exchange carrier (LEC). An integral piece of the circuit is the "last mile," or the circuit running from the LEC to the customer premises. ESF was designed to function as a part of the customer premises equipment (CPE). However, the LEC by mandate cannot poll the CSU that stores the error information. Under the guidelines of the modified final judgment (MFJ), or what we know as divestiture, the LEC cannot go beyond a clearly defined demarcation point. This demarcation is the line termination in the RJ-48, RJ-68, or smart jack —where the LEC stops and the customer takes over. Some of these limitations are falling aside with the deregulation of the telecommunications industry and the Telecommunications Act of 1996. Yet, the local utilities commissions across North America have still held some of the barriers intact. Over time, the change will be finalized, but it is a phased project.

This point, therefore, excludes the LEC from benefits derived from ESF as defined by the AT&T technical reference (54016). To overcome this problem, the American National Standards Institute (ANSI) came up with a proactive approach to ESF: ANSI's standard T1.403 uses the CSU to monitor performance on the T1 line, then puts together an activity report every second and transmits this ESF report back out across the network. This solves the problem but leaves the door open to two sets of standards. As a result, all North American carriers have been migrating to the ANSI T1.403 specification.

Questions

1. When did the Bell System begin to install T1 in the U.S.?
    a. 1955
    b. 1934
    c. 1982
    d. 1960

2. What was the name of the inventor of the PCM technique?
    a. Alexander Bell
    b. Heinrich Hertz
    c. Harry Nyquist
    d. Dr. Watson

3. A T1 carries _____ channels of voice or data.

4. The digital modulation technique that produces the 64-Kbps channel is called ADPCM.   T/F

5. To create the 64-Kbps transmission, we apply the following steps:
    a. Sample the channel at 2x the highest frequency
    b. Quantize the information
    c. Digitally encode the signal
    d. None of the above
    e. All of the above

6. The two framing formats currently in use are _____ and _____.

7. T1s are synchronized in three ways:
    a. Bit
    b. Byte
    c. Frame
    d. CSU
    e. DSU
    f. All of the above
    g. a, b and c only

8. AMI stands for:
   a. Alternating Marked Information
   b. Available Mark Inverted
   c. Alternate Mark Inversion
   d. Any Mark Incident

9. The AMI format creates a bi-polar signal.   T/F

10. Bi polar is shown by _____ and _____ 3 volt pulses.

11. The 1's density rule means that the signal is densely populated with 1's.   T/F

12. Ones density requires that _____ percent of the pulses transmitted will be 1's.

13. The AT&T rule states that in every 8 bits there will be at least ____ pulse(s) and there may be no more than _____ consecutive zero(s).
    a. 1 and 24
    b. 3 and 24
    c. 3 and 8
    d. 1 and 8
    e. 1 and 15

14. The _____ framing format required that the link is tested disruptively.

15. To solve the problem by allowing non-disruptive testing, the _____ format was created.
    a. DS3
    b. D3
    c. D4
    d. ESK
    e. ESF

16. Errors of _____ and ____ occur on the line for various reasons.

17. The T1 can be channelized or non-channelized.   T/F

18. The newer framing format (ESF) uses a CRC-32 to do its error checking.   T/F

19. The beneficiaries of the newer protocols are:

    a. ILECs

    b. Customers

    c. IECs

    d. All of the above

    e. None of the above

20. How many T1s are used to create a T3?

    a. 3

    b. 4

    c. 24

    d. 28

    e. None of the above

The Open Systems Interconnect Model (OSI)

After reading this chapter and completing the questions, you will be able to:

■ Describe the OSI model

■ Converse openly about the seven-layer architecture

■ Compare the differences between the OSI and other models, such as TCP/IP, IBM SNA, and DEC DNA

■ Understand the reasoning for using a model like this for transparent communications

■ Describe the importance of reliable communications processes for moving data

The three-letter acronym OSI (open systems interconnect) appears in several places in this book. No one concept in this industry has been more misunderstood, but that is what happens when several different operations are merged into one.

We first had a telephone industry. Later, we started to call it a telecommunications network—especially as newer services were being supported on this one infrastructure. The merger started when we introduced data processing into the telecommunications industry. Now, we have the convergence network. The data processing industry had already become entrenched in its own jargon and concepts. As long as the data processing function was localized to the mainframe and all transactions were performed in the computer room, no problem existed. However, like all things, this industry evolved. Soon the movement was from the computer room to the desktop, where users wanted connectivity to the mainframe. This was accomplished through the use of specialized wiring systems. Nothing is new here, other than that these special wires were very expensive. The wires had to carry the data from the terminal to the computer and also do the reverse. This was accomplished with the use of traditional communications techniques—by converting the data into electrical energy and carrying it down the wire—and the data was represented in digital form without notice.

Then it happened: Not only did we need connectivity from the desktop to the computer room, we also needed it from a desktop across town or across the country. Now the process was going to change the way we conducted business. The data communications industry became the next battleground. The data processing people all thought that data processing and data communications should be similar enough so that they would control the deployment. The telephony people felt that this computer stuff was a pain anyway, so they were content to let it reside in the data processing arena.

However, some problems existed with this whole situation. To send the data across town or across the entire country, it would be necessary to use a device called a modem. Recall that we talked about this in an earlier chapter, but there the modem was used to make the data look like voice. As long as the data looked like voice, the data folks wanted to send it back to the telephony department, especially when they didn't understand or care to understand how this analog network functioned.

Thus, the marriage of the three techniques began back in the late 1950s and into the 1960s. The evolution was slow because the telephone monopoly controlled the delivery of the transport system. The data processors were looking for a way to make the network digital to avoid the digital-to-analog and the analog-to-digital conversions. This seemed like too many steps, and as each step was taken, there was a risk of introducing errors into the data stream.

Things rolled along nicely, but the data processing evolution kept going from the mainframe environment to one leaning toward distributed computing. Organizations were cropping up that would offer smaller-scale computers (midi[1] and mini) that could handle very specific functions and off-load this process from the mainframe. Once again, this started the ball rolling. Many of the computers in use at the time were not compatible with

---

[1]A mid-range computer, such as a departmental or branch office system, made by the computer manufacturers like DEC and Data General, etc.

each other. This led to a new set of predicaments. As the smaller computer companies were competing with the mainframe world, two major players were doing battle: IBM and DEC. Each had its own hardware and software platforms. Now organizations began to move computers from different manufacturers into their buildings. No problem: These were very specific application processors, so there need be no conflict. That was true, but a user who needed access to the mainframe and the specialty machine now required two separate sets of wires run to the desk and two different terminals on top of the desk. This is reminiscent of the situation portrayed the historical section of this book, where the interconnection of various telephone companies would not work and users needed two or three phones on their desks to intercommunicate. The battle was being fought over compatibility rather than technology. The problems were just starting.

First, let's take another look at this from the perspective of the managers of the computing systems. In Figure 15-1, the organization had a mainframe that was based on architecture created by the manufacturer—in this case, IBM. The hierarchy of this architecture allowed various connection arrangements based on the device's level on the planes of the architecture.

Figure 15-1
The hierarchy in a mainframe environment

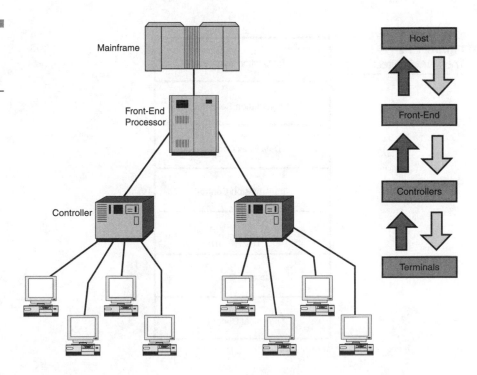

Figure 15-1 shows how the transfer of information among and between users would take place. Things worked pretty well because IBM had everything in place: They delivered the hardware, the software, the connections, and the talent to make everything work together. This was all based on a proprietary and closed architecture called *systems network architecture* (SNA). Figure 15-2 shows the architecture in its stack. This is a seven-layered architecture that IBM created to make everything work in harmony. Using this structure, IBM would fix something that did not work—for a fee, of course.

Later, as the specialty machines appeared, the provider used a separate approach. This provider was created as a result of spin-offs from IBM. The founders of this particular company (DEC) were upset with the strategy and direction that IBM used. Therefore, they created their own offshoot company to offer lower-end machines to the customer, but at more reasonable prices and in a more open environment. DEC, of course, being an offshoot of IBM used a lot of similar approaches. Let's face it: When an engineer or manager leaves one place of employment, it's tough to leave behind all learned information, so the cross-pollination of ideas and goals took root. In the design and rollout of their products, DEC introduced their

Figure 15-2
The SNA architecture

Transaction Services
Presentation Services
Data Flow Control
Transmission Control
Path Control
Data Link Control
Physical Control

Figure 15-3
DEC's DNA
architecture

own closed and proprietary architecture (shown in Figure 15-3), called Digital Network Architecture (DNA), that just happened to have seven layers. These seven layers were based on DEC hardware, software, connections, and talent to make everything work in harmony. Sounds familiar, doesn't it?

Progressive end users who had embarked on a multivendor approach in meeting their computing needs would be faced with two separate architectures to work with. The third aspect of this is that many users wanted to be connected to both systems. Ultimately, the end user wanted to be able to access these two platforms, hardware, software, applications shared data sets, or whatever from a single device. Moreover, many of the specialty applications that the users wanted required the data that was stored in the mainframe. This meant that the users were re-keying the data from printed reports that came from the mainframe. This left a new set of problems:

- The timeliness of the data was suspect. Because it had to be re-keyed, it could be obsolete before it was ever entered.

- The accuracy of the information was questionable because data entry errors are not uncommon.

- The cost of the information was now more expensive because the input was done at least twice.

- The frequency of the input was becoming exponential because as soon as the data was printed out from the mainframe, it could be obsolete as a result of changes made by other users. Unfortunately, this was changed in the mainframe, but the update in the specialty machine was not automatic.

Therefore, the scenario became almost comical. Here's an illustration to make this concept easier to understand. This is a hypothetical situation— all names of people and companies are used only for the purposes of this example. Do not try this yourself, as it was tested by professionals who are skilled at ducking the issues.

Let's use an example of an organization that has two suppliers of computing platforms. One is an ABC mainframe; the other is a DEF BAX. The company has users attached to both machines, and has received complaints about the connections. Users are getting confused when they try to log on for sessions on both machines. The MIS manager decides to go to the vendors and ask whether a way to provide transparent connectivity exists. The dialogue goes something like this:

IS Mgr.:   Hello, ABC? I've got this ABC mainframe where the users are attached using a 333X terminal. I also have a DEF BAX system and my users are using a VL2000/3000 type terminal to connect to the BAX.

ABC: Yes, what can we do for you?

IS Mgr.:   Well, what I'm trying to do is let my BAX users log onto the mainframe and view or manipulate the data on the ABC host. When the need dictates, I'd also like for my users to pull the data from the host and move it over to the BAX where the user can modify or delete the data. Then, when they are done, they should be able to save it back to the original data set on the host.

ABC: So you want your users to access the data on the host, use it, modify it, or whatever. Then you want that data saved on the host so that others can see it and use it. Is that correct?

IS Mgr.:   That's it exactly. I also want the user to be able to use the same keystrokes on their terminal that my 333X terminals use.

ABC: OK! There's no problem, we have the perfect solution for you.

IS Mgr.:   You do! That's great! This is exactly what I was hoping to hear. What do I have to do?

ABC: It's simple. All you have to do is sell all those DEF terminals and the BAX, then buy all ABC terminals and hosts. You'll have full transparency and everyone will enter the exact same keystrokes.

That's not exactly what the IS manager was hoping to hear. So off to DEF. The dialogue will be somewhat the same:

IS Mgr.:   Hello, DEF? I have these two systems, one a BAX using VL2000/3000 terminals serving a special application. I also have this ABC mainframe that is serving some of my back office functions like accounting, billing, inventory control, and so on. What I'd like to do is provide seamless and transparent connectivity between the two computers and let any user access any data from the terminals at their desk. This can be a VL2000/3000 or a 333X. Do you have a way of handling this for me?

DEF: You have a BAX and an AB who?

IS Mgr.:   An ABC host.

DEF: Oh, this is easy. We have these requests all the time and we help our customers through this arrangement very easily. As a matter of fact, we can do it all for you.

IS Mgr.:   You can? This is great. I knew you folks would come through for me. What do I have to do?

DEF: It's really quite simple. Sell all those other devices, buy more BAXs and VL2000/3000s. It will work transparently and everyone will love it!

Once again the dilemma: What was the IS manager to do? Fortunately others had already gone through this problem and a new supplier had emerged: the third-party manufacturers of "black boxes."[2] The box was not black; the name referred to the fact that no one really knew what it did. It was a protocol converter. All the user knew was that if somebody on one system typed the normal way at a terminal, the commands and data typed went into the black box as DEF and came out the other side as ABC, and vice versa. These protocol converters were not inexpensive; but they were certainly a more attractive option than the other choices that the IS manager got. So, the IS manager bought a third-party converter and attached it to both machines. With a connection to each machine, the converter sat in the middle. This is shown in Figure 15-4, where the two hosts are connected to the converter. All is solved. Or is it?

---

[2] Black Box was the name given to any device when we did not really know what was going on inside; it just did what it was supposed to do. The reference to black box is not to the Black Box Company in Pittsburgh, PA, who offers several excellent products and services.

Figure 15-4
A black box was used
to create
transparency.

DEF - BAX

Protocol Converter

ABC

DEF

ABC - Mainframe

After the installation, things appear to be working fairly well. Then one day they start to go awry. The IS manager calls ABC and asks if anything different has been done with the system or code. The converter worked fine yesterday, but today nothing seems to be functioning. ABC, of course, responds that it has done nothing. It would, therefore, suggest it must be those other folks. Now, the IS manager goes to DEF and gets the exact same response. So, it must be those others. Finally, off to the third-party supplier, who of course suggests that it has done nothing different so it must be those others. The result of all this is shown in Figure 15-5. This is called the finger-pointing routine. Point and hide is really what happened.

Even if nothing went wrong, things might not be exactly the same as what the end user accesses at the various machines through protocol converters. The follow-up to this is that the code sets and command lines might be different. Specifically, in a 32XX world, the end user might go through the following keystrokes to perform a function:

■ To repaint a screen with a blank accounting form, press the CMD key, which is located at the upper left corner of the keyboard, using the left index finger.

Figure 15-5
When a problem occurred, the finger-pointing started, leaving the IS manager at a loss.

- At the same time, press the F9 key using the right index finger.
- Voilà! The new screen appears with the blank form ready to go.

To perform the same function from a VL2000/3000 device in the same host, the user might do the following:

- Press the ESC key, located in the upper left corner of the keyboard, with the left index finger. Because no CMD key exists, a remapping of the keyboard must take place.
- At the same time, press the F9 key with the right index finger.
- At the same time, press the shift key with the left thumb. The shift key is on the lower left side of the keyboard.
- At the same time, press the ALT key with the right thumb. The ALT is located at the lower right side of the keyboard.
- At the same time, press the space bar with your right big toe. The space bar is located at the bottom center of the keyboard.
- Voilà! You now have the screen repainted with the blank form ready to be filled in! Figure 15-6 shows what this might look like.

Figure 15-6
Using protocol
converters was not
that transparent.

Obviously, by now you have recognized that this is strictly in jest. There are past ills in the industry, but they have not been this bad. The issue was that transparency in connectivity, communications, and use of the data was not to be had easily. The result was that the users put pressure on their coordinating committees in the industry to come up with a resolution. In 1978, the International Organization for Standards (ISO) was asked to come up with a solution that would allow the transparent communications and data transfer between and among systems regardless of manufacturer. This was originally thought of as the task of the data communications devices. Thus, a new committee was formed to evaluate how this might happen. Everyone in the industry held their breath. What form of solution would be achieved? Because this was a committee made up of users, vendors, and manufacturers of the systems as well as standards members, what could be expected? The result was to come several years later, with what we now have come to know as the ISO OSI reference model. No, they did not just reverse the letters of the organization; this stands for the open systems interconnect reference model. It is a seven-layer architecture, just like the other two architectures that already existed (SNA and DNA)—two of the member companies of the committee were IBM and DEC. This seven-layered architecture is shown in Figure 15-7. The seven layers will be covered in more detail later, but are listed here:

■ The application layer sits at the very top of the model. This is the direct interface with the application used when requesting a service. This layer provides communications services to the end user.

Figure 15-7
The OSI reference
model

- The presentation layer sits below the application layer and provides a service to the application layer. This is where formatting, code conversions, data representation, compression, and encryption are handled for the application.

- The session layer, located under the presentation layer, is responsible for the establishment and maintenance of connections to a process between two different users or systems. The control of the direction of data transfer is handled here.

- The transport layer is right below the session layer. The transport layer controls the connection for error recovery and flow control. It is responsible for assuring error-free data delivery end to end in a cost-efficient manner.

The next three layers deal with the network-specific issues of the communications process. Whereas the upper four layers deal with the end-to-end communications and data transfer, the bottom three layers are concerned with the node-to-node connection. This portion of the network may be provided by a single entity (such as a carrier, PTT, or third-party communications company).

- The network layer sits just under the transport layer and is responsible for the switching and routing of the connection. Also, this layer is responsible for taking the data that is to be shipped from node to node, not end user to end user, and breaking it into smaller pieces to accommodate the transmission system. Congestion control, alternate routing, and other such connectivity services are handled here. The network layer provides establishment of the connection, transfer of the data, releasing the connection, and in some cases, the transfer of data in a connectionless service.

■ The data link layer is responsible for the delivery of the information to the medium. It will create frames of information, if required, and send the frames along to the wires. Additionally, this layer is responsible for the reliability of the information and error checking on a node-to-node basis.

■ The physical layer that sits below the data link layer is the actual electrical or mechanical interface to the physical medium. In this layer, we have the physical pieces and the necessary components based on the dependency of the medium. This layer is responsible for transmitting the bits onto the guided medium (wires). It specifies various physical portions such as the voltage levels, the pins to use in placing the voltage onto the link, and whether the signal will be electrical or photonic (fiber) or modulated onto a nonguided (radio)-based service. We will see how all of these pieces tie together in later text.

Even with all of the effort that was placed on creating this set of protocols and the entire architecture, many industry and end user groups were somewhat frustrated. They wanted a single solution to provide the transparent communications between systems of different manufacturers; and what they got was still another seven-layer architecture. They were amazed that the standards committees would do such a thing. In reality, this was the best way to provide the solutions, but it took a while to sink in. The seven layers are independent of each other; even though they provide services to the upper layer and rely on the lower layer, some freedom still exists. This is important because in the event that any protocol suite in one of the seven layers needs to be changed, the rest of the architecture will remain intact. A single solution would not have done that.

Figure 15-8 compares the three seven-layer architectures—the OSI as a base, the SNA, and the DNA—to see how they line up against each other. In fairness to both DEC and IBM, their architectures were in place before the OSI model was created; therefore, they cannot be expected to be the same. DEC, over the years, has changed the architecture of its DECNet protocols

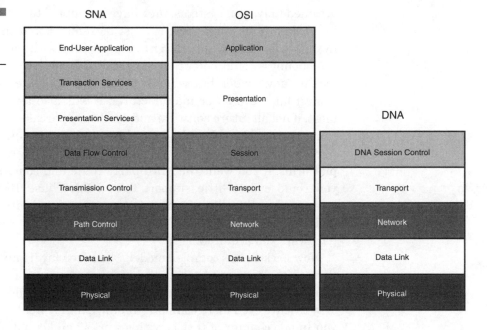

Figure 15-8
Comparing OSI,
DECNet, and SNA

to be more consistent with the OSI. However, IBM has basically done nothing over the past 27 years to change. IBM felt that it already had the single largest and most widely accepted architecture installed at all of the Fortune 1,000 companies, so therefore there was no need to change what already worked. So, even though the OSI architecture was developed around 1978, it was not totally accepted until 1984, and there have been very few implementations of it. In 1988, it was finally ratified as a true standard. More implementations were seen overseas than in North America.

Part of the reason was the cost of moving over to a new architecture. The U.S. government wanted a standard applied to all of their purchases in the past. In an effort to initiate OSI acceptance and implementation, the GSA specified a modified version of the OSI reference model. If you wanted to sell something of a computing or data communications nature to the government, you had to comply with their modified version. It was called the Government Open Systems Interconnect Profile (GOSIP). Yes, you guessed it, the U.S. government was responsible for creating gossip.

(Authors comment: Wait a minute; that was GOSIP, not gossip! Let's try to keep these things straight.)

This model has been the reference on which many of the changes of the past 20 years have been based. Although very few manufacturers have attained fully open systems, they have attempted to use the OSI as a model for their future compliance. It must be remembered that there was little incentive for any manufacturer to comply fully with the OSI model because the openness could potentially jeopardize future revenue streams. Not to pick on any vendor, but when you bought a computer system using SNA from a large computer manufacturer, it was also an unwritten rule that most, if not all future software and hardware purchases would be from that same vendor. If you bought from that vendor, you were assured that your purchases would fit seamlessly into your existing hardware and software platforms. If you went the third-party route and something did not work, you could expect little support from IBM. Thus, IBM's future revenue streams flowed from the proprietary nature of their architecture. If a completely open attitude and platform were introduced, it would work with any hardware you acquired.

Now back to this complex model. The seven layers always confused even those with a rigorous background in the data processing or data communications industry. Furthermore, these folks took 5- and 10-day workshops, only to leave even more confused than when they went in. How can we show you in one chapter of text how this works and keep it simple? We assume that you are likely a novice or getting into some new portion of the industry, and that this is your reference manual. So, let's try it with our usual method: a story. We can hope that by the time this works through, you will have a basic understanding of the function of the model and each of the layers as they play into the industry. Here goes!

Figure 15-9 shows a situation where two people (Don and Bud) are thinking about moving to a new area in a suburb of a major city. There is no subdivision yet; but there is a lot of property that can easily be broken down into perfectly sized lots, all with a great view.

These two players meet with a builder who owns the land and asks for their respective lots, which just happen to be right next to each other. The builder agrees to build both Bud's and Don's houses at a certain price.

Now that the agreements have been reached, both parties decide that they'd like their houses rather quickly. So, they both go back to the builder and ask that the process be accelerated. The builder, of course, will balk at the idea of doing the job too quickly. However, perseverance wins out and the two potential homeowners get the builder to cave in and speed up the construction.

The result is that in two weeks, the houses are ready to go. Now Bud and Don can move in. Immediately, a couple of things become apparent. Because

Figure 15-9
Building on new
subdevelopment
areas

the houses were built so quickly, the builder did not have time to notify the local incumbent local exchange carrier (ILEC) or competitive local exchange carrier (CLEC) that the owners were moving in. So, the two owners take possession, but they have no form of telephony service. Here are Don and Bud, living next door to each other without a means of communicating. What options do they have?

Immediately, they both call the local telephone company (ILEC or CLEC) and are told that the installation of facilities in their new area will take 6 to 12 months. This is too long for next-door neighbors to be without a communications method. So, they consider their options and come up with the choices shown in Table 15-1. The option is shown in the first column, and the pros and cons are in the other two columns. These are not all-inclusive; we have limited our list to a few options.

In the figures illustrating the table results, benefits and losses are associated with the communications options. Therefore, Don and Bud decide to model their communications device after the service that they really wanted—the telephone. The two neighbors aren't going to go out and build a central office. After all, they really just want the convenience of speaking

Table 15-1

Summary of
Communications
Options

Option	Benefits	Deterrents
Use a megaphone and yell out the window from one house to the other (see Figure 15-10).	• Easy to install • Relatively short distances • Can be implemented immediately	• What if one person isn't home? • What if Bud wants to talk to Don at 2:00 a.m.? • Loss of transmission due to distances. • Noisy for other neighbors in the area. • Total lack of privacy.
Throw pebbles at the window, when the receiver hears the pebbles on the window, open the window and yell out (see Figure 15-11).	• Pebbles are readily available. • The method of signaling each other is straightforward.	• Given the distances, the throw will take some effort. This can cause damage. • In inclement weather, this can be inconvenient and awkward.
Use a flashlight and send the signals in Morse code.	• Easy to use • Quick communications	• Don doesn't know Morse Code. • During daylight hours, the sun may diminish the light. • Batteries can fail.
Go next door and visit.	• Easy to accommodate	• Weather may make this difficult.
Have our conversations during the visit.	• Doesn't cost anything	• What about those 2:00 a.m. conversations? • The inconvenience will outweigh the benefits.

with each other. So, they decide to build on a model. Let's use the OSI model and make sure that this all ties in while we provide transparent communications.

Bud comes up with the idea that he and Don need to send their information across a medium. The earlier options used the airwaves as the medium; but weather conditions and other factors limited this. Therefore, both neighbors agree to use a physical medium. They decide to install a piece of everyday common household string between both of their houses. This is shown in Figure 15-12, where the string is run in a direct line of sight between both parties. The string is laid out and the two parties are connected with the medium.

Figure 15-10
A megaphone isn't a good choice, but it could work.

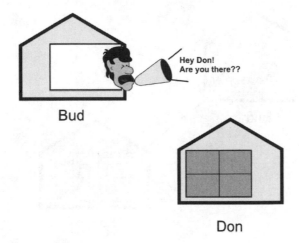

Figure 15-11
Throwing pebbles (or rocks) may not be a good alternative.

Given that the physical string is now attached, can the two parties communicate? It is somewhat obvious that something is still missing. Therefore, the neighbors decide that they have to use the model to handle their next step. Don comes up with the idea that they need to address the physical medium with some electrical or mechanical interface (layer 1 of the OSI). They decide that an electrical interface is not applicable because they do not have an electrical conductor in the string. So all they need is a mechanical interface. Don suggests that each neighbor attach a tin can on his end of the link to build this interface. Using everyday household tin cans

Figure 15-12
A piece of ordinary
string produces a
physical connection
(medium).

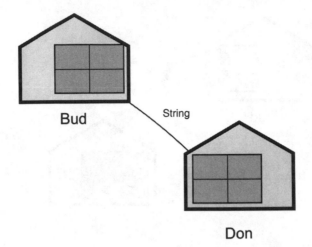

on both ends of the string, Don and Bud have now addressed the bottom layer of the OSI model (see Figure 15-13).

A problem has arisen with this arrangement. To make this all work properly and transparently, everyone must build the connection in the same way. Bud has attached the string through the side of the can, whereas Don has attached the string to the bottom of the can. Although this might work, when you pull the string tight, the can at Bud's end is in an awkward position. This means that the two have to agree on how they will connect the two cans to the string to make this work more efficiently. The agreement is that they will both take an empty can, punch a hole through the bottom, and then attach the string from the outside of the can, through the hole in the bottom, and knot it off inside the can. Then, they will pull the string tight to get a good connection. Now, the bottom layer of the OSI is handled.

The strings are now attached the same way; so can the parties now communicate? Well, maybe! Bud decides to test it out; so he picks up the tin can

Figure 15-13
Two tin cans are used
to satisfy the
mechanical interface
(layer 1 OSI).

on his end and starts to talk to Don. Don is preoccupied with the television set and does not hear that the communications system is being used. The whole conversation is wasted thus far. So, the parties need a means of using the link. They build a protocol that will solve this problem. First, the two parties agree that they should have an alerting mechanism to let the other party know that a conversation is requested. They decide that when one party wants to talk to the other, the originating party will grab the can on his end and yank on it three times. This will cause the can on the other end to rattle around. When the called party sees the can bouncing around, he will know that the party on the other end wants to talk. To use the data link (layer 2), Bud and Don establish a protocol called the yank and rattle. One end yanks the string, causing the can on the other end to rattle. Now they have overcome this obstacle.

We can skip by layer 3 of the model for now. Is it obvious why? Look at Figure 15-14, and it should become fairly clear. The strings are attached to both parties directly. The connection is a point-to-point private line. No switching or routing decisions need to be made, because the connection always goes to the same location. Therefore the network layer doesn't apply per se, so it will be transparent. Now, the neighbors have the necessary connection and the alerting mechanism; so they should be able to communicate without much ado, correct? Maybe not, but see what happens.

Bud now decides that he wants to talk to Don. So, Bud picks up the can and yanks three times. This causes Don's can to bounce around on the other end, which alerts Don that Bud wants to talk to him. Kind of like a ringing

Figure 15-14
The point-to-point connection doesn't need a network layer. No switching decisions need to be made.

Bud

Don

phone, isn't it? So Don jumps up and grabs the can, picks it up, places it to his mouth and says, "Hello." At the same time, Bud is yelling into the can on the other end of this connection for Don to pick up: "Don. Hello, Don, are you there?"

Are these two parties communicating? No, they are not. Both have the can to their mouths; and no one is listening. If both parties are talking and no one is listening, then the information transfer is nil. So, a new set of protocols is required. Let's introduce the transport layer in the OSI model now. Because this whole idea is Bud's, the neighbors agree that whenever Bud wants to speak to Don, or whenever Don wants to speak to Bud, after the can has been rattled a couple of times, Don will always pick the can up and place it to his ear. Bud, on the other hand, will always start the conversation off by placing the can to his mouth. Now, the problems already encountered are handled. So, we should be able to communicate without any further complications, right? Here is the transmission process as it has been defined.

Bud: (Yanks the string).

Don: (Picks up the can on his end and places it to his ear because that's the rule).

Bud: "Hi, Don! Can I borrow your lawn mower today?"

Don: (Takes the can from his ear and places it to his mouth and begins responding) "No way, you told me last week that you were going to finally buy your own."

Bud: (At the same time Don is responding) "I know I told you last week that I was going to buy my own, but I haven't had a chance to get to the store yet."

Now, both parties are talking at the same time. After a given amount of time, they will probably both be listening at the same time. The communications flow is not working properly. So, they have to add a new set of protocols to allow the orderly transfer of the information. The problem stems from the half duplex nature of the link. Only one transmitter/receiver is on each end. Two possible solutions exist. These are as follows.

First, a new string could be run between both parties. On this new string, Don and Bud will attach two new cans, just as they did for the first connection. Each can will be labeled T or R. The T can on Don's end will be connected to the R can at Bud's end, and vice versa. Now, when an alert comes in, each party will pick up the two cans at his end. The T can will be placed in front of each party's mouth, and the R can will be placed in front of each

Figure 15-15
Two separate cans allow simultaneous transmission or reception, not the converse.

party's ear (see Figure 15-15). Now, there are two separate transmission paths, one for transmitting and one for receiving. This is probably the best option, but Bud and Don are reluctant to do this because it adds the complexity of maintaining two strings between their houses and requires twice as many cans on each end. This will take up too much space in their homes.

The alternative to this communications dilemma is the use of a set of rules (protocol) that will define the session layer (the control of the data transfer between the two ends). The session layer will work like this. Because this is Bud's idea, whenever Bud or Don yanks on the string, Don always listens first and Bud always talks first. The problem occurs when the transmitting end is done sending and wants to await the reply: The two parties need to know how to time this out properly. So, Bud will talk first (Have you noticed that Bud talks a lot?). When Bud finishes his statement, he will use an "over" protocol. When Don hears the word over, he will take the can from his ear and place it to his mouth. At the same time, Bud will take the can from his mouth and place it to his ear. Then, Don finally gets a chance to talk. When Don finishes, he will say "over," and the process will reverse back to the beginning, and so on.

Now the two parties have the ability to communicate with each other. Essentially, they can send their information back and forth as they had planned. Now that this whole scenario is established, you have probably noticed that a couple of layers were missed in the OSI model. These would be handled transparently by Don and Bud because they are working with the same communications protocols. However, let's go back and look at these layers to see how they will play out under our scenario. The three we have yet to address are the network, presentation, and application layers. So, we shall complicate the issue by introducing the following add-on needs.

Just as Don and Bud get the communications working by the rules established, a new neighbor, Helen, moves in next door to Don. This is going to happen all around the neighborhood; and we should be prepared. Helen is neighborly and decides that she might have a need to speak to Don and Bud from time to time. The rules already in place can be used to provide the connectivity between all three parties—Figure 15-16 shows this. To set up communications between Helen and Don, a string can be run between the two houses and cans attached to the string. The rule will be as follows: Because Don was here first, Don will always speak first and Helen will listen, regardless of whom rattles the can. The "over" protocol can also be used to provide the session layer, and so on. Now, Helen also needs to talk to Bud, but, as the figure shows, in order for this to happen, they need to run the string from Helen to Bud. This is not a problem for Helen or Bud. As a matter of fact, we can even color-code the cans (red for Don, blue for Bud).

This scenario is a problem for Don. In order for Bud and Helen to connect the string to each location, the string must go in one side of Don's house, pass through and exit the other side to connect to Bud. Don will therefore have to leave his windows open on both sides of his house at all times for this to work. Don doesn't like this idea, so he offers to become a network layer relay point. The process, as shown in Figure 15-17, will work this way. When Bud wants to speak to Helen, he will pick up the one can that is associated with this communications system. He will then yank the can, causing Don to pick up and immediately listen. Bud will then say, "Don, this is

Figure 15-16
Adding a third party
may complicate the
process (for Don).

Bud   Don   Helen

Figure 15-17
By using the relay point, we satisfy the bottom three layers of the model.

a call for Helen." On hearing this, Don, who has two cans and strings, will grab the other can that is connected to the string to Helen's. Don will yank the can, causing Helen to pick up the can and listen. Don speaks first on this connection, so this is fine; he has a can to his ear from Bud and the other can to his mouth leading out to Helen. When Don knows that Helen is on the link, he will say, "Stand by for a message from Bud." At this point, Bud will speak to Don, who in turn will automatically relay everything he hears to Helen. Now the routing of the information is accommodated. The network layer is met, of sorts.

A problem exists with this whole scenario that isn't as obvious. Helen only speaks German. Bud only speaks English. Now the problem: If Bud speaks English into the can connected to Don, how do we make the format or language conversion into something that is usable and understandable to Helen? Luckily, when Don was in school, he took German 101. He didn't excel; but he has a working knowledge of the language. Now, when Don hears Bud say, "Good morning, Helen," in English, Don will relay the information out through the other can in German as: "Guten Tag!" When Bud finishes and says, "over," the process switches. Bud takes the can from his mouth and moves it to his ear. Don takes the can connected to Bud and moves it from his ear to his mouth; at the same time, he takes the can connected to Helen and moves that one from his mouth to his ear.

Helen in turn moves the can from her ear to her mouth and begins to speak or respond. When Helen responds with "Morgen, wie geht's?" Don hears it and converts it to Bud as "Morning. How are you?" So it goes. The presentation layer has just been addressed to accommodate the format or protocol (language) conversion so that transparent communications can take place. The only layer in this case is the applications layer that has not been addressed. What is the application in this regard? Chit-chat: "I just called to say hello!"

By now, you should have an understanding from this simplistic comparison of how the process works through the OSI model. Furthermore, the importance of this all taking place transparently should be obvious. If we had to go through the trials and tribulations of information transfer every time we placed a call, this would be far too cumbersome. The next time a connection to another neighbor is needed, the same rules can be applied.

We already have a simplistic network here, so let's draw it to a conclusion by introducing a couple of other players. Mary moves in behind Bud. There will be a need for Mary to communicate with Bud, Don, and Helen. Rather than trying to run strings all around the neighborhood, we'll just use our relays and rules already in place. So, Mary connects a string to Bud. Communication to Bud is simple. To reach Don, the call will go through Bud to Don; to reach Helen, the call will go through Bud and Don to ultimately get to Helen. One added complication is that Mary only speaks French. Therefore, when Mary says "Bonjour." to Bud, he repeats the information to Don as "Good morning." Don then finally sends it to Helen as "Guten Morgen." Now, Roy moves in behind Don. The neighbors run a connection between Don and Roy—no problem. Roy only speaks pig latin; but that's okay because Don can deal with it. Now, when Mary wants to speak to Roy, she calls through Bud in French, which Bud converts to English and sends on to Don. Don receives the message in English and converts it to pig latin for Roy. The connection is sent through and routed/switched depending on the intended target location. Helen, as you recognize, is left out of this conversation, but she has no need to be connected. The result is shown in Figure 15-18: The connection is routed and switched transparently between and among the neighbors. Don has also become very similar to a central switching system and service provider. Now for voice or data, the telecommunications network is built to handle communication from any user to any other, regardless of the language (format and protocol) or origin of creation (manufacturer). This is what the OSI model was designed to do for us.

Is it here? Partially. Work continues on the standards, especially in how this can all be achieved. Many manufacturers are implementing OSI compatibility in different ways. That's okay, but it might lead to some kludges. The issue is not how the arrangement is created, but the opportunity to have a universal set of rules and protocols that everyone can build to. That is what the OSI reference provides.

That description is probably more than most of us need to know about this. However, we should at least be aware of just what the reference was meant to do for the industry as a whole. If we substitute our players in the previous example, then we can have an organization using a computer platform manufactured by Company Bud. This is connected to or through a

Figure 15-18
The layers can all be
met through this
network.

computer manufactured by Company Don and ultimately sharing and
swapping information with a computer manufactured by Company Helen,
and so on . . . The communications network might well be used as a point-
to-point, point-to-multipoint, or switched dial-up service. Protocols and services such as ISDN, X.25, switched 64 Kbits/s, and leased-line T1 have been
applied, so that the connectivity arrangements adhere to those of the tin
cans and string. Yes, some of the cans might be larger or rounder than others. As long as the same rules apply for electrically and mechanically
attaching to the string (wires, light beams, and radio waves), then this
should all work.

Other Network Architectures

Using the OSI as the reference is fine. It will be the basis of all future development. Other architectures were in existence or sprung up during the wait
for the ubiquitous implementation of OSI. We might never see the end; but
we will see variations and improvements over the OSI as it applies to
vendor-specific architectures or proprietary applications. Here are some of
the more common models:

- SNA, which is now over 27 years old and has undergone very few
  modifications from the original architecture.

- DEC Net. As covered, this is also 25 years old, but has gone through several revisions in an attempt to create openness.

- TCP/IP, a set of protocols that works on a different architecture developed back in the late 1960s and deployed more in the early 1970s for the government. Now it is the protocol for the Internet and the primary set of protocols that LAN, metropolitan area network (MAN), and wide area network (WAN) users are implementing for openness and robustness in their networking needs.

SNA

We have already discussed the SNA world earlier in this chapter. Therefore, the continued discussion of this architecture will concentrate on the subtleties of the SNA to OSI comparison. In 1974, IBM introduced its architecture called Systems Network Architecture (SNA). SNA defines a structure and all of the protocols required to implement a network in which a wide variety of computers, software, and terminal devices can interact and provide a very high degree of network efficiency. Some of the characteristics that were introduced with the SNA concept are as follows:

- Application software uses a standard interface for communications, leaving the software network and device transparent and independent.

- All of the data links can use the same set of rules, called link control procedures.

- Applications can exchange data with each other.

- All applications can be intertwined to allow multiprocessing capabilities.

- Regardless of the location, different devices can access any application on any host.

Various techniques exist for local area data transport through recommendations and implementations by the vendors. Remember that the installations were merely recommendations to move data across a cable system between any two stations on the localized data transmission facility. Networking, whether local area, metropolitan area, or wide area, requires higher-level protocols to manage the transfer of information and make it usable and understandable. Without these higher-level protocols, nothing is guaranteed.

The function of SNA is to augment and supplement the local area network. Imagine that the LAN actually existed under a different name prior to industry acceptance of the term LAN. In the earlier days, this was implemented in the hierarchical networking format provided by SNA, which was introduced in 1974 and changed on a limited basis only. IBM felt that there existed an infrastructure in the major organizations that did not require change. The goal of SNA was to introduce the structure and protocols required to implement a network in which a wide variety of computer hardware, software, and terminal devices could interact and provide a high degree of efficiency and utilization of the network. SNA represents several characteristics of the architecture; for example:

■ Applications software uses a standard communications interface and maintains network and device independence.

■ All data links in SNA use the same link control procedures.

■ Applications can exchange data between and among each other, allowing the use of multiprocessing services.

■ Different types of devices can access applications in different hosts, regardless of the location.

These characteristics of SNA function to work cohesively in any implementation from IBM. SNA, therefore, details the specifications for the devices and nodes on a network and the logical path between these nodes. Both paths and nodes are arranged in the hierarchy using several layers of protocols. This is organized to facilitate the distribution of processing under a common control for the nodes. Furthermore, it is structured to provide flexibility and robustness in routing on the paths.

SNA Components

Each device in an SNA network, from the individual dumb terminal to the host computer, functions with a certain level of control, depending on its position in the hierarchy. It will then operate under the control of the device at the next level up. Terminals, for example, function under the control of the cluster controller. The controller functions under control of the front-end processor and the front-end functions under control of the host. This is the true hierarchical concept IBM introduced 20 years ago.

The *network addressable unit* (NAU) is any segment or code that emphasizes the device to a network, program, or device. Basically, three different types of NAUs exist, as follows:

- The systems services control part (SSCP)
- The physical unit (PU)
- The logical unit (LU)

The SSCP

The SSCP functionally resides in the communications access method of a mainframe computer, or the control program in a midrange computer. Figure 15-19 shows a representation of this control part. This function controls the addressing and routing tables, the name service to address translation services, the routing tables for the network, and all instruction sets that deal with these entities. The SSCP establishes the communications con-

Figure 15-19
The SSCP works as the communications software and manages the network. It will control the setup and teardown of connections between users.

nection between nodes in the network, provides the informational flow control and queuing services for network efficiency, and selects the route for the nodes to communicate with each other.

The Physical Unit

IBM defines the physical unit as a single device on the network. Figure 15-20 is a representation of the PU. In a host computer and a front-end communications processor, this is implemented in software. In a terminal device (less intelligence applied in these), the physical unit is implemented in firmware.

IBM defines the PUs as follows:

- Type 1 is a dumb terminal or a printer.
- Type 2 is a cluster controller (3274) for the terminals or a batch terminal.

Figure 15-20
The physical unit is a supervisory function controlled by the SSCP.

- Type 3 is under study.

- Type 4 is a communications controller such as the front-end processor (37X5).

- Type 5 is a host computer with a system services control part (SSCP).

In SNA, the SSCP controls the physical unit. Each PU is treated as a physical entry point on the network between the network and one or more logical units.

The Logical Unit

The logical unit is the basic communications entity in SNA. The LU is a port where end users access the SNA network. Figure 15-21 shows this access method. Two LUs communicate through what is called an *LU-LU session*, a temporary connection where data can be exchanged on the basis of some mutually agreed upon protocols. The layers of SNA, shown a little differently in Figure 15-22 than in previous versions of the architecture (not to change but to clarify the architecture), build on each other from bottom up. Every SNA node contains the bottom two layers shown in this figure. These two layers—the data link control (DLC) and the path control (PC)—combine as what is called the path control subnetwork.

This is the basic method for the movement of information from a source to a destination node. Sometimes, this can involve passing through intermediate nodes. The LU, which resides in the SNA nodes, consists of the upper three layers in Figure 15-22 and uses the data transport capability of the path control subnetwork.

Figure 15-21

The logical unit is a port where end users access the SNA network.

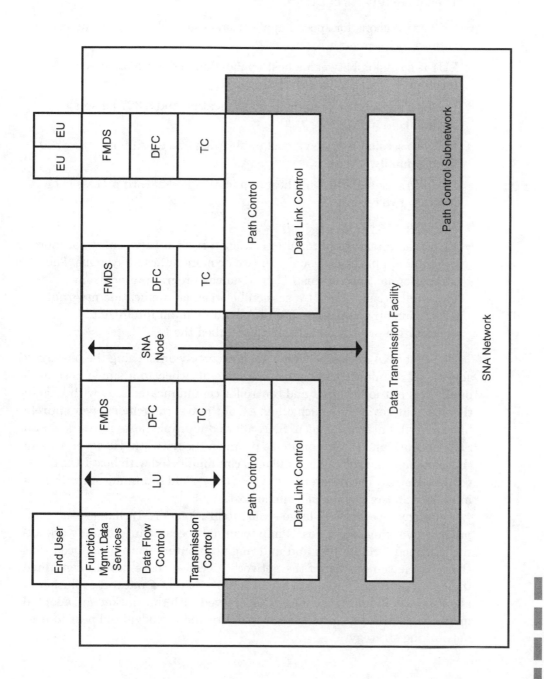

Figure 15-22
The SNA architecture shown differently

The different types of LU are

- LU0 are sessions for special applications where IBM or the end user defines the parameters.
- LU1 is a session between a host application and a remote batch terminal.
- LU2 is a session between the host application and a 3270 display terminal.
- LU3 is a session between a host application and a printer in the 3270 display family.
- LU4 is a session between a host application and a word processor, or between two terminals.
- LU5 is under study.
- LU6 is an intersystem communication, a session between two or more different applications, usually in two or more different systems. The more common type of this LU is advanced program-to-program communications (APPC), a session between an application program in a host and an application program residing in an intelligent workstation or terminal. This is also called the LU6.2.

The first SNA networks were simple tree networks, using the hierarchy shown. All terminals and controllers were attached to a single host computer. LUs in the terminal and controller communicated only with LUs in the host, but never with each other. All of these arrangements were purely hierarchical. Later versions of SNA allowed multiple hosts to reside on an SNA network and communicate as peers on the network. However, LUs in the terminals and controllers still only communicated with host LUs, never with each other. The difference was that they could communicate with LUs in multiple hosts instead of a single host.

Later advances in very-large-scale integration (VLSI) changed the computer networking strategies. Dumb terminals became intelligent workstations. Personal computers and midrange computers were introduced that changed the complexion of the network. Because these devices contained their own processing and storage capability, it was a natural evolution to allow for distributed processing. SNA evolved with the market and adopted more of a peer-to-peer processing capability and the advanced peer-to-peer networking strategy.

Digital Network Architecture (DNA)

Digital Network Architecture, by Digital Equipment Corporation (now acquired by Compaq Computer Corporation), is the model and architecture for the functions of DECNet. DECNet is a system of communications software and hardware that enables DEC's operating systems and components to function in a network with other DEC systems and is open enough to communicate with systems manufactured by others. DECNet is a group of computers with equivalent DEC software and communications hardware that connect with physical channels or lines. Each computer implemented in a network with DECNet software is called a *system*.

DNA defines standard protocols, interfaces, and functions that allow DECNet systems to share data and access various resources, programs, and functions. DNA currently has two separate stacks of protocols, one supporting proprietary protocols and interfaces on a DEC environment and the other supporting the protocols defined in an open systems environment (OSI model). Using a layered approach, DNA is functionally grouped into services and functions based on the layers associated with DECNet. Functionally, DNA is broken down into the following:

- User functions
- Network functions
- Communications functions

Using a slightly different view of DECNet compared to the OSI model than was shown earlier, DNA is shown in Figure 15-23. Two separate stacks are shown here: The first is DEC's version; next to that is the function served by this layer. The labeling on DNA is different than that on the OSI, indicating that DECNet is not 100 percent compatible with the OSI reference. This was demonstrated when DEC introduced its DECNet Phase V. This met with only moderate interest and limited implementation in the industry.

DEC has introduced a family of products and services over the years to allow access to and from DEC computing platforms and other manufacturers' platforms.

Figure 15-23
The DECNet
comparison shown
differently

OSI	DNA	Function		
Application	User	- File Transfer - Down-Line Loading - Virtual Terminal - Remote Resource Access - Remote Command File - Submission		
	Network Management			
Presentation	Network Application			
Session	Session Control	Task to Task		
Transport	End Communications			
Network	Routing	Adaptive Routing		
Data Link	Data Link	DDCMP Point-to Point Multiport	x.25	Ethernet
Physical	Physical			

Internet Protocols (TCP/IP)

While the industry and standards bodies wrestled with openness in the communications and computing arenas, another evolving set of protocols emerged. This is also a layered architecture composed essentially of four layers. A result of a government contract to look at the internetworking of computers in the event of a national disaster, the protocols emerged from the original Advanced Research Projects Agency Network (ARPANET). Developed by Bolt, Beraneck, and Newman of Cambridge, this simple but robust set of protocols was geared toward linking systems in an open architecture. The transmission control protocol with Internet protocol (TCP/IP) continued its evolution from the original ARPANET to what we know as the Internet. The TCP/IP architecture is shown in Figure 15-24. This is a four-layer stack that deals with the equivalent seven-layer architecture of OSI, SNA, and DNA.

Actually, the TCP/IP is quickly becoming the most widely accepted set of protocols in the industry. Included in all forms of the UNIX operating systems and now the protocol of choice in many LAN-to-WAN environments, it is the "middleware" for interconnectivity. The two most prevalent features

Figure 15-24
The TCP/IP protocol
stack architecture

of this protocol stack are its ability to work with just about any environment because it can use application program interfaces to emulate most services on other architectures and its ability to "packetize" the data and send it out.

IP

Internet Protocol (IP), performs a packetization (called *datagrams*) of the user data to be sent between and among the various systems on a network. When a large file is sent down the protocol stack, the IP function is responsible for the segmentation and packetization of this data. Then a header is placed on the datagram for delivery to the data link. The routing and switching of this data is handled at the IP (network) layer. To be somewhat simple in our analogy, IP is also a dumb protocol. When a datagram is prepared for transmission across the medium, IP does not specifically route the call across a specific channel. Rather, it just puts the header on the datagram and lets the network deal with it. Therefore, the outward-bound datagrams can take various routes to get from point A to point B. This means that the datagrams are not sequentially numbered as they are in other protocols. IP makes its best attempt to deliver the datagrams to the destination network interface; however, it makes no assurances that

■ The data will arrive.

■ The data will be error free.

■ The nodes along the way will concern themselves with the accuracy of the data and sequencing, or come back and alert the originator that something is wrong in the delivery mechanism.

This might sound strange in a networking environment, but it allows robustness to be achieved. The nodes along the network merely read the header information and route the datagram to the next logical downstream neighbor. This means that if anything gets corrupted on the network, the node will not know where to send the datagram, so it will throw it away. The network will not send a message back to the originator and let it know that the datagram did not get delivered. Another possibility is that the nodes along the network can send the datagram out on the basis of the best route (based on some costing algorithm or the number of points to pass through). Yet, in the transfer of the datagrams, if one of these routes is busy or broken, the datagrams will be rerouted around the problem to another node. This has great possibilities; but it can lead to a problem.

It is possible, in the IP routing of a datagram, that it can be sent along the network in a loop (see Figure 15-25). The routes might set up in a loop fashion, and the datagram will be circulating on the network like a spinning top. This doesn't cause concern if it is only one datagram; but if it were a general occurrence, the network could get quite bogged down with data-

Figure 15-25
IP can send data into a loop, meaning it will not reach the destination computer. The switches could send the data around and around.

grams spinning around. Therefore, IP has a mechanism in its header information that allows a certain amount of "hops" or what is called time to live (TTL) on the network. Rather than let an undeliverable datagram spin around on the network, IP has a counter mechanism that decrements every time the datagram passes through a network node. If the counter (usually 16 hops or less) expires or gets set to 0, the node will discard the datagram. As you might imagine, if the network can throw away datagrams, we should be alerted when this happens. This is not part of the IP protocol; it does not tell the originator that a datagram has been discarded. Additionally, datagram number four (just an example) was spinning around the network for several hops and was finally discarded. Yet numbers five, six, and seven go through the network without ado. Thus, the later datagrams arrive at the destination, but datagram four is gone. IP does not have a mechanism to know that this has happened, and has no numbering sequence to put everything back in order. Why would anyone favor such a dumb protocol? It is this robustness to deliver the datagrams across the network and throw away bad or undeliverable datagrams that helps to improve the efficiency of network utilization.

TCP

No network manager or administrator would accept not knowing whether data gets delivered across the network. Therefore, working together with IP is the *transmission control protocol* (TCP). TCP provides the smarts to overcome the limitations of IP. Here, the controls will be put in place to ensure that the reliable data stream is sent and delivered. At the sending end, TCP puts a byte count header on the information that will be delivered to the IP protocol layer. This is encapsulated as part of the data in the IP datagram. The receiving end, when it gets the datagrams, is responsible for putting the data back into its proper sequence and ensuring its accuracy. If things are not correct, the byte count acknowledgment (ACK) or nonacknowledged (NAK) message is sent back to the sending end. The sending end receiving a NAK will resend the bytes necessary to fill in the blanks. Furthermore, TCP holds all of the later received bytes (datagrams five, six, and seven from the previous example) until it gets datagram four resent. Thus, it buffers the data at the receiving end. This makes data reception and accuracy the responsibility of the end user (node), not the network responsibility. This is to prevent the network from getting bogged down if errors or loops are occurring. The network is, after all, a transport system, not a computer processing function.

Using TCP/IP, the network operates efficiently; and improvements are being seen every day as the quality of the circuits is improved with all of the fiber-optic backbones being installed. Therefore, the movement in the past ten years has been heavily toward TCP/IP and the Internet.

Questions

1. What does OSI mean?
   a. Open Systems Interface
   b. Only System Interface
   c. Open Systems Interference
   d. Open Systems Interconnect

2. What organization is responsible for creating the OSI?
   a. ITU
   b. ISO
   c. IBM
   d. IEEE

3. What year was the model ratified?
   a. 1978
   b. 1988
   c. 1974
   d. 1983

4. When the OSI model was being developed, it was to solve some of the problems we experiences between:
   a. IBM and DEC
   b. Sun and HP
   c. IBM and Data General
   d. DEC and Data General

5. What organization created the Government Open Systems Interconnect Profile?

   a. International Telecomm Union

   b. CCITT

   c. US government

   d. IBM

6. The OSI model has how many layers?

   a. 11

   b. 6

   c. 7

   d. 4

7. IBM's SNA has how many layers?

   a. 5

   b. 7

   c. 6

   d. 4

8. When DEC created their architecture, what did they call it?

   a. DECnet

   b. DNI

   c. DNA

   d. Digital Networking Standards

9. What layer did we eliminate when we used a point-to-point leased line?

   a. Application

   b. Transport

   c. Network

   d. Data Link

10. What layer is responsible for the electrical and mechanical interface?

   a. 4

   b. 1

   c. 3

   d. 2

11. What layer performs the transparent transmission of information between the two ends?

    a. 7

    b. 6

    c. 4

    d. 5

12. What layer is responsible for translation and protocol conversion?

    a. Application

    b. Presentation

    c. Network

    d. Transport

13. IBM's layer 3 is called Path Services.   T/F

14. The application layer in SNA is called user services.   T/F

15. The best way to handle data transmission is to let the data processing people handle it.   T/F

16. When the world began to evolve to OSI, what happened?

    a. It was widely accepted.

    b. Few people implemented it.

    c. The U.S. government made everyone abide by it.

    d. The North Americans began to replace their IBM systems.

17. Why do we need the model anyway?

    a. It adds more cost to the price of a system.

    b. It provides for transparency in our networks.

    c. It guarantees nothing.

    d. It seemed like a nice thing to do.

18. What is the replacement protocol suite that the U.S. government and the rest of the world is now implementing?

    a. DNA

    b. TCP/IP

    c. SNA

    d. GOSIP

19. How many layers does the TCP/IP protocol model have?

    a. 7

    b. 5

    c. 4

    d. 6

20. IP guarantees delivery and reliability of the data.   T/F

The Internet

When you have completed the reading and the questions, you will be able to:

- Discuss what the Internet is and what it is not
- Understand what all the hype is about in the communications industry
- Discuss the components of the Internet
- Converse about the protocols used and the services available
- Recognize how the Internet protocols are changing
- Understand why IP has changed in its acceptance

Are you on the Net? For an increasing percentage of the world's population (nearly 300 million users as of 2001) the answer to this question is yes. The Internet is a social as well as a technological phenomenon. A huge number of people otherwise unfamiliar with data processing have nonetheless gone out and bought computers, modems, cable modems or xDSL technologies, and other required paraphernalia. Then, they proceeded to hook up to and actually use a resource based on technologies that, if asked about, they could describe in only the most general terms, if at all.

With some qualifications, the Internet ultimately may be one of the few innovations that actually justifies the hype associated with it. Often described as a "network of networks," it provides a path to incredible amounts of information, much of it free for the taking (free if you don't count the basic network access costs). The continuing price of access is reasonable ($19.95 per month for a dial-up account in North America). So many people have figured this out, in fact, that the Internet has quickly become overloaded to the point that it is sometimes essentially unusable. This chapter attempts to provide you with a basic understanding of just what the Internet really is, why you should care about it, the main types of capabilities the Internet provides, how to go about acquiring and using those capabilities, and where the Internet may be going.

A Little History

Back during the Cold War, the U.S. government instigated the construction of the Defense Advanced Research Projects Agency network (DARPAnet). Initially, it only connected a few key government research laboratories and a few universities under contract to the government for various research projects. Over time, additional universities were added. In addition, companies dealing with the government were connected (see Figure 16-1). Some overseas institutions were also added, making this network international. The bandwidths connecting all these institutions were continuously increased to support all kinds of communications (see the following for more details). In reality, the Internet (as we now know it) started out as a 56-Kbps data communications network used to connect these sites together. When the rollout started, the backbone was immediately increased from 56 Kbps to a T1 (1.544 Mbps) transmission system. Later, in the late 1980s, it evolved again to a T3 backbone.

In theory, all of these institutions were connected only to support research associated with the U.S. government. In reality, most provided access to all members of their organizations. Moreover, in the universities' case, that included students. Those students took the knowledge of how this service worked out into the world when they graduated. Somewhere along the way, the *D* in DARPAnet was dropped when people realized that the types of research and other activities on the network went well beyond "defense" and supporting military research.

The service that was most used at that time was electronic mail (e-mail). It was much less sophisticated than the capabilities used today. In fact, most implementations of the time sent only the text of a message, the

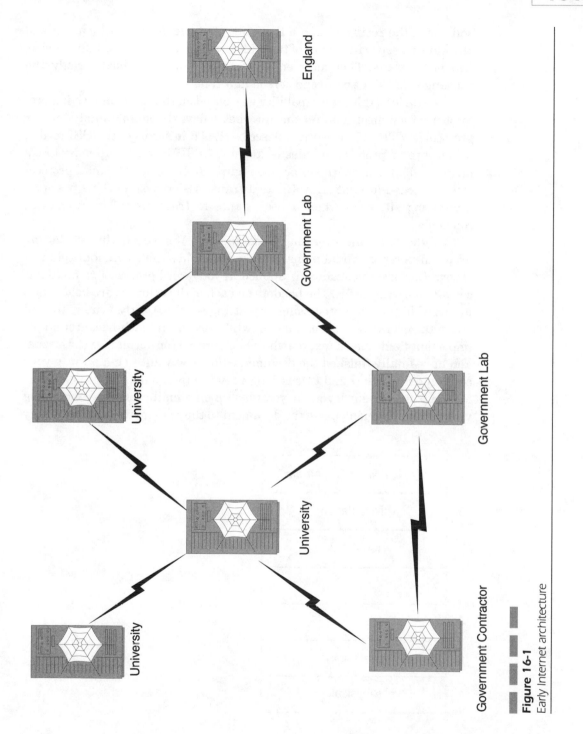

Figure 16-1
Early Internet architecture

address of the recipient, and a text subject string with no attachments of any kind, no separate names of the addressees (versus just their addresses), and no copy-to's. This rudimentary form of e-mail enabled strictly the exchange of ASCII text to one person at a time.

Nevertheless, this mail capability was based on the same underlying protocol used for most mail on the Internet today: the simple mail transfer protocol (SMTP). If one were to describe SMTP in terms of the OSI model, it is a layer 7 protocol. It rides on top of TCP/IP, just like other protocols mentioned later in this chapter (see Figure 16-2). The SMTP mail protocol was developed around an ASCII text transmission system. This poses an interesting situation when a user wants to transmit information to a colleague.

Has the following ever happened to you? You spend the whole day preparing a report. Great pains are taken to build a table with four columns of text. Background shading is applied in your word processor to highlight certain fields in the file. The headers on each of the columns are bolded and italicized in the word processing formatting service. Lastly, you lay this all out with reverse text for emphasis (white text on a black background for important fields, black text on white background for normal text). Eureka! You have finally finished the document. Now you want to e-mail it to your colleague for review and discussion. A few compliments are also expected for the fruits of your labor. So, you type up an e-mail message announcing your accomplishment, paste the document to the mail message, and let it fly

Figure 16-2
SMTP is a layer 7 protocol.

7	SMTP, FTP, HTTP, others
6	(presentation)
5	(session)
4	
3	
2	(data link)
1	(physical)

TCP/IP

through the Net. Soon you call your colleague and ask what he/she thinks about it. Alas, you are told it is garbage! No, the text is not garbage, but the format of the document that arrives is garbage. The formatting has all disappeared. No longer is the table and column format intact. The bolding and shading have also disappeared. Moreover, the text is all over the place, indented where it shouldn't be, and so forth. You are crushed! What happened? After all that work, the other end thinks the document is trash. Well, let's analyze what happened.

Today, word processing systems use an extended ASCII code set. That means that an 8-bit code set is used to format the document in current packages. The Net, on the other hand, was built on a true ASCII code set (7-bit ASCII). As a result, when you transmit the document, the receiving device is looking at the seven bits (not eight) and interpreting the information using a different language. The result is what shows up. To solve this problem, other protocols like file attachments (MIME and Binary) are used in the mail programs on the market today. Relief at last!

The other major layer 7 protocol in use both then and now is the file transfer protocol (FTP). As its name implies, FTP is used to move files from one system to another across a TCP/IP-based network. FTP can be used not only by humans, but also by programs; that is what makes it a layer 7 protocol rather than just an application program. (This is also true of SMTP. If a program sends mail, the program is sometimes referred to as "mail enabled.") However, whereas now most Internet access software has GUI-based FTP built in, systems in the early days had only a command-line interface (similar to DOS, although generally on UNIX-based machines). Calling it user-hostile would be charitable.

Incidentally, most modern PC-based operating systems (Windows 9x, Windows NT, and OS/2) still provide command-line FTP as part of their base package (along with TCP/IP). However, because few people know how to use it (or need to), the vendors do not promote this feature in their marketing materials. To see it, simply start a DOS window, type FTP, and press the Enter key. Or, another way in a Windows 9X system, use the Start button, and then click on the Run command. When the Run window pops up, type FTP and press the Enter key. This launches the core protocol and you can then enter the destination address you want to transfer the files to. It is actually simpler than it seems, but we have become addicted to the GUI interfaces, so we do not like all that complicated typing and command-line interfacing. HELP should list the available commands; the HELP command, where command is one of the choices, should provide you more information on individual commands. QUIT returns you to DOS.

Several additional layer 7 applications were commonly used until the World Wide Web became popular and are still probably used by those not enamored of the Web. Among these are the picturesquely named Gopher and Finger. Gopher is a text-based ancestor of the Web; a Gopher client, like a Web browser, jumps from Gopher site (server) to site retrieving text-based information at the command of its user. Finger is a method of identifying users of UNIX systems. Because most Web users do not have or need UNIX accounts, its usefulness is less now than it was in the past. Other search capabilities include Ph, WAIS, and Veronica.

All of these capabilities and services were used by thousands of people for many years before anyone used the expression "the Web." Nevertheless, you should not feel left out. Compared to the Web, none of these capabilities were packaged in a user-friendly fashion. Moreover, the types of information available via these services were not generally of interest to typical users. After all, the R in ARPAnet did stand for research.

Structure (Who's at the Center—and Why)

Obviously, the backbone is critical, but it's just a start. The vast majority of Internet users (both companies and individuals) are not part of the backbone. Moreover, the backbone providers are generally not in the business of providing end-user (or end-business) connections, other than to their own personnel and customers. Instead, a group of intermediary companies called Internet Service Providers (ISPs) has sprung into being. The commercialization of the Internet by the Clinton and Gore administration in the U.S. created this new ISP business. In 1992, the decision was made to commercialize the Internet as the Information Superhighway. Soon thereafter (1994-1995), the emergence of the ISPs exploded. It is your friendly local ISP that you go to get a connection to the Internet. ISPs themselves connect to the backbone directly, usually for a fee (which is recouped, month by month, from customers like you).

Note that underlying all this is the assumption that actual physical interlocation circuits are still provided by either local telephone companies or interexchange carriers. When a backbone provider, or ISP, *is* an interexchange carrier, it acts in a dual role. Otherwise, such providers and ISPs construct rooms full of routers, modems, DSUs, and so forth, and use their local telco to connect up, both among their own locations and to the Internet backbone itself, or to other backbone providers in the case of the central organizations.

We generally divide ISPs into two categories: regional (sometimes called local) and national (see Figure 16-3). These backbone providers are now called national access providers (NAPs) and they have national access points (NAP), which they call points of presence (POPs). Confused? Actually, the national category should really be called international. See the section on gaining access for more information on these providers. Current 2001 statistics point out that over 4,500 registered ISPs are available in North America. Unfortunately, none of these ISPs is making any money. We will see a feeding frenzy in this market before long, as the larger companies begin to gobble up the little ISPs.

Why the Hype?

It is reasonable to describe the Internet as a peer-to-peer network. This means that, as long as things are set up properly, any computer on the Net can communicate directly with any other computer. What do we mean by *any computer*? Any computer in the world with a connection to the Internet and a properly configured suite of TCP/IP software can participate fully in any service for which it and its users have authorized access.

Of course, in practice, performance considerations may limit what one can actually do with any particular computer. Essentially, by buying computer equipment costing under $1,000, ordering a dial-up telephone line (the extra line can cost as much as $30 a month), and signing up with a local Internet service provider for about $19.95 per month, an individual or an organization can gain full access to the Internet. The ISPs and computer manufacturers have teamed together and now offer free computers (not really powerful, but they do the job) if you subscribe with the ISP for three years. Specific providers like Microsoft Network or America Online (AOL) are the larger providers of this service.

And it's not only for access to information. In addition to pulling information from the network, individuals can publish information to the network. To do this effectively, one must have access to a computer that is connected to the network full-time (that is, 24 hours per day). However, many network providers (ISPs and others) are more than happy to provide

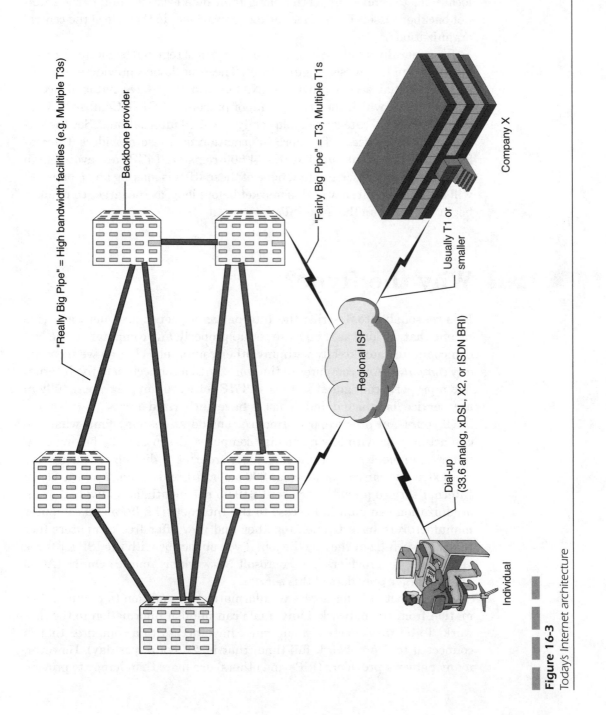

"Really Big Pipe" = High bandwidth facilities (e.g. Multiple T3s)

Backbone provider

"Fairly Big Pipe" = T3, Multiple T1s

Company X

Usually T1 or smaller

Regional ISP

Dial-up
(33.6 analog, xDSL, X2, or ISDN BRI)

Individual

Figure 16-3
Todays Internet architecture

Figure 16-4
Web hosting using a
remote Web hosting
service

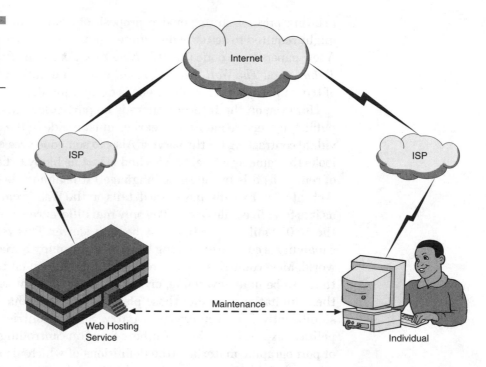

shared access to such full-time-connected computers for a nominal fee (as little as $10 per month, specifically for this publishing capability), or in some cases as part of a basic Internet access fee (see Figure 16-4).

Everybody as a Publisher

The invention of the printing press made it possible for a large number of individuals and organizations to publish their ideas and information to the world at large. The "free press" is an ideal in the U.S., and mostly one that still is a reality. However, with few exceptions, practical and economic limitations usually constrain the geographic areas to which print media is spread. It is an axiom in the newspaper business that "all news is local." Only a tiny percentage of the world's population ever sees much detail about what is happening outside the borders of its own country—even in countries without significant limitations on newspapers. After all, how many people in the U.S. read *The Times* of London? Setting up an actual printing press is an expensive proposition, not to mention the logistical might required to actually distribute a paper worldwide on a regular basis. A few papers have done this (the *New York Times*, the *International Herald Tribune* and *The Wall Street Journal* come to mind), but the total number of truly international publications is quite limited.

However, on the Internet, there is no particular reason why the shared publishing service mentioned earlier must reside in the country of the individual contracting for the service. Also, to someone accessing that service, it looks the same as a local service and is just as likely to be accessed (as long, of course, as it is in the same language!) It is almost as easy to maintain a Web site (later we discuss more details on the Web) from 10,000 miles away as it is from five miles away. The only real difference between the two is that the 10,000-mile connection may be a bit slower. This remote maintenance capability is currently causing heartburn for many bureaucrats around the world. Most countries have some kind of limitation on the types of content that can be made available, or published, on the Internet. In most cases, these limitations parallel those placed on print media, but the rules vary significantly from country to country. Some countries focus on limiting political expression, whereas others focus on controlling the dissemination of pornographic materials (the definitions of which also vary widely). Still others prohibit the propagation of hate materials. In addition, of course, many attempt to block more than one of these.

The problem is, of course, that any one individual or organization that wants to publish information banned in its home country can simply select a network provider in a country that does not block the particular type of information desired. Thus, because the U.S. does not block most forms of political expression, opposition parties from around the world and of all political persuasions can publish from the U.S. to the world with impunity. Likewise, at least one Scandinavian country places few limits on what might elsewhere be described as pornography. No evidence is needed in the home country to betray the originators to local authorities.

To prevent such uncontrolled international communications from circumventing local rules, some countries are considering an attempt to monitor all electronic traffic across their borders, but the Internet is a phenomenon that reaches down to the level of individuals, rather than just companies and other organizations. Unless a country is willing to give up the benefits of having the individuals in its population gain reasonable access to the Internet, monitoring all such traffic is a manifestly impossible scenario, even for the most automated countries in the world (such as the

U.S.). Of course, the threat of enforcement can sometimes be an effective deterrent if the penalties of being caught are harsh, even if the probability of being caught is small. After all, the U.S. Internal Revenue Service can audit only a tiny percentage of the taxes due to the United States government, but by and large people pay taxes anyway.

One can see, however, that the ability of individuals and organizations to communicate with the world has been increased by orders of magnitude by the ubiquity of the Internet.

Commercial Opportunity?

Where do you shop? Chances are that most of your shopping is done at physical storefronts or malls within a few miles of your home. Perhaps you also shop from catalogs that reach you by *snail mail* (that is, the post office). What chance does a small vendor located thousands of miles away from you have of marketing products to you? Until the Internet became available, the vendor had very little chance. That vendor could publish nice color catalogs and mail them out. Many small companies have done just that, and have become large companies by doing so. A good example of this is L.L. Bean. However, this is an expensive route to take; the production of a good catalog is a costly effort, and postage is very expensive if a large number of pieces are to be distributed. The point here is that the cost of even trying is high.

Enter the Internet. Literally tens of millions of people either have or will have access soon, and, with minimal investment (a few thousand dollars), a vendor can in theory reach all of them. A nice potential market, wouldn't you say? Many think the answer to this question is a resounding yes! However, there are a few flies in the ointment, depending on your point of view.

Currently, one can attempt to reach potential customers via the Internet in several ways:

- Send out a large number of electronic messages (the electronic equivalent of junk mail, referred to as *spam* by those who would prefer not to receive such transmissions).
- Place advertising for products and services on others' Web sites.
- Create a Web site (see the following) to describe products and services, and perhaps to actually take orders for those same products and services.

Spam

What is your definition of junk mail? Do you like to receive it? Do you often purchase products as a result of receiving it? We didn't think so. Although people who receive small amounts of postal mail might like receiving anything at all in their mailbox, most would prefer it to be a bit more specific to the person than typical junk mail. Likewise, although new users of the Internet *(newbies)* may initially be excited by messages in their electronic inboxes with titles like ****!!!!*Make big money stuffing envelopes!!!!*****, after the fifth, tenth, or hundredth such message, things become tedious very quickly. The risk that something worthwhile is buried among the garbage is always present. Although the delete button is always there, it takes some time to filter out the spam, and time is usually in short supply.

The good news is that with a small expenditure of money and a little applied intelligence, one can greatly reduce the amount of spam that one actually sees. Products, both for regular e-mail and for newsgroups, are available that are capable of filtering out unwanted messages (see Figure 16-5). For example, Qualcomm's Eudora Pro e-mail program can select e-mail and delete it before reading it on the basis of an unlimited set of user-specified character sequences, whether those sequences appear in a message's subject, in the main body of text, or as part of the sender's name. If you never want to see a message containing the word "toner" in the subject (many scam artists try to sell copier and printer toner via the Net—we

Figure 16-5
Filtering programs dump spam in a trash can.

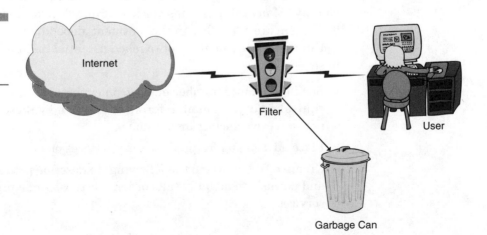

Internet

Filter

User

Garbage Can

have no idea why), you don't have to. Anawave's Gravity, a sophisticated newsgroup reader program, has similar filtering capabilities. On the other hand, as P. T. Barnum said, "there's a sucker born every minute," and the law of large numbers says that if you send out thousands of such messages, at least a few suckers are going to read them and respond. Because the cost of sending out spam is so much smaller than the costs associated with paper mail, it is likely that people will continue to send it out.

A number of organizations have attempted to limit spam in various ways. Some ISPs (for example, CompuServe and America Online) have rules against their own users generating spam; if discovered, a spam sender on those networks will find him- or herself without an ISP. This is helpful, but only partially successful. Literally hundreds of other ISPs are available, at least a few of which exist primarily for the purpose of supporting spam senders. It's not illegal, just very annoying (except to those senders, of course). The United States Congress has considered legislating against spam. Unfortunately, this is one of the areas where the social aspects of the Internet phenomenon come to the fore. Spam is just a form of communication. One person's junk e-mail is another's shining opportunity, or so it is said. Moreover, in the United States, at least, strong constitutional protections counter most attempts to limit communication, particularly via legislation. If one regards Internet mail as a faster alternative to the post office, then spam can be considered unavoidable. At least in the case of the electronic version, methods are available to automatically handle a portion of it, no recycling required.

Web Advertising

One of the distinguishing characteristics of computers is that, if programmed correctly, they can aid in focusing transmission of commercial messages (that is, advertising) to only those people most likely to be receptive to those messages. The Internet embodies a number of ways to advertise to its users. One, mentioned above, is spam. But spam is a sledgehammer approach; by definition, it is not focused. Other, much more subtle approaches, are available. One approach is using "banner ads"—colorful, sometimes animated rectangles on Web pages, similar to magazine ads, but with a significant difference: When clicked on, they normally change the user's current Web page to one on the advertiser's Web site. This is referred to as a *link*. Banner ads are usually placed (for a fee, of course) on sites with a lot of traffic; thus, they are the Net equivalent of putting up a poster for some kind of product or service in the window of a supermarket.

Web Site

Another way one can advertise one's wares on the network is to create a Web site. Creating a Web site is more than just a way to advertise (see Figure 16-6). A Web site puts your corporate or personal image up close and personal in front of any Web user who wants to access it. Unlike spam, however, the creation of a Web site can be very expensive. On a per-user basis, it may not be expensive compared to print advertising; however, the skills as well as the resources involved in creating a Web site are completely different. What does it take to create a Web site? Here are just some of the requirements. For one thing, you need a computer; an ISP may provide one for you if that's the way you'd like to go. An ISP can provide either a dedicated computer—one that is just going to be your own Web site—or a shared (sometimes referred to as a virtual Web site) computer, in which case your Web pages share the computer, the disk space, and so on of a number of other Web sites. Two categories of computers, or rather operating systems, tend to used for Web sites: UNIX computers and Windows NT computers. In practice, any computer that runs UNIX, such as a Sun, IBM RS

Figure 16-6
Sample home page
for a company

Welcome to

Widgets Inc.

- Product Catalog

- Locations

- Technical Support

- Links to Related Sites

Comments? E-mail webmaster@widgetsinc.com

6000, or any other computer capable of running some variant of UNIX can be used. Windows NT and now Windows 2000 computers are increasingly popular because they are somewhat easier to manage; however, the size of the Web site you can create tends to be larger with a UNIX computer. Now the implementation of Linux-based systems is becoming the norm because of the simplicity and cost of the software. In addition, the movement against Microsoft, the NT platform, is now greeted with mixed results.[1] Linux seems to be a movement all of its own as we approach the new millennium. At least it seems easier to create larger sites with a UNIX/Linux computer than with a Windows NT-based machine.

You need much more than just a computer, however. To create a Web site, you need connections to the Internet that require an ISP (discussed elsewhere in this book) and a way to create the pages. Initially, when the Web first came into being, one created Web pages by using a text editor where pages were defined in hypertext markup language (HTML). Markup languages have been around for quite some time. They are distinguished from what-you-see-is-what-you-get (WYSIWYG) systems because they are text. Markup languages use what are called tags. A tag is a word surrounded by angle brackets (<tag-goes-here>) that tells the system processing the markup language what to do with text that immediately precedes or follows the tag. Markup languages are particularly useful for manipulating truly large amounts of text in a consistent way. If you are going to use a WYSIWYG system, then everybody working on a project must have an entire series of standards defined in excruciating detail. For example, normal paragraphs have to be a certain point size, headers have to be a certain point size, and so on, and every individual must know how those work and set their WYSIWYG editors accordingly. With a markup language, instead of saying exact point size for heading, you would say "heading 1." That will be a tag. Of course, although the WYSIWYG editor requires a great deal of specification of detail, a markup language requires the user to know all of the tags. Because HTML is a relatively new language, not many people initially knew those tags. This is one of the main reasons why so-called Web masters command such high salaries. The creation of a Web page is not inherently difficult; however, it requires a skill set that is completely new and therefore rare—at least so far. A fair number of businesses have had Web pages created, then examined what was created and realized that

---

[1] Many people are anti-Microsoft. Therefore, they go out of their way to avoid using the products and software produced by that company.

maintenance is not all that difficult, at least at a conceptual level. In any case, now a large number of tools enable Web maintainers to take at least one large step away from the HTML coding that was required until recently. In addition, a number of editors focus on the HTML coding, but have point-and-shoot selections for the various tags so that you don't necessarily have to memorize all of them.

There is a major additional element here. For example, it is very easy to create a basic newsletter document; however, a really good newsletter requires skills far beyond just the use of a word processor, no matter how sophisticated that word processor is. Page layout skills, an understanding of design elements, and of course an understanding of subject matter are all required. In the case of a Web page or site, a significantly larger number of factors must be taken into account. For example, there is always a temptation with modern tools to create strikingly beautiful Web pages with all kinds of wonderful graphics. However, graphics of any size require a considerable amount of bandwidth or network capacity to be moved out to the people who are going to view them. Most people still access the network via dial-up lines (2001 figures indicate 85 percent). For the most part, those lines at the moment max out at 33.6 Kbps. Some faster speeds are available, but it is a mistake to design a Web page for popular use and then not take into account the vast majority of people who do not have fast connections to the Web. The 56 Kbps modems discussed earlier do not produce fast enough connections for very busy Web sites or dense graphic images. Large files only frustrate visitors of a Web site and chase them away forever. This problem is sometimes aggravated by the fact that companies typically have dedicated, higher-speed connections to the Internet and the Web. By higher-speed, in this case, we mean as fast as a T1 circuit or 1.544 million bits per second. Very large companies have T3s or 45 million bits per second. Connect these to a local area network in a developer's area and the people who are doing the testing on the Web site will see all those lovely pictures positively snap onto their screens. Those same graphics, however, will take a long time to reach a typical dial-in user's screen. The Web is not referred to as "World Wide Wait" for nothing. Of course, now that cable modems and DSL services are reasonably priced, users will see a ramp up in the ability to download files and Web sites much faster. Remember, however, that only 15 percent of the population is on these higher speed connections.

The cost of a Web site varies radically. At the low end, it is possible to get an account on America Online and create a Web site for no extra cost. We are talking about $20 per month or so. But for this price, the amount of storage you get is minimal—two or three megabytes—and you do all the work yourself. All you have is a facility. Moreover, anyone who is serious about providing a Web site for access by many other people probably does not want to put it on America Online or CompuServe. The focus of these providers is serving individual users; they're not really set up to provide excellent Web site support. They are changing, but are not yet there. These companies (AOL, CompuServe, and Prodigy) are charted as online service providers, not ISPs. Many other companies have gone into business to do just that—notably many ISPs. The real cost of setting up a Web site is not the network; it's the computers themselves, which for high-capacity machines could easily cost in the tens of thousands of dollars, possibly even the low hundreds of thousands for a single high-capability server. Some of the more frequently accessed sites are *hit* (accessed) literally millions of times per day. One doesn't want to use a low-end PC to handle something like that. The other major cost is people time. We mentioned previously that the skills aren't all that rarified, but they are still rare. Because of that, people who really know how to do a good job on a Web site still command premium rates. A typical high-end Web site will not come into being for less than $50,000 to $100,000 up front; it can easily cost several times that. Also, there are continuing maintenance costs. One of the most common phenomena seen on the Web today is that a company, possibly very well funded, spends the bucks to create a Web site, puts it online, and gets buried by the number of accesses coming in initially. Those accesses will taper off unless at least two things happen:

1. The Web site is kept up to date. That doesn't mean just current information; it means that the Web site undergoes a perceptible change, whether it's in content or layout, on a continuing basis. People won't come back frequently if, when they come back, they don't see anything new.

2. Enough bandwidth is ensured for the site to handle the actual number of users accessing it. Bandwidth in this context is not just the network access; it's also the capability of the server. As with many other environments, everyone typically blames the network itself when access is slow. More often than not, it turns out that the slowness of the access is due to the undersizing of the server's capabilities.

Advertising, of course, is not the only reason to create a Web site. Many companies, like Amazon.com, for example, have created a Web site that is an entire enterprise. Of course, the site has advertising, but it also has a great deal of content regarding products or services for sale. In the most complete cases, products and services are actually for sale directly via the Web.

Sounds like a major opportunity, right? It could be. Billions of people now routinely access the Web on a daily basis. That's a large pool of potential customers. However, people are in some cases still reluctant to put the necessary information on the network to make real purchases. Both of the major vendors of Web browsers, Netscape and Microsoft, have addressed this concern by incorporating something called a secure sockets layer (SSL) into their browsers, as have the people who created Web sites that actually sell products and services (see Figure 16-7). SSL is pretty good, but because very few people understand that the encryption is present, we believe that it will take some time for Web sales to really take off. It doesn't help that the Web is really slow at times. Often, it's quicker to pick up the telephone and call a vendor than it is to try to go through all the text entry to purchase products and services on the Web.

One should be aware that the Web is almost a science fiction kind of environment. One of the characteristics is that things change rapidly. Web pages come and go, companies appear and disappear, and the features of individual Web pages, as mentioned above, change rapidly. There are some ways to try to keep on top of this. One is to use searchers. A few services or Web sites specialize in helping other users find Web sites. Paradoxically, these services or searchers are free. How do they do it? They accept a great deal of advertising, and this advertising is focused in a way that occurs in no other medium. The Web sites that provide searchers pay attention to what individuals search for, and, based on what those individuals request, different advertising appears along with the responses to the searches. The technology used by these companies is amazing. They have enormous databases that are kept up to date on a continuing basis via automated

Figure 16-7
Secure sockets layer (SSL) provides an end-to-end secure virtual link.

Vendor Web Site

Secure Sockets Layer

Browser Shopper

searchers that go out themselves and collect information from everywhere on the Net. Those databases are then indexed and used for searches for users. The searches are amazingly fast. Of course, to an individual who does not realize what's going on behind the scenes, the searches may not be so amazing. A typical search may return 20,000 results. That would be daunting, but at least in Excite's case, the results are sorted in a descending order according to the likelihood of satisfying the request.

Protocols

We're going to get a little technical here for a moment. TCP/IP was defined elsewhere in this book. TCP/IP is a collection of protocols. The base protocols described by the letters TCP/IP refer to the lower three or four layers of the OSI model. Some layer 7 protocols ride on top of TCP/IP. Among these are FTP, Telnet, simple mail transfer protocol (SMTP), and simple network management protocol (SNMP). Newer protocols like the real time protocols (RTP) and network time stamp protocols (NTP) ride at layer 7.

FTP stands for file transfer protocol. When you use a browser to access a list of files or updates to programs on a Web site, when you actually click on an icon or link to retrieve a file, there's a better-than-even chance that the file is being retrieved using FTP. FTP is not the protocol used for routine browser operations, but the major browsers do incorporate the capability of moving files around using FTP. FTP existed long before the World Wide Web. Most operating systems come with software that enables you to use FTP directly without using a browser. However, FTP typically has a command-line interface in such an environment. If you are comfortable with the C: prompt, then you might want to use FTP in cases where you have problems getting the browser to work properly. A few GUI-based FTP implementations are also stand-alones rather than integrated into a browser. This could be very useful in cases where you're going to spend some time doing nothing but retrieving files, for example, from a vendor's support site.

Telnet (not Telenet) is a means to sign onto a remote system network directly as a user of that system (see Figure 16-8). This is not the same as using the World Wide Web, although the physical infrastructure is the same. When you use a browser to access a Web page, every time you click on a link, you send a request for a specific set of information to a specific Web

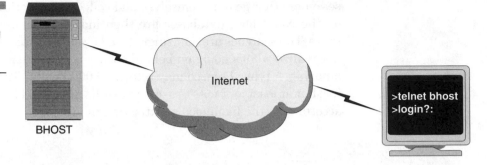

Figure 16-8
Telnet allows signing
onto a remote
computer.

site. That Web site, if it can, sends back just the information you requested. Generally speaking, it then completely forgets it had anything to do with you. No "conversation" takes place: Each exchange is a stand-alone transaction. In the case of Telnet, however, you sign onto a remote machine. To do this, you have to have an account on that machine, although some machines, notably in university environments, may allow you to sign on anonymously or even create your own account. Usually, if you are trying to sign onto a system anonymously, you use the user ID "anonymous" and a password consisting of your complete e-mail address. The software normally does not check the latter; rather, it's just a courtesy and a convention that you comply with in order to get the free service that you're about to use. With the popularity of the Web, Telnet is not a facility you are likely to need on a regular basis. However, if a vendor gives you access to a system for some reason, you may need to access it using this approach. To use it, go to the prompt on your operating system and type Telnet [space] and the name of the system you wish to access. You can also tell Telnet a specific IP address of the form nnn.nnn.nnn.nnn. FTP can also be used to access a remote system in the same way, with the same address and convention.

Telnet enables signing onto a remote computer. SMTP stands for simple mail transfer protocol. You will probably not use this protocol explicitly; however, if you use Internet mail (for example, the mail that is provided as part of Netscape), then you are using the SMTP protocol. As mail protocols go, SMTP is pretty simple. This has caused some problems because it does not in and of itself incorporate ways to send attachments, particularly not binary or program-type attachments. However, a number of vendors have come together, built software, and established conventions that allow these capabilities.

Although among the least sophisticated mail environments in the world, SMTP mail is sort of taking over the world. Why? Because SMTP is built into pretty much all systems that use the Internet. It is the kind of mail that you get when you sign up with an ISP.

The form of an SMTP or Internet mail address is **name@node.extension**. For example, the Internet mail address of one of the authors of this book is **bud@tcic.com**. Until recently, the list of extensions was very short: only about eight or so. Agreements have since been made that will probably significantly increase the number of suffixes. A whole structure of these is beyond the scope of this book.

One of the major successes in the area of intervendor cooperation was the creation of a couple of standards for including attachments with e-mail. The preferred one of these is called Multipurpose Internet Mail Extensions (MIME). A MIME attachment can include just about anything that can be represented in digital form. Moreover, most of the more sophisticated e-mail software packages can automatically create MIME inclusions without users having to go through several steps. MIME extends the format of the Internet mail to allow non-U.S.-ASCII textual messages, nontextual messages, multipart message bodies, and non-U.S.-ASCII information in message headers.

SNMP stands for simple network management protocol. Although this protocol is integral to the management of the Internet, most users will never be involved with it because it is used by people operating the Internet rather than by end users. We will not go further into this topic in this book.

The World Wide Web (or is that world wide wait??) is just a virtual structure running on top of the basic Internet itself. All of the things that were there before the World Wide Web are still there; however, the vast majority of Internet users are not aware of them because the Web itself is so much easier to use. Browsers (and therefore the Web, which really just consists of browsers and Web sites talking back and forth) use a protocol called hypertext transfer protocol (HTTP). One of its key characteristics was mentioned earlier, but bears repeating: Exchanges (or transactions) based on HTTP are "stateless." This means that unless special measures are taken, Web sites do not maintain true "conversations" with users of those Web sites. Every time you access a Web site—that is, every time you get a page from a Web site—the Web site recognizes the request from you, responds to it, and forgets about it. You may be thinking, "But many Web sites that I interact with do seem to keep track of what's going on from one screen to the next." You are correct; they have figured out ways to do this, but those ways don't use the basic HTTP capability; they use some additional capabilities that are built into browsers. The developers of the major browsers realized that this was a problem that had to be solved. What happens is that when a Web site wants to retain some contacts to an exchange, it causes the browser to create something called a *cookie* on the user's local disk drive, somewhere on a directory below the browser. Cookies can either be line entries in a file of cookies, or they can be one per file; Netscape maintains a file of cookies. A cookie is just a sequence of information that the Web site places on the local disk to retain some information. It may have the user's name and ID, and possibly some information that the user filled in on a form on the Web site. One very common use of a cookie is to retain an ID and password that is granted to the user as part of the exchange with the Web site in order to allow the user to get into the Web site in the future without having to go through an elaborate sign-on procedure. Thus, cookies can be very beneficial to efficiency and user satisfaction. However, there has been a fair amount of concern that cookies can also be used to compromise the privacy of individuals. Some people do not want a Web site to retain information about them, especially without telling them about it. Discussions are under way to address this concern. By the time you read this, enhancements may be made to browsers that enable them to tell the user when information from a cookie is about to be used. In practice, we don't believe that users will make heavy use of this capability because it will really slow down accessing Web site services.

Naming Standards

Naming on the Internet starts with a URL, an acronym for Uniform Resource Locator. A URL is the address for a resource or site (usually a directory or file) on the World Wide Web and the convention that Web browsers use for locating files and other remote services. Many things exist on the Internet, such as files or Web pages. Things on the Internet follow a general format. This naming format is *protocol://node/path/filename.type*. Breaking this down, *protocol* will be something like HTTP or FTP. *Node* can be a number of different things. In the case of a Web site, the node name often starts with *www*, but it does not have to. An example of a node name would be **www.excite.com**. In the case of a Web site, there may not be anything after that. In fact, it has an implied file name because the file name *index.html* is the default file name if one is not specified. But it is routine to try and locate a company's Web site by typing **http://www.company-name.com.** More often than not, you will be successful with this syntax. A more elaborate example for the name of a file on the Internet is Netscape's search location. That address is **http://home.netscape.com/search/ index.html**. Note a couple of things here: Netscape does not use the *www* syntax at the beginning of its node name. It doesn't have to; it's not a requirement. A single-level path appears below the node name: *search*. This could be multiple levels, but in this case, it is not. Finally, Netscape has specified the default file name: *index.html*. Again, this isn't required, but it is sometimes nice to show what the defaults are.

Another service is integral to the Internet, although not obvious to Web browser users. It is, however, a critical component at this point, and is used routinely and frequently by Web browsers. This service is a distributed naming service called Domain Name Services (DNS). Like many of the other protocols mentioned, it has been around for much longer than the Web. DNS is the protocol or service that allows you to specify the name of a Web site instead of the Internet address of that site. The Internet providers maintain a complex infrastructure of DNS servers or computers on a continuing basis. Web browser users access DNS service frequently during a session. Every time a user clicks on a Web link or pointer, the browser makes a request to a DNS server that is defined as part of the TCP/IP software on the user's machine. The DNS client accesses the DNS server— possibly several servers—in order to get the TCP/IP address that corresponds to that name. Let's face it, when you type in **http://www.tcic.com**, the servers don't have a clue how to get there. You see, we used a naming convention that is easily understood and remembered by a human. However, the IP protocol uses the decimal delimited numbering convention (that is, 10.122.5.12) to find its nodes. The DNS is used to convert the English language names into IP names. It then passes that address back to the rest of the IP software in order to allow it to make a direct access out to that Web site server. Not only that, but once a Web page is being retrieved, many links that constitute the page may be within that Web page. When you retrieve a page, you don't just get a bunch of stuff in one file; rather, in most cases, intrasite links are built into the page that retrieve images and tables and other objects that are part of the page. There may be multiple retrievals and accesses to DNS servers during the retrieval of a single Web page. This can really slow things down if the network itself is not moving quickly. But if it weren't there at all, maintenance of these sites would be much more difficult because everything would have to be coded with Internet addresses instead of readable names. That's why when you set up your computer, you may or may not have to give it an IP address (it gets one anyway, but sometimes it's dynamically assigned); however, you absolutely must have a DNS address, usually two, in order to provide a backup. There is a way to assign DNS addresses dynamically, but not everyone uses it yet. The ISP provides these DNS addresses.

When we say that you may not have an IP address, but one can be assigned dynamically, it becomes confusing for some people. So here we go again! When you log onto an ISP server, the server uses a protocol called Dynamically Assigned Host Configuration (DHCP). Whew! What that means is that every device needs an IP address in order to send or receive information, mail, or whatever. Many people (particularly dial-in users) only need that address when they log on. So, when you call into your local ISP, your PC and modem go through a handshake with the server. At that point, the server assigns an available IP address (from a pool of numbers) to your PC for the duration of this call. As long as you stay logged on, you use this address. As soon as you log off (hang up) your address is released and placed back into the pool. Next time you log on, you will probably get a new address for this connection. The address is dynamically (on the fly) configured (selected) and assigned by the host (server). TaDa!

Gaining Access

To gain access to the Internet, you need an Internet service provider (ISP). ISPs come in two flavors, regional and national; also, one might consider an international category. National and international carriers tend to be very well known companies. Such organizations as AT&T, CompuServe, and IBM fall into this category. They have access points, or points of presence (POPs), all over the world. Interestingly, CompuServe is probably the most pervasive service, but the others are also up there. It would be worth your while, if you travel, to check into the dial-in services for these services before choosing an ISP. It is a major factor. All have an 800 number access, but it tends not to work terribly well over long distances because you are going through the dial-up network and, as has been mentioned elsewhere, the dial-up network was not really designed for data.

Regional ISPs tend to have slightly lower access charges than the international ones. This is probably because of the additional cost of those international circuits. Another possible advantage of a regional ISP is that, in the region it focuses on, it probably has more dial-in points than the national carriers. So if one of the dial-in points (or numbers) has a problem, you can use an alternative one in your area. The national and international

ISPs are really gunning for your business. They have in most cases brought their prices down to very close to those of the regional carriers. Moreover, they do have the advantage of providing dial-in points across the country and even around the world.

Another factor in selecting an ISP is less obvious than the number of dial-in points. This factor is the ISP's connection to the backbone of the Internet itself. The number of simultaneous users an ISP can effectively handle is directly related to the speed of its connection into the Internet. We discuss high-speed circuits elsewhere in this book. An ISP that has only a T1 connection to the Internet really does not have enough capacity to handle significant numbers of people. This is not normally a problem with the national and international ISPs; however, it is a real consideration when selecting among regional carriers, of which often several are available in any given region. Normally, you probably want to use an ISP that has at least a T3 (a big pipe) connection and perhaps several T3 connections to the Internet. This ISP connection to the Internet factor is particularly important if you are selecting an ISP on behalf of a medium to large company, as opposed to just an individual. A company with hundreds or thousands of individuals connecting to the Internet simultaneously can put a really big load on an ISP. It may increase the ISP's total traffic by a double-digit percentage if it's just a regional ISP. The moral of the story: do your homework.

Another consideration in selecting an ISP is the variety of connection alternatives for the user to the ISP. Obviously, dial-up will be supported, but straight dial-up, at the writing of this book, only reaches speeds of 33.6 Kbps upline to the Net, and as much as 53 Kbps downline from the Net. That's a lot faster than speeds in the past, but it isn't nearly as fast as some available alternatives. Another alternative available now is xDSL. xDSL, sometimes referred to as just DSL (this stands for digital subscriber line), represents a variety of technologies that, as a class, deliver megabit-per-second speeds to homeowners. However, an ISP has to have a special connection to your local telephone company in order for you to access the ISP using xDSL. As a practical matter, xDSL will only be available in limited locations for the next few years. It may not take off if other services become generally available like ISDN, but xDSL has the potential to take off because it provides higher bandwidth than just about any other service to individual homes at a tiny fraction of the cost of equivalent services. Other means of connecting to ISPs involve dedicated circuits, switched 56, or even Frame Relay. You have to decide what you need and what you are willing to pay for, but you also have to check with the ISP to find out what it is willing to accept.

Figure 16-9
Two ISPs provide
backup.

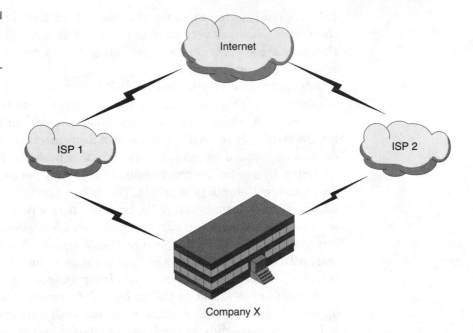

If you are selecting an ISP for a business, two ISPs may be better than one (see Figure 16-9). We mention diverse routing elsewhere in this book. Several ISPs over the past couple of years have had total failures for hours at a time. If you are going to purchase a service like this for your business users, then, as with any other service, you need to consider what happens if the provider fails. One way to handle this is to purchase service from two different ISPs. Another way is to use an ISP that can provide redundant dedicated connections into your business. Don't forget to arrange for diverse routing from your location to the ISPs as well. This may involve, for example, getting circuits to two different central offices, something that the telephone companies tend to resist, but it is still is a good idea if you can swing it.

Some of the other miscellaneous things to consider when selecting an ISP include factors that you might consider when selecting any vendor. Among these are optional services, prices for those services, what support and coaching is available for setting up the use of the ISP, and a hidden gotcha that you really should consider. The key question is, will the ISP still be in business a few months from now? It doesn't take very much equipment to set up an Internet ISP, and many individuals have taken advantage of this fact. We are not recommending that you automatically discriminate against a small ISP; in fact, some of the best ones out there are small organizations. Nonetheless, you may not be comfortable dealing with a very small company, if only because you may have concerns about its ability to handle growth. Again, do your homework.

Internet Futures

Many people are concerned that the Internet will experience spontaneous self-destruction due to its speed of growth. We mentioned earlier that change happens rapidly on the Internet. In fact, a concept called *Internet time* is in common usage. It is difficult to quantify Internet time, but it means that things that one would expect in other environments to take years, take only months or even days on the Internet. A good example of this is the speed at which, for a while, Internet browsers were being revised by their producers. Even now, Netscape releases new beta versions of its Netscape browser on a very frequent basis, sometimes as frequently as once every couple of months. It says something that a high percentage of the people who use browsers on the Internet are actually using beta versions of those browsers just to get the latest features that are being taken advantage of by the sites that they access.

However, we were talking about the growth of the Internet. The two major concerns regarding the growth of the Internet are

1. The traffic levels will grow to the point where things will bog down completely.

2. The number of nodes or computers on the network will exceed the number that can be handled by the addressing scheme.

Actually, in many respects, portions of the Internet have already run out of gas as far as performance is concerned. For good reason, the Web is described as the "World Wide Wait." All the major backbone providers are adding capacity at a very rapid clip. It remains to be seen whether they can keep up with demand. After all, the growth eventually has to taper off a little bit because it is unlikely that more than one computer can be used by every man, woman, and child. Once everybody has a computer, we're limited to the growth of the population. Moreover, the population has not been growing nearly as quickly as the Internet has. Of course, that point may not be reached for a while, so in the meantime, we may experience a fair amount of pain. We can't predict whether the Net will self-destruct. We suspect that it will go through phases of slowing and speeding as new capacity comes online and new facilities become available on the network, bringing in new users and increasing the use by existing users. Many of the manufacturers are now hyping the Optical Internet, meaning that the capacity of fiber Optics will enhance the Internet for the foreseeable future. That is of course, if some of the ISPs buy it!

As far as the network address availability is concerned, we're happy to report that the powers that be on the Internet have defined a new standard —IPv6. Going into the details of the IPv6 protocol is really beyond the scope of this book. Suffice it to say that IPv6 will not have any problems with the number of nodes that it can address any time in the next decade. Not only that, but the designers have done a good job of stripping out unnecessary overhead in order to make this protocol inherently slightly faster than the existing IPv4 protocol now in use on the network (version 5 was a specialty protocol that never received general usage). The main question is not whether IPv6 can handle the number of addresses that it will have to handle, but rather how quickly can it be brought online. Naturally, migration issues arise because millions of people are running software that does not support IPv6 at this time. A certain amount of backward compatibility is built into the new protocol; but we suspect that the people operating the network will have to dance very quickly to get from where they are now to where they want to be in a smooth fashion. IPv6 will be a ten-year migration from the older version Ipv4.

Voice over the Internet

Lately, the hype in the industry is the convergence of the voice and data transmission systems. This is nothing new; we have been trying to integrate voice and data for years. However, a subtle difference exists with today's convergence scenarios:

- In the beginning, the convergence operation mandated that data be made to look like voice; then it could be transmitted on the same circuitry. Circuit-switched voice and data used the age-old techniques of a network founded in voice techniques.

- Now, the convergence states that voice will look like data and the two can reside in packetized form on the same networks and circuitry. Circuit-switching technologies are making way for the packet switching technologies.

These changes take advantage of the idle space in voice conversations, where it has been determined that during a conversation, only about 10 to

25 percent of the circuit time is actually utilized to carry the voice. The rest of the time, we are in idle condition by either

1. Listening to the other end
2. Thinking of a response to a question
3. Breathing between our words

In this idle capacity, the compression of voice can facilitate less circuit usage and encourage the use of a packetized form of voice. Data networking is more efficient because we have been using data packeting for years through packets, frames, or cells.

The use of a packet-switching transmission system enables us to interleave voice and data packets (video too) where idle space occurs. As long as a mechanism exists to recoup the information and reassemble it on the receiving end, it can use bandwidth more efficiently. It is just this bandwidth utilization and effective saving expectations that has driven the world into a frenzy over packetizing voice and interleaving it on a data network, especially the Internet. Carriers have been told that by packetizing voice, they can get an 11 fold increase of traffic (and subsequent revenues) on the existing wires they have today. Can you imagine any carrier turning this down?

A note on the cost of voice and data communications is probably in order here. Currently, the drive is to have free voice on a data network. In the early years of data communications, data was always given a free ride on the voice networks. Telecommunications managers diligently fine-tuned their voice networks and allowed the data to run over the voice networks during the off-hours (after hours). This use of the circuitry was paid for through the dial-up voice communications. This method of providing data over the voice networks crept into some of the business hours when real-time communications were needed. However, many times the voice TIE-lines and leased lines (point-to-point circuits) usually had some reserve capacity. Therefore, the data was placed on the point-to-point circuits that were justified by voice. As the competition in the telecommunications market heated up, we saw the costs for a minute of long distance drop from $.50–.60 per minute in North America down to an average cost today of about $.05–.07 per minute.[2] This significant drop in cost has been the result of competition and technological enhancements. At the same time, the data

---

[2] It still amazes the authors that in 2001, many small business and residential customers are paying as much as $.20–.25 per minute for long-distance calling. This means that the consuming public is not looking for the deals and the carriers are not offering them as much as they say.

convergence took advantage of this falling cost factor. Meanwhile, the data was migrating from a point-to-point technique on a dial-up connection to a more robust packet form of transmission using X.25 or IP packet-switching techniques. The cost per bit of data transmission was dropping rapidly. Then, the introduction of the Internet came to the commercial world. With the commercialization of the Internet in the early 1990s, the culture and the cost factors changed at an escalating pace. The cost of data transmission has been touted as being free on the Internet, the only cost being the access fees. However, the cost of data networking has been rapidly declining on private line Intranets, drawing the attention from both a public and a private networking focus. This convergence has everyone looking for free voice by interleaving voice on the data networks. We agree with the scenario and would not attempt to detract from this goal. However, the other side of the equation is that the circuit-switched networks are continually driving the cost per minute for voice down. Closely aligned to this paradigm is the fact that the North American long-distance companies are now offering specials in their service.

Voice over the Internet Protocol (VoIP)

The public telephone network and the circuit-switching systems are usually taken for granted. Over the past few decades, they have grown to be accepted as almost 100 percent reliable. Manufacturers built in all the necessary stopgaps to prevent downtime and increase lifeline availability of telephony. It was even assumed that when the commercial power failed, the telephony business continued to operate. This did not happen accidentally, but through a very concerted development cycle jointly by the carriers and the manufacturers alike.

Access to a low-cost, high-quality worldwide network is considered essential in today's world. Anything that would jeopardize this access is treated with suspicion. A new paradigm is beginning to occur because more of our basic communications occur in digital form, transported via packet networks such as IP, Asynchronous Transfer Mode (ATM), and Frame Relay. Packet data networking has matured over the same period of time that the voice technologies were maturing. The old basic voice and basic data networks have been replaced with highly reliable networks that carry voice, data, video, and multimedia transmissions. Proprietary solutions manufactured by various providers have fallen to the side, opening the industry to a more open and standards-based environment. In 1996, there was as much data traffic running on the networks as there was voice traffic. Admittedly, industry pundits are all still saying that 90 percent of the revenue in this industry is generated by voice applications. This may be an accounting problem because on average, 57 percent of all international calls originating in North America going to Europe and Asia are actually carrying fax, not voice. Yet, they are considered dial-up voice communications transmissions because of the methodology used. Moreover, the voice market is growing at approximately three to four percent per year, whereas data is growing at approximately 30 percent per year. Because data traffic is growing much faster than telephone traffic, there has been considerable interest in transporting voice over data networks (as opposed to the more traditional data over voice networks). Support for voice communications using the Internet Protocol (IP), which is usually just called *Voice over IP or VoIP*, has become especially attractive given the low-cost, flat-rate pricing of the public Internet. In fact, toll-quality telephony over IP has now become one of the important steps leading to the convergence of the voice, video, and data communications industries. The feasibility of carrying voice and call-signaling messages over the Internet has already been demonstrated. Delivering high-quality commercial products, establishing public services, and convincing users to buy into the vision are all still in their infancy. The evolution of all networks begins this way, so there is no mystique in it.

IP telephony will also have to change somewhat. We will expect it to deliver interpersonal communications that end users are already accustomed to using. These added capabilities will include (but not be limited to):

- Calling line ID (CLID)
- Three-way calling
- Call transfer
- Voice mail
- Voice-to-text conversions

Users are very comfortable with the services and capabilities delivered by the telephone companies on the standard dial-up telephone set using the touch-tone pad. IP telephony must match these services and ease-of-use functions in order to be successful.

IP telephony will not replace the circuit switched telephone networks overnight; they will coexist for the near future. Analysts expect that in 2003, the amount of IP telephony will account for three percent of all voice traffic domestically, and approximately ten to 15 percent of international traffic. This amounts to 50 billion minutes of traffic, so it is consequential. One must be prepared for both alternatives to carrying voice in the next decade. Thus, the differences between the two opposing network strategies will be ironed out and the world may shift into a packet-switched voice network over the next decade.

Quality of Service

One of the arguments against IP-based telephony today is the lack of quality of service (QoS). The manufacturers and developers are working to overcome the objections by producing transmission systems that assure a quality of service for lifeline voice communications. Mission-critical applications in the corporate world will also demand the ability to have a specified grade of service available. The CTI applications with call centers that are Web-enabled, and interactive voice recognition, response, and other speech activated technologies will demand a quality of service to facilitate the use of these systems. Each will demand the grade and quality of service expected in the telephone industry.

Another critical application for IP telephony will be the results of quality of voice transmission. Noisy lines, delays in voice delivery, and clicking and chipping all tend to frustrate users on a voice network. Packet data networks carrying voice services today may produce the same results. Therefore, overcoming these pitfalls is essential to the success and acceptance of Voice over IP telephony applications. Merely installing more capacity (bandwidth) is not a solution to the problem; it is a temporary fix. Instead, developers must concentrate on delivering several solution sets to the industry such as those shown in Table 16-1.

The QoS requirements for IP telephony can therefore be summarized as shown in Table 16-2, which considers the layered approach that vendors will be aggressively pursuing. IP telephony datagrams entering the network will be treated with a priority to deliver the QoS expected by the end user. The routers and switches in the network will assign a high priority marking on each datagram carrying voice, and treat these datagrams specially. Queues throughout the network will be established with variable treatments to handle the voice datagrams first, followed by the data datagrams.

Given the differences, why should we even consider the use of IP telephony? If the IP telephony world is only going to account for three percent

Table 16-1

Different
Approaches
to QoS

Strategy	Description
Integrated Services Architectures (Int-Serv)	Int-Serv includes the specifications to reserve network resources in support of a specific application.Using the RSVP protocol, the application or user can request and allocate sufficient bandwidth to support the short- or long-term connection. This is a partial solution because Int-Serv does not scale well because each networking device (routers and switches) must maintain and manage the information for each flow established across their path.
Differentiated Services (Diff-Serv)	Easier to use than Int-Serv, Diff-Serv uses a different mechanism to handle the flow across the network. Instead of trying to manage individual flows and per-flow signaling needs, Diff-Serv uses DS bits in the header to recognize the flow and the need for QoS on a particular datagram-by-datagram basis. This is more scalable than Int-Serv and does not rely solely on RSVP to control flows.
802.1p Prioritization	The IEEE standard specifies a priority scheme for the layer 2 switching in a switched-LAN. When a packet leaves a subnetwork or a domain, the 802.1p priority can be mapped to Diff-Serv to satisfy the layer 2 switching.

Table 16-2

QoS Requirements
for IP Telephony

Layer Addressed	Technique	Variable
1	Physical Port	Variations of port definitions, or the prioritization of port interfaces based on application
2	IEEE 802.1p Bits	Dedicated paths or ports for high bandwidth applications, but very expensive to maintain
3	IP addressing	RSVP protocol (Int-Serv) DS bits in the IP header (Diff-Serv)

of domestic traffic by 2003, is it worth all the hassle? The answer is a mixed bag, but overall the efficiencies of VoIP outweigh the need to develop better control mechanisms to satisfy the telephony industry.

SIP is a new text-based Internet signaling protocol to be used for establishing real-time calls and conferences over IP networks, as defined by the International Engineering Telecommunications Foundation (IETF).

H.323, the call signaling protocol defined by the International Telecommunications Union (ITU-T) in 1996, was the first industry standard defined for IP telephony and multimedia communications over packet networks. Because of the overlap between the scope of SIP and H.323, work is currently underway to define interworking between the two protocols. Both H.323 and SIP are call-signaling protocols that define mechanisms for call routing, call signaling, capabilities exchange, media control, and supplementary services. Next generation networks will have to deliver end-to-end interoperability across multiple protocols.

Session Announcement Protocol (SAP)   The session announcement protocol controls the advertising function by announcing to either one user (unicast) or multiple users (multicast) that a session has been established. This announcement also serves to facilitate the invite from a SIP protocol where a user can be invited to join and participate in a call.

Real Time Streaming Protocols (RTSP)   Real Time Streaming Protocols (RTSP) takes advantage of streaming which breaks data into many packets sized according to the bandwidth available between client and server. When the client has received enough packets, the user's software can be playing one packet, decompressing another, and downloading the third. The user may start listening almost immediately without having to get the entire media file. Both live data feeds and stored clips can be the sources of data. RTSP acts as a "network remote control" for multimedia servers. The delivery mechanisms are based solely on the Real Time Protocol (RTP). RTSP has been designed to be on top of RTP to both control and deliver real-time content. Real Time Streaming Protocol can also be used with the Resource Reservation Protocol (RSVP) to set up and manage reserved-bandwidth streaming sessions.

One can see that the use of multimedia (voice, data, and video) on the Internet opens the door for a myriad of new protocols. These are but a few.

Questions

1. What is the Internet?
   a. A government network
   b. A network of networks
   c. The geeks network
   d. A U.S.-based network

2. Who really invented the Internet?
   a. Al Gore
   b. The U.S. government
   c. D-ARPA
   d. Bill Clinton

3. When we use the Internet, the core protocols are TCP and IP.   T/F

4. The Internet was developed initially for the transfer of what types of information?
   a. Video and multimedia
   b. Voice and streaming audio
   c. E-mail and small file transfers
   d. Virtual terminal and Telnet

5. When we talk about IP today, what version are we referring to?
   a. 4
   b. 5
   c. 6
   d. 8

6. Why do carriers want to include voice over the Internet?
   a. Reduce lines
   b. Save time
   c. Make more money
   d. It's a trendy thing to do

7. What does DNS stand for?

   a. Domain Network Service

   b. Domain Name Convention

   c. Domain Name Servers

   d. Digital Naming Systems

8. When we refer to the Web, what are we talking about?

   a. A spider web

   b. The World Wide Web of computers

   c. Web-based mail services

   d. Web naming

9. HTTP means a way to move files using the Hyper Text Transfer Protocol.   T/F

10. IP stands for

    a. Internetwork Packets

    b. Internet Payloads

    c. Internet Protocol

    d. Interworking Protocols

11. An IP address is converted by the DNS from English language to a decimal delimited number.   T/F

12. By the year 2003, it is expected that the Internet will be carrying _____ percent of the voice.

13. The best way to handle a file transfer is to use the MIME protocol. T/F

14. By 2003, estimates are that _____ minutes of voice traffic will be carried.

15. How can people get access to the Internet?

    a. Through the local computer hardware stores

    b. Through the local banks

    c. From an ISO provider

    d. Through the local or regional ISP

16. If a user wants to get access at high-speed, what inexpensive telco option is available today?

    a. DSL

    b. Dial-up modems

    c. B-ISDN

    d. T3

17. Normally, the user will use _____ ISP.

    a. Three

    b. Two

    c. One

    d. Four

18. What companies are now competing with the local telco for access to the ISP?

    a. Long-distance dial-up

    b. Cable TV

    c. Gas and electric companies

    d. All of the above

19. The typical fee for access to the Internet for a dial-up user is $49.95 per month.   T/F

20. The cost of a computer to access the Web is now under $1,000.00 in the U.S.   T/F

Remote Access and Virtual Private Networks (VPNs)

After reading this chapter and completing the questions, you will be able to:

■ Explain why a virtual network is used

■ Discuss the means of accessing a VPN

■ Describe the components of a VPN

■ Explain where a VPN is used for remote access

■ Discuss the security issues and forms of protection

When we use the Internet or the Intranet, risks to the security of our data arise. To solve the security problem, a virtual private network (VPN) is used for traveling and remote users to send or receive their information with less concern. This means that someone out there must create a VPN.

Don: Wait a minute, Bud! What the heck is a VPN?

Bud: Funny you should ask that Don, I was just about to explain, but you were a bit too quick on the trigger for me. So please sit back, fasten your seatbelt, and let me explain.

By definition, a VPN is a virtual private network. Let's take the pieces of a VPN and describe them one at a time:

■ **Virtual**   Virtual means almost, not quite, or not real. (Don: Hmmmm.) Real circuits are physical. You can see them, touch them, and "kick the tires." Virtual circuits look like they are there and act like they are there. They do everything as though they are there, but they really are not there.

■ **Private**   Private means that it is dedicated to a specific organization or individual and not available to the public.

■ **Network**   A network is the grouping of circuits that connect the various locations between and among each other.

> Don: So, Bud, to summarize this definition, a VPN is a network that looks like a real network, acts like a real network, and does everything that a real network does, but it's not really there.
>
> Bud: You got it, Don!
>
> Bud: Let me take this one step further, Don. I am going to use an analogy again in the form of a story.

If I were to talk to the readers of this book collectively and ask them if any of them ever saw a virtual image, they would probably say no. Some might say yes thinking that virtual reality is what I am addressing. Nevertheless, that is still not the answer I wanted.

I can tell you that I have seen many virtual images! As you know, I do a lot of public speaking. Recently, I got to a city where I was scheduled to conduct a two-day training class. When I arrived in the late evening, I realized that I had to prepare for the coming day where I would need to speak all day, which meant that I had to prepare by lubricating my vocal chords. Unfortunately, when I arrived so late, the restaurant was closed so I had to go to the lounge area in the lobby of the hotel for a drink.

When I sat at the counter area (the bar), I ordered my first drink. I consumed that one pretty quickly, and then had another. Half way through my third round, I glanced up from where I was sitting. There, in front of me, was a virtual image staring right at me! I quickly threw my head to the right to look away but to no avail. Another virtual image staring straight at me was on my right. Finally, I spun in my seat all the way around to the left. Yes, you guessed it: another virtual image was staring at me. By now, I was unsettled so I called the operator (attendant-bartender) over and said, "Hey, what did you put in my coffee? Everywhere I look I see an image staring at me." The bartender just looked at me and went about his business.

Don: What happened after that Bud?

Bud: Well, you see Don, what was happening was that everywhere I looked I saw me! (Don: Wow, that *is* a scary thing!)

Bud: Enough of that Don, let me continue. You see, the lounge area where I was sitting was surrounded with mirrors on all the walls. Every time I looked up I saw an image of me. Actually, it looked like me. It was dressed like I was dressed. It moved when I moved. (See Figure 17-1 for this image.) However, it was not really me, I was in the room and the images were in the walls. That is what a virtual image looks like.

Now, back to a virtual network. It looks like a network, it acts like a network, and it does everything a network does. But, it is not a real network; it is only an image of a network and is only present when you need (or use) it. Other times, it isn't there! Now, Don, does that make sense? (Don: ZZZZZZZ) Don! Don?

Let's get back to our use of a virtual private network. If we want to use the Internet, for example, everyone cautions us that a hacker, a cracker, or a salami attacker might capture our data and compromise its security. (Don: Aaaagggggghhhhh.) Hey Don, I don't make the names up, I just tell you what they are called.

Anyway, if we want to assure that our data is secure on the Internet, we can create and use a VPN. This means that we can actually carve a tunnel

Figure 17-1
The virtual images

through the Internet to carry our data, and we are the only users of this piece of the Net. All other users are sending their data across the Net, but our data is running inside these secure pipes, as shown in Figure 17-2. We have an actual extension of our private networks (like a LAN-to-LAN connection) that encompasses links across the public networks like the Internet. We use the capability to send and receive data between two computers as though they are connected with a dedicated private line (point-to-point link), even though we are using the shared resources of the Internet. This is shown in Figure 17-3 where we create the logical connection as though we had a private line.

To create the emulation of a dedicated circuit, the original data packet is encapsulated (put in an envelope) in another packet that carries the routing information while the data packet inside the envelope is encrypted. That way, if anyone sees the data traveling down the wires, they cannot read what is in it.

VPNs enable workers to work from home or remotely access their corporate data on the road while traveling and logging in from a hotel. This gives employees and partners remote access to their network resources as though they were in the office. From the user's view, the VPN is just a point-to-point connection between his or her computer and the company server that he or she just happened to dial up (in some cases, this is dedicated for a home

Figure 17-2
The secure pipe in a VPN

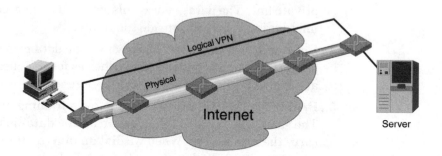

telecommuter who never travels). The infrastructure being used is transparent to the user because the data logically travels across a dedicated link. This form of connection can be used geographically anywhere with branch offices, international partners, or anyone else we choose to allow access. By using the public Internet and the private Intranet, we can combine the best of all the features available and extend them across the world. A router on the public Internet using a VPN logically looks like a dedicated wide area network (WAN) link to the organization.

Components of the VPN

When using a VPN, we incorporate many pieces of a jigsaw puzzle. Each piece serves its own function to provide the interoperation and the security necessary to create a true service. The pieces include

1. **VPN server** This is a computer that enables and accepts VPN connections from VPN clients. The server can provide a remote access (dial-up) connection or a router-to-router connection. The main gist is that the server must allow the creation of a VPN, allow the remote user to log on, establish a VPN connection, and be flexible enough to satisfy the number of simultaneous connections that we feel are necessary.

2. **VPN client**   The VPN client is a computer that initiates the VPN connection. Usually a piece of shim software is used that creates the VPN and includes necessary security procedures.

3. **Tunnel**   This is the virtual piece of the network that carries the data. Not all tunnels carry secure data, but they all try to carry data on a private link. The data is encapsulated inside a new envelope so that the information is invisible inside the tunnel.

4. **Connection**   This is the place where the data gets scrambled and jumbled (called encrypted). Many choices for the encryption technique are available and selected on user preference.

5. **Protocols**   We saw that OSI layer 2 is a framing protocol for the link. The same holds true in this case; we need a data-link layer protocol to carry the information. When we dial up into the Internet, for example, we transmit our IP datagrams (packets). However, what we do not see is that we use a layer 2 protocol called the point-to-point protocol (PPP) to frame the IP datagrams and carry them across the dial connection. In a VPN, we see protocols that include the point-to-point tunneling protocol (PPTP) and we now have Layer 2 Tunnel Protocol (L2TP). In a Windows™ environment, the use of PPTP is currently more prevalent, but the movement is toward L2TP.

6. **Networks**   The network connection is either a dial-up connection, the Internet, or another IP-based network.

All of the components are shown in Figure 17-4 where they come together and form the basis of our VPN.

Figure 17-4
Components of
a VPN

Remote Access

The new culture of workers demands flexible hours, more say in setting their career goals, more access from remote, better training, more chances to experiment, and the opportunity to be empowered. We all know that the knowledgeable workers today demand more access. They want the capability to work *when they want, where they want, and how they want!*

This new generation of workers needs to be empowered to get things done by a new set of rules. No longer do they feel that they should be confined to a specific workplace or specific hours. Instead, they feel that they need to have more quality time at home for a number of reasons. Thus, they feel that they should have access whenever they desire or need it from wherever they happen to be at the time. The challenge they create for the telecommunications and information technology groups is to be able to control the access while fostering the creativity. (Author's note: Please remember that this book is about the enabling technologies of voice and data convergence.)

These workers may also be the type that works all day in the office. Nothing says that they always have to be away from the office; their absence may be a casual thing. Because of other commitments such as day care, children's sports, carpools, and so on, they may have the need to leave the office at a specific time. Yet, these same workers want to get onto the network after hours and continue to work. This may occur in the late evening or the wee hours of the morning. Depending on their work habits and their tolerance, these workers will work more than an eight-hour day if access is available to them. These new workers will expect the organization to meet their demands and give them the rights and privileges of being a remote worker or else they will move on to another organization.

The following list shows the major categories of workers and access methods:

- **Virtual office** (road warrior)   Employees are constantly on the move and carry their offices with them, literally on the shoulders. This could be a road warrior, salesperson, or an executive or manager who is often traveling for meetings.

- **Extended office** (after-hours day extenders)   These employees work away from the office after hours or on weekends.

■ **Home office** (telecommuter) Employees working at home either daily or at least a couple of days a week.

■ **Satellite office/hotel office**
A just-in-time concept for workspaces, in which employees who need a workspace for a limited, temporary time can reserve one for a period of (usually) a few hours to several days. This also works for visitors from other locations and two people sharing a single job and workspace.

The Pressure Is On

The pressure is on for organizations to attract and retain the knowledgeable worker; the remote access programs will help to satisfy this new worker. With over 800,000 information technology (IT) worker vacancies in the industry, the pressure to find and retain good workers is tremendous. This is also true in other departments of an organization, such as

■ Marketing

■ Sales

■ Advertising

■ Human resources

■ Accounting and finance

■ Facilities

It really doesn't matter which department; all suffer from the same lack of skilled workers (or any workers for that matter). Some organizations are recruiting people without the necessary skills and are actually trying to groom their own qualified workers. This is at great expense. Therefore, finding and accommodating access for a new pool of remote workers helps the situation.

Other organizations are trying to recruit from abroad, but are having little success. In fact, employees allowed in with work visas in 1999 amounted to 150,000. However, the government cut the number in 2000 to 117,000. This puts added pressure on finding qualified workers and retaining them. Many telecommunications companies (CLECs and IECs) hire people who were flipping burgers last week and now selling high technology data communications products this week.

Companies, who have a program in place to accommodate these workers, have shown that their retention rates have soared and conversely the turnover rate has dropped dramatically, as seen in Figure 17-5.

Remote Access Defined

Remote access means that the user may wish to gain access to our systems, resources, and data from just about anywhere. The new knowledgeable worker may prefer to work from home, from a hotel while traveling, from a remote site (branch office), or from office space set aside for them in other office buildings (remote hoteling).

While using this access, the organization must supply the necessary provisions to secure the connection for remote access through a virtual private network as we described earlier. Using recent breakthroughs in remote access technologies, from analog modems to high-speed digital connections, companies can simulate the office environment for workers at any location.

Figure 17-5
As retention rates increase, costs decrease.

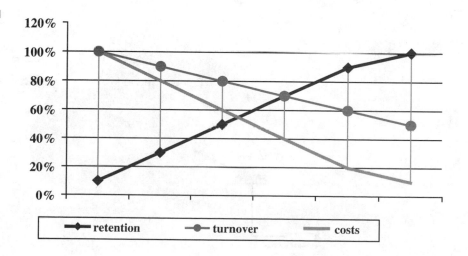

All varieties of organizations and all sizes of firms can benefit from adding remote access to their workplace solutions. Examples of organizations that can benefit from the remote access include

- Law firms
- Schools
- Public agencies
- Call centers
- Police departments (dispatchers, reporters)
- Banks
- News agencies
- Printing businesses
- Retail organizations
- Insurance companies

It's not just technology companies that can benefit from the use of the technology. Granted, many of the high-technology companies have been the pioneers in dealing with and implementing the remote access services. Remote access has gone through several evolutions. These can be categorized as the following:

1. The first choice was a single line dial-up modem into a modem on a server, which is shown in Figure 17-6.

Figure 17-6
The single line modem and access

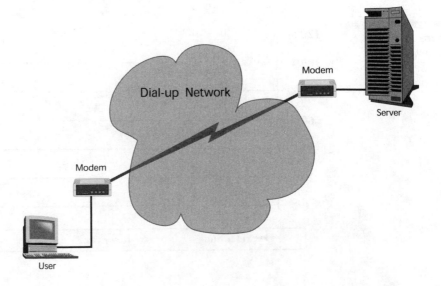

2. The second choice was the modem pool, which resulted from the need to access remote hosts and remote services. A combination of a terminal server and a modem pool were used to facilitate this interface. These configurations were implemented in corporations and universities with branch offices and home workers who needed access to computing resources from remote locations. This is shown in Figure 17-7.

3. Next came LAN access with integrated modems. Computing access began to shift from a single access method to multiple access for corporate LANs connected to remote branch offices. This also led to the implementation of digital modems. Figure 17-8 shows the LAN access method.

4. Multi-card systems were next in the evolution. These systems are characterized by a central processing architecture with integrated modems and networking. These systems also provided for a higher scale of connectivity. They worked with DS1 connections.

5. The distributed processor came next. Carrier class systems were developed as switches in the mid-1990s that offer DS3 connections or 672 channels of connection.

What was once considered communicating over a modem now encompasses support for users over VPNs. If you plan to work with or provide

Figure 17-7
Modem pool

Figure 17-8
The LAN access
method

remote access for users, the numbers of users are increasing at an alarming rate. CATV or xDSL technologies at the remote site (home, branch office, satellite office, and hotel room) now offer new opportunities for high-speed remote access and VPNs, as shown in Figure 17-9. If you are planning to support remote access, then you must be sure that the Remote Access Server (RAS) supports VPN or has an upgrade path to support VPN.

Security Issues

Turning to security, the remote access system must have integral security to protect the network and users from unauthorized access and penetration. Network security is an extremely important issue for network administrators and one that must be addressed in remote access services. We have all heard about the teenaged hackers who have been creating havoc in the data processing and Internet business, as shown in Figure 17-10. These young hackers break into systems for the sheer pleasure of challenging the system and showing their prowess with the modem. And it works; they do it every day. Who can forget that teenager in Montreal called "Mafia boy?"

Figure 17-9
New technologies at
the remote site offer
high-speed access.

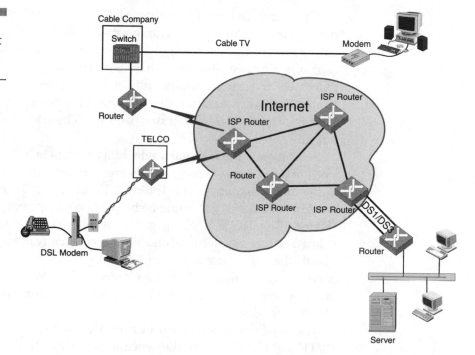

Figure 17-10
The hacker
continuously
attempts to break in
to networks.

Therefore, we have to consider these issues before opening a door. We must start with different techniques such as VPNs, encryption, authenticating servers, and secure firewalls. Remote access for users sitting in a distant site requires that they know how to use the system, so training is extremely important. Additionally, a firewall service will offer a bastion router capability to filter the packet, the protocol, or the user ID and address. Figure 17-11 illustrates firewalls. These systems will help to keep out unwanted guests.

Security must also be ensured while the data is in transit. Therefore, we need to use a form of encryption so an eavesdropper cannot listen in on our data and intercept it. The Internet Engineering Task Force (IETF), an Internet standards governing body, has a working group called IP Security (IPSec). The IPSec working group is defining standards and protocols related to Internet security and VPNs specifically. Everyone has a concern about the risks associated with sending and receiving confidential or mission-critical material on the Internet. Therefore, tools are being developed to provide the safeguards and prevent the newsy articles we read about every day.

The typical protocols used in a remote access server (RAS) have been PPTP and L2TP because they encapsulate PPP. All the RAS needs to do is decapsulate PPP traffic from a VPN and it can process it like any other PPP data. Figure 7-12 is a representation of the PPTP packet. PPTP uses a TCP connection and a generic routing encapsulation (GRE) to encapsulate PPP frames.

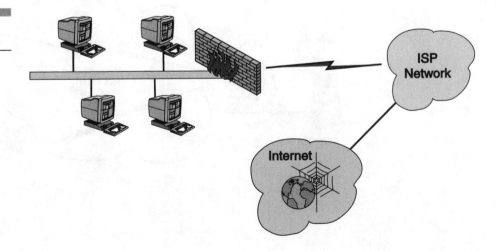

Figure 17-11
Firewalls

Figure 17-12
The PPTP tunnel
packet

| Data Link Header | IP Header | GRE Header | PPP Header | Encrypted PPP Payload (IP Datagram, IPX Datagram, NetBEUI Frame) | Data Link Trailer |

IPSec is gaining in popularity now that standard has settled down. The preferred way to handle remote access and a VPN for the future is through IPSec. IPSec transport mode is clearly going to become the dominant method of securing VPNs and remote access including those that use PPTP and L2TP for tunneling.

Now that we have defined remote access and VPN, we can look at securing the access because everyone reading this is probably thinking: "Not on my network!" particularly if you are in a senior management or information security role. This is not unusual because people are nervous about opening up an entry into their networks from remote. It sounds like a great idea to the remote user who doesn't have to worry about the consequences, but to those responsible for the security and administration in the organization, it is a nightmare. The following discusses some of the security protocols people use.

PAP and CHAP as Part of the PPP

Password Authentication Procedure (PAP) and the Challenge Handshake Authentication Protocols (CHAP) do little for security. In fact, PAP and CHAP are part of the basic PPP protocol suite and fall short in providing a true security procedure. These schemes do not address issues of ironclad authentication and integrity or eavesdropping. The PAP and CHAP are rudimentary procedures used to log on to a network, but hackers and crackers easily defeat both.

L2TP Recommended by Microsoft and Others

Layer 2 Tunnel Protocol (L2TP) is another variation of an IP encapsulation protocol. Encapsulating an L2TP frame inside a UDP packet creates an L2TP tunnel, which is shown in Figure 17-13. This in turn is encapsulated inside an IP datagram, whose source and destination addresses define the tunnel's ends. Because the outer encapsulating protocol is IP, IPSec protocols can be applied to this composite IP packet, thus protecting the data

Figure 17-13
L2TP packet

that flows within the L2TP tunnel. Authentication Header (AH), Encapsulated Security Payload (ESP), and Internet Security Association and Key Management Protocols (ISAKMP) can all be applied in a straightforward way.

Layer 2 Tunnel protocols are an excellent way of providing cost-effective remote access, multiprotocol transport, and remote LAN access. It does not provide cryptographic robust security. We believe that L2TP should therefore be used in conjunction with IPSec for providing secure remote access. L2TP supports both host-created and ISP-created tunnels.

A remote host that implements L2TP should use IPSec to protect any protocol that can be carried within a PPP packet. IPSec offers a variety of advantages:

- IPSec is widely supported by the industry including Cisco, Microsoft, Nortel Networks, and so on.

- This universal presence ensures interoperability and availability of secure solutions for different types and kinds of end users. In addition, all IPSec compliant products from different vendors are required to be compatible.

- IPSec provides for transparent security, irrespective of the applications used.

- IPSec is not limited to operating system-specific solutions. It will be ubiquitous with IP. It will also be a mandatory part of the forthcoming IPv6 standard.

- IPSec offers a variety of strong encryption standards. The key design decision to support an open architecture enables easy adaptability of newer, stronger cryptographic algorithms.

- IPSec includes a secure key-management solution with digital certificate support. IPSec guarantees the ease of management and use. This reduces deployment costs in large-scale corporate networks.

- IPSec used in conjunction with L2TP provides secure remote access client-to-server communication. L2TP alone cannot provide for a totally secure communication channel. It typically provides coverage only at the ends of the established tunnel.

Two major drafts are in IPSec: Authentication Header (AH) and Encapsulated Security Payload (ESP). They are defined as follows:

- **Authentication Header (AH)** Used to provide connectionless integrity and data origin authentication for an entire IP datagram (authentication).

- **Encapsulating Security Payload (ESP)** Provides authentication and encryption for IP datagrams with the encryption algorithm used determined by the user. In ESP authentication, the actual message digest is inserted at the end of the packet (whereas in AH, the digest is inside the authentication).

AH provides only data integrity and ESP, formerly only encryption, now provides both encryption and data integrity. The difference between AH data integrity and ESP data integrity is the scope of the data being authenticated.

AH authenticates the entire packet, whereas ESP doesn't authenticate the outer IP header. In ESP authentication, the actual message digest is now inserted at the end of the packet, whereas in AH, the digest is inside the authentication header.

The major drawback to packet-filtering techniques used in firewalls is that they require access to clear text, both in packet headers and in the packet payloads. When encryption is applied, some or all of the information needed by the packet filters may no longer be available. For example,

- In transport mode, ESP will encrypt the payload of the IP datagram. See Figure 17-14.

- In tunnel mode, ESP will encrypt the entire original datagram, both header and payload. See Figure 17-15.

Figure 17-14
Transport mode

| Data Link Header | IP Header | Authentication Header | Encapsulating Security Payload | Data | Data Link Trailer |

Figure 17-15
Tunnel mode

| Data Link Header | IP Header | Authentication Header | Encapsulating Security Payload | IP Header | Data | Data Link Trailer |

In IPSec-based VPNs, packet filtering will no longer be the principal method for enforcing access control. IPSec's AH protocol, which is crypto-graphic robust, will fill that role.

By using IPSec techniques, we introduce up to five different forms of encryption and digital signatures. These will be sufficient to delay any access to the data and by the time the code could be broken, the data will have little value. Authentication is also a very effective tool that challenges the caller and requests a key-coded response. In a security dynamics environment, a challenge and response can be issued by default every 30 seconds or by user variable to effectively manage the logged on users.

Part of the IETF IPSec standard is the definition of an automated key-management scheme, which includes the concept of a Public Key Infrastructure (PKI). PKI is an open community of Certificate Authorities (CAs), which in most cases, uses a hierarchical model to construct trust associations where none had existed before.

A PKI is important when setting up a VPN between your corporate network and a business partner or supplier because it requires a secure key exchange from a third-party CA that is trusted by both VPN nodes. The mandatory automated key-management scheme defined by IETF IPSec for IPv6 is Internet Security Association and Key Management (ISAKMP/Oakley) with Simple Key management for IP (SKIP) defined as optional. Encryption and key management is shown in Figure 17-16.

A VPN solution that supports automated key-management either by using one of the competing VPN deployment techniques enables security administrators to easily create, distribute, and revoke VPN encryption keys securely using the PKI system. Isn't that what you really need? It is com-

Figure 17-16
Encryption and key
management

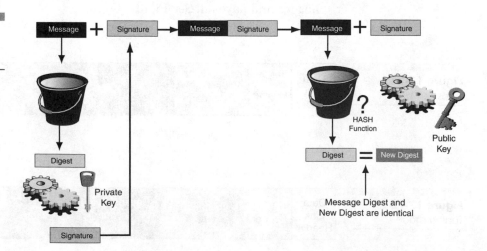

monly known that supported industry standards will ensure application interoperability. Moreover, administrators implementing a VPN face enormous security issues caused by a lack of standards. One of the most important aspects of the IPSec working group is the IPSec standard itself, which is defining the overall IP packet structure and security associations relative to VPN communications.

The IPSec standard dictates that prior to any data transfer occurring, a Security Association (SA) must be negotiated between the two VPN nodes (gateways or clients). Another major benefit of the IPSec efforts is that the standardized packet structure and security association within the IPSec standard will facilitate third-party VPN solutions that interoperate at the data transmission level. However, it does not provide an automatic mechanism to exchange the encryption and data authentication keys needed to establish the encrypted session, which introduces the second major benefit of the IPSec standard: key management infrastructure or PKI.

The IPSec working group is developing and adopting a standardized key management mechanism that enables safe and secure negotiation, distribution, and storage of encryption and authentication keys. A standardized packet structure and key management mechanism will facilitate fully interoperable third-party VPN solutions.

Other VPN technologies that are being proposed or implemented as alternatives to the IPSec standard are not true IP Security standards at all. Instead, they are encapsulation protocols that tunnel higher-level protocols into link-layer protocols. The key technologies that comprise the security component of a VPN are

- Access control to guarantee the security of network connections
- Encryption to protect the privacy of data
- Authentication to verify the user's identity as well as the integrity of the data

The final critical VPN component is enterprise management, which guarantees integration of VPNs into the overall security policy, centralized management from local or remote console, and scalability of the solution. For example, in some highly secure networks, it is important to make sure your remote networking solution is compatible with a range of third-party security devices, such as

- RADIUS (authentication, authorization, accounting)
- Third-party security devices (SecurID)
- CHAP/PAP

- Dial-back
- Centralized user lists
- Password aging
- VASCO data security

Integrated at the VPN point of access, user authentication establishes the identity of the person using the VPN node; this is because an encrypted session is established between the two locations. The user authentication mechanism allows the authorized user of the VPN system access to the system, while preventing the hacker from accessing the system. Some of the common user authentication schemes are

- Operating system username/password
- S/Key (one-time) password
- RADIUS authentication scheme
- Strong two-factor token-based scheme

The strongest user authentication schemes available on the market are two-factor authentication schemes. These require two elements to verify a user's identity: a physical element in his or her possession (a hardware electronic token) and a code that is memorized (a PIN number). Some cutting-edge solutions are beginning to use biometrics mechanisms such as fingerprints, voiceprints, and retinal scans. However, these are still relatively new and expensive.

When evaluating VPN solutions, it is important to consider a solution that has both data authentication and user authentication mechanisms. Currently, some VPN solutions provide only one form of authentication. Because of this, VPN solution providers that only support one of the two authentication mechanisms typically refer to authentication generically, without qualification of whether they support data authentication, user authentication, or both. A complete VPN solution supports both data authentication (also known as the digital signature process or data integrity) as well as user authentication (the process of verifying VPN user identity).

Various cryptographic techniques can be used to ensure data privacy of information transmitted over an unsecured channel such as the Internet, as in the case of a VPN. The transmission mode used in the VPN solution determines which pieces of the message are encrypted. Some solutions encrypt the entire message (IP header and data) while others will encrypt only the data. The four transmission modes used in VPN solutions are

- **In-place transmission mode** Typically, a vendor-specific solution where only the data is encrypted. Packet size is not affected, which in turn ensures that downstream transport mechanisms are not affected.

- **Transport mode** Only the data is encrypted and the packet size will increase in size. This mode provides adequate data privacy for node-to-node VPNs.

- **Encrypted tunnel mode** The IP header information and the data are encrypted with a new IP address created and mapped to the VPN end points providing excellent overall data privacy.

- **Non-encrypted tunnel mode** Nothing is encrypted which means that all data transported is clear text. This is not an effective solution for data privacy.

Oddly enough, some VPN solutions do not perform any encryption at all. Instead, they rely on data encapsulation techniques such as a tunneling or forwarding protocol for data privacy. Not all of the tunneling and forwarding protocols use a cryptographic system for data privacy. This means that it would transmit all data in the clear, leaving one to wonder how non-encryption-based solutions can provide any form of data privacy protection a critical requirement for a virtual private network. Unfortunately, the industry terminology itself may be contributing to some of this confusion. To clarify this issue, one must look specifically at what transmission mode is being used. As with the qualification between data authentication and user authentication, transmission modes should be distinguished between encrypted and non-encrypted. If a VPN solution does not provide any form of encryption for data privacy, then this solution is more appropriately called a virtual network (VN) because there is nothing private about the network.

Questions

1. What does VPN mean?
   a. Very Personal Network
   b. Virtual Private Node
   c. Virtual Private Network
   d. Virtual Public Network

2. Who can benefit from the VPN service?

   a. The road warrior

   b. The lollygagger

   c. Your local hotel

   d. The Internet Service Providers

3. When a VPN is installed, a risk is no longer associated with using the Internet.   T/F

4. What are three types of organizations that can benefit from remote access?

   a. _____

   b. _____

   c. _____

5. When a packet filter is used, we call it a _____.

6. The components of a VPN include the following:

   a. VPN server and client

   b. Connection and network

   c. Protocols and tunnels

   d. None of the above

   e. All of the above

7. What is the remote access service user who calls in after hours?

   a. The road warrior

   b. The satellite office user

   c. The day extender

   d. The pain in the neck

8. What device initiates a VPN connection?

   a. The VPN server

   b. The ISP network

   c. The VPN tunnel software

   d. The VPN client

9. What services can add new opportunities to provide high-speed access? _____ and _____

10. Remote access can be achieved from:

    a. A person's home

    b. Anywhere in the world

    c. A remote office

    d. A local hotel

    e. All of the above

11. The _____ protocol handles the PPP protocol.

12. What are two of the four modes of handling IPSec?

    a. L2F and L2PT

    b. LTTP and L2TP

    c. Tunnel and transport

    d. AH and ESP

13. How many different types of encryption are available in IPSec?

    a. Two

    b. Five

    c. Three

    d. Four

14. What is the motivation behind installing and using VPNs?

    a. Remote access

    b. Dial-up communications

    c. Money

    d. Security

15. IPSec in conjunction with _____ provides secure remote access client-to-server communication.

16. _____ guarantees the security of network connections.

17. Encryption protects the _____ of data.

18. Authentication verifies the user's identity as well as the _____ of the data.

19. Some cutting-edge solutions are beginning to use _____ mechanisms such as fingerprints, voiceprints, and retinal scans.

20. The two very basic security methods used in PPP are:

   a. PPP and PPTP

   b. PAP and CHAP

   c. ISAKAMP and SKIP

   d. PPP and SLIP

Intranet

After reading this chapter and completing the questions, you will be able to:

■ Explain what the Intranet is

■ Discuss the differences between the Internet and Intranet

■ Describe the applications that can be used

■ Deal with the geeks

■ Follow along in a conversation about the function of the Intranet

■ Fill in the checklists that are used to determine the application for an Intranet

With all of the hype and fanfare about the Internet that has surfaced since the early 1990s, many organizations have spent inordinate amounts of money to use and facilitate access to the wide area through the World Wide Web (WWW). These organizations saw the benefits of providing the capabilities of remote access and catalog information access for customers to log onto their Internet-based server. Using a graphical user interface (GUI), organizations have allowed customers to pick up information and dispense or print it locally. This eliminates many of the costs associated with mailing flyers and catalogs. Customers can print their own catalogs as opposed to waiting for information to come through the postal system. Beyond the savings of the catalog printing, companies also save on postage by using this distribution method.

With the emphasis on electronic access to document information and delivery through an architecture called the *Internet,* large corporations began to view this as an opportunity to support their internal client/server architectures. Therefore, these larger organizations began to use the same tools and techniques consistent with those already available on the Internet to build an *Intranet.* The Intranet is an internal Internet, so to speak. As more and more users within organizations moved away from the terminal device (dumb terminal) and became more PC savvy, they began looking for the ability to conduct and transact business online. The Internet enabled this as a transport vehicle for most of the consumers' access capabilities. The Intranet provides the same capabilities and features inside the organization. The desktop device can be used with a Web browser to scan for information that will reside on a large Web-based server that is for exclusive use by internal organizations. Moreover, organizations can blend the combination of both Intranet and Internet services on a single server-based platform, as long as isolation and separation can be maintained. This is where much of the current spending and emphasis is now placed. Users are becoming pros on the Internet, so they are also becoming internal pros at managing, maintaining, and using their Intranets.

Organizations have been impressed with the ease of use and deployment capabilities of the Internet and have seen it as an opportunity to change the way the internal infrastructure works. By using Web servers, Web browsers, and hypertext-based applications, organizations are employing the same technology as their own internal business communications tool. These organizations have discovered that the same features that facilitate the Internet architecture and make it attractive for inter-enterprise communications make it an excellent technology for intra-enterprise communications. In particular, very large organizations that have various application servers, hardware platforms, and multiple sources of information (such as on mainframes) can now use this Intranet server capability to provide a single user interface on a hardware-independent platform. With the various categories of operating systems and hardware systems (PCs and Macs), organizations can now take advantage of the ability to merge the hardware platforms into a single homogenous network.

This movement toward Intranet technology is heavily supported by other industry trends. For example, TCP/IP, the protocol used throughout the Internet (and developed for the Internet), has become the de facto standard as a multivendor protocol in many corporate networks because of its robustness and its simplicity. Simple mail transfer protocol (SMTP) is rapidly becoming the popular standard for internal e-mail systems. Moving away from the proprietary architectures of the past, organizations now use the SMTP and POP server capabilities to facilitate and allow access for users who want to surf an internal Net as well as navigate and access all organizational data housed on different computers and operating system software. The browsers used to do this enable users to get away from using the old command-line interface, which was cumbersome and platform-specific. Users were faced with the challenge of remembering varying keystrokes and organizational needs to be able to talk to different computing systems such as IBM3270 platforms and UNIX. Beyond the TCP/IP platform and protocols, users have simplified access to e-mail systems through the use of the point-to-point protocol (PPP), which allows them to access Internet resources as well as internal mail system information, using a remote serial communications connection. These two simplification protocols have really expanded much of what takes place in an office today.

With the use of a single point-and-click arrangement within an organization, the information residing on an IBM mainframe, a UNIX server, a Novell or NT server, or a PC-based LAN or any other computing platform can be accessed through the same easy-to-use arrangement. This enables universal access to data on the different systems as well as different applications. In a sense, Internet and Web technology is playing much the same role as the proprietary solutions such as the groupware technology used on Lotus Notes or Novell's GroupWise services. The Web server's capability to provide access to a variety of information—even the multimedia applications, files, and video streams—enables it to act much like a Lotus Notes database, yet it can cost much less when an open interface as opposed to when the proprietary interface is used. In the future, the Intranet technology can be expanded to incorporate all collaborative functions and broader support for the multimedia technology. A significant amount of work has been done in most organizations to provide collaborative computing capabilities between various departments. For example, in an advertising or marketing department, much has been done to interface and to integrate the dynamic work group capabilities between artists, freelancers, copywriters, and final editors. Using a single GUI-based environment, these organizations and departments will have access to each other's information or any work in progress. Each of the users will have access to the data so that they can manipulate or view status on a project under way. This creates a much more dynamic environment within the organization without extensive retraining and application-specific programs on everybody's desk. Much of the time and cost associated with the development of a new campaign or advertising literature is accrued in the back-and-forth information flow between these various groups, both externally and internally. By deploying the information through an Intranet, the information can be made readily accessible and available to anyone at any time. The delays in getting the information back and forth between the responsible persons continually extend market delivery from inception to final product. The use of Intranet technologies will pare down the development cycle by days if not weeks. The cost of transmitting or faxing documents, or expressing packages both domestically and internationally can be reduced significantly with an Intranet.

Issues

The use of the Internet technology inside the organization on the Intranet therefore gives credence to the fact that electronic access and delivery services should be deployed using these types of capabilities. From an external communications perspective, the benefits are very clear. Because organizations will deal with many parties who use the Internet, it provides a common method of handling external connectivity. Because it is also widely used by organizations and individuals throughout the world, it provides an excellent platform for future growth within any organization. The costs associated with transmitting information from the Intranet to the Internet can be easily justified on the basis of the simple-to-use dial-up communications technology. In many cases, a local call will allow access to either the Internet or Intranet and therefore allow users to share information regardless of where they are in the world. Most of the commercial online services provide links to the Internet. Internet services are typically inexpensive. Over time, it would be safe to say that the organization would be able to reach virtually any computer with a modem from an Intranet to the Internet.

Another key advantage of this technology is the use of the Web browser. Web browsers tend to be somewhat platform independent and offer the same look and feel to a user regardless of the hardware or operating system. These can typically be purchased inexpensively at local computer stores or downloaded free to individual users. They are usually built into many of the systems (such as the Windows 9X/2000). Based on a hypertext technology, Web software is generally very simple to use. This makes it a natural platform for internal user applications such as directories, employee information bulletin boards, news and highlights within the organization, and access to the data warehouse. The costs associated with a training program and with introducing users to a proprietary operating system versus the cost of learning to use a Web browser are significantly different. The Web browser software is much less expensive to implement and requires much less user training regardless of whether the software is on a PC, Mac, or now the newer Net PCs.

For Intranet users, an internal Web site used to distribute corporate information to employees to accommodate day-to-day business operations makes sense. The organization can develop a team concept for production methods from inception to final product development. By using the Intranet, these team members can easily be kept up to date on product status, project meeting notes, and other incremental information based on a project at hand. This will empower employees to share business data using the same friendly Web browsers that they use to access their external information over the Internet. Moreover, the Intranet will enable linkage between various business units in an organization so that those employees can easily navigate throughout the available data for more complete information at any time.

This approach also facilitates another important element within the organization: off-site access by employees. By building a common set of Internet-based access and delivery mechanisms, the organization can enable remote users (either road warriors or employees working at home) to easily access the information resources. Off-site employees could use the Internet connections to pull down company data and information, send e-mail, or upload new business information at a moment's notice. In other cases, mobile employees and home-based employees can access faster, more highly secured links directly to the internal Intranet while still having the Internet accessible to them.

The Architecture

The ideal access mechanism concerns itself primarily with an infrastructure, which includes the following areas:

- External access
- E-mail
- Directory services

- Security
- Archival systems
- Web services
- Fax servers

Figure 18-1 is a graphic representation of how the Internet and Intranet might work. In this figure, the LAN within the organization is shown at the left. Many different organizational departments can be attached through these different LAN servers. A high-speed backbone infrastructure would be used to link all the servers and the departments together. Just to the right of the server backbone are several different components, called *Intranet servers*, which would now be used to interlink these different departments. The Intranet servers can be one or many servers plugged into the network for access by various departments. These servers function like warehouses, storing much of the corporate information and providing all users with the rights and privileges assigned to access corporate information with the GUI. The browser would enable the connection to the various hosts based on an IP addressing scheme used internally within the organization. Beyond the Intranet servers would be a mail server that serves the entire enterprise. This mail server would run the standard SMTP and POP protocols to supply electronic mail internally as well as to provide a gateway capability to the external world. The enterprise mail server as well as the LAN itself would be attached through a high-speed router connected to a device called a *firewall*. Note that extending off the router is another connection called a *customer Web server*. This Web server would be internal to an organization but allow customers to access electronic document interchange (EDI), order entry, or inventory and status on projects under way. This would be an internally protected Web server using password and log-on capabilities to secure and protect the information as well as provide a barrier to keep users from getting onto the LAN itself. The firewall is in the center of the Intranet, and all access through the firewall is to the router.

Just to the right of the firewall, we see a *marketing server*, which would be optional. This marketing server might be something that enables customers to dial in or contact the organization from a front-end perspective. This marketing server would provide the public with access to catalog information that the organization offers to the consuming public. In the event an organization or an employee accessing the network needed to reach any of the other servers remotely, the marketing server would pass the information through to the firewall for access to the backbone network.

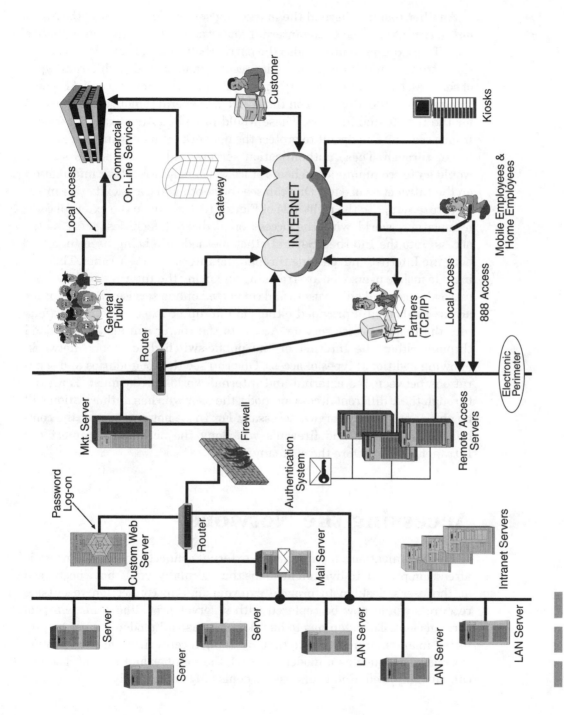

Figure 18-1
Internet and Intranet integration

Another router is beyond the marketing server. This router is the *external router*, as opposed to the internal router as shown on the left of Figure 18-1. This external router is also the barrier between the outside world and the Intranet. On this router, specific access is made based on different types of services. Note that hanging from the bottom of that router is a LAN operating at 10 or 100 Mbps and on that LAN are several remote access servers for the remote dial-in users. These would provide authentication services from a security standpoint to protect the network from allowing just anyone to get through. These authentication servers and remote access servers would let telecommuters and home office workers access all the information on the Intranet as needed. One can see the depth and complexity this infrastructure setup. To the right side of Figure 18-1, we have the external communications world with the access on dedicated facilities (such as T1 access) into the Internet. Several other methods are being used to access both the Internet and, passing through the Internet, the Intranet. This can include mobile users who are traveling and using the Internet as the access method or general public users and connected online services. Several other access methods are provided either on dial-up or leased-line connections into the remote access servers. Access to the router can also be provided through either the Internet or the public-switched telephone network, allowing additional types of access. One can see that boundaries and separations between the external and internal worlds are a must. However, through these different access methods, the user who has authorization will be able to access any service necessary. For those not authorized, the combination of routers and firewalls will deny the access and protect the Intranet, and therefore the company data.

Accessing the Network

At this organization's main location, external connectivity for end users is already improved. Individual modems that normally would have been used at the user's desktop to provide external dial-up connection to outside resources would now be replaced with a server providing a modem pool arrangement. This step has to be taken because all modems must be protected in an environment like this. By using a centralized modem pooling arrangement (such as a modem server), the number and type of modems can be minimized. End users use modems only occasionally, so the pooling makes the resources available as needed, but eliminates the need for a one-to-one ratio. This approach will provide improved price performance as well as the authentication via some token-based access security mechanism.

Because this approach eliminates the need for employee traffic to pass through the Internet firewall, it provides greater accessibility and flexibility for the organization's resources. The employee can use the Internet if desired, but will be limited to e-mail and access to a small number of pre-defined services. Traveling (nomadic) employees outside the organizational headquarters can be given an 800/888/877/866 number to remotely access the server, or they can use a local Internet point-to-presence (POP) if they so desire. By taking this structured approach, the organization will reduce its reliance on costly and disparate means of access. This approach is also more secure because it consolidates external network access via only one of two methods: the firewall or the remote access authentication server. Consolidating access should make external links easier to monitor and manage. Using the Internet brings along reduced costs.

Another benefit to this approach is consolidation and centrally manageable IP address translations. If the organization chooses to use a high-end addressing system internally (such as a class A address) but at the Internet use a class C externally, address translation will be required at the Internet firewall. Remote access servers will dynamically assign internal class A addresses to individual users when they dial into the organization so that no address translation will be necessary for these devices. A standard procedure to follow when approaching this translation need is the use of RFC1597.[1] Figure 18-2 provides a general description of how this address translation can work. With RFC1597, the entire organization will use a private network with a class A address (10.XXX.XXX.XXX, which has not been assigned or registered to any organization). However, the only access to the Internet would be through the firewall hosts that perform the address translation between the internal network address and one or more of the registered class C addresses (YYY.YYY.YYY.XXX). To the outside world, every host on this network will appear to belong to one or more of the organization's class C networks.

The firewall host will maintain an address translation table with an entry for each of the internal hosts that require the Internet access. One

---

[1] RFC is a Request for Comment issued by the Internet Engineering Task Force (IETF) describing how a service should work.

Figure 18-2
The IP address
translation

Internal Non-Registered and
non-routable
Class A Address

Network
Address
Translation
Gateway Hosts
(Firewall Host)

Class C Addresses
(each @ 256 Hosts)

Company Intranet

Internet

alternative for each host or user is to preregister its internal address with
the firewall to be assigned an external compatible address; adding an entry
to the address table will permit up to 256 hosts to have inbound and outbound Internet access. Alternatively, the address translation function in the
host or firewall could be dynamically assigned one of the 256 class C
addresses at the time of connection through the firewall. A dynamic host
controlled protocol (DHCP) enables this capability. Now, any IP messages
outbound from the Intranet to the Internet will pass through the gateway
host function. The gateway host will swap the source address (from the
internal to the external Class C address) but leave the destination address
alone. For any messages inbound from the Internet to the organization, the
gateway host will swap the destination address from the registered external class C number to an internal private class A address but leave the
source address alone. In this approach, no ambiguity exists regarding the
destination address. This will permit standardized packet-level gateway
access to the Internet as opposed to only application-level gateway functionality or use of a cumbersome dual log-on procedure. This strategy
enables the organization to migrate gradually to the newer IP version 6
addressing standard, converting internal addresses before changing external addresses (or vice versa).

Intranet: The Logical Evolution

One can imagine an organization with hundreds of sites located and dispersed around the country or the world. Thousands of employees need access to each and every database for timely information on policy changes, personnel guidelines, training materials, company directories and phone books, product and pricing information for sales organizations, and general dissemination of information. Where individual work groups and departmental requirements provide for secure, unlimited access to their data, the organization now has a need to share this information with all employees on either a wide-open or a limited basis. Some information must remain confidential, but this can also be facilitated. Each geographic region within an organization typically has its own separate databases and servers and provides its own reporting functions that should be shared with the corporate headquarters. In the past, these reports and databases would be transmitted via electronic means. During the transmission, a conversion process would take place that might eliminate formatting. Manual conversion and translation processes for reformatting are labor-intensive and time consuming. Beyond that, if the information is not electronically transmitted, then a hard paper copy must be transmitted via fax or through the postal service. In either case, this hard paper copy would then have to be reentered into the computer database at the corporate headquarters. One can imagine the amount of time and money that is lost in this manual processing of information when disparate systems exist. The risk of error when data is re-keyed is also included. The disparity in systems occurs because each regional or geographic location may well have installed its own hardware and software operating systems on a site-by-site basis as opposed to a global infrastructure on a corporate-wide basis.

Traditionally, organizations have always had multiple policy and procedure handbooks, printed materials, newsletters, and pricing catalogs produced at some centralized location. All of the printed materials are time consuming and expensive to produce and do not necessarily generate revenue in their form and format. Guaranteeing that this information is transmitted or shipped across the country (or the world) in a timely and reasonable fashion has always been a headache. Consider all the costs associated with this, such as the data gathering coming from multiple sites with all of the associated feedback cycles necessary to ensure accuracy, the production process in terms of printing and typesetting and final production, and then the distribution, whereby boxes of materials are packaged and shipped at great expense using surface or air transportation. If all of this could be done electronically on a common, user-friendly interface, the organization would naturally want to consider this.

When viewing today's cost-cutting environment and the need to do more with less, one can hardly afford to eliminate all of the communications necessary. However, the staff (being limited) will not have the time to manage and administer all of the various informational tools necessary to run the organization. In today's competitive environment, timely access to the information is probably more mission critical than ever in the past. A solution to this would be to have a broadcast e-mail system and send the information out to all employees. However, this method is inefficient because users and employees will view the mail at different times or they will scan the mail and not necessarily note the changes that are being introduced. As the mail is being sent out, the information is concurrently generating multiple stored messages in everybody's mailbox, consuming hard disk space as well as producing a directory or mailbox that is being jam-stuffed (comparing it to the in box in a person's office). If, in fact, the mail is starting to stuff the boxes, users can only access, approach, and view a certain amount of information when needed. When information is not needed, the mail will either be discarded or filed for later retrieval. This, however, creates another scenario: "Where did I file this one?"

As a means of overcoming some of these problems and pitfalls, the Intranet was the logical solution to produce a cost-efficient and timely approach to the distribution of information. Using the WWW technology, the *intraprise* has become the global perspective. The server providing the WWW interface is at the foundation of the Internet. Organizations that built their WWW sites store and update information electronically on this WWW server attached to a LAN. As information changes, the server content can be updated with the new or revised data. This allows the organizational employees to access information in a timely and consistent manner and provides accurate information to all employees without the expense of typesetting, printing, distributing, and mailing all the changes. In a very large organization, multiple servers may well exist on the different LANs spread across the country. However, if employees need a price list from a group that is located halfway around the world, they need only access the WWW server to research and gather the data using the GUI. Using the point-and-click method, the employee will find the host (the server) and access the information for immediate viewing. In the event that a printed copy is needed, the file can be downloaded to the local printer on the LAN and be immediately available to the user in hard copy. This prevents the need for having multiple manuals, price lists, and catalogs sitting on people's desks, rarely accessed or used. When the information is needed, it is there; however, when it's not, it doesn't need to be stored on the bookshelves.

For highly confidential information, security on the World Wide Web offers numerous advantages for the internal exchange of information. As an example of this, an organization can restrict information to certain users or departments, such as human resources and financial data, enabling users to access the information securely. This can be done using the Internet as an external backbone and the Intranet as the internal backbone linking the two sites together. In this scenario, the human resources department of a large organization can share ladder plan strategies, salary planning information, personnel reviews and files, or any other type of data in a secure method. In any case, the server would be far easier to configure, use, and manage. Individual home pages can be set up for each of the departments or functional areas. This would enable an easy-to-use interface on a home-page-by-home-page basis. Additionally, when corporate information needs to be distributed, the home page can provide video and audio downloads to discuss notes or special considerations by providing separate interface information.

Is It for Everyone?

Clearly, organizations that have multiple locations spread across the country and hundreds or thousands of employees are a good fit for this Internet/Intranet technology. Because of the disparity and the distribution necessary to keep information flowing, the Intranet becomes a logical choice. However, more and more applications are being developed and Intranets are being deployed for smaller organizations with a handful of sites and possibly 50 or less employees. This is particularly true when dealing with the *virtual office*. The virtual office enables the small office and home office[2] locations to access information through either dial-up access or Internet access into the main headquarters infrastructure. This prevents home office users from having books stacked all over the place. Instead, when the information is needed, the home office users need only access it through their Intranet. Several other applications may tie into the Intranet. An example of this would be the computer telephony integration (CTI), as

---

[2] SOHO—small office and home office

described in Chapter 12, linked together with the home page or the Intranet so that a home office worker can call a specific telephone number and, if the home user's telephone number matches an approved access number, readily access information available on the Intranet. This would imply that CTI is used both at the home office and the corporate office. Combining features and services through these telecommunications techniques creates accessibility of information regardless of where the worker is.

What this means is that the Intranet, once viewed as the large corporate infrastructure, can now move down into the smaller organizations in much the same way it is used in the larger ones. The real name of the game is communications capability. By linking services together through a communications infrastructure, organizations have the ability to provide access whenever, wherever, and however they choose. Printing resources can be consolidated and locally provided based on Intranet technology and the dial-up or remote access services. Therefore, the Intranet is a logical evolution and a good fit for both the large and small organization that needs to provide timely, accurate, and efficient information regardless of the employee location. One can see the benefits and challenges of building an Intranet within an organization by comparing it to some of the higher-end cost solutions provided by the proprietary vendors already offering services. Is it any wonder that many manufacturers of these proprietary solutions have now adopted the name Intranet as part of their business solution packages? Intranet will be one of the major communications infrastructures that will roll through the turn of the century. If an organization has not yet begun to deploy this architecture, it may well be in a position of not having the information readily available and lose its competitive edge. Organizations prosper and grow through a competitive edge and technology accomplishes this.

The Full-Service Intranet

Companies like Microsoft and Netscape have a vision of how organizations can use standard Internet technologies to deploy fully functional ubiquitous communications access for information sharing and applications built on top of open networking technologies and on an open network-based application platform.[3]

---

[3] From Netscape Communications, Inc. (now AOL)

The full-service Intranet is a concept that was first envisioned in early 1995 and that was talked about throughout 1996, and ultimately became a reality in late 1996 and early 1997. A full-service Intranet is supposed to include the capability to run a TCP/IP network inside an organization that provides connectivity to all the people and all the information. Ideally, this increases productivity and provides navigational services through the computing environment on a seamless-based network. This full-service Intranet takes advantage of all the open standards and protocols that emerged as a result of the Internet. When an open standards interface is used, applications and services such as e-mail, groupware, security systems, archival systems, database access, management, and directory services can all be more powerful than they are when run on traditional proprietary systems. Because of the openness in this architecture, end users can reap all the benefits of the cost, platform support, flexibility, and independence from operating systems and vendors and gain the ability to leverage their products and data as a single entity.

Actually, the model is really described in terms of services rather than protocols and standards. Services are provided as a direct result of the interface to all the software and applications. Because Intranet software runs across a client and server architecture, a common network environment spans even heterogeneous networks. Therefore, the services provide users with the abilities of looking up any information, sending and receiving mail, searching directories, using facsimile servers, and providing access to the outside world via the Internet. They also create custom application development from a myriad of third-party providers for sales automation, help desk functions, and financial applications (such as loan calculators and mortgage calculators), and take advantage of all of the capabilities of replication and security. The intent of the Intranet is to make integrated technology (IT) simple and easy to use and to simplify the process of building and managing a network for the IT professionals. A quick note: all industries are facing a potential shortage of qualified and talented IT professionals. In 2000, the industry experienced over a 35 percent shortfall in IT skills. Using the capabilities of the Intranet to manage technologies far more simply, we can overcome the limitations and shortfalls in talents in the future.

Companies like Netscape (now AOL) envision their services of an Intranet in four basic categories:

- Information sharing and management
- Communications and collaboration
- Navigation

■ Application access

Beyond the user services, the full-service Intranet, as portrayed by Netscape, also includes four major network services:

■ Directory

■ Replication

■ Security

■ Management

The services provided by a full-service Intranet will drive the network to a focal point of business computing. The days of old, where the desktop PC was dominated by a command-line interface and proprietary operating software, are just that—old. Using an open architecture and the navigational browsers, an end user sitting at a desktop PC will have the basis of being able to access any piece of information. As a result, network-centric environments can be created. Some of the features and capabilities of these environments are as follows:

■ They are easy to use and implement; they avoid the need to replace all hardware systems and operating software.

■ They encompass all of the existing investments on desktop computers, mainframes, applications, and databases.

■ They provide a network that has interoperability and internetworking capabilities. This enables users to directly address and access any associated equipment existing in the Intranet.

■ Written once—read by many: the capability to write a document or information and distribute or replicate it across the network to multiple servers so that it can be read and accessed by many different locations either simultaneously or on an ad hoc basis.

■ They are centrally managed so that ease of use and operational stability can be accomplished within an Intranet.

■ They are generally lower in cost; using a simple, robust set of applications and the Web browsers provides for less expensive communications infrastructure. This avoids the need to buy separate proprietary and domain-based software and operating systems that can be very expensive.

■ They have flexible operational capabilities: the ability to use individual vendors and operating systems on an open standards-based platform.

- They are proven and mature, as evidenced by the several major Fortune 100 companies that have deployed an Intranet on an enterprise or an intraprise environment.

Applications

When you really think about it, it would be difficult to list all of the applications that could fit on an Intranet. However, the obvious applications that most folks will attempt to integrate and deploy includes such things as

- Database access
- Online financial transactions
- Inventory analysis
- Order entry
- Company newsletters
- Job posting and opportunities
- Corporate-wide public relations announcements

Although these are the primary applications that have been implemented and used extensively by organizations, a wealth of other opportunities could exist, including the routine day-to-day operations that an organization may also need to provide resource sharing. When one thinks of the day-to-day operation, it takes just a little imagination to realize how the integration of the databases can supplement these operations. But taking that a step further, online forms provide for things such as

- Expense report submission and printing
- Help desk functions
- Frequently asked questions about technology
- Questions regarding medical expenses or coverage
- Educational opportunities or training classes available within the organization
- Outside educational courses that are approved and accepted by the organization
- Supply ordering and forms
- Maintenance requests for internal or external facilities-based applications

- Security issues, such as application for a new security card
- Automotive expenses
- Travel requests
- Overtime production and scheduling

When one thinks of the applications that could be put on an online form, whereby an end user within an organization using the Intranet can access the forms and fill them out in a user-friendly fashion then submit them directly to the corresponding department, the possibilities become endless. Updating directories, maintenance of policies and procedures, suggested changes in operations, or any other application could all become part of the Intranet capability. For example, think of how, if a user notices operation inefficiency, an online suggestion box could be directed to the quality control group or to senior management for administration and action. All of the possibilities that require employees to fill out extensive forms and store paper everywhere within the organization could become electronic applications on the Intranet. Using these capabilities, the organization could save a fortune in printing and distribution costs alone. Mail handling through an organization for interoffice communications is an expensive proposition. By using the electronic distribution, the amount of mail handling personnel might be equally reduced, supporting the Intranet in its truest distribution form. This book is not trying to encourage the reduction of operating personnel, but rather the use of people already on board in a more productive manner. An inordinate amount of waste in an organization surrounds filling out and submitting the appropriate forms. Studies have been done around the world showing that the cost and preparation for documentation and administrative handling, postage requests, and things of that nature is excessive and redundant. This multiple handling of paper and documents impedes getting the job done. By routing the appropriate form electronically throughout an organization, the handling can be minimized and the work can be done efficiently. This is the goal of the Intranet.

Getting There from Here

Creating an internal World Wide Web application and an Intranet site, although low in cost and a minimal investment, is still a challenge regardless of who is chosen to do it. Although it will be easy to implement with little training and equipment needed, some decisions should be made before the product is rolled out. The basic system should consist of a server with an operating system and some Web server software. Assuming that the organization already has PCs in place, the client investment is probably going to be relatively insignificant. One can imagine that most users will either have an Internet Explorer or Netscape browser already on their PCs, as this has become quite common. In many cases, browser software is already included in the operating system on PCs purchased today. That being the case, client software is probably simple enough to deploy and implement. As a matter of fact, one would hope that in developing the client access to the Intranet, multiple browsers could be used, depending on what is already on the end user's desktop device.

At the server, the rule of thumb is that server hardware with sufficient memory and disk space to run one of the operating systems such as Windows NT/2000, Windows 95/98/ME, and/or UNIX depends particularly on the preference and in-house expertise. The department responsible for the Intranet will need to configure the hardware with LAN cards, if not already installed, for a TCP/IP connection over the network to the clients. In many cases, more organizations are opting for either the Windows NT or Windows 95/98 interface because of ease of use and their open architecture. This is not an endorsement or a directional statement, merely an observation.

The Web server software will enable the organization to manage the internal presence on the Intranet. The correct server software will provide the functionality required to set up and manage home pages and develop the content base in hypertext markup language (HTML), as already discussed in the section on the Internet. Furthermore, the Web server software will also use the capability to provide search engine capabilities and integrate with internal corporate databases and back-office functionality.

The client browser can launch a variety of applications, access the databases, and retrieve information from across the Internet or Intranet. Client software is also required to generate the HTML code so that it can be added and converted on a document-handling basis. It is very easy to develop the content for a Web using one of the inexpensive authoring tools, including Microsoft's Internet Assistant (a freebie). Depending on the organization's requirements, you can also take advantage of numerous other tools available, including the graphics, software, and packages to convert frame maker documents into HTML as well as integrating text retrieval and indexing software, links to database management systems, and server configurations or management tools.

Therefore, the decisions appear to be fairly straightforward and simple. However, the decisions still required include such things as

- Should the server run a UNIX/LINUX, NT/W2K, or Windows 9X/Me operating environment?

- Do employees require access to all information or just certain subsets of it?

- Do employees need access to the databases such as SQL?

- Should information be made available to all employees or just certain employees or departments? If only a small percentage of the employees require the access, how will data be secured from others reaching or accessing it?

- What form of security will be used to secure the Intranet from the Internet?

- Does the firewall exist or will one need to be purchased? In either case, is the expertise available to install and maintain the firewall database?

- Will multiple browsers be used? If so, what types of access and support, such as HTTP, gopher, FTP, or Telnet, will be required? Does the server support these various protocols?

- Will multiple home pages be installed on the same server? If so, how easy will they be to manage and maintain?

- Is remote administration a requirement?

- Who will be installing the server? Will this be IS, IT, or LAN administration? How easy will it be to install?

- What type of interface will the server use? Will it be intuitive enough and easy to use?

- What type of search engine and text retrieval is supported on this server?

- What addressing schemes does the server support?

- Who will set up the home page and maintain it? Is a Web master available or is training required?

- Who has responsibility for managing the content? Will this be the marketing group, technical support, or a separate Web master?

- Are there special configuration requirements on your hardware platform?

- Will online help and support be available? Who will script it, support it, and maintain it?

- Under what group or department will the Intranet reside? Is this IS/IT?

- How will users request updates or access to information that may not already be available to them? Is this an application of the Intranet because of its online form?

- How does management support play in this whole scenario? Is management convinced that an Intranet will have benefit?

One can clearly see that the decisions and the implementation of an Intranet, although simple, still require some thought before installation is attempted. Management must support the idea and make the decision on how the process will take place.

Other Issues

Other issues must be dealt with as the organization places all of its data on an Intranet accessible to all. When users can access the data, will they be able to edit and delete or just read it? What would be the scenario if a disgruntled employee decided to go onto the home pages and destroy them? These issues are a little more sensitive, but they must be addressed. By placing all of the corporate data and access to that data on an Intranet, productivity will be improved; however, one must not go into this with rose-colored glasses and think that all problems can be solved on a single platform. The issues of security, manageability, and recoverability in the event of loss or destruction of information must also be addressed. The appropriate groups must be assigned and selected before a deployment is started. As users progress and roll out the access to the data, a flexible approach must also be used. If things aren't exactly the way they should be, then the infrastructure has to be put in place to react and adapt very quickly. If the form or format of the data is not readable by all browsers (many versions of browsers are available on the market today) or if the data is not capable of being downloaded due to incompatibility of some systems, then these issues must be resolved quickly. The Intranet is an exciting opportunity for many organizations to quickly link all of their databases and information on a single hardware-independent platform, but it could pose problems and frustrations if not approached correctly.

Other issues might address the bandwidth available on the LAN or WAN. Normal word processing documents that might be significantly smaller in a word processing system may increase in size when all of the GUI information is included. Any GUI will clearly increase the size of the files, including graphic interchange format (GIF) or Joint Photographic Experts Group (JPEG) files, tagged image file format (TIFF) or even bit map images. As the size and the complexity of the document increases, one must decide how the bandwidth will be handled. Will this involve an upgrade to the entire infrastructure on the LAN? Opportunities exist to provide for higher throughput capabilities on the LAN by going from 10 to 100 Mbps. Another opportunity is to leave the 10 Mbps at the desktop and use a switched hub inside a telephone closet. It involves some hardware implementation and deployment, but this can be kept to a minimum if planned properly. The worst-case scenario would be to deploy the Intranet and discover that the capacity and throughput is not available. Users will not accept the same throughput that they see on the Internet. When dialing into the Internet with modem speed communications in the kbps range (28.8–33.6 kbps), users tend to accept slow response and slow downloads. However, on the local area network (LAN), if that same throughput and response were made available to the users, they would burn down the MIS department. Therefore, on the higher speed LANs at 4, 10, or 16 Mbps, the capacity assumes that the LAN is not already bogged down. If the GUIs and pictures increase the network demands, the response could be slowed down significantly. Therefore, it behooves the administrator to analyze and understand in advance the capacity and actual throughput currently on the LAN. If, in fact, an Intranet will be deployed, the necessary upgrades to the LAN will have to be considered as part of the budgeted items.

Again, this is not a condemnation of the Intranet, but merely a caution that tools do exist and capabilities can be provided so long as the appropriate bandwidth is available to support them. Refer to the sections on LANs, Ethernet, and token ring for more details on the throughput capabilities and the response times for the LAN.

Questions

1. What is an Intranet?
   a. A part of the Internet
   b. An external connection to the corporate network
   c. An internal Internet
   d. A LAN

2. Using a _____ creates the same look and feel of the Internet.

3. The predominant protocol that supports the Intranet is:

   a. Novell

   b. IBM SNA

   c. UNIX

   d. TCP/IP

4. To move away from proprietary architecture and systems, organizations now use _____ and _____ servers to surf the internal Web.

   a. Novell and DEC

   b. SMTP and POP

   c. IBM and Microsoft

   d. TCP and IP

5. The internal flow of information between groups has been slowed down by using the Intranet, but the access and ease of use make up for that. T/F

6. The Intranet provides a common method of handling external connectivity.   T/F

7. The Web browser provides the _____ interface to facilitate point and click access.

8. The architecture concerns itself primarily with the overall access to the following areas (select all that apply):

   a. Accounting

   b. External access

   c. Mail systems

   d. Financial

   d. Fax servers

   f. Directory services

   g. Web services

   h. Management networking

   i. Security

9. A useful benefit of RFC 1597 in Intranet technology is the use of:

   a. Access to the rest of the world

   b. IP address translation

   c. Web browsers

    d. E-mail

    e. Directory services

10. Using the WWW technology, the _____ has become a global perspective.

    a. Intraprise

    b. Enterprise

    c. Exercise

    d. Extraprise

11. What device will maintain a translation table with an entry for each internal host needing Internet access?

    a. DNS server

    b. LDAP server

    c. Microsoft SMS server

    d. Firewall

12. What protocol on the Intranet and the LAN will support the assignment of an IP address?

    a. ARP

    b. RARP

    c. ACP

    d. DHCP

13. Some of the applications that will run well on the Intranet include (select all that apply):

    a. Accounting and bookkeeping

    b. Expense reporting

    c. Ordering supplies

    d. Catalog distribution

    e. Marketing materials

    f. Human resources ladder plans

    g. Corporate long range plans

    h. Travel requests

    i. Executive summaries

    j. Payroll files

    k. CTI

14. The Intranet became a reality in what years?

    a. 1990–1991

    b. 1996–1997

    c. 1998–1999

    d. 1994–1995

15. Netscape sees the Intranet technologies supporting all except which service?

    a. Information sharing

    b. Network design

    c. Communications

    d. Navigation

    e. Collaboration

    f. Application access

Packet Switching Technologies (X.25)

After reading this chapter and completing the questions, you will be able to:

- Understand the concept of packet switching
- Discuss the benefits of packet switching over circuit switching for data communications
- Identify the components of the packet switching networks
- Discuss the process of switched virtual circuits
- Relate to the degree of reliability from this packet concept

We have spent a considerable amount of time in past chapters covering the pros and cons of the dial-up telephone network. Keep in mind that when the network was originally fashioned, it was designed as an analog voice telephone network. Restating this position, it was a network that was designed to carry voice communications only.

In the late 1950s, the thought of carrying data communication began to blossom. New needs to move information from a user to a mainframe computer system rapidly emerged. Therefore, the industry was challenged to create a device that would enable a terminal in a remote office (across town or across the country) to communicate with a central computer system, in other words the mainframe. This was not a major problem because many other systems (Telex, TWX, and so on) were already in place to carry low-speed data communications. Dial-up modem communications on the telephone network were already moving about rapidly. Most users were transmitting their data across the dial-up telephone network at relatively low speeds, such as 2,400 or 4,800 bits per second. Only in rare cases did speeds of 9,600 bits per second come into play. The data transfers and host access applications being used on the network were rudimentary.

A problem existed, however, with data transfer. In Chapter 13, we discussed the problems that could be experienced on the dial-up telephone network. Because the use of a modem implies that an analog data transmission is used, all of the problems inherent in analog communications were present. For voice, the analog systems posed no major problem. If a human does not understand part of a conversation, the problem is easily rectified. We merely shout, "What?" into the phone, and the conversation is immediately retransmitted—that is, the person on the other end repeats what was just said. If the line is too bad (full of static, snap, crackle, and other noises), then the two humans agree to hang up and replace the call, hoping for a better connection.

Data Communications Problems

In the data communications world, things were different. Back in the early days of data transmission, transmission protocols were not as sophisticated as they are today. Consequently, if a data transfer was attempted, the overhead was significant. Refer back to the section on overhead in Chapter 13 and you will see that in the case of an asynchronous transmission, employing an ASCII code sent over the dial-up telephone network used approximately 40 percent overhead. This was a tremendous burden in data transfer. When you apply a 2,400-bit-per-second transmit mode with 40 percent overhead, the net data rate is only around 1,440 bits per second.

Again, if you think back to the earlier chapters discussing voice communications, the cost per minute for a voice (or data) call was $0.50 to $0.60. This overhead on the call meant that approximately $0.20 to $0.24 per minute was automatically lost and transmitted nothing usable. This problem became more pronounced as the data needs grew. Adding to the problem, the network was highly unreliable for data transmission. You can only imagine how frustrating it was to set up a file transfer of 2 megabytes of information.

Transmission protocols that were rudimentary in their approach to handling data transfers were still limited. During the data file transfer, if the end user had 1.5 megabytes transmitted over the network, timing was critical. Transfer of a 1.5-megabyte file at 2,400 bits per second would take a significant amount of time. As a matter of averaging this out, the connection would take approximately 83 minutes (without the associated overhead). In reality, the time could be 116 minutes (close to 2 hours). Now imagine this: the first 1.5 megabytes of this 2-megabyte file got through in 116 minutes, and then the inevitable happened. The line failed for any number of reasons. Whether a poor connection existed or the network degraded over time, the result was the same. The call disconnected three-quarters of the way through the transmission. Clearly, this would pose no problem today. By redialing the far end and establishing the connection, one could pick up the transmission where it left off. This was not so back then. If the call disconnected, the protocols could not pick up in the middle of a data set and begin where it left off. As a matter of fact, everything had to be scrapped and the whole file had to be retransmitted. This was not only frustrating, but expensive too! After 116 minutes of transmission at $0.50 per minute, you would have just scrapped $58.00.

The Data Communications Review

This scenario was more the norm than the exception. Users were easily frustrated with the data communications system and dreaded using a modem. Clearly, the industry had to do something about the problem. In the late 1960s, the International Telegraph and Telephone Consultative Committee (CCITT) (now called the International Telecommunication Union [ITU]) commissioned a study group to look for a resolution to this and many other problems. The study group arrived at several initial findings:

- The network was unreliable. Further, the use of data transmission across the analog network was at risk.

- The rollout of digital services was still very limited, and the service was primarily a carrier service.

- Other systems, such as message store and forward, although more reliable than straight dial-up connections, still became congested delivering messages at customer demand. Therefore, the network could delay delivery for hours if not days because of the congestion factor.

■ Other services did not offer any reliability, regardless of the delay.

The response to this whole study was the recommendation to use a packet switching transport system, which would guarantee the reliable delivery of data, break the data down into more manageable pieces, deliver the data at the convenience of the network, sequentially deliver the information, and recover from any failures that might occur on the link without requiring retransmission of the entire file.

Packet Switching Defined

Packet switching was born to accomplish these goals. To define packet switching, we will use the following guidelines.

Packet switching is a means of taking a very large file of information (data) and delivering it to a piece of hardware or software. From this interface, the hardware or software breaks the information down into smaller, more manageable pieces. As these pieces are broken down, additional overhead is applied to the original segment of data. This overhead is used for control of the information. Because the information is segmented, the packet service inserts the telephone number of the addressee, along with the segmentation number (packet #1, packet #2, packet #3, and so on) so that the data can be reassembled at the receiving end. Once the overhead is attached to the segmented data (now called a packet), the packet is transmitted across a physical link to a switching system that reads the address information (telephone number) and routes the packet accordingly. This establishes a virtual connection to the distant end, and each packet is sent along the same route as the first packet. The system uses a connection-oriented transport based on a virtual circuit.

That is quite a definition to work from. Using this as a starting point, the rest should be easy to break down and discuss. Actually, we can packetize the definition and work at explaining it piece by piece.

What Is Packet Switching?

As already mentioned, packet switching is a means of breaking down the larger data files into more manageable pieces. The following is an example that might make the concept a little easier to comprehend.

The Packet Switching Analogy

For the sake of describing this concept, visualize a meeting with all of your peers in the industry. You have all been called into a local meeting to discuss a matter of extreme importance. The U.S. postmaster general asked that you meet regarding a serious problem. The problem is that more and more people (like you) are using other types of delivery services for various articles (mail, packages, and so on). This, of course, detracts from the revenues of the U.S. Postal Service (USPS). Therefore, the postmaster general has an offer to get you back as a customer for your routine deliveries. The scenario plays like this:

Postmaster general We know that you have some concerns about using the U.S. Postal Service. Therefore, in order to get you back as a customer, we are willing to hold the price of a postage stamp at $0.33! Yes, the rumors are true that the cost of a stamp will rise again, but if you'll sign an agreement here today, we will hold the rate at the $0.33.

Author How many of you would sign an agreement to stay with the Postal Service for all of your delivery needs? Just as we thought, this was not enough to move you.

PG OK, let's sweeten the pot. Not only will we hold the price of the stamp at $0.33; if you agree to give the USPS 100 percent of your mail, we'll lower the cost of a stamp to $0.25 and hold that rate for five years. This I guarantee.

AU Some people will be moved to sign this agreement now! Many of us think in terms of business needs and money is always a decision factor. Only a few of the audience will bite this time. This leaves many more people that have not committed. Now for the PG's next move . . . .

PG Okay, folks, here's my last offer. I will drop the price of a stamp to $0.25 and hold it there for five years. In addition, I guarantee that any letter you drop in a USPS mailbox will be delivered anywhere in the country overnight! Now how many of you will sign the agreement?

AU By now you are worn down and will sign on the bottom line. This is an attractive offer. For five years, you get cheaper postage and overnight delivery guaranteed. How can you lose? So you go ahead and sign.

PG   Now that you've all signed on the bottom line, we have a contract that you will use the USPS for all of your mailing and delivery needs. However . . .

AU   Watch out! Here it comes.

PG   In order to do all of the things we contracted to do, I have to give you the conditions of this agreement. You never asked, so I can assume that overnight delivery at $0.25 per letter is what concerns you the most. To meet the terms of our agreement, the conditions are

■ All mail that you wish to send through the USPS must be placed in a standard #10 business envelope. (This is shown in Figure 19-1.) The envelope will be a white 9 1/2 × 4-inch solid (no windows) business envelope. No other envelopes will be used. We don't want to see the holiday red or green, no Mother's Day orchid color, no big seasonal envelopes for birthdays and Valentine's Day, and so on.

■ In each of these business envelopes, you can only put one sheet of paper (standard U.S. business page of 8 1/2 × 11 inches). You can print on it

Figure 19-1
The standard
business envelope
will be used.

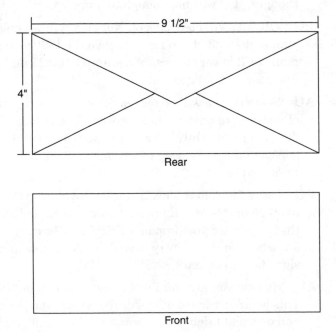

Rear

Front

front and back, but you must still limit the contents to only one page per envelope. (See Figure 19-2 for the standard page letter.)

■ For those of you who have a major pamphlet, book, or other document to mail, the solution is easy. If the pamphlet has 200 pages, you merely have to send 200 envelopes. This means that at each end you will hire a person to handle the process. On the sending end, the postal clerk in your organization will take the pamphlet apart and stuff one envelope at a time with one of the pages. This will require a total of 200 envelopes and stamps ($50.00). The mail clerk will then add some overhead to the envelope, such as

- A *from* address, to be placed in the upper left corner of the envelope

- A *to* address, to be placed in the center of the envelope

- A $0.25 postage stamp or meter imprint, to be placed in the upper right corner of the envelope

- A page number (1 of 200, 2 of 200, 3 of 200, and so on), to be placed in the bottom right corner of the envelope, to assure that the pages stay in order

AU   How are you doing? Are you still with us? Does this sound like a workable solution just to save a few dollars? Will you really save that money? Probably not! But let's continue; there's more.

Figure 19-2
The standard page for letters shall be 8 1/2 × 11 inches. You can print on both sides of the page.

Figure 19-3
The completed business envelope has all the necessary information. Note the numbering system on the bottom right corner.

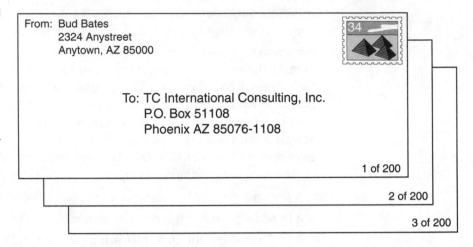

PG   Once the letter is ready for delivery to the USPS (see Figure 19-3 for the final envelope), your mail clerk has to drop these into the mailbox or at the post office. Your job is partially done. At the mailbox, a new set of sequences will begin:

- When the postal employee comes along, the envelopes will be stacked up and checked (counted) to make sure that all of the envelopes are there. If the postal clerks find that an envelope is missing, they will search around for it in the mailbox. If this proves futile, they will contact the mail clerk in your organization and ask that a new copy of the missing envelopes be generated. This of course means that the mail clerk must keep a copy of every page until we accept the envelopes and determine that none are missing.

- If none are missing or if one was missing but has been replaced, the mail clerk will receive an acknowledgment from the postal employee. The mail clerk can now discard all of the spares that were held (called buffering).

- Before the acknowledgment is given to the mail clerk, the postal employee will do a couple of things. Once the envelope count is confirmed, the postal employee will open each and every envelope and read all of the information to ensure that the information contained inside is intact. If something has happened to the page (shown in Figure 19-4), we merely alert the mail clerk to give us a new copy. Also, as the information is read and validated, the postal

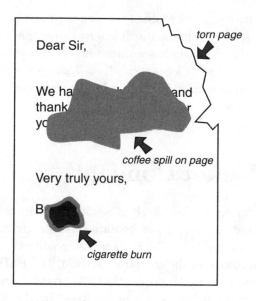

Figure 19-4
Many things can happen to destroy the integrity of the printed page.

employee will make a duplicate of each page of information and store it in a holding bin.

- After these steps have been completed, the acknowledgment will be sent to the company mail clerk, who empties the holding bin at the originating location (flushes the buffer). Now the USPS is responsible for the letter and the integrity of the information. The letter will be passed on to the next location in the chain.

- At each step along the delivery trail (mailbox to post office to plane to receiving post office and so on), the information will be counted, opened and read, copied and accepted. The previous holder of the information will be given an acceptance before destroying the copies. If the system breaks down anywhere along the line, the holder of the stack need only go to the previous location and request a new copy.

- At the end point (your location), the process will end. A mail clerk at the receiving end will count all the envelopes, open and read them, and accept them one at a time. But in this case, the mail clerk will finalize the process by putting the page in each envelope back in the original order until the pamphlet has been reassembled.

- Your organization has just received overnight delivery of the letters, with guaranteed integrity of the information and sequential arrival.

AU   By now you are probably saying to yourself, "These authors have been sniffing too much laser printer toner while preparing this book." This whole scenario sounds too complex to be real, doesn't it? But this is exactly how X.25 packet switching works. The process is a little simpler, but the concept is the same. How does this sound now?

The Packet Concept

Packet switching works like this scenario. If an organization has large amounts of data to send, then the data can be delivered to a packet assembler/disassembler (PAD). The PAD can be a software package or a piece of hardware outboard of the computer system. The PAD acts as the originating mail clerk in that the originating PAD receives the data and breaks it down into manageable pieces or packets. In the data communications arena, a packet can be a variable length of information, usually up to 128 bytes of data (one page in the example). Other implementers of X.25 services have created packets up to 512 bytes, but the average is 128. The 128-byte capability is also referred to as a *fast select*. The packet switching system can immediately route the packet to a distant end and pass data of up to 128 bytes (1,024 bits).

Overhead

To this packet, the PAD then applies some overhead as follows:

- An opening flag that is made up of 8 bits of information. Using a standard high-level data link control (HDLC) framing format covered in the chapters on data and LANs, the opening flag is a sequence of 8 bits that should not be construed as real data. (This is an envelope.)
- A 16-bit address sequence that is a binary description of the end points (the from address).

Control information consists of 8 bits of data describing the type of HDLC frame that is traversing the network (this is a notation on the envelope that describes the information inside). These can be supervisory, unnumbered, or information fields. To be more specific, these break down as follows:

■ **Information (I)** Used to transfer data across the link at a rate determined by the receiver and with error detection and correction.

■ **Supervisory (S)** Used to determine the ready state of the devices receiver is ready (RR), receiver is not ready (RNR), or reject (REJ).

■ **Unnumbered** Used to dictate parameters, such as set modes, disconnect, and so on.

Packet-specific information follows the HDLC information. The packet information will consist of the following information (this information is similar to the *to* address and the designation of the routing that will be used, such as first class, book rate, and so on):

■ **General format identifier (GFI)** 4 bits of information that describes how the data in the packet is being used: from/to an end user, from/to a device controlling the end user device, and so on.

■ **Logical channel group number (LGN)** 4 bits that describe the grouping of channels. Because only 4 bits are available, only eight combinations are used.

■ **Logical channel number (LCN)** An 8-bit description of the actual channel being used. The theoretical number of channels (ports) available is 2,048. Channel groups break down the logical channels so that the numbers play out (Table 19-1). Although the number of logical channels can be 2,048, most organizations implement significantly fewer ports or channels.

Table 19-1

Summary of Logical Groups and Channel Numbers

Type	Logical Group	Logical Channel	Number of Channels
PVC	0	1–255	0–255
PVC	1	256–511	0–255
Incoming-only	2	512–767	0–255
SVC	3	768–1,023	0–255
Two-way	4	1,024–1,279	0–255
SVC	5	1,280–1,535	0–255
Outgoing-only	6	1,536–1,791	0–255
SVC	7	1,792–2,047	0–255

The next overhead elements consist of the *packet type identifier* (PTI), an 8-bit sequence that describes the type of packet being sent across the network. Six different packet types are used in an X.25 switching network. These packet types define what is expected of the devices across the network. Table 19-2 shows the packet types. Note that the packet types have different uses, so their binary equivalent is shown for purposes of differentiation.

The variable data field is now inserted. This is where the 128 bytes of information are contained in the packet. The 128-byte field is the standard implementation, but as mentioned, it can be larger (as much as 512 bytes).

Following the information field is the *Cyclic Redundancy Check* (CRC), a 16-bit sequence that will be used for error detection and/or correction. Using a CRC-16, the error detection capability will be approximately 99.999995 percent. This is to ensure the integrity of the data; rather than having to deliver information over and over again, the concept is to deliver reliable data to the far end.

The closure of the packet is the end of frame flag. In the HDLC frame format, this denotes the end of the frame, so the switches and related equipment know that nothing follows. The switches then calculate all of the error detection and accept or reject the packet on the basis of the data integrity.

Table 19-2

Summary of the Packet Types and Identifiers

Packet Type	Description	Packet Type Identifier
Incoming call	Call request	00001011
Call connected	Call accepted	00001111
Clear indication	Clear request	00010011
Clear confirmed		00010111
Data		xxxxxxx0
Receiver ready		xxx00001
Receiver not ready		xxx00101
Reject		xxx01001
Interrupt indication	Interrupt request	00100011
Interrupt confirmation		00100111
Reset indication	Reset request	00011011
Reset confirmation		00011111
Restart indication	Restart request	11111011
Restart confirmation		11111111

Summary of Packet Format

Figure 19-5 is the actual HDLC frame format used for the packet of information. In this case, one can look at the fields and recheck what each field represents through the sequencing information. Users intimidated by this process can relax; the equipment that generates the packets across the network will do this.

The Packet Network

Figure 19-6 shows a typical network layout. The cloud in the center of the drawing represents the network provided by one of the carriers. From our discussions in earlier chapters, the obvious network configuration is that each of the designated carriers has its own cloud. Actually, each cloud interconnects to the clouds provided by other carriers so that transparent communications can take place. Once the cloud is established, the next step is to provide the packet switching systems (called packet switching exchanges or PSEs). These are nothing more than computers that are capable of reading the address and framing information. The PSEs then route the packet to an appropriate outgoing port to the next downstream neighbor. In many cases, these PSEs are connected to several other PSEs.

Thus, the carrier provides a meshed network, as shown in Figure 19-6. The packet switches can select the outbound route to the next downstream neighbor on the basis of several variables. The selection process can be the circuit used least, the most direct, the most reliable, or some other predefined variable. This again is the magic that takes place inside the cloud. Now that the network cloud and the packet exchanges are in place, the next step is to connect a user.

The User Connection

Users sign up with the carrier of choice and let the carrier worry about the physical connection. As shown in Figure 19-7, the user connection into the cloud is through a dedicated or leased line. The carrier notifies the LEC and orders a leased line at the appropriate speed (in the leased line, this can be up to 64 Kbps on digital circuits). The original network connections back in

Figure 19-5
An HDLC frame is used to carry the X.25 data to the network. Note that the packet is layer 3 and encapsulated into the data link frame.

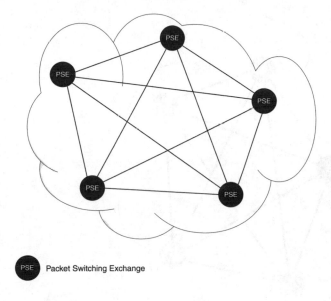

Figure 19-6
The typical X.25 network is a meshed network. The cloud represents the network.

PSE   Packet Switching Exchange

the initial rollout of X.25 services were on analog lines at up to 9.6 Kbps. Either a modem was provided by the carrier at the customer end, or the customer purchased and provided it. Now that the modem is attached at the customer end, the circuit is terminated in a port on the computer (PSE). This is the incoming port that can be used as a permanent virtual connection or as an incoming-only channel. This is part of the addressing mechanism inside the packet where the PSE reads the packets' originating address. The incoming-only channels are the channel numbers assigned to each customer.

The next step follows the connection where the customer must initiate the PAD function, as shown in Figure 19-8. Remember that the PAD is the hardware or software installed to break the data into smaller pieces, attach the overhead, and forward the packetized data to the network. In the reverse order, the PAD is responsible for receiving the packets, peeling off the overhead, and reassembling the data into a serial data stream to the data terminal equipment, whether it is a terminal or host computer. So the PAD's function is crucial. If a software package is performing the PAD function, then the customer must purchase (or license) the software and install it. If the solution is a piece of hardware, the options are different. The customer might buy the PAD and install it, or the carrier might provide and install it. This hardware can be rented, leased, or sold by the carrier. Now the connection exists on one end of the cloud.

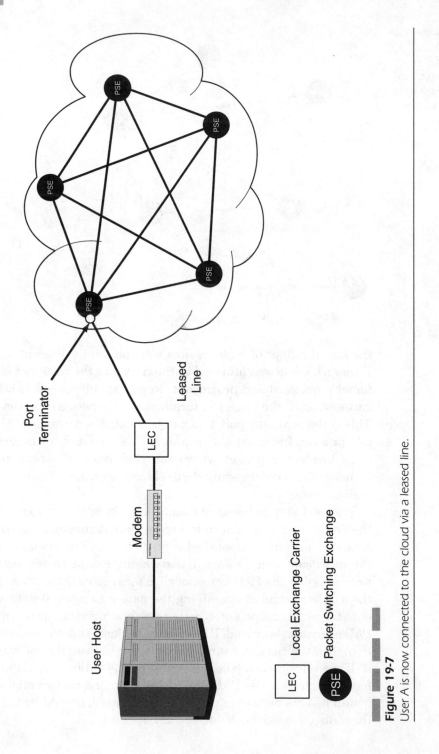

Figure 19-7
User A is now connected to the cloud via a leased line.

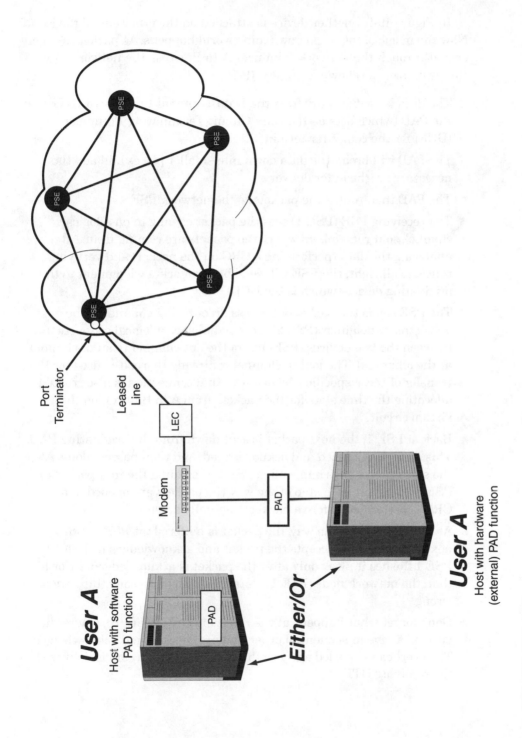

Figure 19-8
User A can have a hardware or software PAD function.

In Figure 19-9, another device is attached on the other end of the cloud. Now the magic of the packet switching world happens. As packets are generated through the network from user A to B across the network, several things happen, as shown in Figure 19-10.

■ The data is sent serially from the Data Terminal Equipment (DTE) to the PAD (which acts as the Data Circuit-Terminating Equipment [DCE] for the computer terminal).

■ The PAD will break the data down into smaller pieces and add the necessary overhead for delivery.

■ The PAD then routes the packets to the network PSE.

■ The receiving PSE (PSE 1) sees the packet coming in on a logical channel, so it remembers where the packets are coming from. After analyzing the data (performing a CRC on the packet) and verifying that it is all right, the PSE will send back an acknowledgment to the originating device (which is the DCE).

■ The PSE sends the packet out across an outgoing channel to the next downstream neighbor (PSE 2). This establishes a logical connection between the two devices (PSEs) from the out-channel to an in-channel at the other end. The logical channel is already there; it is used for the transfer of these specific packets. A virtual connection is also created, allocating the time slots for the packets from A to B to run on the virtual circuit.

■ Back at PSE 1, the next packet is sent down from the originating PAD. This again is analyzed and acknowledged, and then passed along. At the same time this is happening, PSE 2 is sending the first packet to PSE 3. Again, at each step of the way the packets are opened and a CRC is performed before a packet is actually accepted.

■ At each PSE along the way, the packet is buffered (at PSE 1) until the next receiving PSE accepts the packet and acknowledges it (PSE 2). PSE 1 flushes it away only after the packet is acknowledged. Prior to that, the network node (PSE 1) stored it just in case something went wrong.

■ Don't forget what happens at the receiving end (device B), where the packets arrive in sequential order and are checked and acknowledged. The overhead is peeled away so that a serial data stream is delivered to the receiving DTE.

Figure 19-9

A second user, B, is attached to the cloud.

Figure 19-10

Serial data sent to the PAD are packetized (A/B) and then sent across a virtual circuit to location B. B can return responses (B/A) on a duplex circuit.

■ This process continues from device A through the network to device B until all data packets are received. Every packet along every step of the link is sent, accepted, acknowledged, and forwarded until all get through. This is the guaranteed delivery of reliable data properly sequenced. The logical link that is established between devices A and B is full duplex. The two devices can be sending and receiving simultaneously.

You can see from the packet delivery process that the packet switching process has benefits. However, nothing is perfect. The overhead on the packet, the buffering of multiple packets along the route, the CRC performance at each node along the network, and the final sequenced data delivery all combine to present the risk of serious delays. What you receive in integrity and reliability can be offset in delays across the network. You must always weigh the possibilities and choose the best service.

Benefits of Packets

The real benefit to this method of data delivery ties into the scenario presented in the beginning of this chapter. Remember the problems with the dial-up telephone network and the risk of sending three-quarters of a file transfer only to have a glitch in the transfer? Using the packetized effort, if a glitch occurs, the network might have from 7 to 128 outstanding packets traversing the links. Therefore, instead of scrapping the entire file, the network automatically recovers and resends the packets that were lost or corrupted. This means that the users would save time and money on an error-prone network. Again, the risk of congestion and delay on the network might cause others to look for alternative solutions.

Other Benefits

Beyond these benefits, other benefits can be achieved from the use of the dedicated link into the network. As Figure 19-11 shows, the link is not solely for one user at a time, nor is it for two specific locations. When the organization uses a packet switching network, the users might need to have multiple simultaneous connections up and running. Therefore, the PAD will

Figure 19-11

Multiple duplex connections can run simultaneously on the same circuit.

act similarly to a statistical time division multiplexer (statmux). The stat-mux capability allows multiple connections into the single device, and will sample each of the ports in a sequential mode to determine whether the port has anything to send. If a packet has been prepared, the statmux will generate the call request (initiate a call) to the network. The connection will be created and the data will flow. This assumes that no problems are being experienced on the network.

As a new user logs on and generates a request to send data, the PAD will set up this connection. Packets will be interleaved across the physical link between or among the various users. One can imagine that not all devices will transmit at the same rate of speed or have the same amount of two-way interactive traffic. Therefore, the statmux function of the PAD interleaves the packets based on an algorithm that enables each device to appear as though a dedicated link is available to it. The use of a statmux will be a benefit because it will enable users to employ the expensive leased link to the maximum benefit of the organization. This requires fewer physical links and takes advantage of the dead time between transmissions and so on.

Figure 19-12 shows a series of sessions running on a single link, all interleaved. It also shows that packets are not specifically interleaved in the order of A, B, C . . . Instead, they can be interleaved on the basis of the flow or delivery method used, such as A, B, A, B, C, B, A . . . Herein lies the added benefit of packet switching—the user achieves the necessary data throughput without having a dedicated resource that is only periodically used.

Advantages of Packet Switching

Many people consider packet switching to be the most efficient means of sharing both public and private network facilities among multiple users. Each packet contains all of the necessary control and routing information to deliver the packet across the network. Packets can be routed independently or as a series that must be maintained and preserved as an entity. The major advantages of using this type of transport system are

- Shared access among multiple users, either in a single company or in multiple organizations
- Full error control and flow control in place to provide the smooth and efficient transfer of data
- Transparency of the user data

Figure 19-12
Packets are interleaved to various locations on the same physical link. Different virtual circuits are used to get the packet to its destination.

- Speed and code conversion capabilities

- Protection from an intermediate node or link failure

- Pricing advantages: because the network is used by many, the prices are on a per-packet, rather than per-minute, basis.

Other Components of Packet Switching

Although the primary components of packet switching have already been discussed, others are available. As the evolution of the X.25 standard continued in the early 1970s, several different implementations were enhanced. This includes devices or access methods that you should understand. These are summarized so that you can appreciate how these pieces all work together. Some of these added pieces include

- The ability to dial into the packet-switching network from an asynchronous modem communication. Although packet switching (a la X.25) is a synchronous transfer system, the need for remote dial-up communications exists. Therefore, the standards bodies included this capability in one of the enhanced versions of the network. As shown in Figure 19-13, a dial-up connection can be made from a user. In this case, the asynchronous communication will be a serial data transfer to a network-based PAD. The PAD will accept the serial asynchronous data, collect it, segment it into packets, and establish the connection to the remote host desired. In this case, the connection is now across the X.25 world, synchronously moving packets across the network. This uses an X.28 protocol to establish the connection between the asynchronous terminal and the PAD.

- The PAD-to-host arrangement is controlled by the X.29 protocol. Control information is exchanged between a PAD (X.3) and a packet mode DTE or another PAD (X.3). This is shown in Figure 19-14. In this case, as the communication is established between these devices, the X.3 PAD will set the parameters of the remote device. This could be the speed, format, control parameters, or anything that would be appropriate in the file transfer. The X.29 parameters can also provide keyboard conversion into network-usable information.

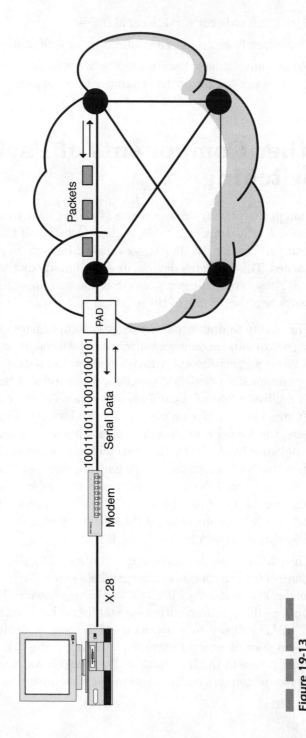

Figure 19-13

Asynchronous dial-up terminals can dial into the X.25 network through a PAD on the network.

Figure 19-14
The X.3 PAD can set the remote host parameters to handle the asynchronous user.

■ The internetworking capability of an X.25 network uses a protocol called X.75. Although this should be user transparent, the network needs the X.75 parameters to provide a gateway between two different packet networks or between networks in different countries. In each case, the gateway function is something that should only concern the network carrier. However, as more organizations install their own private network switching systems, the need to interconnect to the public data networks rises. Therefore, the internetworking capability is moving closer to the end user's door. Figure 19-15 shows a representation of an X.75 interconnection.

The X.25 Numbering Plan

The X.25 numbering plan takes advantage of the worldwide numbering plan designed by the CCITT International Telecommunications Union Telephony Standardization Sector (ITU-TSS). It is known as the X.121 worldwide network numbering plan for the public data networks. This was a design for public networks only. However, in most of the world this is acceptable because only one public network exists that is controlled and operated by the Post Telephone and Telegraph (PTT) organizations.

In the United States, however, the proliferation of both public and private networks is completely different. Looking at all of the players involved today in the carrier community, you can see that easily 300 networks could exist publicly. Couple that with the private organizations that can add packet switching to their networks and want to access public networks, and the number can expand exponentially.

Applications for X.25 Services

No single solution fits any transport system. Therefore, the variations of the X.25 capabilities are as numerous as the organizations using them. However, if you think in terms of the overall use, the following can be applied.

If a user organization has data to transfer between or among a limited number of locations and the data transfer will be continuous (such as 8-12-24 hours per day) or the files are constantly very large, the use of X.25 might or might not apply. In this case, the connection will likely be a leased

Figure 19-15

X.75 interconnectivity protocols enable different networks to communicate.

line between two hosts (for example) and the data transfer will be constant. The leased line is an expensive proposition unless the volume of data justifies the connection full time. A data transfer will use very little time to initiate a session between hosts or end-to-end devices because they are physically connected together.

If, on the other hand, a user organization has multiple locations (10, 20, 30, and so on) and only needs to establish a connection occasionally during the day (twice or three times, perhaps), and the data is batched in a large transfer that will take 1 hour, then a dial-up circuit might be appropriate. In this case, the cost associated with a leased line would likely be unjustified. Therefore, a dial-up modem communications will be a better solution. The time it takes to generate a connection and handshake between the modems can be approximately 1 to 2 minutes. As a portion of the data session, the call setup is insignificant. Again, the dial-up communications will be a possible solution.

If, however, an organization has many (50, 100, 200, or 1,000) locations that must pass information to a central computing platform, and the amount of data is relatively trivial, then packet switching might be the most appropriate solution. In this case, let's use a department store that has 100 locations spread around the country. The stores use a point-of-sale (POS) system to run the registers and perform inventory and other associated data processing functions. Each night, the store must communicate three pieces of information back to the home office: the amount of daily sales, the amount of money deposited in the local bank for transfer back to corporate, and the items totally out of stock and in need of immediate replenishment. The entire data transfer in this example will be approximately 10 seconds.

It would not be prudent to spend the money to lease data lines to each of the 100 locations. The expense could never be justified. Even in a multipoint circuit environment, this will be too expensive.

A dial-up connection would be inappropriate because at 1 to 2 minutes of setup and handshake, it will take longer to establish the connection than to actually transmit the information because only 10 seconds' worth of data will be transferred. Also, the amount of time lost in sequentially dialing 100 locations with the associated timing and handshakes would be far too great to get all the calls through in a reasonable amount of time. Therefore, the packet switching arrangement would be more appropriate.

Using the packetized data, several devices can be simultaneously generating packets of information to the host and transmitting the nightly information across the network. Different logical connections will be established and the packet reassembly process will take its due course to deliver the required information in the appropriate form.

An organization that has nightly or periodical information to transfer is a prime candidate for packet switching. Other forms of information transfer that could be performed by a packet switching service are

- Transactional processing, such as for automated teller machines (ATMs)
- Process control information, such as for electrical distribution, oil drilling, and chemical production facilities
- Database inquiries
- Credit card approvals
- Motor vehicle registration information
- Signaling system seven (SS7) messages for call setup and teardown
- File transfers where reliable and guaranteed data delivery is required
- Money transfers, such as on the SWIFTE network

One can see that many of these organizations can take full advantage of the packetization of the data streams and still conduct the normal day-to-day business activities.

Other Forms of Packets

As an industry accepted standard, X.25 is the most widely installed and accepted form of data transmission. This is a worldwide standard, and the interconnectivity solutions defined have created a usable form and format throughout the world. In later chapters of this book, we discuss other forms of data transmission. However, these are emerging forms of packet switching (fast packets) that are not ubiquitous. Other forms of transmission might or might not be in use in third-world countries. Speeds are limited and facilities to transmit at various other means might not yet exist. Therefore, the X.25 standard has become the industry norm.

Still, other forms or variations of packet switching exist today. One is called fast select, which is a single packet transfer (rather than a sequentially numbered series of packets) where only one packet needs to be sent. This can be applicable in a UNIX world where a single character is sent across the network to a UNIX host. It would be inappropriate to have a group of packets sent across the network when all that is needed is a single packet. Another use of such a system is in credit card approval. The single packet that gets generated is limited by the data needs, such as

■ The credit card number

■ The expiration date of the card (optional)

■ The ID number of the vendor requesting the approval

■ The dollar amount of the transaction

In this case, because only a very limited amount of information is required, it can all be contained in a single packet. The network does not use the sequential transfer as it does in X.25, nor does the reliability check take place on the network. Instead, the POS equipment packet is acknowledged when the main credit clearinghouse sends back an acknowledgment. If something is corrupted in the transfer of the packet, the vendor must retransmit the entire transaction. This is a sporadic type of data transfer and works well for the most part. Delays do occur, but mainly as a result of the clearinghouse computers being busy.

Still another form of packet switching, called a *datagram*, is used in the industry. A datagram transfer is a form of packet switching. Typically, the datagram does not follow the same virtual circuit concept. Every packet is sent across the network and can take a different route to get from point A to B. Also, a datagram is not checked at every node along the route; only the header (or address) information is checked for the location of the destination. As each packet is received, it is scanned for the destination address and then immediately routed along to the next node. No CRCs are done on the data. It is not the network's responsibility to guarantee the integrity of the data; that will be left to the receiving device using a higher-level protocol. With this concept of a different path for each packet, the idea of sequentially numbering the packets is lost. The network treats every packet as its own entity (or as packet number one). If a packet is lost or something else happens, the network does not care. The sequencing and reassembly of the data back into its original form is handled by the receiving end's higher-layer protocols. An example of this is Transmission Control Protocol with Internet Protocol (TCP/IP). IP packets are datagrams that are segments of the original data stream. It works at the layer 3 of the OSI model, as covered in Chapter 15. As a network layer protocol, IP's only concern is to break the data down into packets and make its best effort to deliver the packets.

TCP, at the receiving end, is responsible for reassembling the data back into the serial data stream and ensuring the integrity and sequencing of the information. TCP is not a network layer protocol; it works at the higher layers of the OSI model (transport and above). TCP/IP is the mainstream of the Internet and has been widely adopted as the protocol stack of choice in many LAN and WAN arenas. Because of its robustness and ability to deal with the packetization of the data, more organizations are using TCP/IP as their WAN protocol. TCP/IP is not without its problems, but the advantages far outweigh the disadvantages. The industry as a whole, and the vendor community in particular, has recognized the importance of TCP/IP in the mainstream of products. Just about every LAN network operating systems (NOS) vendor now supports the use of TCP/IP. From a physical network and data link layer, TCP/IP will run on most any topology. It is supported by the hardware suppliers of network interface cards (NICs).

Questions

1. What is the purpose of packet switching?
    a. To break the packets down for the heck of it
    b. To gain more reliable data transfers
    c. To get more revenue because the rates are charged on a packet by packet
    d. Because everyone else is doing it

2. What is the designated protocol name for packet switching?
    a. X.75
    b. X.29
    c. X.25
    d. X.400

3. When we send data in packets, the packets are counted byte by byte.   T/F

4. The organization responsible for creating the packet switching protocol is:
    a. Internet Engineering Task Force (IETF)
    b. Institute for Electrical and Electronic Engineers (IEEE)
    c. International Telecommunications Union (ITU)
    d. Internet Service Providers (ISP)

5. When the carriers offer X.25 packet switching, they are typically called:

   a. PDN

   b. VAN

   c. WAN

   d. PSTN

6. Packet switching uses a combination of switched and permanent virtual circuits.   T/F

7. The sharing of the circuit is done through a technique called:

   a. Packet switching

   b. Frequency division multiplexing

   c. Statistical time division multiplexing

   d. Time division multiplexing

8. The highest rated speed for packet switching is:

   a. 56 Kbps

   b. 2 Mbps

   c. 128 Kbps

   d. 64 Kbps

9. The X.25 packets are encapsulated inside a _____ frame for transmission.

   a. SDLC

   b. HDLC

   c. PPP

   d. BDLC

10. Whenever a packet gets transmitted, it is either _____ or _____ along the way.

   a. Ack or nak

   b. Sent or received

   c. Held or discarded

   d. Ack or rak

11. Packet switching is a hold and forward technology.   T/F

12. The sequencing of a packet is not important in X.25.   T/F

13. X.25 uses a _____ transmission mode.
    a. Half-duplex
    b. Simplex
    c. Redirection
    d. Duplex

14. Packets can be interleaved on the same physical circuit, but must be destined to different locations.   T/F

15. When the packets are received, they are checked and _____ before being forwarded.

16. Holding the packets in temporary storage is called:

    _____.

17. Benefits of packet switching include (choose all that apply):
    a. Less expensive data
    b. More reliable data
    c. Faster date transfers
    d. Reduced delay
    e. Guaranteed delivery

18. The numbering plan used by the packet switching is:
    a. PDN
    b. E.164
    c. X.121
    d. X.75

19. X.75 is used as a packet switching technology to provide:
    a. TCP/IP interfaces
    b. Internetworking
    c. Packet transparency
    d. Packet delay

20. The use of packet switching has been replaced by circuit switching.   T/F

Local Area Networks (LANs)

After reading this chapter and completing the questions, you will be able to:

- Explain what a LAN is
- Understand the concept of using a LAN
- Discuss the various means of creating a LAN
- Openly recognize the topologies
- Explain the difference between a LAN and WAN

What Are LANs?

The digital data communications technologies covered up to this point can function over essentially arbitrary distances. Whether at 1 mile or 10,000, they will work about the same. Nevertheless, certain data communications functions would be much more useful (for example, file sharing and transmission) if higher speeds could be used than those generally available on a wide area basis. What if some slick optimization and engineering techniques were used to radically improve communications performance, at least for short distances? The productized answers to these questions are local area networks (LANs).

In the early 1980s, a new device made its way to the desktop. IBM introduced the PC, a single-diskette system that was functionally a terminal device that just happened to have its own intelligence. The single-floppy diskette was sufficient to run the entire system and still provide the user plenty of storage space. The second version of IBM's desktop computing system (PC) was a dual-floppy disk system, where one diskette was used to run the operating system for the machine and the other floppy was used for the data storage. Not much exciting happened during this era, but some people felt that the single- and dual-diskette systems were too limited and awkward to use. The industry had no problems. Then, it happened!

The third evolution of the PC introduced by IBM had a hard disk. The disk operating system was stored on the hard disk, so the machine could operate without the user playing around with those floppies. This in itself was a major improvement, but this version of the PC was a bit pricey ($5,000 to $6,000). Furthermore, management and information systems personnel had to reckon with a different situation. The hard disk had a total capacity of 10 megabytes. These professionals knew back then, just as you and I would know, that no one would ever need 10 megabytes of hard disk space all to him- or herself. Therefore, a new sharing of resources was needed. The first LANs had resource-sharing capabilities, so five users could share that 10-megabyte disk. Hence the LAN was born. Because the LAN was hard disk sharing, it was typically set up in one department and localized. The actual LANs started out as serial port connections where users were daisy-chained together to access the disk.

A little later on, the introduction of the laser printer (Hewlett Packard's [HP's] wizardry) led to a new problem. One specific user in the department might have a laser printer, whereas others had a dot-matrix printer. In the early 1980s, this dot-matrix output was nothing to write (or print) home about. Therefore, everyone wanted a personal laser printer rather than a dot matrix. Clearly, management did not want to spend $5,000 for every employee to have his or her own laser printer. The LAN was the resource-sharing service, so the printer moved onto the network.

What is a LAN? Originally, the industry defined local area networks as data communications facilities with the following key elements:

- High communications speed
- Very low error rate
- Geographic boundaries
- A single-cable system or medium for multiple-attached devices

■ A sharing of resources, such as printers, modems, files, disks, and applications

Let's examine these one at a time.

High Communications Speed

At the time (the 1970s), use of communications speeds above 1 Mbps on either a wide or local area basis was exceedingly rare, other than on terminals locally connected to a mainframe. Therefore, high-speed communications meant transfer rates in the millions of bits (or megabits) per second. Even then, it was obvious that submegabit speeds would become a significant speed limit unless they could be vastly increased.

Nevertheless, why not simply use the existing WAN protocols for LANs? They certainly can be used this way. The reason, in a word, is overhead. One major source of overhead in WAN protocols is their routing capabilities. These range from relatively simple (for example, IBM's SNA, which traditionally requires much human intervention to establish or change routes for network traffic) to extremely complex (for example, Digital's DECNet, which can generally figure out where to send something without any assistance at all). But regardless of their sophistication, they add overhead that is not required in a LAN. Thus, LAN protocols eliminate routing overhead by functioning as though all nodes are physically adjacent. Another source of overhead is error checking, which is covered in the following paragraphs.

Most LAN technologies currently in use provide maximum communications speeds well above 1 Mbps. Table 20-1 provides a summary of the typical speeds available from the various approaches. We look at the more

Table 20-1

Summary of Major Architecture Speeds

LAN Name	Typical Speeds
Appletalk	256 Kbps
Arcnet	2.5 Mbps
Token Ring (original)	4 Mbps
Ethernet	10 Mbps
Token Ring (updated)	16 Mbps

common of these transport systems individually in later chapters. For the moment, we are interested in the products that produce these speeds.

AppleTalk is the only true LAN that falls below 1 Mbps in the table. It is nonetheless popular due to its excellent ease of configuration (not to mention that it comes free with every Macintosh!).

Very Low Error Rate

An error rate is the typical percentage of bits that can be corrupted on a regular basis during routine transmissions. As mentioned in the discussion of protocols, error checking ensures that such damaged bits are retransmitted so that applications never see the errors. But the data link protocols in use for wide area networks must contend with much higher error rates than would normally be experienced using LAN technologies.

Wide area analog communications typically experience one error in somewhere between 10^5 and 10^6 bits transmitted. A very low error rate is at least two orders of magnitude better than this or one error in 10^8 transmitted bits. Several technologies meet this challenge.

In a typical WAN protocol stack, error checking takes place at multiple-stack levels. At each level, error checking requires both additional bits in the transmitted frames and additional processing time at both ends (at the sending end, to create the error-checking bits, and at the receiving end, to determine whether any errors occurred). If some of that error-checking overhead can be eliminated because of fewer errors to catch, higher speeds can be achieved more easily, which, not coincidentally, is another of the prime characteristics of a LAN.

The physical elements of a LAN do not depend on the vagaries of the telephone companies' facilities. Those elements are digital and are designed specifically to deliver high-speed communications with very low error rates. Thus, the higher levels of the protocols can be relied on to handle the few errors that do creep in. Most LAN protocols do little or no error checking, and this is one of the design elements that permits their higher speeds.

Geographic Boundaries

A LAN is bounded by some geographic limitation. (Otherwise, by definition it would not be local.) Engineering considerations and physics impose this limitation; vendors did not impose it by fiat. The technologies employed to meet the other requirements (especially the requirement for high speed at a low error rate) tend to preclude more wide area transmission capabilities.

The geographic limitations of the various LAN technologies are expressed in different ways. A maximum distance usually exists from one node (or connected, network-addressable computer) to the next, expressed in tens or perhaps hundreds of meters. A maximum distance usually exists from one node to any other network node, typically hundreds or a few thousands of meters.

Network technologies that only reach up to the bounds of a single campus, or group of collocated buildings, satisfy these specific limitations. However, as we will see, a number of new technologies and connectivity options have worked together to mitigate the distance limitations significantly, which applies to LANs as they were originally defined and designed.

Single Cable System or Medium for Multiple Attached Devices

One of the less obvious, but nonetheless essential, characteristics of a LAN is that all devices on it are viewed and, to all intents and purposes, function as being adjacent. This implies that no special routing capabilities are required for communications traffic from one device to another; just put the information on the LAN, and it will reach its destination. To put this into the International Standards Organization (ISO) context, no routing functions should be required for a LAN to operate.

To accomplish this feat, all the devices must reside or appear to reside (from the point of view of an attached device) on a single-cable system. Thus, each end-node-to-end-node link is also functionally a point-to-point link. No routing choices need be made if every machine you can talk to is right next door. All signals from all devices propagate throughout that cable system. In reality, the LAN is a broadcast multipoint circuit on which all devices have equal access.

Different types of LANs accomplish this function in different ways. Some of the ways are covered in this chapter; later chapters focus specifically on Ethernet and token ring signaling.

A LAN by Another Name

The previous definition of a LAN focused on the components used to provide connectivity among communicating devices. In fact, LANs initially tended to be configured to provide computer-to-computer communications on a more or less egalitarian, or many-to-many, basis. However, the rapid development of network operating systems (NOSs) gave rise to a different, although related, definition of a local area network.

What Do Users of LANs See When They Use the Network?

Configurations vary widely. However, when a user turns on his or her workstation, it normally runs a number of programs automatically until the user is prompted to enter identification (user ID) and a password. This is called *logging in*. If you ask the user (with, of course, precise grammar), "Into what are you logging?" he or she will answer, "I'm logging into the network, of course!"

Logging into a bunch of wires? Well, not exactly. Because security and access to services is typically (although certainly not always) provided for a given user from a single file server, users often perceive and refer to that server as the network or the LAN. Managers of those servers often go along with this usage in order to avoid confusion—or because they believe it to be the only definition anyway. For single-server shops, this causes no problems. In fact, not surprisingly, many of the NOS vendors also use the term LAN in this way. It is what they sell, so one cannot fault them for focusing attention on what to them is the important component of the environment.

However, referring to a server as a LAN can cause quite a bit of confusion in certain cases. Consider the case of having multiple servers on a single-wiring facility. This is certainly a reasonable thing to do, particularly if the servers provide different types of services. Is each a LAN? Are they all, collectively, the LAN? If someone logs into one of these servers from a different cable plant (connected using methods described later in this chapter), which LAN is he or she on?

Alternatively, consider the individual responsible for the design and implementation of the wiring plant, together with the connectivity devices described in the following paragraphs. This person will most likely refer to the wiring plant as the LAN. In this usage, LANs provide connectivity among devices, including servers. This book generally refers to the wiring plant together with the active devices providing connectivity as the LAN. File servers are just one category of servers, albeit an important one.

Why Are They Used?

For many, the answer to "Why use LANs?" is "How could we work without them?" Nevertheless, business operated for centuries without LANs and automated data processing functioned successfully for more than a decade without them. What changed?

Performance

One major change was the increasing popularity of minicomputers (not personal computers: the development of LANs predates that of personal computers). Mainframe communications architectures had been optimized for use of large numbers of terminals. In fact, a special category of communications hardware (front-end processors) was developed in order to off-load the additional work necessary to manage such terminals.

In the minicomputer environment, however, front-end processors could not be used; the minicomputers were not built to handle the high input/ output speeds necessary to service such processors. Instead, terminals were directly connected to serial communications boards, printed circuit boards with multiple RS-232 connections that plugged directly into the backplanes or buses of those minicomputers.

Minicomputers are designed to respond immediately to certain requests for services called *interrupts*. Every keystroke on terminals connected in this way generates an interrupt on the associated minicomputer. Interrupt is exactly what happens; all processing ceases for an instant while the single keystroke is processed. You can easily see that, as additional terminals are added to a minicomputer, the amount of substantive processing accomplished (versus that required merely to receive characters from attached terminals) decreases rapidly!

If the communicated information from the terminals could be presented to the minicomputers more efficiently (in groups without generating one interrupt per keystroke), the minicomputers could serve far more terminal users. A new input/output method was needed.

Wiring

Another issue, again in the minicomputer environment, was the snarl of wiring that communications was generating in computer rooms throughout the world as well as in buildings containing those same terminal users. Before local area networks, almost every logical (non-wide area) connection from a terminal to a computer required a separate set of physical wires from the terminal all the way back to the computer. Even if not every terminal needed access to every computer, this type of wiring was common. Figure 20-1 shows the spiderweb of wires that would be required to link the various devices together. This is expensive to install, difficult to manage, and inefficient in the use of ports and facilities.

Data switches, or data PBXs, were alternatives, but they could only support lower speeds, and to configure them economically, they still had to be large and centrally located, much like the computers! Such devices helped, but they were not an optimal solution. But what if a network device could be used to consolidate the terminal wiring? Terminal servers are LAN devices that can perform such a function (Figure 20-2).

This might not look all that much better than the previous figure. Nevertheless, terminal servers can be located near the terminals, with one long cable back to the main computer system instead of one per terminal. In a real business setting, this greatly simplifies terminal wiring. A terminal server can enable any given terminal to have more than one session active simultaneously, either with one or several destination computers. If a new computer is added to the environment, only the authorizations change; no wiring other than the new computer's connection to the LAN is required. Best of all, the way LANs are implemented on minicomputers eliminates the interrupt-per-keystroke problem. Naturally, the sessions need to be responded to; however, a much smaller percentage of the minicomputer's resources are devoted strictly to communications functions.

Not only did these terminals generate wiring snarls, but sites with multiple minicomputers were also common. Suppose you had six computers, each with a need to reach all of the others on occasion. You could easily end up with a network-wiring diagram like the one shown in Figure 20-3. The wiring nightmares were so bad that many organizations joked that if the wiring was pulled out, the building would probably fall to the ground.

Imagine what a mess this would be if 8, 10, or 20 computers had to be connected! However, if you used a common cable system, you might get something as the setup depicted in Figure 20-4. Clearly, this is an improvement, but the real question is: is it easier to manage? You bet! In addition,

Figure 20-1
The typical wiring
scenario in a
multicomputing
environment

Terminals

Figure 20-2
The use of a terminal
server eliminates the
wiring mesh.

Terminals

Terminal Server

Terminal Server

the number of components required, and therefore the cost, decreases geometrically.

Initially, local area networks were developed to address these problems. Other issues, such as the sharing of printers, were initially not of concern; that issue came later. Connection of terminals to the minicomputers provided access to the printers on those computers as well as WAN communications resources on those computers.

Figure 20-3
The minicomputer
connectivity requires
the same form of
wiring mess.

Figure 20-4
A single cabling
structure might be a
better approach.

Shared Resources

Much of this progress occurred before personal computers were generally available. With the advent of personal computers, additional requirements surfaced. A general need appeared for resource sharing where the resources were not connected to a central computer. One of the two primary resource categories that were first shared was a printer. High-quality printers were initially quite expensive; management was understandably reluctant to provide one laser printer for each user of a personal computer. Printers could be connected in three general ways:

- To a central server, perhaps providing file services as well as print services
- To a user's computer, enabling others to use that computer at the same time the user was using it
- Directly to the LAN by themselves, if the specific printer had LAN capability

The other major resource first shared was file services. File services provide a PC user with the ability to reference files on another machine (the server) as though those files were actually located on the user's PC. Why not have them on the user's PC? This is for several reasons.

- *Initially, large disks were also very expensive.* The cost per megabyte was lower for larger disk drives, making sharing of such drives economically attractive.
- *The larger drives were also much faster.* Network managers, in some cases, could actually provide better disk input/output performance across the network than the user would experience if the information were on a local drive.
- *Users do not back up data.* Yes, there are exceptions, but a manager would be foolish to assume that his or her users are among them. If information is stored centrally, then it can be backed up under management control rather than relying on users to protect their data.

The observant reader might ask at this point, "Why not just use a mainframe or minicomputer as before?" This is a good question. Perhaps the answer is that the applications becoming available on PCs were so much more functional and attractive (remember user-friendly?) than those applications users had access to on larger computers. Moreover, PC spreadsheets easily implemented many functions that hitherto could not be automated because of central IS departments' backlogs. Users were going to use their PCs anyway. Consequently, methods had to be found to support the users and their PCs properly and economically.

As network offerings matured, additional shared resources became common:

- Database servers
- Application servers
- Communications servers
- Backup servers

Database servers provide centralized processing capability optimized for efficient handling of databases. In practice, this typically means that they have large, very fast disk drives. Some mainframe environments also dedicate machines to handling databases. The difference in this case is that such a mainframe would typically cost well over $1 million; a minicomputer or PC in the same role will typically cost less than $500,000, sometimes less than $100,000.

One of the particularly useful capabilities of a LAN is to enable companies to provide individual processor configurations optimized for specific functions. The capability to provide such servers goes a long way to justify the extra management effort involved in managing LANs.

Application servers are machines dedicated to handling specific applications. Such a server might be marketed together with a specific application by a value-added reseller (VAR). Such a configuration can be used in either of two basic ways: via terminal access (as with mainframes, but for one application suite only) or a client/server approach.

Communications servers enable the centralization of external communications facilities and hardware. Modern communications server capabilities include the capability to provide both in- and outbound modem pools (either separated or shared) along with routers and gateways that serve an entire user community. Without such servers, it is not uncommon to see a configuration involving one modem per PC user. Centralizing a modem pool enables the acquisition of faster, better modems, and more efficient use of them (if only a percentage of the user population will be using a modem at any one time).

Backup servers enable the off-loading of backup functions, which would most likely otherwise reside on file servers. Because the failure of a file server is typically the single most disastrous possible occurrence in a LAN environment, it does not make sense to make the file server the primary backup device (the unit with an installed tape drive). If the server fails (because of a failed power supply, for example), it becomes somewhat difficult to restore the data to another machine.

LANs are not limited to these categories of servers; these categories are just the most frequently implemented. Other possibilities include scanner servers and facsimile servers. Additional functions will most likely evolve over time.

Distributed Systems

The term *distributed processing* predates LANs. However, LANs make it much easier to implement. What is distributed processing? It is not simply spreading functions out among multiple computers, although many people believe that is all there is to it. Distributed processing has a few basic premises:

- Do the work close to where the results are required (minimizing communications costs, a key objective of distributed processing).
- Dedicate a processor(s) configured appropriately to its specific functions.
- Use cheaper MIPS (a raw unit of processing power that is generally less expensive when purchased in smaller units).
- For robustness—the capability to continue key functions in the presence of failures—this provides a certain degree of redundancy. Do not have just one processor in any given function category.

Of course, distributed processing is also designed into wide area networks (WANs), but enabling computers to communicate at high speeds among themselves is much easier to accomplish in a LAN environment.

Client/Server Architecture

Client/server design is, depending on one's viewpoint, either an extension or a subset of the distributed processing design. Whereas distributed processing typically begins with the premise that all computers are created equal at least insofar as their communications patterns—client/server design uses a more asymmetric model. But more subtle differences arise.

The basic premise of client/server design is similar to that of distributed processing: dedicate a processor(s) configured appropriately to its specific functions. But in this case, a certain amount of predefinition is applied. Specifically, it is usually assumed that precisely two processors will be involved for a given application: a desktop PC used by a human being (the client) and one other machine (the server). The division of labor between these two can be assigned in many ways. Many books have been written on the subject, so it is not pursued in this book. However, we mention the general approach because, in most cases, a critical characteristic of client/server design is high-speed communications between clients and servers, speed that can only be easily accomplished via LAN technologies.

Scalability

A key benefit often provided by both distributed systems and client/server architectures is scalability. Roughly speaking, scalability is the capability to increase the power and/or number of users in an environment smoothly without major redesigns or swapping out of equipment and software. In a mainframe environment, upgrade paths often looked like the chart shown in Figure 20-5.

Figure 20-5
The function of capacity over time when dealing with the mainframe

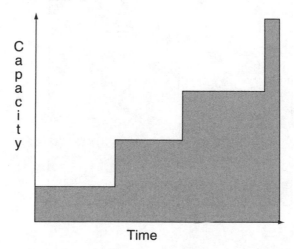

With smaller individual machines linked together with LANs, capacity upgrades tend to look more like the next chart shown in Figure 20-6. In this chart, the capacity is added in smaller increments, as user-needs dictate.

The key difference is that, with smaller machines, each upgrade is less expensive and the added capacity is readily available. Each upgrade is less financially traumatic, so when the need arises, it is usually easier to make the appropriate acquisitions. With mainframes, each upgrade is a big bite, and it takes a while to exhaust the new capacity once you have it. Because each upgrade costs a lot, justification usually takes a while, often resulting in demand exceeding capacity until the approval comes through for an upgrade.

Scalability is more an argument in favor of many small processors rather than specifically for LANs. However, the easiest way to connect those processors is with a LAN.

How They Work

A LAN environment includes, at a minimum, nodes and wiring. We first cover what makes up a node.

Figure 20-6
Capacity for smaller-based machines over time

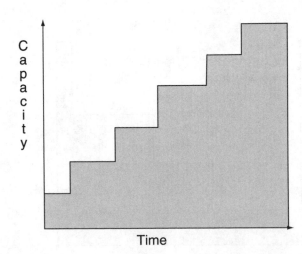

Node Configuration Elements

A LAN node is a computer that has a unique network address. This address consists of a sequence of letters and numbers (or possibly just numbers) that, just like your postal address, identifies the node so that messages sent to it can be delivered to the correct device. LAN nodes comprise certain basic elements (Figure 20-7). The key components of the LAN include the following:

- Processor (computer, possibly but not necessarily including a keyboard and monitor, and so on)
- Software
- LAN network interface card (NIC)
- Medium, whether it is a cable or wireless

The processor can be just about any computer currently available. The software and NIC, however, deserve more discussion.

Figure 20-7
The basic components of a LAN

LAN Software for LAN Nodes

Every LAN node requires a complete, functional implementation of the International Standards Organization's (ISO's) Open Systems Interconnect (OSI) model. This does not mean that the specific software is the ISO standard software; rather, it means that all the functions described in the OSI model must be addressed in one way or another. With the exception of part of layer 1 (the physical layer), all of the OSI functions are accomplished in software, so it should be no surprise that most LAN software involves not one, but several software modules that collectively enable a node to communicate.

At the bottom layer of the protocol stack (of these software modules) is certain software that is built into the NIC (in read-only memory [ROM]) as part of the physical layer. This is generally invisible to the user, or even to the installer, but it is critical. When installed, the onboard NIC software executes in the same address space used by other software on the node; thus certain address space might have to be set aside by the node so that other programs do not step on the software. This might be handled directly by the node's operating system, or it might have to be addressed directly by the installer.

The next layer of software is the network driver. This software is the go-between or interface between the rest of the software on the node and the NIC. In the world of PCs, two prevalent standards are used for this software: Network Distributed Interface Standard (NDIS, from Microsoft) and Open Data Interface (ODI, from Novell). These standards define not how the software drivers operate, but the standard approach for the other software on the computer to interact with the NDIS or ODI drivers.

It is the NIC manufacturers' responsibility to provide such drivers with their interface cards. Providing such standard software is much more difficult than you might assume. As with all of the other software on a node, the NIC interface software runs under the operating system supporting that node. Computers, especially personal computers, can run many different operating systems. A different driver implementing a given interface standard is required for each operating system. If a vendor supports both ODI and NDIS (and most do), it doubles the number of modules to be provided. Nowadays, the PC-based systems include all of the necessary protocols to support either network card driver. An example is Windows 9X, which has all the necessary drivers for both NDIS and ODI.

The province of network operating systems, such as Novell's NetWare, IBM's LAN Server, and Banyan's Vines is above the level of the driver software. Because the driver standards insulate these environments from the hardware, all of these NOSs can support several different types of LANs. The NOS software on a node provides two major functions:

■ It provides all of the communications functions specified in the OSI model above level 2.

■ It intercepts and satisfies resource requests on the node for resources that would normally appear on the node but instead are to be provided via the LAN (file access, communications access, and so on).

These resource requests can originate directly from the keyboard (a user types a file from a server disk to the screen) or from a program (a word processor program retrieves a document from a remote server). Such requests are normally satisfied so transparently that the user or requesting program is completely oblivious to the fact that a LAN function occurred.

LAN NOS software is typically priced on a per-active-user basis. At this writing, such prices vary widely depending on the NOS as well as the volume of such licenses. They can range from being free, to as high as close to $300 each. Fortunately, when this pricing structure is used, the server software does not normally have any additional charge.

LAN Network Interface Cards

Network interface cards (NICs) typically fit into an expansion slot on a computer. In some cases, however, the network interface is built into the computer in the factory. The latter approach usually results in a lower overall cost but can reduce or eliminate the opportunity to change or upgrade the network interface later. Functions performed by a NIC include the following:

■ Provides a unique LAN address for the node that is built in by the manufacturer.

■ Performs the link-level functions with other nodes appropriate to the physical connection (such as, fiber optics) and protocol (such as, Ethernet) used on the particular LAN.

■ Accepts protocol frames of information at full LAN speed and buffering (storing) them on the card until the computer is ready to process them.

■ Recognizes, examines the address information, and ignores received protocol frames that are not addressed to the node in which the NIC is installed.

■ Responds to certain management signals on the network—these might be inquiries as to the status of the card or recent communications loads imposed on it, or commands to stop communication on the network. (The latter might arrive if the card fails in such a way as to begin placing spurious traffic on the network.)

Like NOS software, NICs vary widely in price. Factors affecting price include

- How many NICs are purchased (volume discounts)
- The type of LAN to be supported (Ethernet, token ring, and so on)
- Management capabilities, if any
- Glitzy add-on features provided by the NIC manufacturer
- Buffer size
- Speed
- Bus type

The last three—buffer size, speed, and bus type—bear more discussion.

All NOS node software functions parallel to other software on a node. For example, the computer does not stop doing word processing when LAN communications occur. Thus, the node can get quite busy on occasion, perhaps so busy that frames arriving across the network might not always be dealt with promptly. However, those frames continue to arrive at the NIC at the rated speed of the LAN (for example, if Ethernet, that speed is always 10 Mbps). What happens if the bits pile up in the NIC? If the buffer on the NIC fills and more bits continue to arrive, some bits will be lost ("dropped on the floor" in the vernacular). Obviously, the more buffer on the NIC, the less likely this happens.

An interaction occurs between needed buffer space and the speed of the node. If the node's speed is well matched to the LAN, then minimal buffers are needed. If the node is much slower than the LAN's rated speed, then larger buffers might be desirable. Smaller buffers will result in retransmissions of the data from the sender, reducing the overall throughput of the LAN.

The speed of the NIC is also a factor. However, does not the NIC communicate at the defined speed of the LAN? It does, on the LAN side. However, the speed with which it communicates to its node (the local speed) is independent of the LAN speed. The part of the NIC doing local communications might or might not be as fast as the node receiving the information. If it is not that fast, then the NIC is a communications bottleneck. If overall performance is not satisfactory, this is one possible cause.

The type of bus in the node can also have a major effect on the local NIC speed. We are not speaking of the LAN bus, which is described later, but rather the internal architecture of the node. In the case of IBM-compatible personal computers, at least four different types of buses are currently available:

- Industry standard architecture (ISA)
- Microchannel (MC) (almost obsolete now)
- Extended industry standard architecture (EISA)
- Peripheral component interconnect (PCI)

ISA is generally slower than all but the slowest LANs, no matter how fast the node processor or the NIC is. All of the other types can easily keep up with most LAN speeds, provided that the NIC internal speed is also fast enough.

Most other (non-IBM-compatible) nodes can accept data more quickly than most LANs can deliver it. Therefore, if a bottleneck occurs at the node, it will usually be either the LAN itself or the NIC.

Topologies

The word *topology* is used in at least two different ways when discussing local area networks. Unfortunately, speakers rarely identify which of the two meanings they are using. Even worse, they often muddle the two meanings together. We try to distinguish the two meanings by qualifying the term into physical topology and logical topology.

Physical topology constitutes the way one lays out the wires in a building. The major physical topologies include

- Bus
- Ring
- Star
- Combinations of the above (tree, double ring)

Logical topology describes the way signals travel on the wires. Unfortunately, logical topologies share much the same terminology as physical topologies. Signals can travel in the following fashions:

- Bus
- Ring
- Star (or switched)

So, is there any difference between physical and logical topologies? Emphatically, yes! As we will see, most of the logical topologies can be used on most of the physical topologies. Thus, you can use bus communications techniques on a bus or star; ring communications techniques on a bus, ring, or tree; and star communications techniques on a bus or star. Confused? Read on—we sort the main variations out one at a time.

Physical Topologies

The bus physical topology has the following key characteristics:

- All locations on the communications medium are directly and electronically accessible to all other points.

- Any signal placed on a bus becomes immediately available to all other nodes on the bus without requiring any form of retransmission.

Physical bus topologies are usually drawn as a line with nodes attached, as shown in Figure 20-8. Note that the bus is a single high-speed cable with

Figure 20-8

The layout of a bus topology

Ethernet

all devices connected to it. But as you will see when we cover media, some buses do not require any wires at all.

The ring physical topology has the following key characteristics:

- Each node is connected to only two other nodes.
- Transmissions from one node to another pass via all intervening nodes in the ring.

Complete failure of a node, together with its NIC, can (in theory) cause the entire network to fail. We say "in theory" because in practice, ring NICs are designed to fail "open;" traffic continues to pass.

Rings are typically drawn as shown in Figure 20-9. Variations to this ring are covered in greater detail in Chapter 22.

Some types of rings (for example, fiber distributed data interface [FDDI]) have additional active devices to construct the ring itself (Figure 20-10). This architecture is not a perfect circle as we think of it, but it is still a ring.

Figure 20-9
The typical physical ring as it evolved

■■■ ■■■ ■■■ ■■■
Figure 20-10
The FDDI uses a
different type of ring.
Not all rings are laid
out in perfect circles.

The star physical topology has the following key characteristics:

■ Each node connects to a central device with its own wire or set of wires.

■ The central device is responsible for ensuring that traffic for a given node reaches it.

■ Data might or might not pass through multiple nodes on the way to its destination, depending on the specific capabilities of the central device.

Star topologies often are drawn something like the one shown in Figure 20-11.

Note that, although some type of device is always at the center, star diagrams do not show it often. It depends on whether the focus of the diagram

Figure 20-11
The typical star
network layout

is the nodes or the way the network is built. In the latter case, the diagram would look like the variation shown in Figure 20-12.

Logical Topologies

As mentioned earlier, logical topologies include bus, ring, and star (or switched). A logical bus operates with each transmission visible to every other node on the LAN. The easiest way to do this, of course, is with a physical bus; all devices connect to the same wire.

But consider the user of a star physical topology. If the central device instantly retransmits every frame it receives from one wire out to every other wire, how can the individual devices detect whether they are on a physical bus or physical star? Do they care? The answer to both questions is a qualified no. A certain amount of engineering goes into building such devices. However, Ethernet, for example, was originally designed to function on a physical bus. Nowadays, almost all Ethernet installations consist of physical stars.

Bus topologies require a method of handling collisions—times when two or more nodes attempt to transmit at the same or overlapping times. Different methods are used with different protocols.

A logical ring consists of a network where any given transmission passes from one device to another in a fixed sequence until it reaches its destination. It is naturally most obvious on a physical ring. However, it also can be implemented on a physical bus or a physical star. In the case of a physical bus, although all devices see all transmissions, each transmits on the common medium in a fixed sequence, sending packets only downstream. An advantage of this tightly-disciplined line protocol is that a collision can never occur; all devices know their turn and follow it. On the other hand, it can be quite a while until one's turn arrives.

A logical star cannot be built on a physical ring or bus; it requires a central device to make intelligent choices as to the disposition of each frame, sending the frame only to the correct destination. Ethernet switches, a relatively recent development, operate in this fashion. Collisions cannot happen in this environment, although buffer overruns in the central device can occur if it is not quick enough to keep ahead of the frame arrival rate.

Mixed Topologies—The Real World

As we will see in later chapters, ideal designs as described previously have never stopped engineers from building what will work. Token rings are really stars, Ethernet is also usually a star, and the fiber distributed data interface (FDDI) is the first real ring that was widely implemented. It uses the variation shown with devices building the ring. The following is a brief list of some of the more popular LAN protocols, with notes as to their topologies:

Ethernet and token ring   A later chapter discusses these protocols.

LocalTalk   This Apple protocol uses a bus physical and logical architecture. Its contention management approach is called carrier sense with multiple access and collision avoidance (CSMA/CA). All devices listen continuously to media (carrier sense). Multiple devices connect to the same media (multiple access). When a device wishes to send a packet, it sends out a very small precursor packet requesting permission. Because the packet is very small (and is only sent out in the first place if the medium is idle), it is unlikely that it will collide with another packet. Presuming that it doesn't collide, all other devices are now on notice that the real packet is coming, so they do not step on it with their own transmissions. This is LocalTalk's approach to collision avoidance.

Manufacturing automation protocol (MAP)   MAP uses a token-passing bus. The token-passing bus is designed to have the benefit of the bus (high bandwidth) and the predictability of the ring (token passing). All devices hear each device's transmissions. However, every device transmits to the next in a fixed sequence, thus completely avoiding collisions, but lengthening the average time until any given device receives its turn to transmit.

Asynchronous transfer mode (ATM)   ATM is both a late-model LAN and a WAN technology. It is designed to complement the LAN by performing noncontention LAN emulation. This means that the ATM will look like a star and provide dedicated bandwidth to each device on the network. In reality, the older LANs (now called legacy LANs) will not be sharing a single-cable system and competing for the bandwidth as they do today.

Peer-to-peer versus server-based   This is an area of network design that sounds as though it is a topology-related subject, but it is really not. Peer-to-peer and server-based are two different approaches to designing network operating systems and applications. Entire volumes have been written on both approaches; we briefly summarize and distinguish between the two approaches in the next few paragraphs.

Peer-to-peer networks afford users great flexibility because every node can potentially function as a server. In practice, this means that relatively small shops can set up many or all of their computers to provide file and other services to all other computers. In principle, this is an egalitarian and flexible approach. In reality, it can quickly turn into a nightmare if not managed carefully.

The problem is that managing any server properly requires that a certain amount of time and expertise be focused on that task. Users, not unreasonably, tend to focus their efforts on their own jobs to the exclusion of network management functions. If a user's machine is configured as a server and the user does not manage it, who does?

Another problem with this approach is that server functions consume computer and input/output resources (time). If you as a user are also providing services to other users, your local performance will be directly affected by the load others put on your machine. Because a major benefit of personal computers is that the power on your desktop is yours alone, peer-to-peer configurations can quickly cause frustration because of degraded performance, unless each machine has more power than is needed solely to satisfy its assigned user.

Having given some of the more serious drawbacks of peer-to-peer environments, it should be stated that thousands of small businesses, who use this technology, function well. The key is that they are small enough that the disadvantages described never become serious enough to outweigh the advantages. Some of the advantages of peer-to-peer NOSs include the following:

- Any system can be configured as a server, providing effective group access to any files desired, no matter where those files reside.

- Typically lower cost-per-node, partly because of lower software costs and partly because of the elimination of the need to purchase high-powered dedicated servers.

- Reduced management costs, partly because some management functions typically do not get performed, but also because these systems are designed to be more easily managed than the dedicated server systems.

Server-based networks predominate. Their advantages and disadvantages are partly the flip side of those listed in the peer-to-peer discussion. But two should be emphasized:

■ Server-based networks can be and typically are tuned so as to support larger numbers of users (anywhere from 20 to 300) on a single server. The management effort involved to support such numbers is much less on a per-user basis than would be the case if a peer-to-peer approach were used for such a large user base.

■ Although it seems a self-fulfilling prophecy, the very large numbers of installations of server-based systems (especially NetWare) have resulted in an appropriately sized base of people expert in the configuration and management of such systems. Also, that same installed base has attracted many creators of after-market software products that complement and extend such environments, a far larger selection than is available for the peer-to-peer products.

Internetworking

Internetworking refers to the connecting together of two or more networks, either LANs, WANs, or a mixture of the two.

The creators of LANs designed them to be truly local. This was not an arbitrarily-imposed design restriction; by not requiring a LAN to be capable of wide area communications, the engineers could take advantage of a much more controlled environment. This control enabled the use of techniques that, although not practical over a wide area, could deliver far higher communications performance than WAN communications of the day, as well as reliability orders of magnitude faster than those same WAN communications.

However, as expected, a demand soon materialized for the capability to provide LAN-type communications (that is, fast, having a lower error rate, and using typical LAN protocols) over areas wider than those originally envisioned as being supportable by LANs. And engineers, as expected, came up with not one, but several ways of accomplishing this. All involve the use of additional devices that, in varying ways, take a LAN signal and send it further than the original LAN specification allows.

Terminology is important at this point. We cover four types of devices that provide such extended LAN connectivity. The first type, repeaters, is considered to extend the reach of a given LAN. As such, using repeaters is not technically internetworking, although we describe it in this section because it nonetheless involves extending the reach of LAN technology in a given environment. All three of the other technologies—bridges, routers, and gateways—are considered to provide connections among or between different LANs, thus providing true internetworking capabilities. The reason for this division between repeaters and the rest should become apparent as we cover the devices in more detail. We begin with the simplest of the devices and continue on to more sophisticated products.

Repeaters

Repeaters are relatively unintelligent connections between two LAN segments of the same type (Ethernet, token ring, and so on). A repeater is sensitive to the traffic's content only at the ISO level 1 (physical) layer. An Ethernet repeater will transmit any traffic that can be sent on Ethernet, a token ring repeater will send on all token ring traffic, and so on. Repeaters satisfy only three key functions:

- Distance
- Electrical isolation
- Media conversion

Bridges

Bridges are intelligent connections between two LANs of the same type. They operate at layer 2 of the OSI reference model (data link). The bridge is responsible for linking the two segments or LANs together and transparently passing frames across the link to each other. No form of choices is used, and no format or protocol conversions or any other services are available other than providing the physical and logical paths between the two networks or segments.

The bridge can be intelligent, providing filtering and forwarding services across the link. A filter is used if an addressable device is on the network that is sending the frame. This is so a frame of information does not get sent across the wires to another segment or network that has no need to see the frame. Forwarding takes place when the bridge sees a frame that is addressed to a node on the other side of the link.

Routers

Routers are devices that connect two LANs where multiple paths exist (or a single path exists on a dial/leased line basis). Working at layer 3 of the OSI model (routing, or network layer), the router will be responsible for ensuring that the data gets to its destination. Several considerations about this decision process arise as the router is more sophisticated; therefore, it is more complex to manage. However, this added complexity brings significant gains to the users who are looking to internetwork their LANs. Many large organizations now use routers in their backbone network to connect segments (departments, floors on a building, and so on) together with alternative paths to get from one LAN segment to another. The feeling is that the resiliency is worth the added complexity.

Gateways

Gateways connect two networks of different types (such as, a LAN to an X.25 network). These operate at higher levels of the OSI model: ISO levels 4–7 (transport, session, presentation, and application). In effect, the gateway handles everything above the network layer in the OSI model. The controlling portion of a session, the format and protocol conversion to make all things common, and the actual application interface reside in the gateway's domain for interconnectivity.

Benefits of using gateways include an initial cost savings, high performance, and high flexibility and scalability.

LAN Switching versus Nonswitched

When discussing driving habits, some people say, "Speed kills." This may be true, but in the case of networks, lack of speed can kill. Networks can be designed in many ways, but one of the most popular and straightforward ways is to design a backbone whereby a high-speed path is present for

Figure 20-13
A backbone
architecture

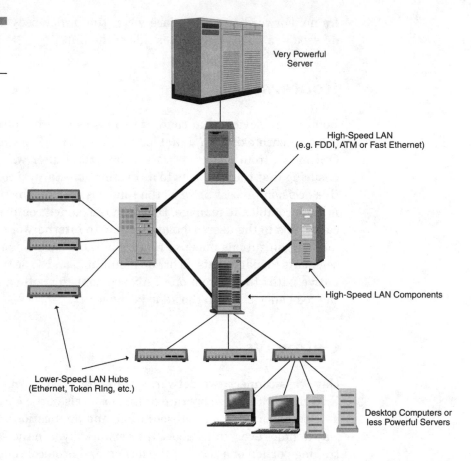

Very Powerful
Server

High-Speed LAN
(e.g. FDDI, ATM or Fast Ethernet)

High-Speed LAN Components

Lower-Speed LAN Hubs
(Ethernet, Token RIng, etc.)

Desktop Computers or
less Powerful Servers

high-speed requirements at a central point (topologically speaking) and all subsidiary networks connect to that backbone. See Figure 20-13. Several assumptions accompany this model. One is that a need arises for connections between either the subnetworks or from each of the subnetworks to that central backbone, possibly for server or application access. These assumptions are not necessarily valid. For example, if the business primarily uses local area networks to provide office automation capabilities, an entire series of islands of automation may exist where it doesn't matter that they are islands. We certainly don't want to be loading applications across the wide area; and if all you are doing is loading applications and storing such data as word processing or spreadsheet information, then you really don't need a backbone to connect up with disparate networks.

In many cases, however, backbones are required, so speed is important. The technologies suitable for high-speed backbones are described later in this chapter. At this point, we are talking about a way to deliver somewhat higher speed to desktops or for small backbones.

The typical office automation network designer has to make a choice about where various components reside. The major components are data and applications. Ideally, we believe that data ought to be stored centrally, whereas applications ought to be executed from the desktop. Why? It's a matter of performance. The internal bus speeds of even medium-speed desktop computers far exceed the capabilities of cost-effective local area networks. Loading applications takes a long time, relatively speaking. When you have many people doing this simultaneously, it can bury a network. You can pay the money to upgrade in the way we will describe, but an easier approach is to distribute the applications to the desktop. But, you say, that is a maintenance nightmare! In the past, it was. Applications are available today that will distribute software to the desktop in a very cost-effective and efficient manner. It is not necessary to touch every desktop in order to install or update applications if one has LAN connectivity to those desktops from a distribution server.

We realize, however, that not every company has installed such software-distribution capabilities or is convinced that this is the way to go. So what do they do when the performance penalty of loading applications from servers to all the desktops begins to bury their networks? Wouldn't it be nice if they could simply change the central equipment in the network and get a speed kicker? In fact, they can do exactly that.

With older technology such as coaxial Ethernet, this wouldn't work. But the technology we're going to discuss, switching, does provide a speed boost, a real capacity boost, without necessarily touching the desktops in any way.

The key fact to remember is that most local area networks employ shared media. Generally, when we refer to shared media, we mean Ethernet hub-based LANs (shown in Figure 20-14) and token rings. Even though both topologies in modern networks are wired with radial or star-type wiring, the equipment at the center (as discussed elsewhere in this book) causes every node in a ring or Ethernet segment to see all of the traffic generated by all the other nodes. They are designed this way, and it is a good way to design a network for many reasons. However, when the traffic starts increasing, everybody sees all of the increases. That's a problem. How do we address it? We replace the central piece of equipment, an Ethernet hub or a token ring MAU, with a corresponding switch.

Figure 20-14
Shared LAN—packets
go everywhere.

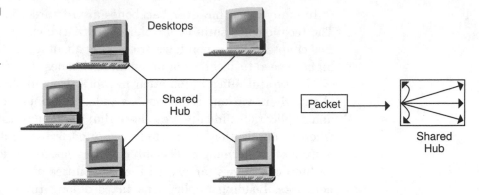

The job of a switch is twofold:

■ It has to make the traffic on the wires to the devices to which the switch is connected look exactly the way it was before, from the point of view of the connected devices because we are not planning on changing the electronics in those devices.

■ It examines every packet coming in on every wire and, on a packet-by-packet basis, directs those packets outbound to only the port or circuit where the packet has to go.

This may sound like routing, but it happens at a much lower (and therefore faster) level of the architecture than that at which routing takes place. Whereas routing is done at the middle levels on such protocols as IPX or TCP/IP, switching is done at layer 2, the media access control (MAC) layer. It's done on the basis of the hardware addresses of the connected network devices; therefore it's very fast. But the speed alone is not what creates the major benefit. The major benefit is that the only traffic that is put on a wire going to a device is traffic destined for that device (plus broadcast traffic, unfortunately—see Figure 20-15). So, that wire only sees traffic to and from that device; this means that, in effect, the wire now has the full-rated bandwidth of the network dedicated to just that device and the connections it's talking to; that bandwidth is no longer shared. Whereas before we might have had an Ethernet running at 10 Mbps and 30 devices sharing that bandwidth, now each device sees 10 Mbps coming to its doorstep and no other traffic is present to degrade that. This is a major performance upgrade.

This has some limitations, however. For one thing, this is not necessarily a good way to upgrade server connectivity. If you think about it, you will

Figure 20-15
Switched LAN—
packets go only to
correct destination.

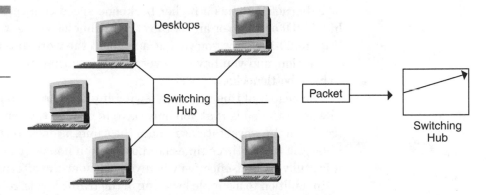

realize that the connection going into the server is still 10 Mbps, or 16 Mbps in the case of token ring. Traffic on wires going to workstations without a switch would have a lot of traffic that really wasn't designated for those workstations when using either Ethernet or token ring. But in a typical small network, all of the traffic is either going to or from the server if only one is present. Giving it a switched connection doesn't really help much because all of the traffic is still going to have to appear on that circuit (Figure 20-16). A better way to go is to have a switched hub for either token ring

Figure 20-16
Switched
connections don't do
servers much good.

or Ethernet that has a higher backbone speed connection into something like FDDI or ATM, or any of the other technologies we will talk about later (Figure 20-17). Now you've upgraded both the workstations and the server connection, and you have an overall increase that means you're less likely to have bottlenecks.

The beauty of this approach (switching to improve connectivity capacity to workstations) is that you only have to change the central hub. The electronics in the workstations remain the same, as does the wiring. Even if the hubs cost two or three times per port what a nonswitching hub would cost, it is still very cost-effective when you consider the alternatives.

In addition to a simple lowering of the traffic levels, collisions are usually avoided in this approach because no other devices on any particular segment are trying to get in at the same time. Put another way, the segment becomes a single wire connecting, or virtually connecting, two devices talking back and forth through the hub without any interfering traffic to get in the way.

A couple of interesting variations on this are being marketed. One is full-duplex Ethernet. If you recall, Ethernet is actually a half-duplex medium. Only one packet can be on the wire at a time, and it, of course, is going only

Figure 20-17
Upgrading the
server's connection to
ATM

in one direction, or at least it is only destined for a device that is in one direction along the wire. On the other hand, full-duplex Ethernet, if it is switched, changes this in such a way that the devices can communicate both ways simultaneously over what is still a 10Base-T-type wiring cable run (Figure 20-18). Unfortunately, this approach requires a replacement of the network interface card in all machines participating in the network. Therefore, it does not result in a cheap upgrade, but it gives you potentially double the capacity on the connections to the workstations and/or servers compared to even what switched Ethernet can provide. But beware! In many cases, the amount of traffic on the network going from the workstations to the central site is truly minimal when compared to the traffic going toward the workstations. Putting in the technology that provides equal transmission capacity in both directions sounds great, but if you really don't need much more than a tiny fractional increase on the overall capacity on one of the directions, then in effect you are creating capacity that will never be used—and paying a pretty penny for it. One place where full-duplex technology could be valuable is video conferencing on the local area network. There you are sending video signals bidirectionally, generating a great deal of bandwidth requirements. But in general, we don't feel that full-duplex local area network technology has much of a future, at least for desktops.

The next variation is more of a topological variant than a technological one. Switching technology was described in the preceding paragraphs in the context of delivering full bandwidth to individual desktops. But in many cases, workgroups need greater connection speed to a backbone. Moreover, many companies cascade Ethernet hubs in order to gain connectivity

Figure 20-18
Standard Ethernet is half duplex; full-duplex Ethernet works two ways at once.

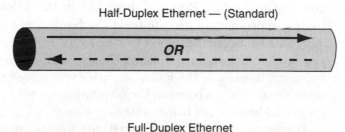

Half-Duplex Ethernet — (Standard)

OR

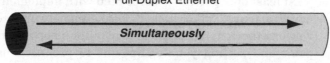

Full-Duplex Ethernet

Simultaneously

Figure 20-19
Cascaded, shared
hubs

benefits while minimizing wiring costs (Figure 20-19). The problem, of course, is that the connections become much more heavily loaded as one moves up the upside-down tree hierarchy that Ethernet uses for its physical configuration. Ethernet could be considered a poor man's backbone, where, at the lower end of the tree, we insert whole nonswitched Ethernet hubs for workgroups rather than individual workstations (Figure 20-20). It's a much less expensive approach than using the much faster technologies that are described later. Of course, one doesn't get the major speed increases that these other technologies can deliver, but this solution may suffice for a while.

Switching can be used with other protocols, especially token ring, FDDI, and any of the fast Ethernet described in the following paragraphs. Of course, some vendors need to build the hardware, but vendors are amazingly ambitious, and we expect that you will be able to buy almost anything you want in a switching variant. Those ports will cost more, but adding switching to some of the following faster technologies in some cases could make the difference between those technologies being acceptably fast for a given backbone or not being quite fast enough.

At least one "gotcha" is associated with implementing switching technology. In a shared (nonswitched) local area network technology such as token ring or Ethernet, it is possible to monitor a network by connecting up at any point and setting your equipment to promiscuous mode. This requires

Figure 20-20

Switched hubs—a lightweight backbone

special software, but most modern NICs can do this. Although some consider this a security risk, it is extremely beneficial for network-management purposes. If one wishes to monitor the level of traffic on a network or examine packet contents to figure out why things aren't working properly, this becomes a valuable characteristic in an architecture. Switching technology defeats this capability. Because the only packets that go onto a wire are those destined for that wire, a PC connected up in promiscuous mode will still only receive packets addressed to that PC; packets going elsewhere only go to those other locations. Some network devices have special monitor ports that actually provide all the traffic seen on the backbone of those devices. However, not all hubs and routers have this capability. It is a recognized problem, and we do expect hardware vendors to address it over time.

As mentioned previously, switching technologies are sometimes used in order to provide a moderate upgrade in speed in an environment that is running out of gas. They are an alternative to changing technologies and installing something like a fast Ethernet or one of the other higher-speed technologies. So the question is: does it make sense to switch or use something else like a fast Ethernet? We believe that a mix of technologies will, in most cases, provide the biggest bang for your buck. Because of the elimination of collisions in a switched Ethernet environment vis-à-vis a shared

Ethernet environment, switched Ethernet provides a significant improvement in to-the-desktop bandwidth. In fact, few applications would demand more than clear-channel 10-Mbps bandwidth. An example might be full-motion, uncompressed video teleconferencing. However, the vast majority, including downloads of application programs, can easily be satisfied with clear-channel 10-Mbps Ethernet. This cannot be said of shared Ethernet, which runs out of gas at a much lower level of utilization and hits that utilization level much more easily. Now, the 100-Mbps Ethernet in an auto-detect mode can use either 10 Mbps when attached to a 10-Mbps switch or 100 Mbps when attached to a 100-Mbps switch. As the industry evolved, the introduction of the 1-Gbps Ethernet changed the way we perceive the use of the bandwidth.

However, we do not believe that switched Ethernet is a major backbone technology except in the smallest environments. Regarding the use of switched Ethernet in order to provide server connectivity is a case-in-point. A better approach is to use switched Ethernet as the lowest-level connectivity solution in an architecture and connect those switched Ethernet workgroups or switched token ring workgroups to a higher-speed backbone technology, perhaps one of those discussed elsewhere in this book.

Questions

1. What is the reason for installing a LAN?

   a. Making a network.

   b. Sharing resources.

   c. Because everyone else is doing it.

   d. It is cheap.

2. When the first LANs were used, they were both _____ and _____ laid out.

   a. Physically and topologically

   b. Physiologically and topologically

   c. Physically and logically

   d. Physically and mentally

3. The three basic forms of a LAN are:

   a. Ring, bus, and star

   b. Ring, star, and hub

   c. Star, spoke, and wheel

   d. Physical, logical, and topological

4. The need for a LAN began in:

   a. 1990

   b. 1980

   c. 1996

   d. 1974

5. Data switches, or data PBXs, were alternatives, but they could only support:

   a. IBM data

   b. Lower speeds

   c. Higher speeds

   d. Dial-up connections

6. One of the less obvious characteristics of a LAN is that all devices on it are viewed and function as being:

   a. Equals

   b. Subservient

   c. Adjacent

   d. Tangent

7. Ethernet is actually a _____ medium.

8. Every keystroke on terminals connected to a main computer generates a:

   a. Letter

   b. Interrupt

   c. Symbol

   d. Flag

9. If each node is connected to only two other nodes, we are looking at a:

   a. Bus

   b. Star

   c. Spoke

   d. Ring

10. _____ are machines dedicated to handling specific applications.

11. The user can always be counted on to back up his/her data.   T/F

12. The use of a _____ server helps to share modems.

13. Peer-to-peer networks afford users great flexibility.   T/F

14. The card placed inside the PC is called:

    a. The LAN card

    b. The Network Interface Card (NIC)

    c. The server card

    d. A token

15. Server-based networks can be and typically are tuned so as to support anywhere from ___ to ____ users on a single server.

    a. 1–50

    b. 10–100

    c. 20–300

    d. 50–60

16. Routers are sophisticated; therefore they are more complex to:

    a. Design

    b. Install

    c. Purchase

    d. Manage

17. The NIC card provides a unique LAN address called the:

    a. Big Mac

    b. Apple Interface

    c. LAN address

    d. MAC address

18. LAN switches operate at layer _____ of the OSI model.

    a. One

    b. Two

    c. Three

    d. Six

19. The device that spans the upper layers of the OSI model on a LAN is called:

    a. Bridge

    b. Router

    c. Repeater

    d. Gateway

20. Printers are never addressable devices on a LAN.   T/F

Ethernet

After reading this chapter and completing the questions, you will be able to:

- Describe the Ethernet
- Discuss the various speeds associated with Ethernet
- Understand how an Ethernet frame is created
- Discuss the use of carrier sense multiple access with collision detection (CSMA/CD)
- Describe the throughput constraints
- Recognize a switch or a hub in a closet

Ethernet was the first commercial approach to using a local area network (LAN) on a bus topology. Ethernet is the most commonly used LAN technology today, accounting for more than 83 percent of the installations worldwide. Although certain recently developed technologies are faster, Ethernet still enjoys continued popularity and growth for a number of reasons:

- For its speed: it is by far the least expensive networking approach.
- Its various standards supporting a wide variety of media are sufficiently well defined so that products from multiple vendors can be mixed and matched with a reasonable expectation that they will work well together.

- Ethernet equipment exists to enable virtually any intelligent device to connect to an Ethernet.

- A variety of interfaces still exist for dumb terminal interconnection through terminal servers.

- It is fast enough for the vast majority of applications in use today, despite what we hear in the press or from the vendor community.

- The Ethernet standards continue to evolve to keep pace with other LAN techniques.

The Ethernet standard(s) defines an approach to building a contention-based LAN on a bus topology. As originally defined and implemented by Xerox, Intel, and Digital Equipment Corporation (the DIX design), the bus appears to be a single straight cable system to all connected devices. The cable is available to multiple users at the same time, even though only one user at a time can send data if a shared bus is installed. We present these concepts in more detail in the rest of this chapter.

A note on standards: the Institute for Electrical and Electronic Engineers (IEEE) is responsible for the standards setting and administration for LANs. The committees associated with setting these standards are called the 802 committees. Technically, the LAN protocol implemented most widely and still referred to as Ethernet is actually defined in the 802.3 standard; it is not precisely the same as either of the two Ethernet standards (I or II) defined by the Xerox-Intel-DEC triumvirate. However, most equipment currently available can support both standards; also, in most cases, the devices can interoperate on the same media. In any case, most people, when not attempting to be particularly precise, refer to 802.3 as Ethernet. We do also.

Concepts

Ethernet uses several concepts in producing and carrying data across the LAN. These concepts separate the Ethernet from other data transmission systems. The following concepts specify the operating characteristics.

Bus—CSMA/CD

The human ear is much better at picking out a single voice from among multiple simultaneous speakers than any electronic receiver is at selecting one signal from among many. Thus, every LAN using a bus (a shared medium) design must incorporate a contention management or arbitration mechanism that results in only one signal being present at a time. No matter how many devices share the medium, they have to wait their turn. Otherwise, signals on the cable would conflict like voices on the floor of a commodities exchange, but with less profit. Ethernet uses a contention management approach called carrier sense multiple access with collision detection (CSMA/CD) to ensure that devices speak politely, one at a time. CSMA/CD is designed to provide equal use of the network for all attached devices. CSMA/CD actually breaks down into three meaningful two-word terms.

Carrier Sense   All stations listen to the cable continuously. Many non-Ethernet signaling approaches send a single unvarying signal (a carrier) and impose variations on it based on the desired information to be transmitted, whether data, voice, or music. Examples include AM and FM radio as well as television. Ethernet is different in that Ethernet nodes do not send out any signal at all unless they have something to say—kind of like Mr. Ed, the talking horse. Therefore, when stations monitor the cable, they are listening for the presence of a carrier signal, whether modulated or not. If a device that wants to transmit detects a carrier on the cable, then it knows that another device is either preparing to send, is sending, or has just finished sending information onto the cable. In any case, the waiting device will hold back until the carrier signal vanishes.

Multiple Access   If no one is using the cable, any of the network devices attached to the Ethernet can transmit data onto the network at will; no central control is present, nor do we have a need for any. This is a more powerful design element than it might appear to be at first blush. Networks degrade (or experience reduced performance) in different ways, depending on their design. One factor that does not in and of itself degrade an Ethernet is the attachment of hundreds of devices. (The theoretical limit of the number of addressable stations on the network is 1,024, although most networks only have 30 to 35 nodes attached.) Because the wire is truly idle, unless a device is transmitting, only active devices impose any load on the network. Thus, a myriad of devices can be connected, so long as most of them are not transmitting at any one time.

Of course, there is a potential fly in this ointment: if all those attached devices need to transmit a lot of data, great congestion will ensue. However, this might be acceptable for some networks—not the congestion, but the threat of it. Some networks are built to support primarily word processing, an occasional file transfer, and perhaps some electronic mail. With such networks, the light load per machine enables many devices to be present without degrading the network. Networks that will experience much traffic at all per device must be engineered more carefully, perhaps by being divided up into multiple bridged segments.

Collision Detection   In the event that two devices attempt to transmit at the same time or even during overlapping time intervals, a collision will occur.

Think of two people simultaneously beginning to speak at a cocktail party. If they both continue to speak, neither will be understood. This might be fine for a New Yorker, who can talk and listen at the same time, but for the type of network under discussion, it can be devastating. On an Ethernet, if a collision occurs, the data is lost and each system must retransmit. However, retransmitting immediately will only cause the exact same result —a new collision.

At the cocktail party (if the attendees are reasonably well behaved), both speakers will stop as soon as they become aware of the problem. On an Ethernet, the first device that detects the problem will stop the regular transmission and send out a special jamming signal, which tells all attached devices that a collision has occurred. Every device will hear the jam signal because all devices continue to listen to the network even if they are transmitting.

At the cocktail party, each speaker hesitates a moment, then tries again. The person who hesitates the shortest time gets the word in edgewise, while the other waits for the next opportunity. On an Ethernet, any device that was attempting to transmit at the time the jam signal arrives will assume that a collision occurred. It will therefore calculate and wait a semirandom amount of time. What is semirandom? Each device uses a preprogrammed backoff algorithm to wait a certain period of time before retransmitting. The individual devices will therefore wait different amounts of time. The calculation (algorithm) is an attempt to generate a random number, but the (guaranteed unique) address of each device is a part of the calculation. Thus, the amount of time waited in such circumstances will always be different for each involved device, ensuring that the next attempt by the device that waits the shortest time will succeed—well, almost.

The problem is that the only devices that apply the waiting algorithm are those that experienced the collision. Any other device that has occasion to transmit will only follow the standard Ethernet approach (listen, then transmit). If a new participant decides that it is time to transmit, it could do so just as the fastest waiter in the previous group finishes its wait and goes ahead with its second try. If this happens, another collision will occur.

You might well ask, "How does anything ever make it through an Ethernet?" We must emphasize that all of the shilly-shallying described in the previous paragraphs happens in a small number of microseconds. And remember, unless devices attempt to transmit at almost exactly the same time, collisions will not happen; the second device waits its turn, then transmits.

Nonetheless, if you understand how the collision detection and avoidance mechanism works, it should be no surprise that as the number of communicating devices attached to an Ethernet increases, the number of collisions also increases. In practice, close management is indicated when steady traffic on an Ethernet exceeds about 30 to 40 percent of the 10-Mbps capacity of the network. This really means that an Ethernet with an average number of users on it will yield an effective throughput of approximately 3.3 to 4 Mbps. This assumes a mix of 30 to 1,000 terminals, or 30 to 35 PCs, 6 computer-aided design (CAD) workstations, or 2 minicomputers. In all of these examples, we are using averages; however, the authors know of organizations that have supported 1,000 terminals on a large Ethernet. The difference was the type of work being performed. If all the work is word processing, as you might find in a legal business environment, then the demands on the network will be minimal. Yet, put five to six CAD terminals on the network and things will definitely be different. These five to six terminals will saturate the network and be prone to collision.

Half Duplex

If you have ever seen a fast typist using a terminal connected to a mini-computer via Ethernet, you might have concluded that Ethernet is a full-duplex protocol. However, Ethernet is actually a half-duplex protocol. It is so fast, though, that it is functionally full duplex. Although no more than one frame can occupy the wire at a time—and in the case of a typist, it is possible that each 64-byte frame might actually include only 1 byte of data in each direction—the frames are moved back and forth so quickly that to a human being it looks as if the typing and the receiving of characters are simultaneous.

If two files were copied, one from node A to node B and the other from node B to node A, at exactly the same time, the flow of frames in both directions would intermingle so that it would once again appear that the transmission was going in both ways simultaneously. Nevertheless, because at any one instant only one frame can occupy the wire at a time, the medium is actually only half duplex.

Bandwidth

Ethernet was created in the beginning to operate at 10 Mbps. Making all implementations run at the same speed has some advantage: no significant speed matching is required when connecting multiple Ethernet segments, even those built using different media.

However, although all Ethernets run at 10 Mbps, not all devices on an Ethernet actually communicate at 10 Mbps. This concept is difficult to grasp, but it is important. Every node connected to an Ethernet incorporates an interface capable of receiving from and transmitting onto the Ethernet at 10 Mbps exactly. Otherwise, it does not comply with the Ethernet standard. Nevertheless, that interface card might not communicate to its own node at 10 Mbps. After all, a percentage of existing desktop PCs cannot even accept data at 10 Mbps through their internal buses! Although this number is declining, the evolution is one that must be considered. Sometimes the interface card is not built to interface with the node at a high enough speed; in other cases, the card could go faster but the node could not. This inability to keep up with the nominal speed of the Ethernet itself is one major source of performance problems, especially if the slow interface is found on a server. Think of people who still have the old Intel 286, 386, and 486 chipsets in their PCs.

As with all protocols, not all of the bandwidth on Ethernet is actually available for carrying application-related data. Some bits are required for overhead functions. Ethernet supports a variable-length frame; the minimum frame length is 64 bytes, and the maximum frame size is 1,518 bytes. The variation results from changing the amount of data transmitted. In the Ethernet (actually 802.3) protocol, 18 bytes in each frame are dedicated to overhead, as shown in Table 21-1.

Table 21-1

Composition of
an 802.3 Frame

Function	Bytes	Description
Destination address	6	Ethernet address of the node to which the frame is addressed
Source address	6	Ethernet address of the sending node
Length	2	Indicates the number of bytes of data in the next (data) field
Data	46–1,500	The payload—the actual data being transmitted
CRC	4	Cyclic redundancy error detection bytes

Destination Address

Both the destination and source addresses are 6-byte fields, usually represented in hexadecimal format: for example, BB-BB-BB-BB-BB-BB.[1] Every Ethernet interface on a LAN receives and processes all frames transmitted on the LAN. The main job of the receiving interface is to compare the destination address in each received packet with its own address. If the addresses match, the frame is delivered to higher protocol layers at the node for further processing and eventual handoff to an application. If the addresses do not match, the frame is dropped on the floor; that is, it is discarded.

Source Address

As mentioned elsewhere, every Ethernet node contains an interface device. Today, these are mostly built-in or installed at the factory; other times they are provided as part of an add-on printed circuit board that implements the interface. Every single one of those devices worldwide contains (or should

---

[1] In our normal numbering system, decimal or base 10, the digits 0 through 9 are used to count. Note that even though we call it base 10, and it has 10 digits, no single digit represents the quantity 10. Each position (ones, tens, hundreds, and so on) in a number contains a decimal digit (that is, 0 through 9) indicating how many of a power of 10 ($10^0 = 1$, $10^1 = 10$, $10^2 = 100$, and so on) goes into that number. Thus, the number 264 is four 1's plus six 10s plus two 100s.

contain) a unique 48-bit Ethernet address, usually stored in programmable read-only memory (PROM). Every company that wishes to manufacture such Ethernet devices applies to the IEEE (in the past, Xerox performed this function) for a unique 3-byte code. As the company manufactures the interfaces, it burns in its 3-byte code into the first 3 bytes of the 6-byte address of that device. The other 3 bytes of the address are normally assigned sequentially, one per device, but can be assigned in whatever way the manufacturer wishes. The only requirement is that every device has a different 6-byte address. If properly followed, this system guarantees that every manufactured Ethernet device will have its own unique 6-byte physical address.

Apparently, at least one Far East manufacturer has broken this approach to guaranteeing address uniqueness. It acquired chip designs for Ethernet interfaces and then proceeded to manufacture them, one after another, with identical addresses. If more than one of those interfaces were installed on the same local area network, they would be unable to communicate, either with each other or with other devices.

Other variants to this rule occurred when users were allowed to assign their own 3-byte extensions on the addressing mechanism. This allowed a network manager to assign specific addresses to servers, sometimes in a sequence that made sense to the manager for the appropriate LAN. However, this led to some complications where the manager would assign two identical addresses to the devices on the network, which led to conflicts. Most installations today have the standard addressing that comes on the card because of the past problems with this process.

Length

Valid lengths for Ethernet frames are from 64 to 1,518 bytes inclusive. The length field in the frame indicates only the number of payload bytes, and that value can range from 46 to 1,500 bytes inclusive. Notice that a frame cannot contain fewer than 46 bytes of data. What happens if the sending device provides fewer bytes to be transmitted? The controller will add *pad* bytes to bring the overall frame size up to the minimum length of 64 bytes. The undersized frames are called *runts*. If a runt gets onto the cable, the interface cards will accept the frame and determine that it is too short, thus, discarding it immediately.

Why is there a minimum length? The minimum frame length and the capability to detect collisions interact. Each medium supported by the Ethernet standard has a defined maximum length for any one segment.

One factor that goes into determining that length is the need to ensure that a device transmitting a frame onto the segment will still be listening if a collision occurs and will recognize that the collision happened to its own transmitted frame. Devices stop listening for their own collisions a very short time after they finish transmitting. Therefore, once a device begins transmitting, it must continue to do so long enough for the most distant device to receive at least the beginning of the frame, plus the time required to receive a jam signal from that distant device if such an event occurs.

If the minimum frame size were smaller, then the defined maximum segment sizes would also have to be shorter. To enable longer-than-specified segment lengths, the minimum frame size would have to be increased, requiring additional pad characters and reducing the efficiency of the Ethernet protocol. The 64-byte minimum cannot be claimed to be ideal; rather, it is an engineering judgment call by the original designers of the Ethernet protocol. If installers adhere to the rules regarding segment lengths, no undetected collisions can occur.

Data

This is the frame's payload, the reason the frame is being transmitted in the first place. The data can be up to 1,500 bytes, although it does not have to be arranged in 8-bit octets (bytes); actually, it can be any pattern of up to 12,000 bits (that is, $8 \times 1,500$). In most cases, the actual number of application-related bytes carried will be smaller than this because some of the 1,500 bytes will be used by higher-level protocols for their overhead bytes, sometimes many more per frame than are required by Ethernet itself. The average size Ethernet frame is judged to be between 300 and 350 bytes. If a frame exceeds the maximum length of 1,518 bytes (1,500 payload and 18 overhead), the frame is considered a giant. Giants will also be discarded by the receiving interfaces.

CRC

The *cyclic redundancy check* (CRC) digits enable the receiving node's Ethernet interface to determine whether a frame was received intact or not. If not, the frame is discarded. If the interface is one of the more expensive available, it might also keep track of the number of frames discarded in order to facilitate management and detection of network faults. Error checking was covered earlier in this book.

Components

Speaking generally, the components used to implement a LAN tend to be similar across implementations; an interface must be built into (or added to) each node. Each node must have driver software installed that communicates between the node's (network) operating system software and the interface, and the interface must be connected to the network medium. However, when one delves a little deeper, significant differences appear among LAN architectures and even among variations in the same LAN architecture, such as Ethernet.

For example, Ethernet is probably supported over more different types of media (with truly standard implementations) than any other LAN protocol. The detailed piece parts, as well as design considerations, vary greatly depending on the specific medium.

The rest of this chapter covers the various components that can be used to build an Ethernet. We also mix in some design information and rules. Before getting down into the details, though, we would like to indicate what happens to people who violate the rules. Actually, most organizations do not have network police. However, many network installers and users wish they did. Generally speaking, two kinds of consequences can result when LAN design rules are violated. The network doesn't work. Obvious, right? What could be worse? What could be worse is the alternative: a network that does work . . . sort of.

The designers of the various LAN standards (not just Ethernet, of course) attempted to specify standards that would result in *robust networks* —networks that could continue to operate in the presence of certain kinds of problems. But, TANSTAAFL—"there ain't no such thing as a free lunch." If a network does have some kind of problem and continues to operate anyway, that operation is usually somewhat degraded. In Ethernet's case, for example, intermittent short circuits appear as collisions to users. No data is lost, but overall performance can be slow. Out-and-out failures are often much easier to diagnose and repair.

10Base5

This is a good time to explain the naming standard used for the various Ethernet substandards. Bear in mind that committees defined these. Each term is made up of three parts. The first part (in this case, 10) indicates that the network runs at 10 Mbps. The second part (Base) indicates that the network is a baseband network (see the 10Broad36 section). The last part (in this case, 5) indicates some physical component of the cabling system. In the case of 10Base5, it indicates that one segment can reach up to 500 meters (1,640 feet) in length. We explain the variations in these terms as we cover each of Ethernet's supported media.

Ethernet was originally defined to operate over a particularly heavy type of coaxial cable, one thicker than most individuals' thumbs. People in the industry often referred to it as orange hose—a particularly apt name because of its usual color. A more conventional term for the 10Base5 medium is thick wire coax or thick wire Ethernet.

10Base5 Piece Parts   As with any LAN, every attached device must have a network interface card (NIC). In the case of thick wire, the NIC has a port called an *attachment unit interface* (AUI), a nine-pin interface designed to connect to a transceiver cable (sometimes also referred to as a drop cable).

The transceiver cable can extend up to 50 meters (164 feet), but usually is much shorter, somewhere between 2 and 10 meters. This cable is not Ethernet cable; it is not coaxial, but rather multipin, similar to RS232 but with fewer wires. The transceiver cable plugs into a transceiver.

Transceivers include the component for a combined transmitter and receiver. Minimum spacing between transceivers on the cable is 2.5 meters (8.2 feet). When using the orange Ethernet cable, black marks appear on the cable to indicate the appropriate spacing between the taps. If you do not adhere to the distance limits, other problems can occur. Ethernet transceivers are also sometimes referred to as taps or sometimes vampire taps.

Vampire tap is most descriptive. Thick-wire Ethernet taps can be attached to the orange hose without interrupting the network. Inserting two sharp points into the cable, one deep enough to reach the core, the other stopping at the braid, does this. (A special tool is usually used to predrill the holes.) The tap clamps onto the cable with the two points sunken into the cable. The design might seem somewhat baroque, but the ability to add or remove devices from an active network was a significant advance in network technology at the time Ethernet was first designed.

Not all networks, not even most other Ethernets, require separate transceivers, so it would be worthwhile to indicate their function at this point. Ethernet transceivers perform several important functions:

- Physical access to the main LAN cable
- Media conversion from coaxial to multistrand cable

■ Electrical protection and isolation in both directions (LAN to NIC and vice versa)

But transceivers are essentially passive devices; the protocol smarts reside in the NICs.

Thick wire is the only Ethernet medium that must be configured as a physical bus. As mentioned earlier, thick wire can be configured in segments up to 500 meters long. Up to three segments can be connected in series using two Ethernet repeaters. If more segments are so connected, the (very small) delays unavoidably introduced by the repeaters might foul up the collision detection part of the protocol.

Up to 100 direct physical attachments can be made to one segment, although far more network devices can be attached through other ways than that. Up to 1,024 network addresses can reside on a segment or set of segments connected by repeaters. As with the other rules, violators of this configuration rule might be punished by undetected collisions.

Barrel connectors are small passive devices used to connect two pieces of coaxial cable to make a longer one. Barrel connectors are not defined parts of the Ethernet standard. They can be used, but the rules for segment lengths simply apply to the aggregate length built up of smaller wire pieces; that is, a 500-meter length can include one or more barrel connectors, but it still is limited to 500 meters.

Terminators are also small, passive devices. However, unlike barrel connectors, terminators are defined Ethernet components and are essential to proper operation of a 10Base5 Ethernet. Every 10Base5 segment must have precisely two terminators installed, one on both ends. One and only one of those terminators must be properly grounded. We used to tell students that this was required to ensure that the bits do not fall out of the wire. But actually, in a matter of speaking, terminators are intended to ensure that the bits do fall out of the wire; improperly terminated coaxial cable ends can reflect transmissions back onto the wire, interfering with themselves and/or later transmissions and generating unnecessary collisions.

Configuration of 10Base5 Parts

Setup Designing 10Base5 networks is relatively simple, but installing them is less so. If only one segment is needed, typical configurations include those shown in Figure 21-1.

Note a few characteristics of the 10Base5 cable layouts:

■ No loop is created; the cable forms a line, however bendy.

Figure 21-1
Typical 10Base5 cable layouts

- The cable is strung in such a way that all parts of the building are within reasonable transceiver cable reach.

- The cable is continuous and is most likely not configured to take advantage of any existing cable troughs. In fact, it is probably placed in the ceiling.

- The 500-meter segment length limitation applies to the length of the cable on the reel; how it is laid out does not affect the length limitation at all.

- Everything that attaches to a 10Base5 cable connects via a transceiver that is clamped to the cable or via something else that is attached via a transceiver. The cable ends never plug into anything but the appropriate terminator.

- If more than one segment is required, the segments connect, as shown in Figure 21-2.

Figure 21-2

Connecting 10Base5
segments

Because of the complexity of the layout, the differences in building designs, and the difficulty in using this thick-wire coax, this has become a throwback in the installation business. No new 10Base5 networks are being installed these days, so we will not go into great detail on their possible layouts. But it is a good idea to expand on the two-repeater rule because it applies (sometimes in modified form) to other Ethernet topologies as well. The rule says, in effect, "Thou shall not configure an Ethernet such that traffic must flow via more than two repeaters to get from any node to any other node." This seems straightforward, but at least one subtlety is not obvious. If two repeaters are configured so that the cable between them has no other drops (not even one), then for purposes of the two-repeater rule, those two repeaters each count as one-half of one repeater. Thus, the two add up to one. An Ethernet can thus have up to four repeaters in series without violating the two-repeater rule. Figure 21-3 illustrates a configuration with three repeaters.

Figure 21-3

Three repeaters
complying with the
two-repeater rule

The two-repeater rule is not as onerous as might be the case. It is possible to configure a 10Base5 network with an almost arbitrarily large number of segments. For example, consider the comb configuration shown in Figure 21-4. No single packet must traverse more than two repeaters to reach anywhere on the network, although seven repeaters are in the configuration. Each segment can still be 500 meters; the opportunity to connect a great many nodes is available with such layout, if necessary. Nodes can be placed on any segment, although in practice, the top segment, which is connected to all seven repeaters, is often designated as a backbone and reserved for repeaters and perhaps network-monitoring equipment. The drawback is that whenever a single frame is sent, it will be sent across every link on the network, causing possible congestion throughout the LAN.

Changes   Changing connections to a 10Base5 network is simple; simply unplug or plug in components as needed, adhering to the configuration rules. No special software configuration is required for new nodes; removed nodes require no closeout procedures to remove them from any tables or anything else. (This simplicity might or might not extend to the upper layers of the protocols used on the Ethernet.)

However, physical access to the main cable itself is required. In an office environment, the main cable is typically strung in the ceiling, with transceiver cables leading to individual offices, so moves and changes can be

Figure 21-4
Comb 10Base5
layout

Repeaters

Figure 21-5
To move a station is very complex. It requires going above the ceiling. The drop behind the wall may not lend itself to removal.

Tap

Cables run on J-hooks

Plenum Space

Electric

Ceiling Line

quite an effort. For this reason and others, 10Base5 is rarely installed anymore. Figure 21-5 shows how accessing the cable and the need to add a drop cable from the ceiling to the device can be problematic.

10Base2

10Base5 wiring is extremely difficult to work with and costly on a per-foot basis. With improving technology, companies determined that by applying some engineering smarts, they could design a new Ethernet standard (still 802.3) for use on a much lighter, flexible, and less expensive type of coaxial cable. 10Base2, also often referred to as thin wire or cheapernet, is specified to run on RG-58A coaxial cable. This cable is almost identical to cable that you probably have running into your home for cable television. However, the configuration of 10Base5 and that of 10Base2 have quite a number of differences.

10Base2 Piece Parts As with the other 802.3 media, 10Base2 requires a network interface card (NIC) in each node. However, the NIC is much smarter and the tap is much simpler (and less expensive) than in a 10Base5 configuration. Also, no transceiver cable is required or even allowed; instead, the tap, called a *T connector*, plugs right into the back of the NIC. The T connector splits the signal on the cable, enabling it to continue on and also sending a copy directly into the connector on the NIC—a coax connector of the same type as on the other two sides of the T connector. A T connector looks something like the example shown in Figure 21-6.

T connectors have advantages and disadvantages compared to transceivers. They are far less expensive, about one-tenth the cost. They can be added or removed from a 10Base2 daisy chain in seconds, much more quickly than a 10Base5 transceiver. However, unlike with 10Base5, T connectors are inserted in line in the coaxial cable; if a T connector is to be added or removed, the entire cable will be down for a few seconds while the change is being made. This is true even if the T connector is being added to the end of the cable. Once a T connector is added to the cable, unplugging it from or plugging it into its attached node does not disrupt the cable so long as the T connector itself remains in the cable. For this reason, many installations preconfigure many T connectors in each daisy chain to avoid later disruption.

The minimum distance between T connectors is 0.5 meters (1.6 feet). One 10Base2 segment can be up to 185 meters (607 feet) long, much shorter than a 10Base5 segment. As with 10Base5, every segment must end with a terminator, in this case one designed for 10Base2. As you can see in the next section, how the coax is terminated and how it is laid out are different when compared with 10Base5.

Figure 21-6
The 10Base2 T connector

Configuration of 10Base2 Parts

Setup   10Base2 is supported in two different kinds of configurations and is also often used in a third configuration not originally envisioned in the specification. The three configurations can briefly be summarized as follows:

- Star with daisy chains
- Pure star configuration
- Daisy chain bus

The original specification for 10Base2 was a star configuration, with each radiating spoke as a daisy chain bus. Such a configuration might look like the example in Figure 21-7.

A *multiport repeater* (MPR) takes every signal it receives on one daisy chain and sends it out over all of the other daisy chains to which it is connected. Up to 27 T connectors (some vendors support up to 30) can be installed on each daisy chain; the number of ports on the MPR limits the number of daisy chains. The last T connector on each daisy chain must have a terminator on one side. The MPR is an active device; it plugs into AC power. As such, it is grounded through its power cord and therefore provides an electrical ground for each attached segment. Thus, no separate ground is

Figure 21-7
10Base2 using a
multiport repeater

required (or indeed allowed) for the individual segments. Note that each daisy chain is plugged directly into a port on the MPR; the cable end at the MPR does not require a T connector.

This MPR configuration of daisy chains is very cost-effective compared to 10Base5. However, wiring and maintaining it is rather onerous. Until the last few years, using this approach for wall-plate installations (vs. just running the cable along the floor) was very difficult and often subject to frequent outages as individuals interrupted connections, disrupting the entire daisy chain. More recently, special wall plates have come onto the market that simplify such wiring; however, they are quite expensive. 10Base2 installations can also use a pure star configuration, as shown in Figure 21-8.

With only one T connector (and therefore only one Ethernet node) per cable, the per-port cost of a 10Base2 pure star is much higher than the daisy chain approach; the cost of the MPR itself is spread across far fewer devices than with the previous configuration. Nonetheless, the star has two major advantages over both the daisy chain and 10Base5:

■ Because it is no longer a physical bus (although it is still a logical bus), it can use the physical communications paths installed in buildings for

Figure 21-8
10Base2 pure star

the purposes of telephone wiring because telephone wiring is also star configured.

■ Because each node is on its own cable, cable faults generally do not affect other nodes through the MPR.

Vendors officially support both of the two previous 10Base2 configurations. However, vendors do not support the following configuration. The pure daisy chain bus (Figure 21-9), without use of any repeater, was not contemplated by the specifiers of the 10Base2 standard (perhaps because the opportunity to sell equipment to implement it is minimal). The biggest problem with it is that, although every Ethernet segment is supposed to be grounded, daisy chains without repeaters usually are not grounded in practice.

Because such networks are by definition very small (not to exceed 30 T connectors), the problems brought on by grounding them improperly usually do not cause major interruptions. Certainly, this is probably the least expensive type of Ethernet configuration on a per-port basis that supports more than two nodes. All of the cabling components together (except the NICs and software) can be assembled for about $10 to $25 per Ethernet node total in most cases.

Changes   Removing a node from any 10Base2 network is simple; just unplug the T connector from the back of the NIC, leaving the T connector in the cable. Adding a node to either of the daisy chain configurations is more difficult. If dealing with preterminated coaxial cable lengths, adding a node requires at least one additional cable length and a T connector.

The problem is not so much acquiring the materials as it is getting at the portion of cable to which the new cable length is to be added. In addition, unless the new connectors are used (and these must be preinstalled), the entire daisy chain is down until the new T connector is inserted and connected.

The pure star approach is typically precabled to every work location, like normal telephone wiring. With the appropriate use of patch panels at a central location, moves and changes in such an environment are easier than

Figure 21-9
10Base2 daisy chain
bus without repeater

moving telephones. (Normally, telephone moves involve telephone number changes; Ethernet moves require only connecting the new location up to any active MPR port.) Locations not requiring Ethernet connectivity do not have their coaxial cable runs connected to an active MPR port. If 10Base-T wiring had not been invented, the 10Base2 approach might have become much more popular.

10Base-T

10Base-T defines a standard for running Ethernet over unshielded twisted pair (UTP) wiring. The prospect of using existing, in-place (but unused) telephone wiring provided much of the impetus for the development of this standard. Many organizations had already been using some of the existing wiring in their buildings after the breakup of the Bell System in 1984. What actually happened was that Bell came along and told users that the in-house (station) wiring was theirs. Bell would no longer be in the in-house wiring business and would not maintain the wires as they had in the past. Realizing that the number of wires in the building just for the telephone systems was extraordinary[2] and that installing new wiring was expensive, many organizations saw the opportunity to use the existing spare telephone wires to run their higher-speed LAN connections. However, in practice, little of the wiring that was in place (when the standard came out) could meet Ethernet performance requirements. Even if these wires could meet the standards, the vendors required that they be certified. This meant that the vendor would send in a team of wiring experts who would test and certify each cable run. In reality, it was more expensive to certify the existing wiring than to install all new wires. This proved to be a catch-22 for the end user.

Nonetheless, the much lower wiring cost of 10Base-T (primarily because of the lower cost of telephone wiring as opposed to coaxial cable), as well as the availability of people who know how to work with UTP wiring, has made this cabling approach extremely popular. The vast majority of new installations today use 10Base-T for horizontal (that is, to the desktop) wiring.

---

[2] Back then, Bell used to install a 25-pair cable to every desktop, even if only a single pair was needed. This enabled them to avoid having to rewire when a phone was changed or moved.

The possibility of running Ethernet over UTP excited many companies before the actual standard was developed. Several vendors, including Synoptics,[3] DEC, and others came out with Ethernet-over-UTP variants before the 10Base-T standard was finalized. These variants worked, but naturally, it was impossible to intermix components from these vendors to build an Ethernet-over-UTP configuration. Most of the vendors did, however, have the integrity to guarantee free conversion, or at least plausible migration paths, from their proprietary hardware to hardware compliant with the 10Base-T standard when the latter became available.

This promise does not mean, of course, that all customers bothered to take advantage of such upgrades when they became available. You might find yourself dealing with an existing UTP-based Ethernet installation with which you have had no previous involvement. If so, we suggest you verify that the hardware is indeed 10Base-T compliant rather than an older proprietary variant before blithely assuming that added 10Base-T hardware will integrate properly.

10Base-T Piece Parts 10Base-T NICs are functionally similar to 10Base2 NICs. That is, no separate transceiver is required as with a 10Base5 architecture. The connections are quite different, however. Ethernet UTP wire is terminated at each end with an eight-pin modular RJ-45 jack (only four pins are used). The modular jack plugs directly into the NIC; no T connector is required. Each cable supports only one Ethernet node, as with the pure star thin net approach. See Figure 21-10 for a representation of the 10Base-T environment. At least category 3 wire must be used (see Chapter 43 for more information on categories of UTP wire). Its length must not exceed 100 meters (328 feet).

A 10Base-T hub (sometimes also called a concentrator) is usually required. This is another version of the LAN in a box. The box or hub is the backbone network, whereas the horizontal run to the desktop is the drop. The only exception is if only two devices are to be connected; two 10Base-T devices can be linked via a crossover 10Base-T cable. 10Base-T hubs are functionally identical to multiport repeaters, although some vendors provide sufficiently fast central hubs that the two-repeater rule can be slightly relaxed.

---

[3] Synoptics later merged with Wellfleet (a router manufacturer), creating Bay Networks. Bay was acquired by Nortel in 1998.

Figure 21-10
The 10Base-T
connection

10Base-T hubs (and, to a large extent, other hubs as well) come in two broad categories:

- Work group hubs, sometimes referred to as stackable hubs
- Backplane chassis, sometimes referred to as concentrators

Work group hubs are relatively inexpensive (as low as $200 to $300) devices that typically support 12 or 16 connections. If they incorporate Simple Network Management Protocol (SNMP) management agents, the cost increases by several hundred dollars. Work group hubs, by definition, have very few options in their configurations. Nevertheless, their low cost and simple environmental requirements (they can be mounted in a rack or simply placed on a table or on the floor) make them extremely popular.

Chassis-based concentrators offer great modular flexibility. Such devices consist of a power supply, some control logic, and several slots into which interface boards can be inserted. Each interface board can support several 10Base-T cables, often 12. Depending on the manufacturer, other boards might be available to support different types of networks out of the same chassis. Those other network types (for example, token ring) might be interconnected to the Ethernet board either via an additional interface board just for that purpose or via an external device not inserted into the chassis.

10Base-F (Fiber)

Newer uses of various cabling systems have always been explored. The fiber-optic medium has caught everyone's attention because of the declining costs of the glass and the electrical characteristics (that is, the freedom from electrical and radio frequency interference and the isolation from electrical components being nonissues) of the fiber. When users discovered that the fiber could be used inexpensively in the backbone network, they were thrilled. If they could use a high-speed medium that was impervious to the electrical, mechanical, and radio frequency interference, then the network could be stretched to areas that were previously unavailable. Furthermore, none of the grounding and bonding issues that come with copper cable were issues on the fiber network. When the Ethernet standard ramped up to higher speeds (100-Mbps Ethernet, for example), the fiber would support these higher speeds with ease. Thus, the backbone saw more implementations with the 10Base-F installed.

The 10-Mbps standard was still used in the backbone network, but UTP wiring was still the least expensive proposition for wiring to the desktop. Therefore, a medium changer is required. In the closets where the LAN will run from floor to floor or from closet to closet, fiber is used. At the hub, ports exist for the connection from hub to hub via the fiber backbone. Inside the hub, the electronics are present to convert the fiber backbone to a copper station drop, or, in more precise terms, from the light to the electrical pulses needed for the copper. Figure 21-11 shows a typical configuration of the 10Base-F environment. This could be extended to the desktop, but, as already stated, the cost of putting fiber cards acting as transceivers in a PC or workstation is too steep for the average user. Therefore, this is done in a mixed environment.

10Broad36

Some networks have been built based on a broadband coaxial cable in the backbone. This might be more prevalent in a campus area (such as a college, corporate park, or hospital) where multiple buildings are interlinked. The use of the broadband cable was an expedient to support the needs of the organization's voice, data, and video needs because all of these components were analog transmissions that were connected between buildings. Therefore, the broadband backbone cable (such as a CATV cable) was used when the Ethernet was introduced. Customers who needed to link multiple buildings together were constrained by the 500-meter distance limitations of the Ethernet baseband coax. Even with the two-repeater rule, the most that the cable could be extended was 1,500 meters, just under a mile. Although this might sound like a lot of cable, which should reach just about anywhere, the one mile of cable gets used very quickly when it needs to be snaked through ceilings, up and down from the ceiling heights, and so on.

Figure 21-11

The 10BaseF uses fiber in the backbone, but converts to copper to the desk.

Therefore, the existing broadband cable offered a significant distance increase to Ethernet users who had to exceed the distance allowances. Using a 10-Mbps transmission speed on a broadband cable, the distance limitations were increased to 3,600 meters. This is a sevenfold increase in the distances over which the cable could be run. So the vendors came up with a solution to the distance and the medium needs for the end user. Broadband cable inherently is an analog transmission system. Special devices called frequency agile modems (FAMs) were attached to the cable to modulate the electrical signal onto the carrier. The cable is normally broken down into various channels of 6 MHz each. Using a bridging arrangement, two channels could be connected together as a 12-MHz channel and used to transmit 10-Mbps Ethernet on this coax. This created more flexibility in overall networking ability because the Ethernet, as stated in the beginning of this chapter, has been implemented in a variety of media.

Digital Equipment Corporation (DEC) was a supporter of this form of connectivity in their DECNet on Ethernet from the onset. Others also came up with the necessary piece parts to use the broadband cable systems for the 10-Mbps Ethernet standards. This has also been accepted as a connection under the IEEE standards committee. See Figure 21-12 for a cable using the broadband Ethernet connection.

An innovation from a spin-off of DEC called LANCity, Inc. has produced a device or a concentrator called *channel works* that enables direct connection to a CATV operator's cable system to deliver 10-Mbps Ethernet connectivity across the cable. In this regard, the channel works product is supposed to be able to garner up to 83 separate Ethernets on a single cable. The primary application has been to link multiple buildings in a metropolitan area network (MAN) for government, schools, universities, and hospitals that have multiple buildings all across town. This has been a pretty well-accepted innovation in many communities. LANCity was later acquired by Bay Networks, which in turn was acquired by Nortel in 1998. One of the most widely used CATV interfaces for the cable companies as they roll out Internet access is through the use of these channel works boxes. Now a new cable modem standard to bridge a PC onto a CATV and access the Internet is becoming very popular.

Fast Ethernet

Why Do We Need Fast Ethernet?   As described elsewhere, the uses of local area networks have changed over the years. Whereas in the past the

Figure 21-12
A broadband (CATV)
application using 10
Mbits/s on coax

primary use was for movement of files and access to data by applications, a frequent use of local area networks now is to load applications from servers. Also, the character of those applications has changed. The executables themselves have moved into the multiple megabyte range, and in some cases, graphic files are also now in the millions of bits. This means that faster networks are needed. Another factor driving the need for speed is larger, higher-resolution monitors. A modern 1,024 × 768 monitor displays slightly over 1 million bits for one screen's worth of information. That would require, ideally, slightly more than one-tenth of a second to traverse an Ethernet. In practice, it would take considerably longer. One-tenth of a second may not sound like a great deal, but on a small network of 10 users, a whole second might be eaten up just by the one screen to each user. In practice, it would be worse because contention would slow things down.

Some applications are considerably worse than this. Large, high-resolution graphics files make some environments entirely unsupportable by a standard Ethernet. For example, the size of a single digitized magazine cover can approach 70 megabytes. Bottom line: we need more speed.

The culture of the workforce has also changed considerably. The days of just typing ASCII text characters on a screen have gone. With Internet and Intranet access, the user now does more information processing. Moreover, that information is represented through a GUI, in which the graphics interfaces are denser. The amount of data traveling across our networks is rapidly becoming exponential. The 10-Mbps Ethernet was pushed aside in favor of the 100-Mbps Ethernet. Some organizations have moved to a 10-Mbps switched Ethernet as a means of forestalling the change of all the NIC cards in the PCs. This makes sense, but only begs for the actual upgrade later. Now newer switches and hubs are auto-detecting where a mix of 10- and 100-Mbps Ethernet NIC cards can be used on the same network. This complicates the issue slightly, but also gains time for the changes that are inevitable.

Many computer manufacturers are now installing 10- to 100-Mbps Ethernet cards directly in the PCs when they are made. This saves the LAN administrator from having to buy the cards separately. A minor issue is associated with the manufacturers installing these cards. Not all NIC cards are created equal. Many are made with special features and functions not available to others. Therefore, some conflict could occur on the LAN when these mixed variations are all on the same network. The other problem is that the computer manufacturers who install the NICs usually require special drivers for their machine. Thus, a user must be aware that differences will arise and the price we pay for free LAN cards is the added burden of keeping on top of the myriad protocols and drivers required.

As the convergence of voice and data caught on in the industry during the late 1990s, the move is to incorporate voice, data, and streaming video at the desktop on the LAN. Given the limits of the 10-Mbps Ethernet with the specifications discussed earlier, the movement to 100 Mbps was escalated.

The term Fast Ethernet is primarily used today to refer to a technology described as 100Base-T. In 1996, when the technology was introduced, Fast Ethernet actually referred to several technologies. This creates some confusion. One of the technologies was switched Ethernet. Switched Ethernet is described in another chapter, but generally speaking, Fast Ethernet no longer refers to switched 10-Mbps Ethernet. Likewise, full-duplex Ethernet, at least the full-duplex variation of 10Base-T, is no longer referred to as Fast Ethernet. Just as with 1,200-bps modems, which once were described as high-speed, the advent of better technologies has resulted in changing the terminology used to describe the older technologies.

Only two technologies really deserve the name Fast Ethernet. Of the two, the vast majority of analysts have declared 100Base-T the winner. The other is 100VGAnyLAN. We'll discuss both technologies in this chapter, but make no mistake; 100VGAnyLAN is dead. We'll also briefly describe Gigabit Ethernet, a technology that was standardized in 1998.

100Base-T   When developers were trying to determine what the successor to Ethernet should be, they had two basic choices: try to stick to the basic technology as closely as possible, just increasing its speed, or try to make fundamental improvements to solve flaws that had become more obvious over time. Two camps developed, one taking each approach. The winning camp is the one that took the first approach. Their product was 100Base-T. The good news about 100Base-T is that the frame size and characteristics are identical to those in standard Ethernet. It uses CSMA/CD and in general can be understood and managed by network administrators and software in the same way that 100Base-T could be managed. The bad news is that collisions still occur, and the product still taps out at considerably less than the nominal 100 Mbps that it is supposed to be able to handle. One might describe it as *Ethernet on steroids*. The actual throughput on a 100Base-T is about 33 to 40 Mbps if using a hub and about 60 Mbps if using an Ethernet switch.

It is, however, the most popular replacement for standard Ethernet by far. This is due largely to good marketing, but something should definitely be said for not having to do major retraining of your network administrators and technicians. In 1998, 50 percent of all new LANs installed were at the 100-Mbps rate. In 1999, that number jumped to almost 67 percent. This varied between the shared bus concept in a hub and the switched version using a switch. Regardless, the costs, although higher than 10-Mbps NICs, are sufficiently attractive to merit the installation regardless of whether the speed is needed at the desktop today.

Like the original Ethernet, 100Base-T supports several media. Notably absent from this list is coaxial cable. Both standard copper wiring and fiber are supported. As with all high-speed technologies, the copper implementation has severe distance limitations. Most of the high-speed technologies do not support end devices more than 100 meters away from their central electronics locations; Fast Ethernet is no exception.

Fast Ethernet can be handled on three variations of copper wire. The first is category 3 UTP (unshielded twisted pair). If you are going to use category 3, however, you must use four pairs of twisted-pair wiring. This is an extremely unpopular option. It is not difficult to see why. Although many installations have some copper wiring available, it is extremely unusual to have four pairs that are unused. If one is going to have to put in new wiring, there is no reason to put in anything less capable than category 5. In addition, Fast Ethernet on category 3 only supports half-duplex operation. If Fast Ethernet is used in half-duplex mode on four pairs of either category 3 or category 5 wiring, it is described as 100Base-T4.

The second copper variation supported is category 5 UTP. In the case of category 5, Fast Ethernet can operate in either half or full duplex on two pairs of wire rather than the four required for category 3. Operating on two pairs, Fast Ethernet is referred to as 100Base-TX. This is by far the most popular implementation of Fast Ethernet.

The third variation supported on copper for Fast Ethernet is shielded twisted pair (STP). Generally speaking, STP should only be installed in special cases where the potential interference either to or from the network is an issue. STP is much more difficult to install, with more demanding grounding requirements than UTP. It doesn't increase speed, nor does it improve usage of the pairs in the cable. As far as network performance is concerned, it works the same as on UTP.

In addition to copper wiring, 100Base-T is supported on fiber. As with category 5, fiber supports both half- and full-duplex operations. Why might you use fiber? It doesn't improve the speed. The reason is fiber's general superiority over copper, as described elsewhere in this book. In the case of Fast Ethernet, the main reason to use fiber would be to extend the available distances. Fast Ethernet over copper, as mentioned earlier, only reaches 100 meters to the desktop. A more severe limitation is that distances between copper-connected Fast Ethernet hubs must not exceed 5 meters (Figure 21-13). The use of fiber considerably relaxes these limitations.

As with standard Ethernet, the way the wiring (either copper or fiber) can be used varies. Buyers must select among shared, switched, and/or full-duplex use of the media and obtain the right electronics to install at both ends of the cable. The default is shared half duplex. One should be aware that just as in standard Ethernet, the contention experienced with a shared half-duplex configuration means that in no case, except a two-user network, will you be able to count on actually getting anywhere near the 100-Mbps nominal performance of a Fast Ethernet. However, that should not usually be a major problem. Just as with standard Ethernet, medium or even large work groups can be set up that still get a significant performance improvement over standard Ethernet by using shared half-duplex Fast Ethernet.

Figure 21-13
Copper-connected
Fast Ethernet hubs
have to be close!

Fast Ethernet Hub

If copper
5 meters maximum

Fast Ethernet Hub

If what you're doing is building a backbone, you probably want to use switched full-duplex Fast Ethernet. This will deliver close to the rated 100-Mbit performance to each node, and it costs considerably less than the available alternatives (FDDI and ATM are the ones that come to mind). Note that for anything but shared half duplex, one must use either category 5 UTP or fiber cabling. Naturally, the cost of the electronics involved to deliver switched or full duplex is considerably more than that for shared half duplex—in fact, three to five times the cost of the less expensive approach.

Changing your network over to Fast Ethernet has been made much easier than it might have been by clever manufacturers that have addressed the problem. Because all Fast Ethernet implementations are based on either copper or fiber, the cabling is done in a star or radial configuration; no physical bus topologies need apply. This means that in theory and in practice, each node can be upgraded individually. The manufacturers build the central electronics (hubs, switches, and so on) with the capability, in most cases, to handle either 10- or 100-Mbps Ethernet on a port-by-port basis. This means that better electronics can be swapped at the central location, the network can be brought back up, and one-by-one, individual users' machines can be upgraded (Figure 21-14).

Better than this, however, is the advent of dual-speed NICs. Several manufacturers make NICs that operate at both 10 and 100 Mbps. These are

Figure 21-14
Implementing Fast
Ethernet — 10/100
hub

described as 10/100 cards. But any given computer can run at only one speed at a time—why do we need the dual speed? Most environments upgrade individual computers in groups; it is rare to replace all of the computers in an environment at one time. Often, they are replaced one at a time, as users' needs change. With 10/100 cards, a company can make a long-term decision to move toward 100Base-T without having to upgrade all the central hubs. The company can upgrade the desktops and then upgrade the hubs as it makes sense to do so. In most cases, the 10/100 cards automatically sense the speed of the connected wire (that is, of the central electronics port) at the time the PC is booted.

A changeover plan could be developed in one of two ways. One plan would be to replace all of the NICs in desktops over time with 10/100 cards. These cards are not significantly more expensive than standard Ethernet cards. Once all of the cards are replaced, then replace the central electronics with 100Base-T switches and hubs, reboot all the desktops, and you are done. The second approach would be to replace the central electronics with switches and hubs with units that have 10/100 ports. These are more costly, but give a degree of flexibility that isn't available in the first scenario; not all desktops have to be upgraded either. Once the central electronics are all upgraded, one can begin upgrading the desktops. In a pinch, some desktops can be upgraded in parallel, although this complicates the management efforts.

100Base-T Performance Expectations The most obvious alternative to implementing 100Base-T is switched 10Base-T Ethernet. Surprisingly, the latter may, under some circumstances, deliver better performance than shared 100Base-T. One may think that this is an unfair comparison; however, the costs are similar, whereas the cost of switched 100Base-T is probably much too high for desktop use in most cases. So we will consider switched 10Base-T and shared 100Base-T as alternatives.

It all boils down to the numbers. In an environment with small work-groups (fewer than 20), shared 100Base-T will probably deliver much better performance to the desktop than shared Ethernet could. Why? With 100Base-T, each user will average at most 5 Mbits of capacity on the hub if all are active simultaneously. But in most real-world scenarios, not all users are truly simultaneously active. In the typical case, fewer than 10 percent of the users are doing anything on the network at any given instant. Ten percent of 20 people is two people. These two active users, in most cases, would share 100 Mbps of capacity, or 50 Mbps each, which is obviously better than switched Ethernet's delivery of 10 Mbps at best to each user. However, let's cook the numbers a little differently. If 100 users are on a switched Ethernet segment, each will still get 10 Mbps delivered to the desktop all the time. Fast Ethernet at 100 Mbps, in the worst case, will deliver only 1 Mbps to the desktop. If 10 percent of users are active at a time, then each will get about 10 Mbps. In practice, contention on the 100-Mbps hub will reduce that by 20 to 30 percent. In this case, switched Ethernet might be a better choice than the Fast Ethernet.

A major decision factor is the type of work the users are doing. If each is doing network-intensive activities on a continuing basis that can be satisfied by a 10-Mbps pipe, switched Ethernet is probably the technology of choice. On the other hand, if the user population makes sporadic use of the network, but each use tends to benefit from a truly high bandwidth (editing large graphic files is an application that comes to mind), then 100 Mbps (or higher) would definitely be the better choice because each user would experience close to the maximum capacity when needed, if it's only lightly used.

100VGAnyLAN Back before 100Base-T had established its market share, a group of technically oriented companies including Hewlett-Packard felt that the second approach to upgrading Ethernet—improving its flaws as opposed to just increasing its speed—was the better approach. The result of their efforts was 100VGAnyLAN. This technology, like the Betamax VCR, is clearly superior to its competitor (100Base-T). Unfortunately, as with the Betamax, it didn't win over the market. One can still buy 100VGAnyLAN products; however, the system is regarded by most as an also-ran.

100VGAnyLAN had much to recommend it. Its designers chose to eliminate the CSMA/CD method of allocating capacity. Instead, it uses what is called a demand-priority allocation scheme, where each NIC notifies its corresponding hub that it has something to send. The hub pays attention to these notifications and solicits the input once notified. It is also possible to designate high-priority traffic, such as video, enabling a better pattern of performance for such traffic in this technology.

100VGAnyLAN also had the capability to support either Ethernet or token ring traffic. This traffic cannot be on the same hub, but one can use the same kind of hubs for both, significantly reducing the complexity of a LAN implementation environment. The rules for cascading 100VG hubs are no more restrictive than those for standard Ethernet and considerably more flexible than those for 100Base-T. As with 100Base-T, the cable running out to the workstations can be 100 meters long; however, the distance between hubs also can be 100 meters, 20 times the limitation of 100Base-T.

100VGAnyLAN has some disadvantages, partially explaining its failure in the marketplace. For one thing, its initial specification required four pairs of unshielded twisted pair wiring, no matter which category was being used. Another disadvantage is more political than technological. Since the beginning, Ethernet has used CSMA/CD as its media allocation scheme, 100VGAnyLAN does not. It uses demand priority. In fact, this is an advantage; however, purists in the Ethernet camp have attacked 100VGAnyLAN on this basis. It is a poor reason not to use the technology; however, enough advocates of Ethernet went the other way because of this that it seriously and adversely affected 100VGAnyLAN's market share. Very few vendors subscribed to the 100VGAnyLAN technological specification. At this point, it is really only enthusiastically supported by Hewlett-Packard, and even HP has moved on to support 100BaseT.

Gigabit Ethernet Although we do not know of anyone who alleges that full-duplex switched 100Base-T is insufficient to handle any likely desktop requirement, if one puts together enough high-speed desktop LANs, the backbone to serve them needs to be a better technology than that desktop LAN technology, whatever it is. Moreover, if the use of voice, data, video, and multimedia finally becomes a reality on a single architecture, then the need for more than 100 Mbps to the desk may become a reality. Gigabit Ethernet was developed with the goal of providing these applications to the individual user in the future. In 1998, products were introduced before the standards had been adopted. As with many new technologies, some vendors came out with products early and promised to change or upgrade those products, at no cost to the initial implementers, to whatever the standard becomes. This allowed the vendors to get a leap on the market and assure their market share before others could get there. So the question is, when would you use Gigabit Ethernet and when would you not?

Like 100Base-T, Gigabit Ethernet comes in half- and full-duplex variations. In its half-duplex implementation, it has some very severe limitations regarding delivery of actual capacity. An interaction occurs in all Ethernets between minimum packet size and size in terms of radius of the actual maximum network configuration. The smaller the minimum frame size, the smaller the maximum radius of the network. This relationship is compounded in a bad way by increasing the speed of the network transmission. Because the goal in upgrading to a faster variety of Ethernet is to keep the same frame size limitations, the radius of the Gigabit Ethernet without using a special technique is limited to about 20 meters, which is obviously impractical. The designers implemented a special technique that involves transmission of a special signal in any case where a frame smaller than 512 bytes is transmitted on a Gigabit Ethernet. This means that for large frames (those associated with large file transfers), Gigabit Ethernet might actually deliver close to its full speed. However, many networks being used by human beings as opposed to machines generate a large number of small frames averaging only 300 to 350 bytes. In the worst case, such a network, even if implemented on Gigabit Ethernet, would experience performance a little better than that delivered by 100Base-T in its full-duplex incarnation. The technique creates a 200-meter network diameter. This limitation means that any network implementer needs to seriously analyze what kind of traffic is going to be carried by that network and evaluate the likely bandwidth to actually be delivered by Gigabit Ethernet.

Gigabit Ethernet also did not provide quality of service (QoS) guarantees, although the proponents of Gigabit Ethernet are working to provide QoS-like services. This means that even though its nominal speed is very high, it still is not an ideal technology for satisfying isochronous type traffic (such as video). The new standards for the 802.3Q are designed to handle QoS features for Gigabit Ethernet.

If one implements full-duplex Gigabit Ethernet, the issue regarding distance pretty much disappears. Gigabit Ethernet requires the use of fiber. Two kinds of fiber are available: multimode and single mode. Multimode should be able to reach up to about 550 meters, whereas single mode should be able to reach distances approaching 3 kilometers.

One other caution: Most of the Intel-based servers in service are generally incapable of accepting or transmitting information at speeds significantly greater than those that can be provided by 100Base-T. Thus, hooking a server directly to a Gigabit pipe would not necessarily deliver improved performance over Fast Ethernet. Higher-end UNIX servers can deliver performance two to four times the above, but even they cannot yet receive or transmit information at true Gigabit speeds. Backbone components (routers, and so on) also are just now coming on the market that can handle speeds in this range. Therefore, simply buying Gigabit devices and dropping them into the network is not likely to be a successful strategy.

Gigabit Ethernet does promise to be a less expensive technology than ATM. In cases where backbones can be successfully implemented with Gigabit Ethernet, it may be more cost-effective. However, ATM is available at speed ranges that are at least competitive with Gigabit Ethernet. With the additional capabilities of ATM and its large (carrier-based) installed base, ATM is probably the preferred technology for high-capacity backbones at least for the next couple of years.

Just when we thought it was safe to come out of the LAN closets and use the technologies, with the knowledge that Gigabit Ethernet is coming along to deal with bandwidth issues, the next in a series of evolutionary steps emerged. Now the talk is focused on 10-Gigabit Ethernet. Nortel Networks announced their strategy in 1999 with the use of 10-Gbps Ethernet over Synchronous Optical network (SONET) OC-192-based networks. The 10-Gigabit Ethernet standards are still emerging, so many vendors are coming out with their own proprietary solutions to satisfy this demand. Once again, this places the buyer at risk when the standards finally get approved sometime in 2003-2004.

This 10-Gigabit strategy also points out that the end user may not need this speed yet, but the carriers (telcos, ISPs, and new providers) will be looking for this throughput. If a carrier chooses to offer 1 Gbps to a consumer (large organization), then the 10 Gbps is necessary for the provider to guarantee the QoS and the effective data rates. This is particularly true when serving the ISPs and Internet Telephony Service Providers (ITSPs). Through the use of Metro Area Networks running on SONET standards and using Dense Wave-Division Multiplexing (DWDM) on the fiber systems, the carriers will be delivering 1-2-54 or 10 Gbps Ethernet.

Virtual LANs

In a traditional shared media network, traffic generated by a station is propagated to all other stations on the local segment. For a given station on shared Ethernet, the local segment is the collision domain because traffic on the segment has the potential to cause an Ethernet collision. The local segment is also the broadcast domain because any broadcast is sent to all stations on the local segment.

Ethernet bridges and switches divide a network into smaller collision domains, but they do not affect the broadcast domain. In simple terms, a *virtual local area network* (VLAN) can be thought of as a mechanism to fine-tune broadcast domains.

A VLAN is a collection of switch ports that make up a single broadcast domain. A VLAN can be defined for a single switch, or it can span multiple switches. VLANs are logical entities created in the software configuration to control traffic flow. Membership in workgroup segments can be determined logically instead of by user location, and moves, adds, and changes can be easily configured as the network evolves.

IEEE 802.11 Wireless LANs

The IEEE 802.11 standard defines the physical layer and media access control (MAC) layer for a wireless local area network (WLAN). The standard defines three different physical layers for the 802.11 WLAN, each operating in a different frequency range and at rates of 1 Mbps and 2 Mbps. In this section, we focus on the architecture of 802.11 LANs and their media access protocols. We'll see that although it belongs to the same standard family as Ethernet, it has a significantly different architecture and media access protocol. The IEEE 802.11 represents the first standard for WLAN products from an internationally recognized, independent organization. The IEEE manages most of the standards for wired LANs. We saw the standards at work when we reviewed the Ethernet (802.3) and the Token Ring (802.5). The WLAN standard (802.11) represents an important milestone in WLAN systems because customers can now have multiple sources for the components of their WLAN systems. Some applications are still available where the existing proprietary data communications are a good fit because they may optimize some aspect of the network performance. However, 802.11 compliant products expand the users' options.

802.11 LAN Architecture The principal components of the 802.11 WLAN architecture are shown in any architectural drawing. The fundamental building block of the 802.11 architecture is the cell, known as the *basic service set* (BSS) in 802.11 parlance. A BSS typically contains one or more wireless stations and a central base station, known as an *access point*

(AP) in 802.11 terminology. The stations, either fixed or mobile, and the central base station communicate among themselves using the IEEE 802.11 wireless MAC protocol. Multiple access points may be connected together (using a wired Ethernet or another wireless channel) to form a so-called *distribution system* (DS). The DS appears to upper-level protocols (such as, IP) as a single 802 network, in much the same way that a bridged, wired 802.3 Ethernet network appears as a single 802 network to the upper-layer protocols.

How It Will Be Used in End Applications?   The IEEE 802.11 standard defines the protocol for two types of networks: ad hoc and client/server networks.

- An *ad hoc network* is a simple network where communications are established between multiple stations in a given coverage area without the use of an access point or server. The standard specifies the etiquette that each station must observe so that they all have fair access to the wireless media. It provides methods for arbitrating requests to use the media to ensure that throughput is maximized for all of the users in the base service set. IEEE 802.11 stations can also group themselves together to form an ad hoc network—a network with no central control and with no connections to the outside world. In this case, the network is formed on the fly simply because mobile devices have found themselves in proximity to each other, have a need to communicate, and find no pre-existing network infrastructure (such as a pre-existing 802.11 BSS with an AP) in the location. An ad hoc network might be formed, for example, when people with laptops meet together (in a conference room, a train, a car, and so on) and want to exchange data in the absence of a centralized access point. A tremendous recent increase in interest in ad hoc networking has occurred, as communicating portable devices continue to proliferate. Figure 21-15 illustrates the ad hoc network.

- The *client/server network* uses an access point that controls the allocation of transmit time for all stations and enables mobile stations to roam from cell to cell. The access point is used to handle traffic from the mobile radio to the wired or wireless backbone of the client/server network. This arrangement enables point coordination of all of the stations in the basic service area and ensures proper handling of the data traffic. The access point routes data between the stations and other wireless stations or to and from the network server. Typically,

Figure 21-15
The ad hoc network

WLANs controlled by a central access point will provide better throughput performance. Figure 21-16 illustrates the client/server approach.

Physical Layer Implementation Choices The physical layer in any network defines the modulation and signaling characteristics for the transmission of data. At the physical layer, two RF transmission methods and

Figure 21-16
The client/server approach to wireless LANs

Ethernet used to connect multiple APs

Legend:
AP=   Access Point
BSS=   Basic Service Set

one infrared are defined. Operation of the WLAN in unlicensed RF bands requires the spread spectrum modulation to meet the requirements for operation in most countries. The RF transmission standards in the standard are Frequency Hopping Spread Spectrum (FHSS) and Direct Sequence Spread Spectrum (DSSS). Both architectures are defined for operation in the 2.4-GHz frequency band typically occupying 83 MHz of bandwidth from 2.400 GHz to 2.483 GHz.

- Differential BPSK (DBPSK) and DQPSK is the modulation for the direct sequence.
- Frequency hopping uses two to four levels Gaussian FSK as the modulation signaling method.

Different frequencies were approved for use in Japan, the United States, and Europe and any WLAN product must meet the requirements for the country where it is sold. The physical layer data rate for FHSS system is 1 Mbps. For DSSS, both 1-Mbps and 2-Mbps data rates are supported. The choice between FHSS and DSSS will depend on a number of factors related to the user's application and the environment that the system will be operating.

Infrared Physical Layer   One infrared standard is supported which operates in the 850nM- to 950nM-band with peak power of 2 W. The modulation for infrared is accomplished using either 4- or 16-level, pulse-positioning modulation. The physical layer supports two data rates: 1 and 2 Mbps.

Direct Sequencing Spread Spectrum (DSSS) Physical Layer   The DSSS physical layer uses an 11-bit Barker Sequence to spread the data before it is transmitted. Each transmitted bit is modulated by the 11-bit sequence. This process spreads the RF energy across a wider bandwidth than would be required to transmit the raw data. The receiver reverses the RF input to recover the original data. The advantage is the reduced effects of narrowband sources of interference.

The IEEE 802.11 protocol can also use a short request to send (RTS) control frame and a short clear to send (CTS) frame to reserve access to the channel. When a sender wants to send a frame, it can first send an RTS frame to the receiver, indicating the duration of the data packet and the ACK packet. A receiver that receives an RTS frame responds with a CTS frame, giving the sender explicit permission to send. All other stations hearing the RTS or CTS then know about the pending data transmission and can avoid interfering with those transmissions. An IEEE 802.11 sender can

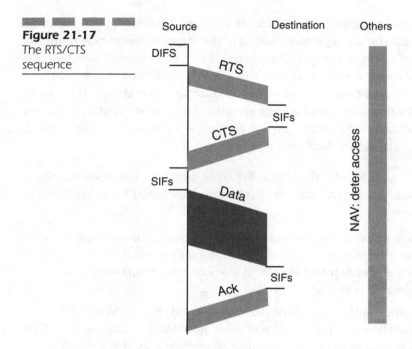

Figure 21-17
The RTS/CTS
sequence

operate either using the RTS/CTS control frames or can send its data without first using the RTS control frame. Figure 21-17 shows the RTS/CTS sequence.

The use of the RTS and CTS frames helps avoid collisions in three important ways:

1. Because all stations within the receiver's vicinity will hear the receiver's transmitted CTS frame, the CTS frame helps avoid both the hidden station problem and the fading problem.

2. Because the RTS and CTS frames are short, a collision involving an RTS or CTS frame will only last for the duration of the whole RTS or CTS frame.

3. When the RTS and CTS frames are correctly transmitted, no collisions should occur involving the subsequent DATA and acknowledge (ACK) frames.

Frequency Hopping Spread Spectrum (FHSS) Physical Layer   The FHSS physical layer has 22 hop patterns to choose from. The frequency hop physical layer is required to hop across the 2.4-GHz ISM band covering 79 channels.

Each channel occupies 1 MHz of bandwidth and must hop at the minimum rate specified by the regulatory bodies of the intended country. A minimum hop rate of 2.5 hops per second is specified for the United States.

Each of the physical layers uses their own unique header to synchronize the receiver and to determine signal modulation format and data packet length. The physical layer headers are always transmitted at 1 Mbps. Predefined fields in the headers provide the option to increase the data rate to 2 Mbps for the actual data packet.

The MAC Layer Unlike the 802.3 Ethernet protocol, the wireless 802.11 MAC protocol does not implement collision detection. This is because of a few reasons:

- The ability to detect collisions requires the ability to both send (one's own signal) and receive (to determine if another station's transmissions are interfering with one's own transmission) at the same time. This can be costly.

- More importantly, even if one had collision detection and sensed no collision when sending, a collision could still occur at the receiver. This situation results from the particular characteristics of the wireless channel.

Given the difficulties with detecting collisions at a wireless receiver, the designers of IEEE 802.11 developed an access protocol that aimed to avoid collisions (hence, the name CSMA/CA), rather than detect and recover from collisions (CSMA/CD).

First, the IEEE 802.11 frame contains a duration field in which the sending station explicitly indicates the length of time that its frame will be transmitting on the channel. This value enables other stations to determine the minimum amount of time (the so-called network allocation vector, [NAV]) for which they should defer their access.

The MAC layer specification for 802.11 has similarities to the 802.3 Ethernet wired line standard. The protocols for 802.11 use a protocol scheme know as carrier sense multiple access collision avoidance (CSMA/CA). This protocol avoids collisions instead of detecting a collision like the algorithm used in 802.3. It is difficult to detect collisions in an RF transmission network, which is why collision avoidance is used. The MAC layer operates together with the physical layer by sampling the energy over the medium transmitting data. The physical layer uses a clear channel assessment (CCA) algorithm to determine if the channel is clear. This is accomplished by measuring the RF energy at the antenna and determining the strength of the received signal. The best method to use depends upon the levels of interference in the operating environment. The CSMA/CA protocol provides options that can minimize collisions by using RTS, CTS, data and acknowledge (ACK) transmission frames, in a sequential fashion.

Communications is established when one of the wireless nodes sends a short message RTS frame. The RTS frame includes the destination and the length of message. The message duration is known as the *network allocation vector* (NAV). The NAV alerts all others in the medium to back off for the duration of the transmission. The receiving station issues a CTS frame, which echoes the sender's address and the NAV. If the CTS frame is not received, it is assumed that a collision occurred and the RTS process starts over. After the data frame is received, an ACK frame is sent back verifying a successful data transmission. A common limitation with wireless LAN systems is the hidden node problem. This can disrupt 40 percent or more of the communications in a highly loaded LAN environment. It occurs when a station in a service set cannot detect the transmission of another station to detect that the media is busy. Figure 21-18 shows the hidden node.

With the emphasis now on Voice over IP telephone applications, the 802.11 standard enables the interconnection of the traditional PBX and LANs as shown in Figure 21-19.

Figure 21-18
The hidden node

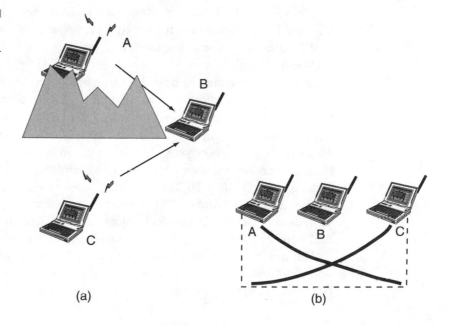

(a)

(b)

Figure 21-19
The wireless LAN and
PBX integration

The 802.11b standard now enables the transmission of 11 Mbps on the wireless LANs with new speeds being promised every day. We hear that the wireless standards will support up to 52 Mbps in the future.

What is next? Who knows where this is all leading? However, the talk of offering 1 Gbps to the desktop for the convergence of voice, data, video, and multimedia has become commonplace since the introduction of these two high-level steps.

In the hexadecimal, or base 16, numbering system, we also use the digits 0 through 9 to count. But we need six additional symbols to represent the values 10 through 15 (we have no need for a single symbol for 16). Hexadecimal uses the capital letters A through F to represent the values 10 through 15, respectively. Each position in a hexadecimal number contains a hexadecimal digit (0 through F) indicating how many of a power of sixteen ($16^0 \times 1$, $16^1 \times 16$, $16^2 \times 256$, and so on) goes into that number. Thus, the hexadecimal number 264 is four 1's plus six 16s plus two 256s or, in total as represented in the decimal numbering system, 612. The hexadecimal number BB is eleven 1's plus eleven 16s, or a total of 187 decimal.

The natural internal numbering system used in most data processing and communications equipment is binary, or *base 2*, using only 1's and 0's. Network addresses (and many other items in data communications and data processing) are usually represented in hexadecimal notation because of the ease with which it can represent or be converted into 4-bit binary (base 2) numbers, as follows:

- Hex digit   0   1   2   3   4   5   6   7   8   9
                    A   B   C   D   E   F
- Binary value   0000   0001   0010   0011   0100   0101   0110   0111
                    1000   1001   1010   1011   1100   1101   1110   1111
- Decimal value   0 1 2 3 4 5 6 7 8 9 10 11 12 13
                    14 15

Because it only takes one hexadecimal digit to represent any possible single 4-bit binary value (as illustrated in this example), and 1 byte equals 8 bits, it takes exactly two hexadecimal digits to represent the contents of 1 byte.

Questions

1. What three companies originally formed the Ethernet standard?
   a. IBM, DEC, and Xerox
   b. Intel, DEC, and IBM
   c. Intel, Xerox, and DEC
   d. Intel, DEC, and IEEE
2. The original speed for Ethernet was designed at _____.
3. The use of a _____ was the first cabling system used.
   a. Thick wire fiber
   b. Thin wire coax
   c. Thick wire coax
   d. Thin fiber
4. The Ethernet operates at the following speeds:
   a. 10, 50, 100
   b. 10, 100; 1,000
   c. 100; 1,000; 100,000
   d. 1, 10, 100

5. The Ethernet specification that used thin coax is called _____.

    a. 10Base5

    b. 10Base2

    c. 100Base10

    d. 10BaseF

6. The 10 broad 36 standard is designed around which other industry?

    a. The telephone companies

    b. The cable TV companies

    c. Corporations

    d. The ISPs

7. When using a 10/100 card, the hub will _____ sense the speed of the card.

8. Regular 10-Mbps Ethernet will deliver approximately what throughput?

    a. 10 Mbps

    b. 6–8 Mbps

    c. 3.3–4 Mbps

    d. 5–6 Mbps

9. The contention standard is called:

    a. CSMA/CA

    b. CSMA/DC

    c. CSMA/CDR

    d. CSMA/CD

10. The IEEE standards committee is called the _____.

11. The Ethernet standard is called:

    a. 802.1

    b. 802.5

    c. 802.11

    d. 802.3

12. The wireless standard will deliver between the following speeds:

    a. 1-2 and 10

    b. 1-2 and 11

    c. 1-2 and 52

    d. 1-10-100

13. The minimum size frame in an Ethernet network is _____ bytes.

    a. 46

    b. 64

    c. 128

    d. 1,500

14. The frame carries a payload of between _____ and _____ bytes.

    a. 64–1,518

    b. 46–1,500

    c. 64–1,500

    d. 46–1,518

15. The length indicator indicates the actual _____.

    a. Frame size

    b. Payload size

    c. Address size

    d. Data and overhead length

16. A frame that is too large is called a _____.

17. When we link segments together, the rule is no more than ____ repeaters.

    a. Three

    b. Seven

    c. Four

    d. Two

18. 100 Mbps Ethernet is also called _____.

    a. 100BaseT

    b. 100VGAnyLAN

    c. 100Base4

    d. Fast Ethernet

19. Wireless LANs use the following contention algorithm:

    a. CSMA/CD

    b. CSMA/CC

    c. CSMA/CA

    d. TRS/CTS

20. The future network speed that is currently being worked on for the metro networks is called:

    a. 10-Mbps Ethernet

    b. 1,000-Mbps Ethernet

    c. 10,000-Mbps Ethernet

    d. 100-Mbps Ethernet

Token Ring LANs

After reading this chapter and completing the questions, you will be able to:

- Discuss what the Token Ring LAN is about
- Determine the differences between a ring and a bus
- Understand the benefits of Token Ring
- Discuss why everyone is moving to Ethernet from Token Ring
- Understand IBM's philosophy in creating the Token Ring Networks
- Discuss the throughput of the rings

Token Rings

Another access method that can be used in a local area network (LAN) is the token-passing concept. The *token-passing concept* is an access method that was initially developed to work on a physical and a logical ring. Remember, LANs are used in both physical and logical topologies. A *topology* is the layout of the physical wiring plan to provide a single shared cabling system. If you think about some of the constraints and limitations of the bus topology covered in the previous chapter, the issue is the collisions that can occur on a network. The issue that seems to arise in the discussion of the topology of the physical Ethernet is that the signal (information) has to propagate (travel) down to the ends of the cabling system. At the ends of the system are terminators (no, not Arnold Schwarzenegger) that absorb, or remove, the electrical pulses from the cable. This means that in order to send information and be assured that the information reaches its destination, the transmitting device can only use 50 percent of the time to generate the information onto the wire. The other 50 percent of the time allotted to this device is devoted to listening to the cable to make sure the signal makes it all the way to the ends without colliding with some other device's data. This would appear to be somewhat wasteful because only a 50 percent duty cycle is allowed. To overcome this situation, the use of a ring topology was introduced. Along with the topology, a collision avoidance scheme was also introduced. If a device wants to transmit, it must have a permission slip to do so. The permission slip is in the form of an electrical signal, called a *token*, which travels around the network constantly. Only one user will be on the network at a time; only one token is needed.

The IBM Token Concept

In 1984, IBM announced plans to produce a set of network interfaces that adhered to the IEEE 802.5 token-passing concept. This access method was IBM's defense against the use of Ethernets. As you will recall, Digital Equipment Corporation, Intel, and Xerox produced Ethernet as the network topology and access method of choice. With the proliferation of LANs in the industry, IBM had not endorsed the Ethernet, yet had no counter for a networking environment other than Systems Network Architecture (SNA). To arrive at an IBM-stamped LAN, the token-passing ring was announced. In 1985, the Token Ring LANs were beginning to appear. End users who had not changed over to the bus topology were waiting for the IBM LAN. They immediately went for Token Rings: after all, "no one ever got fired by buying IBM." So a new set of boundaries was established. Users were in one of two camps, either supporting or criticizing peer implementations of the LAN topologies. IBM created a new approach in defense against the Ethernet supporters. Many of the IBM systems would not work on an Ethernet, so immediately a new connectivity solution was introduced to support the big iron and the in-between hardware. The range of devices from the desktop, in either an industry standard architecture (ISA) or a microchannel architecture (MCA) to the mainframe computing platforms, could all be introduced to the LAN.

IBM's version and the standardized IEEE version of tokens included the use of a deterministic system. By using a single token, the network allows only one device at a time to transmit. Therefore, the risks and problems associated with the CSMA/CD LANs are eliminated. Each device gets its fair share of use on the network. In order to do this, the devices are allotted time to use the token as it arrives.

Initial Layout

In the beginning days of the Token Ring, the cables were installed as a physical ring. Figure 22-1 shows the actual layout of the cabling. In this initial layout, each device installed on the ring is connected to the physical and closed ring of wires. Wires run to an inbound slot on a device—actually to the network interface card (NIC), which is now called a token interface card (TIC)—then out to an outbound side of the device. This means that every

Figure 22-1
The physical ring connects each device with a wire-in/wire-out arrangement—a closed circle is created.

device has a wire-in/wire-out connection. This is done on a four-wire cable. As the devices are attached to the network, they are wired from the upstream neighbor and to the downstream neighbor. This continues around the LAN until the circle is closed.

Problems Encountered

Nothing ever works the way we want it to all the time. Unfortunately, several problems arose with the use of this system of wiring devices together physically. These include, but are not limited to, the following:

Lack of Power

When the devices are wired together, the electrical signal (or data) runs down the wires through one device to the next. This means that the electricity comes into the TIC card, is read, and then regenerated to go out to the cable. However, this implies that the TIC card must be active at all times. When users on the ring finished their daily activities or if they did not come into work, a problem was created. In both of these cases, the user's device (PC) was not powered on. The TIC card that is installed inside the PC in an expansion slot draws its power from the PC. However, if the PC isn't on, the TIC card is dead, which means that the LAN is down (Figure 22-2). This left many LAN administrators in a quandary because the problem was not initially obvious. Administrators spent many hours running around the building looking for the cause of the problem on the LAN.

Lack of Connection

After an end user has waited for connection to the LAN for what he or she perceives as forever, the LAN administrator finally gets the wires installed, the PC configured, and the software loaded. This usually happens during off-hours or on weekends. At any rate, the user comes into the office on the following day. Initially, the end user is ecstatic about finally being connected to the LAN. However, this wears off quickly, and the user then decides that the device is not located in a convenient location. Therefore, the user picks up the PC and moves it across the room to another location in the office or

Figure 22-2
If the power to the
PC is off, the LAN
does not work.

Figure 22-2
If the power to the
PC is off, the LAN
does not work.

work area. Unfortunately, as shown in Figure 22-3, this also pulls the wires out of the wall and the jack. The broken wires render the LAN unusable because electrical continuity is lost. The LAN must be wired as a closed circle so that the electrical current will flow around the wires consistently.

Constant Changes

The last scenario involves the dynamics of the networking environment. After a LAN administrator painstakingly sets up the network, the inevitable happens. A new user must be added to the network. Sometimes this can be quite simple, yet other cases require an entire new layout of the wiring system to reach the new user. In any case, the result is the same. The LAN administrator has to cut the connection and run the wires from the existing termination on a PC to the new one added to the network. This means that the LAN is out of service or down for the time it takes to get the new wires run and connected. Only when everything is put back into the physical ring will the network be back up again. This is shown in Figure 22-4, where a new user must be added.

Figure 22-3
If a user moves the
PC, the wires can be
broken. The LAN is
down.

Obviously, the results of these scenarios leave one conclusion: the LAN is down a lot! Something had to be done to preclude this from continually happening. IBM decided to create the LAN in a box concept.

The Solution to Physical Problems

To overcome the downtime and the lost credibility, the evolution to a centralized network began. IBM developed a modification to the physical structure of the ring. Using a version of a star network, they introduced the multistation access unit (MAU). Figure 22-5 illustrates a multistation access unit that was installed in a star configuration in a telephone closet. The ring was now a physical star and a logical ring. Physical defines the structure of the wiring, whereas logical defines the signal (energy) flow. Using a basic telephony concept, wires were no longer pulled from device A to B to C to D to A as they had been. Instead, they were all pulled from location X. A single cable from X to A, X to B, and so on was used. This created some other unique characteristics.

Figure 22-4
If constant changes are required, the wires between A and B must be cut and run to E. The LAN is down.

Figure 22-5
The MAU uses a physical star but a logical ring. This LAN in a box helps to overcome the downtime problem.

Additional capabilities of the newer Token Ring networks enable the self-healing of a cable or device problem. Using the physical ring from MAU to MAU, if the cable gets broken (Figure 22-6), the electronics running the ring are intelligent enough to close off the ring and reverse itself. This creates a far better approach to keeping the LAN up and running than what was used in the past. If the cable is cut or disconnected, the LAN senses the open condition, drops a shorting bar, and loops the transmit and receive wires together. The resulting network is shown in Figure 22-7. Although this is not a perfect solution, it does help to keep the uptime needs of the organization closer to the design and intent. Because the ring closes and reverses itself, designing the cable lengths is very important. What used to be a short connection between MAUs has now doubled in length because the signal must run on a longer cable to get from device to device. Distance limitations are still a factor insofar as the signal must run on the wires. By reversing the wires, the cable distances are doubled. This merely means that the LAN administrator must be cognizant of this limitation.

The original Token Ring topology was delivered at 4 Mbps. Distances of wires run from device to device could not exceed a total length of 1,600 feet. Newer rings operate at 16 Mbps, but the distance was cut in half for a total cable run of 800 feet. Too many organizations realized that this distance limitation was in the way. To solve this problem, IBM included a repeater

Figure 22-6
If the physical ring (MAU to MAU) is cut, the electronics in the MAU can close the ring by dropping a shorting.

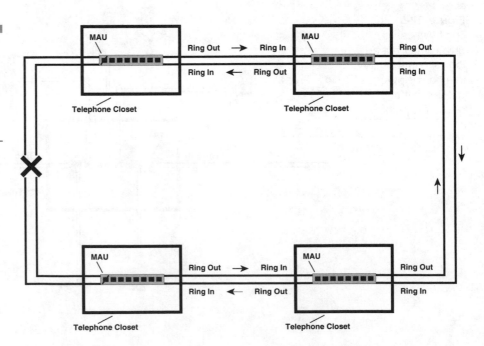

Figure 22-7
The resultant network is a closed loop around the problem.

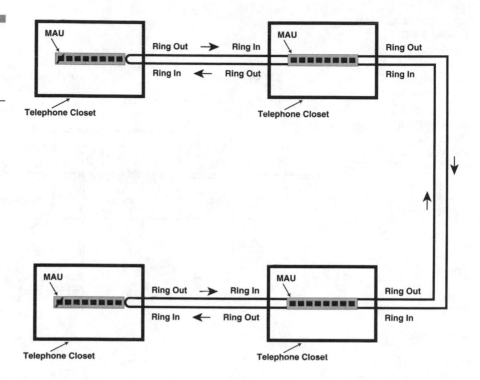

function in the MAU so that each port on the MAU (Figure 22-8) would regenerate the signal and overcome the risk of signal loss. The MAU typically had only eight ports, as shown in the figure, plus a ring-in and a ring-out port. This enables multiple MAUs to be hooked together in a ring fashion and enables more than eight devices to be clustered into a single logical ring.

Further, each of the ports in the MAU also includes electronics in the componentry that have shorting bars. A shorting bar allows for a single (or multiple) device to be unplugged from the network without causing the network to go down. The original, as you recall, required that all devices be physically operating and plugged together in order to work. Now users can unplug a device or power it off without risk to the network.

Cable Types Used

When IBM introduced the Token Ring, a second part of the network design was the introduction of the structured wiring plan. To ensure that the

Figure 22-8
A repeater function is included in the MAU to overcome the distance limitations. Unplugged PCs are bypassed with shorting bars in the MAU.

networks would operate in an office or factory environment, different types of cables were introduced. The cable types enabled various environmental and operational conditions to exist. This was not an inexpensive cabling solution, but if one wanted the IBM seal of approval, the IBM cabling system had to be used. Table 22-1 shows the variations of the cabling. This wiring included the typical twisted pairs similar (but different) to telephone wiring. Telephone wiring existed in buildings for years and many LAN administrators thought that a simple installation would be to use the existing telephone wires. This led to devastating results. Cables reflect energy. They also act like antennae and draw in electrical energy. Unless the wires are protected from each other (bleed off of energy) and from other sources of disturbances in a building (such as electric motors, electrical welders, fluorescent light ballast, and so on), the results will be degradation of the network and corruption of the data. IBM introduced shielded wires to preserve the integrity of the data and prevent the influx of noise onto the cable. Thicker wires were also used. Instead of the traditional telephone wire, which is very thin (26 American wire gauge [AWG]), IBM used a thicker wire (22 AWG). In some cases, a fiber solution was also recommended to carry the higher speed data. The cabling design included both stranded and

Table 22-1

*Summary of the
IBM Cable Types*

IBM Type	Number of Wires and Type
1	Two pairs of shielded solid core 22 AWG
2	Two pairs of shielded solid core 22 AWG and four pairs of unshielded solid 22 AWG
3	Four pairs of unshielded solid core 22 AWG
5	Fiber-optic cable, multiple strand
6	Two pairs of shielded, stranded 26 AWG
8	Flat cable to go under carpets
9	Two pairs of shielded solid core 26 AWG

solid conductor copper cables, shielded and unshielded, and varying gauges. IBM was attempting to accomplish a one-stop shopping arrangement for all of an organization's cabling needs. Many felt that this was overkill typical of IBM. Furthermore, the pricing for such a cabling system left many organizations with sticker shock after being quoted installation prices in excess of $1 million. This cost was greater than anyone ever could have imagined, especially when everyone was accustomed to using the less expensive telephone wiring.

Although this was a very expensive and bulky wiring scheme, some organizations installed this system nearly 10 years ago and are still supporting the original and the upgraded capacities and speeds on the same wires. To prevent problems with radiation and cross talk, IBM also used a device called a *media filter*. The purpose of the media filter was to reduce or eliminate the interfering emanations from the wires that would cause corruption of the data. These, again, have worked for the duration.

Shielding of the cables when higher data rates are being used is important. However, the shielding is dependent on proper grounding. The ground wire should be connected to a proper building ground. The building ground should have a good, solid earth ground. This is a possible problem for all types of buildings and subsequently can cause problems on the LAN. If the LAN wiring is not properly grounded, disruptions are likely to occur. If the building ground is suspect, a certified engineer should check it and correct any problems. Old ground rods corrode or deteriorate, losing the proper depth to maintain a good ground. Installers like to use a cold-water pipe to tap the ground, but fail to recognize that many buildings now use plastic pipes, not copper, eliminating the ground. One must be very specific in requesting a proper ground.

Speeds

As already mentioned, IBM's first version of the Token Ring operated at 4 Mbps. Many of these rings are still in use today, nearly 10 years after the announced product. The industry and the Ethernet proponents scoffed at the slower-speed network when they heard of the limited speed. They perceived the situation this way: IBM was so desperate to get a network out into the marketplace that they shortchanged the user. Most people did not recognize the significance of the deterministic rather than CSMA/CD network access control. A well-installed Ethernet operating at 10 Mbps will support up to 1,024 nodes and yield approximately a 40 percent net throughput. This equates to about 4 Mbps of effective utilization. In actuality, the Ethernet yields about 3.3 Mbps. The main reason for this difference is the propagation time, the potential for collisions, and other timing delays that are prevalent on the bus. If collisions begin to occur, the backoff algorithm used by each of the NIC cards prevents either of the two conflicting devices from transmitting until a period of time passes. If continued collisions occur, the backoff algorithm used by the NIC cards becomes exponentially longer and longer. This means that more devices than can use the cable at a given time are waiting to use the cable.

Conversely, the deterministic nature of the ring using a token-passing access control does not have the same problems. No collisions will occur because only a single token exists and only one device can transmit when it controls the token. Consequently, the ring can be more effectively used. The effective throughput of a 4-Mbps token-passing ring is approximately 3.3 Mbps. This parallels the performance of the Ethernet even though the raw speeds are different. Furthermore, IBM's second version of the Token Ring card introduced a higher rate of speed. Operating at 16 Mbps, the faster speed using a deterministic access control method yields approximately 12 Mbps. These speed comparisons are shown in Table 22-2 as a quick reference in the event that this issue ever has to be reviewed. Because two camps always exist, pro or con on Ethernet or Token Ring, this one point is usually a neutralizing factor. Therefore, we want it to be clearly understood and visible for future reference.

Table 22-2

Comparing
Effective
Throughput
on LANs

Access Method	Raw Speed	Effective Throughput
Ethernet CSMA/CD	10 Mbits/s	3.3 Mbits/s
Token-passing ring	4 Mbits/s	3.3 Mbits/s
Token-passing ring	16 Mbits/s	12.0 Mbits/s

Media Access Control Layer

As with any LAN, the token-passing ring requires certain access control methods. To summarize from earlier discussions, the LAN really operates at the bottom two layers of the OSI model: the physical layer and the data-link layer. The data-link layer is subdivided into two parts: the media access control (MAC) and the logical link control functions. A Token Ring can be shown (Figure 22-9) as it stacks onto the model. This comparison shows that the following apply:

■ The physical link deals with the physical structure of the cabling system and the access method used at the physical layer. This is labeled layer 1 in the figure.

Figure 22-9
A Token Ring as it
stacks onto the
model

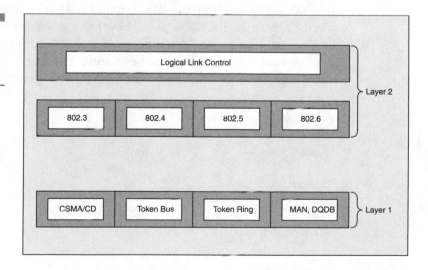

- The data-link sublayer, called the media access control layer, shows the access control in support of the IEEE and the International Telecommunication Union (ITU) model for access control.

- The logical link control (LLC) brings the various topologies together in a common format. The LLC represents the upper portion of layer 2 of the OSI model.

In each of the cases, the other forms of LAN access methods are shown in the same layers of the model. Layer 1 deals with the forms shown in Table 22-3.

The Types of Frame

The Token Ring uses three different types of frames in its ongoing operation. These three frames are determined by the service that they provide on the network:

- The token
- The frame
- The abort message

We will look at each of these and their purpose so that the differences can be seen more clearly. In many ways, users who support this infrastructure consider the Token Ring the most popular network concept (whether this is true or not). The ills of the past Ethernet concept were addressed on the ring so that less confusion resides on the ring, and troubleshooting, maintenance, and diagnostics can all be simpler. The word "simpler" might frustrate many network administrators, but the intent is to simplify the

Table 22-3

Comparing Standards and Topologies

Topology/Class	IEEE Standard
Ethernet	802.3
Token-passing bus	802.4
Token-passing ring	802.5
DQDB, CATV services	802.6

detection of errors and the resolution of problems. We (Don and Bud) differ in our opinions about which of the two network strategies is better and why. Obviously, the intent of this book is not to steer any user to a specific product or service, but toward a better understanding of what each service does. From this perspective, the control placed on the Token Ring yields a better management scheme. The network facilitates the use of the cabling system in the way it was designed to be used. Now back to the frame formats. Our intent is not to bog the discussion down with a lot of bits and bytes. But if you don't understand what the ring is doing and what the reasoning behind it is, then the whole situation becomes a moot point. Again, the differences are significant in the way they operate; the functionality that they serve is similar.

The Token

The token is made up of 24 bits of information (three octets). The three octets define the start and stop sequence within this frame. A token will traverse the network constantly, even if no traffic exists. See Figure 22-10 for the frame format of the token as we continue through this discussion. The first octet in the token is the start delimiter (SD). It is made up of a combination of good bits and violation bits (in the way we produce digital pulses in this case, called Manchester Coding). The reason for the good and bad bits is to differentiate a token from real information. Therefore, the start delimiter is a unique set of 1's and 0's that can be differentiated by all devices on the network as being the beginning of a token. These eight bits are always formed in the same way.

Skipping to the third octet in the token is the end delimiter (ED), which contains a combination of good bits and bad bits. Much like the start delimiter, the end delimiter is used as a specific sequence to signal the end of a

Figure 22-10
The token is a 3-byte sequence that moves around the network.

token. Again, this is a unique combination, so no confusion arises about what is being presented to the network.

Now back to the middle octet in the token. This octet is called the access control (AC) byte, which really equates to the working portion of the token. The 8 bits are made up of a series of working bits that define what is happening inside the token (Figure 22-11). Bits 1 through 3 in the access control byte are marked as priority (P) bits. Each device (or node, as they are called) on the network has an assigned priority by the system administrator. Because it has 3 bits, a total of eight priorities can be used on the network, working from 000 through 111. In order of succession, 000 will be the lowest-priority device and 111 will be the highest-priority device. In order for a node to transmit information on the network, it must have the token (of course, the token must be free). The device must have equal or greater priority than the token in order to use it. This will enable certain devices to have a higher priority to send information than others. An example of this might be that the server on the network would have a higher priority than a regular low-end user who only performs word processing functions. This is not a caste system, but a means of providing service and controls on the network so that one device cannot take over the network.

The fourth bit is called the token (T) bit; it signals what is present, a token (T = 0) or a frame of data (T = 1). Two possibilities exist as the token comes around: it is either a free token or a busy token containing user information. This token bit can establish the capability to let the server use the token more often than an end user, thereby enabling all others on the network to gain access to the server and receive their information. You can only imagine how the performance would be viewed if the server has to wait to send a file, save a file, and so on. Everyone on the network would think that

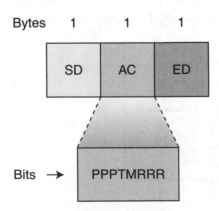

Figure 22-11
The access control byte format

the network is performing slowly, and in reality, it would be. Regardless of the reason, if the user does not get an instantaneous response, then the network is slow. No other options exist.

Bit number 5 in this AC byte is used as a monitor (M) bit for network token control. Think of this bit as a traffic cop on the network. A device on the network is assigned the responsibility of monitoring what happens on the network. When a token is sent around the network, it would not be wise to let it circle around and around continuously. Therefore, the monitor station is responsible to see that this doesn't happen. The transmitting station (sender) sets the M bit in the token to a 0. As the token goes by the active monitor, it sets the M bit to a 1. If the monitor station receives an incoming priority token or a frame with the M = 1 set, it knows that the transmitting station did not take the information off the network after a round trip. The monitor station then takes the token off and cleans it up. Then it issues a new token to be used on the network. Only one token is still on the network at this point. To prevent any major problems on such a network, the monitor station is set up to handle the problems with tokens on the network. Thus, if something happened to the monitor, one or two neighbors are designated as the standby monitors to take over the responsibility (Figure 22-12).

Figure 22-12
One or two devices will be selected as standby monitor nodes. The monitor node is usually a high-priority node.

Monitor Node

Alternate
Standby Monitor Node

Standby Monitor Node

Bits 6, 7, and 8 of the AC byte are allocated as reservation (R) bits. Remember the priority levels? Well, if a server or any other device has information to send across the network and it has a high priority, it can reserve the token for its use on the next pass around the network. These 3 bits are assigned for use so that a single device cannot control the network and send frame after frame of information, denying access to all other stations on the network. Therefore, as the token goes by, the NIC inside the node will set the reservation bits and request the next available token. Certain constraints can be placed on the network where a single node might only be allowed one use of the token, after which it must release the token. Other higher-priority devices might be allowed to use the token two or three times before relinquishing control. It is through these bits in the access control field that this is implemented so that other devices have a fair share of network usage. This was a well-thought-out plan for the network.

The Abort Sequence

Figure 22-13 shows the abort sequence that is used in the Token Ring network. In the event that problems exist on the network, the nodes are designed to recognize the problem and discard the token. The abort sequence includes the capability to read the start delimiter and the end delimiter, place them together, and issue this to the network by the detecting node. This alerts all nodes on the network that the problem exists. Things that can go wrong will go wrong. This can include such problems as data corruption, lost tokens, time-outs, address problems, and so on.

The Data Frame

Above and beyond the token format, the ring carries a frame of information known as the *data frame* (Figure 22-14). This frame has a variable length based on the data inside. It is comprised of the following pieces:

- The start delimiter (SD) in the token frame
- Access control (AC)

These constitute the first 2 bytes of the data frame. Following these 2 bytes come

- The frame control (FC) byte, which indicates the type of data in the frame

Figure 22-13
By placing the start
and end delimiters
together, a node
detecting a bad
frame will alert all
other nodes that a
problem exists.

Figure 22-14
The data frame
layout in a Token
Ring (802.5) network

- The destination address (DA) of the token, a definition of where the frame is being sent. The destination address is 6 bytes (48 bits) long.
- The source address (SA), the indicator of where the frame came from or who sent it. This address is also 6 bytes long.
- The data, the field where the actual information being sent is provided. It can be just information, or it can also contain such information as MAC or LLC information or routing information. This enables all physical and data link overhead to be contained inside the data packet

transparently. The data field is a variable amount of information that can be up to 4,048 bytes on a 4-Mbps network and up to 16,192 bytes on a 16-Mbps network.

- The frame check sequence (FCS) is a CRC-32 error-detection pattern that checks the validity of the information in the FC, DA, SA, data, and FCS bytes. Using a 32-bit CRC, the error-detection capability is better than 99.99995 percent. If a single bit error occurs in the transmission of the frame, the frame will be tossed out. This is fairly stringent, but must be used to ensure the integrity of the data on the network.

- The end delimiter (ED) from the original token. This is a single byte of information.

- The frame status (FS) byte, which indicates the status of the actual frame. In this byte control, mechanisms are used to determine what has happened since the transmitting station initially sent data.

Figure 22-15 shows the various bits used in the FS byte. There are reasons for this technique. First, the figure shows that the byte is composed of a sequence that mimics *ACxxACxx* where

- The receiving device uses the *A* bits to indicate that the destination address was recognized.

- The receiving device uses the *C* bits to indicate that the information (data) was copied.

- The *x* bits are not used and therefore ignored.

- The *A* and *C* bits inside the FS byte are important for the overall control of the network.

Because the transmitter is using a one-way cable transmission system, the information is sent out onto the wire. The sender must know that the

Figure 22-15
The frame status byte includes the A and C bits. A is used to designate a recognized address (to a receiver) and C is used to designate the data has been copied.

data arrived at the desired location. However, because this is a one-way system, the only indication to the sender occurs if the receiver sends back a return receipt requested notification. This is where these bits come in to play. If the sender does not receive the frame back (in the full circle) with the *A* and *C* bits set properly, then the message must be retransmitted. However, if the *A* and *C* bits are properly set, the transmitter knows that everything worked according to plan. Therefore, the transmitter will remove the information from the network, free up the token, and send it back onto the network for another device's use. Note that two *A* and *C* bits are in this byte. The frame status byte is not checked by a CRC; therefore, as a check and balance on this arrangement, the two *A* and two *C* bits must be identical. Table 22-4 shows the combinations of the *A* and *C* bits inside the frame status. If an *A* or *C* bit is set to a 0, it is not recognized or used, whereas if set to a 1, it means that everything is okay.

The following scenario will hopefully summarize the use of a Token Ring network simply. We recognize that many readers are seeing this information for the first time and that many of the framing formats and control sequences are complicated and confusing. Sometimes the information needs to be read and reread. Therefore, we attempt to use the network as best we can through an analogy. The process is fairly straightforward, but the concept can become quite complicated if you do not have a basic understanding

Table 22-4

Summary of the Frame Status Bits Being Used

Pattern of Frame Status Byte	Explanation
00xx00xx	Nothing was recognized or copied. The station may be out of order or turned off or the frame discarded.
10xx10xx	The receiver recognized its address and responded, indicating that it is on the network. However, the receiver did not copy the information. The data CRC may have been corrupted or some other problem may have occurred.
01xx01xx	If this happens, you have a major problem. The addressee did not respond to the frame of data, but somehow it copied the frame. This is theoretically not possible, or a promiscuous device could be present that set the *C* bits but received someone else's data. It is time to call the Cybercops!
11xx11xx	The addressee recognized that the information was for it, and the data was copied. Everything worked the way it was intended to.

of what is taking place. So, fasten your seat belts and enjoy the ride around the ring.

Case Example

We wish to set up a Token Ring, so we establish the number of users who need to be connected. As we begin the process, we use an older format of physical and logical ring. Therefore, we find that we have five users that need to share the resources on the network. As shown in Figure 22-16, we run the cables from device to device. In this example, we have a wire connected to the in port of the NIC card at station A. The second wire is connected to the out port of the NIC in device A, but the out wire runs to the in port of device B. At device B, we run the out wire from B to the in port at C. From C, we run the out port wire to the in port on device D. At D, we run the out port wire to the in port wire at device E, and at E we connect the out port to device A. Now we have a physical ring. The circle is closed and continuity exists between and among all devices.

Figure 22-16
The physical and logical ring in place—a 4-Mbits/s ring is created and devices/nodes are tagged as functions require.

Next, we install the LAN drivers in each of the PCs to basically let each PC know how to use the NIC card that has been installed in the expansion slot. The card has several components, including the electrical connection to the backplane on the PC, a chip set that operates at 4 Mbps, buffers to hold the data, and a framer that will take the necessary data to be transmitted around the network in chunks. (Remember that in a 4-Mbps Token Ring, the frame can be as large as 4,048 bytes.) Next, we select device A as the monitor station and B as the backup (or standby monitor). We begin by assigning the connected device D as a file server. Now we are just about ready to begin the process.

As each device is powered up, the 6-byte address is recognized as being the card's location. So the card's CPU recognizes its own address. At the physical layer, we now have full connectivity.

When we load up the network operating system (NOS), we also build a database of the network devices attached to this ring. This will also be the time that we grant certain rights and privileges to the individual PC, including the services that can be accessed, the priority of the individual PC, its address, and the upstream and downstream neighboring information.

Next, we begin to operate the network. User A wants to send information to the file server. Therefore, user A begins by using a save command on a file in word processing. The PC and its operating components (whether in DOS, Windows, or other) send the information to the NIC card for delivery to the file server. The NIC card stores the data in a buffer. Next, the NIC central processing unit (CPU) formats the data into a frame of information. Figure 22-17 shows the data being prepared into a frame (envelope). The NIC stuffs 4,048 bytes of information into this envelope. For all intents and purposes, this equals two pages of information. The two pages of information have been inserted into the empty envelope.

Figure 22-18 illustrates the addressing information that is placed on the frame. We now have a frame that is just about ready to go. More information must be attached to this packet, such as the permission slip referenced earlier in this chapter. The permission slip comes from the network.

The NIC monitors the incoming port to see whether anything is coming down the wires. It waits for the token to come down the path to collect the data. Now the NIC sees the token coming in on the in port and grabs the information. In a very quick analysis, the NIC determines that the token has other information attached to it. Unfortunately, the token comes by, but it is busy. This is a service where only one token at a time will be available to use. Therefore, the NIC just passes the busy token along through the out

Figure 22-17
The process of preparing a frame for transmission—the frame is formatted by the NIC and stored in a buffer until the node can send to the server.

Figure 22-18
The NIC inserts the addressing information and performs a CRC on the information in the frame.

port back onto the network so that the information can get to its designated address. The NIC now waits for the token's next pass.

Here it comes again. This time the NIC grabs the information and determines that the token is free (Figure 22-19). The NIC does several things:

1. It grabs the free token and makes it busy by changing a bit field in the AC byte.

2. It appends its data to the token, starting with the frame control, the destination address, the source address, the information field (4,048 bytes), and the frame check sequence.

3. The end delimiter and the frame status bytes are behind this information.

4. Now the NIC sends the frame out to the network. As the frame is moving down the wire, the next NIC located at device B sees the token coming and grabs it.

Figure 22-19
The NIC grabs the free token and appends the data frame. Note the sequence.

① The NIC sees the inbound frame, examines it and sees it's busy, then sends the entire frame back out to the network.

② The NIC sees the free token on the next pass so it inserts the buffered frame into the token and sends it out to the network destined for the file server.

5. NIC B then reads the token and sees that this is a frame, so it checks the destination address. Realizing that the frame is not for B, it immediately sends the frame directly back on the network to its downstream neighbor. The process continues through C.

6. As C sends the frame out to the network to D, things change. The addressee is the file server at D. So when D gets the frame, it reads the information and sees that the destination address is D.

7. D now makes a copy of the frame and stores it in memory on the card. Now D sets the A (address recognized) and C (frame copied) bits in the frame status byte to 1.

8. Leaving the entire frame intact and having modified the A and C bits, D sends the frame back out to the network, where it will go through device E, then on to device A (the originator).

9. When A receives the frame back, it analyzes the frame and sees that the A and C bits have been set to 1 (return receipt requested). Therefore, A strips off the frame field, sets the token as idle, and sends the free token out to the network for the next station waiting to transmit to use. A node typically only gets one use of the token and then must wait for the next pass before using the token again.

10. The process restarts all over again, depending on the source and destination addresses used.

As you see, this can be an efficient use of a network service. The larger the network gets, however, the more the devices will be waiting to transmit rather than transmitting. Growth and latency on these networks will slow the network down by 1 bit time per node attached. Therefore, when IBM introduced its souped-up Token Ring network at 16 Mbps, the frame size increased by fourfold and two tokens were allowed to exist on the network. This should be helpful in keeping things moving quickly.

Not much changed over time since the second version of the Token Ring. When a user needed more than 16 Mbps, then the migration on a ring was to FDDI (discussed in Chapter 24). These NIC cards are significantly more expensive than the Ethernet cards (regardless of the speed). Table 22-5 provides an example of this cost. These numbers are representative of the costs for the cards today.

One can see where the industries got a little confused about why they should buy IBM's version of LAN. In fact, at the end of 1999, the Token Ring

Table 22-5

Comparing Cost
of NIC Cards

NIC Card Type	Speed	Cost per Card in $
IBM Token Ring	4 Mbps	$295
IBM Token Ring	16 Mbps	$495–695
Ethernet	10 Mbps	$10–19
Ethernet	10/100 Mbps	$25–50
Ethernet	100 Mbps	$45–50
Ethernet	1,000 Mbps	$350–450
ATM	50 Mbps (full duplex)	$400

amounts to approximately 12 percent of all LANs installed worldwide (compared to 80+ percent Ethernet). The largest corporations in the world use the Token Ring and based on their data needs, price is not the issue.

Therefore, the Token Ring presence was diminished by the pricing model for smaller LANs and for smaller organizations. In 1998 and 1999, a task force got together with the express intent of developing the 100- and 1,000-Mbps Token Ring to keep pace with the evolution of the Ethernet. Some progress has been made, but more work needs to be done before a standardized fast token arrives on the market.

Moreover, the emphasis that IBM took was on the ATM NIC cards at the desktop. ATM was initially developed to deliver 50 Mbps full-duplex service to the end user. IBM conducted separate studies and determined that the end user did not need 50 Mbps full duplex. Instead, the end user only needed 25.9 Mbps full duplex. IBM recommended this change to the ATM Forum and the ITU. This recommendation was met with much resistance, and finally the ATM Forum and ITU accepted a modified version at 12.8 and 25.6 Mbps throughput for ATM to the desktop.

While this activity was under way, Bay Networks (who acquired Centillion Switch Company) slipped into the lead of suppliers of the IBM token concept.

Questions

1. What company invented the Token Ring Network?

   a. DEC

   b. Intel

   c. IBM

   d. Xerox

2. What year did the Token Ring come out?

   a. 1999

   b. 1985

   c. 2000

   d. 1974

3. What was the original speed for the Token Ring?

   a. 3.3 Mbps

   b. 10 Mbps

   c. 16 Mbps

   d. 4 Mbps

4. What is the effective rate of speed in the Token Ring network?

   a. 4.0 Mbps

   b. 12 Mbps

   c. 3.0 Mbps

   d. 3.3 Mbps

5. How large is the data field in the 4-Mbps frame?

   a. 4,096 bytes

   b. 4,048 bytes

   c. 4,068 bytes

   d. 16,192 bytes

6. What was the solution to the downtime?

   a. IBM sold off its business.

   b. Centillion networks were created.

   c. The MAU was produced.

   d. The Ethernet took over popularity.

7. What is the main drawback to IBM Token Rings?

    a. The cost

    b. The proprietary nature of the LAN

    c. The complexity of the setup

    d. All of the above

8. When the token is sent around the ring and a device copies the data, the _____ fields are filled in.

9. How many tokens are on a 4-Mbps ring?

    a. As many as the number of terminals

    b. Two

    c. None

    d. One

10. When the monitor bit is set, the token must come around the network within a specific timeframe.   T/F

11. If the token does not come around, the monitor sets the abort message.   T/F

12. When the token is corrupted, the downstream neighbor:

    a. Creates a new message

    b. Begins to beacon

    c. Passes along the original data without the AC bits set

    d. Drops the frame off the network

13. When IBM wanted to speed things up, the new LAN was created using:

    a. 25.6-Mbps cards

    b. 25.9-Mbps cards

    c. 16-Mbps cards

    d. 12-Mbps cards

14. The frame for the faster Token Ring network is _____ bytes.

15. IBM has gotten out of the Token Ring business.   T/F

16. When a NIC card is preparing to send, it must:

    a. Hold the data in a buffer

    b. Insert the MAC address of the destination device

    c. Insert its return address

    d. All of the above

17. What is the effective data rate of the 16-Mbps ring?

    a. 16 Mbps

    b. 13 Mbps

    c. 12 Mbps

    d. 10 Mbps

18. When a device wants to use the ring, it sets the:

    a. Frame bit

    b. Monitor bit

    c. CRC bits

    d. *A* and *C* bits

19. The actual token consists of _____ bytes.

    a. 4,068

    b. 128

    c. 46

    d. 3

20. The CRC-32 used on the ring assures us of _____ percent reliability.

Baseband versus Broadband

After reading this chapter and completing the questions, you will be able to:

- Discuss the differences between baseband and broadband communications
- Understand the way the baseband modulates its signal
- Compare the baseband and broadband LANs for speed and application
- Determine which cable has the better throughput given the applications
- Discuss the benefits of the baseband and broadband systems

When LANs were first emerging in the late 1970s, they were called local nets. These local networking services and techniques would be the foundation of the LANs of the future. Two opinions were formed as to how these services might be provided. In earlier discussions in this book, we said that two factions existed in the industry: the voice and the data communications factions.

Whenever a voice person became involved in the picture, all data needs were satisfied by the traditional data communications techniques. This meant that the voice analog dial-up or leased-line services were installed. After that, a modem was used to convert the digital signals of a computer into the analog signals of the voice world for transmission. The same method was used for local and long-haul communications needs. Most voice people felt comfortable with the use of modulation techniques on the link.

However, whenever a data communications person became involved, the picture changed. Most of what was installed in the data world evolved around the single largest player in the industry: IBM. IBM's strategy was to use a coaxial cable to enable high-speed communications for computing platforms. This included the hierarchical structure of the SNA world. We've already covered most of these concepts in past chapters, so by now the acronyms should be familiar. At any rate, the coaxial world was introduced to overcome the limitations of the noisy twisted pair wiring that the voice folks always used. This coax was traditionally used in a baseband arena. A single cable was extended to the end-user device (3270 terminal, 3274 controller, or other). Nothing else needed to be done because IBM would directly apply the electrical voltages on the coax for propagation down the wire to the next hierarchical device. This was a baseband application of the cable, so a nonmodulated approach was used. Electricity was directly applied to the cable and it propagated (ran) down to the ends unchanged.

Another faction that cropped up in the industry came from the *radio frequency* (RF) proponents. The use of radio-based systems was also prevalent in the industry prior to this era. Therefore, the radio folks looked at the need to send simultaneous signals down a medium to an end device. They began to use RF techniques to carry multiple data signals. Where localized communications was the only requirement, the RF folks decided to apply some of the characteristics of the CATV business in the local data communications business. Local nets were set up with the use of a broadband communications capacity, the equivalent of CATV, to support the need for multiple, simultaneous data streams on a single medium. The voice half of the business favored this approach because a modulation technique (such as, modems) was used.

Baseband and Broadband

Baseband and broadband are two different types of signaling that can be used on a wire. We are speaking of the basic electrical waveforms that are injected onto the medium. Nevertheless, do not tune out at this point just because you are not an electrical or radio engineer (or even if you are)! We cover these methods in the context of benefits and choices rather than instructing the reader on the design and construction of the associated components. The emergence from the local nets into a formalized LAN arena introduced a new battleground between these factions in the industry: those who felt comfortable with the use of a baseband service (the data communications groups) and those who felt more comfortable with the use of a higher-speed communications channel capacity (the voice communications, broadband RF, and electrical engineers). The stage was set for the next set of arguments. In the early 1980s, this was a hot battle, with each side claiming that it had the best solution and that the other side did not know what it was talking about.

Many organizations had to take this decision to a very high level of management for approval. When you think about the concept, why was management bothered with these complex decisions? All management wanted was a communications solution that met the organizational needs without wasting money. Management was asked to decide on a technical decision that it was not qualified to make. Hence, outside consultants were brought in to assist with the decision process. Unfortunately, the external consultants were equally split in their recommendations. We have seen cases where management brought in a consultant at the recommendation of the baseband side of the business. Then a management consultant was brought in from the broadband side of the business. Management now had two recommendations, each different, so a third (independent) consultant was brought in to be the tiebreaker. What a waste of time and money!

Let's look at some of the differences between these two concepts. First, let's review the fundamental motivations that were used in determining whether to use a LAN or other connectivity arrangement.

Motivations Driving the LAN Decision

If you go back to when these decisions were being wrestled with, some historical perspective will help you to understand the argument in its basic form. When local nets and the ensuing LANs were being researched, the fundamental needs were clear.

The number of terminal users in the late 1970s and early 1980s was limited. Many very large organizations had a total number of terminals based on a 50:1 or 100:1 ratio. Only one terminal device was available for every 50 or 100 total employees. This might have been a shared device among users or a common function (data entry) whereby all employees brought their data to a keypunch operator for input/output.

The industry was claiming that by the mid-1980s the terminal ratio would be closer to 10:1 and closing in on 1:1. Office automation would mandate that the deployment of such terminal devices would be required for every "knowledge worker." The alternative to massive wiring to support this increasing population of users was to use a form of the backbone system with easier connectivity to a central computer, rather than "home runs" to the host from the user terminal. However, the use of a LAN to replace or simplify the cabling nightmare and the expanding population went far beyond this. The following is a group of other reasons for installing a LAN on a single-shared medium. Table 23-1 summarizes the primary motivations for considering the LAN.

Data Rates

Local cable runs or dial-up communications normally handled the original data rates for terminals. The newer terminal devices that use bit map overlays, graphical user interfaces, and the density of the data require much higher data speeds than were previously available. The LAN is designed to support much higher throughput speeds than traditional dial-up communications and local cable attachments.

Interconnection

Older terminals were hard-wired back to the host, or controller, or were connected by a dial-up line. The use of a LAN moves away from the concept of a central computer control into a distributed control architecture. This enables a server to support users locally and only connect to the host when necessary. This interconnectivity is a function of the LAN. Figure 23-1 shows the other problem with interconnectivity. A user might need to access three different computers; therefore, a terminal attached to each was required. The lack of desk space was a problem, and the cost of such a solution was exorbitant.

Table 23-1

Primary Motivations
for Considering
the LAN

Reason	Discussion
Data rates	The original data rates for terminals were normally handled by local cable runs or dial-up connections. The newer terminal devices that use bit map overlays, graphical user interfaces, and the density of the data require much higher data speeds than what was available. The LAN is designed to support much higher throughput speeds than traditional dial-up communications and local cable attachments.
Interconnection	Most terminals were hard-wired back to the host, or controller, or were connected by a dial-up line. The use of a LAN moves away from the concept of a central computer control into a distributed control architecture. This enables a server to support users locally and only connect to the host when necessary. This interconnectivity is a function of the LAN. Figure 23-1 shows the other problem with interconnectivity. A user may need to access three different computers; therefore, a terminal attached to each was required. The lack of desk space created problems, and the cost of such a solution was exorbitant.
Integrated resources	Voice, data, text, and video were all on separate networks and wiring schemes, as shown in Figure 23-2. The LAN was touted as the first solution to integrate all these into a single infrastructure. Although this is not still a reality, except in limited tests, the concept of a single access to any service was a motivation to consider LANs, as shown in Figure 23-3.
Compatibility issues	Various access and protocol stacks were used. The LAN was to provide a common interface for access to any connected service. The operative phrase was common communications among various vendors. LAN interfaces were to be highly intelligent, so that it did not matter what the need was as long as the common path could be established.
Cost implications	As previously mentioned, the cost of separate systems and wiring solutions was exorbitant. The LAN single connection was to provide this at a much more reasonable rate to the organization.

Integrated Resources

Voice, data, text, and video were all on separate networks and wiring schemes (Figure 23-2). The LAN was touted as the first solution to integrate all these into a single infrastructure. Although this is still not a reality, except in limited tests, the concept of a single access to any service was a motivation to consider LANs (Figure 23-3).

Figure 23-1
The cost for a separate terminal connection to each computer was high.

Figure 23-2
Four separate wiring systems were used to provide appropriate services. This is an expensive, nonintegrated solution.

■■■ ■■■ ■■■ ■■■
Figure 23-3
An integrated
solution with a single
cable was the ideal
goal of a LAN.

Compatibility Issues

Various access and protocol stacks were used. The LAN was to provide a common interface for access to any connected service. The operative phrase was common communications among various vendors. LAN interfaces were to be highly intelligent, so that it did not matter what the need was as long as the common path could be established.

Cost Implications

As already mentioned, the cost of separate systems and wiring solutions was exorbitant. The LAN single connection was to provide this at a much more reasonable rate.

Table 23-2 represents the cost comparisons of the alternatives. In this table, we use example prices only because the actual connections and services go beyond what we can address for every organization. The numbers

Table 23-2

Comparison of
Costs for a Single
versus Multiple
Cabling System
Connection

Needed Connection	Separate Connection	LAN Connection
Voice, twisted pair to the PBX	$ 500	
Data terminal, coax cable 327X device	$1,000	
Word processing connection to a specialized system or minicomputer on a coax or twisted pair	$ 450	
Video connection on a coax CATV cable	$ 500	
Voice, data, video, and word processing integrated on a LAN		$ 800
Total	$2,450	$ 800
Differences		($1,650)

are generic, but roughly approximate to what was found in an organization back then. We looked at the cost of wiring a voice connection to the PBX, a data terminal via coax to the host, a text-based terminal to a word processing system (specialized or minicomputer), and a video connection. Then we compared this to the LAN connection costs that were offered in the past.

This was an appropriate comparison, but a problem emerged with this philosophy. The various systems being offered in the LAN arena would not support all of these services on a single cable system. The reasons for this argument are as follows:

■ Voice, although a baseband system, is a two-way simultaneous conversation, full duplex. Although we saw that voice operates primarily as a half-duplex service, the need to be fully duplexed is always there. Conversations are built around the need for two people (or more) to interact as they would in a face-to-face conversation. The LANs would not specifically allow this in the Ethernet and token-passing ring installations; they are baseband.

■ Both voice and video require a constant bit rate of transmission. They are not data communications transport. Voice and video are not easily packetized or placed in frames like data. Data and LANs deal with more variability in their need to transmit, but can suffice for the packetization or framed format of transport. If an integrated cable is used, various streams will be required on the cable simultaneously in a full- and half-duplex method. This was formerly not an available service because baseband LANs are primarily one-way transmission systems.

- As this was a shared cable system, the use of the cable by a single user at a time on the entire bandwidth was not appropriate. Voice does not need 4, 10, or 16 Mbps. Video can use this much, but we have already compressed this into much smaller bandwidth requirements. Hence, the baseband LAN was only perceived as a single transport for data, not voice and video. This underpinned the benefits of a fully integrated solution.

Three ways were available to provide the integrated solution, which included the following.

The PBX

Integrated PBX solutions were being touted for their robustness in the business environment. Because most organizations already had a telephone system, the PBX manufacturers were pushing their wares as the solution for voice, data, and other needs. However, the PBX was limited in its capability to handle the higher speeds integral to the LAN desires and data transport. Digital PBXs were still relegated to the 64-Kbps digital or 9.6-Kbps analog dial-up connections. The PBX players were quick to state that the average LAN transmits at 4 or 10 Mbps, one-way. However, the digital PBX can handle much higher aggregated speeds than a LAN. Voice is two-way, so the PBX has a two-way simultaneous connection. Table 23-3 shows how the PBX suppliers were touting their bandwidth capacities.

Although you might argue with the numbers, the PBX makers also conducted studies and found that most computer systems were limited to 64-Kbps data transfer rates, and that the average user needed no more than that. We have to give them credit for trying! PBXs introduced one added risk that everyone noticed right away. The system was a centralized architecture, which meant that all of the associated risks of a single box on a network were present. Further, this was a digression from the distributed architecture that the LAN players were trying to accomplish.

Table 23-3

PBX Manufacturers'
Comeback to Their
LAN Service

Item	PBX	LAN Bus	LAN Ring
Number of users who can be simultaneously wired	10,000	1,000 in Ethernet	260 in token ring
Maximum speed per connection	64 Kbps	10 Mbps	16 Mbps
Two-way benefits	64 Kbps	Not available	Not available
Total number of users communicating at once	5,000*	1	1
Number of users times aggregated bandwidth	640 Mbps†	10 Mbps	16 Mbps
Capability to handle video	Yes	No	No

*This assumes that 5,000 users can simultaneously call the other 5,000 users in the system, meaning that 50 percent of the people can call the other 50 percent.

†This number is derived from the following: 5,000 users transmitting and receiving at 64 Kbps is 128 Kbps times 5,000 connections or 640 Mbps. This is arguable, but the companies were in the running and hyped what they had to offer.

Baseband Cable Systems

As mentioned in earlier chapters, an Ethernet and token ring normally use baseband signaling. Baseband signaling is actually rather simple in concept. Devices using this technique place a digital (square waveforms—that is, 1's and 0's) signal directly on the attached medium (the cable). Only one device can communicate at a time on a baseband system. There is no means for allowing two devices to originate a signal on the medium during overlapping time intervals. If two devices did try to transmit simultaneously, both digital signals would instantly be garbled beyond recognition. In the case of a bus network, several elaborate methods are used to ensure that transmitters have the medium to themselves (refer to the Ethernet discussion). In token ring and star networks, any given cable has only two connected devices following rigid protocols; no conflict arises (refer to the token ring discussion).

As with any digital signal, the square waveforms degrade over distance somewhat more quickly than would be the case using analog transmission techniques. However, so long as baseband networks are engineered within their designed distance limitations, they experience a very low level of errors.

Figure 23-4 shows a representation of the degradation of the square wave. Distances are limited in a coax cable system such as the Ethernet. Specification for a thick-wire Ethernet is 500 meters. Yes, repeaters can be used to extend the distances, as seen in the Chapter 21. Two repeaters can extend the linear distance to approximately 1,500 meters (just under a mile of cable). However, this is still a single-user access at a time on the entire bandwidth available. The degradation of the signal is only one part of the equation.

A key characteristic of actual baseband network standards is that they have generally been designed to enable a by-the-numbers design approach. If one uses standardized components and stays within the specific guide-lines, the networks should work fine (barring failed components, of course). Also, the equipment, because it only deals with one signal at a time, costs less than digital broadband components. Proponents of the baseband sys-tems were diehards in their assessment that this was the least expensive and the most robust operation to meet the needs of the LAN for the future. Realizing that these LANs were being built for the transport of data only, these people felt that there was no need to do anything else. Xerox, of Eth-ernet acclaim, was one of the single largest proponents of the baseband approach. This was natural because Xerox was in that market. However, several comments made by Xerox as an organization led people to believe that this was the technology that they would live and die on.

Several issues must be taken with the idea of the single bus topology or the token ring topology that permits only one user at a time to send in one direction. Much has already been said about how the network works in the Chapters 21 and 22. Therefore, we will concentrate on the differences

Figure 23-4
The square wave degrades over distances, limiting the overall LAN length.

Well-formed
Digital Signal
(individual packets,
one after another)

Baseband Medium

Attenuated and
blurred (rounded)
Digital Signal

between baseband and broadband. We are not trying to suggest that a choose-or-not-choose approach is covered here. We will merely try to cover all of the issues in an unbiased fashion. The following paragraphs describe some counters to the arguments that always surface.

Baseband Is Cheaper Than Broadband and PBX Solutions

Although this is a valid argument, the jury never sits for a global statement in this industry. Whereas the Ethernet cards are very inexpensive and the ancillary equipment pieces such as hubs and twisted-pair wiring are inexpensive today, the PBX prices for 64-Kbps transport have also dropped through the floor. Secondly, CATV has been in use for longer than we can remember. The parts are also available and mass produced. Thus, a per-tap arrangement makes this a somewhat moot point because the cost per drop is about the same. If we look at the token ring services, the MAUs and the token ring cards are more expensive, as seen in the previous chapter. A 16-Mbps token ring card can cost upward of $695, and the MAU can be as expensive as $600 to $700 for an eight-port tap into the baseband LAN.

Baseband Is a Very Scalable LAN Service

In fact, it is not as scalable as one might be led to believe. More than 20 years have passed since the initial baseband LANs were first contrived. Only recently has the ability to take the baseband from the 10- or 16-Mbps speeds to the 100/1,000-Mbps range been available. A baseband service addresses a fundamental need. The speed constraints are not suitable for the application of trying to merge voice and video on the LAN. Therefore, a full-duplex LAN in either Ethernet or token ring is now an option. The addition of voice and video will demand duplex and higher speeds, otherwise the network will quickly come to a grinding halt.

Baseband Is Highly Efficient

Any protocol that we add onto any topology and medium can be efficient. The use of baseband, Ethernet, and token ring in particular has a certain amount of overhead. These protocols tend to make the baseband decision different than you might think. As we saw in the Ethernet discussion, frames have minimum sizes. This is so the systems attached to the baseband cable can see the timing and listen to the information during specific time slots. All data transferred must abide by the rules or the system doesn't work. The overhead and the wait-until-it's-your-turn-to-send approach make the 10-Mbps throughput drop to approximately 3.3 to 4 Mbps. That happens to be 60 to 67 percent inefficient.

Therefore, the argument for the baseband system is not as straightforward as you might believe. The heavier the load on a baseband system, the greater the efficiency loss. For example, a 10-Mbps Ethernet typically yields a net throughput of only 3 to 4 Mbps. The larger the population of users or the density of the data, the greater the risk of collisions. Figure 23-5 illustrates an example of the collision. If I send peanut butter and you send jelly, halfway down the cable we collide. Now you have jelly in my peanut butter! This isn't what I sent, so it must be discarded and resent. In a baseband token ring, things are more deterministic, but the greater the population on the network, the greater the waiting time to finally transmit. See Figure 23-6 for a small-scale look at the performances of CSMA/CD and token-passing rings.

Figure 23-5
The denser the data or the greater the number of users, the greater the likelihood of collisions.

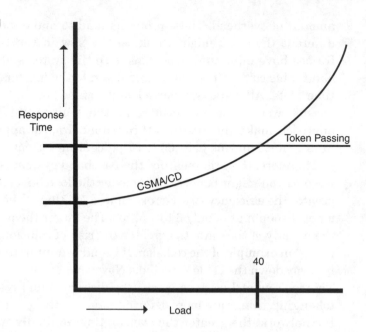

Figure 23-6
This is a comparison of load and response time for baseband networks. Token passing is a smoother degradation, whereas CSMA/CD works efficiently at lower loads.

Broadband Cable Systems

The term *broadband* is used in several different ways in the communications industry. Descriptions of two of these uses are

■ Any wide-area communications channel of significant bandwidth. *Significant* in this case is used to mean any circuit whose capacity equaled or exceeded 56 Kbps. Some analog facilities fit this description. Now, if a circuit is not at least a T1 (1.544 Mbps), it is rarely referred to as a broadband facility. In fact, many of the T1 services and below are referred to as *narrowband*; T1 up to T3 are called *wideband,* and everything above the T3 level is referred to as *broadband.* Like anything else in this industry, all of this is according to your own interpretation. Analog wide area facilities, of whatever capacity, are rarely referred to as being broadband.

■ Any one of a specific set of service offerings from common carriers (SMDS, T1 and T3, ATM, frame relay, SONET, and so on). It is the specific technique of using coaxial cable to carry multiple channels over LAN distances.

This last description is the one discussed in this chapter. We have spent a lot of time throughout this book defining the applications, uses, and definitions of baseband, yet little time discussing broadband communications. Therefore, we finally delve into the subject now. Although most people do not think in terms of baseband and broadband, they exist for significant differences and reasons. To fully understand the broadband communications, we use a CATV system as a comparison.

The LAN arena has always argued that baseband was the simplest and least expensive solution to installing a network. Fundamental differences exist with such a global statement. Furthermore, the broadband communications on a cable system is perceived as an inferior product offering.

Broadband signaling on coaxial cable is one method of designing a local area network. It is unique in several respects:

- Multiple signals coexist simultaneously (actually at the same time, not just appearing as though they are happening at the same time because of speed).

- Broadband signaling is inherently analog, but digital signals can nonetheless be sent using it, just as digital signals can be sent over the public telephone network.

- It uses many components originally designed for a completely unrelated industry—cable television.

- It is not plug-and-play like, for example, Ethernet and token ring.

- It is targeted primarily at industrial environments because it runs only on coaxial cable, a medium more resistant than most (not counting fiber) to interference by industrial processes (such as, arc welders).

Cables that use broadband signaling function like a superhighway with a few hundred lanes, all divided by solid, double yellow lines (with no breaks). Each lane carries traffic more or less independently of traffic in other lanes. If traffic drifts across lanes, accidents will occur that disrupt traffic. However, this doesn't normally happen because buffers separate the lanes (the double yellow lines provide some physical spacing, although not so much as to be wasteful).

Broadband LANs are based on the same underlying technology as cable television. To understand this, you only need to consider a typical CATV system in a hotel or large apartment complex. The building is served from some transmission system located outside the confines of the physical plant. This serving end of the cable is called a *head end*. From the head end, the television signals are distributed along the cable and the cable forks as necessary to cover all locations. Many TV signals are on the cable at the same time. The user of the cable interface unit (the TV in this case) selects a particular channel from the whole list of available channels on the cable. This is done by tuning into a specific frequency, which is what you do when you use the infrared remote control changer (Figure 23-7). The set is then tuned to the channel designator selected on the remote controller. The TV does this by tuning in on a specific frequency range or a frequency band. Because television channels need to carry a lot of information in the form of motion video (albeit one-way broadcast video), the bandwidth of the channel has been allocated a 6-MHz capacity (6 MHz or 6 million cycles per second). The interval from the lowest to the highest frequencies passed on this channel is 6 MHz. The channels are run next to each other similar to the way the telephone network operates. Channel 2, for example, on a CATV might operate on a frequency band of 48 to 54 MHz. Channel 3 will operate at 54 to 60 MHz. Standard cable systems have an immense amount of bandwidth available to them.

As the TV signals propagate down the cable, they will lose some of their strength. This loss of power is similar to that which occurs on the telephone network and is called *attenuation*. If the signal drops below a certain threshold, it becomes difficult to separate the signal from the electrical noise always present on the cable. Of course, when this happens, the signal quality, or the output, to the TV drops and a low-quality TV picture is produced. To overcome this problem, an amplifier is placed at certain intervals along the cable. The amplifier boosts the signal strength so that it can continue to move along the wire in a usable manner.

Although only a single physical cable is present, a number of channels can be present on the cable simultaneously. This is accomplished by sharing the frequency spectrum of the cable and assigning different frequency

Figure 23-7
The remote controller causes the cable box and TV to tune to a new channel. All channels are on the cable at one time, but only one can be viewed.

Infrared controller tunes TV to a new channel

ranges to different channels. This was covered earlier in the chapter on data communications and is called *frequency division multiplexing* (FDM). A broadband cable communications system operates exactly like this CATV system, and even uses the same types of cable and connectors. A counter to this FDM technique is the division of the cable not divided into frequency bands but into time slots. This is called *time-division multiplexing* (TDM); with this, each station can grab the entire bandwidth of the cable, but only for a very short period. The cable is currently capable of carrying up to 750 to 950 MHz, depending on the vintage in use. Early cable systems using the FDM techniques divided the channels into a number of dedicated logical channels as strictly an alternative to twisted-pair wiring. This FDM technique did not address the interconnectivity solutions required by a LAN. Past innovations have allowed a time-division multiple access (TDMA) within an FDM channel. A single cable can service a large amount of terminal communications. On this same cable, but on different FDM channels, data circuits, voice channel, and video signals can all coexist.

Modern systems enable multiplexing on two separate dimensions. The channels are separated by FDM, and in a specific frequency band, the channel can then be shared via TDMA among multiple users. The most common of the TDMA access methods on a broadband cable has been the CSMA/CD developed by Xerox Corporation for Ethernet.

The considerable raw bandwidth of the cable is divided into many individual channels, each wide enough to carry one digital signal. However, the underlying structure of the network is different. On a broadband network, a single-head end device receives every broadcast signal on one of two major sets of channels, and then retransmits the same signal on the corresponding outbound channel. Figure 23-8 illustrates broadband bandwidth allocations.

The actual cable runs might look something like those in Figure 23-9, a sample broadband cable layout. This diagram provides a clue as to why small proportions of Ethernets are implemented on broadband cable plants; they are too complicated!

Because it is a truly multichannel medium, broadband cable permits a surprising variety of applications to reside on a single cable plant. On one cable, a company can carry security video signals, terminal channels for mainframe access, one- or two-way video signals for classroom use, and Ethernet. Ethernet? But Ethernet is baseband!

Well, yes, Ethernet is baseband. Baseband signaling, as stated, requires a dedicated channel on which one frame at a time is placed. But the Ethernet can use multiple media. Why not carve out part of a broadband cable's

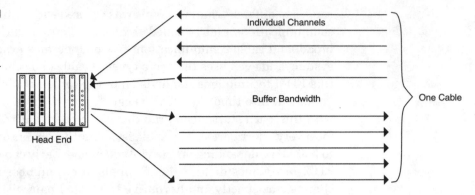

Figure 23-8
Broadband
bandwidth allocation

Figure 23-9
Sample broadband
cable layout

bandwidth for an Ethernet (or even several Ethernets—up to three at once are supported)?

Broadband cables in the CATV world have an inherent difference; they are designed around delivering the TV programming on a single cable in a unidirectional flow. All signals come from the CATV head end. A couple of variations are allowed to turn this cable into a bidirectional transmission; these are as follows:

- Using a single cable, a midsplit arrangement can accommodate two-way simultaneous transmission. A midsplit divides the cable into separate pieces. A portion of the cable, called a *reverse direction*, is used to send signals to the head end from the transmitting devices.

The rest of the cable, called the *forward direction*, is used to send from the head end to the receiving devices. Figure 23-10 shows this arrangement. A portion of the cable is allocated for a guard band to prevent the overlap between the channels. The head end's job is to receive the signals from the devices on the reverse direction, change the frequency, and send the signal back out to the cable on the forward direction.

■ The second choice is to use a dual cable system. In this case, the entire spectrum of a single cable is used in the reverse direction to the head end. The second cable is used for the forward direction from the head end to the devices attached to this cable. Figure 23-11 shows a

Figure 23-10
The midsplit cable

Head End

Figure 23-11
A dual cable can be used to get the full bandwidth in a system in each direction.

summary of how this will look. For those of us who remember the Wangnet approach, Wang used a dual cable system. Each of the frequencies was split up to provide services and utility bands for connecting other devices such as Ethernets to their broadband cable system.

Broadband is inherently an analog signaling method. Because video cameras, for example, are also analog devices, a signal from a video camera (or video recorder) can be directly transmitted onto a broadband cable channel in red, green, blue (RGB) format. No conversions are required, as shown in Figure 23-12. Voice signals and conversations can also be modulated onto the broadband cable easily. In the case of a PBX on a site or campus, voice tie lines can be used (Figure 23-13). Dedicated high-speed data links can also be set up on a broadband cabling system. Further, telemetry and paging circuits can be modulated directly on and off the cable. Finally, Ethernet and other digital technologies are indeed implemented on broadband cables.

But additional hardware is needed. From earlier chapters, you might remember another situation where digital signals were required to travel over an analog network, in that case the public telephone network. As in that case, to transmit digital signals over a broadband network, we must use special modems in addition to all the normal components required to implement a cable television system. Broadband modems are called frequency agile modems (FAMs). Because frames are sent on one frequency and received on another frequency, they must be agile.

Figure 23-12
Video can be modulated directly onto the broadband cable without any conversion.

Figure 23-13

Voice-grade tie lines
can be sent directly
across the broadband
cable.

However, all of the typical voice, data, video, and LAN services can be applied in some form onto the broadband cable. This was one of the motivating factors in making the decision to go to a LAN, wasn't it? The ability to create an integrated cabling solution for all of our communications needs has quite a bit of merit. Yet, unfortunately or fortunately, baseband cabling persevered and became the norm. Some of the reasons for this are the complexities of managing and maintaining the system. Table 23-4 summarizes the capabilities of using a broadband cabling system.

What more can we ask a single cabling system to do? Everything that we need to accomplish on a single site can be performed and modulated onto a single or dual cable system. Yet the opponents of this cabling scheme have a tendency to disparage it and claim that it is foolish to even consider it as an alternative.

Table 23-4

Summary of What
Can Be Run on the
Broadband Cable

Voice tie lines such as four-wire E&M
Logical connections of 3270 terminals to the cable and to the controller
CAD/CAM
Video conferencing
Closed-circuit security systems
Building management systems such as energy management, security, alarms, and so on
LAN a la Ethernet

One significant disadvantage to broadband (as opposed to baseband) is that it must be installed by technicians qualified in radio technology. Moreover, as with all radio technology, it must

■ Be periodically checked to ensure compliance with FCC regulations.

■ Be returned when significant changes are made to the configuration, particularly when additional taps, which would cause added loss, are placed on the cable. The use of more amplifiers might also be required.

In short, it is more of a hassle than baseband technologies. Thus, the baseband war won. Both sides of this equation have had some strong arguments. In a large campus environment, broadband might carry a lot of benefits, whereas on a department-by-department basis, installation and maintenance of baseband was less of a problem, so this was the preferred route to follow.

Baseband versus Broadband

Why use one over the other? Baseband should be your default choice because of its simplicity and lower cost. It is far more widespread; parts and service are much more readily available.

As with any default, a number of factors might push someone in the direction of other solutions. Those needs that might mandate selection of a broadband rather than a baseband solution include

■ A cable television plant (with available bandwidth) is already in place in the facility to be wired (thus helping to limit costs).

■ Video signaling is also required for a significant portion of the locations to be wired.

■ Several separated Ethernets (but no more than three) are required, and which Ethernet a drop is to be on might change. (This reason is weaker today than in the past; such a configuration can now easily be accommodated with Ethernet hubs and appropriate 10BASE-T wiring.)

■ The distances to be covered are longer than those that other Ethernet cabling can support, but within those supported by broadband.

■ The network is to be installed in a highly electrically noisy environment—for example, on a factory floor. (Fiber is an alternative solution to broadband that should also be considered in such cases.)

Questions

1. Coax cables were initially and traditionally operated as:
   a. Baseband
   b. Broadband
   c. Dial up
   d. Video

2. Baseband uses a _____ approach to propagating the signal.
   a. Modulated
   b. Demodulated
   c. Nonmodulated
   d. Fully modulated

3. Baseband communications is:
   a. Analog
   b. Digital
   c. Half duplex
   d. Full duplex
   e. A and C
   f. B and D

4. Although a baseband system, this service operates as a two-way simultaneous transmission, full duplex.
   a. LANs
   b. Data
   c. Voice
   d. Video

5. With a baseband system, how many devices can communicate at a time?
   a. 2
   b. 1,024
   c. 1
   d. 12

6. Digital PBXs were still relegated to 9.6 Kbps data only.   T/F

7. Digital PBX systems cannot be used in lieu of a LAN.   T/F

8. In a baseband network, multiple signals coexist simultaneously on the cable.   T/F

9. Broadband cables use a modulation technique called:

   a. TDM

   b. FDM

   c. QPSK

   d. AM

10. Broadband cables have very large amounts of bandwidth.   T/F

11. Baseband cables operate at approximately:

   a. 10 MHz

   b. 450 MHz

   c. 20 MHz

   d. 900 MHz

12. Cables that use broadband signaling function like a _____ with a few hundred lanes, all divided by solid, double yellow lines.

   a. Narrowband road

   b. Wide area network

   c. Metropolitan network

   d. Superhighway

13. All of the typical voice, data, video, and LAN services can be applied in some form onto the broadband cable.   T/F

14. The CATV systems operate as baseband LANs when we connect an Ethernet.   T/F

15. CATV systems can carry highly reliable data because:

   a. They are operated by a CATV company.

   b. They are shielded cables.

   c. They can act as an antenna.

   d. Data was designed to run in between the channels.

Fiber Distributed Data Interface (FDDI)

After reading this chapter and completing the questions, you will be able to:

- Discuss the meaning of fiber distributed data interface (FDDI)
- Understand what the speeds are when using an FDDI
- Determine the benefits of using the FDDI network
- Understand the use of a ring topology in the campus area network (CAN)
- Discuss the difference between the normal token ring concept and the FDDI concept

When we discussed the speed of the LANs as we looked at the Ethernet and token ring topologies, we were specific in terms of what can be expected. The older Ethernet operates at 10 Mbps, whereas the initial version of the token ring operates at 4 Mbps, with an updated version operating at 16 Mbps. These speeds were fine when the LANs were first introduced, but as we approach the end of the century, LAN throughput is becoming a potential bottleneck. The speeds were initially introduced and shared among 20 to 30 users to perform word processing, small spreadsheets, and the like. However, as the LANs ballooned in the industry, with devices appearing on nearly every desk, and the applications became more intense, the 4-, 10-, and 16-Mbps capacities were clearly signaling that a problem was looming.

More users are sharing more data on a single cable. We could use a subnetworking technique to buy time, but this introduces smaller networks competing for a shared bandwidth. Furthermore, the more we subnetwork, the more pieces on the network can fail. Consequently, the industry set out to develop a much faster network arrangement. The result was a technique known as *fiber distributed data interface* (FDDI). FDDI was designed under the auspices of ANSI as a high-speed, highly reliable data transport. The significance of the FDDI standard is that it is a national standard supported by the entire data communications industry. Because it is a national standard, FDDI workstations, computers, and other peripheral devices work together regardless of the manufacturer. Moving away from the limitations of a 10-Mbps bus and the high-end 16-Mbps ring, FDDI was designed to have an effective throughput of 100 Mbps. Using a fiber-optic backbone and a deterministic token-passing approach, the technology overcomes the constraints of the older systems. This is not a panacea for all LANs, but a stepping-stone into higher-speed digital communications. Certain strengths and limitations should be noted when considering FDDI. It is not for everyone, yet for those organizations that have exhausted the throughput capabilities of the LAN, FDDI might offer some breathing room.

FDDI Design

When ANSI first started this long and arduous task back in 1988, the goal was to overcome more than just the throughput problems. Surely, a higher speed capability was an earnest desire, and at 100 Mbps, no one would argue that a 6- to 10-fold increase in throughput was not warranted. However, other constraints were also concentrated on; these are summarized in Table 24-1, which looks at the limitations of the bus and the rings of old combined. These were the targets for the standards committees and should be presented right up front.

To overcome these and many other limitations, the FDDI standard was written and technology was developed to address each of these areas. Therefore, FDDI is designed to do the following:

- Support higher data rates at up to 100 Mbps.

- Work in a deterministic token-passing environment, preventing collisions.

- Support attachment of up to 1,000 addressable nodes.

Table 24-1

*Summary of
Existing Topology
Problems and
Limitations*

Topology/Item	Limitation
Bus speed	10 Mbps with effective throughput of 3.3–4 Mbps
Ring speed	4 Mbps with effective throughput of 3.3 Mbps 16 Mbps with effective throughput of 12 Mbps
Bus attachments	Up to 1,024 addressable nodes, but limited by cable lengths of 1,500 meters
Ring attachments	72 addressable nodes on unshielded twisted pairs and 260 addressable nodes on shielded twisted pairs depending on distances
Unshielded twisted pair	Error-prone due to wire characteristics and electrical and mechanical interference
Shielded twisted pair	More expensive, bulky, and subject to ground loops
Bus and ring topologies	Subject to disruptions from cable breaks and other cable-related problems
Bus topology	Collisions when the network is 40 percent busy, resulting in less throughput

- Extend the distance of the ring up to 200 km (approximately 124 miles) for a single ring and 100 km (approximately 62 miles) for a dual ring.

- Provide robustness, in that a dual ring can be used as a backup or to wrap around after equipment and cable failures.

- Use optical fiber as the preferred medium to overcome the physical limitations of electrical and mechanical interference.

- Provide spacing of up to 2 km (approximately 1.25 miles) between repeaters.

Using the parameters listed, FDDI was born. You might expect that the industry and LAN administrators jumped for joy. Unfortunately, this did not happen. FDDI received a cool reception. The single largest reason (one we have stated over and over) was money! FDDI was just too expensive for most LAN administrators to implement. As FDDI was introduced, a card operating in a high-end server could be purchased for $15,000 to $23,000. The individual cards that were designed to work in a PC or PC-based server sold for $1,500 to $2,000. Can you imagine what the cost for a 100-user LAN might be? For the sake of keeping it simple, we have summarized the costs

Table 24-2

Summary of Costs
for a PC Equipped
for the LAN
Connection

Item	Cost
Change to PC, Intel-based PIII × 4/100 or Pentium 700-MHz with 64MB RAM, 20.0-GB hard drive, single floppy, and SVGA monitor	$2,500
LAN interface card Ethernet	$ 99*
LAN interface card ring (4/16)	$ 295
Cables and connectors	$ 25
Total	$2,624–$2,820

*This is an either-or decision with the Ethernet or the token ring card. Thus, the range of costs for the PC is included with either option.

in Table 24-2. At the time FDDI came to the desktop, the PC hardware costs were rapidly dropping. The table summarizes the cost of a typical PC.

From a cost of $2,600 to $2,800 for the PC, reduce the incremental charge of the NIC card ($99 to $295) but add the cost of an FDDI card ($1,500 to $2,000) and you would double the cost per device on the network very quickly. Now, using this example, a price comparison is shown for different-size networks, with the resultant differences shown in Table 24-3.

Table 24-3

Summary of Cost
Difference in a LAN

Number of Users	Cost/PC Std NIC 2,600	Cost/PC FDDI 4,600	Difference
10	26,000	46,000	20,000
20	52,000	92,000	40,000
30	78,000	138,000	60,000
50	130,000	230,000	100,000
100	260,000	460,000	200,000
250	650,000	1,150,000	500,000
500	1,300,000	2,300,000	1,000,000
1,000	2,600,000	4,600,000	2,000,000

A true picture of the financial implications can be painted this way. The table brings the reluctance factor home nicely.

Can you imagine the way management would feel if we were to request a LAN using FDDI and show the cost of a 100-user network? The PC-based solution with a standard NIC card is $200,000 less than the FDDI solution. What would be the benefit of an added $200,000 in investment? But wait! There's more. The prices listed are examples only, so we should make sure that all the costs are associated with this comparison. We didn't add the differences for the server connection, the wiring differential, and the concentrators (MAUs) that work in the closet. So, taking this one step further, these costs must be considered. To do so, we summarize the cost per connection as listed in Table 24-4 (by now you see we are getting cost crazy).

We are not trying to dissuade the reader from looking at the FDDI solution, but are trying to make sure that a true picture is painted. Thus, if we take that 100-user LAN we dealt with in the previous example and add to the cost of that LAN, the variation (Table 24-4), a comparison of the LAN to the FDDI, now totals up differently (Table 24-5). This is for comparative purposes only, so that a set of numbers can be used. The actual prices will be completely different when you look at the building and work group specifics in your own network. Having said that, we continue our comparison.

This is a shocking result because the actual cost to use the FDDI is double that of a regular twisted-pair LAN. So why use it? Well, let's back up a little. We have been using a 100-user LAN with Ethernet operating at 10 Mbps. For only twice the investment, we get a 10-fold increase in the throughput! Regardless of what management has to say, this type of effective throughput has some benefits. This is especially true when

Table 24-4

Additional Costs of Installing FDDI to the Desktop above Regular LAN Connections

Item	Cost Per Port/User FDDI	Totals
Servers for 100 users, 2 used	2 FDDI cards @ $15,000	$30,000
Wiring for fiber to desk, with connectors, etc.	$50,000 for station wiring $14,000 for backbone wiring, $4,000 for connectors	$68,000
MAUs (called concentrators) for FDDI backbone	4 @ $500	$2,000
Total difference		$100,000

Table 24-5

Truer Comparison for the 100-User LAN with FDDI

Original Cost of Connectivity	Added Costs for FDDI	Cumulative	Total
100-user LAN, hardware, etc. at $2,600 per station	0	$260,000	
Cost of wiring for normal LAN at $350 per port/station	0	$ 35,000	$295,000
100-user LAN, hardware, etc. with FDDI to the desk	$200,000	$260,000 plus $200,000	
Cost of wiring for fiber to the desk and fiber backbone, connectors, etc. from Table 24-4	$100,000	$100,000	$560,000
Difference for 100 users			$265,000

mission-critical applications reside on the LAN, when CAD/computer-assisted manufacturing (CAM) or graphics applications are running, or when heavy database and spreadsheet activity is resident. A bit more on the graphics applications: when you are running a network operating system from any manufacturer and you combine a graphical user interface (GUI) (such as Windows), you have added to the density of the data through the GUI. To further compound the issue, when users are using Windows on the network and they use a screen saver, they have all just added an immense amount of graphics on the LAN. Many administrators saw their 4-, 10-, and 16-Mbps LANs grind to a snail's pace, only to find that the GUI and screen savers were the culprits. Meanwhile, back to FDDI: this would help to significantly reduce this problem.

FDDI Configuration

As we mentioned, FDDI is designed to run on a token-passing ring operating at 100 Mbps. The fiber used is a 62.5-μm center core with a 125-μm outer cladding. This constitutes a multimode fiber system. Other multimode fiber sizes can be used, but the specification states 62.5/125 as the transmission medium. The fiber is configured as a single ring (Figure 24-1).

Figure 24-1
FDDI on a single ring topology

The single ring uses two strands of fiber to provide the resiliency of the ring to heal itself in the event of a cable problem. An optional second ring (Figure 24-2) can be installed. The second ring will be used as a backup to the first in the event of a major failure. When two rings are used, they operate in a dual counter-rotating manner. This means that they transmit the data in different directions. If dual rings are used, then four strands (or fibers) are run to each station. An alternative to a full dual ring architecture can be used for critical applications and for critical user groups. Figure 24-3 shows this alternative, where a single ring and a dual ring are intertwined. The single-ring users are noncritical, whereas the dual-ring users are more critical and downtime cannot be tolerated.

Stations on the fiber can be connected differently because of these options. They can be

- **Single attached stations (SAS)**   These devices are noncritical and are attached only to a single ring.

- **Dual attached stations (DAS)**   These devices have the circuitry and componentry to be attached to dual rings.

Figure 24-2
FDDI dual ring is
operational.

Figure 24-3
A mix of single ring
and dual ring can be
linked together.

A definition is in order at this point because we have a tendency to intermingle words in this industry. We talk about critical and noncritical users.
Then we introduce the concept of a station. Other times we talk about
nodes. Are they the same? The answer is no. These terms have some subtle
and logical differences in their definitions. Let's try it this way.

A *user* is any workstation, PC, server, or other device used to perform
work. A *station* is an addressable device on the network. This is the closest

proximity to a user there is. The user is human and the station is the mechanical device. However, because it is an addressable device, the station can either input data into or extract data from the FDDI.

A *node* is an active device on the network. The node can be a repeater or a device that completes the passing of information around the FDDI network. A node is non-addressable. All stations are also nodes, but all nodes are not stations.

Now, isn't that crystal clear? A node on the network can be a concentrator, the equivalent of a MAU or a multiport repeater. When we refer to attaching users either singly or dually to the FDDI, we are referring to the station. However, the physical attachment is likely through a node (a concentrator).

FDDI on the OSI Model

You knew this was coming! Where does all of this fit in our model? When we looked at the LAN architecture, we stated that the LAN typically works at the bottom two layers of the OSI model (physical and data link). Therefore, because we are really dealing with a LAN that is "on steroids" to get it up to a faster 100 Mbps, it should be obvious that the FDDI standards also deal with the lower layers of the OSI. Figure 24-4 shows this reference.

Figure 24-4
The FDDI stacks up against the bottom two layers of the OSI model.

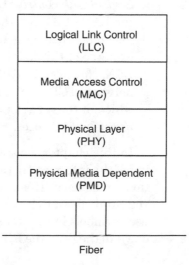

At the physical layer, the FDDI is broken into two separate sublayers, as follows:

■ The *Physical-media-dependent* (PMD) sublayer is at the bottom. The PMD is responsible for such things as the specifications of sending and receiving the signals; making sure that the proper power levels for the light are applied; and specifying the physical cables and connectors used.

■ The *Physical layer protocol* (PHY) is designed to be media independent. This means that this upper portion of layer 1 doesn't care what the cables are. It does define the coding of the information to be sent, the decoding of the signals that arrive, the timing on the network, the status of the lines (wires or fibers), and the framing conventions.

The data link layer is again a sublayered architecture. The two sublayers and their responsibilities are

■ *Media access control* (MAC) sublayer protocols define the rules for formatting the frame of information to be sent/received, error checking, handling the token on the FDDI, and managing the data link addressing. Some of this is contained in what is called *station management* (SMT). SMT is responsible for managing the station attached to the FDDI. It provides the rules for node configuration, statistics gathering on errors, recovery in the event of an error, and managing the connections.

■ *Logical link control* (LLC) is, as always, the common control function of the LAN. It defines the protocols to be used in the upper layers of the model because most LANs these days use multiple protocols. An example of this is a LAN running Novell Netware 3.X or 4.X. On this LAN, Novell's SPX/IPX protocols are prevalent, but depending on the network, TCP/IP might also be running on the network. LLC manages which of these two stacks is used in delivering the information to the upper-layer devices.

In this chapter, we stated that the PHY layer is responsible for the coding of the information, the timing on the network, and the framing conventions to be used. This is a fairly sophisticated set of responsibilities. When you think about it, this is heavy stuff. The coding is a classic example. FDDI uses symbols in the transmission of data onto the cable. To send the pulses down to the fiber, the PHY is responsible for performing a 4B/5B coding conversion. Four bits (4B) of information are delivered to the PHY. The PHY converts these 4 bits into a 5-bit (5B) symbol. This provides some synchronization (timing) on the FDDI and makes use of the extra bits inserted into the symbol by ensuring that enough pulses (1's) are used to keep the power of the light on the fiber. If too many 0's are present, then the equipment on the fiber will get amnesia and lose its place. If that happens, the equipment will have to resynchronize (time) between ends. No data will be transmitted while the systems are trying to retime, so a disruption will occur. Along with this creation of symbols, the FDDI uses electrical characteristics that are called nonreturn to zero inverted (NRZI). The use of 1's and 0's will occur with a transition from the 1's. The provision of the symbols enables the transition to occur on a regular basis. This is all taken care of through the standards and specifications. Figure 24-5 shows the process as the actual data goes through the 4B/5B and the encoding being used in the NRZI format. For the actual data throughput, the 4B/5B encoding provides a transmission rate of 100 Mbps on a 125-Mbaud link. A binary 1 is equal to a pulse of light; the light is on. A binary 0 is equal to no light; the light is off.

Building on this discussion, the MAC layer is responsible for the construction of the frames at the sending side and the interpretation of the frames at the receiving side of the link. It is also responsible for sending frames to and receiving frames from the LLC, repeating frames like the token ring process. A number of other functions occur at the MAC layer, but

Figure 24-5
The encoding and decoding process at the physical layer

a crucial one to be aware of is that it provides access to the ring using a timed token protocol. A station on an FDDI network can send information after it detects an idle token. To do this, the station must do the following:

- Capture the token.
- Remove the token from the ring.
- Send the data (this can be a single frame or multiple frames).
- On completion of transmission, put the token back onto the network so another station can send.

After transmitting information onto the network, it is the sending station's responsibility to perform the cleanup operation by removing its own information from the ring. As the data makes a full circle and comes by the sender, the sending station will remove the data from the ring. If something is corrupted or changed, the MAC layer will not try to solve the problem. The LLC or higher layers are responsible for error recovery, not the MAC layer.

The timing of the token passing on FDDI is different from a typical ring topology. A timed token-passing concept is used. This means that as a station is ready to transmit its information, synchronous slots are made available to the station. When the station sends all of its data frames, if it does not have any more reserved synchronous traffic to send (the synchronous traffic is the guaranteed bandwidth necessary for the particular station), it can use the extra time left over to send asynchronous traffic. Asynchronous traffic is referred to as random arrival or a bandwidth of demand capability for excess services, not the start/stop communications process commonly used in data communications. Each station has a small clocking mechanism (a stopwatch) to determine how long it will take the token to go around the ring (rotation) and pass by again. On the basis of this timing sequence, the station can determine how long it can hold the token and transmit its information. Once the station determines the timing, it sends all of its synchronous data on the network. If any spare time is still left over, the station can send its asynchronous traffic.

The FDDI Frame

You knew that we would discuss this piece, so here it is. The FDDI uses a frame size of 4,500 bytes, which is different than the size of the other LAN

Table 24-6

Comparison of
Frame Sizes Based
on LAN Type Used

LAN	Frame Size
Ethernet 10 Mbps	1,518 bytes
Token ring 4 Mbps	4,048 bytes
Token ring 16 Mbps	16,192 bytes
FDDI 100 Mbps	4,500 bytes

frames we have already discussed. Table 24-6 shows a comparison of the frame sizes based on the LAN type used. This is for comparative purposes, so that the size of the frames can be seen to work for the FDDI and other LANs.

The actual frame consists of similar size and structures of the existing LANs, but some subtle differences appear. This is a mechanism that transmits the data around the network. The frame will be broken down into several components, as shown in Figure 24-6. The token for FDDI prior to data is shown in Figure 24-7. This is not unlike the token used in a

Figure 24-6
The FDDI frame

	P	SD	FC	DA	SA	Data	FCS	ED	FS
Bytes	6	1	1	6	6	0≤4500	4	1/2	2+
4B Symbols	12	2	2	4 or 12*	4 or 12*	--	8	1	3+

* Some variation here based on
whether 16- or 48-bit address

Figure 24-7
The FDDI token

	P	SD	FC	ED
Symbols	≥12	2	2	1

Table 24-7

Summary of
Abbreviations Used
in the FDDI Frame

Abbreviation	Description
P	*Preamble* is a presynchronization pattern that is made up of at least 6 bytes consisting of all 1's. The 6-byte (48-bit) minimum is broken down into twelve 4-bit patterns to create the 5-bit symbols (4B/5B).
SD	*Starting delimiter* is made up of 1 byte (8 bits) to indicate the start of a frame. When using the 4B/5B symbols, the starting delimiter is divided into two 4-bit patterns and converted into two 5-bit symbols.
FC	*Frame control* is a 1-byte sequence broken down into two 4-bit sequences and encoded into two 5-bit symbols
DA	*Destination address* is a 6-byte address that becomes twelve 4-bit patterns and is encoded into twelve 5-bit symbols
SA	*Source address* is a 6-byte address that is broken down into twelve 4-bit patterns and then encoded into twelve 5-bit symbols
DATA	The data that is being carried: amount varies from 0 up to 4,500 bytes. This is broken down into the 4-bit patterns and encoded into the 5-bit symbols.
FCS	*Frame check sequence* is a CRC-32 computed from the FC through the FCS. This is a 4-byte sequence (32 bits) or 8 symbols.
ED	*Ending delimiter* is the signal to indicate the end of the frame. This is a 1-byte pattern that goes through the same 4B/5B sequence.
FS	*Frame status* has at least 12 bits or three 4-bit patterns consisting of three pieces of information. The first is the E bit that will be used to denote whether an error occurred in the frame. Next, the A bit signifies whether the address is recognized or not. The third is the C bit that indicates whether the information was copied. The EAC will be repeated at least two times as a check for errors because no CRD is performed on the frame status.

token-passing ring. After all, FDDI is a token-passing concept operating at higher speed. Table 24-7 lists the actual frame codes for reference. It would be wise to refer to this table when reviewing the figure so that the abbreviations will be easier to understand.

The frame definitions resemble those of a standard token-passing ring frame, with the exception of the preamble. The preamble is designed to set the timing and synchronization of the frame for each of the devices.

Synchronization

Because timing arrangements are used on an FDDI, it is critical that all devices keep the appropriate clocking mechanism. The PHY defines the clocking arrangement for the network. Every FDDI station on the network has its own independent clock. The receiver is designed to synchronize its clock to the incoming data and use its clock to decode the data taken off the network. It then retransmits the data with a new timing (clocking) that is generated by the local station. Sounds complex, but it is really quite simple. This keeps the network operating efficiently. The preamble in the beginning of the frame is designed to have pulses to create the clock synchronization. This again keeps everything in good working order. It should be noted that the bulk of the networks using the FDDI systems operate with almost no errors and that the performance of the components is exceptional. This is a highly reliable networking service.

FDDI Applications

The primary application of FDDI is in the backbone for many LANs. This high-speed backbone is used to connect a group of lower-speed LANs, such as token rings and Ethernets. Although other ways of using this FDDI network are available, users see it as a means of extending the LAN into a campus area network (CAN). Using a high-rise as one example, the backbone service is achieved. Figure 24-8 shows a group of individual LANs, operating with various speeds and topologies, connected to the FDDI backbone. This is where the FDDI standards shine. FDDI is topology and protocol independent when connecting these other services. The high-rise idea works nicely in many older buildings where the cables might be in elevator shafts, running close to electrical closets, or in proximity to other forms of interference (electrical, mechanical, or radio) that would corrupt the data on a copper-based backbone. Further, where riser space is at a premium, fiber is less bulky and offers a reliable connection between floors without taking up much cable or wall space. Moving out from the backbone in the high-rise, the FDDI can also be used in the CAN. In this particular case, the fiber is immune from electrical hazards such as lightning spikes and so on. This means that the typical protection normally used on copper cabling between buildings and the grounding and bonding requirements required by local fire and electric codes are nonissues. FDDI stands to provide the higher

Figure 24-8
Various speeds on
topologies can
connect to the FDDI
ring.

throughput between these buildings on a campus because the extended distances provide greater flexibility. Working on the 62/125 -μm fiber and providing up to 2 km between repeaters extends the distances over those of conventional LANs.

Figure 24-9 is a representation of the campus connection. The cables require far less conduit space, so one positive is that added ducts will likely not be required. Another positive is that if the outer conduit runs are stuffed with existing copper wiring, the fiber can be laid in electrical con-

Figure 24-9
A campus
environment with
FDDI as the host
connector.

Figure 24-9
A campus environment with FDDI as the host connector.

duits, which might be far less packed. If need be, fiber can be run through the same right-of-way with water pipes—something we could never do with copper. The water pipes can act as grounds and attract electrical spikes. Too many applications have been hindered because of the lack of bandwidth and connectivity in the past. FDDI offers the opportunity to overcome these limitations.

Figure 24-10 shows another variation of the application for FDDI. This case uses the FDDI as a collapsed backbone arrangement, where multiple closets in a high-rise or a campus can be linked with the fiber and an FDDI interconnection can support the higher-speed throughputs. The ability to bridge and route traffic across the FDDI is another positive. Because FDDI is protocol independent, one or two different brands of equipment can be attached to the fiber ring. The types of bridges and routers are summarized in the following sections.

Figure 24-10
The collapsed
backbone with FDDI
in a high-rise

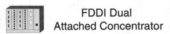
FDDI Dual
Attached Concentrator

Encapsulating Bridges

The data from the bridge (frame) are inserted directly into an FDDI frame and remain transparent to the network. As long as the addressing mechanisms are addressable, little concern is raised about the use of an encapsulation technique. Although the FDDI nodes will not be concerned with the frame format, the stations attached to individual LANs will be. If encapsulation on FDDI is performed, the frame must be delivered to a station that can read the frame format.

Translating Bridges

The data from a bridge (a frame) are stripped of the overhead that is associated with the original network topology and reformatted with new overhead to make the frame 100 percent FDDI compatible. This enables various equipment and topologies to coexist on the network harmoniously. Translation is more expensive than encapsulation, but the differences are becoming minuscule.

FDDI in the Metropolitan Area Network (MAN)

Developments in the local exchange carriers' areas have indicated that FDDI has the robustness and reliability to be delivered in the metropolitan area. The LECs moved ahead with plans to offer 100-Mbps throughput across their fiber rings in the major metropolitan areas. A particular scenario includes what is going on in the nation's capitol. In some cases, Bell offers 100-Mbps Ethernet and plans to move to gigabit Ethernet in the metropolitan areas. However, the gigabit Ethernet may also carry FDDI frames. Bell is providing an FDDI ring throughout Capitol Hill to interconnect LANs in various government agencies and buildings across the town. Figure 24-11 shows this form of a metropolitan area network (MAN) with the MAN in place. The LECs have been using some conservative -

Figure 24-11
FDDI in the MAN

approaches in their deployment so that they do not overstate their offerings or create a bottleneck. Table 24-8 summarizes the differences of the FDDI standard and the way many of the LECs will offer this service.

FDDI Recovery

Clearly, the LECs and users alike will be careful to overcome risk where possible. Yet when placing an FDDI into service, the risk is exponential; all of the traffic on the network becomes supercritical. The FDDI provisions call for the ability to select how the network will be used and recovered. FDDI provides a bypass option so that a failed component on the network will be bypassed, preventing downtime on the network. Figure 24-12 shows the ability to perform the bypass of a failed component. Using the aforementioned dual counter-rotating ring topology provides an optical bypass capability in the node electronics. If a station is not powered on, as was the case in the token ring problem lists, then the optical bypass allows the network to continue to operate. This is one solid way of guaranteeing fewer problems on such a network.

Also, stations attached to the ring can be single-attached stations or dual-attached stations. The single-attached stations are not perceived as mission critical. If a problem occurs with a cable break, the ring can close itself off and go around a problem. However, if the ring has multiple complications or failures, disaster will strike. With deeper pockets in the FDDI world, a user can take advantage of dual-attached stations that are connected to both the primary and secondary FDDI cable.

Table 24-8

Comparison of FDDI Standards and LEC Implementations

LEC	Standards
Multimode 62/125 -μm cabling, optional single-mode fiber 9/125 μm	Multimode fiber 62/125 μm Specs are completed for single-mode fiber.
500 stations	1,000 stations
100 Mbps using single or dual ring	100 Mbps with a single ring, optioned at 200 Mbps with dual ring
100 km maximum distance either ring	200 km maximum distance with a single ring, 100 km with a dual ring
Repeaters spaced up to 2 km apart	Repeaters spaced up to 2 km apart

Figure 24-12
A dual counter-rotating ring in healing wrap bypasses problems.

FDDI-II

Whereas FDDI is designed for the bursty nature of our data needs, no other alternative was available for other packet forms of transfers. Voice and video are considered to have a constant bit rate, whereas data transmission is considered to be a variable-bit-rate service. Therefore, you could not attempt to put these other telecommunications services on the FDDI as originally specified. Newer specifications have been written to accommodate the voice and video needs of organizations. This is designed to give native throughput on a LAN-to-LAN connection, as well as packetized isochronous services such as video and voice.

Clearly, FDDI-II was destined for greatness. Or so we thought! The evolution of FDDI-II has been slow in coming, partly because of the relative slowness of the standards bodies. However, the issue now is: will it ever come about? With the evolution of switched multimegabit data services (SMDS) and asynchronous transfer mode (ATM), other alternatives to the FDDI-II standard are available. Many customers are looking at ATM as a better way to handle the integration of voice, video, data, and LAN traffic. Whereas FDDI only gives the user a total of 100 Mbps, ATM starts at

50 and 155 Mbps and aggregates the bandwidth up into the 2.4+-Gbps rates of today. When you need added bandwidth, ATM allows you to add another card that increases cumulative bandwidth up to the new rate added. FDDI will remain a shared resource for the future, so the cumulative bandwidth without any form of subnetworking will remain at 100 Mbps. You only need to wait a few short years to see whether these two transport systems are complementary or competing service offerings.

Questions

1. What organization is responsible for the FDDI standards?
   a. IBM
   b. Microsoft
   c. ANSI
   d. OSI

2. When the FDDI was first planned, it was to compete with the ____.
   a. 100-Mbps Token Ring
   b. 10-Mbps Ethernet
   c. 100-Mbps Ethernet
   d. ATM

3. What topology does FDDI use?
   a. Logical star but physical ring
   b. Physical star but logical ring
   c. Physical ring and physical star
   d. Physical ring and logical ring

4. The SAS stands for:
   a. Single added station
   b. Source and signal
   c. Signal attached source
   d. Single attached station

5. What is the effective data rate of the FDDI?
   a. 125 Mbps
   b. 10 Mbps

    c. 100 Mbps

    d. 90 Mbps

6. The signaling rate of an FDDI is:

    a. 100 Mbaud

    b. 50 Mbaud

    c. 10 Mbaud

    d. 125 Mbaud

7. The FDDI is a direct replacement for IBM's 16-Mbps token ring.   T/F

8. The frame in an FDDI carries a payload of:

    a. 1,518 bytes

    b. 16,192 bytes

    c. 4,500 bytes

    d. All of the above

9. The maximum payload of an FDDI frame is 4,500 bytes.   T/F

10. FDDI uses a 4B/5B coding techniques to prepare the data for the link.   T/F

11. The FDDI uses a _____ to represent the data in the frame.

    a. Symbol

    b. Byte

    c. Bit

    d. Frame

12. The use of FDDI is strictly limited to the CAN.   T/F

13. What layer is typically responsible for error recovery?

    a. MAC

    b. PHY

    c. LLC

    d. PMD

14. The two types of bridges used in FDDI are _____ and _____ .

15. It is critical that all devices keep the appropriate _____ mechanism.

Switched Multimegabit Data Services (SMDS)

After reading this chapter and completing the questions, you will be able to:

- Describe the SMDS concept
- Understand where SMDS is used
- Determine what the carriers were trying to achieve
- Understand how the SMDS switching concept differs
- Discuss why SMDS is on limited use and time

The following information deals with a service rather than a technology, but we will probably bounce between the two fields in such a definition. The use of high-speed data transfer has been around in various forms, and the last few chapters discussed ways of moving data across a network faster and more efficiently. These are goals in the industry that are never totally achieved. As soon as an enhancement is developed, the industry says, "That was good, but I want it faster, better, cheaper now!" We have mentioned catch-22 environments throughout this book, and this is one of them. We ask for services to be faster, and when this is delivered, we want them to be faster yet! Switched multimegabit data service (SMDS) is in a similar situation, in that it is a service that delivers the data throughput at a very high rate of speed by today's standards. Yet everyone has looked at it and said, "too little."

So, back to the drawing board. One quick word of caution for the reader at this point: SMDS and some of the other high-speed communications services and technologies we are discussing go beyond the scope of a voice/data primer. We need to discuss these because the techniques are already available and many of the industry gurus toss the acronyms around. Therefore, it is important for a user to have a general overview of the SMDS concept. Unfortunately, this can become quite detailed and technical. We can't do much about it, so bear with it and someday it will all make sense.

What Is SMDS?

As already mentioned, SMDS is a service provided on a high-speed communications channel to support what is called a *metropolitan area network* (MAN). A MAN is defined under the ANSI and IEEE specifications for an 802.6 network arrangement. In many cases, the user needs to provide connections between LANs in a major metropolitan area. This had been done in the past with leased lines, such as 56-Kbps and T1 lines. The use of a leased line was limited in a couple of ways.

First, the leased line might not have enough speed to connect various LAN-to-LAN services. If a user is running a 4-, 10-, or 16-Mbps LAN, the T1 will limit the throughput to 1.536 Mbps, leaving the possibility of severe congestion at the network interface. This has been the single largest concern in the industry. The 56/64-Kbps channels were even worse as far as throughput. A 4-, 10-, or 16-Mbps LAN trying to send data frames from LAN to LAN would certainly become congested and produce significant delays in the transfer of the data.

Secondly, the costs of the leased lines are not insignificant. If the network shown in Figure 25-1 is connected with a full-meshed arrangement and four locations require a total of 12 leased access lines (as in this case), the cost of a T1 at a representative cost of $700 per link per month would be $8,400 monthly, or slightly over $100,000 per year. Other ways of providing this connection are available, but in each case, if the network were configured with fewer links, the congestion would become exponentially more severe. Using a 56- or 64-Kbps link to each of the locations does not achieve the desired end result, so we will not go into the math on this type of linkage.

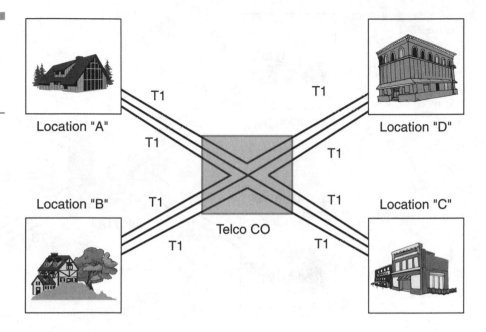

Figure 25-1
A meshed T1
network requires too
many access lines,
which creates a very
expensive network.

What if congestion is really bad? In this case, the user was faced with a dilemma. T1 was not all that attractive pricewise, but the only other choice to get more bandwidth between the sites was to step into a T3. Providing connectivity with a T3 would come at an astronomical price. In many parts of the country, the cost of a T3 access to a central office is more than $7,000 per month. The cost now to connect these four locations in a meshed network (Figure 25-2) would approximate $84,000 per month, or $1,000,000 annually. Few organizations can afford this form of connectivity.

Adding to the problems of too much or too little bandwidth, the excess capacity of a T3 would be wasted in most cases because this is a localized form of communications. Although you could multiplex voice and other data transfers onto this network (at the T3 level), the cost of the multiplexers would likely be exorbitant. Additionally, the cost to place a call or to transfer data to these local sites would be either free or very inexpensive. It would not be prudent to try to force this traffic onto the T3 when a less expensive technique already exists.

These results left users and LAN administrators in a bind. No reasonably priced service was available that would provide native LAN connectivity and throughput, yet the demands of the networks and resources were

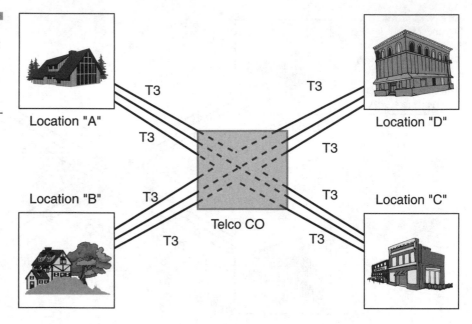

escalating. To conquer this problem, several of the standards bodies began to look at alternatives. This includes ANSI, Bellcore (now Telcordia technologies), and the IEEE in the United States.

SMDS is another form of high-speed public connectionless packet switching. As such, the SMDS services handle the transfer of data across a MAN at rates of 4, 10, 16, or 34 Mbps. Users can commit to a burst rate that guarantees them the throughput they require. Because SMDS is a service and not a technology, the data delivery is at whatever rate the subscriber signs on for. This service is designed to assist users in building network connections that require high-speed linkages without the added overhead and costs associated with fixed capacities. Therefore, it is a shared resource between and among various organizations in a metropolitan area. The connectivity can be intracompany or intercompany. As a LAN-to-LAN service, SMDS uses a connectionless orientation. The users do not have to dial up or be connected directly to each other. Like the LAN, the frames or packets are sent out across the network with a destination address. All units on the network read the frame, but only those devices that are addressed copy the data.

The Local Environment

The local exchange carriers (LECs) are noticeably absent from the discussions of the higher-speed services in this book. Most of the higher-speed connections have been through the links provided by the interexchange carriers (IECs). Even in the case of leased lines, where the IEC must use LEC facilities (Figure 25-3), the IEC is still in control of the service. Most of our networks are wide-area-network (WAN)-based. Therefore, as a result of the divestiture in 1984, the LECs have been restrained from participating in this arena. Where the LEC did provide the local loop to the customer premises for the IEC, the LEC prices were considered too expensive. The tariffs did not allow for the negotiation of better prices because LEC services are supposed to be universally applied to any customer. The IECs in turn began to suggest ways to bypass the LEC connection, such as through the CAPs and CATV companies. These competitors are covered in earlier chapters. Consequently, the local environment for MAN services was limited and options were not readily available.

Bellcore developed the specifications of SMDS in the local arena for the Regional Bell Operating Companies (RBOCs) that fund the Bellcore

Figure 25-3
Even though the WAN physically passes through the LEC office, the connection is logically transparent to the user/IEC.

Table 25-1

Status of RBOCs
Supporting SMDS

RBOC	Status
Ameritech (now SBC)	Adopted and available
Bell Atlantic (now Verizon)	Adopted and available
Bell South	Adopted and available
PIacTel (now SBC)	Adopted and available
SouthWestern Bell (SBC)	Adopted and available
U.S. West (nw Qwest)	Adopted and available

research and development efforts. Just about all of the RBOCs have endorsed the use of SMDS (Table 25-1).

Using SMDS as a shared service among many users, the LECs now have an alternative to the competitive arrangements. Furthermore, as SMDS is being developed, the LECs are offering these services as value-added services rather than having the costs rolled into the embedded base pricing structure. This means that the services are not tariffed the same and that competitive pricing and special deals can be had. SMDS is designed for applications that are bursty in nature, requiring a burst of bandwidth for short periods of time. These applications do not need committed capacities and bandwidth all the time, but when they need it, they grab it and use it. Unfortunately, SMDS is designed for the data traffic carried on LANs, not for the higher-density, quality graphics and interactive video applications that are emerging. These applications will be addressed in the future. SMDS does support interactive sessions between users, so all is not lost under the restrictions and constraints of an SMDS network. Thus, the interactive applications that can be supported in a localized environment include

- Computer-assisted design (CAD)
- Computer-assisted manufacturing (CAM)
- Source code transfer from host to host
- LAN-to-LAN native transfers
- Imaging services (magnetic resonance imaging, document imaging, and so on)
- Publishing services (compound documents)

Technology Used in SMDS

We have stated that SMDS is a service and not a technology, so we should also say that SMDS uses a technology called *distributed queue on a dual bus* (DQDB) to handle the transfer of the information. As a technology, DQDB is straightforward; it distributes the ability of users on the network into queues, and it uses dual bus architectures that are unidirectional (one-way) each. In LANs, most of what we discussed is a unidirectional data transfer. This architecture uses a controlled sequencing on a fiber-optic cable. However, the primary implementations have been single-direction transfers (one cable transmits one way, while the second cable transmits the opposite direction). Using a distributed queue, a group of time slots is allocated on the network. Each device that wishes to transmit data across the cable must wait its turn for a queue slot. When the queue slot becomes available, the transmitter can send data.

The SMDS Goal

The goal of SMDS, then, is to provide the high-speed data transfer for customer systems and yet preserve the customer equipment investments. Too many systems and services in the past have required the use of *forklift technology*. When you needed more, you brought in the forklift and removed the old equipment. Then the lift brought in and plunked down the new equipment. This did not meet the user needs, nor did it encourage the migration to the higher-speed communications services until the equipment had been fully depreciated under IRS and financial rules. A second goal of SMDS is to enter the workplace as quickly as possible. If no incentive exists, then everyone will take a wait-and-see attitude. If users are not encouraged to implement SMDS, they will seek other avenues of providing the services—meaning competitors. The LECs don't want this to happen; they want in as fast as possible. If they are the first providers and meet the needs quickly, users will be less likely to go out and seek other alternatives. Furthermore, if the SMDS proliferation can be rolled out quickly, users can switch to higher rates of speed in the future as they are developed. In the future, SMDS will carry up to 150 Mbps in the MAN.

Access Rates to SMDS

As mentioned, this is a primary service offering from the LECs. As such, the access rates delivered today deal with the transport services of the past. This means that two basic platforms are available for accessing an SMDS network: T1 (1.544 Mbps) or T3 (44.736 Mbps). Unfortunately, there is little in between. However, the LECs have been offering this access at very attractive rates. Many of the LECs around the United States and the PTTs around the world (18 countries have already adopted the SMDS standards) are rolling out the service and the products. In the European marketplace, the PTTs are delivering speeds of 2 Mbps (called E1), 34 Mbps (E3), and 140 Mbps (E4), or 155 and 622 Mbps on what is termed synchronous digital hierarchy (SDH). These higher speeds are still in beta, but will be the thrust of the future.

The LECs that have been aggressively pushing this service have come up with some very attractive rates to encourage its use. In the East, the LECs offer unlimited usage of the network with T1 access for around $500 per month/per site. This eliminates the need for the meshed network and provides a single connection into the network for on-demand bandwidth up to 1.5 Mbps (Figure 25-4).

Figure 25-4
The revised network provides access up to T1 speeds on demand. This is much less expensive, but it can be very robust.

Location "A"

Location "D"

SMDS

Location "B"

LEC Network

Location "C"

Accessing the MAN

Next, look at the access method shown in Figure 25-5. The LEC will install a twisted-pair (four-wire circuit) T1 access for the lower-end user or a fiber loop for T3 access. Variations are shown in which the LEC can run a fiber to the door and will deliver any rate on that fiber. Still another variation is the use of a fiber ring into the customer premises where a T1 or T3 access can be provided. If fiber is not available to the door, the LECs might bring the fiber to the curb and deliver a metallic link (coax) into the customer location at T3 speeds. These are all variations of the same service provisioning that are dependent on what the LEC has available to use. In the future, SMDS might well wind up on microwave radio if that alternative is already in place. However, the primary method will be deployment across a fiber-based network.

Figure 25-5
Various options are available for the LEC to deliver access into the SMDS network.

Once the local loop is installed, the customer will use a high-speed router at T1 or T3 speeds. An interface called the SMDS network interface (SNI) will be used as the connection at the customer location. Just a quick note: many of the LECs have been delivering SMDS service to the customer premises and providing the router. It seems that they have no means of controlling the data that is sent across the fiber and that if the customer provides the router, they have no means of stopping the customer from adding cards in the router, thereby grabbing additional bandwidth for free. Because this is a value-added service and not covered under the normal tariffs, it can be accomplished. The demarcation point (DEMARC) on the fiber has now moved beyond the entrance of the customer's building into the equipment. The DEMARC will now be at the high-speed interface on the router card. With the SNI, the customer attaches to the router (Figure 25-6). The link might be on a single thread or a ring using a dual thread; it doesn't matter. The customer equipment, such as a LAN or a host computer, is then connected to this network. Access to the network is achieved using a DQDB technique. The access using DQDB through the SNI then proceeds out to a switching system in the network. Protocols are written to provide the interswitching systems services to make this all transparent to the end user. MCI/WorldCom announced plans to provide connections on a long-distance basis with Bell Atlantic (Verizon) and Pacific Bell (SBC), creating a true cross-country SMDS network. Figure 25-7 shows this process with the intercarrier interfaces in place. In the event that the LECs choose to connect to another service, called asynchronous transfer mode (ATM), the overlay of SMDS will be directly onto an ATM network. Once again, this will be transparent to the end user.

Figure 25-6
Customer connection at the DEMARC may change depending on who provides the router. The SNI is the interface between customer and LEC.

Figure 25-7
IEC-to-LEC arrangements are now falling into place, taking SMDS across the WAN. The intercarrier interfaces have been defined.

The IEEE 802.6 Architecture

As with this entire book, we attempt to cover all the bases from a brief overview of the techniques, systems, and services to more detailed discussion. It is fitting, therefore, to explain just how the SMDS and DQDB work together in an architecture of protocols and services and how they stack up against the IEEE 802.6 standards and protocols. The architecture is shown in Figure 25-8 with the dual bus at the physical layer and DQDB at the link layer, as they compare to the OSI model. Note that four different services are sitting on top of the DQDB (data link layer). The first is a medium access control-to-logical link control service, still working at the data link layer. The second of these services is a connection-oriented service. The third is a provision for isochronous service (such as voice, video, and so on). The fourth service is termed *other* and is under study for future use. The MAC layer contains several services.

Figure 25-8
The IEEE 802.6
standard architecture

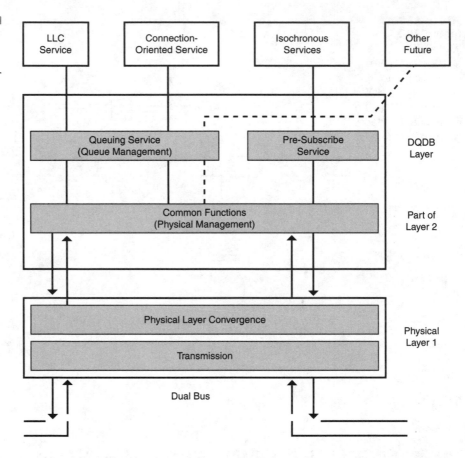

The DQDB Architecture

Logically, the DQDB is structured as a dual bus, although in many cases it might also be in the form of a ring. Figure 25-9 lays out the dual bus architecture. Two separate unidirectional buses are present. Each transmits in one direction, but when combined, they create a full-duplex operation. The buses are labeled *A* and *B* to provide the necessary full-duplex operation between any two nodes on the network. An LEC lays out the cables in one of two ways. The cables can be laid out with a head end in two different nodes (Figure 25-10). In this case, the head end of each of the buses appears at different locations, signifying the direction of the bus. In Figure 25-11, the two head ends of the dual buses are located in the same end point,

Figure 25-9
The dual bus
topology as defined

Figure 25-10
The open bus is one
way to lay out
the MAN.

establishing a looped arrangement. This resembles a ring, but in reality, it does not create the ring because both ends of the fiber are open-ended, meaning they are not closed off into a physical ring. Using either physical installation, the provision exists to recover the network in the event of an equipment failure or a problem on the fiber, such as *backhoe fade* where the cable gets cut. A break in the cable on the open bus architecture is healed, as shown in Figure 25-12. The network will automatically reconfigure itself as two separate networks. The system in Figure 25-13 uses a looped architecture; if a failure occurs, the network will bypass the failed component or cable and reconfigure it into what constitutes an open bus. These robust arrangements ensure more availability and more user satisfaction.

Figure 25-11
The looped bus has both head ends in the same location.

Figure 25-12
In an open bus, a cable break results in the formation of subnetworks into two networks.

Figure 25-13
The closed loop
overcomes cable
breaks bypassing the
failed cable. It looks
like an open bus.

Figure 25-13
The closed loop
overcomes cable
breaks bypassing the
failed cable. It looks
like an open bus.

The MAN Access Unit

Similar to a multistation access unit (MAU) on a LAN, each node on a MAN
has an access unit called a MAN access unit. To avoid confusing the user, we
will refer to this as an access unit instead of a MAU. Each access unit is
attached to both buses. The access unit can support a single node or act as
a concentrator handling multiple inputs from a cluster. The access unit is
used to read and write into the DQDB slots at the rate of 8,000 samples per
second. The buses have a slotted queue arrangement. As the access unit
reads or writes into these slots, it can deliver information, read information,
or request time on the network by reservation. The 8,000 samples per second means that the network is timed to all of the synchronous time-division
multiplexing systems in use for voice and data transmission, as well as the
synchronous optical network (SONET) standards. Figure 25-14 is a graphic
representation of the functionality of the MAN access unit. The nodes read
and copy data from the slots created in the queue. They gain access by writing to the slots.

The DQDB protocol is straightforward and based on a counter system.
The counter system is used on each bus to determine whether a slot is

Figure 25-14
The MAN access unit
reads/writes to the
bus 8,000 times a
second.

Figure 25-14
The MAN access unit reads/writes to the bus 8,000 times a second.

available to be reserved or written into. The DQDB node reserves slots on one bus in order to use the slots on the second bus. Every time a slot comes by with a reservation tagged to it, the node increments a counter. It also watches the other bus and decrements its counter with every slot that goes by empty. Essentially, the node reserves slots on one bus to be used on the other. It sends a reservation request so that all of its upstream and downstream neighbors know that it wishes to send information. Then it begins to count the number of empty and reserved slots as they go by. When the counter equals zero, the node knows that it can now send its data. This is a form of carrier sense multiple access with collision avoidance (CSMA/CA) that prevents a problem from occurring when nodes try to send data at the same time. Figure 25-15 shows a sample of what happens on the bus from the access unit.

Because this is called distributed queue on a dual bus, it should stand to reason that each node maintains a list of queues for each bus. Although these two queues operate identically, they are kept separate from each other. This creates a deterministic approach to the dual bus that is very similar to a token-passing arrangement. To prevent any one node from saturating the network, provisions are in place to periodically send empty queue slots onto the network so that this deterministic MAN can be achieved. No one node is allowed to reserve all the slots on the network; slots are negotiated based on quality of service (QOS), which equates somewhat to a throughput rate. You buy the throughput you need, and you pay for the QOS that you want.

Figure 25-15
When unit 1 wishes to send, it counts the reserved slots on bus B, and then it decrements the counter on bus A until a slot is available.

The Data Handling

A fair way to get into data transfer on a MAN is to understand the formulation of the data units. The 802.6 can accept data up to 9,188 bytes (octets) long. Then a three-step process is used to break the data down into more manageable portions. The end result is that the data will be transferred across the network in the slots (queues) at 53 bytes of information at a time. We will take the description of this process slowly to try to keep it going smoothly. It is analogous to ATM, which is covered later, but it is not the same. To prepare the data for transfer, the equipment is used to define the protocol data units of up to 9,188 bytes. Several convergence layers (processes) act on the data to make it more manageable. The layers they are handled in define these processes. Think of this as slicing and dicing the data into smaller chunks, similar to the X.25 transport.

Segmentation and Reassembly

Within the DQDB layer, the media access control convergence produces a segmentation and reassembly process (SAR). This process takes a very large frame of information and breaks it down into smaller pieces that can be put back together at the receiving end. If we start at the top (Figure 25-16), a large frame (MAC layer) of information is delivered from the logical link control unit. In this case, it might be a bridge, router, or LAN interface. At this stage, the header and trailer information is added to the MAC layer information. This is called an initial MAC protocol data unit (IMPDU). The IMPDU is then chopped up into fixed-length segments called derived MAC protocol data units (DMPDUs), and header and trailer information is attached to it. The numbering of these DMPDUs is handled by the relative position in the slicing and dicing process. The DMPDU can be a beginning, a continuing, or an ending protocol data unit. The numbering is just that—a beginning, continuing, or ending unit. As you can see from Figure 25-16, the data units prepared for the slots in the DQDB format will be 53-byte segments. This will include 44 bytes of payload (the data) plus 7 bytes of header and 2 bytes of trailer information. This fixed-length segment is then sent across the DQDB in a time slot.

Figure 25-16

As the MAC layer frame (9,188 bytes) is delivered, a header and trailer are added to create the IMPDU. Then it is sliced and diced into segments, and the header info is added, creating a slot (53 bytes).

The SMDS Data Unit

The encapsulation of an SMDS data unit is very similar to the way the data is transferred across the network. First, up to 9,188 bytes of data is delivered to the interface equipment. Then the process begins of slicing and dicing the data into smaller pieces that will wind up in the 53-byte slots using an SMDS interface protocol (SIP). Figure 25-17 shows this process from the beginning. The 9,188-byte data unit, plus the associated overhead, is added to the data unit. This is a layer 3 SIP-PDU. Table 25-2 describes the abbreviations of the information contained in the layer 3 SIP-PDU. You might want to keep this available as you review the diagram.

Table 25-2

Summary of Fields in the Layer 3 SIP-PDU

Abbreviation	Length	Description
RSVD	8 bits	Reserved
BEtag	8 bits	Beginning and ending tag
BAsize	16 bits	Buffer allocation size (length)
DA	64 bits	Destination address (to)
SA	64 bits	Source address (from)
X+		Ignored by the network
X+HLPI	6 bits	Higher-level protocol ID
PL	2 bits	PAD length (if used)
X+QOS	4 bits	Quality of service
CIB	1 bit	CRC presence indicator bit (indicates the presence or absence of CRC)
HEL	3 bits	Header extension length (describes the header extension)
X+BRDG	16 bits	Bridging
HE	96 bits	Header information
PAD	0–24 bits	Padding or filler
X+CRC32	0–32 bits	Cyclic redundancy check (if used)
L	16 bits	Length (must agree with the BAsize)

SOURCE: © 1991, Bell Communications Research, Inc.

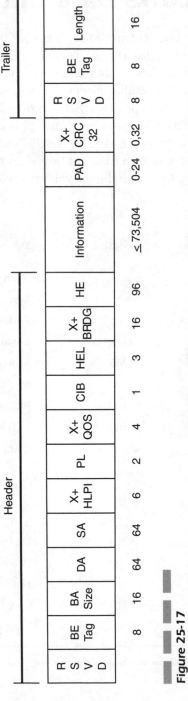

Figure 25-17
The SMDS frame (9,188 bytes) is similarly converged. The overhead is shown in this graphic for the SIP level 3 PDU.

The layer 3 SIP-PDU then gets broken down into smaller pieces by going through another process that breaks the data into layer 2 SIP-PDUs. The layer 2 SIP-PDUs will be broken down into 44 bytes of data and an additional 7 bytes of header and 2 bytes of trailer information. This is shown in Figure 25-18. Table 25-3 is a summary of the abbreviated definitions for this figure. Again, you might wish to keep this available as you review the framed format in the graphic.

This slot or segment is then delivered to the physical medium for transport across the network (layer 1 SIP-PDU). The physical layer is divided into two pieces or sublayers called the physical layer convergence process and the transmission system.

Figure 25-18
The layer 3 PDU is segmented into layer 2 PDUs at 53 bytes.

Table 25-3

Summary of Abbreviations for the Layer 2 SIP-PDU

Abbreviation	Length	Description
AC	8 bits	Access control
VCI	20 bits	Virtual channel identifier
PT	2 bits	Payload type
PP	2 bits	Payload priority
HCS	8 bits	Header check sequence (a CRC on the header)
ST	2 bits	Segment type (beginning, continuing, or ending)
SN	4 bits	Sequence number
MID	10 bits	Message identification
PL	6 bits	Payload length
PCRC	10 bits	Payload CRC

SOURCE: © 1991, Bell Communications Research, Inc.

SMDS in a LAN Environment

Enough of the bits and bytes for now. When using a LAN-to-LAN in a metropolitan area, the concern is how to transmit the information transparently. Most LANs use some protocols that provide for the reliable delivery of the actual data. In many LANs today, the protocol of choice is TCP/IP. If we stack this up on an architecture, we need to see where the pieces all fit together. Figure 25-19 shows a LAN architecture running TCP/IP. This stack uses the TCP portion of the stack to guarantee reliable data transfer at layer 4 of the OSI model. The IP is a packet-switching protocol working at layer 3 of the OSI model. IP breaks the data down into smaller chunks for delivery across a network, then hands the packets down to layer 2 of the OSI, which is the data link layer. This is where we can enter the SMDS world by using the equipment to transfer the data across the network. At the data link layer, the stack deals with the three SMDS interface protocols (SIPs). The data will be segmented into slots, or 53-byte segments, and will be prepared for transmission across the network. The stack is at the center of all this. This is where the convergence takes place, using the original TCP/IP data and sending it across the network in SMDS format. At the

Figure 25-19
Typical LAN running
TCP/IP into SMDS

receiving end, the data is reassembled and sent back up the protocol stack to be delivered in a usable and understandable format.

Information Throughput

As mentioned earlier, the user will subscribe to an element of throughput. The phrase used in the SMDS world is *sustained information rate* (SIR). This is very similar to the frame relay term called the *committed information rate* (CIR). The SIR is based on a rate of service called classes. Five classes of service are defined for use depending on the application being served. Table 25-4 shows the classes of service. These SIRs closely match the LAN throughput speeds that we are familiar with today. In several cases, we have discussed the use of 4, 10, or 16 Mbps. Two other speeds exist. One is 25 Mbps, which is a LAN speed several vendors will be offering in the future, supporting IBM's efforts to get LANs at ATM speeds. Although ATM is defined as a 50- or 155-Mbps rate today, IBM has conjured up the notion that a full-duplex LAN operating at 25 Mbps will yield an effective LAN speed of 50 Mbps: that's ATM. This is a supported speed by the standards bodies; the ATM Forum, IBM, and 32 other companies introduced this service and the chip sets necessary to deliver this speed. It will likely become a de facto standard in the future. The last SMDS class of service supports 34-Mbps throughput. The intent of classes of service is to provide control over how much information any node can place on the network as well as to prevent or control congestion on the network.

Table 25-4

Summary of SMDS
Classes of Service

Access Class of Service	SIR
1	4 Mbps
2	10 Mbps
3	16 Mbps
4	25 Mbps
5	34 Mbps

The use of SMDS and the DQDB formats and protocols can deliver a myriad of services across the MAN. In the future, new capacities will be added. Whereas today the MAN is defined to provide LAN extension services, the ability to add other services will be introduced in the future. The current use of SMDS in the industry includes the following:

- LAN-to-LAN in a metropolitan area
- Intra- and intercompany document transfer and sharing
- Collaborative processing and development
- Host-to-host transfers
- Direct access storage device (DASD) mirroring
- Disaster recovery planning for remote hot site

Questions

1. The letters SMDS stand for:
   a. Station Message Detail System
   b. Storage Message Distribution System
   c. Switched Multimegabit Data Services
   d. Switched Message Data System
2. What group has responsibility for SMDS?
   a. ISO
   b. IEEE
   c. ITU
   d. EIA/TIA
3. What are the rated speeds for SMDS?
   a. 34 Mbps
   b. 16 Mbps
   c. 25 Mbps
   d. 10 Mbps
   e. None of the above
   f. All of the above

4. Which technique is used to distribute the services?

   a. DQDB

   b. DCRR

   c. SMDS

   d. LAN

   e. MAN

5. SMDS is limited to work in the LAN only.   T/F

6. SMDS is the most popular transmission system endorsed by the RBOCs.   T/F

7. SMDS uses a _____ cell concept.

   a. 54-byte

   b. 1,500-byte

   c. 53-byte

   d. 9,188-byte

8. ATM and SMDS are the exact same service; they are just called by different terms.   T/F

9. The IEEE assigned the following standard for SMDS service:

   a. 802.3

   b. 802.6

   c. 802.4

   d. 802.5

10. With SMDS, users can commit to a burst rate that guarantees them the throughput they require.   T/F

11. SMDS is another form of high-speed public connectionless:

   a. Circuit switching

   b. Local switching

   c. Packet switching

   d. Time-division multiplexing

12. SMDS uses a _____ to sample its data.

   a. TDM

   b. STDM

   c. FDM

   d. ATM

13. Logically, the DQDB is structured as a _____, although in many cases it might also be in the form of a ring.

    a. Single piece of wire

    b. Redundant ring

    c. Dual counter-rotating ring

    d. Dual bus

14. One service on SMDS is the provision for _____ service (such as voice, video, and so on).

    a. Pleisochronous

    b. Synchronous

    c. Asynchronous

    d. Isochronous

15. Each node on a metropolitan area network (MAN) has an access unit called a:

    a. MAU

    b. MAN

    c. Hub

    d. Switch

Frame Relay

After reading this chapter and completing the questions, you will be able to:

- Describe frame relay
- Understand the rationale for using frame relay services
- Describe the addressing techniques of frame relay
- Discuss the benefits of using the protocols for higher speed data
- Understand where frame relay fits in the overall OSI model

One of the data transport systems developed in 1992 is a high-speed packet switching technique called *frame relay*. Frames of information are generated by most all of the data communications processes today. Although we call them by different names, such as *packets, frames,* or *cells,* they all are just a means of transmitting a specific amount of information across a network. When first introduced, frame relay was met with mild enthusiasm. This is not to say that it is not an efficient means of transferring the data, merely that the industry was confused about what the intended goals would be.

What Is Frame Relay?

Frame relay is a high-performance, cost-efficient means of connecting an organization's multiple LANs and Systems Network Architecture (SNA) services with various techniques. Like the older X.25 packet switching services, frame relay uses the transmission links only when they are needed. Essentially, the virtual circuit concept applies here as much as in any other network service.

The customer rents or leases a physical circuit into the cloud, as shown in Figure 26-1. This circuit is terminated onto a port in a computer system. The computer system (switch) recognizes where the connecting ends of the wires are located and uses the full set of wires when the customer has traffic to pass into the network. Thus, a virtual circuit connection is established into the cloud for future use as the customer's needs dictate. Because the connection is not always "nailed up," other customers connected to the same network supplier can also transmit traffic across the same physical pairs of wires within the cloud. Additionally, like private line connections, frame relay transports data very quickly, with only a limited amount of delay for network processing to take place.

When comparing frame relay to the X.25 services, much less processing is required inside the switches. Therefore, the reduced processing enables the transport of data much more quickly. By eliminating the overhead in each of the processors, the network merely looks at an address in the frame and passes the frame along to the next node in the network.

Figure 26-1
The customer leases/rents a dedicated circuit into the cloud and terminates it on a port.

Why Was Frame Relay Developed?

Major trends in the industry led to the development of frame relay services. These can be categorized into four major trends as follows:

- *The increased need for speed across the network platforms within the end user and the carrier networks.* The need for higher speeds is driven by the move away from the original text-based services to graphics-oriented services and the bursty, time-sensitive data needs of the user. The proliferation of high-speed LANs being deployed has shifted the paradigm of computing platforms. The demands of these services will exceed by hundreds to thousands of times the data transport needs of the older text-based services. Users demand connectivity and speed to assure quick and reliable communications between systems. Fortunately, the bursty way we conduct business allows the sharing of resources among many users who thereby share the bandwidth available. To accommodate this connectivity, some changes had to be made to the overhead intensity. One way to accommodate the reduced overhead is to eliminate some of the processing, mainly in the error-detection and correction schemes.

- *Increasing intelligence of the devices attached to the network.* The use of data transfer between and among devices on the network has moved many of the processing functions to the desktop. The capacity to move the information around the network must meet the demands of each attached device. Increased functionality must be met with increases in the bandwidth allocation for these devices.

- *Improved transmission facilities.* The days of "dirty" or poor-quality transmission lines required the use of overcorrecting protocols such as X.25 and SNA. Because the network now performs better, a newer transmission capability is needed.

- *The need to connect LANs to WANs and the internetworking capabilities.* Today's users want to connect LANs across the boundaries of the wide area. Users demand and expect the same speed and accuracy across the WAN that they get on the local networks. Therefore, a newer transport system to support the higher speed connections across a wider area was needed.

The Significance of Frame Relay

As an analog transmission system, the old network was extremely noisy, producing many network errors and corrupting data. When data errors were introduced, a retransmission was required. The more retransmissions that were necessary, the less effective was throughput on the network. In fact, several years ago, the use of a 4800-bps transmission service on the analog dial-up network might well have produced an effective throughput of only 400 bps after all the errors and retransmissions. To solve this problem, the network introduced the X.25 services, also called *packet switching*. The X.25 was originally designed to handle the customer's asynchronous traffic. Frame relay was designed to take advantage of the low-error, high-performance digital network and to meet the needs of the intelligent, synchronous use of the newer and more sophisticated user applications.

Compared to private leased lines, frame relay makes network design much simpler. The private line network shown in Figure 26-2 requires a detailed analysis to set all the right connections in place; this further accentuates the traffic-sensitive needs of the user network. The meshed network uses a series of connections that are N-1 points with links running from site to site. Therefore, if 10 sites exist in the network, nine links will run from each site to every other site. This allows for speed of connectivity, but the network costs are much higher. Further, depending on the nature of the data traffic, the bursty data needs of a LAN-to-LAN or LAN-to-WAN con-

Figure 26-2
A leased line network requires more detailed analysis depending on the communities of interest.

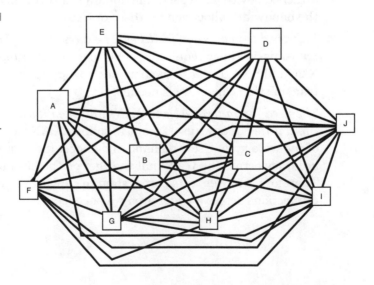

Figure 26-3
A single access is all
that's needed into the
cloud.

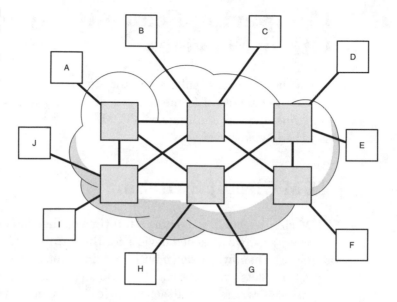

nection are not required full time. We therefore spend significantly more of the organization's money to support the meshed leased line network.

In Figure 26-3, single frame relay access from each site is provided into the network cloud, instead of nine in the earlier network. Data transported across the network will be interleaved on a frame-by-frame basis. Multiple sessions can run on the same link concurrently. Communications from a single site to any other site can be handled using the predefined network connections of the virtual circuits. In frame relay, these connections use *permanent logical links* (PLLs), more commonly referred to as *permanent virtual circuits* (PVCs). Each of the PVCs connects two sites just as a private line would, but in this case the bandwidth is shared among multiple users rather than being dedicated to the one site for access to a single site. Using this multiple-site connectivity on a single link reduces the costs associated with customer premises equipment, such as CPU ports, router ports, or other connectivity arrangements. Because fewer ports are required, fewer connection devices are required; therefore, the customer saves money.

Because the PVCs are predefined for each pair of end-to-end connections, a network path is always available for the customer's application to transport data. This eliminates the call setup time associated with the dial-up lines and the X.25 packet arrangements. The connection is always ready for the devices to ship data in a framed format.

Comparing Frame Relay to Other Services

When the network suppliers and the standards bodies were attempting to define the benefits of frame relay services, they looked at a comparison of the time-division multiplexed (TDM) switched circuit and the packet switched network services.

TDM Circuit Switching

TDM circuit switching creates a full-time connection or a dedicated circuit between any two attached devices for the duration of the connection. TDM divides the bandwidth down into fixed time slots in which there can be multiple time slots available; each with its own fixed capacity. This is shown in Figure 26-4 where each attached device on the network is assigned a fixed portion of the bandwidth using one or more time slots. When the device is in transmit mode, the data is merely placed in this time slot without any extra overhead such as processing or translations. Therefore, TDM is

Figure 26-4
TDM switching forces the transmission into a fixed-capacity time slot, and the channels are virtually wasted.

protocol-transparent to the traffic being carried. Unfortunately, when this attached device is not sending data, the time slots remain empty, wasting the bandwidth. A high-speed device on the network can be bottled up waiting to transmit data, while idle capacity cannot be allocated to this device. TDM is not well suited for the bursty data that are becoming the norm in today's organization.

X.25 Packet Switching

Because TDM had its limitations, a newer service was created that allowed the bandwidth to be allocated "on the fly." Instead of simply putting the data into a fixed time slot, smaller pieces of data called *packets,* containing the source and destination address information as well as other control functional information, are used. When data bursts are sent, multiple packets are generated and routed across the network based on the address. The network creates a virtual circuit from each source to each destination to keep track of the packets on each connection. This is shown in Figure 26-5 where multiple virtual circuits can be active on a line at the same time. This is a statistical time-division-multiplexing (STDM) scheme. STDM analyzes past usage to interleave more packets to the heavy users and fewer packet slots

Figure 26-5
Multiple connections on virtual circuits are active on the line simultaneously.

to the light users. The major drawback to this scheme is the penalty paid in speed of delivery. Guaranteed data delivery and integrity were prerequisites for the development of the X.25.

The standards bodies attempted to use the best of all systems. Taking the features of the switched network and the packet services, they arrived at frame relay to meet the needs of the user. This comparison took into account the following service connections:

- **Speed** The dial-up digital networks now support high-speed connections of up to 2.048 Mbps. X.25 networks only support speeds of up to 64 Kbps. The decision was made to use a digital connection of up to 2.048 Mbps.

- **Network setup delay** Call setup time on a switched network is relatively low. This is also true for the X.25 network in general terms. However, as network congestion builds up on the X.25 switched circuits, extensive delays occur. The PVC allows this because the call setup time is eliminated.

- **Routing** The routing of the switched network is static. When one sets up a switched call, the routing is used once to establish the link. In case of a network delay or a failed link, the user must reestablish the call through a new dial sequence. The X.25 network is robust in that if a problem occurs on the link, the packet nodes in the network immediately reestablish the connection with the next packet. Therefore, the suppliers and standards bodies opted for the robust and dynamic call setup with very low delay.

- **Signaling** In the switched network design, the signaling is also static in that it is used only in the initial setup or teardown of the call. Therefore, if the call is interrupted, the signaling disappears. In the packet switched networks, the signaling is dynamic; it is contained in every packet and thus is easily reestablished. The standards bodies opted for the dynamic signaling arrangements of the packet switched networks.

- **Bandwidth** In the circuit switched networks, the bandwidth is fixed. If you dial up a 56-Kbps circuit, you get a full 56 Kbps whether you need it or not. However, the variable length of a packet allows for use of much less than the maximum of 56 or 64 Kbps. The disadvantage here is that the speed cannot exceed the range of 56 or 64 Kbps. Therefore, the standards bodies opted to arrive at a dynamically allocated bandwidth-on-demand concept.

■ **Costs** Circuit switched services are relatively low priced. The costs per minute are very reasonable. Pricing approximates $0.50 per minute for a switched data service at T1 speeds well below the costs that you might expect. In the packet switched services, the expense is very low, priced at a cost per kilopacket. The only issue here is what the best method of call processing will be if frames are routed across a PVC.

The network suppliers are now offering frame relay access and use on an individual case basis. They might require a nondisclosure agreement before they will submit a proposal for pricing a frame relay network. This was initially a turnoff for customers who were interested in pilot programs introducing frame relay for the WAN connections. The problem was solved through the creative pricing arrangements, and now frame relay is becoming more readily accepted.

In Table 26-1, the issues and comparisons from this information are summarized. This is how the standards bodies arrived at the service offerings of frame relay.

Service levels with frame relay are also a concern before critical data is placed on the network. The level of service is something that must be seriously considered. Response time across the network should equal that of a dedicated line. However, the use of a frame-based service must be carefully designed with the speeds that will deliver the desired response time. Table 26-2 shows a comparison of what can be expected from the use of a frame relay network. This assumes that the appropriate speeds are used and that

Table 26-1

Comparing Frame Relay Services to Switched and Packet Services

Offering	Circuit Switched	Packet Switched	Frame Relay or Fast Packet
Speed	64 Kbps 2.048 Mbps	64 Kbps maximum	0–2.048 Mbps
Delay	Low	Low to high	Low
Routing	Static (call by call)	Dynamic (packet by packet)	Dynamic (frame by frame)
Signaling	Static (session)	Dynamic (packet)	Dynamic (frame)
Bandwidth	Fixed	Variable, Dynamic	Dynamic
Costs	Low	Very low	Variable (low to very high)

Table 26-2

Expected Service
Delivery with
Frame Relay

U.S. Domestic Network Service Levels	Values
Percentage of availability	Node to node: 99.99% End to end: 99.85%
Bit error rates expected	Approximately 10^{-8}
Block error rates expected	Approximately 10^{-5}
Burst rates	To access channel rates or CIR
Burst timing	≤ 2 s if available
Delay on network	≤ 20 ms average
Average round-trip network delay	≤ 400 ms maximum depending on CIR
Data rates	0–2.048 Mbps, varies by vendor
Maximum number of hops	4–5 depending on network

the number of hops allowed in the network is kept at a minimum. The number of hops is the number of nodes the frame must pass through within the network to get to the end. This table shows what can be typically expected from the use of this service.

Frame Relay Speeds

Frame relay was designed initially to start from 64 Kbps up to 1.544 Mbps in North America. Speeds of 2.048 Mbps were approved in the rest of the world. This speed is based on using T1 or E1 access links. A small company came along and introduced speeds of 50 Mbps. This company, Cascade Communications, broke all the barriers. Cascade wanted the network to be robust, not limited to old data rates.

When designing a frame relay service, the speed of access is important both prior to and after installation. The customer must be aware of the need for and select a specified delivery rate. Assigning the speed from both an access and a pricing perspective can be done in various ways. For small locations, such as branch offices with little predictable traffic, the customer might consider the lowest possible access speed. The frame relay suppliers offer speeds that are flat-rate, usage-sensitive, and flat/usage-sensitive combined. The flat-rate service offers the speed of service at a fixed rate of speed, whereas the usage-based service might not include flat-rate service, but a pay-as-you-go rate for all usage. The combined service is a mix of both offerings.

Carriers now call this burstable frame relay. The customer selects a committed information rate (CIR). The CIR is a guaranteed rate of throughput when using frame relay. The CIR is assigned to each PVC. Each PVC is assigned a CIR consistent with the average expected volume of traffic to the destination port. Because frame relay is a duplex service (data can be transmitted in each direction simultaneously), a different CIR can be assigned in each direction. This produces an asymmetrical throughput based on demand. This enables added flexibility to meet the customer's needs.

However, because the nature of LANs is that of bursty traffic, the CIR can be burst over and above the fixed rate for two seconds at a time in some carriers' networks. This committed burst rate (Bc) can be up to the link rate, but many of the carriers limit the burst rate to the speed of the CIR. When the network is not very busy, the customer could still burst data onto the network at an even higher rate. The burst excess rate (Be) can be an additional speed of up to the channel capacity, or in some carrier's networks, it can be 50 percent above the committed burst rate, but only for one-second increments. Combining these rates, an example can be drawn as follows:

$$\text{CIR} + Bc + Be = \text{Total throughput}$$

$$128 \text{ Kbps} + 128 \text{ Kbps} + 64 \text{ Kbps} = 320 \text{ Kbps total}$$

Some carriers will not allow any bursts across the network. Rather, they require that the maximum throughput be limited to the committed information rate. What we are emphasizing here is that no standard offerings exist. Remember to ask, rather than assume that all frame relay networks are the same.

The variable PVC arrangement with differing CIRs is a flexible arrangement. However, care must be taken in regards to this arrangement because a fee is associated with the port on the switching node within the network that can be substantial. The CIR rates can vary in 4-, 8-, or 16-Kbps increments, so there is a lot of flexibility in the selection process.

Guaranteed Delivery

When a committed information rate is used, the guarantee is that the network will make all efforts to deliver traffic (frames) at the CIR, but bursts are another situation. As you send data frames into the network, they will follow the same logical connection in sequence. Therefore, there should be no out-of-sequencing and no loss of frames. Unfortunately, there is no real guarantee! Frames can be lost, discarded, or delayed while en route. When using the burst rate or the burst excess rate, the network will make its best attempt to deliver the frames, but no guarantees are made.

As each frame bursts out through the network, it is marked within its overhead with a *discard eligibility bit*. This means that as the network nodes attempt to serve higher rates of throughput, the frames are given a designator by the end user equipment. This designator lets the other hops on the network know that if the network suddenly begins to get congested, the frames riding the network beyond the CIR can be discarded and other customer frames within the CIR will have priority. In essence, the network provides some breathing room for users by expanding and contracting based on how busy it is. The less busy the network, the higher a customer can burst without risk.

Because the network will only make its best attempt to deliver the data, the end user equipment must be intelligent enough to recognize that frames have been discarded. In Figure 26-6, the frame format is shown with the setup of the bytes in the header information, creating the discard eligibility setting. In this framed overhead, other pieces of information are also contained. Designators in each frame that are set by the network nodes along the path alert the nodes and customer equipment when congestion is occurring. The forward explicit congestion notification (FECN) and a back-

Figure 26-6
The frame format used in frame relay

ward explicit congestion notification (BECN) are used for this purpose. These are shown in the framing overhead.

Another piece of the frame layout is the data link control identification (DLCI) that marks the PVC addressing scheme. The FECN and BECN, along with the DLCI, are parts of the 2-byte sequence. Encapsulated in the frame after the header is the *user data,* a variable-length frame of user information that can carry up to 1,610 bytes. Cascade also changed the rules for the initial payload. When Cascade introduced a frame relay switch, it could handle payloads of up to 4,096 bytes. The 4,096 bytes were sufficient to satisfy the IBM data needs. The initial 1,610-byte payload can carry a full Ethernet frame with some overhead. The IBM token ring uses a frame of up to 4,048 bytes.

The bytes are not important at this point, but the variable length is. Because this is a variable, the processing of the data across the network has some inherent delays. For this reason, the packet switching networks have received a negative image. The X.25 and the frame relay networks have timers and delimiters that the nodes must use to process the data across the network. These are set to certain parameters to allow frames or packets to be transmitted at differing sizes.

Along with the variable-length data frames, the trailer in Figure 26-6 represents the overhead associated with the error checking (frame check sequence). However, when transmitting data across the network, buffers must be allocated to receive the frames. Because the data are variable, the full-size buffer must be allocated to receive a frame. This happens even if the frame is only half-full. The switch cannot process the data until the beginning flag and the ending flag are received and the CRC is calculated on what is in between. Therefore, added buffering is required for this system to work. Variable works in some cases, but in others it introduces extra overhead and latency.

However, the frame relay nodes across the network only perform the error-checking of the addressing; they don't check the user data contained inside. Each node on the network only checks the address and passes the frame along the predefined path (the PVC) to the next node. Nowhere is the data verified. Data integrity is the responsibility of the end devices that perform error-checking and retransmission requests. When the frame relay system emerged in the network, the digital world was already well in place. Because you can expect fewer errors from the transmission medium, then the intense error-checking at each step along the network can be eliminated and save valuable transport time.

Advantages of Frame Relay Services

The benefits and advantages of frame relay services are many. At a minimum, these will include the following:

Increased Utilization and Efficiency

The network uses frame relay services to enable the user network to "breathe" when necessary and to dynamically allocate the bandwidth in real time. The support of multiple connections simultaneously enables multiple sessions to be online concurrently. The nature of the bursty data transmissions on our applications does not require the full-time allocation of bandwidth. This enables shared resources on corporate LANs in remote sites.

Savings Through Network Consolidations

Data from various sources can be applied to the network in various ways, such as SNA traffic from the host, LAN bursty traffic from the desktop devices, and traffic from other application-specific devices. The use of a single connection to support all of these connections at various speeds and at variable times enables the end user to consolidate services and therefore save money. Frame relay enables the user to save on transmission and switching costs.

Improved Network Up-Time

Network down-time is a phrase that will make even the most staunch data processing person shudder. The use of a frame relay service into the virtual cloud enables the reestablishment of the network connections within the cloud automatically. The only single point of failure that really remains is in the local loop or last mile. Up-time can achieve 99.9 percent availability on a network of this sort. Furthermore, only a single connection is required. The customer can reduce the equipment costs for the interface equipment (DSU/CSU, routers, mux ports, and so on) because the number and type of interfaces can be limited to one.

Improvements in Response Time

With direct logical connectivity to the multiple locations on the network, a single interface improves the response times. Limiting the number of hops that the frames will traverse through, along with eliminating the call setup time, vastly improves response times. The allocation of bandwidth to support the bursty data needs also improves the response times, especially when a burst rate can be accommodated. Frame relay is a reliable transport protocol for high-performance and fast-response interconnections of intelligent end user devices, providing the highest ubiquitous speed, lowest overhead protocol standard available for the WAN.

Easily Modifiable and Fast Growth

The logically connected PVCs can be adjusted easily through the network administration group of the carrier. New PVCs can be assigned on a single link quickly, or existing PVCs can be increased in capacity up to the access channel capacity needed to support the dynamics of the organization's transport needs. With the PVC concept, a virtual connection is created quickly and without major modifications to the network.

Standards-Based

Frame relay falls into the ITU-TSS and the ANSI standards infrastructure. The interoperability between various switching platforms has been proven, and it is a logical progression toward the future switching services for broader bandwidth services, such as ATM, enabling a smooth transition to these newer, emerging services.

Services Available

The following services and protocols are usually readily available from the carriers, enabling the transparent flow of data across the network. Those that are not will be added as the network services proliferate and the interfaces are developed to support the various service offerings.

TCP/IP and Novell IPX/SPX

Using the packet-level routing capabilities of the frame relay network through a certified or type-accepted router (the word internationally is *homologated*), any type of data can be transported. Some routers might not support all of the protocols needed within an enterprise's network. The particular router to support the specific protocols is normally determined by the carrier in its recommendations for the network connections. In the event a customer does not have a router capable of internetworking with the suggested network or other pieces, the carriers are in a position to rent, lease, or sell the specific routers that will work on their networks. The routers support a variety of LAN topologies such as Ethernet, token ring (at 4 or 16 Mbps), and FDDI.

CCITT X.25 Protocol

Convenient interfaces to the X.25 networks are being introduced to enable a customer to connect to and transport data to sites that might not have the frame relay services available. The X.25 interface can connect the host-computing environment to the network interface across a public packet switching service, and then into an X.25 gateway on the public network (see Figure 26-7). Packets of data also can be rerouted across the frame relay network through the router at the customer location (see Figure 26-8).

Facsimile (CCITT Group III or IV) Traffic

The X.400 protocol electronic messaging service for domestic and international messaging services can be accommodated by the carrier or through the interfaces at the customer location. Facsimile traffic is extremely time-sensitive, and the packetized fax has not been truly developed.

The Major Players

The two major standards players in the specification and support of frame relay services are the International Telegraph and Telephone Consultative Committee (CCITT) and the American National Standards Institute

Figure 26-7
Access to frame relay
can be through the
public packet
switching service to
an X.25 gateway.

(ANSI). Together, they have defined a standard data (packet mode) interface for ISDN networks and frame relay services. The basics of frame relay were actually developed in CCITT blue book I.122 (*Packet Mode Bearer Services*) in 1988. The speed at which frame relay was developed from that point on has been directly attributable to the demand for a simple, easy-to-use, high-performance service for LAN-to-LAN connectivity. Additional standards are covered in the following paragraphs.

Others

In 1989, StrataCom (now a Cisco Company), Digital Equipment Corporation (now Compaq), Northern Telecom, Inc. (Nortel), and Cisco Systems began a joint development effort to specify added frame relay services

Figure 26-8
An alternative is to
use X.25 on a
customer's router that
redirects the packet
onto frame relay.

under the auspices of the Frame Relay Forum. Their efforts were specifically geared toward addressing the needs of LAN-to-LAN communications, including the need for a local management interface (LMI). The collaboration of these groups led to the publication of a joint specification for the first implementations of frame relay by numerous vendors in 1990. Portions of that specification were adopted by CCITT and ANSI for inclusion in the standards. The standards that are associated with the frame relay services are shown in Table 26-3.

In 1988, ITU approved Recommendation I.122, "Framework for Additional Packet Mode Bearer Services," which is part of a series of ISDN-related specifications. ISDN developers had been using a protocol called the link access protocol with D channel (LAP-D) to carry signaling information on the D channel of ISDN (LAPD), as defined by CCITT Recommendation Q.921. LAPD has characteristics that could be useful in other applications, such as a provision for the multiplexing of virtual circuits at level 2 in the frame level (as opposed to level 3 in the X.25 networks). Therefore, I.122

Table 26-3

*CCITT and ANSI
Standards Involved
with Frame Relay
Services*

ANSI Standards	
T1.606	Frame Relay Architectural Specification
T1.618	Data Transfer Protocol
T1.617	Signaling Specifications (Control Protocol)

CITT Standards	
I.122	Framework for Providing Additional Packet Mode Bearer Services
Q.922	ISDN Data Layer Specification for Frame Mode Bearer Services (LAP-F)
Q.931	ISDN User-Network Interface Layer 3 Specification (Blue Book)
Q.933	ISDN DSS1 Signaling Specification for Frame Mode Bearer Services

was written to provide a framework outlining how such a protocol might be used in applications other than ISDN signaling.

What the Standards State

To fully understand how frame relay works, the following three areas must be incorporated in the networking technology:

- The basic data flow of frame relay
- The interface signaling used at the network/user interface
- The internal operation of a frame relay network

The frame relay standards define an interface and the flow of the data, not the whole network. The internal operation of the network depends on the vendor's implementation of goods and support services.

The Basic Data Flow

In most popular synchronous protocols, data is carried across a communications line based on very similar structures. The standard HDLC frame format is used in a myriad of these protocols and services. Frame relay

Figure 26-9
The standard HDLC
frame format used
for SNA, X.25, and
so on.

makes a very slight change to the basic frame structure, redefining the header at the beginning of the frame (2-bytes long).

The basic frame structure for other synchronous protocols is shown in Figure 26-9. In this case, the HDLC frame header consists of an address and control information. For frame relay, the header is changed, as shown in Figure 26-10, which uses the 2 bytes (octets) to define the following pieces:

- **Data link connection identifier (DLCI)**   This identifier uses up to 1,024 LCNs.

- **Command/response bit (C/R)**   This is not used in frame relay.

- **Extended address bit (EA)**   When set to 0, it extends the DLCI address.

- **Forward explicit congestion notification bit (FECN)**   This is set in the frames going out into the network toward the destination address.

- **Backward explicit congestion notification bit (BECN)**   This is set in frames returning from the network to the source address.

- **Discard eligibility bit (DE)**   This bit is used by the source equipment to denote whether the frame is eligible to be discarded by the network if the network gets congested. When set to 1, it indicates that the frame is eligible to be discarded during a congestion period.

- **Extended address bit (EA)**   When set to 1, it is used to end the DLCI.

Figure 26-10
The change is in the
HDLC frame for
frame relay.

Interface Signaling for Control

When frame relay was first proposed to the standards bodies, the concept was fairly straightforward: keep the network protocols simple and let the higher layer protocols at the other end of the link deal with any problems. The networks would need to have a signaling mechanism to address several areas:

- Allowing the network to notify devices when congestion exists and becoming aware of the status of the permanent virtual circuits (PVCs)

- Guaranteeing throughput and equality for all users on the network, so that a single user would not occupy the network and deny others their just access

- Creating the opportunity to expand the services and features of the network in the future

Therefore, the standards players had to incorporate the use of a signaling system to solve these issues. Some of them make use of certain bits within the 2-byte header. Others use certain DLCIs as the interface control mechanism. Unfortunately, these mechanisms add to the complexity of the frame relay network, so the actual use of the signaling mechanisms is optional. However, if a vendor chooses not to implement the signaling, other complications can arise. The effective throughput of the network, the expected versus actual response times on the network, and the efficiencies gained from frame relay might all be lost.

Internal Networking

All of the standards and modifications define what is supposed to happen at the frame relay interface, normally called the user-to-network interface (UNI). How well the network performs is also determined by what happens inside the cloud. Unfortunately, the standards do not attempt to specify how to determine this. Some of the functions that occur within the cloud include

■ Determining the path for the PVCs in use

■ Estimating when congestion is building up, and deciding what to do to stop it

■ Responding quickly to mitigate the congestion when it does occur

■ Deciding which frames to discard when this becomes necessary

■ Providing guaranteed rates or quality of service levels to users

■ Establishing or permitting multiple levels of priority traffic

■ Providing the correct throughput levels of service

■ Effectively monitoring performance and producing reports on statistics, routes, and so on

Voice over Frame Relay

Because frame relay is easy to set up and conceptually is a fast packet relay concept, it enables users to build virtual connections from just about anywhere to anywhere. The industry has moved away from point-to-point leased line connections and has rolled out a frame relay virtual network in lieu of the leased lines. Much of this is because the virtual network provides for a robust connectivity solution at a less expensive cost. It is from this robust network that a data network emerged. Frame relay initially was developed around a packet switching data communications need, especially for LAN-to-LAN traffic; however, more users began to look at the cost benefits of using frame relay as a WAN technology. What resulted was the question, "If data is cheaper, why not voice or fax?"

Consequently, the industry started to look for a means of carrying voice on a frame relay network. Some of the considerations used in looking at voice over frame relay include the following:

■ Frame relay travels across the public switched telephone network, so the provider does not have to dedicate specific loops across the long-distance portion of the network and maintain specific copper connections. Therefore, it is less expensive, because the overlay to the public switched telephone network can be used for multiple customers.

- Frame relay virtual circuits afford a variability in bandwidth with the bursting capabilities already discussed. A typical frame relay capability specifies both the committed information rate (CIR) and the committed burst rate.

- Many organizations have excess capacity available; therefore, carrying packets of voice inside the frames is straightforward.

In view of the capabilities of the committed information and the committed burst rates, vendors are more able to flexibly and dynamically allocate the capacities without having excess service remaining idle. Consequently, vendors have been beefing up the backbone networks using high-speed ATM so that the capacity is readily available to provide the services necessary. Therefore, when discussion about using frame relay to carry voice communications occurred, the carriers were not overly distraught. However, their caveats were acknowledged and acted on.

Frame relay is good for bursty traffic, as opposed to the sustained information rates of voice. Frame relay guarantees only on the committed information rate, not on the bursting rates. If voice is to be used on frames, the risk of frames not arriving at their final destination still exists. If voice frames are discarded, lost, or even delayed, there is no mechanism to go back for retransmission. The retransmission requirement would be activated when something arrives out of cycle, and the receiver on the far end (the user) would have to use a self-correcting method (*"What?"*). It is through the request for retransmission that a new frame would then have to be retransmitted, but it would not be one small frame of information; it could very well be a complete sentence or discussion. This, of course, does require some fine-tuning on a network before much voice is run across frames.

If an organization chooses to run frame relay, the likelihood is that it will use compressed voice. Several standards have been adopted to provide voice over frame relay, not to mention the G.723A and G.729 ITU standards for voice compression techniques. The G.729 standard offers what most people consider the best compromise in both speed and compression to preserve voice quality. This is typically done at 16 Kbps and is the direction the majority of the users are heading. Clearly, the idea of getting a free ride for voice on a data network is a novel one. For years, the data has always traversed the network as a free ride behind voice communications. Therefore, this change in concept and ideology brings a whole new perspective on the use of voice communications. If voice can ride for free and the data network can still sustain the amount of information processing that must take place, then this is worth considering.

International

It is now becoming increasingly possible and common for small start-up ventures to enter into and define a segment of the marketplace. Due in part to equal access and deregulation in the United States and the forthcoming international agreements to standardize, deregulate, and in some cases privatize much of the world's telecommunications infrastructure, open communications will continue to create opportunities for growth in almost all segments of the telecommunications marketplace. Organizations, working on an international network, have begun to deploy voice over frame relay services.

In many cases, communication capabilities will be offered in two differing approaches: either usage-sensitive or flat-rate pricing. Under the usage-sensitive approach, the organization will dial into a public switch using the local seven-digit telephone number, and from there pass the traffic of the internationally placed call through the switch to a FRAD. This FRAD would then use an incorporation of an IP translation so that the frame relay packets could be routed to a far-end FRAD or router for retranslation at the far end. Because the local user is dialing into a local PBX-type port, the traffic can be captured for billing purposes on a cost-per-minute basis. One can expect that this cost-per-minute pricing scheme will be significantly less expensive than running a circuit switched dial-up telephone call to the same international locations.

On the other hand, organizations (third parties) are now considering the use of flat-rate pricing. Using a flat-rate schedule for a single monthly access fee, the clients will have dial-up voice, fax, and data access to and from a number of the world's business centers without incurring any additional long-distance cost regardless of the time of day or the length of call.

As international marketplaces emerge, the cost of frame relay services will continue to drop. As this drop in price occurs, the use of frame relay will become more attractive to carry voice communications. If today's current technology allows for $0.50 per minute between the United States and Japan, for example, the frame relay services might well be offered at $0.10 to $0.15 per minute. Only the larger organizations, which have sustained traffic needs between the same two end points, would benefit from going to their own private frame relay services to carry their own voice. Instead, the small to midsize companies might see benefits from the use of the public switched frame relay access for carrying voice and fax in particular. But then later data communications will be the normal evolution, so that organizations will try to converge and integrate all of their technologies onto a single dial-up communications medium. Sounds like the voice network, doesn't it?

Advantages

The chief advantage of this application revolves around the way it is priced. Comparatively inexpensive, a frame is priced by bandwidth and by permanent virtual circuit (PVC) access point. It is not distance- or usage-based as a norm. This is of critical significance when evaluating the potential for the usage-based voice that would be carried.

It is also estimated that approximately 80 percent of Internet servers run on frame relay. This is partly because of its low cost, particularly among Internet access suppliers who provide service on a monthly access fee with unlimited usage. This has been incorporated in the general strategies of the frame relay deployment.

A second key advantage is that the communications network suppliers carry the frame relay services over the existing infrastructure. Much of the upgrade, maintenance, restoration, repair, and other concerns about managing a network are the responsibility of the frame relay carrier as opposed to the end user. This removes most of the networking burden from the end user. Just about everything between the sites is domed, operated, managed, and maintained by the communications provider, removing all of that responsibility from the end-user organization.

Disadvantages

The prime limitation to frame relay has been the capability to transmit time-sensitive applications (such as voice, fax, and video) due to the burst transmission characteristics of the system. The original design was for a data communications network where these time sensitivities were not as critical. Furthermore, outside the United States, the acceptance and availability of frame relay has been somewhat sporadic. A number of countries still do not offer frame relay access or service capabilities, limiting where frame relay can be used.

Questions

1. Frame relay is included as a member of the _____.
   a. Fast packet switching family
   b. Cell relay family
   c. Circuit relay family
   d. Dial-up telephone network

2. Frame relay was developed by a group of four vendors, including:
   a. Cisco, IBM, Compaq, and NT
   b. Dell, Bell, IBM, and DEC
   c. DEC, Cisco, Stratacom, and NT
   d. Bell, Cisco, Stratacom, and DEC

3. When using a frame relay service, the user selects the _____ that he or she needs for speed.
   a. Bc
   b. CIR
   c. Br
   d. Be

4. Frame relay was introduced in what year?
   a. 1990
   b. 1991
   c. 1992
   d. 1993

5. When using the CIR, a customer then specifies the locations where the _____ is logically connected.

   a. SVC

   b. PVC

   c. SNA

   d. TCP

6. Frame relay and X.25 can interwork together in countries where frame is not available.   T/F

7. Frame relay is a stepping stone toward the B-ISDN and ATM architectures.   T/F

8. The address is called the _____.

   a. IP address

   b. SNA address

   c. Data link connection identifier

   d. Logical channel number

9. The traffic congestion notifications are called the _____.

   a. FECE and BECE

   b. FEBC and REBC

   c. FEA and BEA

   d. FECN and BECN

10. Traffic can be sent out at the Bc rate for ____ seconds.

11. When designing a network between 10 sites, how many links are needed into the cloud?

    a. 9

    b. 10

    c. 90

    d. 100

12. What are the typical access link speeds used in North America?

    a. 2.048 Mbps

    b. 56 Kbps

    c. 64 Kbps

    d. 1.544 Mbps

13. When the variable payload was initially introduced, it contained up to
    _____ bytes.

    a. 2,096

    b. 1,610

    c. 1,518

    d. 4,048

14. Incremental rates are possible in frame relay, varying from 4, 8, and 16
    Kbps steps.   T/F

15. The Be rate can be sent into the network at any time without concern.
    T/F

16. Frame relay was designed to operate in the _____.

    a. LAN

    b. MAN

    c. WAN

    d. CAN

17. The normal type of traffic placed onto the network is our time-sensitive
    data.   T/F

18. Voice over Frame is not possible because the compression does not
    accommodate the delays.   T/F

19. Fax over frame relay is possible today.   T/F

20. Frame relay will be replaced as soon as ATM becomes more
    available.   T/F

Integrated Services Digital Network (ISDN)

After reading this chapter and completing the questions, you will be able to:

■ Describe ISDN

■ Discuss what ISDN really means to the telecommunications industry

■ Understand why ISDN was initially developed

■ Describe the various services available in ISDN networking

■ Understand why people feel that it was too little too late

The integrated services digital network (ISDN) is one of the carrier product offerings designed to support what the carriers perceive as the customers' need for the transport of information. Simply stated, ISDN is a mechanism that enables the on-demand transport of voice and nonvoice services on a call-by-call basis. ISDN was conceived in the 1970s and then produced in the early 1980s by the world's telephone companies as the next-generation network. The existing voice networks didn't deal well with data. One had to use modems to transmit data, the data rates were only around 4800 to 9600 bps, and the connections (worldwide) were unreliable. ISDN is based on all-digital transmission, using state-of-the-art technology to allow access to the raw bandwidth that the carrier believes is

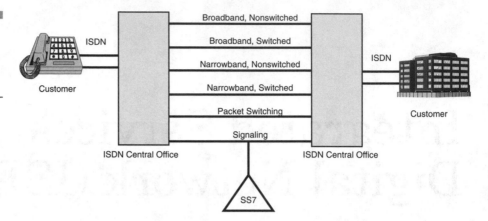

Figure 27-1
ISDN provides a mix
of current and future
services to the
customer.

needed by the customer. In Figure 27-1, the basis of ISDN is shown as the combination of present and future services.

The industry as a whole is somewhat in a state of turmoil. Many users feel that their needs for ISDN have not yet materialized. Some feel that it is too little too late. Still others feel that ISDN is part of the future, allowing the flexibility and the capability to address present and future needs for telecommunications services.

ISDN Defined

ISDN, as defined by the ITU-TSS, is a network service, evolving from the telephony networks, that provides end-to-end digital connectivity to support a wide range of services, including voice and nonvoice services, which users will have access to through a limited set of standard multipurpose interfaces.

Proponents of ISDN state that the services include the capability to

- *Transmit the name and number of the calling party to your telephone before you answer the call.* This would be of some interest to the residential user as a means of screening calls. Today these features are provided without ISDN because of enhancements made to the central office switching systems. Features and functions that were earmarked for ISDN are now delivered on the plain old telephone service (POTS) networks. Think of the benefits to any telephone-intensive business as an incoming call delivers the customer's information (phone number, contact person, account status, and so on) as the agent answers the call.

■ *Allow access to multipoint and dial-up voice and data conference calls from the desktop.* The use of voice and data calls through digital technology will be at a rate of 64 Kbps. You can get a customer on the phone, access a database, and display your marketing information on his terminal, PC, or other device all at the same time.

■ *Choose the services to be provided on a line-by-line basis, with access to various services as needed.* The use of voice, data, and video conferencing can be allowed on a call-by-call basis.

■ *Use the same line to transmit telemetry information without interfering with the ongoing voice and data calls in progress.*

You can imagine the impact these features would have on the industry as a whole if the need for the labor-intensive resources that are becoming scarce at an alarming rate were to be reduced further by technology. Therefore, ISDN is a series of products and services designed by the carriers for the users to increase the productivity and contain the costs associated with doing business. Wrong!

No doubt, these enhancements offer a variety of applications that will only be limited by the user's imagination. However, the truest concept of ISDN is that it is a transport vehicle that delivers the digital data (voice and data services). It is not a product, and it is not a package of hardware offerings from the suppliers.

How do users perceive the usefulness of a network topology and the ensuing benefits that can be derived? For many, the offerings of ISDN today match what can be done today without ISDN. For example, the caller ID display, which equates to automatic number identification (ANI), can be accomplished today using the central office digital switching technology that's already there. Another example would be the use of ISDN for telemetry purposes; by using a dial-up modem and some mechanical interfaces, the same function can be accomplished.

So why all the hype? If everything can be done using existing technology, why do we even need ISDN? The answer is obvious. Once you look at the possibilities of using the same lines and interfaces that you have today, integrated across the network on call-by-call basis, you can eliminate the need for special lines dedicated to specific applications.

Who Is Making the Rules?

The ITU is the responsible body for the development of ISDN standards on a global basis. ITU's emphasis will be to ensure that ISDN will be just as ubiquitous as the present-day public switched telephone network (PSTN) when fully deployed, if ever. Because ISDN is an enhancement to the PSTN, this should pose no great threat. However, the ITU has also expressed the need for portability in the deployment of ISDN in its universal state. This means that an ISDN terminal should be capable of being plugged into an ISDN anywhere in the world and still provide full features and functions. This creates a dilemma for the ITU because the PSTN really hasn't achieved the same portability on a global basis. The interfaces are different, the line-terminating impedances aren't the same, and the signaling is different. So how can the Consultative Committee for International Telephony and Telegraph (CCITT)* expect the evolution of universal access to a network from anywhere in the world?

The name *ITU-T* came about due to the privatization trend separating telephone service from the post office and the general elimination of telegraph service. Because its members were no longer PTTs, the organization couldn't properly be called the CCITT. The CCITT was always a consulting committee to the International Telecommunications Union. So, the ITU-TSS is the Telecommunications Standard subsection of the ITU. The CCITT was comprised of study groups (SGs). Each SG has its own area of expertise. Some of the better known ones related to ISDN are

SG VII	Public data network (X.25) X. series standards
SG VIII	Terminal equipment for telematic services
SG XI	ISDN and telephone network switching and signaling
SG XII	Transmission performance of telephone networks and terminals
SG XV	Transmission systems
SG XVII	Data transmission over public telephone networks
SG XVIII	Digital networks including ISDN

Although they are called standards, the ITU-T technically publishes *recommendations*.

---

*CCITT is called the ITU now, but at the time of specification, it was still called the CCITT. Therefore, some references are to the standards groups of the time.

The ITU has created an ISDN reference model, or a picture, of what an ISDN should look like. This model identifies a series of functional groupings of equipment and reference points where the critical functions must be performed to ensure communication between the groupings. Don't confuse the groupings and functions as different pieces of equipment; rather, they are functions that must be performed. These recommendations were contained in the findings, known as the red book that came out in 1984. Subsequent work has been done on the definition and implementation of ISDN services. The additional information is contained in the blue book, dated 1988. Figure 27-2 is a representation of the ISDN reference model.

Why Do We Need ISDN?

The carriers and vendors would have us believe that we need ISDN more now than ever, and that the only way we can successfully use the all-digital end-to-end capabilities of the network is through the implementation of ISDN. These providers might be correct, but they also have a tendency to oversell the capabilities and possibilities. The most overused and abused term these days is the concept of ISDN. Everyone wants us to believe that the system and network are there today for our unmitigated use of all of the

Figure 27-2
The CCITT ISDN
reference model

V: Interface is between exchange termination and line termination.

U: Interface is peculiar to U.S. only as a demarcation point
   between the line termination and the network terminal.

T: Interface is between network termination 1 (i.e. CSU, MUX)
   and network termination 2 (i.e. PBX LAN, etc.)

S: Interface is between the network termination device (1 or 2)
   and the subscriber equipment, called terminal equipment 1. S is
   also used between the NT and a terminal adapter (TA) which
   allows non-ISDN equipment to be used on the network.

R: Interface is between the non-ISDN equipment and TA.

features and capabilities. Unfortunately, nothing could be further from the truth. In order to implement a digital network at the local loop level, substantial investment by the local exchange carriers is still required. Many carriers have never moved toward ISDN architecture.

Meanwhile, back to the question of why we need ISDN. As the need for higher speed transport increases, the limits of the available analog interface to the LEC and the IEC will be quickly surpassed. More and more users are demanding added call-carrying capacity to move information around the world. The primary areas that will consume bandwidth are additional speed for data communications, the transfer of files from host to host, host to PC, PC to host, LAN to LAN, and LAN to WAN, and access to the Internet. The bulk of the ISDN services being installed are data applications for surfing the Web.

Another need is the demand to transfer graphic information. As the desktop applications communicating complex documents from workstation to workstation are enhanced, even greater carrying capacities of bandwidth are necessary to move these files. The typical multipage, text-based document will be fine, but complex documents that incorporate the use of graphics or annotations with voice, data, text, video, and any other format will require the transmission of files at the multimegabit rates.

Thus, as more complex information is entered into the systems and the demand for greater bandwidth increases, the use of ISDN clear-channel capacity will increase productivity and reduce costs. This doesn't portend that you must have ISDN to send documents at higher speeds. Specific needs will dictate the use of higher throughput and the technology to be used.

The main thrust is that ISDN is supposed to reduce call lengths because of the higher throughput on a dial-up basis. The shorter the call, the less expensive to support it. From the standpoint of the carrier (both the LEC and the IEC), the shorter call duration will aid in providing services to a greater number of users without adding circuit capacity and overbuilding the network. Therefore, the carriers also stand to improve efficiency in the use of their networks, which should reduce their operating costs. This sounds too good to be true; both the supplier and the user will have lower costs! In theory, it should work; the reality remains to be seen. In fact, ISDN usage has increased call durations as users surf the Internet. This causes the LECS a lot of concern.

Now you can probably appreciate why the push is on for the implementation, acceptance, and standardization of the ground rules for this capability. The other obvious benefits of ISDN include

- More flexibility for the user on a call-by-call basis.

- Better control over the network by the carriers.

- All-digital transmission is more reliable and less expensive than analog.

- Quicker setup time on calls.

- Additional services from the carriers, which equates to more revenue.

- Fewer new cable facilities needed in the office and the residence, because multiple simultaneous services can be used over a single two-wire connection at the local loop.

- Analog-to-digital/digital-to-analog conversions become the customer's responsibility.

- Signaling out of band becomes the customer's responsibility.

- Carriers can provide improved network management and maintenance control.

- High-speed facsimile, dial-up video, slow-scan video, Internet access, and packet switching will become more cost advantageous, thereby encouraging more use of these services.

The Overall ISDN Concept

The objective of ISDN was originally introduced in 1979: the evolution of telephony applications that provide digital end-to-end connectivity to support a wide range of services, including voice and nonvoice, through a set of limited multipurpose user interfaces. The reason for this concept was the obsolescence and cost-prohibitive nature of the older analog technology. Since the days when a dial-up voice connection was riddled with crackling and popping on the line, users have been clamoring for the local and long-haul carriers to improve service. The evolution of analog-to-digital transmission techniques significantly improved the transmission of voice and facilitated the ultimate introduction of high-speed data communications. It would be appropriate to summarize some of the telecommunications requirements placed on the networks and carriers. The following are the candidates for integrated digital communications through the evolved networking techniques.

Telegraph

The telegraph was the first electrical communications system to be introduced. It used direct current pulse signals on single-wire earth-return lines, and later on two-wire lines. It was possible to detect signals over long distances by the use of sensitized galvanometers. Transatlantic cables were in use in the mid-1800s. Pulse codes such as Morse code were devised, and operators who were highly skilled could achieve speeds of 30 words per minute. The use of the telegraph and the ensuing delays over the transmission path distorted the actual human side of communications. Unnecessary words were eliminated as an expedient in getting the transmission across the cable. The telegraph introduced the first forms of digital coding and used a protocol to ensure accuracy and the reception of messages.

Telephone

Users could now communicate directly with each other without the need for a protocol or the intervention of a skilled operator to interpret the message. After the operators were removed from the picture, telephone communications needed improvements to allow a novice caller to use the system comfortably over great distances. Automatic switching, an invention necessitated in the network and invented by an undertaker, Almond Strowger, increased the ease of use and the ability of unskilled callers to access other telephones without human intervention.

Telex

The development and manufacture of complex machines prepared the way for the production of delicate mechanisms for telephone switching. At about the same time Alexander Graham Bell was promoting the telephone, the typewriter (invented in 1867 by Christopher Sholes) was finding its way into the office. It took only a small adaptation to use an electric typewriter to send telegraph code for each letter and number on the keyboard. It wasn't until the 1930s, however, that interconnection using the Telex actually expanded without the need for the skilled telegraph operator. One of the reasons this process was slow to be accepted was the protocol needed for the machines to call and answer back with a discrete identity. Telex machines that used a punched tape constituted the first attempt to introduce direct machine-to-machine communications without the intervention of the operator. Many people in the industry thought this was a dead technology, especially because of the proliferation of facsimile and view data terminals. However, Telex is still alive and strong on an international spectrum.

Data Communications

Telex and the telegraph are actually the original data networks introduced into the industry. The term *data communications* became more commonplace after the introduction of digital computers, which encouraged the concept of time-sharing tasks requested by many terminals and devices. Today, the use of data communications over the public switched telephone network is continually on the rise. Speech bandwidth, as provided by the local exchange carriers, has recently come to limit the speed of information flow between communications devices (up to 33.6 Kbps on dial-up analog lines).

Packet Switching

Using a dedicated or a circuit switched facility to communicate information has been one of our primary means of communicating data. Public packet switching techniques were introduced as an evolution of these facilities. Public packet switched networks were modeled after the bursty nature of data communications and the concept that all data calls do not necessarily need simultaneous two-way communication. Several users' packets might be traversing the network on the same virtual link without any degradation of the response or loss of data integrity. This method enables the carriers to gain greater use of their facilities and allows users to communicate at decent rates of speed without the use of dedicated or private lines.

Integration

The use and existence of separate networks to provide the previously discussed services has in some ways been an advantage accessing these network services. However, using separate lines and "access methods" has also been a disadvantage. To access to the various services, the user had to subscribe to a particular network. The user was presented with an overhead and management problem in administering the effective use of each of the facilities provided. Moreover, in periods of peak loading, many facilities were overburdened while others sat idle.

To eliminate this problem, users and suppliers alike began to explore and demand an integrated plan. This plan calls for access, through gateways or other methods, to any service by any user through a common set of lines. The existence of integrated networks will allow for user management of the entire telecommunications function through the single thread to the outside world. This is what the overall objective of the ISDN really is: to provide the user with easy access to multiple services over a single connection to the network. The least important element of the title *ISDN* is the word *digital,* even though it is the digital network that enables this universal and simple access to the wide range of services provided. To meet this objective, the comparisons shown in Table 27-1 must be implemented.

These are no simple tasks. The concept is complex to define and even more difficult to perform. This is particularly true in the regulatory environment here in the United States, where clear lines of demarcation have been established with the divestiture of AT&T from the telephone company subsidiaries.

The ISDN Architecture

ISDN is based on the open systems interconnection (OSI) layered communications model adopted by the ITU. The architecture generalizes the OSI model and applies it to information and signaling transfer and system management. The inclusion of the transmission media in the model highlights the need to evolve ISDN from today's metallic environment in the local loop plant to a fiber-optic environment and on-premises wiring to higher grades of twisted pairs or fiber optics. The system management reflects the market's need for the customer-controllable and easily maintainable systems and services.

Physical View

Two CCITT ISDN user network interfaces are used for connection to end user devices. They are the basic rate interface (BRI), 2B+D, and the primary rate interface (PRI), 23B+D/30B+D (30B+D is the international

Table 27-1

Comparing the
Objectives of ISDN

Locally	Publicly
Duplex operation of simultaneous voice, data, telemetry, and signaling on a single link must exist.	Capacity must exist to independently switch voice, data, telemetry, and signaling information from a subscriber location over a single line.
Transparency must exist on the message content used in the various services.	The capability must be put in place to extract the message address information, check information for validity, and transmit the message information to the desired address.
Operation must take place over the two-wire connection (twisted pair) within the distance limitations and other characteristics of the copper wire.	The ability to access specialized networks (packet switching, for example) and pass message information to and from these networks in a protocol-transparent way must be provided.
Extended areas must be serviced through the use of digital regenerators. The old analog amplification equipment must be removed.	Charges and billing information must be identified and billed across the various services between the providers.
Rapid access and setup times must be available. Power consumption across the line (span power) must be kept at a minimum during idle stages. Setup times must be provided end to end within 2s, replacing the older methods of call setup requiring 6 to 30s.	The capability to address or subaddress the customer premises equipment and ensure proper operation when addressing and connection take place must be provided.
Transmission and timing systems to detect framing and bit timing must be provided in both directions.	Some form of local power to the customer premises equipment from the network switching exchange must be provided. This must be able to switch on local power to "power up/power on" the customer's equipment.
Good error-free performance (a typical error rate of 10^{-7} is expected) must exist.	
Compatibility in interfaces to other forms of digital transmission media such as radio, fiber optics, cellular, and coax must exist.	
Protection must be provided against power cross-connect faults, lightning, and so on.	
Remote equipment must be suitable for mounting independently on premises for integration with customer-provided terminal equipment.	

version of ISDN PRI; it uses an E1 with the framing and signaling channels). These are covered later. However, see Figure 27-3 for the basic rate concept and Figure 27-4 for the primary rate concept. Although the most common PRI configuration is a single D channel per physical facility, multiple links (up to 20) can share a single D channel. This leads to increased information-carrying capacity for the interface. The D channel on one 23B+D can be used to control a number of 24B PRI connections.

Figure 27-3
The basic rate interface (BRI) supports 2B+D.

Figure 27-4
The primary rate interface (PRI) supports 23B+D in the United States and 30B+D internationally.

The PRI offers an economic alternative for connecting digital PBXs, LANs, host computers, and other devices to the network. The BRI brings customers integrated voice and data, as well as advanced voice features. The BRI is a standard interface and offers the user the benefit of multi-vendor compatibility.

To maximize terminal portability and ensure easy change from one network to another, the same BRI and PRI interfaces are used for interconnecting terminals, hosts, digital PBX, and other devices in the premises network. The ISDN architecture includes premises applications processors that provide information movement and management and end customer control features. Examples of some of these features are as follows:

- Voice messaging
- Text messaging
- Message center attendants
- Message detail recording
- Electronic directory
- Traffic data
- Customer station rearrangement

At the network ISDN node, the integrated channelized access is separated into components (either physically or logically, depending on the implementation) and diverted to the appropriate functions. The network ISDN node also provides interconnections to four types of networks:

- Channel switched networks
- Circuit switched networks
- Packet switched networks
- Common channel signaling networks

Logical View

The following areas provide separate logical and physical views of an ISDN architecture. The three areas where logically the network Inter-functions use packet mode, circuit mode, and application services. From a user's perspective, this logical view separates the physical copper cable pair into three distinct methods of accessing the network over the one pair of wires.

Circuit Mode Services

The 1984 CCITT red book defines, in Q.931 (I.451), messages and procedures for basic call setups and disconnects, and it includes a potential framework for supplementary voice services. Carriers use LAPD as the link layer protocol and the extended Q.931 as the network layer protocol for the D channel. The extension furnishes signaling for implementing all of today's Centrex and advanced PBX features in ISDN. New functional messages are added, as well as messages conveying the activation and deactivation of feature buttons and dial feature/access codes. The extended version of Q.931 protocol is being expanded to include functional messages for advanced signaling in the premises network and for features unique to ISDN. For an overview of the message format, see Figure 27-5. This is the HDLC frame format for LAPD messages that will traverse the data channel. ISDN also provides transparent circuit mode services for the transfer of information. Protocols for layers 2 to 7 are supplied by end user devices.

Figure 27-5
The HDLC frame format for LAP-D signaling

The out-of-band signaling infrastructure for the premises network is provided by the D channel in the BRI and PRI. It can also be provided by the public common-channel signaling (CCS) network that transports the user-to-user signaling transparently from one premises switch to another. This extends the benefit of today's CCS network to premises network users and facilitates the interconnection of geographically scattered premises switches.

In the public network, the ISDN user part (ISUP) and the signaling connection control part (SCCP) of the CCITT signaling system 7 (SS7) support end-to-end ISDN features, while the transaction capability (TCAP) supports communications between the network switches and network application nodes.

Packet Mode Services

The ISDN architecture supports packet switched data services on the 16-Kbps D channel and the 64-Kbps B channel, using X.25, X.31, and the LAPD-based packet mode protocol.

X.31 extends X.25 to provide dial-up packet switched services in an ISDN. It uses Q.931 signaling to establish the physical channel connection to the packet handler, after which the conventional X.25 in-band call control is used to establish the logical connection (see Figure 27-6).

Figure 27-6
The Q.931 signaling establishes a physical connection to a packet switching (X.25) handler.

ISDN

PSE

The LAPD-based packet mode protocol is the next step toward integrated signaling. It uses Q.931 signaling to establish the physical and logical connections. The LAPD-based packet mode protocol also decomposes bearer capabilities into building blocks to enable the freedom to distribute functions between the network and the premises system. This allows the tailoring of individual services to application needs.

LAPD layer 2 supports multiple logical links on a single physical link. The minimum-functionality packet switched service uses a portion of LAPD consisting of

- Multiplexing
- Error detection
- Frame delimiting

Other LAPD functions like error retransmission, packet sequencing, and acknowledgment can be performed on an end-to-end basis by end user devices. The LAPD-based packet mode protocol initially supports X.25-like services. Unlike an X.25 service, full X.25 is terminated only by the end user devices; the intermediate switch provides the minimum-functionality packet switching. Consequently, the X.25 services supported by the LAPD-based packet mode protocol have lower transnetwork delays and higher throughput. The LAPD-based packet mode protocol, together with its Q.931 signaling procedure, provides a mechanism for the customer to request services on the basis of application needs on a call-by-call basis. This means that a user can use the signaling channel to establish a voice call on the link at 64 Kbps as an independent action (see Figure 27-7). The call can proceed as normal until the two parties agree to conclude the conversation and mutually hang up, ending the connection between them.

Immediately following this call, the user can now use the signaling system to link the two B channels together and form a 128-Kbps data connec-

Figure 27-7
The user can establish a 64-Kbps voice connection on ISDN in subsecond times. The call will be physically connected until the parties hang up.

Figure 27-8
Immediately after a voice call, the user can signal the network to establish a 128-Kbps connection to a remote host computer.

Idle

Terminator

128 Kbps

ISDN

D Channel

Terminator

tion to a remote host (see Figure 27-8) to conduct a file transfer to the host system. This is called *bonding* the two channels together.

Application Services

The marriage of the terminal and telephone expands the horizon of services that the network must provide. More and more required functions go beyond information movement into information management and its applications. Voice messages are left on recording systems that can be controlled by the end user for playback and editing. Electronic directory services can request that the switch dial a number directly when a button on the phone is pushed. These applications require the higher layer protocols available in ISDN. ITU's recommendations for the various layers are

- X.224 as the transport layer protocol
- X.225 as the session layer protocol
- X.226 as the presentation layer protocol

These are shown in the context of a comparison with the OSI model in Figure 27-9.

Figure 27-9
The ISDN protocols
as they compare to
the OSI reference
model

| Application (being deferred) |
| Presentation X.226 |
| Session X.225 |
| Transport X.224 |
| Network Q.931 |
| Data Link Q.921 |
| Physical |

The Exchange Carrier Networks

The key element in realizing the ISDN exchange carrier networks is the local switch. As long as the carrier (LEC) has a switch that offers the basic interfaces to ISDN, the switch acts as the ISDN node. The switch (typically the end office) will provide simultaneous voice and data services to Centrex and local dial-tone users over a basic rate interface. This switch supports the full range of Centrex voice features using the extended version of Q.931 as well as circuit switched and packet switched data.

In addition, the switch will more than likely support modem pooling for internetworking with non-ISDN data terminals through the public network. Figure 27-10 shows this in a modem pooling arrangement. This moves the services (data circuit switched) onto the network. Users will access these services on an as-needed basis. The network now becomes the service provider instead of just the dial-tone provider.

The switch will also support the end user applications processor environment. This application processor will provide message services, an electronic directory, message detail recording, and traffic data statistics. Using the SS7 transaction capability (TCAP) and the switching services point (SSP), the switch will interact with network databases to process calls (see

Figure 27-10
The exchange office ISDN node can support modem pooling with non-ISDN terminals. The modem can be added to the link from the pool as needed.

Figure 27-11). This will enable the exchange carrier to implement intelligent network architecture and offer such services as virtual private networks, enhanced services, and centralized network control as part of the ISDN capabilities. The use of the primary rate interface connected to the switch will allow the transparent end-to-end transport of user-to-user information for applications such as caller name, security check, and feature transparency.

Additional flexibility can be derived through the use of remote switching modules (RSMs) and subscriber loop carrier (SLC) carrier systems, shown in Figure 27-12. Using these devices, ISDN services can be provided to remote locations. On the network side (IEC), using signaling system 7 (SS7) in conjunction with the ISDN user part, access can be provided. The combination of channel capabilities, circuit switching, X.25 packet switching, and common-channel signaling is derived through a series of ISDN gateways for the inter-/intra-LATA services.

The Interexchange Network

The interexchange carrier network services can be accessed through a major ISDN node either by switched services through the local exchange carrier or directly using private line services. The same four supporting transit

Figure 27-11

Figure 27-11
The ISDN carrier office enables access to a full range of services on the network. This allows call processing and features in an intelligent network architecture.

Figure 27-12
The LEC-to-IEC handoff will function through gateways to combine long-distance circuits/packet/signal switches. Remote areas will be served from the LEC via remote partitions.

components are accessible through the IXC network services. Service functions can be attained through a digital cross-connect system (DCS) supporting circuit mode service speeds of 64, 384, and 1536 Kbps, as shown in Figure 27-13. The use of a packet switching system (IPSS) supports the X.25 packet data network. DACS-based private line services and customer-controlled reconfiguration (CCR) are also provided. ISDN services also add capabilities through network application processors that operate off the common-channel signaling network to provide advanced 800/888/877/866 services, software-defined networks, and so on.

The Premises Network

The premises line of services and products is designed around the full integration of voice and nonvoice applications, as shown in Figure 27-14. Intelligence is also provided through a network gateway or node in an ISDN environment. ISDN-capable PBXs acting as the gateways to the public network, as provided by the exchange carriers, are accessed through the PRI. Using this arrangement, a variety of transport services and facilities can be accessed, taking full advantage of the call-by-call service selection capability of Q.931. Add-on capabilities such as the following will be available through these ISDN-capable PBXs:

- Message center services
- Voice messaging (voice mail)
- Office telecommunications services (OTS)

Figure 27-13
Access to the interexchange carrier network can be made through the LEC or direct to the IEC by bypassing the local carrier. At the IEC network, 384 to 1,536 Kbps can be accessed through a digital cross-connect system (DCS).

Circuit Switched @ 64 Kbps

T1/E1 Switched

384 Kbps Switched

Figure 27-14
A full range of
services will be
available through the
PBX for voice and
nonvoice
applications. The PBX
will use the primary
rate interface.

- Electronic mail (E-mail)
- Centralized management systems
- Least-cost routing (LCR)
- Address translations
- Security
- Feature transparency
- Station message detail recording (SMDR)

Basic Operating Characteristics

The basic structure for ISDN operating characteristics is digitally encoded data using a standard of 64 Kbps as the basic rate and 1,536 Kbps as the primary rate. This is a derived channel using pulse code modulation techniques, the North American standard for digital transmission.

The North American T1 differs from the international or European standard of 30 channels at 64 Kbps, plus overhead of one channel at 64 Kbps, yielding a digital stream of 2.048 Mbps, the E1. Other differences exist in the encoding and compounding techniques that require a translation from North American to European standards and vice versa.

Other rates of bandwidth are used in the ISDN concept. They use fractional portions of the DS1/E1 for speeds higher than the 64-Kbps rate. This is also referred to as multirate ISDN. See Figure 27-15 for a representation of this.

Bearer Services

ISDN works on the principle of transport services known as *bearer services*. The basic operation of the bearer service is the 64-Kbps channel capacity. The bearer service offers the capability to transport digital voice or non-voice services using this standard. Packet services can also be transported across the bearer service at higher rates of speed (up to 64 Kbps).

Figure 27-15
The capability to use various bandwidth requirements through multirate ISDN in a PBX or mux.

Bearer services are divided into two categories. The first is the basic rate interface (BRI), which uses two bearer services at 64 Kbps and one data channel operating at 16 Kbps, with an additional 48 Kbps of overhead, yielding a 192-Kbps data stream over the typical two twisted wires (see Figure 27-16) from the business or residence to the local exchange. The second category is the primary rate interface (PRI), which uses 23 bearer services and one data channel, all at the 64-Kbps per channel speed, yielding a 1.536-Mbps data stream from the business to the local exchange. As mentioned before, this is the North American standard (used in the United States, Canada, and Japan), whereas the international standard uses 30 bearer services plus one data service all at the 64-Kbps rate, yielding a 2.048-Mbps data stream. These framing formats are shown in Figure 27-17.

The primary rate under either the North American or international standard will use existing T1/E1 technology and be the main emphasis for the

Figure 27-16
The actual throughput on the ISDN BRI is 192 Kbps in each direction. Only 144 Kbps in each direction is available to the BRI user in a duplex mode.

Figure 27-17
The PRI format will deliver T1 at 23 B+D and 8-Kbps framing, or the E1 at 30 B+D.

business world. Applications will be based on the use of WATS, In WATS (800/888/877), FX, tie lines, and data lines, all combined into a single primary rate. Because T1/E1 technology has proliferated so much in the United States and the rest of the world over the past few years due to the economics involved, the evolution to a PRI should be simple. The connection through a digital PBX, multiplexer, network node, DCS, or other T1/E1-compatible equipment will require little change in the network and simple card changes in the customer premises network.

Questions

1. What does ISDN stand for?
   a. I still don't need
   b. I smell dollars now
   c. Integrated services digital networks
   d. Innovations subscribers don't need

2. The intent of installing the ISDN networks was to use the services for:
   a. Voice and non-voice services
   b. Dedicated point-to-point data circuits
   c. Digital Telex
   d. Analog data

3. The beneficiaries of ISDN were supposed to be:
   a. Customers
   b. ILECs
   c. IECs
   d. CLECs
   e. All of the above
   f. None of the above

4. ISDN will introduce two services known as:
   a. PRI and B8ZS
   b. BRI and E1
   c. T1 and E1
   d. BRI and PRI

5. The concept of ISDN was to use out of band signaling. T/F

6. The protocol used at layer 2 of the OSI model for the signaling is called:

   a. LAPB

   b. LAPD

   c. LAPP

   d. LAPM

7. The bulk of the ISDN services being installed is for people using the dial up network for voice. T/F

8. The capacity to link multiple channels together is called _____.

   a. Binding

   b. Linking

   c. Super-rating

   d. Bonding

9. The signaling portion of the ISDN network is designed to use the standards of:

   a. SS6

   b. X.25

   c. DSS

   d. SS7

10. PRI services come in two flavors for the U.S. and the rest of the world, described as:

    a. 2B+D and 23B+D

    b. 23B+D and 30B+D

    c. 24B+31B+D

    d. 23D+B and 30D+B

11. The most common user interface is the:

    a. PRI

    b. Multi-rate service

    c. Local loop

    d. BRI

12. The BRI supports a total of _____.

    a. 128 Kbps

    b. 144 Kbps

    c. 129 Kbps

    d. 256 Kbps

13. When the carriers introduced the ISDN networks, they expected calls to be:

    a. More expensive

    b. Shorter

    c. Longer

    d. Less expensive

14. The responsible standards committee for ISDN is OSI.   T/F

15. ISDN was introduced and widely accepted in North America but has barely been used in Europe.   T/F

Asynchronous Transfer Mode (ATM)

After reading this chapter and completing the questions, you will be able to:

- Discuss the concept of cell relay
- Understand why the cells are so important
- Describe the broadband concept with ATM
- Understand how ATM is a precursor to B-ISDN
- Discuss the benefits of using cell relay

A synchronous transfer mode (ATM) is one of a class of packet-switching technologies that relays traffic via an address contained within the packet. Packet-switching techniques are not new; some have been around since the late 1960s. However, when packet switching was first developed, the packets used variable lengths of information. This variable nature of each packet caused some latency within a network because the processing equipment used special timers and delimiters to ensure that all of the data was enclosed in the packet. As a next step toward creating a faster packet-switching service, the industry introduced the concept of *frame relay*. Both of the packet-switching concepts (one [X.25] a layer 3 and the other [frame relay] a layer 2 protocol) used variable-length packets. To overcome this overhead and latency, a fixed cell size was introduced. In early 1992, the industry adopted a fast packet, or *cell relay*, concept that uses a short (53-byte), fixed-length cell to transmit information across both private and public networks. This cell relay technique was introduced as ATM. ATM represents a specific type of cell relay that is defined in the general category of the overall broadband ISDN (B-ISDN) standard. In fact, when we talk about B-ISDN, we are actually talking about ATM.

ATM is defined as a transport and switching method in which information does not occur periodically with some reference, such as a frame pattern. All other techniques use a fixed timing reference; ATM does not: hence, the name *asynchronous*. With ATM, data arrives and is processed across the network randomly. No specific timing is associated with ATM traffic, so the cells are generated as data needs to be transmitted. When no traffic exists, idle cells may be present on the network, or cells carrying other payloads will be present.

What Is ATM?

ATM is a telecommunications concept defined by the American National Standards Institute (ANSI) and International Telecommunications Union (ITU) standards committees for the transport of a broad range of user information including voice, data, and video communication on any user-to-network interface (UNI). Because the ATM concept covers these services, it might as well be positioned as the high-speed networking tool of the 1990s and beyond. ATM can be used to aggregate user traffic from multiple existing applications onto a single UNI. The current version of the UNI is 4.0, which specifies the rates of speed and the agreed-to throughput at the user interface. As shown in Figure 28-1, the ATM concept aggregates a myriad of services onto a single access arrangement.

All of these services can be combined at aggregate rates of up to 622 Mbps today for user traffic. However, the end-user future rates of speed will be in the 1.2 to 2.4 Gbps class. Currently, the carriers are using speeds of 622 Mbps across their backbone networks, but will be deploying the 2.4 Gbps soon. In the future, the carriers will step up to 10 Gbps and higher rates.

Figure 28-1
Multiple inputs are aggregated onto a single UNI.

Broadband Communications

The use of fixed statistical (and synchronous) time-division multiplexing (TDM) services on the telecommunications networks of old had certain limitations. One of these was the restrictive bandwidth available to perform functional transmission. Fixed time slots were used, requiring that amount of bandwidth to be allocated to a specific service at a specified transmission rate. The result was that fixed time slots of 64-Kbps baseband services were delivered to a user network. Where larger amounts of throughput were required, these fixed slots were concatenated together to achieve higher rates of speed (such as 128, 256, or 384 Kbps, and so on). Users want to select and utilize the required throughput rate as needed. This breathing concept makes the service far more usable.

ATM is an outgrowth of B-ISDN standards that are intended to run on SONET. Therefore, asynchronous transfer mode is designed to run on synchronous facilities. *Broadband* is defined as a higher throughput rate of bursty traffic than is traditionally available on the telephone companies' channel capacities. Instead of a 64-Kbps (DS0) channel, the broadband communications handle multimegabit transport starting at the very low end at 1.544 Mbps and progressing upward in *chunks*, or increments, up to 155 Mbps, 622 Mbps, and 1+ Gbps.

The Cell Concept

In the past, using the traditional time-division multiplexing arrangement, bandwidth was provided on a fixed time slot basis. If a user wanted a high-data rate transfer, this fixed time slot limitation got in the way. Using the standard 64-Kbps transmission speeds, you would be able to derive rates based on standards of 64-Kbps chunks. However, this only worked for a channel capacity of 64 Kbps or 1.536 Mbps.

Obviously, this impeded the ability to use bandwidth efficiently and cost the user either money or throughput performance. Something had to be done!

Network suppliers began to look at the inefficient use of capacity. They found that they were consistently overbuilding their infrastructure of links or trunks only to lease it off at lower rates than they should have. These low rates were supposed to make the service more attractive to the end user. However, this overbuilding is expensive because the suppliers were providing service that was only minimally used, and they could not reclaim the bandwidth that sat idle for 8, 12, or 16 hours a day.

Looking at user demands and the suppliers' own financial picture, a new concept emerged: rather than forcing the user to adapt to the constraints of the network, why not let the network adapt to the needs of the user? Thus, ATM was born. ATM gets around the inefficiency of the fixed time slot, rates, and formats of the TDM world by allocating whatever is necessary to the user whenever the user wants it. To do this, the network suppliers looked to the packet-switching world and settled on a service that mimics packet switching. Differences exist, however. Instead of using the processor-intensive slow-speed services of X.25 packet switching (which tops out at 64 Kbps) or the speedier frame relay (2 Mbps or a deviation up to 50 Mbps), a mix of packet/frame technology evolved using a fixed-size cell that offers higher throughput due to efficient use of bandwidth without the overhead of X.25 and frame relay.

The Importance of Cells

These cells can get around the waste of frame relay or other frame concepts. In frame relay, the frames are larger, but variable in length. Admittedly, the variable amount of data in a frame accommodates the burstiness of the data. However, the use of the timers and delimiters places extra constraints on the use of packets and frames. Therefore, if a frame size is set to accommodate LAN traffic, such as an Ethernet frame of 1,500 bytes, the network deals with a frame of the same size. Consequently, the 1,500-byte frame is used, even if only 150 bytes are to be transmitted. In many implementations, a pad function (filler) is used to fill the frame for transmission. The network has been used for a much longer period to send an insignificant amount of data. The use of this frame was only 10 percent efficient. This was done through the fills and the buffering of data until the network switch was sure that all of the data was received before sending it on to the next location in the network. Although the network was handling this partially empty frame, other users who wanted to transmit were delayed, all because the network had to recover timing, framing, and formatting on the fixed time slots. Moreover, when a variable frame size is used, the buffers across the network have to work accordingly. In many cases, the buffers in the frame relay switches are set to expect a full frame of 1,610 bytes (plus the associated overhead). If a switch has a nearly full buffer and a frame arrives, the switch must allocate the full-size buffer for the receipt of the frame. If a full-frame buffer cannot be allocated, the switch throws the frame away. Although the frame may have been partially filled, the maximum buffer cannot be allocated. Therefore, the network is inefficiently used because the data is discarded when it did not have to be. Ultimately, the frame size was extended to a maximum of 4,096 bytes to accommodate IBM token and other frames. This just adds to the complexity of the needed buffer space. The switches on the network have to receive the beginning (opening) flag, buffer the frame until it has everything, and then look for the closing flag before the network can process the data.

On the other hand, a much smaller cell enables the transmitter to break down large blocks of information into more manageable pieces. If the frame used (in this example) is only partially filled, the network need not be concerned. It will only be required to send the 150 bytes of information plus any associated overhead in a couple of cells. Thus, the network performs more efficiently. The processor speed can be used to maximize the throughput and minimize delays across the network. Cells can now be processed very quickly in silicon (chipsets). Many of the ATM switch manufacturers are now using application-specific integrated circuits (ASICs) in the systems to process the cells efficiently and quickly.

Deriving Bandwidth

When these fixed cells are used, another benefit is achieved. Users who needed to transmit 8 Mbps were stuck. Either they would have to settle for a T1 (1.544 Mbps) transmission, which would ultimately cause congestion, or they would have to lease a T3 (44.736 Mbps), which would be too expensive and mostly unused. Again, the fixed time slot arrangement of the TDM world got in the way.

Using a cell concept, the user would transparently send cells interleaved across the network regardless of the amount of bandwidth needed and consequently would get an effective throughput of 8 Mbps.

Cell Sizes and Formats

The standard fixed cell size for ATM is 53 bytes (octets). This comprises 5 bytes of overhead for activities such as addressing and 48 bytes of payload. Figure 28-2 shows the cell. The 48-byte payload will be a variable, depending on the information and control necessary. Several types of cells used could take 4 bytes of the 48 away for control, leaving the user 44 bytes of effective data; another option gives the user all 48 bytes of payload for data. It depends on the implementation and the service run on ATM. Either way, the cell is still fixed at 53 bytes long.

The cell is broken down as follows. Figure 28-3 shows 5 bytes of overhead.

General Flow Control Identifier

The first 4 bits of byte 1 contain what is known as a general flow control identifier (GFC). This is used to control the flow of traffic across the user-to-network interface (UNI) out to the network. The standards bodies are still deciding how to best use the GFC and are not explicit in their definition of

Figure 28-2
The ATM cell consists of 5 bytes of header and 48 bytes of payload.

Figure 28-3
The overhead uses 5
bytes to keep
addressing in order.

its use. Remember that this is only used at the user interface because once the cell goes onto the network-to-network interface (NNI) that is between network nodes, these extra 4 bits will be reassigned for network addressing. The GFC is only used at the entry to the ATM backbone network between the user device and the rest of the network.

Virtual Path Identifier

The next 8 bits of the header are called the virtual path identifier (VPI). A VPI is part of the network address. A virtual path is a grouping of channels between network nodes.

Virtual Channel Identifier

The virtual channel identifier (VCI) is a pointer on which channel (virtual) the system is using on the path. The combination of the virtual path and virtual channel make up the data link running between two network nodes. The VCI is 16 bits long, using the second 4 bits of byte 2, all 8 bits of byte 3, and first 4 bits of byte 4.

Payload Type

Three bits in byte 4 are allocated to define the payload type (PT), which indicates the type of information contained in the cell. Because these cells will be used for transporting different types of information, the network equipment might have to handle it differently.

Cell-Loss Priority

Bit 8 of byte 4 is a cell-loss priority (CLP) bit. The user can define whether or not to discard the cell if congestion occurs on the network. If congestion occurs and the user sets the bit to 1, the network can discard the cell. If the bit is set to 0, then the cell may not be discarded.

Header Error Control

The fifth byte of the overhead is used as a header error control (HEC). This is an error-correcting byte that is conducted on the first 4 bytes of the header. It is used to correct single-bit errors and detect multiple errors in the header information. If a single-bit error occurs, the HEC will correct it. However, if multiple errors occur in the header, it will discard the cell so that cells will not be routed to the wrong address because of errors occurring on the network. The HEC only looks at the header information; it does not concern itself with the user data contained in the next 48 bytes.

The Cell Format for User Data

Once the header is completed, the user information is then inserted (Figure 28-4). As already mentioned, the user field is either 44 or 48 bytes of information, depending on the process used. The following shows how this works.

The Adaptation Layer

The ATM adaptation layer (AAL) is probably the most significant part of ATM. The adaptation layer provides the flexibility of a single communications process to carry multiple types of traffic such as data, voice, video, and multimedia.

Figure 28-4
Once the header is
computed, the
payload is attached.

ATM Cell Overhead

Each type of traffic has varying needs. Voice needs constant data traffic; LAN is bursty in nature; video is time sensitive; data transfers from host to host can be delayed without a problem. It is in this adaptation process that the network can deal freely with varying types of information and only route cells on the basis of the routing information in the header.

Just about any type of transmission will require more than a single cell of information (48 bytes), so the ATM adaptation layer divides the information into smaller segments that are capable of being inserted into cells for transport between two end nodes. Depending on the type of traffic, the adaptation layer functions in one of five ways. These ways are shown in Table 28-1, with various types of information and adaptation layers involved.

The AAL is broken down into two sublayers; the first is the convergence sublayer and the second is the segmentation and reassembly sublayer (SAR). This SAR is similar to X.25 PADs. The purpose of the process is to break the data down into the 48-byte payloads, yet maintain data integrity and pointers for ID purposes. This process of two sublayers produces a protocol data unit (PDU). The convergence sublayer PDU is of a variable length that is determined by the AAL type and the length of the high-layer data passed to it. The SAR-PDU is always kept at 48 bytes to fill an ATM

Table 28-1

Summary of the
Five Different
Adaptation Types

Type	Name	Description
1.	Constant-bit-rate (CBR) services	Enables ATM to handle voice services at DS0, DS1, and DS3 levels. Recovers timing and clocking for voice services.
2.	Variable-bit-rate (VBR) time-sensitive services	Not finalized, but reserved for data transmissions that are synchronized. Also will address packet mode video in a compressed mode using bursty data transmission.
3.	Connection-oriented VBR data transfer	Bursty data generated across the network between two users on a prearranged connection. Large file transfers fall into this category.
4.	Connectionless VBR transfer	Transmission of data without a prearranged connection. Suitable for LAN traffic that is bursty and short. Same reasoning as X.25, where dial-up connection and setup take longer than data transfer.
5.	Simple and efficient adaptation layer (SEAL)	Improved type 3 for data transfer where higher-level protocols can handle data and error recovery. Uses all 48 bytes as data transmission and handles message transfer as sequenced packets.

cell data stream. This is shown in Figure 28-5 as it goes through the process.

As the user data, which can be multimegabyte files, is passed down to the convergence sublayer (CS) process, the data is broken down into variable block lengths. A maximum of 64 KB is used in this process. The large user file is broken down into the 64-KB segments. A header and trailer describing the type and size of the CS-PDU are added. This is then passed on to the next sublayer process.

The SAR then receives the CS-PDU and breaks it down into 44-byte cells (if less than 44 bytes, the rest is padded). Additional overhead (2 bytes of header and 2 bytes of trailer) is added to the SAR-PDU. The simple and efficient adaptation layer (SEAL) uses all 48 bytes for user information, and therefore uses the bandwidth more efficiently.

Finally, the PDU is inserted into an ATM cell with the 5-byte header. Following this, the cell is handed down to the physical cable system.

Figure 28-5
The adaptation process goes through two steps to produce the ATM payload.

ATM Standards Protocols

The development of communications standards takes on a global perspective and coordination. Many standards bodies are involved with the often lengthy task of generating a consensus on implementing a broadband communications technology. These bodies are continually refining and extending the standards, adding more advanced features and capabilities. At each revision of a standard, the cumulative experience with the older implementation is used to update and improve the standard. The older standard implementations remain useful; they are simply built on. The standards process has always been a fine balance between technology and commercial interests. A recent phenomenon among standards groups is the emergence of the forum from various commercial groups. The purpose of the forum is to impact the standards process for a particular communications technology positively. The forum consists of a group of interested carriers and vendors supporting education and implementation activities.

ITU

ITU has recommended that ATM be used in worldwide broadband networks. The first standards were produced in the mid-1980s and provided a basic outline of the service. ATM was chosen as the transfer mode for B-ISDN in 1988, and an initial set of recommendations was agreed on in 1990. These recommendations specify ATM among the protocol suites at the lower layers of the OSI reference mode. Most ATM standards are already specified by the international ITU committee. However, work continues in the area of signaling, call setup definitions, and network management functions.

The B-ISDN protocol reference model, shown in Figure 28-6, is defined in CCITT recommendation I.121 into multiple planes:

- **The U plane**   The *user plane* provides for the transfer of user application information. It contains the physical layer, the ATM layer, and multiple ATM adaptation layers required for different service users (for example, continues bit rate and variable bit rate service).

- **The C plane**   The *control plane* protocols deal with call establishment and release and other connection control functions necessary to provide switched service. The C plane shares the physical and ATM layers with the U plane. It also includes the ATM adaptation layer procedures and high-layer signaling protocols.

- **The M plane**   The *management plane* provides management functions and the capability of exchanging information between the U and C planes. The M plane contains two sections: layer management, which performs layer specific management functions, and plane management, which performs management and coordination functions related to the complete system.

Figure 28-6

The B-ISDN protocol reference model (CCITT)

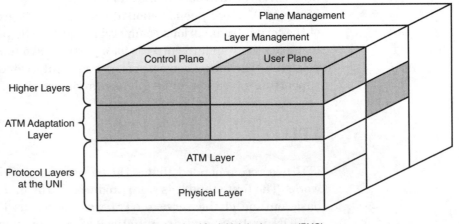

Protocol layers involved for initial deployment (PVC).
Extra layers necessary for switched service (SVC).

Each of these protocols are contained in the user-to-network interface (UNI) protocol architecture. The UNI specification involves the protocols that are either terminated or manipulated at the user-to-network interface. ATM bearer services, defined by both ANSI and ITU, provide a sequence for preserving connection-oriented cell transfer service between the source and the destination, with an agreed-on quality of service (QoS) and throughput. ATM bearer services involve two lower protocols, the ATM and the physical, of the B-ISDN protocol stack. These two layers are service independent and contain functions applicable to all upper-layer protocols. The ATM bearer service at the public UNI is defined as the point-to-point, bidirectional virtual connections at either a virtual path (VP) level and/or a virtual channel (VC) level. The UNIs (private and public) are limited to the physical and ATM layers and high-level protocols required for UNI management.

Rates

Supported U.S. access rates to a public wide-area network supporting cell relay service (ATM) include those shown in Table 28-2.

ATM cells must conform to ITU-T recommendation (CCITT) I.361. Cells are transported to their destination with a level of assurance consistent with a prespecified quality of service (QoS). The actual services provided vary, and service is delivered in a transfer rate of cells per second. Supported transfer rates in the United States range from 150 to 1,470,000 cells per second. The cell/channel control protocols are based on CCITT Q.93B, which is further defined by the ATM Forum.

ATM is a standard based on the overall B-ISDN reference model, as already stated. The ATM-relevant portions of the B-ISDN model comprise the bottom three layers of the B-ISDN protocol stack; the ATM adoption layer (AAL), which is divided into two sublayers; the ATM layer and the

Table 28-2

Basic Rates
Supported on ATM
under U.S.
Standards

Supported Rates
DS-3
STS-1
STS-3c
STS-12c

physical layer, which are also divided into two sublayers. A one-to-one relationship does not exist between the B-ISDN and OSI stacks. However, the three layers (the ATM portion of the B-ISDN protocol stack) are roughly equivalent to the OSI layers 1 (physical) and 2 (data link), as shown in Figure 28-7. Be careful to keep these separate; they are not identical.

ANSI

The ANSI subcommittees active in broadband network standards are T1X1 and T1M1. T1X1 plays a role in SONET rates and format specification, and T1M1 guides the effort to define the standard for operations, administration and maintenance, and provisioning (OAM&P).

The physical-media-dependent (PMD) sublayer deals with aspects that are dependent on the transmission medium selected. The PMD sublayer specifies physical medium and transmission (for example, timing and line coding) characteristics and does not include framing and overhead information. Physical characteristics of the UNI at the user, subscriber, and terminal interface for broadband services (UB, TB, and SB, respectively) reference points are defined in ANSI T1E1 2/92-020 and shown in Figure 28-8. The transmission convergence (TC) sublayer specification deals with physical layer aspects that are independent of the transmission medium specifications. B-ISDN-independent TC sublayer functions and procedures involved at the UNI are defined in ANSI T1.105-1991 and T1E12/92-020.

Figure 28-7

The three layers of B-ISDN closely resemble the bottom two layers of the OSI.

Figure 28-8
The physical access
reference points of
the UNI developed
by ANSI and CCITT
(ANSI)

ATM Forum

The ATM Forum is an international consortium of members that is chartered to accelerate the acceptance of ATM products and services in local, metropolitan, and wide-area networks. Although it is not an official standards body, the forum works with the official ATM standards groups to ensure interoperability among ATM systems. The consortium accelerates ATM adoption through the development of common implementation specifications. The forum's first specification on the ATM user-to-network interface (UNI) provides an important platform on which vendors can design and build equipment. It defines the interface between a router or a workstation and a private ATM switch, or between the private ATM switch and a public ATM switch.

Switches

ATM switches will come in a variety of flavors, speeds, and access ports. At the heart of the switch will be a dual-bus architecture with throughput starting at 622 Mbps on up to 2.4 Gbps and more (see Figure 28-9). Several inputs (starting at 4 and currently up to 16 in the user environment) will match across a matrix of outputs (ranging from 4, 10, or 16 Mbps and more). The ATM switch will process the AAL 3-, 4-, and 5-level services in the enterprise network.

Figure 28-9
ATM switches at the user side will have 4 to 16 ports and support various data streams.

The local switch will handle the switching and routing of cells in a building or department. This local switch will connect to a network backbone switch via an OC-3 (155 Mbps) or less service to start. Faster, higher throughput will become available through upgrades at the backplane level and the number and speed of ports attached. This requires that the switch be scalable and migrateable to the gigabit ranges. Cell switching breaks up data streams into very small units that are independently routed through the switch. The routing occurs mostly in hardware through the switching fabric. The combination of cell-switching and scalable-switching fabrics is a key ingredient of ATM.

Public Switches

The public network ATM switch is a larger, more intelligent version of the customer premises switch. A public switch is capable of handling hundreds of thousands of cells per second and has thousands of switch ports, each operating at rates of up to 622 Mbps. All cell-processing functions are performed by the input controllers, the switch fabric, and the output controllers. In an ATM switch, cell arrivals are not scheduled. The control processor resolves contention when it occurs, as well as call setup and teardown, bandwidth reservation, maintenance, and management. The input controllers are synchronized so that cells arrive at the switch fabric with their headers aligned.

The resulting traffic is said to be *slotted,* and the time to transmit a cell across the switch fabric is called a *time slot.* All VCIs are translated in the input controllers. Each incoming VCI is funneled into the proper output port as defined in a routing table. At the output controllers, the cells are formatted in the proper transmission format. For example, a broadband ISDN output controller provides an interface that consists of a line terminator to handle the physical transmission and an exchange terminator for cell processing.

LAN to LAN via ATM

If all goes according to the plans of vendors, carriers, standards bodies, and users alike, then ATM should have plug-and-play capability. The use of shared-wire, single-bus technology with all stations tapped in might become a thing of the past. As the cable originally snaked from office to office, distances became the bottleneck. When the cable had to be made longer, two pieces were joined together with repeaters. However, a single break in the cable could bring down the entire LAN. The idea of a hub started with the application of a star-wiring topology for Ethernet LANs. Now hubs are becoming the central switching point for the entire enterprise. In the near future, hubs will embrace internetworking switching and multimedia.

The next-generation ATM-based hub will provide an integrated framework (a star-shaped backbone with a high-capacity switch) that provides support for multimedia applications (Figure 28-10). This design eases the task of routing video streams and simplifies network management. As the capacity of a single switch is exceeded, switches will be added to the backbone, and the high-speed intelligent hub will provide a structure to interlink networks.

ATM and Frame Relay Compared

One way to understand the interworking functionality of the two sets of protocols is to compare and contrast their capabilities. Table 28-3 gives an overall summary of the two techniques in use today. One can see a summary of the characteristics of the two service offerings in this comparison. This is not the whole story, but it does give a visual means of seeing the reasons for the popularity of the two techniques.

Figure 28-10
Hubs and switches in
the backbone will
support future
bandwidth needs.

Network Interworking

The network interworking function provides the transport of frame relay
user traffic transparently across the ATM link. It also handles the PVC-
signaling traffic over ATM. As already discussed, this is sometimes called
tunneling through the network. Other times it is called *encapsulating the
traffic*. Regardless of the name it is given, the function provides for the
transparent movement of end-user frame relay information across the ATM
network. The benefit is that with the tunneling or encapsulation formatting, the service is as good as if the end user had a leased-line service
between the two end points. The benefit of this tunneling approach is connecting two frame relay networks across an ATM backbone. This is shown
through the use of the network interworking unit in Figure 28-11. The
interworking function is shown as a separate piece of equipment between
the frame relay and ATM networks, and in some cases, it is just that. However, newer implementations of this architecture place the network interworking function and interfaces inside an ATM switch. Regardless of where
it resides, it is the functionality that is really important, not the location of

Table 28-3

Comparing Frame
Relay and ATM
Characteristics

Characteristic	Frame Relay	ATM
Connection type	Connection oriented	Connection oriented
Connection mechanism	PVC	PVC
Switched access (SVC arrangement)	Yes, but not widely implemented	Yes
Multiplexing arrangement	Statistical TDM	Statistical TDM
Current speeds available	Typically 56 Kbps–2 Mbps; implementations up to 50 Mbps	1.544 Mbps (T1) 12.3 Mbps 25.6 Mbps 34 Mbps (E3) 45 Mbps (T3) 51 Mbps (OC-1) 155 Mbps (OC-3) 622 Mbps (OC-12)
Area served	WAN	LAN CAN MAN WAN
Sequencing of data	No	No
Protocol data units	Variable	Fixed
Protocol data unit size	less than 4,096 bytes	53 bytes
Flow mechanisms	Circuit by circuit	Circuit by circuit
Traffic congestion management	DE bit	CLP bit
Congestion notification	FECN/BECN	Payload type field
Bursty	Yes; defined by B_c and B_e rates	Yes; defined by PCR (maximum burst sizes)
Addressing method	DLCI	VPI and VCI
Address size	10 bits (normal)	24 bits
Standards	Joint development with Frame Relay Forum and ATM Forum, ANSI specifications, ITU standards, and others	

the box. The interworking function will enable each frame relay PVC connection to be mapped on a one-to-one basis over an ATM PVC. In other cases, many frame relay PVCs can be bundled together across a single high-speed ATM PVC. The one-to-one or one-to-many services provide more flexibility.

Service Interworking Functions

The use of a service interworking function takes away some of the flexibility and transparency across the network. It actually acts more like a gateway (protocol converter) to facilitate the connection and communications between different disparate pieces of equipment. Figure 28-12 shows a representation of the interconnection of the service interworking devices across the network. The end user actually sends traffic out across a frame relay network on its own PVC; then it gets passed through the frame relay network to the service interworking function (IWF), where the data is mapped to an ATM PVC. The IWF functionality provides the mapping of the Data Link Connection Identifier (DLCI) to the VPI/VCI, as well as other optional features. The IWF is shown as a separate box, whereas newer implementations will have the dual-mode functionality inside an ATM switch.

Figure 28-12
Frame/ATM service interworking function

Frame relay and ATM can interwork and interoperate through several different techniques. This gives the carrier a sense of comfort, knowing that the legacy systems of the past can still be accommodated. The frame relay investments made in the early 1990s are still viable, and the ATM investments will be around for some time to come. Through the ATM protocols such as Frame User-to-Network Interface (FUNI), end users have the comfort of knowing their networks are not obsolete. One can now see why the networking and service interworking functions are so important. Millions of dollars of investment can still be used, and newer protocols can be deployed without making the entire network obsolete. This is what internetworking is all about.

Questions

1. What does ATM stand for?
   a. Automated Teller Machine
   b. Adode Type Manager
   c. Asynchronous Transfer Mode
   d. Asymmetrical Transfer Mode

2. What organization created the demand for ATM and ensured the acceptance?

   a. ITU

   b. ATM Forum

   c. ANSI

   d. CCITT

3. ATM can support speeds up to 10 Gbps today.   T/F

4. ATM operates at the layer 3 of the OSI model.   T/F

5. The layer sitting on top of ATM that provides for the convergence of data is called:

   a. IP

   b. ATMCS

   c. ACP

   d. AAL

6. ATM is a WAN-only protocol.   T/F

7. One of the ATM speeds supported is:

   a. 175 Mbps

   b. 622 Mbps

   c. 1.9 Gbps

   d. 2.048 Gbps

8. ATM uses a cell payload that is_____.

   a. 53 bytes

   b. 44 bytes

   c. 46 bytes

   d. 48 bytes

9. The cell header is _____ bytes long.

   a. 4

   b. 5

   c. 7

   d. 8

10. The HEC in the header conducts a CRC function on the header.   T/F

11. The complete address of a cell is called the:

    a. VPP/VCI

    b. VPI/VCC

    c. VPI/VCI

    d. VPP/VCI

12. ATM is a connection-oriented service.   T/F

13. ATM was designed for data only.   T/F

14. ATM guarantees certain throughput using an assigned _____.

    a. GoS

    b. PoS

    c. CIR

    d. QoS

15. There are _____ different forms of AAL.

    a. 3

    b. 4

    c. 5

    d. 6

16. The cell size is efficient because it can be processed in silicon faster than buffers.   T/F

17. FUNI is a frame relay specification to work with ATM.   T/F

18. ATM is synonymous with the words B-ISDN.   T/F

19. ATM was invented in _____.

    a. 1992

    b. 1994

    c. 1996

    d. 1998

20. Carriers are not using ATM yet, but they will in the future.   T/F

Digital Subscriber Line (DSL)

After reading this chapter and completing the questions, you will be able to:

- Describe the benefits of using xDSL
- Understand the capabilities of the various types of xDSL
- Discuss the limitations of the local loop
- Describe the modulation techniques used
- Understand why the telcos have been reluctant to offer DSL services over the long run

Although the industry has been scurrying around looking for new ways of transmitting data from the consumer's door, the Incumbent Local Exchange Carriers (ILECs) found new life in their copper cable plant. Clearly, the telcos had a personal stake in finding something that would enable them to continue to use unshielded twisted pairs of wire at everyone's door. The movement to a data communications driver gave them the impetus they needed.

What Is *x*DSL?

One of the major problems facing the ILECs was the ability to maintain and preserve their installed base. Ever since the Telecommunications Act of 1996, the ILECs have faced mounting pressure to provide faster and more accurate Internet access. Therefore, a new form of communications was needed to work over the existing copper cable plant. One of the technologies selected was the use of *x*DSL. The DSL family includes several variations of what is known as *digital subscriber line* (DSL). The lowercase *x* in front of DSL stands for the many variations. These will include

- Asymmetric digital subscriber line (ADSL)
- ISDN-like digital subscriber line (IDSL)
- High-bit-rate digital subscriber line (HDSL)
- Consumer digital subscriber line (CDSL)
- Rate-adaptive digital subscriber line (RADSL)
- Very high-speed digital subscriber line (VDSL)
- Symmetric or single digital subscriber line (SDSL)
- Single-pair high-speed digital subscriber line (SHDSL)

One can see that many variations are available. Each digital subscriber line (DSL) capability carries with it differences in speed, throughput, and facilities used. The most popular of this family under today's technology is asymmetrical digital subscriber line (ADSL).

ADSL is a technology primarily provided by the ILECs because the existing cable plant can support the speeds, which can vary depending on the quality of the copper. The Competitive Local Exchange Carriers (CLECs) are quickly becoming involved in providing *x*DSL now. However, the most important and critical factor in dealing with ADSL technology is the capability to support speeds from 1.5 up to 8.192 Mbps. The ILECs can also support POTS for voice or fax communications on the same line. This means that the ILECs do not have to install all-new cabling to support high-speed communications access to the Internet, which is burning up the wires today.

Asymmetric Digital Subscriber Line (ADSL)

Asymmetric digital subscriber line is the new modem technology that converges the existing twisted-pair telephone lines into the high-speed communications access capability for various services. Most people consider ADSL as a transmission system instead of a modification to the existing transmission facilities. In reality, ADSL is a modem technology used to transmit speeds of 1.5 to 6 Mbps under current technology. In the future, ADSL is expected to support speeds up to 8.192 Mbps. This definition of the higher range of ADSL speeds is one that is yet to be proven; however, with changes in today's technology, one can only imagine that the speeds will be achievable.

ADSL Capabilities

Many of the capabilities being considered with the DSL family are the services for converging voice, data, multimedia, video, and Internet streaming protocols services. The carriers see their future in the rollout of products and services to the general consuming public so they can access the Internet. Table 29-1 shows the theoretical speeds and distances of various ADSL technologies.

Remember that the speeds and distances shown in this table are theoretical. If the copper has been damaged or impaired in any way, the speed and distances will change accordingly (downward), and we all know what condition the wiring is in from earlier discussions in this book. Reality and the actual distances and speeds will most likely be less than those shown in this table. What is most important is the assumption that these speeds can

Table 29-1

Data Rates
for ADSL

Current Data Rate (Mbps)	Wire Gauge	Distance (ft)	Distance (km)
1.5–2.048	24	18,000	5.5
1.5–2.048	26	15,000	4.6
6.3	24	12,000	3.7
6.3	24	9,000	2.7

be established and maintained on the installed base of unshielded twisted pair (UTP) wire. As long as the ILECs can approximate these speeds today, the consumer will most likely not complain.

Modem Technologies

Before proceeding too far in this discussion, a quick review of modem technology is probably in line. Modems, or modulator/demodulators, were designed to move data across the voice communications network. Users still struggle to transmit data across the voice networks at speeds up to 33,600 bps. Even with the newer modems called the *V.90,* which are supposed to operate at 56 Kbps, we still see significant reductions in speed. Although this may seem like high-speed communication, our demands and needs for faster communications have quickly outstripped the capabilities of our current modem services, making the demand for newer services more evident. High-speed modems could be produced, but the economics and variations on the wiring system prove this somewhat impractical. Instead, the providers looked for a better way to provide data communications that mimic the digital transmission speeds we readily accept.

Using the telephone company's voice services, the end user installs a modem on the local loop. This modem is the data circuit-terminating equipment (DCE) for the link. A modem is used to communicate across the wide-area networks, as shown in Figure 29-1. The ILEC installs a voice-grade line on the copper cable plant and allows the end user to connect the modem. The modem then converts the data into an analog signal. There is no magic in modem communications today, but in the early days of data communications, this was considered voodoo science. The miracle of data compression and other multibit modulation techniques quickly expanded the data rates from 300 bps to today's 33.6 Kbps. Newer modems are touted to handle data at speeds of up to 56 Kbps, but few come close to these rates. So, the reality of all the pieces combined still has the consumer operating at approximately 33.6 Kbps.

ISDN-Like Digital Subscriber Line (IDSL)

DSL refers to a pair of modems installed on the last mile of line, which facilitate high data speeds. Network providers use the existing wires and add

Figure 29-1

Modems are installed at the customer's location and use the existing telephone wires to transmit data across the voice network.

the DSL modems to increase the throughput. DSL modems offer duplex operations. The speed of a DSL modem may be 128 Kbps on copper at distances up to 18,000 feet using the twisted pair wires. The bandwidth used is from 0 to 80 kHz. IDSL uses the 128-Kbps full-duplex basic rate interface (BRI). As shown in Figure 29-2, the IDSL technique is all digital, operating at two channels of 64 Kbps for voice or nonvoice operation and a 16-Kbps data channel for signaling, control, and data packets. ISDN was very slow to catch on, but the movement to the Internet created a whole new set of demands. Now more ILECs and the CLECs offer ISDN services. As the deployment of IDSL was speeding up on the local loop, the providers developed a new twist, called *always on ISDN,* mimicking a leased set of channels that are always connected. Bonding the channels together, users can surf the Net at speeds of 128 Kbps. Note that this is a *symmetrical* digital subscriber line.

High-Bit-Rate Digital Subscriber Line (HDSL)

In 1958, Bell developed a voice multiplexing system that uses the 64-Kbps pulse code modulation (PCM). Using the PCM techniques, voice calls were sampled 8,000 times per second and coded using an 8-bit encoding. These samples were then organized into a framed format, using 24 time slots to bundle and multiplex 24 simultaneous conversations onto a single four-wire circuit. Each frame carries 24 samples of 8 bits and 1 framing bit,

Figure 29-2
IDSL line connection
allows 128 Kbps.

Figure 29-2
IDSL line connection allows 128 Kbps.

8,000 times a second. This produces a data rate of 1.544 Mbps. We now refer to this as a Digital Signal Level 1 (DS-1) at the framed data rate. This rate of data transfer is used in the United States, Canada, and Japan.

Throughout the rest of the world, standards were set to operate using an E1 with a signaling rate of 2.048 Mbps. The differences between the two services (T1 and E1) are significant enough to prevent their seamless integration.

However, in the digital arena, T1 required that the provider install the circuits to the customer's premises. The local provider installs a four-wire circuit. Repeaters are spaced at every 5,000 to 6,000 feet. When installing the T1 on the local loop, limitations of the delivery mechanism get in the way. Alternate mark inversion (AMI) consumes all the bandwidth and corrupts the surrounding cable spectrum quickly. Consequently, the providers can only use a single T1 in a 50-pair cable. Figure 29-3 is a representation of this cable layout. This inefficient use of the wiring makes it impractical to install T1s to small office and residential locations. Further limitations require the providers to remove bridge taps, clean up splices, and remove load coils from the wires to get the T1 to work.

Figure 29-3
The typical layout of the T1

Multiplexer

CSU/DSU

Demarcation
Point

Repeater

24 Channels

5-6,000'

24 Channels

(no bridges, taps, load coils, etc. allowed)

Repeater

3,000'

To circumvent these cabling problems, HDSL was developed. HDSL does not require the repeaters on a local loop of up to 12,000 feet. Bridge taps will not bother the service, and the splices are left in place. This means that the provider can offer HDSL more efficiently for 1.544 Mbps. The modulation rate on the HDSL service is more advanced. Sending 768 Kbps on one pair and another 768 Kbps on the second pair of wires splits the T1. This is shown in Figure 29-4.

Originally, HDSL used two pairs at distances of up to 15,000 feet. HDSL at 2.048 Mbps uses three pairs of wire for the same distances. The most

Figure 29-4
HDSL is impervious to the bridge and splices. The T1 is split onto two pairs.

Multiplexer

CSU/DSU

Demarcation
Point

12 Channels

12 Channels

Telco

Repeaterless @ 12,000'
(bridge taps and coils allowed)

recent version, HDSL-2, uses only one pair of wire and is more acceptable to the providers. Nearly all providers today deliver T1 capabilities on some form of HDSL.

Symmetric or Single Digital Subscriber Line (SDSL)

The goal of the DSL family was to continue to support and use the local cable plant. Therefore, providing high-speed communications on a single cable pair became paramount. Most local loops already employ single cable pair today; thus, it is only natural to assume that providers would want this capability. SDSL was developed to provide high-speed communications on that single cable pair, but at distances no greater than 10,000 feet. Despite this distance limitation, SDSL was designed to deliver 1.544 Mbps on the single cable pair. Typically, however, the providers provision SDSL at 768 Kbps. This creates a dilemma for the carriers because HDSL can do the same things as SDSL.

Asymmetric Digital Subscriber Line (ADSL)

SDSL uses only one pair of wires to provide duplex high-speed communications, but it is limited in distance. Not all users require symmetrical speeds at the same time. ADSL was therefore designed to support different speeds in each direction at distances of up to 18,000 feet. Because the speeds requested are typically to access the Internet, most users look for higher download speeds and lower upload speeds. Therefore, the asymmetrical nature of this service meets those needs.

Rate-Adaptive Digital Subscriber Line (RADSL)

Typically, when equipment is installed, assumptions are made based on minimum performance characteristics and speeds. In some cases, special equipment is used to condition the circuit to achieve those speeds. However, if the line conditions vary, the speed will be dependent on the sensitivity of the equipment. In order to achieve variations in throughput and be sensitive to the line conditions, rate-adaptive DSL was developed. This enables the flexibility to adapt to changing conditions and adjust the speeds in each direction to potentially maximize the throughput on each line. In addition, as line conditions change, one could see the speeds changing in each direction during the transmission. Many of the ILECs have installed RADSL as their choice given the local loop conditions. Speeds of up to 768 Kbps are the preferred rates offered by the incumbent providers.

Consumer Digital Subscriber Line (CDSL)

Not all consumers need symmetrical high-speed communication to access the Internet. Furthermore, ADSL speeds are more than the average consumer may be looking for. Lower speed communications capability was developed using CDSL. With other forms of DSL, splitters are used on the line. CDSL was designed to eliminate the splitter on the line. Moreover, speeds of up to 1 Mbps in the download direction and 160 to 384 Kbps in the upload direction are provided. It is expected that the speeds and CDSL will meet needs of the average consumer for some time to come. A universal ADSL working group developed what is called ADSL-lite, also called G.lite. This specification was ratified in late 1998, using the working group's specifications for service delivery to the average consumer. An example of this DSL-lite service is provided by the Nortel Networks' 1-Mb modem.

Very High-Speed Digital Subscriber Line (VDSL)

It was only matter of time until some users demanded higher speed communications than was offered by the current DSL technologies. VDSL was introduced to achieve the higher speeds. In fact, speeds ranging from 13 to 52 Mbps are available, but the distance limitations of the local cable will be a big factor. In order to achieve the speeds, one can expect that a fiber feed will be used to deliver VDSL. This technique will most likely carry ATM (cells) as its primary payload. We can expect some hybrid arrangements to deliver this speed to the door for high-speed data at up to 52 Mbps downward and 1.5 to 6 Mbps upward.

Table 29-2 summarizes the speeds and characteristics of the DSL technologies we have discussed. These are the typical installation and operational characteristics; others will certainly exist in variations of installation and implementation.

Table 29-2

Summary of DSL
Speeds and
Operations Using
Current Methods

Service	Explanation	Download	Upload	Mode of Operation
ADSL	Asymmetric DSL	1.5–8.192 Mbps	16–640 Kbps	Different up and down speeds; one pair of wire
RADSL	Rate-adaptive DSL	64 Kbps–8.192 Mbps	16–768 Kbps	Different up and down speeds; many common operations on 768 Kbps. One pair of wire.
CDSL	Consumer DSL	1 Mbps	16–128 Kbps	Now ratified as DSL-lite. No splitters. One pair of wire.
HDSL	High-bit-rate DSL	1.544 Mbps in North America; 2.048 Mbps in the rest of the world	1.544 Mbps 2.048 Mbps	Symmetrical services Two pairs of wire.
IDSL	ISDN DSL	144 Kbps (64 + 64 + 16) as BRI	144 Kbps (64 + 64 + 16) as BRI	Symmetrical operation. One pair of wire. ISDN BRI.
SDSL	Single DSL	1.544 Mbps 2.048 Mbps	1.544 Mbps 2.048 Mbps	Uses only one pair, but typically provisioned at 768 Kbps. One pair of wire.
SHDSL	Single-pair high-bit-rate DSL	2.312 Mbps	192–384 Kbps	Uses one pair, aimed at small residential customers
VDSL	Very high-speed DSL	13–52 6 Mbps	1.5–6.0 Mbps	Fiber needed and ATM probably used.

Single-Pair High-Speed Digital Subscriber Line (SHDSL)

SHDSL is the newest member of the DSL family being currently standardized at ITU (G.shdsl) and ETSI (TM6) in 2001. G.shdsl targets the small business market. Multiple telephone and data channels, videoconferencing, remote LAN Access, and leased lines with customer-specific data rates are among its many exciting characteristics. Spectrally friendly with other xDSLs, it supports symmetric data rates varying from 192 Kbps to 2.321 Mbps across greater distances than other technologies. SHDSL uses a Trellis Coded Pulse Amplitude Modulation (TC PAM)-based modulation scheme, which is different from the other forms of xDSL. It will operate over a single pair of wires at ranges from 6,000 feet to 20,000 feet (2.3 Mbps to 192 Kbps rates, respectively) on 26 AWG copper. This will produce a 35 to 50 percent improvement in rate at a given range over traditional symmetric DSL and a 15 to 20 percent improvement in distance at a given rate over traditional symmetric DSL. G.shdsl is also known as G.991.2 standard.

The Hype of DSL Technologies

The local providers are extremely excited at the possibility of installing higher speed communications and preserving their local cable plants. No one wants to abandon the local copper loop, but getting more data reliably across the local loop is imperative. Therefore, the ability to breathe new life into the cable plant is an extension of the facilities in place. This also means that they can create a new form of revenue streams from the old copper. Consumers are looking for high-speed access (primarily to access the Internet) for whatever the application. Yet, at the same time, consumers are looking for a bargain. They do not want to spend a lot of money on their communications services.

The providers are trying to bump up their revenues, without major new investments. They would like to launch as many new service offerings on their existing cable plant and increase the costs to the end user. This is a business decision, not a means of trying to rake the consumer over the coals. Yet, a happy medium must be found of providing services and generating revenues with limits on expenses. To do this, the xDSL family offers the opportunity to meet the demands while holding down investment costs. The key ingredient for success is to minimize costs and satisfy the consumer. Make no mistake—if the local provider does not offer high-speed services, someone else will.

xDSL Coding Techniques

Many approaches were developed as a means of encoding data onto xDSL circuits. The more common are carrierless amplitude phase (CAP) modulation and discreet multitone (DMT) modulation. Quadrature phase modulation (QAM) has also been used, but the important part is the standardization. The industry as a rule selected DMT, but several developers and providers have used CAP. It is therefore appropriate to summarize both of these techniques.

Discreet Multitone (DMT) Modulation

DMT uses multiple narrowband carriers, all transmitting simultaneously in a parallel transmission mode. Each of these carriers carries a portion of the information being transmitted. These multiple discrete bands—or in the world of frequency-division multiplexing, subchannels—are modulated independently of each other, using a carrier frequency located in the center of the frequency being used. These carriers are then processed in parallel form.

In order to process the multicarrier frequencies at the same time, a lot of digital processing is required. In the past, this was not economically feasible, but integrated circuitry has made this more feasible.

The American National Standards Institute (ANSI) selected DMT with the use of 256 subcarriers, each with the standard 4.3125-kHz bandwidth. These subcarriers can be independently modulated with a maximum of 15 bps/Hz. This allows up to 60 Kbps per tone used. Figure 28-5 shows the use of the frequency spectrum for the combination of voice and two-way data transmission. In this representation, voice is used in the normal 0- to 4-kHz band on the lower end of the spectrum (although the lower 20 kHz are provided). Separation is allowed between the voice channel and the upstream data communications, which operates between 20 and 130 kHz. Then a separation is allowed between the upstream and the downstream channels. The downstream flow uses between 140 kHz and 1 MHz. As shown in Figure 29-5, the separation allows for the simultaneous up and down streams and the concurrent voice channel. It is on this spectrum that the data rates are sustained. Each of the subchannels operates at approximately 4.3125 kHz, and a separation of 4.3125 kHz between channels is allocated.

Using DMT for the Universal ADSL Service (G.Lite)

Provisions for the high-speed data rates of full ADSL are good, but not every consumer is looking for the high data rates afforded on ADSL. Therefore, the Universal ADSL Working Group decided to reevaluate the need for the end user. They determined that many consumers need downloads of

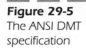

Figure 29-5
The ANSI DMT
specification

0–4 kHz	20 kHz–130 kHz	140 kHz–1 MHz
Voice	Upstream	Downstream

1 to 1.5 Mbps and uploads of 160 to 640 Kbps. Consequently, ADSL-lite specification was designed with these speeds for the future. Initially introduced in early 1998, the specification was ratified in late 1998 to facilitate the lower throughput needs of the average consumer. DMT is the preferred method of delivering G.lite service. There is no way to know if the network providers can support hundreds of multimegabit ADSL up- and download speeds on their existing infrastructure. However, using the G.lite specification can support low-demand users more efficiently. Similar to the DMT used in the ANSI specification, the carriers are divided as shown in Figure 29-6. Note that in this case, the high end of the frequency spectrum tops out at approximately 550 kHz instead of the 1-MHz range with ADSL.

Figure 29-6
The ANSI and UAWG
G.lite spectrum

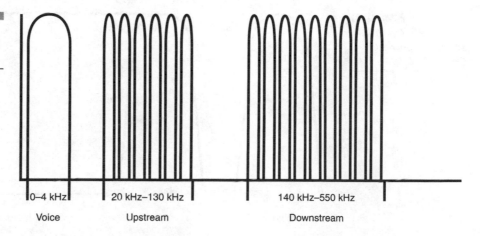

0–4 kHz	20 kHz–130 kHz	140 kHz–550 kHz
Voice	Upstream	Downstream

Carrierless Amplitude Phase (CAP) Modulation

CAP is closely aligned to quadrature amplitude modulation (QAM). QAM as a technique is widely understood in the industry and well deployed in older modems. Both CAP and QAM are single-carrier signal techniques. The data rate is divided in two and modulated onto two different orthogonal carriers before being combined and transmitted. The main difference between CAP and QAM is in the way they are implemented. QAM generates two signals with a sine/cosine mixer and combines them onto the analog domain.

CAP was one of the original proposals for use with ADSL technology. Unfortunately, this was a proprietary solution offered by a single vendor, which turned heads away from acceptance. Figure 29-7 shows CAP's use of the frequency spectrum of the line. Most industry vendors agree that CAP has some benefits over DMT, but also that DMT has more benefits over CAP. The point is that two differing technologies were initially rolled out for ADSL (and the other family members), which contradict each other in their implementation.

CAP uses the entire loop bandwidth (excluding the 4-kHz baseband analog voice channel) to send the bits all at once. The DMT technique has no subchannels. The lack of subchannels removes the concern and problems with individual channel transmission. Most of the RBOCs started using CAP but have since moved on to DMT.

Figure 29-7
The spectral use of CAP

Comments on Deployment

ADSL service is catching on. However, the ILECs and CLECs are dragging their feet. As of late 1998, only about 150,000 ADSL modem pairs were installed in the United States. In contrast, over 800,000 cable modems were installed in residences and businesses across the country. The local owners of the copper loop have to take a more aggressive approach to delivering high-speed services or consumers will go somewhere else. As the market continues to mature and standards continue to develop, the local providers must preserve their infrastructure.

Whereas consumers are reluctant to proceed with ADSL, the HDSL and SDSL services are still very attractive alternatives, offering 1.544- to 2.048-Mbps symmetrical speeds or some variation, as already discussed.

In the future, when high-speed media are installed to the door or to the curb, the logical stepping stone will become the VDSL service, perhaps sometime in 2002 to 2003. Although trials are already under way, too much time passes until the results are complied and analyzed. Therefore, the reality of VDSL for the masses is still a long way off.

Voice over DSL

In general, a Voice over DSL (VoDSL) system functions as an overlay solution to a DSL broadband access network, enabling a CLEC to extend multiline local telephone service off of a centralized voice switch. For example, Jetstream's VoDSL solution allows up to 16 telephone lines and high-speed continuous data service to be provided over a single DSL connection, as shown in Figure 29-8. A VoDSL solution typically consists of three components.

- First, a carrier-class voice gateway resides in the regional switching center (RSC) and serves as a bridge between the circuit-based voice switch and the packet-based DSL access network.
- Second, an Integrated Access Device (IAD) resides at each subscriber premises and connects to a DSL circuit. It also serves as a circuit/packet gateway and provides the subscriber with standard telephone service via up to 16 analog POTS ports and Internet service via an Ethernet connection.
- The third component is the management system.

Figure 29-8
Integrating Voice
over DSL onto ATM
or frame relay

With VoDSL solutions, DSL broadband access networks now have the coverage, capacity, and cost attributes to enable CLECs to deliver local telephone services as well as data services to the small and mid-size business markets. It has already been established that DSL access networks have the right bandwidth to serve the data needs of small and mid-size businesses. With VoDSL access solutions, this is true for serving the local telephone service needs of those subscribers as well.

Some VoDSL solutions are capable of delivering 16 telephone lines over a DSL circuit along with standard data traffic. Because 95 percent of small businesses use 12 or fewer telephone lines, a single DSL circuit provides sufficient bandwidth to serve the voice needs of the vast majority of the market. In addition, if more than 16 lines are required, most VoDSL solutions enable a provider to scale service by provisioning additional DSL connections. In addition to providing the right capacity for providing local telephone service, DSL broadband access networks are very efficient in the way they deliver service. TDM-based transport services, such as a T1 line, require the bandwidth of the line to be channelized and portions dedicated to certain services, such as a telephone line. Even if a call is not active on that line, the bandwidth allocated to that line cannot be used for other purposes. DSL access networks are packet-based, enabling VoDSL solutions to use the bandwidth of a DSL connection dynamically. VoDSL solutions only consume bandwidth on a DSL connection when a call is active on a line. If a call is not active, then that bandwidth is available for other services, such as Internet access. This dynamic bandwidth usage enables providers to maximize the potential of each DSL connection, delivering to subscribers the greatest number of telephone lines and highest possible data speeds.

Because telephony traffic is more sensitive to latency than data traffic, VoDSL solutions guarantee the quality of telephone service by giving telephony packets priority over data packets onto a DSL connection. In other words, telephony traffic always receives the bandwidth it requires and data traffic uses the remaining bandwidth. Fortunately, telephony traffic tends to be very bursty over the course of a typical business day, so the average amount of bandwidth consumed is minimal. For example, over a single 768-Kbps symmetric DSL connection, a CLEC could provide eight telephone lines (serving a PBX/KTS with 32 extensions) and still deliver data service with an average speed of 550 Kbps.

VoATM over DSL

Voice over ATM (VoATM) unites ATM and DSL technologies to deliver on the promise of fully integrated voice and data services. VoATM meets all requirements in terms of quality of service (QoS), flexibility, and reliability because the underlying technology is ATM, a highly effective network architecture developed specifically to carry simultaneous voice and data traffic.

ATM Suitability for Voice Traffic

Sometimes mistakenly associated with VoIP, VoATM is a completely separate technology that predates VoIP. In contrast to IP and frame relay, ATM uses small, fixed-length data packets of 53 bytes each that fill more quickly, are sent immediately, and are much less susceptible to network delays. (Delays experienced by voice in a frame relay or IP packet network can typically be ten times higher than for ATM and increase on slower links.) ATM's packet characteristics make it by far the best-suited packet technology for guaranteeing the same QoS found in toll-quality voice connections.

The ATM Adaptation Layer (AAL), the part of ATM responsible for converting voice and data into ATM cells, enables various traffic types to have data converted to and from the ATM cell and translates high-layer services (such as TCP/IP) into the size and format of the ATM protocol layer. A number of AAL definitions exist to accommodate the various types of network traffic. Those AAL types most commonly used for voice traffic are AAL1, AAL2, and AAL5.

VoATM with AAL1 is the traditional approach for constant bit rate (CBR), time-dependent traffic such as voice and video and provides circuit emulation for trunking applications. ATM with AAL1 is still suitable for voice traffic, but is not the ideal solution for voice services in the local loop because its design for fixed bandwidth allocation means network resources are consumed even when no voice traffic is present. Some equipment manufacturers use AAL5 to provide VoATM and support for variable bit rate (VBR) applications. They also use AAL5 because it is a better choice over AAL1 in terms of bandwidth used. However, the means for carrying voice traffic over AAL5 is not yet fully standardized or widely deployed, and implementations are usually proprietary.

ATM with AAL2 is the newest approach to VoATM. Figure 29-9 shows how AAL2 provides a number of important improvements over AAL1 and AAL5, including support for CBR and VBR applications, dynamic bandwidth allocation, and support for multiple voice calls over a single ATM permanent virtual circuit (PVC). An additional and significant advantage of

Figure 29-9
Voice over ATM with AAL2

AAL2 is that cells carry content information. This feature provides traffic prioritization for packets (cells) and is the key to dynamic bandwidth allocation and efficient network use.

VoATM and DSL

Because DSL links are ready-made for voice and data and ATM excels at carrying varied traffic, using VoATM over DSL over the local loop to the customer is a natural extension of these services. To enable the combination, equipment that supports VoATM is needed at each end of the local loop: a next-generation integrated access device (NG-IAD) at the customer premises and a voice gateway at the CO. The integrated access device concept is shown in Figure 29-10. The integrated devices can use many applications, as shown in Figure 29-11.

The real benefit is that the telephone line that once carried a single phone call for voice, data, or fax traffic can now be expanded to carry data and voice simultaneously on the same pair of wires. Because we use the data protocols (IP), we can multiplex several (16) conversations and Internet access on the higher bandwidth, and still have the lower end (0–4 kHz) available as a full-time fax line. The use of the bandwidth that was once arbitrarily curtailed is now a reality.

Figure 29-10
Integrated access devices

Figure 29-11
Multiple applications
of the IAD

Questions

1. What does DSL stand for?

   a. Direct subscriber link

   b. Digital subscriber loop

   c. Digital speed lines

   d. Digital subscriber line

2. How many flavors of DSL are available?

   a. 5

   b. 6

   c. 7

   d. 8

3. The x in xDSL stands for the speed of the DSL line.   T/F

4. ADSL can support download speeds up to:

   a. 6 Mbps

   b. 8 Mbps

    c. 52 Mbps

    d. 26 Mbps

5. RADSL is usually installed with an upload speed of _____.

    a. 1.544 Mbps

    b. 1.0 Mbps

    c. 768 Kbps

    d. 160 Kbps

6. What distance can ADSL run on a 26 AWG cable?

    a. 8–12 kft

    b. 10–12 kft

    c. 15–24 kft

    d. 15–18 kft

7. The newest family member of the DSL family is _____.

    a. SDLS

    b. SHDSL

    c. CDSL

    d. VDSL

8. The speed of a G.lite service is limited to 1 megabit.   T/F

9. VDSL will bring us download speed of up to 100 Mbps Ethernet.   T/F

10. The ANSI specification uses bandwidth from:

    a. 18–350 kHz

    b. 18–550 kHz

    c. 4–550 kHz

    d. 18–1 MHz

11. The three types of modulation used today are _____.

    a. CAP, MDT, and QAM

    b. CAP, MDT, and TCM

    c. CAP, DMT, and TCAM

    d. CAP, DMT, and QAM

12. Three forms of the xDSL family are psuedo-replacements for T1; they are (select the three):

    a. RADSL

    b. ADSL

    c. SDSL

    d. HDSL

    e. HDSL2

    f. CDSL

    g. Lite

    h. TCAM

13. The use of repeaters is required to run xDSL on the copper cable pairs.   T/F

14. The main types of xDSL use two pairs of wires.   T/F

15. The VDSL service will be symmetrical at 52 Mbps, which is the same as ATM.   T/F

Cable Modem Systems and Technology

After reading this chapter and completing the questions, you will be able to:

- Discuss why the CATV vendors jumped into the data business
- Describe the cable systems they use for data
- Understand the speeds that they offer
- Describe the technique they use to link users on their network
- Discuss what DOCSIS means

In the late 1970s, a major battle arose in the communications and computer industries. Convergence of the two industries was happening as a result of the implementation of local area networks (LANs). In the local networking arena, users began to implement solutions to their data connectivity needs within a localized environment. Two major choices were available for their installation of wiring: baseband coaxial cable and broadband coaxial cable.

The Ethernet Cable

The baseband cable was based on Ethernet development, using a 20-MHz, 50-WΩ coax. Designed as a half-duplex operation, Ethernet enabled the end user to transmit digital data on the cable at speeds of up to 10 Mbps. Clearly, the 10 Mbps was maximum throughput, but was attractive in comparison to the technology of twisted pair at the time (telephone wires were capable of less than 1-Mbps bursty data). Moreover, the use of the baseband technology allowed the data to be digitally applied directly onto the cable system. No analog modulation was necessary to apply the data. It was dc input placed directly onto the cable. The signal propagates to both ends of the cable before another device can transmit. This is shown as a quick review in Figure 30-1. To control the cable access, the attached devices used carrier sense multiple access with collision detection (CSMA/CD) as the access control. CSMA/CD allowed for the possibility that two devices may attempt to transmit on the cable at the same time, causing a collision and corruption of the actual data. Consequently, the cable had to be very controlled.

Figure 30-1
CSMA/CD cable networks are collision domains.

Collision

Ethernet 10 Base 5 Cable

A second alternative at the time was to use the broadband coaxial cable, operating with a bandwidth of approximately 350 MHz on a 75Ω cable. Broadband systems were well known because they were the same as CATV, which had surfaced in the early 1960s. Therefore, the technology was well deployed and commodity priced. Moreover, the 350-MHz capacity was attractive to the computer industry and the communications industry partisans. The issues began to surface quickly regarding the benefits and losses of using each technique. Figure 30-2 shows broadband coaxial cable.

The issue boiled down to analog versus digital and the baseband versus broadband implementations used to achieve this goal. This was a hot issue throughout both industries. The issue included using a broadband cable under the turf of the voice communications departments, whereas the baseband cables were under the primary control of the data processing departments. If one technology was chosen over another, the lines in the sand would be washed away and the convergence of voice and data would force the convergence of the two groups.

The issue was therefore not whether to use a cable, but what *type* of cable to use so that the LAN would fall under the correct jurisdictional authority

Figure 30-2
Broadband coaxial cable

within the organization. Unfortunately, control is not the goal of organizations, access and profitability are. As an industry, too much time was wasted over semantics. However, what ultimately rolled out of the bandwidth argument was that the baseband cable systems were better for the LAN. This was the decision of the 1980s, when all traffic on the LAN was geared to data only at speeds of 10 Mbps and less.

Cable TV Technology

CATV has been around since the early 1960s. It is proven technology. In the early days of Ethernet, Digital Equipment Corporation (DEC) rolled out many systems using baseband (Ethernet) cable. However, some organizations needed more than just data on a large localized network. They worked with two major providers at the time to develop the interfaces for the broadband cable systems to attach an Ethernet to the CATV cable.

DEC developed several working arrangements with various suppliers to provide a frequency-agile modem (FAM) to work on the cable TV systems. The CATV companies did not necessarily own the broadband cable. Instead, this cable was locally owned in a high-rise office or a campus complex by the end user. The cable system provided high bandwidth, but it was very complex for the data and LAN departments to understand. The reason is obvious: the broadband coax operated using frequency-division multiplexing (analog techniques), which was beyond the scope of the LAN administrators and the data processing departments. The voice people knew of analog transmission, but they had a hard time with digital transmission in those days. A silent department was in the crux of all the arguments—the video departments within many organizations stayed out of the fight.

As DEC began to roll out various choices, the average user had to justify the connection of the analog technologies (used as a carrier) with the digital data demands of the LAN. Many organizations consolidated voice, data, LAN, and video on a single cable infrastructure on a campus. The industry came up with a specification for 10Broad36 to satisfy the LAN needs over a coax cable. 10Broad36 stands for 10 Mbps on a broadband cable 3,600 meters long. Figure 30-3 shows a classic representation of the combined services on 10Broad36.

The data industry was distraught because this encouraged the use of an analog carrier system to move digital data. Over the years, however, this has been revisited several times. Wang Computer Company developed a proprietary cable system for connecting Wang systems using two broad-

Figure 30-3
A 10Broad36 cable.

band coax cables. Technologically, the system was sound. However, the price and the proprietary nature of the Wang system forced its demise.

Later in the evolution of this service, the term *broadband LAN* became popularized. Ethernet grew to 100 Mbps and then onto the gigabit range. Justifying this high-speed communication met with resistance until the use of the various fiber and coaxial systems emerged. By taking a quantum leap in the industry, the data and voice departments saw the benefit and need of converging the two services to the desktop and offering voice and video over the LAN. The 10-Mbps Ethernet and coaxial cables could not handle this offering. Moreover, access to the Internet continued with demands to add speed and capacity (voice and video on the Internet). The industry began to seek a new method of bypassing the telephone companies' local loops. A technology already at the door, of course, was CATV. So a new idea emerged: use CATV to support high-speed Internet access and bypass the local loop from telephone companies. Hence, cable modem technology changed the way we will do business in the future.

The New Market

The cable television companies are in the midst of a transition from their traditional core business of entertainment video programming to a position as a full-service provider of video, voice, and data telecommunications services. Among the elements that have made this transition possible are technologies such as the cable data modem. These companies have historically carried a number of data services. These have ranged from news and weather feeds, presented in alphanumeric form on single channels or as scrolling captions, to one-way transmission of data over classic cable systems.

Information providers are targeting upgraded cable network architecture as the delivery mechanism of choice for advanced high-speed data services. These changes stem from the commercial and residential data communications markets. The PC and LAN explosions in the early 1980s were rapidly followed by leaps in computer networking technology. More people now work from home and depend on connectivity from commercial online services (such as AOL, CompuServe, and Prodigy) to the global Internet.

Increased awareness has led to an increasing demand for data service and for higher speeds and enhanced levels of service. Cable is in a unique position to meet these demands. There appears to be no serious barriers to cable deployment of high-speed data transmission.

System Upgrades

The cable platform is steadily evolving into a hybrid digital and analog transmission system. Cable television systems were originally designed to optimize the one-way, analog transmission of television programming to the home. The underlying coaxial cable, however, has enough bandwidth to support two-way transport of signals. Figure 30-4 shows the hybrid network.

Growth in demand for Internet access and other two-way services has dovetailed with the trend within the industry to enhance existing cable systems with fiber-optic technology. Many cable companies are in the midst of upgrading the Hybrid Fiber/Coax (HFC) plant to improve the existing cable services and support data and other new services. Companies are taking different approaches to online service access. For some applications, customers may be accessing information stored locally at or near the cable headend or regional hub such as the @Home services being offered in many cities. This may be temporary until wide-area cable interconnections and expanded Internet backbone networks are in place to allow information access from any remote site.

Figure 30-4
The hybrid data network

Cable Modems

Digital data signals are carried over radio frequency (RF) carrier signals on a cable system. Digital data utilizes cable modems, devices that convert digital information into a modulated RF signal and convert RF signals back to digital information. The conversion is performed by a modem at the subscriber's premises and again by headend equipment handling multiple subscribers. See Figure 30-5 for a block diagram of the cable modem.

A single CATV channel can support multiple data streams or multiple users using shared LAN protocols such as Ethernet, commonly in use in business office LANs today. This is where Ethernet networks can be applied to the broadband coaxial networks. Different modulation techniques are being tried to maximize the data speed that can be transmitted through a 6-MHz channel. Comparing the data traffic rates for different types of modems shows why the cable modem is so popular under today's environment. Table 30-1 shows a comparison of a file download of 500KB using different techniques.

Careful traffic engineering is being performed on cable systems so that data speeds are maximized as customers are added. Just as office LANs are routinely subdivided to provide faster service for each individual user, cable data networks can also be custom tailored within each fiber node to meet customer demand. Multiple 6-MHz channels can be allocated to expand capacity as well.

Figure 30-5
Block diagram of the cable modem

Head End

Customer Location Cable-Modem

Upstream demodulator QPSK – (16 QAM) Freq: 5–65 MHz BW (2 MHz) Rate: 3 Mbps	Upstream modulator QPSK – (16 QAM) Freq: 5–65 MHz BW (2 MHz) Rate: 3 Mbps
Downstream modulator 64 QAM / 256 QAM Freq: 65–850 MHz BW (6–8 MHz) Rate: 27–56 Mbps	Downstream demodulator 64 QAM / 256 QAM Freq: 65–850 MHz BW (6–8 MHz) Rate: 27–56 Mbps

Table 30-1

Comparison of Transmission Speeds—Time to Transmit a Single 500-KB Image (Source: Cable Labs)

Method	Rate	Time
Telephone modem	28.8 Kbps	6–8 min
ISDN	64 Kbps	1–1.5 min
Cable modem	10 Mbps	Approximately 1 s

Some manufacturers have designed modems providing asymmetrical capabilities, using less bandwidth for outgoing signals from the subscriber. CATV companies in some locations may not have completed system upgrades. Therefore, manufacturers have built migration strategies into such modems to allow for eventual transmission of broadband return signals when the systems are ready to provide such service and customers demand it. Table 30-2 provides a representative sample of the way data speeds are provided on cable modems.

Table 30-2 Representative Asymmetrical Data Cable Modem Speeds	Manufacturer	Upstream	Downstream
	General Instrument	1.5 Mbps	30 Mbps
	Hybrid/Intel	96 Kbps	30 Mbps
	LANcity	10 Mbps	10 Mbps
	Motorola	768 Kbps	30 Mbps

Standards

Modems are available today from a variety of vendors, each with their own unique technical approach. These modems are making it possible for cable companies to enter the data communications market now. In the long term, modem costs must drop and greater interoperability is desirable. Customers who buy modems that work in their current cable system need assurance that the modem will work if they move to a different geographic location served by a different cable company. Further, agreement on a standard set of specifications allows the market to enjoy economies of scale and drives down the price of each individual modem. Ultimately, these modems will be available as standard peripheral devices offered as an option to customers buying new personal computers at retail stores. The cable companies and manufacturers came together formally in December 1995 to begin working toward an open standard.

Leading U.S. and Canadian cable companies were involved in this development toward an open cable modem standard. Specifications were to be developed in three phases and then be presented to standards-setting bodies for approval as standards. Individual vendors were free to offer their own implementations with a variety of additional, competitive features, and future improvements. A data interoperability specification will comprise a number of interfaces. The resultant specification is called the Data Over Cable Service Interface Specification (DOCSIS).

Some interfaces reside within the cable network. Several of these system-level interfaces will also be specified to ensure interoperability.

Return Path

The portion of bandwidth reserved for return signals (from the customer to the cable network) is usually in the 5- to 40-MHz portion of the spectrum. This portion of the spectrum can be subject to ingress and other types of interference, so cable systems offering two-way data services have been designed to operate in this environment.

Industry engineers have assembled a set of alternative strategies for return-path operation. Dynamic frequency agility (shifting data from one channel to another when needed) may be designed into modems so that data signals may avoid unwanted interference as it arises. Other approaches utilize a gate that keeps the return path from an individual subscriber closed except for those times when the subscriber actually sends a return signal. Demarcation filters, different return laser types, and reduced node size are among the other approaches, each involving trade-offs between capital cost and maintenance effort and cost.

Return-path transmission issues have already been the subjects of two years of lab and field-testing and product development. The full two-way capability of the coaxial cable already passing most U.S. homes is now being utilized in many areas and will be available in most cable systems soon. Full activation of the return path in any given location will depend on individual cable company circumstances, ranging from market analysis to capital availability.

The spectrum used for the forward and reverse paths is shown in Figure 30-6 as an indication of the frequencies available and the overall management of the system. This also shows that additional 6-MHz channels can be set aside to handle the data traffic on the cable modems and the cables themselves.

Figure 30-6
Frequency spectrum allocated to the cable modems

Applications

Cable modems open the door for customers to enjoy a range of high-speed data services, all at speeds hundreds of times faster than telephone modem calls. Subscribers can be fully connected, 24 hours a day, to services without interfering with cable television service or phone service. Among these services are

- **Information services**   Access to shopping, weather maps, household bill paying, and so forth
- **Internet access**   Electronic mail, discussion groups, and the World Wide Web
- **Business applications**   Interconnecting LANs or supporting collaborative work
- **Cable commuting**   Enabling the already popular notion of working from home
- **Education**   Enabling students to continue to access educational resources from home

The promises of advanced telecommunications networks, once more hype than fact, are now within reach. Cable modems and other technology are being deployed to make it happen. Regardless of the technology selected, the main goal is to get the high-speed data communications on the cable adjacent to the TV and entertainment. This gives the CATV companies the leverage to act in an arbitrage situation, competing with the local telephone companies who have dragged their feet in moving high-speed services to the consumer's door.

The Combined Corporate and End-User Networking Strategies

The use of a single PC on a cable system is okay for the telecommuter (or cable commuter now), but what about the small office or home office where more than a single PC is connected? Figure 30-7 shows an example of various ways the CATV connection can be accomplished. This figure uses an example of local home networking with two PCs connected to a single cable modem. Most of the providers have instructions on how to accomplish this

Figure 30-7
Multiple ways of
connecting to the
cable modem

Cable Router

Cable Modems

Router   10/100 Base Hub

and require a home user (or small user) to download additional software to accommodate the dual connection on a single modem. The second alternative is to have a router connected to the cable modem, such as a branch-office router. The network is attached to the router, and the router is responsible for handling the dispersing of the traffic onto the cable system. This can be a very effective use of the link. Next in the figure is a connection to a hub, such as a 10- or 100BASE-T connection into a LAN hub. CATV providers state this is not supported and will likely not work. However, it has been done and works well for a small office or home office connection. Using the connection directly into the hub from the cable modem makes the modem available to more users instead of just a single PC. The hub will act as a bridging function onto the modem and concentrate the traffic through the individual devices. These configurations all work, but the providers do not support problems if they arise. You are on your own if it does not work.

Security on CATV

When CATV systems are used, they are shared high-speed Ethernet backbone access to the Internet or other connections. One must be aware that on a shared cable, the PC is a peer to all others on the same cable, although they are in physically different locations. With 500 connections, many people will acquire the service from the CATV suppliers. The CATV company installs according to the appropriate technology, not according to security parameters. This is okay because they are merely providing the bandwidth to gain access. It is the end user's responsibility to turn off all the leaks in the local system (the PC). By default, when you run the Microsoft Windows environment and the appropriate networking software, the *shares* on the PC are turned on. The end user must therefore go in and turn them off. This means that if the shared services are not turned off, a user down the street or across the town can double-click on the network neighborhood icon and see all the other PCs connected to the cable. Not only can he or she see the devices, but the user can also double-click on the PC and see the resources available on that PC. From there, when a remote device has double-clicked on your PC, the user can open your drives and see your files. Unless some provisions have been taken to block this access, the intruder (used as a method of entry only) can read, write, edit, or delete your files. Worse yet, while the intruder is on your system, you do not even know he or she is there.

Many users who have cable modem service from the cable companies are not aware of the risks. Worse, the installation personnel on these systems do not totally understand or forget to point out the risks. Therefore, the user leaves the PC on 100 percent of the time, day and night, leaving access to the computer totally available. The cable modem is available 100 percent of the time, making the computer a target for hackers and the mischievous, without the permission or the knowledge of the penetrated computer owner.

Be aware of the risks and find out how to shut these open doors before leaving your computer on the network. Do not assume you are secure just because you shut your system off when not using it. When you do log on, you are exposed, and the perpetrator can get on your system while you are on it too.

Questions

1. In the late 1970s, a major battle arose in the _____ and the computer industries.
   a. Cable TV
   b. Data
   c. Internet
   d. Communications

2. To control the cable access, the attached devices used _____ as the access control.

3. The traditional Ethernet ran on a _____ cable.

   a. Broadband coax

   b. Thin broadband cable

   c. Baseband coax

   d. Thick broadband cable

4. The CATV companies used a _____ as their primary means of carrying their traffic.

   a. Baseband coax

   b. Unshielded twisted pair

   c. Broadband coax

   d. Twinax coax

5. DEC developed several working arrangements with various suppliers to provide a _____ to work on the cable TV systems.

   a. Mux

   b. FAM

   c. TAP

   d. AMP

6. Wang Computer Company developed a proprietary cable system for connecting Wang systems using _____ cables.

   a. Twin

   b. Single

   c. Two

   d. Mid-split

7. A new idea emerged to use _____ for Internet access and bypass the local loop.

   a. UTP

   b. Coax

   c. STP

   d. CATV

8. Digital data signals are carried over _____ signals on a cable system.

   a. CSMA/CD

   b. RF

   c. DOCSIS

   d. CSMA/CA

9. The CATV bandwidth of _____ is used to transmit the Ethernet.

   a. 10-MHz

   b. 24-MHz

   c. 350-MHz

   d. 6-MHz

10. The typical upload speed offered by the CATV companies is:

   a. 128 Kbps

   b. 100 Mbps

   c. 10 Mbps

   d. 1 Mbps

11. Download speeds on the Internet using CATV will yield somewhere around:

   a. 10 Mbps

   b. 5 Mbps

   c. 2 Mbps

   d. 1 Mbps

12. The portion of bandwidth reserved for _____ is usually in the 5- to 40-MHz portion of the spectrum.

   a. Ethernet

   b. Return path

   c. Forward path

   d. Multiuser path

13. The CATV service is very secure.   T/F

14. As many as 2,500 users can be on a single cable leg running in a neighborhood.   T/F

15. In the future, CATV companies may offer up to _____ Mbps to the consumer.

Signaling System 7 (SS7)

After reading this chapter and completing the questions, you will be able to:

- Describe the signaling systems
- Understand what role signaling plays in a network
- Discuss the benefits of out-of-band signaling
- Compare the different types of circuits used in SS7
- Understand the basic call flow through the network using the signaling systems

The preceding chapters of this book have discussed various ways of making a connection across the network and hosting a voice or a data transfer call. A caller's ability to go off hook anywhere in the world today, dial some digits, and then miraculously talk to someone continues to be a mystery. The network's capability to set up the call almost instantly and then tear it down just as fast is what really carries the mystique. How can the network figure out where to send the call so quickly, make the connection, and ring the telephone on the other end? All of this happens in under a second and the user is oblivious as to the intricacies of what occurs. What happens behind the scenes constitutes the backbone of the signaling systems. The networks are now dependent on the capability to handle subsecond call setup and teardown.

Evolution of Signaling Systems

Several signaling systems have been introduced into the telecommunications networks. The current one in use is called *Signaling System Number 7* (SS7) in North America. In the rest of the world, this is referred to *Common Channel Interoffice Signaling System* (CCITT) *Number 7* (CCS7 for short). Although the names are different, the functions and the purposes of the two systems are the same. As always, the North Americans do things one way, and the rest of the world does things a different way. This is an age-old problem, but one that we have learned to deal with and adjust to. The essence of the signaling system boils down to many different factors, but one of the most significant reasons the carriers employ these systems is to save time and money on the network. The carriers are also interested in introducing new features and functions of an intelligent network, as previously discussed. The best signaling systems are designed to facilitate this intelligence in the network nodes designated as signaling devices, which are separate and distinct from the switching systems that carry the conversations.

Pre-SS7

Prior to the implementation of common channel SS7, per-trunk signaling (PTS) was used exclusively in the networks. The PTS method was used for setting up calls between the telephone companies' exchanges. This method continues to be used in some parts of the world where SS7 has not yet been implemented. Admittedly, the number of exchanges using the PTS method is declining. SS7 is gaining in its deployment worldwide. However, the network is always in a state of change and this is no exception. PTS sends tones or multiple frequencies (MF) to identify the digits of the called party. The trunk also provides all of the intelligence for monitoring and supervision (call seizure, hang up, and answer back) of the call. Telephone systems at the customer's location (PBXs), that are not Integrated Services Digital Network Primary Rate Interface (ISDN PRI) compatible, use the PTS method.

On a long-distance call, when a call setup is necessary, each leg of the call repeats the MF call setup procedure until the last exchange in the loop is reached. In essence, the call is being built by the signaling as progress is occurring on a link-by-link basis. As each link is added to the connection,

Figure 31-1
Per-trunk signaling
preceded SS7 but
was slow.

the network is building the entire circuit across town or across the country. Each leg of the call setup takes approximately 2 to 4 seconds, using the configuration shown in Figure 31-1, with a total call setup taking approximately 6 to 12 seconds (at a minimum) from end to end.

This method is inefficient use of the circuitry. Although the call gets to its end destination, several complications could arise. Regardless of the complications, the outcome is the same; the carrier ties up the network and never completes the call. Hence, no revenue is generated. This inefficiency costs the carriers a significant amount of money. Therefore, something had to be done to improve this method of call establishment. The call-establishment part of the connection could take as much as 24 seconds, and then time out and never get to its destination. However, the carrier tied up parts of the network without getting a completion. This is no big deal when discussing one call. However, when a network carries hundreds of millions of calls per day, this accumulated lost time is extensive and expensive.

Introduction to SS7

The ITU-TS developed a digital signaling standard in the mid-1960s called Signaling System Number 6 (SS6) that would revolutionize the industry. Based on a proprietary, high-speed data communications network, SS6 later evolved to SS7. SS7 has now become the signaling standard for the world.

The success of the signaling standards lies in the message structure of the protocol and the network topologies. The protocol uses messages, much like the X.25 and other message-based protocols, to request services from other entities on the network. The messages travel from one network element to another, independent of the actual voice and data that they pertain to, in an envelope called a packet.

The first development of the SS6 in North America was used in the U.S. on a 2,400-bps data link. Later these links were upgraded to 4,800 bps. Messages in the form of data packets were used to request connections on voice trunks between central offices. Placing 12 signal units (of 28 bits each) assembled packets into a data block. This is similar to the methods used today in SS7 architectures.

SS6 used a fixed-length signal unit (28-bit signal units), but SS7 uses variable-length signal units. The most recent version of SS7 uses a 56-Kbps data link throughout North America, whereas SS7 runs at 64 Kbps in the rest of the world. The differences in the speeds between 56 and 64 Kbps results in the fact that the local exchange carriers have not yet fully deployed the use of B8ZS[1] on the digital circuits. Consequently, the 56 Kbps is an anomaly in the SS7 networks. Further, the North American carriers were still installing SS6 through the mid-1980s (even though it was invented in the 1960s) while SS7 deployment began in 1983, leaving two separate signaling systems in use throughout North America.

SS6 networks are very slow, whereas SS7 networks are much faster. The use of a full-DS-1 (1.544-Mbps) data link is still being considered in the North American marketplace.

Purpose of the SS7 Network

The primary purpose of SS7 was to access remote databases to look up and translate information from 800[2] and 900 number calls. This lookup process has several benefits because the carriers do not have to maintain a full database at each switching node, but they know how to get to the remote database and find the information quickly. The second purpose of the SS7 network and protocols was to marry the various stored program-controlled

---

[1] For a discussion of B8ZS, see Chapter 14.

[2] Now the addition of 888, 877, and 866 area codes are included.

systems throughout the network. This enables the quick and efficient call setup and teardown across the network in 1 second. Moreover, this integration provides for better supervision, monitoring, and billing systems integration. Additional benefits of the SS7 network were geared to replacing the SS6 network, which as of today is well over 30 years old. Like anything else, the networks have served us well, but need upgrading on a regular basis due to technology changes and demands for faster, more reliable services.

SS7 networks enable the introduction of additional features and capabilities into the network. This makes SS7 attractive to the carriers so they can generate new revenues from the added features. SS7 also enables the full use of the channel for the talk path because the signaling is done out of band on its own separate channel. This is more efficient in the call setup and teardown process.

What Is Out-of-Band Signaling?

Out-of-band signaling is signaling that does not take place in the same path as the conversation. We are used to thinking of signaling as being in band. We hear a dial tone, dial digits, and hear ringing over the same channel on the same pair of wires. When the call connects, we talk over the same path that was used for the signaling. Traditional telephony used to work this way as well. The signals to set up a call between one switch and another always took place over the same trunk that would eventually carry the call.

In early days, out-of-band signaling was used in the 4-KHz voice-grade channel. Figure 31-2 shows the 4-KHz channel. The telephone companies used band-pass filters on their wiring to contain the voice conversation within the 4-KHz channel. The band-pass filters were placed at 300 Hz (the low pass) and at 3,300 Hz (the high pass). The range of frequencies above the actual filter is 700 Hz $(4,000 - 3,300 = 700)$. In this additional spectrum, in-band signaling was sent down the wires outside the frequencies used for conversation. Actually, the signals were sent across the 3,500- and 3,700-Hz frequencies. Although these worked and were not in the talk path (out of the band), they were limited to the number of tones that could be sent. The result was also a limit to the states that could be represented by the tones.

Out-of-band signaling evolved to a separate digital channel for the exchange of signaling information. This channel is called a signaling link.

Figure 31-2
Out-of-band
signaling

Signaling links are used to carry all the necessary signaling messages between nodes. Thus, when a call is placed, the dialed digits, trunk selected, and other pertinent information are sent between switches using signaling links, rather than trunks, which will ultimately carry the conversation.

It is interesting to note that although SS7 is only used for signaling between network elements, the ISDN D channel extends the concept of out-of-band signaling to the interface between the subscriber and the switch. With ISDN service, signaling that must be conveyed between the user station and the local switch is carried on a separate digital channel, called the D channel. The voice or data that comprise the call are carried on the B channel. In reality, the out-of-band signaling is virtual because the signaling information is actually running on the same path as the B channels. Time slots on the same physical paths separate the signaling and the conversational data flows. Therefore, the signaling is virtually out of band although it is physically in the same bandwidth.

Why Out-of-Band Signaling?

Out-of-band signaling has several advantages that make it more desirable than traditional in-band signaling:

- It enables the transport of more data at higher speeds (56 Kbps can carry data much faster than MF out pulsing).
- It enables signaling at any time in the entire duration of the call, not only at the beginning.

■ It enables signaling to network elements to which no direct trunk connection is available.

The SS7 Network Architecture

If signaling is to be carried on a different path than the voice and data traffic it supports, then what should that path look like? The simplest design would be to allocate one of the paths between each interconnected pair of switches as the signaling link. Subject to capacity constraints, all signaling traffic between the two switches could traverse this link. This type of signaling is known as associated signaling. Instead of using the talk path for signaling information, the new architecture includes the connection from the signal switching point (SSP) to a device called the signal transfer point (STP). It is then the responsibility of the STP to provide the necessary signaling information through the network to affect the call setup.

When necessary, the STP will send information to the signal control point (SCP) for translation or database information on the routing of the call. The pieces combined to form the architecture of the SS7 network are described in Table 31-1 and shown in Figure 31-3 with the connection of the overall components.

Figure 31-3 shows a typical interconnection of an SS7 network. Several points should be noted:

■ Paired STPs perform identical functions. They are redundant. Together, they are referred to as a mated pair of STPs.

Table 31-1

Components of SS7 Networks

Component	Function
Signal switching point (SSP)	SSPs are the telephone switches (end offices and tandems) equipped with SS7-capable software and terminating signaling links. They generally originate, terminate, or switch calls.
Signal transfer point (STP)	STPs are the packet switches of the SS7 network. They receive and route incoming signaling messages toward the proper destination. They also perform specialized routing functions.
Signal control point (SCP)	SCPs are the databases that provide information necessary for advanced call-processing capabilities.

Figure 31-3
*SS7 architectural
beginnings*

- Each SSP has two links (or sets of links): one to each STP of a mated pair. All SS7 signaling to the rest of the world is sent out over these links. Because the STPs are redundant, messages sent over either link (to either STP) will be treated equivalently.
- A link (or set of links) joins the STPs of a mated pair.
- Four links (or sets of links) interconnect two mated pairs of STPs. These links are referred to as a quad.
- SCPs are usually (though not always) deployed in pairs. As with STPs, the SCPs of a pair are intended to function identically. Pairs of SCPs are also referred to as mated pairs of SCPs. Note that a pair of links does not directly join them.
- Signaling architectures such as this, which provide indirect signaling paths between network elements, are referred to as providing quasi-associated signaling.

SS7 Interconnection

The actual linkage enables the local exchange offices to send the necessary information out of band across the signaling links. SS7 therefore uses messages in the form of packets to signal across the network through the STPs. This enables the full use of the talk path for information exchange and the messaging paths for informational dialogue between the switching systems and the transfer points.

The links are used to pass control and billing information, network management information, and other control functions as necessary without interfering with the conversational path.

Basic Functions of the SS7 Network

The basic functions of the SS7 network include some of the following pieces of information:

■ The exchange of circuit-related information between the switching points along the network

■ The exchange of non-circuit-related information between the databases and the control points within the network

■ The facilitation of features and functions by marrying the stored program control systems together throughout the network into a homogeneous network environment

Further, the SS7 network enables these features to be put into place without unduly burdening the actual network call path arrangements:

■ It handles the rerouting of network traffic in the event of circuit failures by using automatic protection switching services, such as those found in SONET or alternate routing information.

■ Because it is a packet-switching concept, the SS7 network prevents misrouted calls, duplication of call requests, and lost packets (requests for service).

■ It enables the full use of out-of-band signaling using the ITU Q.931 signaling arrangements for call setup and teardown.

■ It enables growth so that new features and functions can be introduced to the network without major disruptions.

Signaling Links

SS7 signaling links are characterized according to their use in the signaling network. Virtually all links are identical in that they are 56-Kbps (or 64-Kbps) bidirectional data links that support the same lower layers of the protocol; the difference is in their use within a signaling network. The bidirectional nature of these links enables traffic to pass in both directions between signaling points. Three basic forms of signaling links exist, although they are physically the same. They all use the 56-Kbps DS0A in North America and 64-Kbps DS0C data facilities in nearly every other portion of the world (except Japan, where they still use a 4.8-Kbps link). The three forms of signaling links are

- **Associated** The simplest form of signaling link is referred to as the associated signaling link, as shown in Figure 31-4. In associated signaling, the link is directly parallel from the end office with the voice path for which it is providing the signaling information. This is not an ideal situation because it would require a signaling link from the end office to every other end office in the network. Some associated modes of signaling are in use, but they are rare.

  One will most often find associated signaling deployed at an end-user location using a single T1 and common-channel signaling. Channel 24 on a T1 is the associated out-of-band signaling channel for the preceding 23 talk channels.

  In some cases, it may be better to directly connect two SSPs together via a single link. All related SS7 messages to circuits connecting the two exchanges are sent through this link. A connection is still provided to the home STP using other links to support all other SS7 traffic.

- **Nonassociated** The nonassociated signaling link arrangement has a separate logical path from the actual voice path, as shown in Figure 31-5. Multiple nodes are usually involved to reach the end destination, whereas the voice may have a direct path to reach the final destination. Nonassociated signaling is a common occurrence in many SS7 networks.

  The primary problem with this form of signaling is the number of signaling nodes that the call must use to progress through the network. The more nodes used, the more processing and delay that can occur. Nonassociated signaling involves the use of STPs to reach the remote exchange. To establish a trunk connection between the two exchanges,

Figure 31-4
Associated signaling

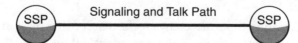

Signaling and Talk Path

SSP ———————————————— SSP

Figure 31-5
Nonassociated
signaling

Signaling Path

STP ———————————— STP

SSP ————————————— SSP

Talk Path

a signaling message will be sent via SS7 and STPs to the adjacent exchange.

■ **Quasi-ssociated** In quasi-associated signaling, a minimum number of nodes are used to process the call to the final destination, as shown in Figure 31-6. This is the preferred method of setting up and using an SS7 backbone because each node introduces additional delay in signaling delivery. By eliminating some of the processors on the setup, the delay can be minimized.

SS7 networks favor the use of quasi-associated signaling. In quasi-associated signaling, both nodes are connected to the same STP. The signaling path is still through the STP to the adjacent SSP.

Figure 31-6
Quasi-associated
signaling

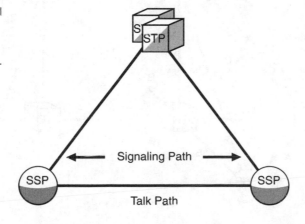

Signaling Path

SSP ←——————→ SSP

Talk Path

The Link Architecture

Signaling links are logically organized by link type (A through F) according to their use in the SS7 signaling network. These are shown in Figure 31-7 with the full linkage in place. The links are described below as supplemental to the figure.

■ **A link**   An access (A) link connects a signaling end point (SCP or SSP) to an STP. Only messages originating from or destined to the signaling end point are transmitted on an A link.

■ **B link**   A bridge (B) link connects one STP to another STP. Typically, a quad of B links interconnect peer (or primary) STPs (the STPs from one network to the STPs of another network). The distinction between a B link and a D link is rather arbitrary. For this reason, such links may be referred to as B/D links.

■ **C link**   A cross (C) link connects STPs performing identical functions into a mated pair. A C link is used only when an STP has no other route available to a destination signaling point due to link failure. Note that SCPs may also be deployed in pairs to improve reliability; unlike STPs, however, signaling links does not interconnect mated SCPs.

■ **D link**   A diagonal (D) link connects a secondary (local or regional) STP pair to a primary (internetwork gateway) STP pair in a quad-link configuration. Secondary STPs within the same network are connected

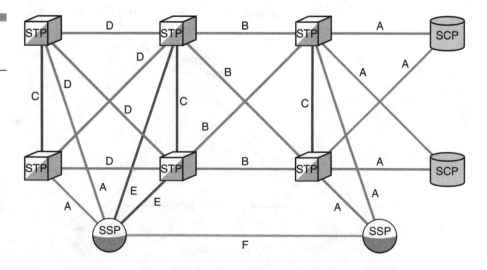

Figure 31-7
The signaling link
architecture

via a quad of D links. The distinction between a B link and a D link is rather arbitrary. For this reason, such links may be referred to as B/D links.

- **E link** An extended (E) link connects an SSP to an alternate STP. E links provide an alternate signaling path if an SSP's home STP cannot be reached via an A link. E links are not usually provisioned unless the benefit of a marginally higher degree of reliability justifies the added expense.

- **F link** A fully associated (F) link connects two signaling end points (SSPs and SCPs). F links are not usually used in networks with STPs. In networks without STPs, F links directly connect signaling points.

Links and Linksets

A linkset is a grouping of links joining the same two nodes. A minimum of one link to a maximum of 16 or 32[3] links can make up the linkset. Normally, SSPs have one or two links connecting to their STPs, based on normal capacity and traffic requirements. This constitutes a one- or two-link linkset. SCPs have many more links in their linksets to handle the large amount of messaging for 800/888/877/866 and 900 numbers, calling cards, and advanced intelligent network (AIN) services.

Combined Linksets

Combined linkset is a term used to define routing from an SSP or SCP toward the related STP, where two linksets are used to share the traffic outward to the STP and beyond. The requirement is not that all linksets be the same size, but the normal practice is to have equally sized groupings of linksets connecting the same end node. Using a linkset arrangement, the normal number of links associated with a linkset is shown in Table 31-2.

Linksets are defined as a grouping of links between two points on the SS7 network. All links in a linkset must have the same adjacent node in order to be classified as part of a linkset. The switches in the network will alternate traffic across the various links to be sure that the links are always

---

[3] The 32 links are typical in proprietary networks using an E-1. Most networks, however, are set-up with 16.

Table 31-2

Configuration of
Linksets

Link Type	Number of Links
A links	Maximum of 16 or 32 links
B/D links	Installed in quads up to a maximum of 8 links
C links	Installed individually up to a maximum of 8 links

available. This load spreading (or balancing) serves many functions. Some of them are

- To be aware when a link fails
- To recognize when congestion is occurring in the network
- To use the links when traffic is not critical and be aware when a link is down before it becomes critical

Routes and Routesets

The term *routeset* refers to the routing capability of addressing a node within the SS7 network. Every node within the network has a unique address. This address is referred to as a point code. The addressing scheme or point code is the major routing characteristic of the CCS7 (SS7) network. The terms routeset and point code are synonymous.

The point code is made up of nine digits broken down into three three-digit sequences. An example of this is 245-100-000. Reading the point code from left to right, we find that

- The first three digits refer to the network identifier (245)
- The next three digits refer to the cluster number (100)
- The final three digits refer to the member number (000)

In any given network, 256 clusters can be present and each can have 256 members. The network number in this case is for Stentor Communications in Canada.

The routing of SS7 messages to a destination point code can take different paths, or routes. From the SSP perspective, the node has only two ways out: one toward each of its mated STPs. From that point on, the STPs decide what routes are appropriate based on time, resources, and status of the network. From the SSP, various originating and terminating (destination) addressing scenarios are defined as follows:

- If the route chosen is a direct path using a directly connected link (SSP1-STPA), then the route is classified as an associated route.

- If the route is not directly connected via links (SSP1-SSP2), the route is classified as a quasi-route.

- All routing is controlled by nodal translations, providing flexible and network-specific routing arrangements. This is shown in Figure 31-8.

SS7 Protocol Stack

The SS7 uses a four-layer protocol stack that equates to the seven-layer Open Systems Interconnection (OSI) model. These protocols provide different services depending on the use of the signaling network. The layers constitute a two-part functionality: the bottom three layers are considered the communications transmission of the messages, whereas the upper portion

Figure 31-8
Routes and routesets

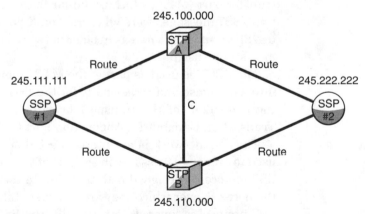

Origination	Destination			
SSP 1 → STP A	2 Routes =	SSP 1 / STP A	SSP 1 / STP B / STP A
SSP 1 → STP B	2 Routes =	SSP 1 / STP B	SSP 1 / STP A / STP B
SSP 1 → SSP 2	2 Routes =	SSP 1 / STP A / SSP 2	SSP 1 / STP B / SSP 2
STP A → SSP 1	2 Routes =	STP A / SSP 1	STP A / STP B / SSP 1

Associate Route	Direct link between origination and destination nodes
Quasi Route	Indirect routing between origination and destination nodes

Figure 31-9
SS7 protocols

of the stack performs the data processing function. See Figure 31-9 for the protocols.

The stack shows that the bottom three layers make up the message transfer part (MTP), which is similar to the X.25 network function. At one time, SS7 messages were all carried on X.25. Now newer implementations use SS7 protocols, whereas in older networks or third-world countries, X.25 may still be used.

The SCCP is used as part of the MTP when necessary to support access into a database and occasionally for the ISDN user part. This extra link is the equivalent of the transport layer of the OSI model supporting the Transaction Capabilities Application Part (TCAP).

The SS7 network is an interconnected set of network elements that is used to exchange messages in support of telecommunications functions. The SS7 protocol is designed both to facilitate these functions and to maintain the network over which they are provided. Like most modern protocols, the SS7 protocol is layered. Functionally, the SS7 protocol stack can be compared to the OSI reference model. Although OSI is a seven-layer stack designed to perform several communications and transparent functions, the SS7 protocol stack is similar but different.

Like any other stack, the SS7 protocol stack is specifically designed for reliable data transfer between different signaling elements on the network. Guaranteed delivery and the prevention of duplication or lost packets are crucial to network operations. To satisfy differing functions, the stack uses various upper-layer protocols, but consistently uses the same lower layers.

Basic Call Setup with ISDN User Part (ISUP)

The important part of the protocols is the call setup and teardown. This next example is shown in Figure 31-10.

When a call is placed to an out-of-switch number, the originating SSP transmits an ISUP initial address message (IAM) to reserve an idle trunk circuit from the originating switch to the destination switch (1a). The IAM includes the originating point code, destination point code, circuit identification code dialed digits, and, optionally, the calling party's number and name. In this example, the IAM is routed via the home STP of the originating switch to the destination switch (1b). Note that the same signaling links are used for the duration of the call unless a link failure condition forces a switch to use an alternate signaling link.

The destination switch examines the dialed number and determines that it serves the called party and that the line is available for ringing. The destination switch transmits an ISUP address complete message (ACM) to the originating switch (2a) via its home STP to indicate that the remote end of the trunk circuit has been reserved. The destination switch rings the called party's line and sends a ringing tone over the trunk to the originating

Figure 31-10
Call setup with ISUP

switch. The STP routes the ACM to the originating switch (2b), which connects the calling party's line to the trunk to complete the voice circuit from the calling party to the called party. The calling party hears the ringing tone on the voice trunk.

In this example, the originating and destination switches are directly connected with trunks. If the originating and destination switches are not directly connected with trunks, the originating switch transmits an IAM to reserve a trunk circuit to an intermediate switch. The intermediate switch sends an ACM to acknowledge the circuit reservation request and then transmits an IAM to reserve a trunk circuit to another switch. This process continues until all trunks required to complete the connection from the originating switch to the destination switch are reserved.

When thecalled party picks up the phone, the destination switch terminates the ringing tone and transmits an ISUP answer message (ANM) to the originating switch via its home STP (3a). The STP routes the ANM to the originating switch (3b), which verifies that the calling party's line is connected to the reserved trunk, and, if so, initiates billing.

If the calling party hangs up first, the originating switch sends an ISUP release message (REL) to release the trunk circuit between the switches (4a). The STP routes the REL to the destination switch (4b). If the called party hangs up first or if the line is busy, the destination switch sends an REL to the originating switch indicating the release cause (for example, normal release or busy).

Upon receiving the REL, the destination switch disconnects the trunk from the called party's line. Next, it sets the trunk's state to idle, and transmits an ISUP release complete message (RLC) to the originating switch (5a) to acknowledge the release of the remote end of the trunk circuit. When the originating switch receives (or generates) the RLC (5b), it terminates the billing cycle and sets the trunk state to idle in preparation for the next call.

ISUP messages may also be transmitted during the connection phase of the call (such as between the ISUP ANM and REL messages).

SS7 Applications

At this point we switch gears and look at some of the applications that are possible because of SS7 implementations. The use of advanced intelligent network (AIN) features, ISDN features, and wireless capabilities all became a reality because of the functions of SS7 integration. Some of the features are listed in the following section; remember they are formulated and possible because of SS7, although they may be part of other systems or concepts. These include

- 800/888/877/866/900 services
- Enhancements in 800/888/877/866 services within call centers
- 911 enhancements
- Class features
- Calling card toll fraud prevention
- Credit card approval and authentication
- Software/virtual defined private networks
- Call tracing
- Call blocking

It is with the SS7 protocols and signaling systems that all these features and functions are possible. Many of the features are possible through the stored program CO switches. However, when we activate features that work across the network (or world), SS7 facilitates the delivery mechanism. Other systems will be introduced in the future to implement more intelligence in the networks, such as the advanced intelligent networks (AINs), but they will require the infrastructure of the signaling systems to enact and carry their messages.

Questions

1. The older signaling system (SS6) was created in 1960s.   T/F
2. SS7 was first deployed in the industry in what year?
    a. 1980
    b. 1982
    c. 1983
    d. 1989

3. The preferred form of associated signaling is _____.

   a. Nonassociated

   b. Associated

   c. Fully associated

   d. Quasi-associated

4. The telephone carriers were still installing SS6 through _____.

   a. 1983

   b. 1985

   c. 1980

   d. 1973

5. The Central Office is now called the:

   a. STP

   b. SSP

   c. SCP

   d. TCAP

6. SS7 uses a _____ layer protocol stack.

   a. Seven-

   b. Four-

   c. Three-

   d. Five-

   e. Six-

7. Out-of-band signaling means that the signals are carried inside the voice channel.   T/F

8. Originally, the carriers used frequencies that carried signaling information using _____.

   a. 300 Hz to 3,300 Hz

   b. 100 Hz to 400 Hz

   c. 3,600 Hz to 3,900 Hz

   d. 3,500 Hz to 3,700 Hz

9. TCAP is the application support for the SS7 networks.   T/F

10. The location where the databases are kept is called:

    a. STP

    b. Database engines

    c. SCP

    d. SSP

11. The ISUP has all the components necessary to handle call setup and teardown.   T/F

12. The protocols used to carry the message are called:

    a. X.25

    b. IP

    c. TCP

    d. MTP

13. The original SS6 used _____ different signaling units.

14. The signaling units used in the SS6 networks were made up of _____ bits.

15. SS7 circuits run on links that operate at:

    a. 1.544 Mbps

    b. 56 Kbps

    c. 66 Kbps

    d. 4.8 Kbps

16. The B and D links are the same functionally.   T/F

17. The routeset and the _____ are synonymous.

    a. Route

    b. Linkset

    c. Point code

    d. Database

18. STPs are usually installed in _____.

    a. The middle of the network

    b. Mated pairs

    c. Stand-alone mode

    d. Half duplex

19. The _____ is used with the MTP when a translation is needed from a database.

   a. STP

   b. SCP

   c. SNMP

   d. SCCP

20. Point codes are made up of _____ digits.

   a. 12

   b. 32

   c. 16

   d. 9

Local Number Portability (LNP)

After reading this chapter and completing the questions, you will be able to:

■ Discuss the key points of LNP

■ Describe the new components of LNP architecture

■ Understand the need for preserving our telephone numbering systems

■ Discuss the differences between the wireline and wireless carriers for LNP

■ Understand why the FCC is so adamant about using LNP

When the breakup of the industry began in 1984, the Federal Communications Commission (FCC) and others had a vision that personal communications services would become a reality. The Telecommunications Act of 1996 took this one step closer to the expectations of the regulators. The ultimate goal was to provide seamless and transparent communications for the consumer, with a choice of providers. No one ever really expected that the local loop would remain in the control of one supplier. Thus, the local competitive market took hold. However, the number plan assignments were rigidly set.

An essential stipulation of the Telecommunications Act of 1996 requires that customers must be able to change local carriers while maintaining the same telephone number. The ability to make numbers portable across service providers is driving significant investment in the network infrastructure for both the wireline and wireless carriers. Although the carriers were not required to reroute calls from their networks to ported numbers until June 1999, the advent of wireline number porting also has had an immediate and significant financial impact. This also impacts the ability to complete outgoing calls between wireline and wireless numbers.

All calls to entire NPA-NXX blocks will require local number portability (LNP) processing to determine if the specific number has actually been ported, increasing the demand on the network resources. Because using the number portability (NP) databases to complete wireless-to-wireline calls will be a technical necessity, providers need to address both the cost and the service issues.

Several other issues are in play at the same time. LNP is only one of the major impacting changes. The wireless and wireline carriers are dealing with the regulatory issues for other scenarios, such as right-of-way issues, physical interconnection problems, the needs of integrating operational support systems, and settlements between the carriers for access and co-carrier charges.

The Three Phases of LNP

The ultimate goal of the Telecommunications Act of 1996 includes the end users' (customers') ability to take their numbers anywhere. This constitutes full location transportability. Of course, we cannot just make such a quantum leap of technology without considering interim steps to minimize confusion.

Consumers do not have a clue about LNP issues. They hear about the ability to use LNP, but do not have any concept of what it means to the carriers. Polls of end users reveal that 80 percent of residential customers would not be willing to change service providers if they have to change telephone numbers. Moreover, 90 percent of business subscribers would be unwilling to change service providers if it involves changing telephone numbers. To foster competition, the idea of LNP was embraced and pushed to the public.

Consequently, we will look at the three steps of LNP to reach an end. The three steps include

- **Service provider portability** The first step in LNP permits the subscriber to keep their current telephone number when they change service providers. Changes in service providers can mean between and among the ILEC, CLEC, wireless cellular, wireless PCS, wireless SMR, and the cable TV providers, to name the most common. Applying initially to the wireline providers, service provider portability will eventually extend to the wireless networks.

- **Service portability**   When a subscriber desires services unavailable through the local-end office, service portability enables the customer to secure these services from another switching system without changing telephone numbers. This enables the customer to change the mix of services available for use.

- **Location portability**   The final step in LNP enables customers to keep their telephone numbers when they move away from a service area covered by the current central office. The farther away the customer moves, the more the technological challenge posed by LNP. Let's use an example of Bud moving from Phoenix to Boston; he wants to keep the number (480) 777-7992. The ramifications of this solution change the entire numbering plan and the geographic boundary of the service providers.

LNP for Cellular and PCS Suppliers

Few carriers reveal their final plans in advance. They will say that they will meet the mandates of the law, but not exactly say how. However, let's look at the impacts on their systems.

Cellular Providers

The cellular industry has been a success story to behold. Over the past 17 years, it has grown from nothing to over 200 million customers. With very few exceptions, the cellular carriers see themselves as a complementary carrier to the ILEC business. Some of this comes from the fact that two parts of the cellular network started when the licenses were issued: wireline carriers meant the ILEC-operated, regulated portion of the cellular network and non-wireline meant the competition. In most cases, the ILECs that operated the wireline side of the business spread out across the country as part of the non-wireline provider (competing for wireless services with their cousins). Therefore, the ILEC side of the business influences the cellular industry heavily. The cellular providers see themselves as complementing the wireline business instead of competing with it.

Personal Communications Services (PCS) and Specialized Mobile Radio (SMR) Providers

These carriers seem to be the ones seeking a niche in the market. As they offer services to their customers, they view themselves as an alternative to the ILEC wireline services and at the same time as complementary. Depending on how the customer reacts, the PCS providers especially will move toward one position. The providers offer the same features and functions as the wireline service providers, including

- Call forwarding (busy or don't answer)
- Voice messaging
- Three-way calling
- Caller ID
- Call transferring

The PCS providers using LNP in their potpourri of offerings are now saying that the customer can use the same number for the home number, the business number, and the traveling number. Why pay for two different lines and service offerings when you can do it all on one telephone (and number)?

Their speech is somewhat convincing, but they fail to mention the cost of the airtime for receiving calls and the added cost for making local calls. However, they are now packaging these services in such a way that they are invisible.

The LNP deadline for wireless LNP implementation in the top 100 metropolitan service areas (MSAs) is November 2002, at least as it stands now. The implication is that the wireless carrier implementations will be fully IS-41 compliant, using an LNP trigger mechanism. In addition to wireline LECs, all cellular, broadband personal communication services (PCS), and certain specialized mobile radio (SMR) carriers must be able to deliver calls from their networks to ported numbers anywhere in the nation by November 2002. Furthermore, those carriers must offer LNP throughout their networks by November 2002, including the ability to support full roaming transparently.

LNP Differences

Wireless carriers handle their customers differently than the wireline carriers do. In general, major differences arise in the way they handle customer care. Some are very good at managing the customer to provide interface; others never see the customer and rarely become involved with solving problems.

The way the infrastructure is established is also a potential problem. The wireless carriers have completely different overlays in the network for rating calls. The wireline carriers have geographically-bounded rate centers, but the wireless carriers have different boundaries. It is normal for a wireless carrier to backhaul a call several miles (or a couple of hundred miles) to process out of its mobile switching center (MSC). The calling area for a wireless carrier is set in a different way.

The wireless carriers' billing systems are different too. In the wireline networks, customers do not pay to receive calls (with the exception of a collect or an 800/888/877/866 call), whereas in the wireless network, airtime is billed for every minute of usage. Moreover, in the wireline network, the caller gets unlimited outbound local calls (for most network providers, except where message units are billed), whereas in the wireless networks, airtime is billed for all local calls. The wireless carriers have been attempting to minimize the visibility by offering packages of X minutes for Y dollars per month. However, in revenue generation, the wireless carriers have the advantage because they pre-bill for the service whether the customer uses it or not. Now, with LNP, they must know where the call is going and how it is actually terminated in order to capture the usage. Most importantly, they need the originating and terminating minutes to bill when the customer exceeds the allotted time in the package. If the wireline carriers offered these packages, we'd be burning down the COs.

Somehow the interface between the wireless and wireline carriers must come together to make this all transparent. Further, the wireless carriers need an interface to the number portability administration center (NPAC), which requires more updates and more SS7 links to facilitate the LNP operation.

What's It All About, Anyway?

LNP is a far-reaching mandate. Because the Telecommunications Act of 1996 ensured competition could be allowed to grow in the local and long-distance markets, we have seen competition in the long-distance market grow and prosper. Therefore, the FCC mandated that in order for new entrants to move into the business of local access, and to foster the competitive spirit, LNP was a requirement.

Few consumers or businesses will take a chance with a new provider, if they have to change numbers. LNP was made available to wireline customers in the 100 top MSAs at the end of 1998 and to the wireless subscribers by 2002. Although the deadline was pushed back to the year 2002, this is not a trivial matter. They want a reprieve for the broadband PCS suppliers to build out their basic infrastructure. They feel that if the LNP issue is to be addressed while these carriers are still building their infrastructure, it will prove to be negative in their market segment. Most wireless carriers say they have something in place, but the choices are varied in the way they will implement this.

Wireless customer-care and billing systems are different from those of the wireline carriers. Even the way they define their rate centers differs widely from that of the wireline providers. The wireless carriers must now make the wireline LNP systems work within the wireless systems, which is no simple matter. Many questions about how the systems will work for the wireless networks and providers are still unanswered. These include

- How will the wireless carriers transfer the line information to the number portability administration centers (NPACs)?

- What happens to the roaming discussed in the earlier chapters?

- How will over-the-air provisioning be handled when LNP is added?

- What will become of the mutual compensation billing systems they use?

- When "calling party pays" becomes a reality, who is billed when the wireless carriers don't have LNP information telling them where the call was actually terminated? For example, calling party pays means that the caller is the one who will be billed for a call, not the recipient of the call (i.e. wireless user). If the number used to be just down the street from me, but has been ported across country, the call is now long distance. If the caller is paying for the connection that means a call that was always local is now long distance. Some form of announcement should be made to advise the caller that they are actually making a long distance call.

Where's the Money?

One of the big issues in complying with the LNP mandates is the fact that the carriers must have a return on investment. The cost implications of building out the network to accommodate the LNP requirements are significant. The FCC recognized this issue when mandating that LNP be implemented between the local providers (ILECs), the CLECs, and the wireless providers.

Several mechanisms will help the carriers recoup their costs. These include the carriers' ability to bill back to the consumer, which started in February 1999. The consumer will pay for the overall implementation, but carriers will never really recoup all their costs because of other regulatory and tariff issues. The local utilities commissions are always dragging their feet when approving any costs passed through to the consumer. Carriers subject to a rate-of-return or a price-cap constraint will be allowed to recover their carrier-specific costs directly related to the installation and operation of LNP. A federally approved monthly charge was enacted to last no more than five years. Costs related to the N-1 querying protocol (used to determine the last carrier before the incumbent carrier) may be recovered from noncompliant carriers or default carriers through a federal tariff for query services. The wireless carriers have considered the option of just paying the ILECs for the LNP services. However, this can be too expensive for them, leaving the other possibilities still available.

However, more is involved than just recouping costs; carriers must also gain revenue. The Gartner Group conducted a study on LNP and found that a substantial amount of money can be made. The domestic local telephone services market, after opening the market to competition with LNP, will result in basic service opportunities of $4.9 billion in 1999 and up to $6.2 billion in 2000. The network access market potential was said to total $4 billion in 1999 and $5.4 billion in 2000. These estimates were based on an assumption that 75 percent of the U.S. population lives in the 100 top MSAs and that 75 percent of all the service revenues will come from the 100 top MSAs. Market-share rates are based on the customer's ability to churn.

The Wireless Carriers' Decision

Carriers have choices on how they will handle the LNP situation. Not every carrier is affected by the services (such as the IECs and the pay-phone providers), but those who are affected can choose their own destiny. They can choose to do one of the following:

■ *Do nothing.* Carriers can remain noncompliant within the guidelines of the Telecommunications Act of 1996 and allow the terminating carrier to perform the N-1 database query for them. A carrier without LNP has no way of knowing whether outgoing calls are dialed to numbers that are ported; therefore, the calls are automatically sent to the carrier who owned the number originally. If it is a number in a ported region, the destination carrier must dip into the LNP database to correctly route the call to the final end point. ILECs are expected to charge $0.001 to $0.008 for this. For a wireless carrier, this can be substantial, with estimates set at $250,000 to $1 million per year, based on very conservative averages. That being the case, the wireless carriers are likely to get on the LNP bandwagon quickly if this is their choice. They will still need 6 to 9 months to implement a decision.

■ *Choose a service bureau.* This is the choice that many of the smaller wireless carriers have expressed the most interest in today. Most of the cellular carriers are already using clearinghouse functionality from service bureaus. The most common are GTE and Cincinnati Bell Information Services (CBIS), who provide reciprocal billing and accounting functions. For a fee, the service bureau will offer the LNP service. If the wireless carrier outsources to a service bureau, minimal upgrades to the wireless carrier networks are required. Some errors are likely to occur because this manual system requires entries into multiple operating support systems (OSSs). Carriers who choose this option have LNP-enabled call routing, but lack the other competitive advantages that go with LNP in full operation.

■ *Choose an internal LNP solution.* This is the most expensive of the choices in the short term, but for the long term, it will be of real benefit. For both wireline and wireless carriers, this is an expensive and complicated solution. The benefits of LNP are that it will take full advantage of the intelligent network (IN), the advanced intelligent network (AIN) features, and/or the wireless intelligent network (WIN) infrastructure. This will give the wireless carrier an edge over the competition by bringing a new level of intelligence into the wireless telecommunications industry and networks.

Basic LNP Networks

The components of LNP are not that much different from the original SS7 networks used for years. The pieces serve different functions; looking at the components in Figure 32-1, we see

- The switching service point (SSP) is the local CO or tandem.
- The signal transfer point (STP) is a packet-mode handler that routes data queries through the signaling network.
- The signal control point (SCP) is the database for features, routing, and global title translation (GTT).
- The local service management system (LSMS) and service order administration (SOA) can be provisioned separately, but when combined, they are referred to as the number portability administration center (NPAC) connectivity.

For wireless providers, the LNP capabilities depend on the MSA served. Even if a wireless network does not support LNP, the wireless provider's methods and procedures should be updated to support troubleshooting for calls placed to ported wireline numbers.

Figure 32-1
Basic LNP network components

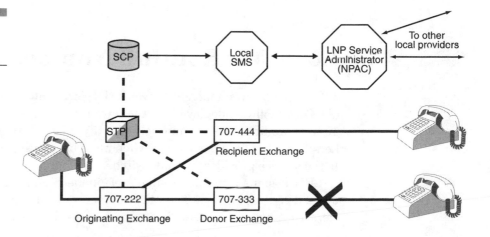

Once wireline networks in the top 100 MSAs have implemented LNP, wireless providers serving the same MSAs need to address wireless end users making calls to portable wireline numbers. Wireless service providers are not required to support LNP routing at this time. Calls for wireless end users to a ported wireline number will complete successfully through the donor network.

LNP Services Administration

A few minor points are at issue:

■ The LECs administer the numbering plan in their regions. The North American Numbering Council (NANC) issued a requirement for a neutral third-party administrator.

■ LNP number administration was limited to regional implementations. Therefore, the NANC directed the INC to develop the guidelines for local routing number (LRN) assignment.

These issues were surmountable, but they did cause minor delays in getting the NPAC services up and running. Many of the wireless providers bought the 10,000 numbers in an NPA-NXX from their LECs. Therefore, they feel they have ownership and proprietary rights to the numbers assigned to them. Furthermore, the inconsistencies in which the plans were applied called for a third party to manage the assignments of numbering plans as well as the LRN assignments.

Location Routing Number (LRN)

LRN depends on intelligent network (IN) or advanced intelligent network (AIN) capabilities deployed by the wireline carriers' networks. LRN is a 10-digit number used to uniquely identify a switch that has ported numbers. The LRN for a particular switch must be a native NPA-NXX assigned to the service provider for that switch.

LRN assigns a unique 10-digit telephone number to each switch in a defined geographic area. The LRN now serves as the network address. Carriers routing telephone calls to end users who have changed from one carrier to another (and kept their same number) perform a database dip to obtain the LRN corresponding to the dialed telephone number. The database dip is performed for all calls where the NPA-NXX of the called number has been flagged in the switch as a portable number. The carrier then routes the call to the new provider based on the LRN.

Figure 32-2 shows the flow of LRN information, which is the same for both a wireline and a wireless provider.

When the caller dials the number (333-3333 in this case), the originating switch (612-222) sends its signaling information (info dialed 333-3333) through the STP to the SCP, which analyzes the route and returns the LRN (612-444-0001). Next, an initial address message (IAM) is forwarded from 612-222 through the STP to the access tandem (AT). The AT translates the LRN and sets up a speech path (trunk) from 222 to 444. Switch 612-444 detects the LRN (612-444-0001) as its address; therefore, the called number and the generic address parameter are swapped. From there, the call is connected (terminated) at 333-3333. The donor switch in this scenario has been uninvolved throughout the process.

Figure 32-2
The basic flow of LRN

LNP Impact on Routing and Rating

As already stated, the wireline and the wireless providers are undergoing changes. Wireless providers have had different billing and rating measures to satisfy their network demands. The ILECs were tied to the regulatory boundaries of the local Public Utility Commissions (PUCs) and the FCC. The impacts for both providers will mean that changes in the way calls are routed, rated for access, and rated for end-user billing will include the use of the LRN in the future. This means that the wireless providers will have to use some inclusions of the LRN differently than they did in the past. The simplest way of doing this (as represented by three major wireless providers) is to use the standard V&H coordinates and then apply from-and-to billing and access ratings to the call. The vertical and horizontal coordinates are used to determine the mileage between two locations (central offices) anywhere in the U.S. for billing purposes.

Using the N-1 architecture, the carriers use the next-to-last service provider to perform the LNP database dip. This will pertain to both wireline and wireless providers. When two IECs are involved, the N-1 query is launched by IEC number two. When only two networks are involved (ILEC and IEC), then the originating service provider is responsible for the LNP query.

Demand for LNP

Local LNP issues will first be addressed in service provider portability. However, as we wait for this to happen, we know that 90 percent of wireless users say they would choose a different carrier if they could keep the same number. This percentage is stated differently than others in this book. All the other studies indicate that more than 80 percent of customers would not be interested in a change if it involved a number change. The wireless carriers are fraught with the fear that the statistic for their networks is that 90 percent would change.

This is a dramatic number in an industry whose biggest problems are churn and fraud. Churn is killing these suppliers in light of the packages that are being offered. The possibility of getting free minutes and/or free local calling from a new supplier is enough to make the wireless carriers' customers jump providers. Long-term contracts are outdated, but were a way to hold the customer for at least some extended period.

Location NP is becoming a bigger issue, and demand is becoming a hotter topic for the carriers and customers alike. However, location portability raises many other issues that have not been fully fleshed out, such as

- Added database dips because of the number of ILECs and IECs that can be involved in a call process.
- 911 public safety answering point (PSAP) administration will become more complicated.
- Rating and billing issues. How do you process a call? Who pays?
- Loss of the North American numbering plan (NANP) geographical significance. In the old days, we knew where a caller was by the telephone number.
- Customer premises equipment (CPE) impacts in the ability to process local versus long-distance calls from a database that must be kept updated. This puts more burdens on the CPE (PBX, key systems, and so on).

New local calling plans will be needed, but they should be separate from the rate center plans in place and regulated today. Possibly, rate center consolidation will be an alternative for number portability from a centralized location and a better way of handling the local versus long-distance calling. Toll alerts may be needed in the signaling network. When a number has been flagged as ported to a new LRN, the network will intercept and advise the calling party that it will be a toll call. This involves more database dips and more equipment to interface in the network. Who pays for this?

Another issue will be that callers will be relegated to make a 10-digit call for all calls, local and long distance, because of the lookup that will be required. Users are already screaming about that; what do providers do to appease this issue?

LNP Operations, Administration, and Maintenance Impacts

Clearly, we can see that all parts of the network are being affected by the implementation of LNP. Many of these issues and impacts are quite costly for the wireline carriers. Looking at all the pieces when we add the MSC in place of the SSP, the impact on the integration becomes far more complex because of the infrastructure differences between the providers. The wireless providers do things differently in many places.

One area is over-the-air provisioning by the wireless carriers. Getting that information to customers who port their numbers to a wireline provider will have to be done through the NPAC. STP and SCP interfaces are using IS-41 and SS7 combinations that work differently from the wireline carriers.

The point is that it can be done at a greater cost to the wireless carrier because of the mobility involved and the database dips that will be required.

Scenarios

These scenarios look at the different choices that may appear in the implementation of LNP by the wireline or wireless carriers. The first, shown in Figure 32-3, is a non-LNP intermediate office using MF trunks between suppliers. The following occurs:

1. The call is placed to the ported subscriber.
2. The originating switch performs an LNP query.
3. SCP replies.
4. The LNP IAM packet is sent to non-LNP tandem.

Figure 32-3
Scenario with a non-LNP office

5. The non-LNP tandem dials over the MF trunk; only LRN is sent (in the called-party ID parameter); the dialed number is lost; and the call fails.

The next scenario, shown in Figure 32-4, deals with a dialed number pulsed to a non-LNP tandem via MF signaling. The following occurs:

1. The call is placed to a ported subscriber from a donor switch.

2. The donor switch performs the LNP query.

3. SCP replies with the LRN.

4. The donor switch sends the dialed digits over an SS7 trunk to a non-LNP tandem (if the donor is provisioned to send only the dialed digits to non-LNP switches—the signal ported number option).

5. The non-LNP tandem sends the call based on the dialed number back to the donor switch. The call will keep going through steps 2 through 5 until the network management system ends the call. (This is message looping—a possible big problem in a wireless network.)

In the third scenario, shown in Figure 32-5, we see the operator services involved in a dial 0 call.

1. The subscriber (708-555-1111) dials 0 and is connected to the Tandem operator services (TOPS) operator.

Figure 32-4
Scenario with non-LNP tandems

Figure 32-5
Scenario with the operator model

2. The operator receives a request to connect to (708) 555-2222 and bill to the originator's station.

3. TOPS determines that the requested number has been ported and sends the LNP query to the SCP.

4. The LNP SCP sends back the response with the LRN (312-225-0000) of the recipient switch.

5. TOPS routes the call to the recipient switch.

6. The recipient switch terminates the call to the ported number, (708) 555-2222.

Occasionally, a database file must be accessed. Using a line information database (LIDB), this scenario follows the flow into and out of the database to determine the location of the called party. The following occurs:

1. Subscriber A (708-232-1111) dials 0-708-555-2222 and the call is routed to TOPS.

2. TOPS sends a bong to the subscriber, requesting the calling card number.

3. TOPS routes the calling card number to the LNP SCP to obtain the correct LIDB point code address.

4. LNP SCP returns the LIDB point code to STP.

5. STP queries the LIDB for calling card validation.

6. LIDB returns calling card validation to TOPS.

7. TOPS routes the billing number to the LNP SCP to obtain the correct calling party service provider (LRN).

8. LNP SCP returns the LRN of the billing number and TOPS populated appropriate automatic message accounting (AMA) module.

9. TOPS routes the called party number (708-555-2222) to the LNP SCP for LRN.

10. LNP SCP returns the LRN of the recipient switch.

11. TOPS routes the call.

Wireless and Wireline E-911

When we think about LNP in a wireline environment, the process is straightforward. The caller places an emergency call from a fixed location, which is easily identifiable. Routing of the E-911 call is to the proper public safety answering point (PSAP) based on a known prearranged location from each telephone. ANI is mapped one to one for all wireline calls using the appropriate callback number and a location from an automatic location information (ALI) database. This is shown in Figure 32-6.

911 calling and routing is built on the limited capability of the centralized automatic message accounting (CAMA) trunks (trunks that were originally used for cost accounting and messaging call information), and the

Figure 32-6
Wireline E-911

CAMA will remain in use for some time to come. This does cause some difficulty for the wireless companies because the need to send more information for wireless 911 calls cannot be met the same way as in wireline calls. Figure 32-7 shows the wireless 911 process using LNP.

Is 911 Iimportant? Nearly 25 percent of all the calls (80,000) per day are from wireless subscribers. This places a great deal of problems on the network.

The Ultimate Goal—2001

The goal by the end of 2001 is to have a fully transparent network that can handle the wireless 911 calls and get to the caller very quickly. Upgrades across the network require that a satellite global positioning system (GPS) be installed at the wireless network interface. The GPS will help in locating the caller and will route to the appropriate PSAP every time. Using the GPS, the feeling is that the caller can be located 67 percent of the time within 125 meters (410 feet) because the call will be routed to the PSAP with the appropriate x, y locator coordinates. The ALI will be updated to

Figure 32-7
Wireless E-911

support both ANI and x, y lookup. The call to the PSAP will arrive with a mapping system showing the x, y coordinates of the calling party.

Benefits of Using LNP and Roaming Capabilities

The benefits of making and receiving calls in a wireless network or a wire-line network are the ultimate revenue generation. When a user on the wireless network is receiving a call today from the wired world (or vice versa), the network uses its own appropriate databases. In this case, the wireless networks rely heavily on their own SCPs, which house the database information of their callers.

Home location registers (HLRs) keep track of all network suppliers' users based on their own network ID. The HLR database has all the appropriate information to recognize the caller by the user electronic serial number (ESN) and mobile telephone number. The database controls the features and functions the user has subscribed to. When a call comes into the network today, the called number is sent to the HLR responsible for the number dialed. These are SS7 messages. The HLR then looks into its database and determines where the caller is located or if the user is on the air.

If the user is located somewhere else, a visiting location register (VLR) entry exists at a remote MSC. The remote end has updated this entry when the user activated the telephone (powered it on and registered) or when an already powered device rolled into range of a cell site from the new location. Then, an SS7 message is sent out to the HLR that the called party is now in someone else's ALI. See Figure 32-8 for the registration process.

If a call is coming in from the network, the SS7 inquiry comes into the HLR, which then sends a redirect message to the remote MSC (the VLR) serving the end user.

Using this roaming capability, database dips are occurring on frequent basis. Many of the wireless networks are already taxing a their databases. They are trying to move more information out to the STP or the local switches rather than constantly hammering into the SCP.

Incoming Calls to an Idle Mobile

Using the IS-41 and SS7 linkage, when a call comes in to a mobile number, the immediate link is to the HLR. The HLR then sends out a query to the

Figure 32-8
Mobile registration

VLR indicating that a call is coming in for the mobile. See Figure 32-9 for the process of incoming calls to idle sets.

The VLR verifies the information and sends back confirmation to the HLR indicating that the call should be steered to the temporary local directory number (TLDN), which is effectively a call-forwarding arrangement. The call is then forwarded to the end-user device, using the dynamically assigned DN.

Once the call is received at the remote MSC, the call is logged into the appropriate billing and accounting system for reciprocal payment and processing. At the end of the month, the billing systems are polled and processed by a service bureau for peering arrangements.

Calls to a Busy Set or a Set That Doesn't Answer

Assume that after the TLDN has been assigned by the VLR and the call has been redirected to the set, the set is busy or does not answer. Now the VLR sends an SS7 message back to the HLR and requests additional information, such as "What do I do now?"

Figure 32-9
*Incoming call to an
idle mobile set*

The VLR then sends out the page to the mobile, but if no answer comes back, then the SS7 message to release the call is sent back to the HLR.

No Answer with Call Forwarding

Assume that the VLR assigned a TLDN to process the call to the called telephone user and then sends out the page, but the caller does not answer. This time the VLR goes back to the HLR for a clarification on the next step. The HLR does a database dip and finds that the called party has call forwarding to another number, such as a business wireline number or a voice-mail system. This information is then fed back to the VLR for processing. The VLR then sends the message back to process the call to the forwarding number, as shown in Figure 32-10. The VLR is completed, and the HLR has provided all the information necessary. The SS7 network now sends the incoming call request to the wireline end office, alerting it that a call is coming in for the forwarded number, and the process continues.

Calls to a Busy Set with Message Waiting

Assume that the call is coming in for a wireless user but the wireless user is on the phone. Now the VLR goes into react mode and assigns a second

Figure 32-10
Call forwarding to a mobile set

TLDN back to the HLR, indicating to forward the call to the new number. The call is then sent to the serving MSC on a separate telephone number reserved for this call. Then, a message is sent through the airwaves to the air interface indicating that a new call is coming (in the form of a beep). The caller can then choose to answer the call or ignore it.

Questions

1. LNP stands for local number portability.   T/F

2. The three types of LNP are:

   a. Location, service, and cost

   b. Location, provider, and number

   c. Service, number, and provider

   d. Wireless, wireline, and provider

3. The mandate for wireless portability is set for _____.

   a. November 2000

   b. November 2001

   c. November 2005

   d. November 2002

4. The new name for the routing is to use a device called a LRG.   T/F

5. LNP will use many of the services and features combined in _____.
   a. SS6
   b. AIN
   c. LRN
   d. NPAC

6. When a switch has ported numbers, it is called the _____.

7. The wireless carriers must provide the LNP services to include

   _____.
   a. Flat-rate pricing
   b. Query
   c. Database dips
   d. Roaming

8. With LNP, carriers must know where the call is going and how it is actually _____ in order to capture the usage.

9. LRN is a _____ number to uniquely identify a switch that has ported numbers.
   a. 10-digit
   b. 7-digit
   c. 3-digit
   d. 5-digit

10. With LNP, the caller pays.   T/F

11. ALI stands for _____.
    a. Automatic line interface
    b. Automatic line information
    c. Allotted link interface
    d. Automatic LNP integration

12. With LNP, the _____ as we know it is going to change.
    a. NANP
    b. NANC
    c. NPAC
    d. NNX

13. All calls to entire NPA-NXX blocks will require LNP processing to determine if the specific number has been _____.

    a. Changed

    b. Charged

    c. Routed

    d. Ported

14. The goal of the _____ includes the end users' (customers') ability to take their numbers anywhere.

    a. FCC mandate of 1999

    b. Modified Final Judgment

    c. Telecomm Act of 1996

    d. Telecomm Act of 1984

15. Who will ultimately pay for the services and features of LNP?

    a. ILECs

    b. IECs

    c. Consumers

    d. Vendors

Cellular and Personal Communications Systems

After reading this chapter and completing the questions, you will be able to:

- Understand how cellular communications works
- Describe the differences between analog and digital cellular
- Converse regarding the call setup process
- Explain the pieces that make up a cellular network
- Understand the concept of PCS

Cellular transmission is the latest and greatest front in the industry. In 1946, Illinois Bell Telephone Company introduced a mobile telephone service that would enable users driving in and around the Chicago area to communicate directly to and from vehicles. Using a radio-to-telephone interface, the telephone companies had a lock on this service. Users lined up by the hundreds if not the thousands to request mobile telephone service.

Unfortunately, this was not as simple as driving up to the telephone company and getting the service requested. Many areas of the country had a 2-year wait as the service rolled out. The reason was simple: radio waves are not intelligent! The telephone companies mounted high-gain antennae on top of high-rise office buildings in the major downtown areas. From there, they would boom out a signal at approximately 250+ watts. This is a very strong signal in any transmission. The antenna was on top of the highest building, and the power output was so great because the telephone companies wanted to get the best coverage possible. The Federal Communications Commission (FCC) had only issued a limited number of frequencies for use in the mobile phone services and improved mobile telephone services (IMTS) networks. Twelve channels were typically allocated in each of the metropolitan areas. Therefore, the channels were limited, and the telephone companies needed to provide the greatest area of coverage possible. All calls within the city had to be routed through the centralized tower because of the limited amount of channels. In this particular network, 12 channels were available. Each channel was used on a high-powered radio transmitter to provide the required coverage. Further, the system operated on a one-way (simplex) basis. Only one side of the call could speak at a time. This was analogous to the older two-way push-to-talk radio systems. The telephone companies were trying to provide coverage in approximately a 25-mile radius from the downtown area. Back in the late 1940s that was sufficient because the workforce was less mobile.

Problems with the AMPS/IMTS

This arrangement worked for short periods, but as newer demands were placed on the system, channel capacity was very limited. Only 12 users could be on the network at one time. The limited number of channels (frequencies assigned by the FCC for this service) led to the frequency reuse planning in the telephone companies.

However, because the telephone companies were also trying to get the greatest coverage, the output signal did not stop at the 25-mile marker. Radio-based communications will travel greater distances as a function of the frequency used and the power output. If you want greater coverage, you need to use a higher power output system and antennae or you have to use more equipment. Even though the signal pattern was designed to provide coverage only in a 25-mile radius, it kept on going beyond the distance planned. This meant that if another system were set up in the nearby area using the same frequencies, the telephone company system would cause interference. As shown in Figure 33-1, another 50 to 75 miles bound the overlap areas. This means that the radio-based system could only use the

Figure 33-1
A map of IMTS
coverage areas and
frequency reuse

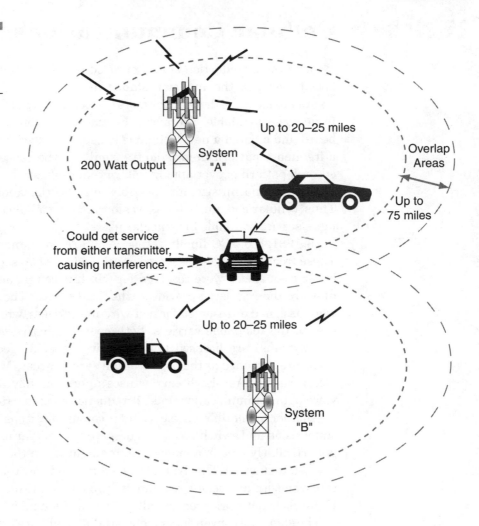

Figure 33-1
A map of IMTS
coverage areas and
frequency reuse

assigned channels every 100 miles apart. The areas around the circle in this figure—the buffer zones—exist to prevent interference. You might recall from the bandwidth discussion earlier in this book that sidebands and frequency band-pass filters are used in the wired telephone world. Essentially the same holds true in the wireless world, where the telephone company allocated the buffer zones so that two conversations would not occur on the same channel. The figure shows that the signal was used in the center (thicker) core, but the overlap areas are shown in the lighter core.

Cellular Communications

Prior to the introduction of an improved telephony service through radio-based systems, the industry standards bodies faced a dilemma. They wanted to meet the demand for more services, but they just did not have the frequencies available. Therefore, the engineers went back to the drawing board and created a new technique called cellular communications. Using a frequency pattern from radio transmitters, the concept produces a honeycomb pattern of overlapping cells of communication. Because these cells can be minimal in size, it is possible to reuse the frequencies repeatedly. Thus, cellular communications was born. The goal of cellular was to make more service available to vehicular users.

In 1981, the FCC finally set aside 666 radio channels for cellular use. These frequencies were assigned or set aside for two separate carriers. The lower frequencies were reserved for wireline companies. Wireline companies are the regulated providers (the local telcos). The higher frequencies were assigned or reserved for non-wireline carriers, which are the competitors to the telephone carriers. Both operating carriers (the wireline and non-wireline) are licensed to operate in a specific geographic area. The areas are classified as the metropolitan service areas (MSAs) and rural service areas (RSAs). Each carrier uses approximately 312 frequencies for voice/data communication and 21 frequencies for control channels.

Another major difference in cellular communications is the use of control supervision and switching of calls to serve the cellular user adequately. This is particularly true in a mobile environment when the vehicle moves from one cell to another. The dynamic switching and control necessary to facilitate a smooth and seamless handoff from one cell to another is paramount. If this does not work properly, all communication may be terminated.

The signal on conventional mobile radiotelephones degraded as the vehicle moved farther away from the base station. This degradation frustrated both the caller and the called party. As the user went beyond an area of coverage, the call would be cut off, further frustrating both calling and called parties.

With cellular communications, when a call is in progress and the caller moves away from the cell site toward a new cell, the call is handed off from one cell to another. In Figure 33-2, this process begins to take place. This is how it works. Once a call is in progress and the handoff from cell to cell becomes necessary to keep it that way, the system initiates a change. As the cellular telephone approaches the imaginary line, the signal strength transmitted back to the cell site will start to fall. The cell site equipment will

Figure 33-2
A call in progress will be handled by the cell in which the user is located.

Call in
progress

B

Overlap
Coverage

A

C

D

send a form of distress message to the mobile telephone switching office (MTSO), indicating that the signal is getting weaker. The MTSO then orchestrates the passing of the call from one cell site to another. In Figure 33-3, the initial sequence begins as a cell site notifies the MTSO that something is going on.

Immediately after receiving the message from the cell site, the MTSO sends out a broadcast to the other cell sites in the area. It requests a determination of which site is receiving the cellular user's signal the most strongly; this is called a quality of service measurement. Each site responds accordingly. In Figure 33-4, the MTSO's initial broadcast goes out across the network.

As the responses come back to the MTSO, the particular cell receiving the signal the most strongly is then selected to accept the call. The MTSO directs the targeted cell site to set up a voice path in parallel to the site losing the signal. When this is ready, the MTSO sends a command to the cellular set to resynthesize, or go to the new frequency. The cellular set then retunes itself to the new frequency assigned to the receiving cell site and

Figure 33-3
The cell site senses
the drop in signal
strength and alters
the MTSO.

Figure 33-4
The MTSO begins its
initial sequence to
prepare for the
handoff.

the handoff takes place. This takes approximately 100 to 200 milliseconds
to enact. Figure 33-5 shows the handoff.

This might sound a little more complicated than it really is. The designers recognized that the original radio systems put out way too much power.
Therefore, frequency reuse was not possible in a 100-mile radius. Using a

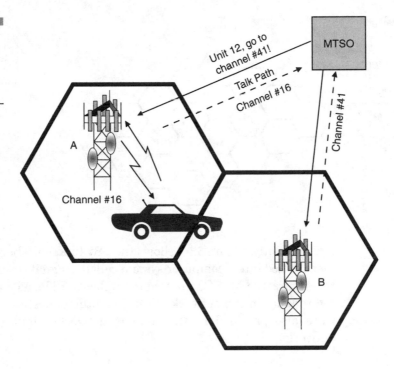

Figure 33-5
The alert goes out to
the cellular site,
advising it to go to a
new channel.

lower power output device, the radius of the radio transmission system is smaller. In fact, the cellular system was designed to operate in a range of approximately 3 to 5 miles. If the power output is reduced to 10 watts, the radio transmission will travel less distance. Therefore, the user must be closer to the equipment to receive the call. To accommodate this, the cellular cells include equipment placed (typically) in the center of each of these overlapping cells. The distance from the radio equipment to the user will be approximately 1 to 2 miles. Therefore, the system should work more efficiently. With only a 10-watt output, the frequencies used in each of the cells can be reused repeatedly. A separation of at least two cells must exist, but that was taken into account. Figure 33-6 is a representation of a cell network with the honeycomb pattern.

The carriers have been getting better at providing this coverage as the years have gone by. Many of the cellular suppliers now have provided for a seamless transition from cell to cell anywhere in the country. To do this, they have developed an interface into another telephone- or landline-based technique called signaling system 7 (SS7). Using SS7, the carriers can now hand a call off across the country without user involvement. It just happens

Figure 33-6
The cellular
honeycomb pattern
is a series of
overlapping cells.

Cellular Network

transparently. Figure 33-7 shows the SS7 linkage, where the MTSO equipment is tied into a computer system called a signal transfer point (STP). In this figure, the MTSOs are tied to duplicate STPs as a means of providing redundancy in the network. With this interconnection, additional features were also provided in the cellular networks similar to the telephone networks.

Meeting the Demand

The capacity to provide communications from a car telephone was easily met but expensive to start. A vehicle-mounted cellular telephone in 1984

Figure 33-7
Cellular equipment
now links to the
backbone network
through SS7 linkage.

retailed for $3,000. However, since then the cost has declined dramatically. Now, in North America, many companies buy the cell phone in the vehicle from the auto manufacturer for a few hundred dollars.

The Telephone (Mobile) Set

The set houses a transceiver capable of tuning to all channels within an area. These are frequency-agile units capable of receiving/transmitting on all 666 frequencies, as opposed to the fixed-frequency units of old. The mobile set is shown in Figure 33-8. The major components of the unit are

- Handset
- Number assignment module (NAM), an electronic fingerprint (a 32-bit binary sequence)
- Logic unit
- Transmitter

Figure 33-8
The cellular unit sets up the calls to the cell site using a frequency-agile capacity to synthesize the necessary frequency.

- Receiver
- Frequency synthesizer (generation of frequencies under control of the logic unit)
- Diplexer—separates transmitter/receiver functions
- Antenna

Cellular's Success and Loss

In 1984, cellular communications became the hot button in the industry. This was the original attempt to add capacity to several systems around the country. In the preceding years, the mobile phone services and the improved mobile telephone services (IMTS) were very limited. Part of the problem was that all systems were analog. Frequency-division multiple access (FDMA) is an analog technique designed to support multiple users in an area with a limited number of frequencies. An analog radio system will use analog input, such as voice communications. Because these systems were designed around voice applications, no one had any thought of the future transmission of data, fax, or packetized data from a vehicle or mobile phone. When cellular was first introduced, the industry experts were predicting that by the year 2000, approximately 900,000 users would be on the network conducting voice telephone calls. After all, it was a voice network designed to carry dial-up telephone calls.

No one was sure what the acceptance rate would be of cellular radiotelephone services. Currently, the U.S. has approximately 200 million cellular users. This was a surprise to the industry experts, who had no idea of the pent-up demand. Approximately 150,000 new users sign up monthly. The problem is not one of acceptance and signing up new users, but a problem of retaining users and encouraging them to use the service more. The churn ratio has been as high as 15 to 30 percent. This is a costly process and one that the providers are trying to overcome. Frustration exists on three counts:

- **The high cost of the service** Depending on the location, the basic monthly service will range from $19 to $129 and the per-minute charge for excess incoming or outgoing calls is $0.25 to $0.70.
- **The possibility of getting poor transmission or reception on the network** This is a design problem that can be fixed.

■ **The lack of available service** The network can get congested very quickly, and if you are paying for the service, you obviously want it available all the time. Users typically don't want to hear about the providers' problems. To overcome this problem, many carriers have split their cells into half and more, just to be able to use the frequencies repeatedly. Figure 33-9 shows where cell splitting has been performed. The graphic shows multiple smaller cells inside a normal cell. This might be over accentuated, but it is primarily a means of showing how this can be accomplished.

Many users sign up for the service but rarely use it; however, this is rapidly changing as the culture of the population and the price change. Users might buy a cellular telephone and keep it for emergency purposes only. This causes concern for the carriers because their revenue is based on usage. Without usage, they have little to no revenue. The capital costs of building the network are fixed and must be recuperated through usage. The carriers are trying to figure out how they can

■ Accommodate more users

■ Encourage subscribers to use more price-sensitive services

■ Generate new revenue

We face a quandary in the industry:

■ The carriers need more users to generate higher revenues to pay off the investment.

Figure 33-9
Cell splitting is required when constant congestion occurs. This helps to use more frequencies in smaller areas.

Average 3 miles; however, in major metropolitan areas, cell splitting will occur. Average can be a few blocks.

Cell Splitting

3 Miles

Original Cell

■ The carriers must continue the evolution from analog to digital systems that will enable more efficient use of bandwidth (frequency spectrum).

■ The need for security and protection against theft is putting pressure on carriers and users alike.

Analog systems do nothing for these three needs per se. Using either amplitude modulation or frequency modulation techniques, which were discussed in the data communications section of this book, to transmit voice on the radio signal uses all of the available bandwidth (or most of it). Distance, noise, and other interference demand power, amplification, and bandwidth to deliver a quality service. This means that the analog cellular carriers can support a single call on a single frequency (specific frequency). As such, the limitations of the systems are in channel availability on a given set of technologies. If you consider the noisy nature of analog signals, you can also determine that quality is a matter of multiple factors, not the least of which will be congestion and atmospheric conditions, as covered in other sections of this book.

Other concerns with analog systems rise from both security and fraud issues. The systems using a single frequency are subject to monitoring, but this is no different from the situation with any other airborne technique. Furthermore, when the analog network can be penetrated fraudulently, we must be concerned. This is not strictly a problem with analog systems.

As mentioned earlier in this chapter, the analog system was designed to provide the benefit of quick communications while on the road. Because this is considered a service that would meet the telephone needs of users on the go, the thought of heavy penetration was only minimally addressed. However, as the major metropolitan service areas (MSAs) began expanding, the carriers realized that the analog systems were limited. With only a single user on a frequency, congestion in the MSA began to be a tremendous problem.

When cell splitting takes place, other issues become problematic for the carriers. The more cells in use because of splitting, the more critical the arrangement of frequencies available to use. Furthermore, as smaller cells are created through splitting, other issues (shown in Table 33-1) become problematic.

This put an additional financial burden on the carriers as they attempted to match need with return on investment. These problems have plagued the industry for quite some time now. As the industry began to

Table 33-1

Some of the
Problems Carriers
Will Experience
with Cell Splitting

Issue	Problem/Symptom
More equipment	Cost issues associated with buying the equipment. A cell site costs in the range of $650,000–$800,000.
Real estate	Getting the space to mount added equipment plus local ordinances in the area. Consumer pressures leading to the not-in-my-backyard syndrome.
Power	Remote generation equipment required that is a cost and a security problem.
Logistical problems	Managing the new sites, new frequencies, and other ancillary services for a much larger equipment base.

search for new solutions, other uses of cellular communications began to crop up, putting an additional load on the service.

The cellular systems were designed for the road warrior driving around with a vehicular telephone. Initial installations were handled in cars and trucks. However, as the technology improved, transportable telephones became nouveau for cellular users. Why should they be required to remain in the vehicle to use the service? Units could be mounted in the vehicle, and when the user got out, the set could be removed and used for several hours of standby operation and 1 hour of online operation. This opened a whole new avenue for service opportunities. The transportables were initially expensive, but prices have dropped to a far more reasonable rate (in the range of $300 to $600). Mobility became more flexible for the cellular user, who was no longer relegated to the vehicle. Figure 33-10 shows the transportable unit. This is still very popular with contractors doing construction, landscaping, and remote facilities work when they roam outside their normal geographic coverage areas. In many cases these phones are used when the contractor is on the periphery of a cell.

Portable hand-held units began the next wave for cellular users. If a set could be removed from the vehicle, why then should it even be tied to the vehicle? If a set could be designed with a rechargeable battery pack, a briefcase model could be made available. Better yet, why not come up with a flip-type telephone or a shirt-pocket telephone? As prices were dropping for the vehicle telephone, so, too, were those for the hand-held telephones. Recently, ads in the trade magazines and local newspapers around the U.S. have been

Figure 33-10
The transportable set took the set out of the vehicle. Up to several hours of standby operation are available, depending on the battery and technology.

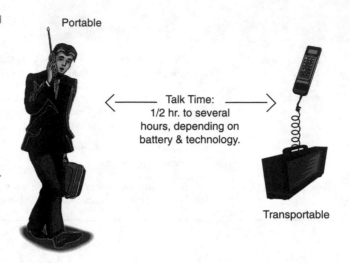

Portable

Talk Time:
1/2 hr. to several hours, depending on battery & technology.

Transportable

offering the hand-held devices for a mere $0 to $15 with a 1-year subscription to the carrier's network. The retail value of these telephones is as low as $360 to $1,500. In order to entice people to buy the phones and use the service, the providers offer the sets at less than retail (loss leader). This has come a long way from the initial days of the cellular networks in 1984.

Features exploded also with the introduction of

■ Voice messaging

■ Redial

■ Display

■ Call forwarding

■ Memory

■ Hands-free operation

Subcompact or shirt-pocket flip telephones caught on. Users became enamored with the technology, and the price was almost too good to pass up. These latest and greatest models have between 0.3 and 0.6 watts of power output; they are totally portable and accessible. Professionals meeting with doctors and lawyers outside their normal office environment like the idea of using a cellular flip telephone. It gives them the ability to be reached at a moment's notice and frees them from the vehicle. These telephones became the talk of many social events.

These evolutions in the analog arena were all driving forces in the use and acceptance of cellular communications. However, as the congestion problem continued to go unsolved, the carriers entered a new era. The whole world has been evolving to digital transmission systems on the local and long-distance scene. This evolution to digital has many benefits for the standard wire-based carriers. These include

- Higher usage
- Better quality
- Multiple techniques
- Digital speeds

Digital Transmission

The cellular carriers continue to step into the digital world. This stems from the perspectives of compatibility and frequency utilization. If users can share a frequency or range of frequencies, then more users can be accommodated on less bandwidth. This has a definite financial impact on the carrier investment strategies. They could support more users on fewer frequencies and require less equipment. Currently, 35 to 40 percent of the cellular and personal telephones are digital. Many carriers still offer analog services as their primary service.

Digital

Digital transmission delivers better multiplexing schemes so that the carriers can get more users on an already strained radio frequency spectrum. Additional possibilities for enhancing security and reducing fraud are also addressed with digital cellular. Again, this appears to be a win-win situation for the carriers. Table 33-2 provides a summary of the key benefits for the cellular carriers' migration to digital communications.

Once the decision was made to consider digital transmission, the major problem was how to achieve the switch, what flavor to use, and how to transfer the existing customer base seamlessly to digital. The options available to the carriers are

- Time-division multiple access (TDMA)
- Extended time-division multiple access (ETDMA)

Table 33-2

Summary of the Key Benefits for the Cellular Carriers' Migration to Digital Communications

Key Benefits of Digital
Less costs overall. Initially conversion will be expensive, but longer range will be less.
More users on the same or fewer frequencies and spectrum.
Better security than offered by the analog transport systems.
Less risk of theft and fraud.

- Code-division multiple access (CDMA)
- Narrowband advanced mobile phone service (N-AMPS)

Carriers and manufacturers are using each of these system types. This creates a split in the industry, depending on the technique chosen and the carrier support. When the network goes completely digital, the telephones purchased by users will have to be changed. Can you imagine the millions of users who are going to rebel against the change of equipment?

Voice Technology and Applications

Because cellular was originally designed for voice communications, all of the development was in the ability to service voice transmissions and applications. Many of the technological aspects have already been addressed. However, just as many applications are available for voice. Some of these include the following:

- **Dial-up calls from and to the user on the road** This is what the cellular network was designed to do. The primary goal of cellular is facilitation of the voice dial-up call without wires.
- **Dispatch services for maintenance and repair crews** Many municipalities are now using cellular communications to notify the crews on the road. Very specific two-way communications can be handled. This certainly beats the disruptive two-way radio systems that were used in the past.
- **Trucker availability** Because truck drivers need to be reached anywhere and anytime, the use of a portable telephone keeps them in touch with the dispatchers. This saves valuable time and money for the

trucker and the company—a savings that hopefully also gets passed along to the customer.

- **Safety and security (accident reporting and 911 services)** The books are full of cases where lives have been saved and emergency response services have been dispatched more quickly thanks to the cellular telephone. The use of a telephone in a vehicle to call 911 (999 in some parts of the world) can get ambulances, fire trucks, and police agencies on the roll much quicker than ever before. No single benefit has proved the value of cellular more than this one.

- **Secondary services for the Coast Guard** Whereas two-way radio-based services were limited and subject to extensive monitoring, the Coast Guard now has a more reliable means of communication without having to go ashore and find a landline.

- **Voice service for police vehicles** Using cellular telephones, police agencies can eliminate the radio patch system that was predominant in day-to-day operation. Motor vehicle registrations, discussions with other officials, and private communications on closed channels all have their unique benefits.

- **Disaster recovery for office or manufacturing locations** Quick reestablishment of voice communications can be handled on a limited basis with cellular telephones. Call forwarding arrangements are easily made to a portable telephone after a building is destroyed. Many of the key players in an organization are highly mobile and therefore benefit from the ability to use the telephone on the run.

- **Replacement for two-way radio applications (such as taxi, ambulance, and other on-demand services)** Two-way radio is difficult to use for the novice. It is noisy, sporadic, and congested in most metropolitan areas around the country.

- **Air phone services** As the nomadic user moves from the office to the vehicle to the airplane, being reachable is still the name of the game. Therefore, a special form of cellular communications will make the traveling executive or salesperson more available.

- **Vehicle scheduling/diversion for dispatchers in a storm, major traffic jam, and so on** The vehicle can be notified to use alternate routes.

- **Fire departments as a backup technology** At a fire scene, things can get quite hectic. Firefighting personnel must always compete for resources and get second opinions from experts. Safety ties in closely with this. The ability to reach a chemical expert regarding the mixing of water with certain materials to extinguish flames makes critical decisions more reliable, as the mixture of water with specific chemicals could produce an explosive reaction. This is not easily discussed on a radio, but it makes sense to use a portable telephone.

- **Supplementing the wires for the non-wired user in an organization**   Within the walls of an organization, catching anyone on the telephone these days is a haphazard proposition. Meetings, social gatherings, and group informal discussions all have a propensity to draw us out of our office areas and away from our PBX or key system. However, taking the cellular telephone with us means that no missed calls should occur in the future.

Facsimile Technology

It was only a matter of time before the users of cellular communications started looking for and finding new applications. A voice application is fine, but supplementing that capability with fax is a natural progression.

Facsimile transmission has been used in the trucking industry for some time. A bill of lading or customs form can be shipped right into the cab of the truck. The advantages of this technique are varied. Other applications, such as sales literature, quotations, medical records, and so on could have strategic and savings benefits. Figure 33-11 shows an example of a fax transmission across the network to a trucker. This particular case involves the arrival of a trucker at a border crossing without all of the appropriate

Figure 33-11
The post-fax scenario enables information to be shipped directly into the vehicle.

paperwork. Assuming that perishable goods are on the truck, the dispatcher needs to get the truck rolling as soon as possible. However, the government needs to see that the appropriate permits, fees, and inspections have been taken care of. Rather than delaying the movement of the vehicle, the trucker can immediately call the dispatcher and request the appropriate forms. When these forms are ready, the dispatcher can simply fax them into the cab of the truck. What was once an overnight and very expensive proposition has been reduced to a few minutes of far less expensive time.

Cellular systems transmit information from sender to receiver. As a mobile unit is transmitting or receiving a fax, handoffs from cell to cell might take place. This handoff might cause a loss of information during the cycle. However, because pixels (dots) are being transmitted, the loss of information will be minimal.

As a facsimile is being scanned, a Huffman and Read (pronounced *reed*) code set is being used. Actually, the facsimile machine is scanning a page of information on a line-by-line basis. During handoff, a 100- to 200-ms delay could occur while the cellular user is handed from one cell to another. For data communications, this is a long time, but fax technology is far more forgiving. The facsimile machine waits for carrier detect and then continues to send. However, any data that was sent during the handoff could be lost. Because the line-by-line scan and transmit is used, all that will be lost is a line of dots. This shouldn't impact the information very much, yielding a high-quality facsimile transmission. This is shown in Figure 33-12, where a line of dots, or one scanned line, has been lost. This is not a major problem because, although the line is lost, the rest of the document is still legible.

Figure 33-12
Interruptions on the circuit do not cause disconnections. A line of dots may be lost during handoff.

Scanning Line

Line lost during transmit

So, using a fax modem allows for a wait time of up to 400 ms—a data communications modem will drop the line if the carrier is lost for greater than 80 ms. A handoff can take from 100 to 200 ms in an average cell. The information should therefore be usable and understandable. Further, as the fax modems communicate to each other, they have the capability to monitor line quality and fall back to slower speeds, if necessary, to get the transmission through.

Data Transmission

Many users say that data transmission does not work on cellular communications. Although this was limited in the early stages, things have gotten much better. The first problems that occurred were with handoff. As a vehicle or mobile set using data services rolled from cell to cell, the handoff would disrupt the call for 100 to 200 ms. This was just enough to disrupt the carrier detect (CD) cycle, so the modem assumed that one of the callers had hung up. Thus the modem would hang up, too! Obviously, this problem could be overcome by having data transmission take place only while the vehicle is stationary. However, that becomes a limitation to communications. As Figure 33-13 represents, when data is disrupted, the modem will fall off and disconnect. This graphic is designed to show the early problems with the wireless transmission services.

Newer data modems for cellular communication use a technique similar to the fax modem. The modem will delay for 400 ms before hanging up. Because the handoff only takes 100 to 200 ms, the modem has time to spare without losing the call. Some data might be affected, but error detection, acknowledgement/negative acknowledgement (ACK/NAK), and cyclic redundancy checks (CRCs) all will come into play in detecting and correcting the errors that occur on the cellular network. See Figure 33-14 for a representation of the data correction problem. Conventional data was always regarded with suspicion on cellular airwaves. Because the modems had to hang onto the line for 400 ms while waiting for the carrier to return, everyone thought that data would only be effective at 2,400 bps. Manufacturers introduced a 9.6-Kbps cellular modem, and others have a 19.2-Kbps cellular modem. Many differences in actual performance and throughput exist. In studies, the actual throughput of a 9.6-Kbps modem is 8 Kbps, and for the 12.2-Kbps modems we get 12- to 14.4-Kbps. We will obviously need much more than that to satisfy the end user.

Figure 33-13
Early implementations of wireless data caused disconnections during cell-to-cell handoff.

Hand-off

Hang-up

Modem

Figure 33-14
Improvements in the data communications prevent the disconnections as handoff occurs.

Hand-off

NAK

Wait 400 milliseconds

Modem

Digital Cellular Evolution

As the spectrum for radio cellular users became more congested, two primary approaches were in the offing:

- Time-division multiple access (TDMA)
- Code-division multiple access (CDMA)

However, standards bodies and manufacturers are all coming up with variations on the use of the frequency spectrum. TDMA was selected. Nevertheless, manufacturers developed an extended TDMA (ETDMA) that will bring more use to the system. TDMA will derive a threefold increase in spectrum use, whereas ETDMA will produce a six- to eightfold increase. The concept is a digital speech interpolation (DSI) technique that uses the quiet times in normal speech, thereby assigning more conversations to fewer channels, gaining up to eight times more capacity than an analog channel. Each move toward digital requires newer equipment, which means more capital investments for the cellular carriers.

TDMA uses a time-division multiplexing scheme where time slices are allocated to multiple conversations. Although TDMA usually deals with an analog-to-digital conversion using a typical pulse code modulation technique, it performs differently in a radio transmission. PCM is translated into a Quadrature phase-shift keying technique, thereby producing a four-phased shift, doubling the data rate for data transmission (actually driving a voice call at 8 Kbps).

Spread spectrum, which was first used back in the 1920s, has evolved from its initial military security applications. Spread spectrum uses a technique of organizing the radio frequency energy over a range of frequencies instead of modulating the frequency. The system uses frequency hopping with time-division multiplexing. One minute the transmitter is operating on one frequency, and the next minute on another, according to some code. The receiver is synchronized to switch frequencies in the same pattern. This is effective in preventing detection (interception) and jamming. Thus, additional security is derived. These techniques should produce 10 to 12 times increased capacity over existing analog systems.

Another possible solution for bandwidth or user expansion is narrowband advanced mobile service (N-AMPS), a technique developed by Motorola. N-AMPS is a channel-splitting technique where channel bandwidths are allocated in chunks of 10 KHz instead of the traditional 30 KHz.

Personal Communications Services

Why require a person to be tied to a pair of wires or to a fixed location with an associated number, when the provider can offer a tie to the individual through an intelligent network that is capable of finding a called party no matter where he or she is? This concept will appear on the mass market at a time when the population is far more mobile than it is now. The use of cordless telephone technology has already made its niche in the industry, particularly in the home, where teens use a cordless telephone as the norm. Security or convenience is not a concern. Service is an issue because the set must be kept directionalized with the base station. The limitation of distance to a 300-foot radius around the base station works fine in the residence. However, this does not work as well in the business environment because of all the concrete and steel around the set.

Therefore, it is only natural that the next logical extension of this service will be to provide unrestricted service and access regardless of where the recipient of the call might be at any time. Consider the ability to use cordless telephony anywhere in the world and the reality of personal communications becomes less a myth and more a fact. Throughout the evolution of wireless communications, users have always wanted the ability to be reached at any time. Unfortunately, the use of earlier systems was always limited to very specific regions, such as major metropolitan centers and the surrounding areas (typically, a 40- to 50-mile radius from the user's home base). This distance limitation led to many complex machinations in the use of paging and radio hand-held systems. The industry finally responded with a more robust application that used satellite and radio repeaters. Now an individual can move out of the home area and be reached virtually anywhere around the country.

Pockets of dead space always exist, but these are limited. Even when two-way improved mobile telephone service (IMTS) was deployed, several limitations were inherent. Limited frequencies, long waiting lists, and expensive service all kept the use of this technology to a minimum. Cellular technology improved the situation, but the cost of the airtime was considered very high. At a time when this cost should have been dropping, carriers and providers of cellular service were raising their rates to compensate for losses because of the high-churn (turnover) rates of customers and because of a new phenomenon: theft and fraud. The legitimate user was penalized for the losses being sustained by the providers.

Now the industry wants to deliver wireless communications in the form of telephony, data, paging, and e-mail applications to the mass market. To do this, a newer concept was needed that enabled rapid deployment of equipment and more diverse coverage of all areas around the country and eventually the world. This would make major investments far less lucrative, so the proposed carriers and providers of personal communications services looked for ways to introduce the technology to the masses with limited investments and large-scale frequency reuse. The resultant discussions being held by these carriers and providers focus on the purchase and installation of microcells and picocells (Figure 33-15). Primarily, the newer carriers are looking at providing much smaller systems and equipment to reuse the frequency spectrum increasingly. The obvious goal is to produce the equivalent of a wireless dial-tone service to the masses (both businesses and residences) for a reasonable, affordable price. As the proliferation of the service continues, the service costs will fall dramatically. One can expect to pay $0 to $20 per month and $0.10 to $0.15 per minute of usage. PCS is still rolling out. Spotty services and coverage areas still prevail, causing some dissatisfaction by users.

This creates a catch-22 situation. The carriers and providers need users to sign up and use the service so that they can deliver more benefits and coverage. Yet, many new users will be frustrated as the deployment takes place and will return to wired dial tone because this is an older, proven technology.

Figure 33-15
A single controller
will be able to
manage up to 96
microcells, with each
cell handling 20 to
25 calls.

Technology

The technology decisions in this arena are equally perplexing. Any attempt to use a narrower band for transmission would only provide a limitation to the services anticipated for use. Consequently, the industry wrestled with the question of what technology to deploy for the future. The costs are astronomical when a nationwide or worldwide network service is installed. Therefore, time-division multiple access (TDMA) and code-division multiple access (CDMA) are being used. Each of the vendors or purveyors of service have taken a different approach. These various technologies are summarized in Table 33-3. In this table, the various options are shown with their respective advances in frequency reuse increases, the comparison of digital versus analog capabilities, the services that might be provided, and the number of suppliers that exist.

One further added comparison includes the use of narrowband advanced mobile telephone service (N-AMPS). This adds a degree of complexity because the variations will not be fully compatible. Therefore, a change in the transmitted signal or the format of the information will be required if an internetworking application is used.

Table 33-3

Comparison of the Technologies Being Considered for PCS/PCN

Technology Capability	TDMA	E-TDMA	CDMA	N-AMPS
Frequency reuse gains	3×	6–8×	10–12×	3–5×
Digital	Yes	Yes	Yes	No
Services to be offered	Voice Data Paging e-mail Internet	Voice Data Paging e-mail	Voice Data Paging e-mail Radio determination Internet	Voice Data Paging
Costs	Low–Medium	High	High	Low
Quality	Fair	Good–Excellent	Good–Excellent	Good

The Concept of PCS/PCN

Visualize how this system might work. The local wired telephone services from the local exchange carriers will still exist. Therefore, the use of the wireless local loop in the dial-tone arena will still use a twisted pair of wires as has always been the case. However, the personal communicator will now act as a cordless telephone in the business or residence.

As shown in Figure 33-16, a cordless telephone arrangement will be set up with a smart terminal. This smart box will enable the user to place a personal communicator in the charging unit at the location. While in the charging unit, the set will act as any cordless telephone. A call coming into the telephone will travel across the local telephone company wires and ring into the network-attached box. When the user picks up the telephone and answers the call, the set will now be cordless. In Figure 33-17, the same scenario will be used, but the most significant difference is the lack of a pair of telephone wires into the business or residence. In this scenario, the set is 100 percent wireless—with a smart interface in the location, a call coming into the business or residence will come in across the airwaves rather than over the wires. The primary difference in this example is the absence of a telephone wire.

Taking this one step further, when the owner of the telephone set chooses to leave the primary location, the set will be taken from the charging unit and possibly clipped onto a belt loop or placed into a pocket (purse, jacket, or other). Wrist-mounted telephone sets will also appear, as shown in

Figure 33-16
The personal communicator placed into a charger or smart box acts like a standard cordless phone when used with telco wires.

RJ-11
Jack

To Telco ⟶

Smart Box

Figure 33-18. AT&T Wireless has a wrist mount that is spring-loaded. When the user opens the set, the hand is cupped around the ear to act as the receiver. Actually, the spring-loaded receiver slips into the palm of the hand and creates a simulation of the normal telephone set. The transmitter is located on the wristband.

As the user leaves the building and steps out into the open space of the neighborhood, the set will immediately begin communicating with a local cell. The local telephone company or another supplier might provide this local cell. However, the cell will be a microcell, possibly mounted atop a light stanchion or telephone pole. In Figure 33-19, the cells are located on top of a telephone pole line. These cells will be wireless to and from the personal communicator set, but the individual cells will be hard-wired along the pole line via fiber, coax cable, or twisted pairs of wire. These wired facilities will be carried back to the telephone company central office. In this particular area, the telephone companies have an edge over their competitors because they already have the poles installed and own the rights of way to these poles.

Figure 33-18
The spring-loaded wrist phone places the receiver in the cupped palm to accommodate full handset operation. The microphone stays at the wrist (Source: Samsung).

Figure 33-19
Once the set is removed from the smart box and the user leaves the locale, an instant communication is established via the microcell to alert the network that the user is mobile.

Smart Box

80–200 feet

TELCO

Communications to Wireless established.

Continuing with the scenario, the user's device will continue to communicate with the local microcell as the user proceeds down a path or walkway. As the user gets close to the boundary of the cell, a handoff will be required from one cell to another. The microcells will only cover a limited distance to begin with, possibly in the range of 80 to 200 feet. This implies that handoffs will happen on a far more frequent basis. As the user continues down the path, the handoffs continue every 80 to 200 feet along the way. As the user enters an area where no poles are present, the microcells are mounted as telepoints along the way. A telepoint is a wireless access mounted atop or on the side of a building. All that is necessary is a close proximity to the telepoint or microcell. In Figure 33-20, the telepoint is mounted on the side of a building, and in Figure 33-21, the microcells are mounted on top of the buildings, each cell serving a radius of 200 feet. Each of these cells will be controlled by a central cell controller, with a cell serving 20 to 25 simultaneous calls and a controller managing between 32 and 64 cells. At some future point in time, these controllers will likely manage up to 96 cells, each

Figure 33-20

When no pole lines are available, telepoints can be mounted on the side of buildings.

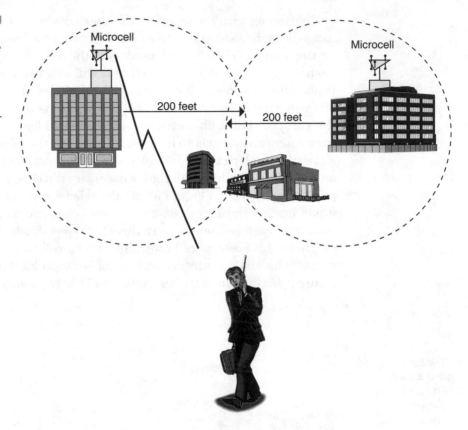

Figure 33-21
Microcells can also be mounted on the tops of buildings, with each cell serving a radius of 200 feet.

controlling 20 to 25 simultaneous calls. This amounts to a single control device managing between 1,900 and 2,400 concurrent calls. Imagine the efficiency of this concept!

Questions

1. What year was cellular first introduced?
   a. 1978
   b. 1984
   c. 1990
   d. 1994

2. The cellular network was used to replace the _____ networks.

    a. AMPS

    b. Two-way radio

    c. IMTS

    d. Walkie-talkie

3. Cell sites operated at approximately _____ miles across.

    a. 10

    b. 7

    c. 12

    d. 3

4. The first cellular phones were made to operate in _____.

    a. Vehicles

    b. Shirt pockets

    c. Briefcases

    d. Wristwatches

5. The AMPS used what technology?

    a. Digital

    b. TDMA

    c. CDMA

    d. Analog

6. Cellular handoff occurs when the user is on the periphery of the cell.   T/F

7. As congestion occurred, one of the first steps to get more utilization was to:

    a. Allow fewer users.

    b. Build more networks.

    c. Perform cell splitting.

    d. Use less bandwidth.

8. When the industry decided to move to digital, the selection was easy and straightforward.   T/F

9. The choices of digital were actually selected between two competing technologies:
    a. TDMA and FDMA
    b. ETDMA and N-AMPS
    c. IMTS and AMPS
    d. TDMA and CDMA

10. The PCS architecture enables more users and less cost.   T/F

11. Future networks will all be driven on TDMA.   T/F

12. Data transmissions operating with modems deliver:
    a. 8 to 19.2 Kbps
    b. 8 to 14.4 Kbps
    c. 8 to 12 Kbps
    d. 9.6 to 19.2 Kbps

13. Fax traffic cannot run over cellular networks because of the handoff problem.   T/F

14. Digital transmission will offer the capability to achieve data at much higher rates.   T/F

15. TDMA helps to achieve a _____ increase in number of users.
    a. 10-fold
    b. 20-fold
    c. 5-fold
    d. 3-fold

Wireless Application Protocol (WAP)

After reading this chapter and completing the questions, you will be able to:

- Describe the concept and purpose of the wireless application protocol
- Understand what role wireless will play on the future of data communications
- Discuss the benefits of using a common protocol for wireless data
- Compare the different choices available to use using WAP
- Understand the basic flow of preparing the transmission

"The Wireless Application Protocol (WAP) is an open, global specification that empowers mobile users with wireless devices to easily access and interact with information and services instantly."—WAP Forum FAQ

Wireless Application Protocol (WAP) is a small application protocol used mainly for small hand-held communication devices like cellular phones and Personal Digital Assistants (PDAs). WAP was originally founded by the cellular equipment giants Nokia, Ericsson, and Motorola and the hand-held device software platform developer Unwired Planet; since then, several dozens of companies, mainly hardware and software manufacturers and network operators, have joined the WAP and are developing all kinds of devices, applications, and services.

WAP is developed to be the standard means of information transportation and Internet service gateway for mobile communication services. WAP is a hardware and software platform and network independent. It uses a lightweight browser, called the microbrowser—client software that can be designed to have minimal footprint and hardware requirements to fit in a very large span of different devices.

WAP has been designed from various currently used Internet standards like HTML, HTTP, XML, TCP, IP, UDP, and TLS. The main points in developing this new protocol were to make it very bandwidth optimized to work as quickly as possible in slow wireless networks (compared to fixed-line networks that conventional protocols are designed for) and flexible to work in small screens of different shapes and various user input devices. Bandwidth requirements are made low by transferring all information as compressed binary and not as plaintext like current similar protocols such as HTTP. Header information is optimized to be small and the page markup language supports making applications small and flexible.

The WAP has been a hot topic in and out of the mobile industry. WAP, as its name implies, is a protocol—a standardized way that a mobile phone talks to a server installed in the mobile phone network. The purpose is to provide the interface between the client device and the server on a mobile network. WAP is hot because

- It provides a standardized way of accessing the Internet from a mobile phone, creating links between the two hot buttons in this industry. By creating a link between the two networking strategies (the Internet and the wireless world), the user has the most accessibility. This creates a dynamic opportunity for the vendor and the end user alike.

- The major wireless vendors including Nokia, Ericsson, and Motorola were the original founders of the WAP Forum and have endorsed the use of the wireless protocols to gain mobile access to the Internet. This also means that they will continue to develop new products and services aimed at satisfying the needs of the user through the WAP architecture. One should feel safe looking down the antenna of a WAP-enabled wireless device (such as a telephone, PDA, Palm, and so on).

- In the year 2000, more than 350 companies were members of the WAP Forum, which show ubiquitous support and development capabilities for the future. One can expect that with this many vendors endeavoring to develop WAP-enabled products, a wide variety of devices and services will be available for the long term. Thus, the investments made today will carry forward into the future.

In the past, the use of mobile information services had not been very successful. Many network operators were disappointed by the actual versus planned results of wireless data. WAP addresses the issues of mobile information as a key ingredient in the overall data connectivity. If all things were perfect, these issues would not exist. However, some detractors feel that the WAP hype is overstated. For example,

- It is difficult to configure WAP phones for new services because at least 20 different parameters must be configured to gain access to a WAP service.

- The number of Short Message Service (SMS)-compliant phones is rather large. SMS is a messaging protocol used as part of the GSM standard. The number of WAP-enabled handsets is small. WAP is a protocol that runs on top of an underlying bearer. None of the existing Global System for Mobile Communications (GSM) bearers for WAP— the SMS, Unstructured Supplementary Services Data (USSD), and circuit-switched data (CSD)—are optimized for WAP.

- The WAP standard is incomplete; even with key elements such as push (proactive sending of information to mobile devices) and wireless telephony included, the WAP 1.2 is not 100 percent complete. Although the standards were approved in 1999 and implemented in 2000, more work needs to be done.

- Many WAP Gateway vendors are competing against each other with the same standardized product. This will lead to consolidation and merger activity as well as place a burden on the vendors. Functionally, they are small fish in a big pond, but there are too many of them. Competition is fierce.

- Other protocols are in the mill and already have strong support as the replacement to WAP.

- WAP services are more expensive to use, especially when using an online circuit-switched data call. Features such as interactivity and selection of more information that are used by the end user will drive the overall cost and online time up. Many WAP users will suffer sticker shock when they receive their first mobile phone bill after using WAP.

WAP Protocol Stack

WAP has a layered architecture, as shown in Figure 34-1. This protocol stack is similar to other stacks shown in this book such as the OSI model, TCP/IP model, and others. The purpose of the stack is to relate to the position on the stack where things happen. This stack is comprised of six basic layers. Each of the layers has a specific role to perform and handle the integration of wireless data and telephony networking.

Wireless Application Environment

The Wireless Application Environment (WAE) defines the user interface on the phone. The application development environment facilitates the development of services that support multiple bearers. To achieve this, the WAE contains the Wireless Markup Language (WML), the WMLScript—a scripting micro-language similar to JavaScript—and the Wireless Telephony Application (WTA). These are the tools that enable WAP-based applications to be developed. WAE is built into the microbrowser program that works much like normal WWW browsers. To summarize these tools, the following points will help to clarify the use of the various protocols:

- WML is the WAP markup language that is similar to the relationship between HTML and WWW. WML is a document type definition (DTD) of extensible markup language (XML) that is a subset of standard

Figure 34-1
The WAP protocol stack
(Source: WAP Forum)

Wireless Application Environment (WAE)
Wireless Session Protocol (WSP)
Wireless Transaction Protocol (WTP)
Wireless Transport Layer Security (WTLS)
Wireless Datagram Protocol (WDP)
Bearers (e.g. Data, SMS, USSD)

generalized markup language (SGML) so it is tag based like the HTML.

■ WMLScript is the WML-integrated scripting language much like JavaScript that can control many functions of the browser and the phone itself by scripts downloaded from the server.

■ WTA is the telephony interface of WAE that can be used to control telephony functions of the device from WML, WMLScript, or the network and to invoke functions by requests from the network.

Wireless Session Protocol

Wireless Session Protocol (WSP) implements session services of WAP. Sessions can be connection-oriented and connectionless and they may be suspended and resumed at will. It is an access point layer that links the WAE to two-session services: a connection-oriented service operating above the Wireless Transaction Protocol (WTP) and a connectionless service operating above the Wireless Datagram Protocol (WDP).

Wireless Transaction Protocol

WTP is the transaction protocol that works between the session protocol WSP and security protocol Wireless Transport Layer Security (WTLS). WTP chops data packets into lower level datagrams and concatenates received datagrams into useful data. WTP also keeps track of sent and received packets and performs retransmissions and acknowledgement sending when needed. WTP operates above a datagram service such as User Datagram Protocol (UDP) to provide a simple protocol suitable for low-bandwidth mobile stations. WTP offers three classes of transaction service:

■ Unreliable one-way request

■ Reliable one-way request

■ Reliable two-way request/respond

WTP supports data concatenation and delayed acknowledgement to help reduce the number of messages sent. This protocol tries to optimize the user experience by providing the information that is needed when it is needed. By stringing several messages together, the end user may get a better feel more quickly for what information is being communicated.

Wireless Transport Layer Security

WTLS incorporates security features that are based upon the established Transport Layer Security (TLS) protocol standard. TLS includes data integrity checks, privacy on the WAP Gateway to the client, and authentication. Similarly, WTLS provides all the cryptography-oriented features for WAP. WTLS handles encrypting, decrypting, user authentications, and data integrity checking. WTLS is based on the fixed-network TLS, formerly known as Secure Sockets Layer (SSL).

Wireless Datagram Protocol

The WDP enables WAP to be bearer independent by adapting the transport layer of the underlying bearer. WDP presents a consistent data format to the higher layers of the WAP protocol stack thereby conferring the advantage of bearer independence to application developers. WDP works as the transport layer of WAP. It processes datagrams from upper layers to formats required by different physical data paths, including bearers that may be GSM, SMS, or CDMA packet data, for example. WDP is adapted to the bearers available in the device so upper layers don't need to care about the physical level. Figure 34-2 shows the physical layer.

Figure 34-2
The physical layers under the WAP stack (Source: WAP Forum)

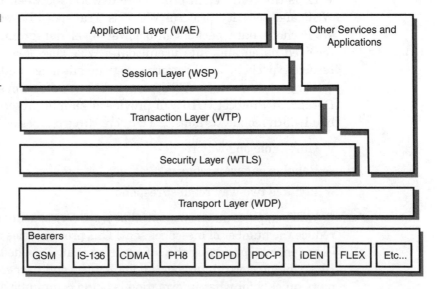

Short Message Service

SMS may not be an adequate bearer for WAP because the protocol is limited to a length of 160 characters per short message. The overhead of the WAP protocol that would be added to an SMS message would mean that even for the simplest of transactions, several SMS messages might have to be sent. Using SMS as a bearer can be time consuming and expensive.

Circuit-Switched Data

Most of the trial WAP-based services use CSD as the underlying bearer. CSD has relatively few users currently; WAP could kick start usage generated by this bearer. However, CSD lacks immediacy—a dial-up connection takes about 10 seconds to connect the WAP client to the gateway. This is the best-case scenario when a complete end-to-end digital call occurs. With analog modem handshaking, the connect time is increased to about 30 seconds.

Unstructured Supplementary Services Data

Unstructured supplementary services data (USSD) is a means of transmitting information or instructions over a GSM network. USSD has some similarities with SMS because both use the GSM signaling path. Unlike SMS, USSD is not a store and forward service. It is session oriented. When a user accesses a USSD service, a session is established and the radio connection stays open until the user or application releases it. Another cause can be a time out that releases the connection. This has more in common with CDS than SMS. USSD text messages can be up to 182 characters long.

USSD has some advantages and disadvantages for deploying services on mobile networks:

- Turnaround response times for interactive applications are shorter for USSD than SMS because of the session-based feature of USSD and because it is not a store and forward service.

- Users do not need to access any particular phone menu to access services with USSD; they can enter the USSD command directly from the initial mobile phone screen.

- Because USSD commands are routed back to the home mobile network's home location register (HLR), services based on USSD work just as well and in exactly the same way when users are roaming.

- USSD works on all existing GSM mobile phones.

- Both SIM Application Toolkit and WAP support USSD.

- USSD Stage 2 has been incorporated into the GSM standard. USSD was previously a one-way bearer useful for administrative purposes such as service access. Stage 2 is more advanced and interactive. By sending in a USSD2 command, the user can receive an information services menu. Therefore, USSD Stage 2 provides WAP-like features on existing phones. USSD could be an ideal bearer for WAP on GSM networks.

General Packet Radio Service

General Packet Radio Service (GPRS) is a new packet-based service introduced on many GSM and time-division multiple access (TDMA) networks starting in 2000. It is exciting as a bearer service because it is

- Always on (no dial-up connection is necessary)

- Fast (up to 170 Kbps in the very best theoretical extreme)

- Supports virtual connectivity

Handset vendors have not confirmed that the direct receipt of GPRS packets on the mobile phone will be supported with the first GPRS terminal offerings. Availability of GPRS mobile terminals is a central question that critically impacts the GPRS business case. Application migration from other non-voice bearers will hinge on the ability to deliver directly to the mobile station.

Two efficient means of delivering and proactively sending (pushing) content to a mobile phone are available:

- SMS, which is, of course, one of WAP bearers

- Having the user maintaining more or less a permanent GPRS (mobile-originated) session with the content server

Unfortunately, mobile-terminated IP traffic might enable unsolicited information like spam to reach the terminal. Internet devices sending unsolicited content may not be chargeable. A worse-case scenario would be that mobile users would have to pay for receiving unsolicited junk content. This is a reason why a mobile vendor may not support mobile termination on their GPRS terminals. However, when they originate the session themselves, GPRS users confirm their agreement to pay for the delivery of content. Users could make their requests via a WAP session, which would not need to be blocked. A WAP session initiated from the WAP microbrowser could be the only way that GPRS users can receive information onto their mobile terminals.

Because all future WAP-enabled phones will support the GPRS, WAP and GPRS will be synergistically tied together. For the interactive, menu-based information exchanges that WAP will handle, circuit-switched data is not immediate enough because of the need to set up a call. SMS, on the other hand, is immediate, but it always uses a store and forward mechanism. Therefore, when a subscriber requests information from his or her microbrowser, the SMS center resources are used in the information transfer. GPRS and WAP are ideal bearers for each other.

WAP also incorporates two different connection modes: WSP connection mode or WSP connectionless protocol. This is very similar to the GPRS point-to-point services, which are connection-oriented or connectionless-oriented. The primary bearer for WAP-based services will depend on availability of WAP handsets and GPRS terminals. WAP will be equally important for the development of GPRS-based applications. Because the bearer level is independent from the application layer in the WAP protocol stack, WAP provides a standardized means to port the same application to different bearers.

WAP Clients and Gateways

WAP uses a client-server philosophy, requiring a microbrowser in the mobile phone and a WAP Gateway connected to the mobile network. However, because WAP requires a larger screen size and more memory, it costs more to produce a WAP handset. Support for WAP in the terminal sets will be the major factor that determines when WAP is a success. Figure 34-3 shows the client-server model.

WAP uses special WAP Gateway proxies to convert data from HTTP to WAP (and back), enabling a conventional WWW server to act as the document origin server. The programs in the WWW server may be written in either WML or standard HTML. The proxy server will convert the standard HTML to WML. The proxy converts the client's WAP requests into HTTP

Figure 34-3
The client-server
model for WAP
(Source: WAP Forum)

requests for WWW servers and Common Gateway Interface (CGI) programs, and then converts their output to WAP formats such as WML and WMLScript, and compresses them for returning them to the client.

The gateway and origin servers may be integrated into a single WAP server that will directly deliver WML data for WAP requests. The server may also include a Wireless Telephony Application (WTA) server that can be directly connected by the mobile data terminal's data bearer layer like GSM or SMS to speed up connections.

SIM Application Toolkit is another wireless protocol that enables a similar functionality set to WAP. SIM Application Toolkit has been available longer than WAP. It is more mature in its development. However, SIM Application Toolkit is a GSM-only technology. SIM Application Toolkit is supported by perhaps 30 percent of the GSM phones. Application developers may support WAP and SIM Application Toolkit and SMS in their gateways. That way the applications and services can be made available to all mobile phone users. Despite the limited installed base of WAP-enabled mobile phones, several vendors manufacture WAP Gateways for network operators, content providers, and application developers. WAP Gateways are installed into the mobile phone network to provide a gateway between the Internet and different mobile non-voice services such as the SMS, circuit-switched data, and GPRS.

Applications

WAP is being used to develop enhanced forms of existing and new versions of today's applications. Mobile data software and hardware suppliers are adding WAP support to their offering, by developing their own WAP interface or partnering with one of the WAP Gateway suppliers.

The WAP will enable customers to easily reply to incoming information on the phone by creating new menus to access mobile services. WAP can help generate additional traffic on the network and therefore revenue for the carriers.

Previously, application developers wrote proprietary software applications and had to port that application to different network types and bearers within the same platform. By separating the bearer from the application, WAP facilitates easy migration of applications between networks and bearers. Like Java, WAP simplifies application development and reduces the cost of wireless application development.

Corporate applications that are being enhanced and enabled with a WAP interface include

- Job dispatch
- Remote point of sale services
- Customer service
- Remote monitoring
- Remote meter reading
- Vehicle location and tracking
- Corporate e-mail
- Remote access to LAN
- File transfer
- Web browsing
- Audio
- Still or moving images
- Home/office automation

Consumer applications that are being enhanced and enabled with a WAP interface include

- Simple person-to-person messaging
- Voice and fax mail notifications

- Unified messaging
- Internet e-mail
- Prepayment
- Ring tones
- Mobile commerce
- Affinity programs
- Mobile banking
- Chat
- Information services

The WAP Forum

According to one research house, over 600 million people will be wireless subscribers at the end of 2001 and more than one billion people by 2005. Accordingly, a "substantial percentage of the phones sold in 2005 will be multimedia enabled" (Source: The WAP forum).

These multimedia capabilities include e-mail and push information to and from the Internet. To guide the development of these exciting new applications, the leaders of the wireless telecommunications industry formed the WAP Forum. WAP is the de facto world standard for wireless information and telephony services on digital mobile phones and other wireless terminals. Carriers representing nearly 100 million subscribers worldwide have joined WAP. This commitment will provide tens of millions of WAP browser-enabled products to consumers by the end of 2000. WAP enables carriers to strengthen their service offerings by providing subscribers with the information they want and need while on the go. The WAP Forum has published a global wireless protocol specification based on existing Internet standards such as XML and IP for all wireless networks.

Enabling information access from hand-held devices requires a deep understanding of both technical and market issues that are unique to the wireless environment. Wireless devices represent the ultimate constrained computing device with limited CPU, memory, and battery life, and a simple user interface. Wireless networks are constrained by low bandwidth, high latency, and unpredictable availability and stability. But most important of all, wireless subscribers have a different set of desires and needs.

The WAP specification addresses these issues by using existing standards and developing new extensions where needed. It enables industry participants to develop solutions that are air interface independent, device independent, and fully interoperable. The WAP solution leverages the tremendous investment in Web servers, Web-development tools, Web programmers, and Web applications while solving the unique problems associated with the wireless domain. The specification further ensures that this solution is fast, reliable, and secure. It enables developers to use existing tools to produce sophisticated applications that have an intuitive user interface. Ultimately, wireless subscribers benefit by gaining the power of information access in the palm of their hand.

Telecommunication professionals have written the WAP specification so that the entire industry, and most importantly its subscribers, can benefit from a single, open specification. Wireless service providers are able to offer a new dimension of service that complements the existing features of their networks, while extending subscriber access to the unbounded creativity of the Web. Handset manufacturers can integrate microbrowser functionality at minimal cost because the WAP specification is open and public. Application developers gain access to a whole new market of information-hungry users, while protecting and leveraging their current investments in Web technology. Subscribers gain real anytime, anywhere information access with a simple and effective user interface, which is available on a variety of networks and devices.

Although the WAP specification solves the transport and content problems of the constrained wireless environment today, the WAP Forum is constantly working to improve the state of wireless information access. The WAP Forum is working with these standards bodies toward a goal of convergence with the HTML and HTTP standards, which are not yet optimized for the wireless environment.

The WAP Forum Goals

The WAP Forum has the following goals:

- To bring Internet content and advanced data services to wireless phones and other wireless terminals
- To create a global wireless protocol specification that works across all wireless network technologies
- To enable the creation of content and applications that scale across a wide range of wireless bearer networks and device types
- To embrace and extend existing standards and technology wherever possible and appropriate

Standards Are Important

The WAP Forum does not develop products, but instead creates license-free standards for the entire industry to use to develop products. Each company's product line can then offer its own unique features, while still conforming to the WAP specification. Because the WAP Forum is not a handset manufacturer, voice-mail vendor, or infrastructure provider, all companies in the telecommunications industry are assured that they are not competing with WAP because WAP does not promote any particular product or product line. Instead, the WAP Forum promotes and supports all companies that are developing products based on the WAP specification.

As much as possible, the WAP Forum seeks to use existing industry standards in its own architecture and design. A WAP Gateway is required to communicate with other Internet nodes using the standard HTTP 1.1 protocol. Furthermore, the specification calls for wireless handsets to use the standard URL addressing scheme to request services.

It is also very important for the WAP Forum's specification to be developed in such a way that they complement existing standards. The WAP V1.0 specification is designed to sit on top of existing bearer channel standards so that any bearer standard can be used with the WAP protocols to implement complete product solutions.

Figure 34-4 shows a WAP phone; the following is the Nokia 7110 using WAP 1.1.

When the WAP Forum identifies a new area of technology where a standard does not exist, or exists but needs modification for wireless, it works to submit its specifications to other industry standards groups.

The WAP Forum currently has several different relationships with other standards bodies:

- The WAP Forum is submitting its specifications to the European Telecommunications Standards Institute (ETSI).
- The Cellular Telecommunications Industry Association (CTIA) has an official liaison officer to the WAP Forum.
- The WAP Forum has established a formal liaison relationship with the World Wide Web Consortium (W3C).
- The WAP Forum is in the process of forming liaison relationships with the Telecommunications Industry Association (TIA) and the Internet Engineering Task Force (IETF).

As new standards emerge, the WAP Forum will continue its active role in ensuring that these new standards remain compatible with the work of the

Figure 34-4
The WAP-enabled phone
(Source: Nokia)

WAP Forum. For example, the WAP Forum will be working with the W3C and IETF to evolve the HTML-Next Generation (NG) and HTTP-NG specifications to better meet the requirements of future wireless network technologies. In addition, the WAP Forum is carefully watching the development of the International Mobile Telecommunications-2000 (IMT-2000, or often 3G) family of standards by the International Telecommunication Union (ITU).

Full Industry Participation

The WAP Forum believes that the best technology standards are only possible with full industry participation. The WAP Forum is therefore open to any industry participant. By encouraging participation across the entire telecommunications industry, the WAP Forum is able to

■ Produce open standards that result from many industry experts working together

■ Develop consensus in the industry for how all the components of a solution will interoperate

■ Produce standards through an open and collaborative process—no one vendor receives favorable treatment and the entire industry benefits from the results

■ Benefit from the innovations of dozens of contributing companies rather than the efforts of only one or two vendors

Bearer Independence

To best address the needs of the widest possible population of end users, the WAP is designed to work optimally with all air interfaces. This principle enables the largest number of service providers, software developers, and handset manufacturers to benefit from one unified specification. Service providers can implement a common solution across their own disparate networks so that every subscriber has the best possible user experience on each network. Applications can be developed using one standard that will work across a variety of networks. Handset manufacturers can use the same software in all of their product lines, reducing development time and simplifying support issues.

By making minimal demands on the air interface itself, the WAP specification can operate on the widest number of air interfaces. It defines a protocol stack that can operate on high latency, low-bandwidth networks such as SMS or the upcoming GSM USSD channel.

Being air interface independent also makes the specification easy to extend to new networks and transports as they develop. As air interfaces become more sophisticated, the services they provide can be designed to comply with the WAP specification, further encouraging the use of one standard across all networks.

Device Independence

In addition to being air interface independent, the WAP specification is also independent of any particular device. Instead, it specifies the bare minimum functionality a device must have and has been designed to accommodate any functionality above that minimum.

Device independence offers similar benefits to bearer independence: applications developed for one standard can operate on a wide variety of devices that implement the specification; network operators gain a consistent user interface for their services across multiple vendors' handsets; application developers do not have to write separate versions of their code for different devices; and service providers can choose any standard-compliant device that meets their own unique market requirements. Device manufacturers are assured that they will have many applications written for their device by implementing the specification, yet are able to add their own brand features above and beyond the minimum standards to make their device unique in the marketplace. Another handset (Nokia) is shown in Figure 34-5.

Interoperability

Service providers must feel secure that their investments will yield benefits in the future. They will not be able to do so until equipment and software offered by different suppliers can be made to work together. The WAP specification has been designed to encourage easy, open interoperability between its key components. Any solution component built to be compliant

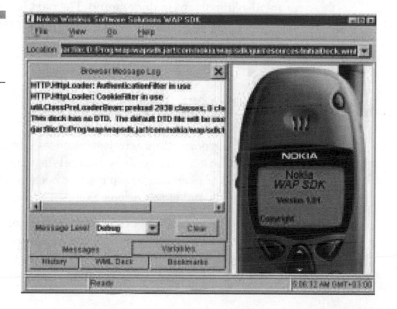

Figure 34-5
The unique WAP
phone
(Source: Nokia)

with the WAP specification can interoperate with any other WAP-compliant component. Service providers can choose equipment and software from multiple WAP-compliant vendors, selecting each piece of the solution that is appropriate for the service provider's particular needs.

Bearer and device independence both help foster interoperability. However, interoperability goes beyond these two principles to require that each WAP-compatible component will communicate with all other components in the solution network by using the standard methods and protocols defined in the specification. Interoperability provides clear benefits for handset manufacturers and infrastructure providers. Handset manufacturers are assured that if their device complies with the WAP specification, it will be able to interface with any WAP-compliant server, regardless of the manufacturer. Likewise, the makers of a WAP-compliant server are assured that any WAP-compliant handset will interface correctly with their servers.

Why WAP?

Providing Internet and Web-based services on a wireless data network presents many challenges to wireless service providers, application developers, and handset manufacturers. Although the obvious limitations are rooted in the nature of wireless devices and data networks, more fundamental differences are also important to understand. The next few sections outline the challenges that must be overcome to make wireless Internet access appealing to the average wireless subscriber.

Market Differentiation

Bringing computing power to a wireless handset opens an extensive new market for information access. This market is very different from the traditional desktop or even the laptop market because the subscriber has a different set of needs and expectations. Some of these differences include

■ **Ease of use** Despite the fact that using a desktop computer has become progressively easier over the last 5 years, a wireless computing device must be dramatically easier to use than even the simplest desktop computer. Computer novices may use these devices.

Furthermore, they will often be used in a dynamic environment where the mobile professional is engaged in multiple activities. Subscribers won't be focused on their handset the way they are when they are sitting in front of a desktop computer. Therefore, the devices must be extremely simple and easy to use. Applications built for these devices must therefore present the best possible user interface for quick and simple usage.

- **Market size** The growth and size of the wireless subscriber market has been phenomenal. The wireless market is enormous; it can afford and will demand optimized solutions.

- **Price sensitivity** Even with today's sub-$1,000 computers, a price difference of $50 between two models is not considered significant. However, a difference of $50 between two mobile handsets is very significant, especially after years of subsidized handset pricing by the service provider. Market studies have shown that a mass-market handset must be priced under $149 to be competitive. A solution must add significant value at a low cost to be effective in this market.

- **Usage patterns** Subscribers expect wireless data access to perform like the rest of their handset. The service should be instantly available, easy to use, and designed to be used for a few minutes at a time. Hourglass icons telling subscribers to wait will not be acceptable.

- **Essential tasks** As soon as professionals step out of the office, information needs and desires change. Wireless Internet subscribers will not want to use their handset to surf the Internet. They will have small, specific tasks that must be accomplished quickly. Subscribers will want to scan e-mail rather than read it all or see just the top stock quotes of interest. Receiving timely traffic alerts on the handset will be essential, whereas the same information may not be as valuable at the desktop. The best applications will give users a comprehensive, personalized summary of important information and will enable them to easily drill down for more detailed information.

Subtle Network Differences

Wireless data networks present a more constrained communication environment compared to wired networks. Because of fundamental limitations of power, available spectrum, and mobility, wireless data networks tend to have

- Less bandwidth
- More latency
- Less connection stability
- Less predictable availability

Furthermore, as bandwidth increases, the handset's power consumption also increases, which further taxes the already limited battery life of a mobile device. So, even as wireless networks improve their ability to deliver higher bandwidth, the power availability at the handset will still limit the effective throughput of data to and from the device. A wireless data solution must be able to overcome these network limitations and still deliver a satisfactory user experience.

Devices Are Definitely Different

Similarly, mass-market, hand-held wireless devices present a more constrained computing environment compared to desktop computers. Because of fundamental limitations of battery life and form factor, mass-market, hand-held devices tend to have

- Less powerful CPUs
- Less memory (ROM and RAM)
- Restricted power consumption
- Smaller displays
- Different input devices (for example, a phone keypad, voice input, and so on)

Because of these limitations, the user interface of a wireless handset is fundamentally different that that of a desktop computer. The limited screen size and lack of a mouse requires a different user interface metaphor than the traditional desktop graphical user interface (GUI).

These conditions are not likely to change dramatically in the near future. The most popular wireless handsets have been designed to be lightweight and fit comfortably in the palm of a hand. Furthermore, consumers desire handsets with longer battery life, which will always limit available bandwidth, and the power consumption of the CPU, memory, and display.

Because a performance gap will always exist between the very best desktop computers and the very best hand-held devices, the method used to deliver wireless data to these devices will have to effectively address this gap. As this gap changes over time, standards will have to continually evolve to keep pace with available functionality and market needs.

Questions

1. WAP stands for:
   a. Wired Application Products
   b. Wireless Application Products
   c. Wireless Adapter Protocol
   d. Wireless App Protocol

2. WAP is used for items like:
   a. PDA
   b. PBX
   c. Modems
   d. Key Systems
   e. Call Centers

3. One of the founders of WAP is _____.
   a. Lucent
   b. Cisco
   c. Samsung Wireless
   d. Unwired Planet

4. WAP is a _____.
   a. Telephone application
   b. Protocol
   c. Data Application
   d. Carrier application

5. The user interface on the phone is called _____.

    a. WAP

    b. WDC

    c. WLL

    d. WAE

6. The WAP markup language is called _____.

    a. XML

    b. HTML

    c. WML

    d. WDP

7. Security is provided on WAP using _____.

    a. WTLS

    b. SSL

    c. TCP

    d. SHTML

8. All future WAP-enabled phones will support _____.

    a. EDGE

    b. GSM

    c. TDMA

    d. GPRS

9. WAP is air-interface independent.   T/F

10. WAP does not use a browser or microbrowser because it is protocol independent.   T/F

3G Wireless

After reading this chapter and completing the questions, you will be able to:

■ Understand how third-generation (3G) wireless will change the course of hand-held communications

■ Describe the motivations to move toward 3G

■ Converse regarding the features and functions of 3G wireless

■ Explain the pieces that make up the new wireless data network

■ Understand the concept of the data transition to wireless

C ell phones are everywhere you look. So are two-way pagers. And soon, wireless hand-held computers like the Palm VII will be everywhere. With this wireless craze comes the desire for greater data access. It's no longer about using a phone to call your stockbroker—now it's about using your wireless device to check your portfolio, receive alerts, and make trades. The Internet and wireless personal devices are coming together. Emerging standards like 3G on the wireless carrier side and the wireless application protocol (WAP) and Wireless Markup Language (WML) on the data side are leading toward a wireless Internet—and every vendor wants to be at ground zero.

In the past, much emphasis has been placed on the use of a wireless telephone set to conduct day-to-day business. The trend in wireless communications exploded after the introduction of cellular communications in 1984. As the industry matured, the demand for more voice users continued to escalate. In 1992, Global System for Mobile Communications (GSM) was rolling out fast in the European marketplace, whereas in North America the networks were divided into digital rollout using Time Division Multiple Access (TDMA) or Code Division Multiple Access (CDMA) technologies. This meant that three different standards were being developed and used heavily throughout the world. Moreover, the analog networks were still fairly prominent using different standards and frequencies. This meant that as an organization began to deploy a wireless strategy in the industry (such as a carrier or a user), compatibility issues continued to play a dominant role in the decision process. One could not just choose what to use without taking into account the possibilities of international demands, local and roaming demands, and the use of the various integrated schemes to satisfy the road warrior. This began to place the burden of selection on the carrier and the end user organization alike.

Competition to be the leader in the industry revolved around the technology selected. Many organizations were getting tied up in knots trying to decide which technology to use. Rather than worrying about the choice of GSM, TDMA, or CDMA, a user should select on the basis of

- Coverage areas
- Pricing plans
- Cost of implementing
- Roaming charges (if any)
- Ease of use
- Long-term usage
- Battery life

Instead of describing the solutions, providers were busy arguing who had the best technology. This led to such an outcry by the end users that the standards committees decided that something different had to be done. This resulted in a study that looked at dual-mode handsets that could be used in digital mode when using the provider's technology decision, and analog mode when roaming between different networks that were not compatible. However, this was only a stopgap measure. More was required, especially when the user might roam between three different carriers. At the same time, analog networks were being displaced by digital networks. The set of

Figure 35-1
Evolution of wireless
standards

standards led to an evolution from first-generation (1G) to 3G wireless over a period of time, as seen in Figure 35-1. The figure also shows that the standards listed include the dial-up voice and the introduction of data on these networks.

Enter the Data

Just as the industry was wrestling with the choices between the use of analog or digital networks and the use of the type of digital (TDMA, CDMA, GSM), another phenomenon started to occur. The use of data transmission began to grow in use and in demand. Users wanted to move away from the circuit-switched data transmission to support packet-switched data because of all the hype of the Internet and the use of packet-switching technologies. Why not have the same efficiencies available on wireless networks? Therefore, the movement was toward data transmission, which was

- Better
- Faster
- Cheaper

To solve this problem, the evolution to 3G wireless standards set the stage to move from circuit data (dial-up) to packet data (IP or X.25). The trend is shown in Figure 35-2 as the movement toward packet-switched

Figure 35-2
The evolution to 3G
wireless data

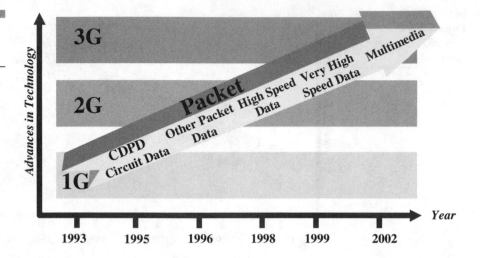

data evolved the industry even more. The packets of data are destined to move us beyond just basic voice calls and slow-speed data transfers. In fact, multimedia applications are actually where the industry is heading. Packet data can handle a variety of data streams and formats; thus it is determined to be the best solution on the road to 3G wireless solutions.

What to Call the Data Systems of the Future

It was not long ago when everyone was surrounded by a single set of terms and definitions. The telecommunications industry was rife with different three letter acronyms (TLAs) that no one understood. Just when we thought it was safe to come out of the telephone closets and use some terms, the industry began creating all new ones for the wireless industry. In Figure 35-3, the evolving data standards on the road to 3G created some rather unique data words and new data standards. These are shown in the figure, but explained in this section. The data speeds for the late 1990s operated at somewhere between 9.6 and 14.4 Kbps (if you were lucky). Later, the industry wanted to raise the bar for data transmission so they created the means of transmitting high-speed circuit-switched data (HSCSD) to operate at

Figure 35-3
 All roads lead to
UMTS.

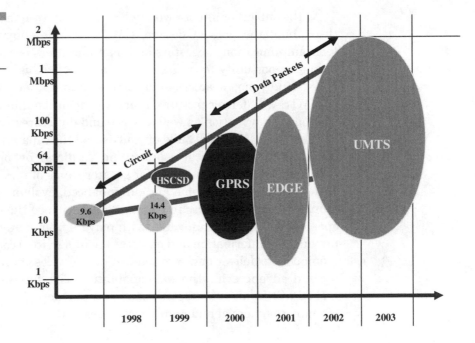

Figure 35-3
All roads lead to UMTS.

speeds of up to 64 Kbps. In 2000, the industry began to test and deploy commercial data speeds as overlays to GSM (internationally and U.S. based, such as VoiceStream) and TDMA (AT&T Wireless) networks using a technique called general packet radio services (GPRS). GPRS is still evolving and being tested to support speeds initially at 28.8 Kbps, but it ultimately should support speeds of 170 Kbps. No sooner will GPRS be installed and the movement will take us to a newer form of data transmission called enhanced data for GSM evolution (EDGE). EDGE is going to ultimately take the speeds up to 384-Kbps packet-switched IP or X.25 data.

The next step in the 3G of wireless communications is to use what is called universal mobile telecommunications services (UMTS). This is true 3G. UMTS is a set of standards designed to carry data at speeds of up to 2 Mbps. The bulk of these standards are designed around the GSM and TDMA architectures because of the proliferation of the technologies (68 percent worldwide use GSM and another 17 percent use TDMA). UMTS is one of the major new 3G mobile communications systems being developed within the framework, which has been defined by the ITU and known as IMT-2000.

As the subject of intense worldwide efforts on research and development throughout the present decade, UMTS has the support of many major telecommunications operators and manufacturers because it represents a unique opportunity to create a mass market for highly personalized and user-friendly mobile access to tomorrow's information society.

UMTS will deliver pictures, graphics, video communications, and other wideband information as well as voice and data directly to people who are on the move. UMTS will build on and extend the capability of today's mobile technologies (like digital cellular and cordless) by providing increased capacity, data capability, and a far greater range of services using an innovative radio access scheme and an enhanced, evolving core network. The launch of UMTS services in the year 2001 will see the evolution of a new, open communications universe, with players from many sectors (including providers of information and entertainment services) coming together harmoniously to deliver new communications services characterized by mobility and advanced multimedia capabilities. The successful deployment of UMTS will require new technologies, new partnerships, and the addressing of many commercial and regulatory issues.

What about the CDMA Folks?

As the industry has been rolling out the TDMA side of the business, the other part of the wireless industry has been moving also. In the CDMA architecture, we found that many of the high-speed circuit-switched data services were good for 19.6 to 64 Kbps already. However, the movement to 3G in CDMA steps through the evolution, all paths lead to 3G.

Before we discuss the evolution of specific products, we need to review the evolution of the IS-95 air interface, which was standardized by the Telecommunications Industry Association (TIA) in July 1993. Networks that utilize the IS-95 CDMA air interface and the ANSI-41 network protocol are branded as cdmaOne networks. IS-95 networks utilize one or more 1.25-MHz carriers and operate within the 800- and 1,900-MHz frequency bands.

The first commercial launch of a cdmaOne network was in Hong Kong in September 1995. Today, cdmaOne has more than 50 million subscribers worldwide. Some key benefits of the IS-95 air interface are soft handoffs (a make-before-break concept that reduces dropped calls) and increased capacity compared to Advanced Mobile Phone System (AMPS) networks. Currently, the cdmaOne product portfolio is designed from the ground up. It does the following:

- Maximizes the advantages of CDMA digital wireless technology
- Incorporates the efficiencies of IP—supports packet data at rates of up to 14.4 Kbps and packet-based transport on the backhaul

The original IS-95-A air interface standard was supplemented with the IS-95-B standard, which includes several improvements for hard-handoff algorithms in multicarrier environments and in parameters that affect the control of soft handoffs. Nonetheless, the primary change in the standard had to do with higher data rates for packet- and circuit-switched CDMA data; data rates of up to 115 Kbps can now be supported by bundling up to eight 14.4- or 9.6-Kbps data channels (14.4 Kbps $\times$ 8 = 115.2 Kbps). Today, some operators in Asia are implementing IS-95-B data with service rates of up to 64 Kbps.

The term 1X, derived from 1XRTT (radio transmission technology), is used to signify that the standard carrier on the air interface is 1.25 MHz— the same as for IS-95-A and IS-95-B. This standard can be implemented in existing spectrum or in new spectrum allocations. The standard also paves the way for the next phase of 3G networks: cdma2000 3X (IS-2000-A).

In brief, cdma2000 1X, which is implemented in existing spectrum allocations,

- Delivers approximately twice the voice capacity of cdmaOne
- Provides data rates of 144 Kbps
- Backward compatible with cdmaOne networks and terminals
- Enhances performance

IS-2000-A/cdma2000 3X

The cdma2000 3X standard was scheduled for completion in 2000. The term 3X, derived from 3XRTT, is used to signify three times 1.25 MHz or approximately 3.75 MHz. The cdma2000 3X multicarrier approach, or wideband cdmaOne, is an important part of the evolution of IS-95-based standards. In all likelihood, IS-2000-A will be followed by supplemental standards that offer additional functionality as the industry evolves. In short, cdma2000 3X

- Offers greater capacity than 1X
- Supports data rates of up to 2 Mbps
- Is backward-compatible with 1X and cdmaOne deployments
- Enhances performance even more

Third-Generation (3G) Wireless

3G systems will provide access, by means of one or more radio links, to a wide range of telecommunication services supported by the fixed telecommunication networks and to other services that are specific to mobile users. A range of mobile terminal types will be encompassed, linking to terrestrial and/or satellite-based networks, and the terminals may be designed for mobile or fixed use.

Key features of 3G systems are a high degree of commonality of design worldwide, compatibility of services, use of small pocket terminals with worldwide roaming capability, Internet and other multimedia applications, and a wide range of services and terminals. According to the International Telecommunication Union (ITU) International Mobile Telecommunications 2000 initiative (IMT-2000), 3G mobile system services are beginning to appear, subject to market considerations. Table 35-1 describes some of the key service attributes and capabilities expected of 3G systems.

On October 13, 2000, former President Clinton executed a memorandum that articulated the need to select radio frequency spectrum to satisfy the U.S.' future needs for mobile voice, high-speed data, and Internet-accessible wireless capability. The Presidential Memorandum established guiding principles for the Executive Agencies to be used in selecting spectrum that could be made available for 3G wireless systems, and strongly encouraged independent federal agencies to follow the same principles in any actions they might take related to the development of 3G systems.

Noting the joint spectrum management responsibilities of the executive branch and the Commission, the Presidential Memorandum directed the Secretary of Commerce to work cooperatively with the FCC with two goals in mind: (1) to develop a plan to select spectrum for 3G wireless systems by October 20, 2000, and (2) to issue by November 15, 2000, an interim report on the current spectrum uses and potential for reallocation or sharing of the

Table 35-1

Summary of 3G
Capabilities

3G System Capabilities	
Support of circuit and packet data	■ 144 Kbps or higher in high-mobility (vehicular) traffic ■ 384 Kbps for pedestrian traffic ■ 2 Mbps or higher for indoor traffic
Interoperability and roaming	■ Capability to interoperate among carriers ■ Roaming services available and transparent device determination
Common billing/user profiles	■ Sharing of usage/rate information between service providers ■ Standardized call detail recording ■ Standardized user profiles
Location and positioning services	■ Capability to determine geographic position of mobiles ■ Report it to both the network and the mobile terminal
Support of multimedia services/capabilities	■ Fixed and variable rate bit traffic ■ Bandwidth on demand ■ Asymmetric data rates in the forward and reverse links ■ Multimedia mail store and forward ■ Broadband access up to 2 Mbps

bands identified at the 2000 World Radio Communication Conference that could be used for 3G systems. These actions were taken to enable the Commission to identify spectrum for 3G systems by July 2001 and auction licenses by September 30, 2002.

3G wireless technology combines two powerful innovations: wireless communications and the Internet. Today's wireless devices are designed to transmit voice and brief text messages and cannot handle digital multimedia and other high-bandwidth Internet content. 3G devices, by contrast, provide high-speed mobile connections to the Internet and other communications networks, giving users full access to the rich content and commercial possibilities of the information superhighway.

Mobile phones and other wireless devices, such as personal digital assistants (PDAs) equipped with 3G technologies, enable users to surf the Internet at high speeds, as shown previously in Figure 35-4. The immediate goal is to raise transmission speeds from approximately 9.6 Kbps to 2 Mbps. However, 3G is not expected to be available commercially in North America

Figure 35-4
PDAs ready to surf
the Web with 3G

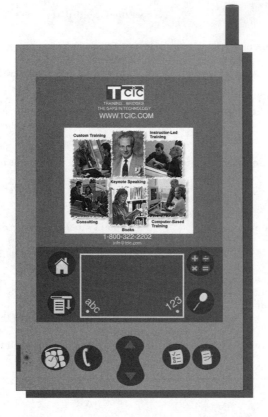

until at least 2003. Many feel that 3G is overhyped, comparing the rollout of 3G to the difficulties involved with creating standards for high-definition TV. Currently, the Internet is not friendly to mobile devices. But over time, the Internet will become more adaptable to mobility.

One of the biggest challenges facing 3G, and one that slowed work on the proposed standard, was negotiation between hardware makers and carriers who had vested interests in wideband CDMA and TDMA/FDMA technologies. This appears to have been overcome with the introduction in late 1999 of a new radio access technology called universal terrestrial radio access (UTRA), which was proposed by the 3G Partnership Project and combines elements of all three techniques. The problem with the UTRA specification is that it appears to give service providers choices for how to implement multiplexing on their systems—and that could mean incompatibility. Currently, five different standards can be selected from to implement a 3G solution from the carriers' perspective. These include UMTS, CDMA 2000, WCDMA, TD/CDMA and UWC-136.

Applications for 3G

Possible 3G applications are even more impressive. According to the International Telecommunication Union (ITU), 3G devices will be compact enough to fit into a pocket or handbag and will integrate the functions of a range of existing devices. The ITU suggests that the 3G device will function as a

- Phone
- Computer
- Television
- Pager
- Videoconferencing center
- Newspaper
- Diary
- Credit card

It will support not only voice communications, but also real-time video and full-scale multimedia via a screen that can be pulled out and flexible. It will also function as a portable address book and agenda, containing all the information about meetings and contacts and able to remind you automatically before an important appointment or automatically connect to an audio or videoconference at a specified time. It will automatically search the Internet for relevant news and information on preselected subjects, book your next holiday for you online, and download a bedtime story for your child, complete with moving pictures. It will even be able to pay for goods when you shop via wireless electronic funds transfer. In short, the new mobile handset will become the single, indispensable life tool, carried everywhere by everyone, just like a wallet or purse is today.[1]

---

[1] International Telecommunication Union, "The Next Generation of Mobile Communications." October 10, 2000.

Although some applications are already on the market, others are still developing. An example of this is the use of the 3G phones for TV reception. Figure 35-5 shows a TV included in a telephone. Can you imagine? Think of a person driving down the road today. Everyone is out to deny us access to cell phones because it distracts drivers from their duties as drivers. Now, instead of being distracted by a phone call, the risk is that we will be watching our favorite talk show host or soap opera on the TV (oops, I mean phone) while attempting to drive to and from work. This is a possibility.

What about the road warrior who is on the go all week long and needs to conduct business? Once again the 3G phones can be used as a videoconferencing device. Now not only will we call our office, we can actually host a meeting while driving down the road. We can see the party (parties) we are having a meeting with. Figure 35-6 shows the videoconferencing capability.

This just adds a new dimension to the overall risk of using cellular phones. First we were told that they cause cancer (a claim that has never been truly proven). Then we could use the phone to download our e-mail. The WAP-enabled phone enabled us to access our e-mail and Web sites, as

Figure 35-5
Television reception
at the handset
(Source: Samsung)

Figure 35-6
The videocon-
ferencing capability
(Source: Nokia)

Figure 35-7
WAP-enabled phones
provide e-mail and
Web access
(Source: Nokia).

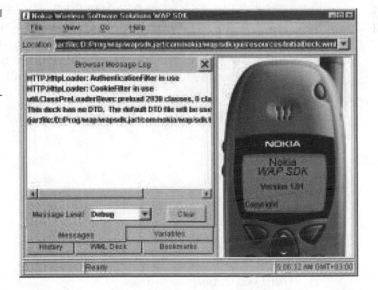

seen in Figure 35-7. What can we do besides make a phone call? 3G architectures were built for these pieces. To handle high-speed data access and
all of the personalized communications needs prepares the network and the
provider to be a one-stop shopping environment.

What Does It All Mean?

The sum of all the pieces is that much work still remains to be done before we see a true 3G architecture, handset, and application working together. Like all other services, the piece parts are forming and being introduced as fast as the vendors can develop them. Many proprietary solutions are creeping into the business (even though 3G is supposed to be an open standard). The applications and the speed are what everyone seems to be concentrating upon. However, 3G was supposed to be a universal standard for all vendors to build to in order to ensure compatibility and interoperability. This is still yet to happen, but there may be hope in the future.

More than 80 percent of all the wireless Internet users in the world are in Asia. Once 3G services are fully deployed in Japan, Korea, China, Hong Kong, and Malaysia, Internet penetration in the Asian region is expected to soar—making China, not the U.S., the largest wireless and Internet market in the world. Moreover, within the next two years, Asia as a whole may far surpass the U.S. with respect to the number of Internet and wireless users. China could have more Internet and wireless users than any other nation, and when combined with other Asian countries such as Japan and Korea, it will become a major force in the two revolutions shaping the new economy: the Internet and wireless technologies.

Currently, the U.S. is still reviewing the requirements for additional spectrum for 3G and is far from offering the types of services on the scale that will be offered abroad.

Questions

1. What does 3G stand for?
   a. Third goal
   b. TDMA generation
   c. TDMA global
   d. Third generation
2. What are the choices (technologies) that the vendors had?
   a. TMDA, CMDA, GSM
   b. FDMA, TMDA, GSM
   c. CDMA, TDMA, GSM
   d. TDMA/TDD, TDMA/FDMA, CDMA

3. What percent of users are on board with GSM?

   a. 68 percent

   b. 75 percent

   c. 85 percent

   d. 12 percent

4. In the future, the handset can be used for (select only one):

   a. VCR

   b. Data terminal

   c. Watch

   d. ATM card

5. In future applications, which application will enable us to see the other end of a call?

   a. TV set

   b. Videoconferencing set

   c. Telephone set

   d. Global positioning system

6. The movement was toward more data transmission at various speeds and the demand for (select only one):

   a. Better data

   b. Faster handset availability

   c. Cheaper quality of services

   d. Higher data error rates

7. What does GPRS mean?

   a. General packet data services

   b. General packet radio system

   c. Generic pocket radio system

   d. General packet radio service

8. For what technology is EDGE suited?

   a. TDMA

   b. FDMA

   c. GSM

   d. CDMA

9. What does the 3X mean in the term CDMA2000 3X?

    a. Third generation

    b. Three times more users

    c. Three separate networks

    d. Three times the normal channel size

10. What is the speed supported by EDGE?

    a. 384 Kbps

    b. 64 Kbps

    c. 170 Kbps

    d. 2 Mbps

Light Systems

After reading this chapter and completing the questions, you will be able to:

- Understand the use of light systems for wireless communications
- Discuss the operation of infrared light
- Evaluate the differences between light and radio systems
- Determine the possible risks associated with the wireless light systems
- Discuss the application of free-space optics

Transmitting light through the air provides another form of wireless communications. This can be an exciting opportunity to provide basic connectivity in a localized area at a very reasonable cost. Infrared light systems have been around for three decades but have never really caught on until recently. Clearly, the need to provide connectivity is the issue in any telecommunications environment. Infrared or laser beams can be considered in the overall corporate strategy if the bandwidth needs are limited to a few channels or if the communications system is being complemented or supplemented with this technique. Operating high in the frequency spectrum of laser beams in the terahertz (trillions of hertz) range, an invisible light beam is focused from a transmitter to a receiver over a very short distance, usually under 1.5 miles. Similar to radio waves, infrared light is subject to specific curtailments and impairments in transmission paths, such as

■ Very limited distances, typically less than 1.5 miles

■ The necessity of a clear line of sight in order to communicate with the other end

■ Limited bandwidth of approximately 155 Mbps. Unguided light systems were introduced in 1999 by Lucent Technologies that will operate at 2.488 Gbps, and it has been promised that we will see 10 Gbps in the near future.

■ Susceptibility to environmental disturbances and limitations, such as movement and electrical disruptions

■ Susceptibility to disruption from fog, dust, heavy rain, and other objects in the path because the fine beam of light might not be able to penetrate these impairments

With this in mind, the use of laser or infrared light still has its benefits. One would certainly have an opportunity to gain benefit under the right conditions. No single technique can be 100 percent effective; each has its own limitations and advantages. This is why so many options are available. Organizations can choose the transport systems that best meet their needs.

Despite the current technical bandwidth limitations, this technology has certain cost advantages and ease-of-use considerations. These factors keep this technology high on the acceptability scale of many users for many applications. The availability of low-powered solid-state laser diodes has opened up many possibilities. Producing cost-effective through-the-air transmission capabilities for voice, data, video, and now LAN traffic at native speeds will enhance a network immensely. Transmission through the air without a cable system infrastructure reduces the need for the right of way that would be necessary with a cable system. Furthermore, the infrared system falls into the category of nonlicensed technology. This removes many of the licensing requirements and associated delays and costs incurred with other systems. For distances of under 2 miles, this technique holds a wide range of exciting possibilities. To use such a system, however, three criteria must be considered:

■ The basic geometry of the system

■ Atmospheric conditions that will affect the transmission

■ Site selection for the installation of the link

System Geometry

As already mentioned, the infrared system is generally used in a point-to-point, line-of-sight application. Some multipoint and repeated systems have been developed, but these are rare. Three elements make up the basic system, including

- The transmitter, where the signal is modulated from its original electrical form into a light beam
- The medium used—in this case, air
- The receiver, which demodulates the light back into its original electrical form

These basic components are shown integrated into a complete laser system in Figure 36-1. In this figure, the components look like bars; this is for representation only.

The data is input into the transmitter, where it is modulated into a light beam. The raw laser beam is a very narrow beam of light (the actual light is referred to as monochromatic) that has very little divergence or spreading. Theoretically, the beam is usable by the receiver in its raw form, but in reality, it is extremely difficult to aim and maintain this raw light beam. Therefore, the raw light beam must pass through a lens that will produce a divergent beam. This helps to solve the initial limitation of the beam itself. However, it also imposes some distance limitations on the transmitted signal. Because the lens creates the divergence, it reduces the distance from the transmitter to the receiver by diffusing the strength of the beam. Safety requirements also limit the output power of the beam. The transmitter generally uses a constant diameter of light, called a footprint, regardless of the distance being used.

The incoming light is focused by a collector, or collecting lens, that sends the received beam to an optical detector. The receiver uses an angle of

Figure 36-1
The basic components of an infrared system

Rear Panel

acceptance (RAA) of approximately 3 to 5 mR to provide a degree of selectivity. The transmit beam divergence angle (TBA) is always greater than the receiver angle of acceptance. The receiver needs a minimum level of incident light in order to demodulate the light back to the original electrical input. Trade-offs in the size, complexity, and cost of the receiver lens limit the range. Figure 36-2 shows the receiver angle of acceptance and the transmitter beam divergence angle.

The setup in the previous paragraph is a one-way, point-to-point system (called a simplex system). However, most applications need two-way communications; for this, a duplex system can be used. To create a duplex system, two simplex systems are coupled together. Figure 36-3 shows the creation of a duplex system. Both systems will operate with lasers of the same wavelength (typically 830 nm). This is an advantage of a light-based system because the lasers do not switch from transmitting to receiving like a radio system would. (Remember that in radio systems, two separate sets of frequencies are used to keep the transmit frequency apart from the receive frequency.) A further feature of focused light transmission systems is that multiple systems can be mounted close to each other without causing interference as long as the angle the systems make with each other is

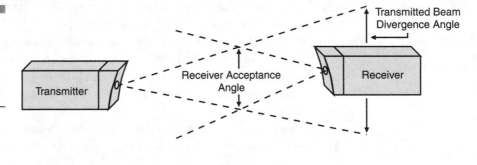

Figure 36-2
The transmitted beam divergence angle compared to the receiver acceptance angle

Figure 36-3
A duplex system is created by linking two simplex systems together.

Figure 36-4
Multiple systems can
be installed close
together without
conflict.

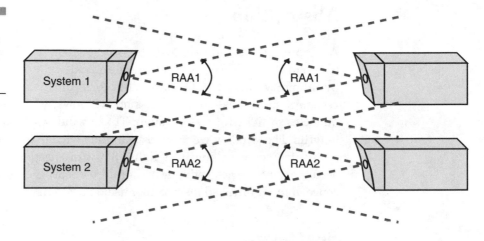

greater than the original angle of the receiver. Figure 36-4 shows the use of multiple systems. Two light beams are transmitted across the same path, yet they are kept separate because the angles of acceptance are different.

Atmospheric Conditions

The effects of atmosphere on light transmission will influence the total overall performance of the system. The severity and the duration of these conditions will affect the distance and performance. All electromagnetic radiation used in any communications system is affected by the atmosphere. However, each of the transmission systems is affected differently, whether it is a low/high-frequency radio, microwave radio, or laser transmission. The wavelength of each transmission determines the effects on the actual transmission. The three most significant conditions that affect laser transmission are

- Absorption
- Scattering
- Shimmer

All three conditions can reduce the energy at the receiver, which will then affect the reliability and the bit error levels. These three conditions are covered in more detail.

Absorption

Absorption is caused primarily by water vapor (H_2O) and carbon dioxide (CO_2) in the air. The density of water and carbon monoxide are conditioned by humidity and altitude. Gases that form in the atmosphere have many resonant bands, called transmission windows, which enable specific frequencies of light to pass through. These windows occur at various wavelengths. The window we are most familiar with is that of visible light. The near-infrared wavelength of light (830 nm) used in laser transmission occurs at one of these windows; therefore absorption is not generally a big concern in an infrared laser transmission system.

Scattering

Scattering has a greater effect than absorption. The atmospheric scattering of light is a function of the wavelength of the light and the number and size of scattering elements in the air. The optical visibility along the path is directly related to the number and size of the scattering particles. The three most common scattering elements in the air that will affect laser beam transmission are as follows.

Fog and smog   Fog appears when the relative humidity of air is brought to an appropriate saturation level. Some of the nuclei then grow through condensation into water droplets. Attenuation by fog is directly attributable to water droplets less than a few microns in radius. The result of the scattering is that a reduced percentage of the transmitted light reaches the receiver.

Visualize the situation of driving a vehicle in dense fog. The headlights on the car are somewhat useless. Try turning on the high beams and see what difference this action makes. The resultant scattering of the visible light from the headlights makes it almost impossible to see. The light is being reflected back at the vehicle as well as being scattered in all directions. This is exactly how fog affects the infrared light beam.

Smog's effects are similar to those of fog, but not as severe. This is because of the difference in radius of the particulate matter. Consequently, fog is the limiting factor in laser transmission performance.

Rain   Although the liquid content of a heavy shower is 10 times the density of a dense fog, the radius of a raindrop is approximately 1,000 times that of a fog droplet. This is the primary reason that attenuation via rain is 100 times less than that via fog. Think about this for a moment; when fog is created, the saturation level in the air is very high, but the droplets are much finer. In rain, although more liquid is falling, the coarse drops don't affect the transmission as much. Visualize that more space is between the drops of rain than between the droplets in fog; therefore the light can get through rain much more easily.

When you are driving in a heavy rainfall, the headlights still penetrate the raindrops and give greater visibility over a greater distance. Even when you turn on the high beams, the distance visibility is better than with the low beams. A certain amount of the light is still being reflected back at the vehicle and scattered in all directions, but more is penetrating the rain. The same results occur with the transmission of the laser beam through the rain. It would take an extremely heavy rain (greater than 5 inches per hour) to significantly reduce the transmission of the laser beam.

Snow The effects of snow on laser transmission fall somewhere between those of fog and rain, depending on the level of water particles in the snow. A very wet snow is close to rain, and an extremely dry snow is similar to fog. Visualize driving through a dense snowstorm. Driving through a heavy, wet snow is like driving through a heavy rain. It is not all that pleasurable, but at least the light penetrates the snow and visibility is achieved. However, when a whiteout occurs, the ability to get the light through the snow is significantly reduced. The light appears to be reflecting right back at the vehicle, rendering all attempts to increase visibility useless. The same effect occurs with a laser transmission.

Shimmer

Picture driving down a long road on a hot day. As you look toward the horizon, it appears that water is on the road. As you look closer, you can see what appear to be heat waves shimmering off the ground. This is the direct result of a combination of factors including

- Atmospheric turbulence
- Air density
- Light refraction
- Cloud cover
- Wind

These factors combined cause disturbances similar to a laser beam passing through the atmosphere. As local conditions begin to combine, shimmer begins to affect the transmission. Shimmer imposes a low-frequency variation on the amount of light reaching the receiver. This variance could result in excessive data error rates or video distortion on a laser communication system. By using simple, proven techniques such as frequency modulation (FM) and automatic gain control (AGC) in the system, the effects of shimmer can be minimized. Moving the equipment several meters above the heat source will also reduce the effects of shimmer.

Site Selection

Proper site selection is an equally important factor. To ensure successful installation and use, several factors must be considered, such as

- Clear line of sight
- Mounting conditions
- Avoiding adverse conditions
- Mounting structures

Each of these factors is important. Diligence must be applied.

Clear Line of Sight

When setting up a transmission system, a clear line of sight is needed. This means that nothing can obstruct the light. The two ends must physically see each other or the system will not work: it is as simple as that. The laser beams should not be directed through or near wires (such as electric wires, telephone, and cable TV). Trying to force the light through tree limbs is not a good idea. As Figure 36-5 shows, getting over cables and wires is important. Allowances must be made for the growth of tree branches over time (Figure 36-6).

The system can be mounted either indoors or out. Figure 36-7 shows the system mounted indoors. The light beam passes through glass. The glass must not have any reflective coating or tinting; these might impair the beam's capability to pass through.

Figure 36-5
Towers may be
necessary to keep the
path above electric or
telephone wires.

Figure 36-6
A clear path must be
ensured for the
transmission.

Adverse Mounting Conditions

Few precautions must be dealt with when mounting the unit. It is important to ensure that the maximum signal strength is received and that the beam is not inadvertently misdirected. These considerations include avoiding heat sources, water obstructions, east-west orientations, and vibration.

Heat sources Heat scintillation (or shimmer) occurs as a result of differences in the index of refraction of air caused by temperature. The air might act as a lens that incorrectly steers the laser beam. The beam should not be directed over exhaust

Figure 36-7
With proper care, the
laser can be used
indoors to pass
through glass.

Reflective Coating

WARNING!
DO NOT USE ON
GLASS WITH REFLECTIVE
COATING.

vents, cooling towers, chimneys, smokestacks, or large air-
conditioning units.

Water obstruction   Water droplets on glass can redirect the light.
To prevent this when using the system indoors, use an awning
above the window. If building codes preclude using an awning,
mount the unit as high as possible on the glass. This will prevent
buildup of water on this section of the glass because the water will
run down quickly.

East-west orientation   The angle of acceptance is designed to be
quite narrow. Any extraneous infrared light passing directly into
this angle of acceptance will be accepted, thus causing errors.
East-west shots that have direct sunlight on the same axis will
cause interference. The sun emits infrared light, and this cannot
be filtered out. Therefore, a system will be blinded for periods
when the sun's axis is the same as that of the beam from the
system.

Vibration   Both the transmitter and receiver deal with very
narrow beams of light. The smallest movement of the transmitter
or receiver can severely limit transmission or reception. The
system could even lose its angle totally, resulting in an outage.

Licensing Requirements

Because infrared and laser beam technology employs wavelengths in the invisible light spectrum, no licensing is required. The use of light fortunately falls into the frequency spectrum that has no regulatory guidelines. The U.S. government has not figured out how to charge for the use of light, nor can they determine how much we use. Therefore, they can't tax it on a usage-sensitive basis. Because the government cannot figure this out, neither can the telephone companies. This, of course, makes it much easier to deal with the technology itself, allowing an organization to place a system in operation quickly.

Unlike radio technology, where the bulk of the frequency spectrum requires licenses and path clearances (with limited exceptions) from the regulatory bodies around the world, the use of light theoretically causes no interference between systems. Thus, use of this spectrum is allowed with little to no coordination effort. So long as the acceptance angle of one receiver does not coexist on the exact same axis with that of another, no problems should occur. This is an attractive feature of light-based systems.

Bandwidth Capacities

The system's bandwidth can cover a myriad of capacities, depending on the configuration purchased. The specific application must be considered in terms of the bandwidth necessary as well. At the high end of the bandwidth, the systems today can deliver as much as 16-Mbps throughput for LAN-to-LAN connections on a token-passing ring network. Point-to-point systems at 155 Mbps are used for LANs and MANs. Thus, one could say that the current bandwidth is 16 to 155 Mbps. However, other systems are designed to meet the needs of the user interface. An example of the capacities is summarized in Table 36-1. In this table, the needs are met by different systems at the capacities required to meet the application. In several of these systems, the pricing is dependent on the actual needs.

Table 36-1

Summary of
Various Systems
Available on the
Market and the
Application Used

Bandwidth	Application
10 Mbps	Ethernet data link
4 and 16 Mbps	Token-passing ring
1.544 / 6.312 Mbps	T1/T2 capacity data/video
4 × 1.544 Mbps	Quad T1 voice/data
RS-232 to 19.2 Kbps	Data transceivers
RS-422A to 2.048 Mbps	Data transceivers
Audio 20 to 20 KHz	Audio services

Applications

As noted in Table 36-1, infrared and laser technologies have several applications. These are addressed in the following section as they pertain to a need for connectivity from site to site. In the following scenarios, a typical customer with two sites (buildings) located approximately 1,000 meters apart, whether on a single campus or in two buildings in the same town, needs to provide various forms of connectivity between these sites. After the customer looks at the alternatives, the choice is between

- A direct burial cable (copper, coax, or fiber)
- A microwave radio system
- An infrared laser system

Although more considerations and information are needed to arrive at any conclusion, the following might play as an active comparison.

The Cable Decision

On looking at the cable scenario, the customer is faced with the extraordinary costs of digging a trench, laying a conduit, and running a cable connection to the two buildings. Additionally, the necessary right of way might be extremely difficult to obtain. The customer decides that a cable-based solution is not appropriate in this situation. Note that another alternative exists: the use of local leased-line facilities from the local exchange carrier (LEC) or a competitive access provider (CAP). However, the long-term leased-line rental costs are not attractive to the customer.

The Radio Decision

Looking at the area and the potential ordinances and variances that would be required in this scenario, the microwave decision is also determined to be feasible only if another alternative cannot be found. Given that certain forms of licensing are required and that a clear path is necessary in a very heavily installed radio area, the costs and time constraints are greater than the customer wishes to endure. The customer is not even sure that investing all this time and effort in the process will result in the granting of a license. Hence, the microwave choice is ruled out.

The Infrared Decision

Because the cable and the microwave choices are not that attractive, the logical choice is to use an infrared system. No licensing requirements are necessary, so the system can be put into action as soon as the acquisition is made. Because no right-of-way constraints impede the process, it can be handled appropriately and quickly. An added benefit is that no monthly recurring charges will occur for the use of the facilities as they would with leased lines. Finally, implementation requires no major tower, power equipment, cable entrances, or other construction projects.

The cost of buying the system is also very attractive because a one-time outlay of less than $20,000 is all that is required. The customer also takes into consideration the fact that if a move from one of the buildings is ever necessary, the system can be packed up and moved along with the rest of the office equipment. Assuming that a clear line of sight can be obtained and that the distance does not exceed the specifications of the system, it can be back into action in a matter of hours. This is not the case with the other options. The infrared laser system is the clear winner in this particular scenario. However, what about the application? Regardless of the application, the same rules apply. However, in this particular scenario, the applications might include the following:

The Use of Infrared Technology to Link Two LANs Together   The technology can link a token ring-to-token ring network together at native speeds. Either a 4- or 16-Mbps capacity can be applied in this example. In Figure 36-8, two LANs are linked together at native speeds. This means that the LANs are connected at the same speed at which the LAN operates. This allows for transparent connectivity at the full-rated speed of the network itself for a price of approximately $35,000 for a full 16 Mbps, or $26,000 for 4 Mbps, rather than slowing the transport down to some lower speed. If a bridging arrangement is used in this example, the total throughput is limited to a speed of 1.544 Mbps or less.

Infrared Laser Technology Used to Link Two Ethernet LANs   Figure 36-9 shows the use of infrared laser technology to link two Ethernet LANs together at a native speed of 10 Mbps. A different system is used in this example, with the native throughput operating at the full-rated 10 Mbps, rather than using a slower bridging arrangement that runs at 1.544 Mbps or less. The system is priced at around $15,000.

In both of these cases, the alternatives to these connections could be leased T1/E1-speed lines at connections slower than the LAN operating speed. This could potentially cause network congestion because the

Figure 36-8

Linking two token ring LANs together at a native speed of 4 or 16 Mbps provides transparent connectivity.

Figure 36-9
Infrared can link two
Ethernet LANs
together at a native
speed of 10 Mbps.

throughput is buffered to accommodate the line speed. Further, the leased line of up to 1 mile from a local operating company (telco) could cost as much as $700 to $1,000 per month. The payback on this arrangement would obviously be dramatic—gaining the additional speed and still paying for the system in less than 2 to 3 years, depending on the system selected. Furthermore, if the native speeds were leased from the local telco, the costs for the services could be as much as $1,800 to $2,400 depending on the speed selected, thereby producing a return on the investment in less than 12 to 16 months. This is for the close-in services. Complete installation of a microwave system could cost as much as $80,000 to $100,000—three to four times the cost of infrared. As can be seen for this environment, the use of the infrared system has some definite advantages.

Connecting PBX to PBX Using a Digital Transmission System   The connection of PBX to PBX using a digital transmission system for tie line capabilities between systems using a quad T1 capability for voice connectivity is another application. Figure 36-10 shows this arrangement with a digital trunk interface connection at each end of the system. In this particular situation, 56/64 Kbps of voice connections are provided with 24 channels on each of the four T1s, resulting in 96 digital voice connections. This would be a prime case for connecting two PBXs in very close proximity to a single network or a means of providing other voice-networked services such as voice messaging, off-premises extension, and so on. For a quad T1 service, the infrared system would price out at approximately $23,000, yielding a net payback time of less than 1 year, given four T1s at $1,000 per month rental from the local telco.

Figure 36-10
Linking PBXs together with up to four T1s for tie lines. DTI cards are used in the PBX to yield up to a 96-PCM circuit at 64 Kbps.

T1/T2 Service Between Two Sites The provision of a T1/T2 service between two sites to provide a 6-Mbps channel or four 1.544-Mbps channels for videoconferencing capabilities at compressed video standards is shown in Figure 36-11. These compression rates deliver superior-quality video compared to the more compressed speeds currently being offered in the industry (such as 256-, 384-, or 512-Kbps video services). This service would cost approximately $15,000, and would certainly deliver a return on investment in less than 1 year.

Infrared High-Speed Digital Dataphone Services Figure 36-12 shows the use of an infrared service to provide for high-speed digital dataphone services (DDS) using a host computer. In this scenario, a DDS service can be replaced with the system between these two buildings, whereby a statistical time-division multiplexer (stat-mux) or a subrate multiplexer can be used to provide several 9.6- to 19.2-Kbps data channels at the remote site. This system would cost approximately $10,000, but a DDS service between these two sites at 56 Kbps could cost as much as $1,800 per month. This would yield a payback in less than 6 months.

Figure 36-11
The infrared system can deliver speeds of up to 6 Mbps (T2) for videoconferencing or four links at 1.544 Mbps (T1).

Figure 36-12
The infrared system
can replace multiple
DDS service for data
connections to a host
computer at 9.6–
19.2 Kbps each.

These examples are merely representative of the types of connections that can be provided at a 1:1 ratio. Clearly, mixing and matching the services on these infrared systems would offer even greater returns on investment.

Can the System Carry LAN Traffic Transparently?

Obviously, the question always comes up as to whether an infrared system can really carry true LAN native speeds. For this to occur, several conditions must be met.

First, the system must have the bandwidth capacity to carry the native LAN traffic. This has been evidenced in these scenarios, where the system throughput is at least 4, 10, or 16 Mbps.

Second, the system might not add significant latency to the network because the entire LAN is based on very specific timing for the delivery of the frames on the network. Should the latency become a problem, the frames will not be delivered in time, causing a discarded frame or a network time-out, which could require resynchronization of the network to recover timing. In either case, transmission speed of the infrared system across the air would approximate 3.3 nanoseconds per meter. A 1,000-meter distance between these systems would add only a 3,300-nanosecond latency to the transport of the frame. Further, the system must modulate the signal onto the medium with some added delay based on the equipment. If a standard delay of approximately 30 nanoseconds is added for the modulation and the demodulation process, then an additional 60 nanoseconds of delay is added. These delays should fall well within the defined tolerance levels of the networks.

Third, the connection arrangement must either fall within the scope of an access to a bridge or repeater for the cable system in an Ethernet world or else be connected as a station or at a multistation access unit (MAU) for a token ring network. Once again, these connections are easily made with the use of the infrared interfaces and the network components.

Advantages of Infrared

The use of infrared technology has advantages. The benefits are quite numerous and should be continually considered whenever a connection is required, rather than immediately ruling this technology out. Many organizations automatically discount this as an old technology not worthy of consideration. The more astute telecommunications person keeps it in mind as an option, at least until some other technology proves to be either better suited for the job or more cost effective. Some of the major advantages of infrared include the following:

- Immune to radio frequency interference (RFI) and electromagnetic interference (EMI)
- Reasonably high bandwidth available
- Secure technology, more so than a radio-based technique
- Cost effective
- Easy to install
- Efficient when dealing with a potential move of the system
- No license required

- Systems can traverse similar paths without interference
- Can be up and running in a matter of hours
- Supports multiple standard interfaces
- Handles voice, data, video, and LAN traffic either separately or on the same system, depending on application

Disadvantages of Infrared

As with any technological invention and use, infrared has pros and cons. The primary disadvantages of infrared are not as dramatic, but should be factored into the equation. Because the use of a light-based system such as this is primarily based on actual need, these disadvantages exist:

- Very limited distances, 1.5 miles at most, depending on the manufacturer and the rate of speed being used
- Concern over the use of a laser in an office environment
- Negative effects of vibration
- Impairment by atmospheric disturbances of reception of the beam from the transmitter
- Risk of exposing cleaning personnel to the light (laser) beam
- Needs for a clear path in a line of sight, regardless of any other condition
- Need for stable mounting because of the sway of buildings, mounts, poles, or trees—very little tolerance can be allowed as a result of the small footprint of the received signal

Fiber-Optic-Compatible Systems

A newer product has emerged on the market that utilizes a fiber-optic system of wave-division multiplexing services with up to four clear channels of pulse frequency modulation video or digital data signals per wavelength window via one multimode fiber. Although this is not a wireless technique, the concept is similar to a development that has been touted as free-space optics. In the conceptual model of this newer service, vendors are creating the bandwidth of a fiber-optic channel capacity across free airwaves: hence the name free space as opposed to capacity inhibited by a piece of glass cable. A standard fiber-based system uses different wavelengths to carry the channels of communication across a glass fiber. The free-space optics system uses a different color of light in a different wavelength to carry various streams of voice, data, or video transmission over short distances. Obviously, because this concept uses laser beams in free space, it is necessary to use low-power output devices. Distances of approximately 3 to 5 miles are being discussed at this time. Some of the applications for this free-space optics system will include, but not be limited to

- Security and surveillance systems
- Multimedia learning over a short distance
- Video multiplexing using NTSC, PAL, and SECAM standards
- Digital data at native speeds
- Digital voice transmission

Low power will be a requirement to prevent any damage from the effects of the laser output in close confines, such as major metropolitan downtown areas. The system will also have to meet the requirements for infrared systems, such as not being too close to pedestrian traffic. However, because the free-space optics system operates in the visible light spectrum, the signal will be less impeded by the various atmospheric conditions that affect the operation of an infrared system.

The system will also be fully modular and easily transportable, as with an infrared system. This will provide the flexibility to set up and operate a transmission quickly. Because this system will use light beams traveling across the airwaves, the licensing issue will not come into play. The bandwidth of these systems will range from approximately 2 to 40 MHz, yielding data rates of up to 16 Mbps for native LAN traffic at the LAN speed. Wavelengths will be 750, 780, 810, and 840 nanometers.

The use of this form of communications medium will obviously offer some very attractive options to end users for access to the long-distance carrier's point of presence (POP) and ultimate access to the long-distance networks. Local area, campus area, metropolitan area, and wide area networks will all have some use of the free-space optics systems. Consider the use of such a system as an alternative to access the long-distance network or as a means of bypassing the local loop in the telephone company arena.

Questions

1. Infrared light systems have been around for _____ years but have never really caught on until recently.

   a. 3

   b. 10

   c. 30

   d. 33

2. Infrared systems typically operate over less than 1.5 miles.   T/F

3. The three elements that make up the basic system include _____, _____, and _____.

4. Normal infrared systems have limited bandwidth of approximately:

   a. 10 Mbps

   b. 50 Mbps

   c. 155 Mbps

   d. 2.488 Gbps

5. Lucent Technologies created a _____ optics system capable of carrying 2.488 Gbps.

6. The three most significant conditions that affect laser transmission are:

   a. Absorption, scattering, and shimmer

   b. Absorption, fog, and smog

   c. Rain, snow, and sleet

   d. Dust, birds, and trees

7. Absorption is caused primarily by water vapor and carbon dioxide in the air.   T/F

8. What is the limiting factor in laser transmission performance?

   a. Smog

   b. Fog

   c. Dirt

   d. Dust

9. Heat scintillation or _____ occurs as a result of differences in the index of refraction of air caused by temperature.

   a. Shatter

   b. Scatter

   c. Shimmer

   d. Smatter

10. Point-to-point systems at _____ Mbps are used for LANs and MANs.

    a. 1.544 Mbps

    b. 10 Mbps

    c. 16 Mbps

    d. 155 Mbps

SONET and SDH

After reading this chapter and completing the questions, you will be able to:

- Discuss the benefits of the fiber standards
- Understand the speeds of SONET and SDH
- Determine what the differences are in WDM and DWDM
- Understand the SONET link architecture
- Explain the basic components of the model

All of the digital transmission speeds discussed earlier were initially set to be carried on the existing wired systems in place at the telephone company and interexchange carrier levels. These systems included microwave, coaxial, and twisted-pair copper wires. As newer fiber-optic systems were introduced, a new synchronous digital hierarchy (SDH) evolved. Throughout the world, SDH was accepted, yet in the U.S. the term *synchronous optical network* (SONET) was adopted. Although the international and U.S. versions of SDH/SONET are very close, they are not identical.

SONET defines a means to increase throughput and bandwidth through a set of multiplexing parameters. These roles provide certain advantages to the industry, such as

- Reduced equipment requirements in the carriers' network
- Enhanced network reliability and availability
- Conditions to define the overhead necessary to facilitate better network management
- Definitions of the multiplexing functions and formats to carry the lower level digital signals (such as DS-1, DS-2, and DS-3)
- Generic standards encouraging interoperability between different vendors' products
- A flexible means of addressing current as well as future applications and bandwidth usage

SONET defines the optical carrier (OC) levels and the electrical equivalent rates in the synchronous transport signals (STS) for the fiber-based transmission hierarchy.

Background Leading to SONET Development

Prior to the development of SONET, the initial fiber-based systems used in the PSTN were all highly proprietary. The proprietary nature of the products included the following:

- Equipment
- Line coding
- Maintenance
- Provisioning
- Multiplexing
- Administration

The carriers (local and long-distance providers) were frustrated with the proprietary products because of interoperability problems, sole-source vendor solutions (which held the carriers hostage to one vendor), and cost issues. These carriers approached the standards committees and demanded that a set of operational standards be developed that would enable them to mix and match products from various vendors. In 1984, a task force was established to develop such a standard. The resultant standard became SONET.

The SONET Line Rates

SONET defines a technique to carry many signals from different sources and at different capacities through a synchronous optical hierarchy. The flexibility and robustness of SONET are some of its strongest selling points. Additionally, in the past, many of the high-speed multiplexing arrangements (DS-2 and DS-3) used bit interleaving to multiplex the data streams through the multiplexers. SONET uses a byte-interleaved multiplexing format. This is a strong point because it keeps the basic DS-0 intact throughout the network, making it easier to perform diagnostics and troubleshooting. Byte interleaving simplifies the process and provides better end-to-end management.

The base level of a SONET signal is called the synchronous transport signal level 1 (STS-1) operating at 51.84 Mbps. The first step in using the SONET architecture is to create the STS-1. SONET specifies a synchronous transport signal (level 1) of 51.84 Mbps, which is a DS3 with extra overhead. The overhead provides diagnostic and maintenance capabilities on each synchronous transport signal (STS). The optical equivalent of the STS-1 is an optical carrier level 1 (OC-1). This is the basic building block for chunks of bandwidth as they are multiplexed together to form much higher capacities. Increments of SONET include the capacities shown in Table 37-1. These transport systems and carrier levels work from the base of a T3 plus overhead creating an STS-1.

SONET goes further than just defining the multiplexed values of speed. It breaks the architecture of the link into three separate steps for purposes of defining the interfaces and defining responsibility. These layers include (a fourth is added to describe the layer-by-layer responsibilities)

- **Photonic layer**   Deals with the transport of bits and the conversion from an STS electrical pulse into an OC signal in light pulses.
- **Section layer**   Deals with the transport of the STS-N frame across a physical link. The functions of the section layer include scrambling, framing, and error monitoring.

Table 37-1

SONET Rates

	The SONET Hierarchy		
Electrical Signal	**Optical Value**	**Speed**	**Capacity**
STS-1	OC-1	51.84 Mbps	28 DS-1 or 1 DS-3
STS-3	OC-3	155.520 Mbps	84 DS-1 or 3 DS-3
STS-12	OC-12	622.08 Mbps	336 DS-1 or 12 DS-3
STS-24	OC-24	1.244 Gbps	672 DS-1 or 24 DS-3
STS-48	OC-48	2.488 Gbps	1,344 DS-1 or 48 DS-3
STS-192	OC-192	9.953Gbps	5,376 DS-1 or 192 DS-3
STS-768 [1]	OC-768	40 Gbps	21,504 DS-1 or 768 DS-3

Other rates exist, but these are the most popularly implemented.

---

[1] The OC-768 rate and STS-768 rate are newly defined. As the capacities are increased, the rates will follow.

- **Line layer**   Deals with the reliable transport path of overhead and payload information across a physical system.
- **Path layer**   Deals with the transport of network services such as DS1 and DS3 between path-terminating equipment.

SONET incorporates each of these into architecture such that overhead and responsibilities are clearly defined. Figure 37-1 shows this layered architecture. Note that the four layers are shown in this graphic. Actually, the photonic and section layers are one, but have been subdivided for clarity in showing the structure. The photonic and section layers deal with the physical medium, or the OSI layer 1 protocols.

The SONET architecture actually consists of three parts:

- The *section* is defined as the transport between two repeating functions or between line-terminating equipment and a repeater.
- The *line* is defined as the transport of the payload between two pieces of line-terminating equipment.
- The *path* is defined as the transport of the payload between two pieces of path-terminating equipment (multiplexers and so on) or the end-to-end circuit.

Figure 37-1
The SONET protocol stack

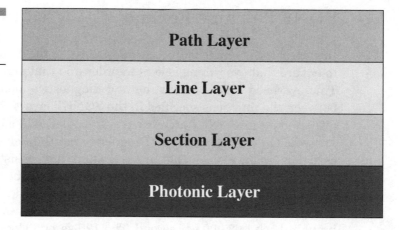

Figure 37-1
The SONET protocol stack

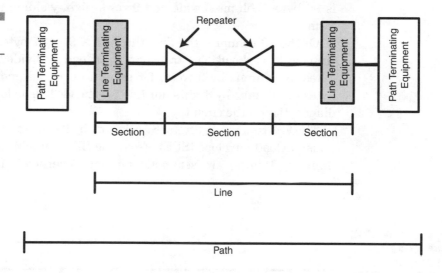

Figure 37-2
The link architecture

This is shown in Figure 37-2, where the pieces are laid out on a plane. The graphic shows how the pieces all work together in a fiber link. The fiber specification is what was originally used in SONET (and SDH internationally); however, newer microwave and satellite termination equipment is being introduced to provide the same capacities and formats. SONET defines the responsibility of the carriers in multiplexing the signal onto the physical medium, as well as the points of demarcation for the various carriers involved with the circuit.

SONET Frame Format

In each of the layers listed, overhead is added to the data being transported to ensure that everything is kept in order and that errors can be detected. This overhead allows for testing and diagnostics along the entire route between the functions specified in the SONET layers. A new frame size is also used in the SONET architecture. The older M13 asynchronous format just couldn't cut the mustard. In order to get the network back to a synchronous timing element, a frame is created that consists of 90 octets (8-bit bytes) across and 9 rows (810 bytes) down. This is the OC-1 frame, or the equivalent of the DS3 frame plus the extra overhead. However, with the change in size, the frequency of frames generated across the network is now brought back to 8,000 per second. The 125-second clocking and timing for the digital network can be reestablished. The frame shown in Figure 37-3 is 90 bytes (columns) wide and 9 rows high, yielding the 810-byte frame format.

Of the 90 columns, the first three (3 × 9 = 27 bytes) are allocated for transport overhead. The transport overhead is divided into two pieces: 9 bytes (3 columns by 3 rows) for section overhead and the remaining 18 bytes (3 columns by 6 rows) for line overhead. This is for maintenance and diagnostics on the circuit.

The 783 remaining octets (87 columns by 9 rows) are called the synchronous payload envelope (SPE). From the SPE, an additional 9 bytes (1 column by 9 rows) are set aside for path overhead. The path overhead

Figure 37-3
The SONET frame

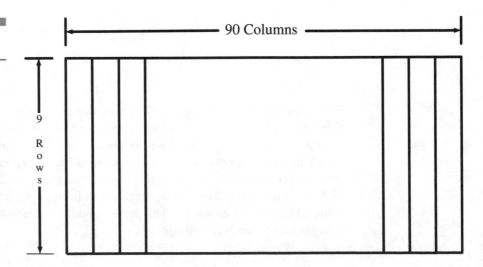

accommodates the maintenance and diagnostics at each end of the circuit —typically, the customer equipment. Thus the leftover 774 bytes are reserved for the actual data transport.

$$(774 \times 8 \text{ bits} = 6192 \text{ bits} \times 8000 \text{ frames per second } 49.536 \text{ Mbps})$$

ATM uses the STS payload as the transport of information by inserting 53 cells into the STS payload. This allows for the fluid and dynamic allocation of the bandwidth available. As it is advertised, ATM starts at 50 and 155 Mbps. To achieve the 155-Mbps rate, three OC-1s are concatenated (kept together as a single data stream) to produce an OC-3C. This works out rather nicely.

While using the SONET specification for carrying the data, cells are mapped horizontally into the SONET frame, as shown in Figure 37-4. However, newer things have occurred since the initial SONET standards were developed. Now SONET operates at speeds of up to the OC-192, which is the equivalent of 192 T3s. OC-192 is 9.958 Gbps of throughput. However, using a dense wave division multiplexing (DWDM) concept (sending different colors of light onto the fiber), we can achieve approximately 32 OC-192s on a single piece of fiber, or 320 Gbps. Moreover, the manufacturers (like Nortel Networks and Lucent Technologies) are rapidly pursuing data rates at 1.6 Tbps* on a single fiber. With these speeds being generated on the fiber, we shall see nearly unlimited bandwidth in the future. This, of course, creates the scenario to offer voice, data, and video on a single access link using ATM and SONET at a fraction of current costs.

One can only imagine where this will all lead. If we can get to 1.6 Tbps, then what about taking the next step to 10 Tbps? If we get to 10 Tbps, then what about stepping up to 100 Tbps? This is the way we have been pushing

Figure 37-4
Cell mapping on SONET

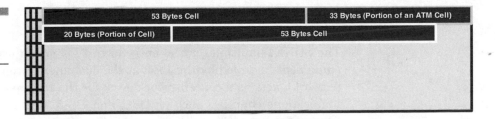

*Terabits per second (1 trillion bits per second)

the carriers and manufacturers alike. They, of course, have been responding in kind.

The use of the higher speed communications methods also leads to a newer transmission rate. Many vendors have announced that by using SONET OC-192, they will deliver 10-Gbps Ethernet speeds across the wide area networks. This becomes a battleground for the various suppliers; the telcos want to deliver gigabit speeds over their ATM backbone, whereas the newer carriers (like Qwest Communications and Level 3 Communications) want to deliver across SONET backbones and they do not care what form is provided.

SONET Topologies

Several different topologies can be used in a SONET network using the various multiplexers. These include the normal topologies most networks have been accustomed to over the years. They include the following:

- Point to point
- Point to multipoint
- Hub and spoke
- Ring

The variations enable the flexibility of SONET in the wide area networks built by the carriers, but are now becoming the method of choice at many large organizations. In each of the topologies, larger organizations are finding the benefits of installing highly reliable interoperable equipment at the private network interfaces and access to the public networks.

Point to Point

The SONET multiplexer, the entry level PTE for an organization (or the equipment installed by the LEC at the customer's premises to access the network), acts as a concentrator device for the multiple lower speed communications channels such as DS-1 and DS-3. In its simplest form, two devices are connected with an optical fiber (with any repeaters as necessary) as a point-to-point circuit. As the entry-level point into SONET architecture, the inputs and outputs are identical. In this environment, the

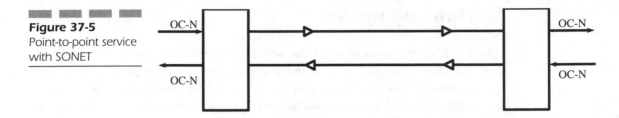

Figure 37-5
Point-to-point service
with SONET

network can act as a stand-alone environment and not have to interface with the public-switched networks. See Figure 37-5 for the point-to-point multiplexing arrangement.

Point to Multipoint

The next step is to consider the point-to-multipoint arrangement. This will use a form of add-drop multiplexing to drop circuits off along the way. In a large corporate network spanning the country (or any subset), a single high-speed link may be employed. The SONET add-drop multiplexer (ADM) is used for the task of dropping circuits out without demultiplexing the entire high-speed signal. In Figure 37-6, the ADM is installed between two far-end locations so that signals can be added or dropped off as necessary. This is a better solution than renting three different circuits between points A-B, A-C, and B-C, which adds to the complexity and cost. By using a circuit from A-B-C with ADMs, the service can usually be more efficiently accommodated.

Figure 37-6
ADMs installed along
the way

Hub and Spoke

The hub and spoke method (sometimes referred to as the star network) provides some added flexibility in the event of unpredicted growth or constant changes in the architecture of the network. A SONET multiplexer can be hubbed into a Digital Cross-Connect where it is concentrated and then forwarded on to the next node. This is used in many larger organizations where regional offices are located and district or branch offices are tied into the network through the hub. Once again the flexibility is available if a major change occurs in the network architecture or in the event of major campaigns in the organization. Hubs will act as the cross-connect points to link the various echelons in the network together. These may be developed in a blocking or non-blocking manner. Typically, some blocking may be allowed. Figure 37-7 shows the hub and spoke arrangement.

Ring

Next comes the real glory of SONET! In a ring architecture, where SONET automatic protection switching (APS) is employed, the best of all worlds comes to fruition. In this topology, ADMs are used throughout the network and a series of point-to-point links are installed between adjoining neighbors. The bidirectional capability places the most robustness into the network; however, unidirectional services can also be installed. The primary advantage of the ring architecture is survivability in the event of a cable cut or a failure in a network node. The multiplexers have sufficient intelligence to reroute or reverse direction in the event of a failure. If more than one

Figure 37-7
Hub and spoke in a
SONET multiplexer
network

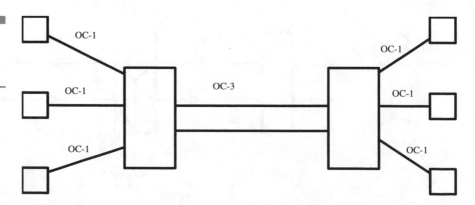

Figure 37-8
Ring architecture of
SONET multiplexers

fiber link is installed, the systems could use alternate paths, but they must recover in milliseconds (which APS on SONET is designed to do). Figure 37-8 shows the ring topology with dual fibers run (bidirectional service) between the ADMs.

While the ANSI committees were working on SONET though, another movement was underfoot. In Europe, the standards committees were also wrestling with the logical replacement to the plesiochronous digital hierarchy (PDH), which is an asynchronous multiplexing plan to create high-speed communications channels. The Europeans came up with a separate multiplexing hierarchy called synchronous digital hierarchy (SDH) in support of the SONET standards.

Synchronous Digital Hierarchy (SDH)

Ever since the standards bodies approved the recommendations for the SDH (and SONET), the services have been effectively used to improve and revolutionize the industry. Significant cost efficiencies and performance improvements have been shown. SDH provides a means for the rest of the world to use the capabilities of fiber-based transport systems and multiplexing architectures to improve upon the older plesiochronous digital hierarchy (PDH), which was inefficient and expensive. The plesiochronous digital hierarchy evolved in response to the demand for plain old telephone services (POTS) and was not ideally suited to deliver the efficient use of bandwidth and high-speed services.

Digital networks continue to expand in complexity and penetration within the carriers' networks and are now moving closer to the consumers' door. High-speed communications prior to the formulation of SDH in 1990 operated at speeds of up to 139.364 Mbps. However, the carriers implemented coaxial and radio-based systems operating at 140 Mbps to 565 Mbps. The networks were severely constrained due to the high cost of the transmission medium (coaxial cable especially). The multiplexing rates used plesiochronous rates, which led to the European PDH. After the development of fiber and the enhancements of integrated circuitry, the newer transmission speeds and complex networking architectures became realistic. In Europe, the evolution and deployment of ISDN also led to the proliferation of the B-ISDN standards, which provides a simple multiplexing technique.

Synchronous Communications

What does synchronous mean anyway? Why is it so important to the telecommunications industry? The easiest way to describe the need for synchronization is that the bits from one telephone call are always in the same location inside a digital transmission frame such as a DS1. In the U.S., telephone calls using digital transmission systems create a DS-0. The DS-0s are multiplexed 24 per DS-1 channel. DS-1 lines are synchronously timed and mapped; therefore, it is easy to remove or insert a call. Finding the location creates an easy add-drop multiplexing arrangement.

Traditionally, transmission systems have been asynchronous, with each network terminal running on its own clock. In digital transmission, clocking is one of the most important considerations. Clocking means using a series of repetitive pulses to keep the bit rate of data constant and to indicate where the ones and zeroes are located in a data stream.

Because these clocks are totally independent, large variations occur in the clock rate and thus the signal bit rate. For example, a DS-3 signal specified at 44.736 Mbps + 20 ppm can produce a variation of up to 1,789 bps between one incoming DS-3 and another.

Asynchronous multiplexing uses multiple stages. Signals such as asynchronous DS-1s are multiplexed, extra bits are added (bit stuffing) to account for the variations of each individual stream and are combined with other bits (framing bits) to form a DS-2 stream. Recall from Chapter 14, "T1 and the T Carrier," on T1 that the DS1 is synchronous. However, the DS-1 is synchronous unto itself, not unto others. Pulse stuffing is used to multiplex up to DS-3 levels. The DS-1s are neither visible nor accessible within a DS-3 frame. DS-3s are multiplexed up to higher rates in the same manner. At the higher asynchronous rate, they cannot be accessed without demultiplexing.

In a synchronous system, such as SONET, the average frequency of all clocks in the system will be the same (synchronous) or nearly the same (plesiochronous). Every clock can be traced back to a highly stable reference supply. Thus, the STS-1 rate remains at a nominal 51.84 Mbps, enabling many synchronous STS-1 signals to be stacked together when multiplexed without any bit stuffing. Thus, the STS-1s are easily accessed at a higher STS-n rate.

Plesiochronous

Plesiochronous means almost synchronous. Variations occur on the timing of the line so bits are stuffed into the frames as padding. The digital bits (1's and 0's) vary slightly in their specific location within the frame creating *jitter*. This occurs on a frame-to-frame basis creating ill timing and requiring some other actions to make everything bear some semblance of timing.

SDH Frame

The SDH forms a multiplexing rate based on the STM-N frame format. The STM stands for synchronous transmission module. The STM-N general frame format works as follows. Similar to the SONET OC-1 (albeit larger), the basic STM-1 frame consists of

$$270\ columns \times 9\ rows = 2430\ octets$$
$$9\ columns\ \times 9\ rows = 81\ octets\ section\ overhead$$

The remaining 2,349 octets create the payload. Higher rate frames are derived from multiples of STM-1 according to value of N. Figure 37-9 shows

Figure 37-9
The STM-1 frame
formats

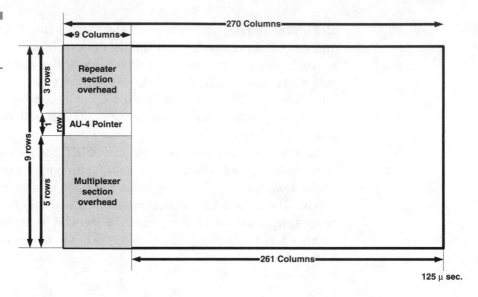

the standard STM-1 frame. This is similar, but also different from the frame in an OC-3.

The typical rates of speed and the appropriate STS and STM rates are shown in Table 37-2.

Only three of the hierarchical levels are actually defined in the standard and are commercially available. These are the STM-1, STM-4, and STM-16.

Table 37-2

Comparison of STS
and STM Rates

Electrical Rate	Optical Rate	Speed
STS-1	STM-0	51.84 Mbps
STS-3	STM-1	155.52 Mbps
STS-9	STM-3	466.56 Mbps
STS-12	STM-4	622.08 Mbps
STS-18	STM-6	933.12 Mbps
STS-24	STM-8	1.244 Gbps
STS-36	STM-12	1.866 Gbps
STS-48	STM-16	2.488 Gbps

As the data are prepared to place in the frame, several different modes of transport are available. At the input, the data flows into a container with a size designation. For example, the C11 is the equivalent of a T1 transport mechanism at 1.544 Mbps. The C12 will carry the E1 transport mechanism at 2.048 Mbps. Another transport is the C2, which is the equivalent of a DS2 operating at 6.312 Mbps. Each of these levels of container is then input into a virtual container (VC level N). This may sound very similar to the SONET virtual tributary (VT). SDH defines a number of containers, each corresponding to an existing plesiochronous rate. The information from a PDH signal is mapped into the relevant container. This is done similarly to the bit-stuffing procedure used in conventional PDH multiplexers.

Next, the virtual containers are mapped and multiplexed within the frame into a tributary unit level N. This completes the input from a container to a virtual container to a tributary unit. The levels are pretty much the same designation, as shown in Table 37-3. The T1, E1, and T2 lines can be mapped and multiplexed into the virtual containers that convert the format needed within SDH. The containers are then aligned with the timing of the system to create a tributary unit (TU).

SDH brings the harmony to the overall multiplexing of the various signals and transport rates. It also acts as the gateway between SONET and SDH structure. It has been over a decade since the actual ratification of the standards, and now more than ever, the benefits are visible. Transcontinental links are now in heavy use across the world on fiber-based architectures.

Table 37-3

Levels of Input as They Map into the Tributary Units

Equivalent	Rate	Input	Mapping	Aligning
DS-1	1.544 Mbps	C11	VC-11	TU-11
E-1	2.048 Mbps	C12	VC-12	TU-12
DS-2	6.312 Mbps	C2	VC-2	TU-2
E-3/T-3	34.368/44.736 Mbps	C3	VC-3	TU-3
E-3/T3	34.368/44.736 Mbps	C3	VC-3	AU-3
E4	139.264 Mbps	C4	VC-4	AU-4

Waves of Light on the Fiber

Ten years ago, the implementation of the OC-48 SONET specification had the industry believing that limitless bandwidth was available. One can just imagine that a mere decade ago the $2.5 \pm$ Gbps capacities of the optical fiber networks was innovative and exceeded our wildest imaginations about how we would ever fill these communications channels. Yet, the industry began to recognize the changes in consumption patterns. Because of the demand for multimedia communications, video WAN started to erode even the highest capacities available. To solve this problem, researchers began to experiment with the use of more than one light beam on the same cable. By using different radio frequencies on a cable TV system, the carriers were able to expand the number of TV channels available to them on the same coaxial systems. Why not do the same things with the various frequencies of light?

Wave division multiplexing (WDM), in contrast, can carry multiple data bit rates, enabling multiple channels to be carried on a single fiber. The technique uses different colors of light down the same fiber to carry different channels of information, which are then separated out at the distant end by a diffraction grating that identifies each color. All optical networks employing WDM with add-drop multiplexers and cross-connects permit this. Dense WDM (DWDM) systems multiplex up to 160 or more wavelengths in the narrow beam window, increase capacity on existing fiber, and are data rate transparent.

WDM was first developed to increase the distance signals could be transported in long-distance networks, from 35 to 50 km to as much as 970 km or more with optical amplifiers. Subsequently companies discovered that DWDM would work in metropolitan networks just as well. These DWDM ring systems can be connected with Asynchronous Transfer Mode (ATM) switches and Internet Protocol (IP) routers. ATM networks are expected to use SONET/SDH physical layer interfaces with OC-12 add-drop multiplexers.

Where normal digital transmission systems use time division multiplexing (TDM) and cable TV analog technologies use frequency division multiplexing (FDM). Wave division multiplexing (WDM) is a combination of the two schemes. The use of a TDM multiplexer breaks the bandwidth down to specific time slots such as those found in SONET-based networks. However, by using the combination of frequency (different wavelengths) and time (time slots), the fiber can be used to carry orders of magnitude more than traditional fiber-based systems. Furthermore, several different wavelengths and colors of light can be used to produce far more capacity.

The Benefits of a Combined Network

By combining the benefits of low error rate and high-speed fiber networks with the strengths and survivability of SONET/SDH and placing the multiple bands of light on a single fiber, we can achieve bandwidth beyond our wildest imagination. In the future, we will likely see a designer's networking strategy where designer bandwidth can be customized on a user-by-user level. My next-door neighbor may want a pipe coming in from the telco on fiber at 1 Gbps, whereas I may want a higher speed communications channel at 10 Gbps. These will all be custom built or demand-activated in such a way as to support our needs for the next decade.

Questions

1. What does SONET mean?
   a. Synchronous opportunity networks
   b. Synchronous optical networks
   c. Standards-based optical networks
   d. Standard optional networking

2. The SONET link architecture is broken into _____ pieces.
   a. 1
   b. 2
   c. 3
   d. 4

3. The point between two different repeaters is called the line.   T/F

4. The end-to-end communications is called the path.   T/F

5. The basic SONET rate called the OC-1 operates at _____.
   a. 34 Mbps
   b. 49.76 Mbps
   c. 51.22 Mbps
   d. 51.84 Mbps

6. The basic rate for SDH is called the _____.

7. The STM-1 is the equivalent to an OC-4.   T/F

8. PDH stands for:

   a. Plesiochronous data header

   b. Plesiochronous data hierarchy

   c. Plesiochronous digital hierarchy

   d. Plesiochronous data header

9. SONET can use ADMs to drop off certain portions of the bandwidth without demultiplexing the entire payload.   T/F

10. The _____ standard uses virtual containers to carry its payload.

11. What is the payload of an OC-1?

   a. 51.84 Mbps

   b. 50 Mbps

   c. 49.53 Mbps

   d. 34.11 Mbps

12. Wave division multiplexing combines the _____ and _____ multiplexing schemes.

   a. Time and space

   b. Frequency and statistical

   c. Frequency and space

   d. Frequency and time

13. WDM can multiplex multiple data streams on the same piece of fiber.   T/F

14. The ability to multiplex as much as 128 or more wavelengths on a piece of fiber is called:

   a. Wave division multiplexing

   b. SONET

   c. Add-drop multiplexing

   d. Dense wave division multiplexing

15. SONET and SDH use a ring topology when _____ is required.

   a. A loop

   b. Add-drop multiplexing

   c. Survivability

   d. Duplex operation

Finances for Telecommunications

After reading this chapter and completing the questions, you will be able to:

- Understand the rationale behind finances for telecommunications
- Discuss the cost and benefit ratio to justify expenses
- Evaluate when a project is a win-win
- Discuss the application of the financial rules

U p until 1980, companies regarded communications expenses for data and voice as the costs of doing business. This was due to many reasons:

- For the first half of the century, only voice communications existed in electronic form.
- The telephone company supplied voice communications capability.
- The telephone company really did not offer a great variety of options to its customers.
- What it did offer worked well, but management could make few choices.

- The telecommunications manager's main responsibility was to place and coordinate orders with the telephone company and to track the bills to ensure that they were correct.

- Because little choice was given in what to order, managing telecommunications was almost an oxymoron.

Also, people who managed communications tended not to have a management point of view. They were not oriented toward providing management with enough information to make business decisions. After all, presenting a telecommunications budget as a fait accompli was much easier than justifying each project individually. This orientation is still seen in many telephone bills rendered by Postal, Telephone, and Telegraph authorities (PTTs); the level of detail seen in a normal bill in the U.S. is often either a separate (priced) service or simply unavailable outside of the U.S.

In the late 1960s, choices began to proliferate. Data communications began to grow as a percentage of the total communications budget. Still, the mentality that regarded communications as an overhead function with little potential to be managed—certainly not a possible profit center—remained in most companies.

However, as more and more companies in the U.S. felt the cold winds of international competition, and as each market niche started to fill up with more and more competitors, every area of expenditure in organizations came under scrutiny. Telecommunications (used to include both voice and data) constitutes a significant expenditure of funds in many companies—an expenditure that tends to increase steadily. In many organizations, this is the second or third largest cost on the balance sheet. As an overhead function, it is a prime candidate for cost control and optimization, especially with the increasing number of ways to satisfy any given communications requirement.

Cost is always an issue no matter what financial position your organization is in. Management expects to achieve the best pricing and value for its dollars. Yet, management still sees telecommunications as an overhead function, a necessary evil. This image must be dispelled. The use of telecommunications as a strategic resource will

- Increase productivity
- Reduce costs
- Improve the bottom line

All you have to do is convince your management of these benefits. Moreover, companies are increasingly becoming aware that telecommunications can be used as a competitive weapon in the marketplace—a method of improving attractiveness to customers and in some cases, a way of directly generating additional revenue. Of course, turning a new set of technologies into a competitive weapon can be much more difficult than it sounds. Nonetheless, it has been done often enough that the very idea no longer sounds as implausible as it once did.

In fact, notwithstanding the brouhaha about the information highway, modem communications technologies should indeed be regarded as means to improve revenues and productivity. However, expenditures on these technologies could be wasted if they do not rest on a sound financial basis. As in any other major capital or expense decision, the financial effects of such choices should be considered before, during, and after the choices are made. In some cases, the dollars involved might drive a decision. It is important to understand when and how to cost justify a decision or perform a comparative financial analysis among several alternatives, in order to prove to upper management that the investment and/or monthly expenditures will appropriately benefit the organization.

Sometimes the benefits are so obvious or overwhelming, or the costs of not making the investment are so horrendous, that no analysis needs to be done. This chapter, in contrast, focuses on the financial aspects that can influence the decision of whether or not to make the investment:

- How do you approach this tender subject without alienating management?

- How do you persuade management that the communications expenditures will generate greater returns than many other forms of expense?

The answer is different in every organization. First and foremost, you have to begin to speak in management's terms. All too often, telecommunications and telephony people want to describe technologies, applications, and state-of-the-art concepts to their management. Unfortunately, jargon and the use of technical terms turns management off. Consequently, when vying for the same corporate dollars as all the other departments, telecommunications tends to lose ground. If you learn the language of business and apply business principles to your purchasing decisions, you will stand a better chance of getting the funds needed to support the organization.

In order to analyze or justify expenditures, two key aspects of the transaction and technology must be identified:

- Benefits
- Costs

The normal hurdles such decisions face in an organization must also be understood in order to perform the appropriate cost/benefit analysis. The rule of thumb is that for every dollar invested (cost =1), we should see three dollars returned in benefits (benefit =3), or a benefit to cost ratio of 3:1. If you can achieve a 3:1 ratio, then the project is usually a winner. If you cannot reach this ratio then the project may be in serious jeopardy.

Benefits

When considering any expenditure, the first step is to identify the expected benefits. Such benefits are normally categorized into hard and soft benefits.

Hard Benefits

Hard benefits are those that can easily have objective and predictable dollar figures assigned to them. Examples of hard benefits might include some of the following ideas:

- Reduce dial-out voice communications costs by $3,000 per month or add voice over a data protocol (such as VoIP, VoDSL, VTOA, and VoFR; all were discussed in earlier chapters).
- Decrease PBX maintenance costs by $500 per month, especially when using a next-generation PBX that uses the IP telephone sets shown in an earlier chapter.
- Avoid a one-time PBX acquisition cost of $150,000 in the next fiscal year.
- Allow direct charge-back of appropriate calls to clients (versus absorbing them as overhead) in the amount of $3,500 per month.
- Avoid the requirement of acquiring a new T1 (costing $4,000 per month) by using the xDSL technologies on the existing wires. An example of this can be voice and telephony over ATM (VTOA) or voice over single-pair high-speed digital subscriber line (SHDSL).
- Reduce travel costs (airline, hotel, and meals) by $8,000 per month.
- Control overnight package shipment costs by avoiding $2,500 in expected monthly bills; using fax servers, e-mail, and FTP servers will help to reduce the cost of external courier services.
- Reduce the cost of dial-in data communications by $5,000 per month.

Each of these examples shares a few key elements. Each states a particular type of expenditure, a specific dollar amount to be saved, and a (usually recurring) time period (typically per month). Most communications and maintenance bills are stated in terms of months, so your savings will usually also be stated that way initially. Ultimately, as you work with the figures, they will be translated into yearly figures as management normally thinks in terms of yearly budgets. This translation also benefits you because yearly savings are normally much more impressive, at least in the case of savings that recur monthly.

Soft Benefits

Soft benefits are results that you expect to be good for the company, but that are more difficult to quantify and sometimes even to identify. The object of this exercise is to make the soft benefits as hard as possible. This will make more sense later on.

Identifying soft benefits is typically a two-pass activity. On the first pass, one simply makes a general identification of areas that are expected to benefit from the planned expenditure. Examples might include

- Improve productivity of call handlers in the customer service area.
- Reduce the time required to add items into inventory.
- Increase the productivity of our consultants by giving them quicker access to reference information.
- Reduce the cycle time required to develop a new product (or troubleshoot a problem in an existing one).
- Diminish the number of errors experienced in information retrieved by our customers when they dial in to our network.
- Optimize the routing of our delivery vehicles.
- Minimize the time to respond to trouble calls.

Any organization would jump at the chance to achieve any of these goals, right? Well, perhaps, but a few questions will probably arise before management signs on the dotted line. Those questions include

- How much money will this save or generate?
- How much do I have to pay now to experience this saving later?
- When is later?

In the following section, we will address how much must be paid, but it is your job to calculate probable savings to be derived from the expenditure you propose. How do you do it?

It is quite possible that the real reason you are proposing an expenditure is to achieve a soft rather than hard saving. That is, you really do not know exactly how much will be saved, but you believe (or your internal client believes) that the change will be a beneficial one. However, you must quantify this belief—wishing doesn't make it so—or convince management to loosen the purse strings.

An additional pass is required to refine the benefit statements. Soft benefits often refer, in one way or another, to improvements in the efficiency of human beings. In the list of benefits, the first, second, third, and sixth items express the hope that such a benefit will occur. Quantifying such benefits is fairly straightforward, although a number of assumptions must be made. Always state your assumptions. You will most likely use a spreadsheet for your analysis. If someone questions or corrects an assumption, you can easily change it and redo the analysis. If your assumptions are not clearly stated, management cannot evaluate how realistic your predictions are.

To quantify the benefits expected from an improvement in productivity, you need to determine or assume the following:

- Exactly what activity is to be shortened? Examples include length of time on a phone call, the average time to travel from one customer location to the next, or the length of time to check one item into inventory.

- How many times does that activity occur per year?

- How much time is to be cut off each occurrence of the activity? For example, if an average new order call takes 5 minutes, the average length of such a call might be reduced by 30 seconds.

- What is the cost (average salary, hourly rate, and so on) of a person who typically performs this activity? This should be a fully-loaded figure; that is, it should include medical benefits, retirement fund, vacation, and so on, if applicable.

The place to start to get this information is the supervisor; however, a trip to human resources might also be required.

Once you have established this, it is time to hit the spreadsheet. Figure 38-1 illustrates a sample calculation based on a proposal to add a computer-integrated telephony function to a PBX. It is assumed that if many of the customers' records can be brought up on screen automatically for

Figure 38-1
A sample calculation on a proposed computer telephony integration (CTI) solution

1	Expected time savings per call (in seconds)	30
2	Annual telephone orders	250,000
3	Expected seconds saved (row 1 × row 2)	7,500,000
4	Expected hours saved (row 3/3,600)	2,083
5	Customer rep salary (fully loaded)	$40,000
6	Customer rep cost per hour (row 5/2,000)	$20
7	Potential savings (row 4 × row 6)	$41,667

customer representatives, then an average of 30 seconds will be saved during each order by speeding the recording of address, telephone, and other customer information that is usually static.

It would be nice to be able to point to row seven and say, "See, this will save us over $40,000! Let's do it!" But this is a raw number. Much remains to be considered before the analysis is ready for management's review. Does management expect to hire additional customer reps? If so, then the number of calls is probably expected to increase. Should you do a 5-year analysis, incorporating a volume growth factor? Would the use of this improvement forestall the additional hires? Would the organization be able to make do with the same number of agents if a 30-second reduction per call is achieved? (This is possible: if you are handling tens of thousands of calls per day and you save 30 seconds on each, it can equate to significant hours of savings.) Refer back to Chapter 8 on traffic engineering, which had a similar example of the savings of time. This includes the ability to save more than just lines, trunks, and other ancillary equipment. It can also account for substantial people savings.

How sensitive is this analysis to changes in the assumptions? You should be able to get accurate figures on an average salary. But how precise is your 30-second estimate? Be prepared with either studies done in your industry that bear out your calculations or perhaps the results of a study done with a stopwatch that shows how much time is used by taking down the information to be avoided. Do not forget that not all calls fit your paradigm; new customers will not be in your database, and many will call from locations other than their own telephone (thus not creating a match-up of their telephone number with the customer records in your database).

Costs

The benefit figures, whether soft or hard, are gross; that is, they identify changes in or avoidance of expenditures, but they do not identify what must be done or spent to realize those savings.

Cost is a relative term. We think of cost as an outlay of dollars. Yet, true costs include both the long-term investments and support, coupled with the returns on investment. This is important to selling concepts to management. Systems in raw dollars cost approximately $700 to $1,000 per station when dealing with PBXs. The long-term dollars over a 5-year period can be three times that. However, if the telephone set is used to produce revenue of $1 million, what is the cost?

Cost and Benefit Calculations

As should be obvious from the name, a *cost and benefit analysis* balances the two key aspects of an opportunity (also known as an investment or, more commonly, an expenditure). The ratio of benefits we derive from each dollar of cost invested produces the benefit to cost ratio (B/C). As discussed previously, hard costs and soft benefits exist. If your goal is to justify an expenditure, you should do your best to turn soft benefits into hard benefits. However, once you have reduced everything to dollars, your work has just begun.

Life Cycles

Contrary to popular opinion, a *life cycle* is not (only) a piece of equipment found at your local health club. Rather, it is a key concept in the analysis of acquisitions of both communications and data processing equipment. It is not applicable to items paid for on a monthly basis, but only to equipment with an expected useful lifetime of several years.

What is an item's life cycle? The answer is not so obvious. It is not the length of time the equipment could successfully operate (if properly maintained). It is not even necessarily the length of time the equipment could provide service more economically than other alternatives. Rather, it is the length of time that an organization can realistically expect to use the item in its planned role before discarding or replacing it. But, you might say, coming up with such a time frame is only slightly more accurate than fortune-telling with a crystal ball! Indeed. The process of determining the life cycle of a piece or category of equipment is one that involves forecasting technology trends, the expected health of the business, possibly interest rates, and other factors. In short, it is largely a matter of opinion.

Nonetheless, you must try to nail down a figure—for financial, operational, and career reasons.

Financial Assume that someone is developing an annual budget for desktop personal computer purchases. For simplicity, we'll assume that a group of 10 users needs to be equipped. A reasonable approximation of the cost of one desktop unit, with software, is about $5,000. If you further assume that each machine will serve productively for an average of 4 years, what should the annual budget be? Ten people times $5,000 is $50,000 in the first year. After that, we'll spend $50,000 every 4 years, or $12,500 per year on average.

But wait! It has just been determined that all of the computers will have to be replaced an average of every 3 years rather than every 4. The startup cost remains the same, but now $50,000 will be spent every 3 years, which is $16,667 per year.

PBXs typically serve for a long time, often as long as a decade or more. However, technology is changing more rapidly than in the past. Assuming that a PBX bought now will still be in service 10 years from now could be a big mistake.

Payback Periods One of the simpler methods of evaluating investments is payback analysis. This isn't tripping someone that hit you in the school-yard 30 years ago. Rather, it is an approach to taking into account the time value of money without actually doing the requisite calculations. However, it does give an initial rough feel for an investment's viability as compared to alternatives.

Notice that we are using the term investment, rather than expenditure, in this section. To have a payback period at all, an investment must bring in, over time, revenue greater than that spent to get the revenue. Otherwise, a negative payback occurs, suggesting that this would be a poor investment indeed!

Payback analysis, also sometimes described as break-even analysis, is straightforward. A revenue stream or periodic savings figure associated with an investment is estimated (for example, $10,000 per year in reduced calling costs achieved by installing a virtual voice network). The costs associated with that stream of revenue are totaled (for example, $20,000 in one-time costs, plus a marginal increase in the cost of access lines to the network of $5,000 per year). A little work with a spreadsheet and voilà! The break-even (B/E) point is 3 years from the date of investment. Table 38-1 shows the numbers used to perform the calculations on the spreadsheet. From this table, we graphed the information shown in Figure 38-2. Note that the graph shows the cumulative figures.

In today's business climate, a 3-year break-even point will most likely not generate intense management excitement.

Notice that with break-even or payback analysis, the time value of money is typically disregarded. When comparing alternative projects with

Table 38-1

Summary of Calculations in a Payback Analysis

Year	Savings	Cumulative Savings	Cost	Cumulative Costs
0	$10,000	$10,000	$25,000	$25,000
1	$10,000	$20,000	$5,000	$30,000
2	$10,000	$30,000	$5,000	$35,000
3	$10,000	$40,000	$5,000	$40,000
4	$10,000	$50,000	$5,000	$45,000
5	$10,000	$60,000	$5,000	$50,000

Figure 38-2
The savings versus costs graphed to show B/E

Break-Even Analysis

- - - - Cumulative savings   ——— Cumulative Cost

similar time horizons, this is not unreasonable. However, when management begins to focus more carefully on your numbers, you most likely will need to create a more rigorous analysis. One way to do that is with return on investment calculations.

Return on Investment Calculations Return on investment (ROI) is where the rubber meets the road in investment analysis. One way to approach ROI is to use an internal rate of return (IRR) analysis. To refer to the help available with Microsoft's Excel spreadsheet, the IRR returns the internal rate of return for a series of cash flows represented by the numbers in values. These cash flows do not have to be even, as they would be for an annuity. The internal rate of return is the interest rate received for an investment consisting of payments (negative values) and income (positive values) that occur at regular periods.

In English, the IRR is comparable to the interest rate your company might get on the money it is considering investing if it put the funds in a bank instead of into your tender clutches. The IRR does take into account the time value of money, so if you include all of the factors, it does provide a good decision tool when selecting among alternative investments.

Any modern spreadsheet should be able to do this for you. Using the previous example, the net initial cost in the first year is $15,000. Each year thereafter has a net savings of $5,000. The IRR for this stream of outgo and income during the first 5 years would be about 13 percent. This is better than passbook savings, but, of course, considerably more risky.

When the analysis of the life cycle concept is mixed in, the results become much more interesting. This is because ROI is intimately tied to the total length of the expected revenue stream. It is a statement of the average interest rate compared to the expected cash flow over the duration of the analysis. Table 38-2 shows how much better the investment looks if a 6-year period is assumed: a 24 percent internal rate of return! On the other hand, if the technology is supplanted in 2 years, we lose money at an annual rate of 23 percent.

▇▇ ▇▇ Pricing Considerations

If you had to plan for a new system today, the world would be at your beck and call. Vendors and carriers alike are in a slump. The sales of equipment, peripherals, and services are all slowing down. Increased pressure is being

Table 38-2

Internal Rate of
Return Analysis

Year	In/Out	IRR
0	−$15,000	
1	$5,000	−66.7 percent
2	$5,000	−23.2 percent
3	$5,000	0.0 percent
4	$5,000	12.6 percent
5	$5,000	19.9 percent
6	$5,000	24.3 percent

applied on the sales forces to increase revenue. This implies that a buyer's market exists, which is true if you know what your needs are and how to negotiate with the vendors.

Unfortunately, many telecommunications and telephony personnel might be good technically but lack the skills to deal with other issues. Thus, you have to understand the pricing schemes and be prepared to wait them out, if necessary, in order to get your best deal. For equipment purchases, many of the vendors use a one-third rule. One-third of the quoted price is for equipment, one-third is for installation, and one-third is for the profit margin. The final third is where you have room to negotiate.

For example, a digital PBX system would cost approximately $750 to $1,000 per line. If you use a 1,000-line system, you can assume that you will pay between $750,000 to $1 million. Request a budgetary price from your vendors and see what they quote. You might be pleasantly surprised, or you might get sticker shock when you read the budgetary price. First, the price might be quoted on a rudimentary scheme of 1,000 lines: 50 percent single-line sets and 50 percent digital multiline sets. So, let's use $750,000.

However, the vendor might also assume that you'll want features and peripheral equipment above and beyond a rudimentary system. Therefore, you might see duplicate central processing units (CPUs), battery backup, enhanced features, station message detail recording (SMDR), enhanced networking, and least-cost routing, among other features. The cost might come in at $1.5 million. How did it get so expensive? What happened? If the vendors start in a position of strength (at $1,500 per line), they have plenty of room to negotiate. They will offer you a 50 percent reduction on initial-station equipment and features right up front. The price dropped only 15 percent to approximately $1,275,000, and you believe you did your job.

However, all that was reduced was the station equipment from its original inflated price! Remember, the system should have started at $1 million. How can the vendors come back and reduce the price even further? They haven't even touched the price or the profit! That's how!

The Decision-Making Process

Once you have determined that a true need exists for the purchase of any communications peripheral or system, the next step is to evaluate everything on both a financial long-term basis and a functional basis. Do not let yourself get trapped into the love-that-technology routine. Too many systems are bought on the basis of emotional appeal rather than company need. This can be the kiss of death.

Some suggestions to follow are

- *Buy only when necessary, but leave plenty of time to start the process.* This gives you the edge on the buying cycle. If you wait too long, then your leverage of time is gone, and you'll have to buy before you get the right deal.

- *Remember the financial picture.* Recruit a team of others from the finance, purchasing, facilities, and legal departments to assist in the decision-making process. Bring them up to speed immediately. Other sets of eyes help to maintain focus and objectivity.

- *Don't get too close to the salesperson.* This is business, not friendship. If things are not going their way, the vendors (salesperson and manager) will go right around you to your management and keep you out of the loop. Control your project and your vendors.

- *Accept no verbal agreements.* Everything must be in writing! A short pencil is worth a long memory. You'd be surprised how many agreements are forgotten after the contract is signed.

- *Keep everything above board.* Don't accept gifts or favors. This can ruin your career. Even if nothing is going on, the perception is what will get you.

Justifying Costs

The justification process does not have one rule. You must learn what the criteria are within your organization. Many organizations use the return on investment (ROI) method or the internal rate of return (IRR) method.

Others use a discounted cash flow (DCF) analysis to authorize expenditures. Many smaller companies might use an emotional decision and justification process. It is really up to the management in the individual organization. So how do you know how to go about this?

- *Get away from the technical role and become more of a business manager.* You need to speak the language of the organization. This can be in financial terms (a universal language) or in production or cost containment/cost reduction terms. Whatever the language of the management, you have to get on that platform.

- *Ask for help.* Find a department manager or peer who has been successful in getting approval for new projects. Go with a winning style.

- *Don't reinvent the wheel.* When you are trying to justify a system, ask others to review your information. They might give you pointers that will help. If a similar-size project has been recently approved for any department, find out what that project manager did. Use a format that is already approved, something that management is obviously comfortable with.

- *If you are not comfortable with the justification process, get a champion or mentor who will run with the project for you.* This could be a senior manager or financial manager. This might be a risk because the mentor or champion might try to take full control after the approval is gained. The projects are usually highly visible, so a lot of credit could be up for grabs.

Maintenance Issues

Maintenance issues should be discussed with the vendor in advance of a purchase decision. You might be replacing a system that has become obsolete or is continually breaking. The last thing you want to do is jump into a decision that might engender the same problems. You certainly do not want to buy a system that is about to be discontinued or that will not be supported before the end of its financial and useful life cycle. Ask the following questions:

- What will the long-term maintenance costs of the system be?
- How much will the maintenance cost in years 2 through 5 and 6 through 10? Can you prepay maintenance at a reduced rate?
- How long is the warranty period? It should be at least 1 year.

- When does the warranty start: after cutover or after acceptance? The two dates can have significant time differences. Is this a moving window?

- What are the normal maintenance periods (9 A.M. to 5 P.M., Monday through Friday) and what will the costs be if maintenance is required during other periods?

- What will the costs be to add one more set? Ten more? One hundred more?

- When or where are the big bumps in price?

- What will the remedies be for nonperformance?

- How will the vendor handle major and minor outages?

- Does the vendor have spares on site? If not, where are they and how available are they?

- How will the vendor keep your system current? At what cost?

- Can you train your own people? If so, for how much? If not, why not?

- What about initial user training, refresher training, new employee training? How often and how much?

- Can you trade in excess equipment? Can the trade be applied toward upgrades and new releases?

Reduced Rates versus Improved Service

What are your objectives for the purchase of a new system: reduced rates or improved service? Many users really never address the issue of their buying motives. If the objective is to reduce rates, then the issues might vary from those surrounding improvements in service. Of course, the best choice is both, but you might have to decide between these two issues.

If reduced rates are the primary objective, you could give up some of the features and niceties of the system. Keep the long-term benefits of a system in mind. Often, reducing rates is a short-term goal that might prove to be more expensive in the long run. If, for example, you choose the least possible expense today by selecting a PBX with all single-line sets, you might experience dissatisfaction from the users. Ultimately, they will begin demanding multiline sets with added features and capabilities. Now you'll have a group of single-line sets in a closet, paid for but not used. Further, the add-on costs for the multiline sets might now be more expensive after the installation.

Improved service will point you in a direction of serving the end user. These are your customers. Although the initial costs might be higher for the services they need or ask for, the long-term capital outlay should be less. The acceptance of a system customized to meet their needs will also go a long way in the overall payback of the system. Increases in user satisfaction, productivity, and revenue are soft-dollar benefits for telecommunications systems. However, they are real values to the organization. Don't lose sight of the total picture.

Sample Calculations

Before you can present your case to management or approve the purchase of the system/service, you have to understand the total cost both in initial outlay and ongoing cost. To do this, you have to gather all the facts. This will start with

- Initial costs, purchases, installation, training, preparation, and so on
- Add-on costs over the period of years, based on system and peripherals
- Maintenance costs
- Human resources needed to operate the system
- The obsolescence factor: how long the system will be adequate

Initial Costs

Assume that you are planning to buy a new PBX that will serve multiple users (1,500 to 2,000). You've done your homework and estimate that the system can be purchased for $1,000 per line. Your initial assessment will be approximately $1.5 to $2 million to purchase the system, installed with a 1-year warranty. This system will be needed in 1 year because the existing system is too small and continually breaks down.

A further analysis should reveal additional costs to include that might not be as obvious, but must be included in the calculations to be fair:

Construction costs for PBX room (30 × 50)	$50,000
Raised flooring	$10,000
UPS system	$20,000
Fire detection/suppression system	$15,000
HVAC add-on tonnage	$20,000
Security system (card key or other)	$15,000
New conduits for new wiring	$25,000
Electrical work	$7,000
Removal of old system	$5,000
Handling of old batteries (hazardous)	$5,000
Training costs (1,500 users @ 1 hr. @ $20)	$30,000
Project management	$40,000
Total	$242,000

The figures are obviously based on some industry averages. They reflect approximately 15 percent additional costs over and above the initial purchase price. These numbers can and should be included in the overall cost analysis for the system because they represent real costs.

Some added long-term costs that should be considered over the life cycle are

Space (rental) $4.00/sq. ft./ann.	$6,000/ann.
Insurance @ 0.50 per $1000±	$8,500/ann.
Spares (parts/sets and so on)	$10,000/ann.
Test equipment	$20,000/one time
Heat/light/utility costs $1.00/sq. ft	$1,500/ann.
Inspection costs for HVAC/fire suppression	$500/ann.
Contingencies (5–10 percent total ann. exp.)	$2,650/ann.
Total other	$29,150/ann.
	$20,000/one time

Be sure to work with various departments to understand the operating costs. These might include

- Purchasing

- Finance

- Facilities

- Insurance

- Safety/security

Add-On Costs

Assuming that the base price for the system is as outlined in the previous example, the add-on prices might include items such as

Automatic call distributor (100 line)	$50,000 (1)
Voice mail/automatic attendant	$80,000 (1)
Modem pooling (simple)	$10,000 (2)
LAN interface (56-Kbps bridge)	$15,000 (2)
T1 direct interface (5 cards @ $2,800)	$14,000 (1)
Station message detail recording	$20,000 (1)
Four-wire E&M T/L cards for V-mail (4 @ $500)	$2,000 (1)
Paging access (excludes speakers)	$12,000 (2)
Power failure transfer (48 lines @ $6,000)	$6,000 (2)
Total add-ons	$209,000*

*Spread over 2 years (166,000 year 1; 43,000 year 2).

By now, you might be getting the feeling that the cost of a telecommunications system is not just something that you pick off the shelf. Nor are the prices simple to calculate because so many other components are involved. You have to look at all of the added costs: for example, construction, maintenance, human resources, insurance, and taxes. This is the only way to truly justify the expense to management. They have to perform these calculations if you do not. Admittedly, they will use the financial department to perform these calculations; but if you have no input in that process, they might use different assumptions and disprove the benefit that you anticipated. Consequently, the onus is on the individual responsible for the technology to prove or disprove. How can management use different assumptions? Look at a simple point that is summarized in Table 38-3. This is how we compare the differences in perceptions.

Table 38-3

Differences of Years Used for a Single Decision

Person Responsible	Number of Years Expected for Considering Numbers
Telecommunications	3-year payback or sooner or information management
IRS	5-year depreciation at accelerated rate
Finance department	7-year straight-line depreciation
Senior management	10-year life (don't want to do this very often)

Questions

1. The B/C ratio describes the following:
   a. Benefit versus control
   b. Benefit versus cost
   c. Banking and control
   d. Basic and conditional

2. A good rule of thumb is to use a _____ ratio.
   a. 1:1
   b. 2:1
   c. 3:1
   d. 4:1
   e. 5:1

3. Prior to 1980, the telecommunications manager's main responsibility was to _____ and _____ orders with the telephone company.

4. In the 1960s, _____ communications began to grow as a percentage of the total communications budget.
   a. Voice
   b. Video
   c. Fax
   d. Data

5. In telecommunications departments, we think of cost as:
   a. A relative term
   b. An outlay of dollars
   c. The total picture
   d. The only issue concerning management

6. Some techniques to reduce the cost of communications include VoIP, VoDSL, VTOA, and VoFR.   T/F

7. True costs ignore the long-term investments and support, as well as the returns on investment.   T/F

8. The IRR stands for:

   a. Internal revenue rates

   b. International regulated revenues

   c. Internal rate of recognition

   d. Internal rate of return

9. Return on investment (ROI) is rarely used in a corporate environment. T/F

10. When considering expenditures, the first step is to identify the expected _____ and _____ benefits.

    a. Current, projected

    b. Solid, sanguine

    c. Hard, soft

    d. Basic, advanced

11. Your objectives for the purchase of a new system should include either:

    a. Reduced rates or improved service

    b. Promotions or rejection

    c. Self-improvement or corporate benefit

    d. Status quo or change

12. Some of the issues you have to understand include the total cost both in _____ and _____ cost.

13. Data you need to collect includes initial costs, add-on, maintenance costs, human resources, and obsolescence factors.   T/F

14. If you are not comfortable with the justification process, get a:

    a. New job

    b. New boss

    c. Degree in finance

    d. Champion

15. The cost of a telecommunications system is not just something that you pick off the shelf. T/F

Cabling Systems

After reading this chapter and completing the questions, you will be able to:

■ Understand the various forms of cabling used in offices

■ Discuss the differences in the TIA categories of wire

■ Describe the benefit of fiber

■ Understand the capacities of coax cables

■ Evaluate the risks associated with each of the systems

Before the development of local area networks (LANs), organizations that needed in-building data communications cabling systems had a limited number of choices. Terminals used RS232C, unshielded twisted pair (UTP), or in some cases (especially block-mode IBM terminals) coaxial cable. High-speed connections in an IBM environment were handled with special in-room cables (maximum distance about 200 feet) called bus and tag cables. (Voice always used unshielded twisted-pair wires—it had no choice at all.)

A key characteristic of these cabling systems is that, in general, a need for a particular cable was met by pulling just enough cable to satisfy that need. The cost of installing such a cable run (to connect one device) typically ranged from about $200 to over $1,000, depending on limitations of and available routes through the existing physical plant. Because moves and changes occur frequently in a business environment, the cabling cost alone for a normal data communications environment would be considerable, even after all of the initial installation was completed. This frequently occurred as soon as the initial installation was completed because move and change activity was frozen or put off until the cables were installed. Frustration existed because users might have gone through one or two moves since the beginning of the installation, but the wires were installed at the original locations. No easy way was available to functionally change in midstream.

When LANs were first introduced on a widespread basis, a new concept —data utility—became popular. Fundamental to this approach was the idea that, given the opportunity, it would be smart to prewire every plausible work location in a building. This prewiring would enable moves and changes to consist of just movement of the user hardware and perhaps some software changes, although some LANs enabled moves with no software changes.

The cabling of the day was either coaxial (in ARCnet's case) or heavy coaxial (in Ethernet's case); nonetheless, the idea of placing a jack in the wall for as-needed connections ("just like the electric company!" was the claim) rapidly took hold. Still, this facility was just for data communications —and only LAN data at that.

About this time, another idea began to gain in popularity: the idea that voice and data communications should be integrated in some way. Just how they would become, and (in many cases) avoid becoming integrated, is another story. However, one area in which apparent integration could be accomplished relatively easily was in wall jacks. One could design jacks with built-in outlets for multiple types of communications. Jacks have been designed with some or all of the following:

- Voice
- Terminal
- LAN (sometimes more than one)
- Video
- Generic analog (In cases where the voice connection is for a digital PBX, analog connections are sometimes also provided to enable analog devices, such as modems, to also gain external access.)

Figure 39-1 shows a typical multipurpose outlet layout. The multiple outlets were designed to be utilitarian so that any need could be met with a single interface at the wall outlet. This was a good and noble goal, but many cases are documented proving that early implementations were not that successful. Obviously, these jacks can become quite crowded. Not so obviously, the jacks only provide the appearance of integration. After all, what is behind the jacks? Typically, each of the cabling types goes to wherever it needs to be. The office walls are neater, however.

A more recent concept is that of structured cabling systems. Typically, these systems are offered by some of the major systems vendors as well as other organizations. Some of the more successful vendors of such systems include

- Lucent Technologies
- IBM
- DEC
- Others (such as AMP and KRONE)

The idea of a structured cabling system is to predefine the type (or types) of cable to be used for each specific purpose. Then wires of all identified types are preinstalled, coordinating the installation in order to save money and provide a consistent and neat physical plant for both current and foreseeable communications (both voice and data) needs. This approach is particularly beneficial when a new building is being constructed. However, buildings with older cabling that did not measure up to modern requirements have been retrofitted on occasion at a substantial cost.

Each vendor of a structured cabling system offers essentially all media. Company management still must decide what requirements might materialize in the future. However, once a company commits to a particular system, the requirements directly drive cable selection, configuration, and installation approaches. Fewer decisions must be made. Vendor installers can work more efficiently because they are familiar with the components of the particular system.

Of course, any given vendor ensures that at least its own products are well supported on its system. For example, when it was introduced, IBM's system had no provision for Ethernet cabling, but DEC's system did offer such an option. In an environment where a company typically buys most of its data processing equipment from one vendor, selection of that vendor's cabling system might make sense. However, if a company wishes to sole-source the entire environment, and thereby have one company to point to when failures occur, then using a vendor's structured cabling system would be an excellent idea. But essentially the same system can be built by independent cabling suppliers at a significantly lower cost. Also, if a multivendor environment exists in the building, the vendor-specific plans limit the opportunities to tie everything together neatly.

Building cabling has vendor-independent standards known as EIA/TIA[1] 568 A/B and EIA/TIA 569. The intent of these standards is to provide, in effect, a highest common denominator. If the standards are adhered to, they should be able to support anything, presuming that the EIA/TIA has thought of it. If you are planning to comply with the EIA/TIA guidelines, you must make your own choices as to media.

All structured cabling standards address two basic types of wiring: vertical and horizontal. Vertical wiring is cabling that connects wiring closets, each of which serves multiple users. Usually, the wiring closets to be connected are each on a different floor. With luck, they will be in the same position on each floor. Figure 39-2 shows a sample of the wiring closets stacked

---

[1] EIA is the Electronics Industries Association; TIA is the Telecommunications Industry Association. These bodies set the standards for the structured wiring systems.

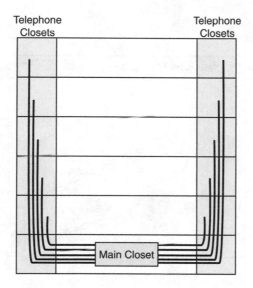

Figure 39-2

The telephone closets are typically stacked on top of each other in high-rise buildings. The vertical wiring feeds to each floor.

above each other in a high-rise office building. Vertical wiring usually runs up and down, hence the name. Vertical wiring is always at least the same bandwidth as horizontal wiring. More often than not, high-speed media is used for vertical wiring because connecting groups of users (with all of their traffic appearing on the vertical wiring) can demand aggregate bandwidths far exceeding those needed to satisfy individual user requirements.

The telephone closets are typically stacked on top of each other in high-rise buildings. The vertical wiring feeds to each floor. Horizontal wiring runs from the wiring closet above the ceiling to the wall jack in each of the office locations. Figure 39-3 is a representation of the horizontal wiring system running to the wall jack. This includes such things as the cable, the drop inside or behind the wall, and the wall plate (jack). In many cases, the horizontal wiring will include the base cord that runs from the wall outlet and plugs into the PC or telephone set at the desk.

Interbuilding wiring also is often a concern to those wiring a campus or multibuilding environment. Like vertical wiring, it must carry high bandwidths (only more so). It also necessitates special requirements, such as resistance to gophers or rodents and other environmental hazards, and presents special problems, such as appropriate grounding when connecting between two different buildings' electrical systems.

The rest of this chapter presents the more likely choices currently available for these types of wiring.

Twisted Pair

Twisted pair refers to telephone wiring. This type of paired wiring usually comes as two solid copper wires, each covered with a plastic insulator and twisted together. It is not the silver satin cable often sold in hardware stores for use with telephones. Silver satin is a flat-wire system where all the wires are laid side by side rather than twisted around each other in pairs. Twisted-pair wiring is often described as shielded or unshielded twisted pair (STP or UTP). UTP (Figure 39-4) has been primarily used for voice communications. It is twisted to reduce induction effects in adjacent wires, otherwise known as cross talk. The more twists per foot, the better the reduction in the cross talk. The twisted-pair wiring is usually sold in various flavors, as shown in Table 39-1. In these pairings, the number of pairs is always important because of basic and immediate needs as well as future needs. The best approach anyone can take when installing wiring to the desk or in vertical distribution is always to add more.

Table 39-1

Typical Number of
Pairs Used for
Installation

Description	Number of Pairs	Used
Analog telephone wiring	2 pairs	1 pair
Digital telephone wiring	1–4 pairs	1–4 pairs
LAN wiring Ethernet 10BASE-T	4 pairs	2 pairs
LAN wiring token ring 4 or 16 Mbps	4 pairs	2 pairs
Horizontal telephone wires	25 pairs	1–4 for individual sets

The wire pairs are typically color coded so that the pairing can be kept together visually, rather than by guesswork. This pairing color code is designed so that a striped wire and a solid-color wire, or a striped wire and a striped wire of the reverse color combination, create a pair; older wiring systems, such as the old telephone wiring in households, use a solid-color wire convention. Table 39-2 shows the more common combinations. The two colors on the wire insulation represent where the convention uses a striped color code (that is, white/blue means a white wire with a blue stripe,

Table 39-2

Color Coding for
Normal Pairings

Pair Number	Color-Coded Pairing
One	White wire/blue stripe and blue wire, or white wire/blue stripe and blue wire/white stripe
Two	White wire/orange stripe and orange wire, or white/orange and orange/white
Three	White/green and green or white/green and green/white
Four	White/brown and brown or white/brown and brown/white

Older analog wiring found still in some buildings uses a four-wire pairing with these color-coding conventions.

One	Red/green Red is the transmit and green is the receive wire.
Two	Black/yellow Black is the battery and yellow is the ground for some sets; if a two-line set is used, then black is transmit 2 and yellow is receive 2.

blue/white means a blue wire with a white stripe). In the reverse wiring, the color code uses the two colors in the reverse; however, the normal pair contains a striped and a solid wire (that is, white/blue is a white wire with blue stripes and blue is a solid blue wire).

If installing a telephone set (for example) that requires one pair, it would be imprudent to run the wires to the set with only one pair enclosed. Otherwise, the first thing that would happen if you chose to change the device hanging off these wires is that you would be confronted with the need to rewire with additional pairs. Telephone systems typically can be used that require from one to four pairs at the desk. Thus, the minimum number of pairs to the desk is four. We have always adopted a standard that a minimum of two each of the four-pair wiring be installed. After all, the cost of adding a few hundred feet of wire at the time of initial installation is only a few cents per foot. If, however, rewiring is necessary, the labor to go back and pull more wires will cost a significant amount (Table 39-3).

UTP is a balanced wiring system. This means that both wires carry similar types of electrical signals and have similar characteristics. No special grounding is required. With the appropriate adapter, UTP can be used to support nonremote terminal traffic that would otherwise require RS232 cabling. Shielded twisted-pair (STP) wiring (Figure 39-5) was endorsed by IBM at about the same time the company released the 4-Mbps token ring.

Table 39-3

Comparing the Difference Between Pulling a Single Cable Twice versus Two Cables Once Shows the Real Dollar Value of Preplanning. The Main Cost Difference Is the Labor.

Item	Cost of Pulling One Cable to Each Desk (each)	Cost of Pulling Two Cables to Each Desk (each × 2)
Materials (4-pair cable, block, RJ45, cross-connect wire, base cord)	$9.35	$18.70
Labor to pull wires, punch down and test	$300	$320
Total cost per run	$309.35	$338.70
@ 50 pulls	$15,467.50	$16,935
Cost for additional installations	$15,467.50	$0 50
Total cost	$30,935	$16,935
Difference		($14,000)

Figure 39-5
Shielded twisted pairs include foil wrap that is connected to a good earth ground.

STP was better for data communications than early UTP was, but only if it was installed correctly. The shield—a foil sheath covering the copper pairs —must be properly grounded. If not, the shield can create a ground loop (Figure 39-6). This situation introduces the possibility that a wiring system will become an antenna, which is worse than if no shielding were used. STP is also more costly than UTP because of the extra foil shielding and because the jacks and plugs cost significantly more than those used with UTP. STP was generally used only for token ring installations, before appropriate UTP grades and components became available. The shield, if properly installed, will provide better cable performance, such as reduced cross talk, protection from grounds and faults, greater signal distances, and protection from EMI and RFI interference.[2]

AT&T (now Lucent) and others experienced many queries from customers as to the transmission characteristics of various UTP offerings. The

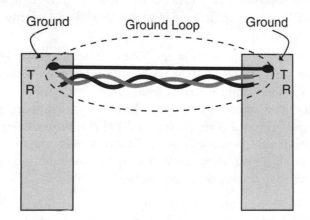

Figure 39-6
If grounded on both ends at different potentials, the shield creates a ground loop. This is worse than no ground at all.

---

[2] EMI refers to electromechanical interference; RFI refers to radio frequency interference. These are the conditions that are introduced into the copper on the twisted-pair wiring.

company's specification sheets provided the desired information, but in a format that only an electrical engineering graduate could understand. To make buying products easier, vendors developed a set of simplified data-grade wire specifications based on the underlying detailed electrical characteristics of the wire. Initially supported by the Underwriters Laboratories (UL), this specification contained three levels numbered 1 through 3. As more wiring products became available and needed, the company extended the grading scheme. Now five defined levels or data grades for UTP wiring are supported by the TIA/EIA, each capable of handling its own requirements as well as those addressed by all lower levels:

- **Level 1**   Sometimes described as barbed wire, this level will handle the requirements of voice communications, called plain old telephone service (POTS), and limited data rates that meet EIA 232-specific data rates (such as 19.2 Kbps).

- **Level 2**   This level is certified to handle the requirements of a 4-Mbps token ring.

- **Level 3**   This level addresses Ethernet's requirements of 10 Mbps on twisted pairs. The specifications from various vendors suggest that this specification will support higher rates, such as 16 and 20 Mbps, but it is not an EIA standard.

- **Level 4**   This level is used for 16-Mbps token ring speeds and the 20-Mbps ARCNet service. IBM is planning to introduce a 25-Mbps token-passing ring concept at duplex arrangements that will be called ATM. The specification is to use level 3 or 4 wiring to support these speeds.

- **Level 5**   This level is certified to function properly at up to 100 Mbps, protocol unspecified, as long as no cable run exceeds 100 meters (328-foot combined runs from the closet to the workstation). The industry is now stating that level 5+ will support up to 155-Mbps speeds that are supported by ATM standards. A level 5E is being endorsed to support gigabit Ethernet over copper cables because the speeds continue to rise and rewiring the building every time a speed increase occurs is too expensive.

The term *level* applies only to the wire itself. The entire system is described as category *n*, where n matches the wiring level. The entire system includes jacks, plugs, and patch panels, in addition to the wiring itself. These components also need to be certified as meeting category whatever requirements. Because category 5 components cost more to install, people sometimes install category 5 wiring with category 3 components. Because replacing the components is much easier than rewiring a building, they expect to replace the components later if required.

Some LAN technologies require 100 Mbps. These include two varieties of Fast Ethernet, as well as a standard for Fiber Distributed Data Interface (FDDI) that runs on category 5 UTP. No matter what LAN topology is used, UTP is almost always configured with a radial wiring plan and rarely as a physical bus. Radial (or star, radiating out from a central point) fits well into building cabling troughs, which in large part accounts for the popularity of UTP data wiring.

UTP offers the lowest medium cost per foot installed. Of available technologies, it is the most limited in distance because of the nature of the medium. Every medium has an inverse relationship between distance and potential speed. The specific ratio varies with the media. For any given speed, UTP has the shortest distance limitation of the media discussed in this chapter.

However, UTP has many suppliers, and installers are familiar with it. Because of its popularity, vendors focus on getting their products to function in this type of physical plant. Unless a company will possibly need speeds greater than 100 to 155 Mbps to the desktop, or will need cable runs to exceed 100 meters, a category-5 installation is likely to handle all requirements for at least the next 5 years. If you are planning a category-5 implementation, however, be sure to have installers who are experienced with category 5 and who have more than just basic telephone wiring experience. Installing category 5 is not particularly difficult, but it is different from the other wiring levels. Specific considerations must be adhered to when installing this type of wiring or all efforts will be for naught. When improperly installed, the category-5 cabling can be negated and functionally provide only speeds based on the weakest link in the system, such as category 1. You can spend a lot of money on the wiring system, only to be left with an infrastructure that doesn't meet expectations; or, retrofits that are expensive might be required to bring the wiring up to standard. This can be a devastating financial burden to the organization.

Twisted-pair wire is typically cabled using standardized jacks and plugs. Originally standardized by AT&T, the designations of these jacks are easily understood codes (such as RJ11, RJ45, and others). We assume that someone found them easy to understand, anyway. In any case, the key differentiating factors among these jacks and plugs are

- How many pairs of wire can terminate on the jack (two, three, or four)?
- How many pairs of wire actually do terminate on the jack?
- How are the pairs assigned?

Every electrical signal path on UTP requires one pair of wires. If two signal paths are required (for example, digital sending and receiving), then two pairs are required. However, those pairs most likely will not be assigned in sequence (for example, left to right or right to left); that would be too easy. As an example, voice wiring on an RJ11 jack (which can hold two pairs of wire and thus handle two analog voice lines) typically uses the center pair of pins or wires on the jack for the first line, and the outer pair for the second line if present. If only one line is to be installed, sometimes the outer pair will not even be present on the jacks and plugs, even though the RJ11 jacks are still used.

Every defined use of UTP (for example, 10BASE-T for Ethernet) includes a very precise specification of which positions will be used on what jack for which transmission path. 10BASE-T is different from token ring, and both differ from the standard for FDDI[3] over UTP, even though all of these are defined on RJ45 jacks and plugs. See Figure 39-7 for a representation of the various ways that the wires can be used in the jacks based on differing standards.

Figure 39-7

The specific number of pairs and the pinouts differ on the basis of use.

---

[3] Fiber Distributed Data Interface (FDDI) was specified on a proprietary cabling scheme using Copper Distributed Data Interface (CDDI). This has not been popular because of the Ethernet speed increases and proliferation.

Coax

Coaxial cable is decreasing in popularity. Before fiber was developed, it was the only practical medium to achieve high bandwidths over distances exceeding a few hundred feet. Whereas a high-speed signal (up to about 100 Mbps) can go via UTP up to 100 meters or so, some forms of coaxial cable can carry signals requiring several hundred Mbps a few thousand meters. The two basic forms of coaxial cable are baseband and broadband. Baseband is used for an Ethernet connection and broadband is the typical cable used in cable TV (CATV) systems. The use of baseband versus broadband systems was covered in Chapter 23.

Coaxial cable is an unbalanced medium; the signal goes through one conductor (the inner core), while the other conductor (the outer braid) functions as the ground. Signals can be converted from a balanced to an unbalanced medium (and back) via use of a special passive device called a balun (balanced and unbalanced), so long as the numbers of required conductors match. This technique is used to supplement coaxial cable with twisted-pair wires as an economic measure. Coaxial ends might be used on a cable run, but UTP wires are used in the middle for the vertical or horizontal run to save money in the wiring of a building. See Figure 39-8 for a typical installation using the balun.

All coaxial cables have the same basic construction. Each has an inner conductive core, usually of copper (usually solid but sometimes stranded). Around the core is the dielectric, an insulating material. Around the dielectric is a second conductive path or sheath, usually in the form of braided copper. This basic construction is illustrated in Figure 39-9 for baseband coaxial cable and in Figure 39-10 for broadband coaxial cable. As with other available media, the underlying construction is varied in many ways to enable customization for specific purposes.

Variations in the thickness of the three key components, as well as in the type or types of covering used, result in a bewildering array of possible cables. Each specific type has a designation (for example, RG58A) that

Figure 39-8
The balun is used to run less-expensive twisted pairs to a coax interface.

Coaxial   Twisted Pair

Balun   Balun

Figure 39-9
The baseband coax
construction

Solid aluminum
sleeve or braided
copper shield

Copper center conductor

Outer Jacket
(PVC or Teflon)

Dielectric foam
polyethylene

Figure 39-10
The broadband coax
construction

Solid aluminum
sleeve

Copper center conductor

Outer Jacket
(PVC or Teflon)

Dielectric foam
polyethylene

completely specifies its characteristics. Each type of LAN or other communications system standard typically includes a specification that designates the types of cable on which that system is supported.

Coaxial cable now is rarely used for horizontal wiring, although Ethernet can use thin-wire coax in this way. The reason is that the cost per port for thin wire is much higher than for UTP. On the other hand, coax is the second best choice (after fiber) for vertical wiring. Its high bandwidth and its capability to handle longer distances fit the requirements of vertical wiring well. Also, it is easier to splice and repair than fiber.

Coax was the first choice for interbuilding wiring in the past—that is, before fiber became generally available. But, with the exception of ease of repair and termination, fiber has now supplanted coax as the medium of choice for external wiring.

Fiber Optics

Fiber optics is the medium of the 21st century and available now. It is a technology everyone seems to be welcoming with open arms. The available bandwidth, the potential flexibility, the range of applications available, and the ring topology that all wide-area carriers appear to be installing lend credibility to the widespread use of fiber. Considering that the technology is relatively new both as regards deployment into private telecommunications networks and by the local exchange and interexchange carriers, the acceptance of the technology is positive.

Fiber can be used both as a wide area and a local area-cabling medium. As a wide-area network (WAN) medium, it has no peer. Essentially all new long-distance cable runs are now built using fiber technologies. Most of the interexchange carriers have adopted a ring topology in their networks. Because the bandwidth is so readily available to them, they can provide automatic reroute capabilities along the reverse route. This is also the way many of the local exchange carriers are going. See Figure 39-11 for a sample layout of a carrier network with a fiber ring. This picture shows the resiliency of a ring in the event of a cable or equipment failure.

The ring topology is only one of the available possibilities. Organizations considering installing private fiber, whether LANs or WANs, must address the issue of which topology should be deployed. The three basic topologies to deliver bandwidth to the user are the star, ring, and dual counterrotating ring network.

The star network is workable as long as a diverse route exists as protection against failure. However, if the star is single threaded, the user and the

Figure 39-11
The carrier networks using fiber rings

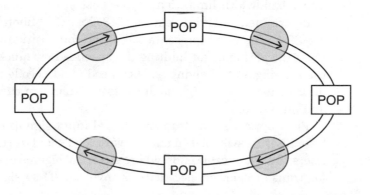

carrier are at risk of failure. The use of a diverse route tends to drive up costs for the use of this topology. Therefore, many users might be concerned about providing only a single feed as their primary route for local service, dedicated services, and access to the point of presences (POPs).

Rings automatically provide the diverse route through a single access point. Vendor and user alike gain advantages by using a ring. In the event of a failure of some component along the way, the ring can be automatically reversed to carry traffic in the opposite direction. Many private users have adopted this technique. The cost is higher, but the risks are minimized. The critical point of failure might be the entrance to the building, the common cable vault where all the services come together. Thus, before choosing to deploy fiber rings, a critical look has to be cast on the total route, and choke points must be eliminated.

The dual counterrotating ring (DCRR) is the latest and greatest idea in the protection of bandwidth. If access into the building can be diverse, and a ring is established with two diverse fiber rings running in two diverse routes to the same location, you have the DCRR. The first ring is installed normally, as any ring might be; the second is run through diverse entrances and along different conduit-, pole-, or direct-buried routes. In addition to being the most expensive solution to the network configuration, this technique is also the most versatile. Information (such as voice, data, graphics, and images) is modulated onto both fibers and simultaneously transmitted to the receiving end. The receiver, getting both transmissions, evaluates the information and selects the best signal for use. In the event that a problem occurs along the way, causing disruptions to the signal, the receiver will receive from only one source. Therefore, the decision to select is null; the receiver uses the only signal it received.

Fiber comes in both glass and plastic varieties. Glass works faster, but for reasonably short distances (up to about 3 kilometers) plastic suffices. The upper bandwidth limitation on the best of the glass offerings has yet to be determined, but it is in excess of 13 Gbps (13 billion bits per second). Figure 39-12 shows a representation of the composition of the fiber. Interestingly, the gating factor limiting the speed is how quickly the electronics at the sending and receiving ends can code and decode the signals. It is less difficult to generate signals much faster than can currently be recognized and processed.

Fiber optic systems transmit digital input signals over modulated light beams (lights switched on and off work for 1's and 0's) that pass through the fibers. Except at cable ends, where electrical signals are converted into light for transmission, no electricity is involved. Thus signals on fiber cannot

Figure 39-12

The composition of
optical fiber

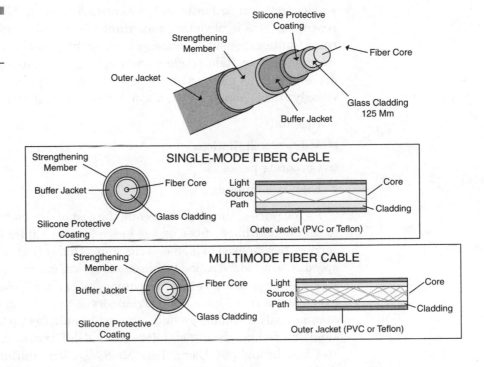

interfere with, transmit, or be affected by any surrounding electromagnetic or electrical signals. This implies that

- Fiber signals are immune to interference.
- Fiber signals cannot generate any electrical interference.
- Fiber signals are (almost) immune to security violations, at least while on the fiber.

Glass fiber comes in two basic types: single-mode and multimode. (All plastic fiber is multimode.)

Single-mode is better. It has no known upper bandwidth limitation.[4] However, it costs more and is generally overkill for non-WAN applications. Telcos and long-distance carriers use it for runs of hundreds or even thousands of miles without needing to use repeaters. The most recent

---

[4] The theoretical limit of single-mode fiber is 100 terabits per second (Tbps), although no means of testing this speed are available.

single-mode transatlantic cable was installed over 3,000 miles without any repeaters. This is obviously important because the repeaters require the same (quite expensive) electronic componentry as the ends. Normally, end users do not include single-mode fiber in their environments, but price decreases in the electronics and fiber are making this far more attractive. Clearly, this is happening in major campus environments such as

- Hospitals
- Military installations
- Corporate parks
- High-rise buildings

As the price of the glass drops and the cost of the electronics moves closer to that of multimode fiber, expect to see far more glass fiber installed. The carriers have moved to high-end electronics today that are specified to carry speed on a standard called synchronous optical networks (SONET). SONET specifies the speeds at which the equipment can multiplex signals from various sources into high-speed carrier services (Table 39-4). Today, we have commercially available products that will multiplex up to 10 Gbps onto the single-mode fiber. Now a standard for SONET is evolving that will yield a 40-Gbps throughput. Using dense wave division multiplexing (DWDM) on the fiber, a capacity of 320 Gbps is possible immediately. However, nothing stops and waits for us to catch up. Therefore, a single-mode fiber with DWDM will soon be offering speeds of 1.6 Tbps (terabits, or trillion bits, per second).

The upper speed limit on multimode cable is currently under 1 Gbps, fast enough for most applications. Table 39-5 shows a summary of the multimode speeds based on the thickness of the glass. This is something that has

Table 39-4

Typical Speeds Currently Specified on Single-Mode Fiber

Single-Mode Fiber									
10 MC Using SONET Standards (the range of thickness is between 8.3 and 10 microns)									
OC1	OC3	OC9	OC12	OC24	OC36	OC48	OC96	OC192	OC255
51.84	155.52	466.56	622.08	1.244	1.866	2.488	4.976	9.953	13.92
Mbps	Mbps	Mbps	Mbps	Gbps	Gbps	Gbps	Gbps	Gbps	Gbps

Table 39-5

Typical Speeds for
the Various
Thickness of
Multimode Fiber

Multimode Fiber	
Microns/Thickness	Typical Speeds
100–140	40–100 Mbps
62.5–125	100–565 Mbps
50–125	466–622 Mbps

been around for some time now, and the thickness of the glass is continually evolving. The various thickness listed in the table is based on just that evolution. The current multimode fiber predominantly employed is 62.5-micron glass with a 125-micron outer cladding. Other standards exist, but the specifications for FDDI and other associated protocols call for 62.5/125. The cable costs are getting to the point of being equal these days, but the electronics for the multimode fiber are significantly less expensive. How long that will continue is a mystery. However, we do know from the previous chapters that the Asynchronous Transfer Mode (ATM), Switched Multimegabit Data Service (SMDS), and other higher speed transport systems are all being used more and more. As this continues and other technologies roll out, you can expect that fiber will become a commodity-priced item.

Applications of Fiber

Table 39-6 is a summary of the driving applications that will cause the proliferation of more fiber in the carrier and in end user networks. Each of these applications can be satisfied by current technologies and transport systems. However, as the need for the integration of various pieces of these applications continues, the current speeds will not be enough. Thus, the computers we know today will demand more speed and larger file transfers. Video to the desktop or onto a LAN will get closer and closer to reality for the masses. The wiring infrastructure must therefore be prepared to support raw bandwidth to the desktop rather than a slower shared medium among multiple users.

Table 39-6

Application
Demands for the
Speed of Fiber

Uses of Fiber Systems

Voice   Although voice does not inherently require the speeds of fiber, it is the multi-plexing of thousands of voice calls onto a single fiber that will aid in the deployment.

Data   Data speeds will continue to increase beyond what we currently use. At dial today, the user can get 28.8 to 56 Kbps depending on the network used. Future speeds in the multi-Mbps range will not be uncommon.

Video   Real-time video requires 243 Mbps, which today is unrealistic and prohibitively priced. However, video to the desk for simultaneous conversations at dozens to hundreds of desks will require much higher aggregated bandwidth than only fiber can deliver.

Computer conferencing   Host-to-host and client-server computing systems are going to demand much more from our communications infrastructure.

Computer-aided design/computer-aided manufacturing (CAD/CAM)   CAD files are getting larger and more complex every day. Newer CAD systems produce three-dimensional, solid graphics. Files that were once a few hundred kilobytes are now hundreds of megabytes. In the future, such files may be gigabytes or terabytes.

LAN to LAN   Transparency across LAN boundaries at speeds approximating 155 Mbps to every desk will obviate all other technological advances and demand the fiber to the desk.

LAN to WAN   Just as LAN boundaries need to be crossed, the wider area will be stressed to keep up with the demands of the future bandwidth.

Host to Host   As already mentioned, large data transfers, real-time journaling, and backup between host computers will keep up the pace on the bandwidth needs.

Multimedia   Linking voice, data, LAN, and video traffic simultaneously will be a big hit in the future. The fiber in the backbone and to the desk will make it happen.

Medical imaging   Teleradiology, telemedicine, and other imaging systems (CAT, MRI, and so on) will demand that the capacities of the fiber be placed to any location and at any desk for on-demand dial-up services.

Fiber Differences

Two types of materials are in any fiber. Both are glass (or both plastic), but with different indexes of refraction. The inner core is actually where the signal is carried; the surrounding material, called the cladding, has a reflective inner surface (by virtue of the different refraction index) that keeps most of the light within the inner core.

Fiber comes in various sizes, which are all very small. The diameters of both types of fibers are measured in microns (a micron is one millionth of a meter). The diameters are always specified with two numbers separated by a slash or dash. The first number is the diameter of the inner core; the other is the outer diameter of the cladding. The most popular and most used multimode fiber's specification is 62.5/125; the generally used monomode fiber has an 8-micron center but a similar outer diameter, so its specification is 8/125.

Fiber is the medium of choice for interbuilding wiring because of its non-electrical nature (eliminating interbuilding grounding issues as well as being, if buried, entirely immune to the effects of lightning strikes) and the great distances it can cover without intermediate repeaters. It is also often used for vertical wiring because of both its bandwidth and its electrical immunity. Its small size also recommends it for this application, especially in buildings with risers that are almost full.

Why Would One Not Use Fiber Wherever Possible?

- The material still costs somewhat more than UTP.
- Fewer people know how to work with it.
- Splicing and terminating remain difficult, although this is improving, with new automated systems developed for the purpose.
- Components using it are not generally available for all types of LANs, although they are for Ethernet.

LANs implemented on fiber do not necessarily operate any more quickly than those based on UTP. For example, Ethernet runs at 10 Mbps. To gain the speed benefits of fiber, a different type of LAN must be used, implying the need for more expensive active components throughout the network. Use of fiber effectively eliminates the upper speed limit for future uses of the LAN cabling; only the active devices would require upgrading to increase operational speeds. Category-5 systems can operate LANs at up to 100 Mbps (but only up to about 100 meters away from a hub), which is faster than most communications managers think they will have to go in the near future.

Questions

1. When local area networks (LANs) were first introduced on a widespread basis, a new concept called _____ became popular.

   a. Voice cabling usage

   b. Data utility

   c. Structured wires

   d. Main distribution frames

2. Early on, high-speed connections in an IBM environment were handled with special in-room cables called _____ and _____ cables.

3. EIA/TIA 568 A/B and EIA/TIA 569 are vendor-independent standards for building cabling.   T/F

4. All structured cabling standards address two basic types of wiring:

   a. Basic and advanced

   b. Vertical and horizontal

   c. Riser and flat

   d. Riser and standard

5. _____ wiring runs from the wiring closet above the ceiling to the wall jack in each of the office locations.

   a. Backbone

   b. Vertical

   c. Riser

   d. Horizontal

6. UTP is a(n) _____ wiring system.

   a. Unbalanced

   b. Balanced

   c. Hybrid

   d. Twin axial

7. Interbuilding wiring also is often a concern to those wiring a _____ or multibuilding environment.

   a. Building

   b. Floor

    c. Multitenant

    d. Campus

8. UTP has been primarily used for _____ communications.

    a. Data

    b. Video

    c. Fax

    d. Voice

9. UTP is twisted to reduce induction effects in adjacent wires, otherwise known as _____.

10. _____ was better for data communications than early UTP was if installed correctly.

    a. Ethernet coax

    b. CATV

    c. Fiber

    d. STP

11. A foil sheath covering the copper pairs must be properly grounded or it can create a:

    a. False connection

    b. Noisy connection

    c. Ground loop

    d. Far end cross talk

12. The medium of the 21st century is _____.

    a. Coax

    b. Fiber

    c. Wireless

    d. UTP

13. Coaxial cable is a(n) _____ medium.

    a. Inexpensive

    b. Balanced

    c. Unbalanced

    d. Twin axial

14. Signals can be converted from a balanced to an unbalanced medium (and back) with a special passive device called a _____.

15. Fiber comes in both _____ and _____ varieties.

    a. Thick, thin

    b. Plastic, glass

    c. Fat, skinny

    d. Single, dual

Planning the Communications Applications

After reading this chapter and completing the questions, you will be able to:

- Discuss the various ways of using the communications systems
- Understand that organizations are developing more dependencies on communications systems
- Discuss the benefits associated with the process
- Understand the components that link together in a communications system
- Link all the pieces together in your own applications

U p to this point, we have covered many of the facets and components that comprise a communications system. From the very beginning we promised to make this as nontechnical (engineering) as possible. We have included pricing models in some cases or have looked at the use of the systems in pieces that can become the overall infrastructure for other connections. We have spent a good deal of this book discussing the pros and cons of the pieces where possible. But the real icing on the cake comes from the actual use of these systems and technologies. We plan to put together a few lists that will show services and capabilities of a telecommunications-oriented person. From there, we can then let you use your imagination in either selling the product, installing the pieces, financially justifying the projects, or just using the services of networks. The issues are not going to be all-inclusive; instead we are going to give you the model upon which to build. The structure is to assemble enough information in which to evaluate and formulate an action plan. Whole books could be written for this subject, but we want to at least provide some rudimentary guidelines for you to proceed.

Starting Point

Let's start off with a scenario. You are a new person to the communications business. You have just taken your first position in an organization. Management has tasked you with coming up with an assessment of what you can do for the organization. You now have to come up with a game plan.

After taking a new position, it usually works to take two to six weeks (this depends on the size of organization) to learn just what the pieces are. During this time it helps to get the feel for the system.

Step 1: Make a Phone Call Anywhere in the World by Picking up Any Phone and Dialing It.

1. Are you on a key system or a PBX?

2. Are any policies and procedures in place that describe who can make a call internationally?

3. If procedures are in place, what roadblocks prevented or allowed the call to go through?

4. Find out if any tools are in place that will track the telephone call by:

Date of call
Name (or extension) of caller
Time of call
Dialed number
Cost and allocation
Duration of call
Approvals needed, if any

5. What procedures would you recommend if you had a free hand at reestablishing the procedures?

6. Before you react, do you understand the operation well enough to make a change?

7. Is an equipment log and inventory available for the key system or PBX?

8. How old is the equipment?

9. Are maintenance logs kept? Are they available?

10. What revision level and date of purchase is the system?

11. What is the current revision level of the vendor's product?

All too often people step into a new position and try to make changes immediately because they feel that they must produce and justify their selection. Unfortunately, they do this before they really understand the operation or the company's business. Assume that the company's primary business is selling products and services to international markets. Would this knowledge change your decision? Therefore, take a few weeks to learn the business. Then start to amass the information.

Step 2: Make a Data Connection.

1. Sit behind your PC and connect to the server on your LAN.

2. Peruse the network and see how many servers exist on your LAN. (You can use the Windows network neighborhood icon on your Windows desktop, if you are running on that platform.)

3. Make some notes about the following:

How many network devices can you see on the network?
How many can you log onto (can you share files, directories, or printers from any other user?)
If you can access these devices, can you open files and read/write to/edit, or delete the files? Are you supposed to have this privilege?
Can you add or delete protocols on the LAN?
Can you get a list from your PC on the protocols used and the shares in place?
Are file and printer sharing turned on?
Connect to the Internet from this PC.
Can you access any sites from the Internet?
Can you send and receive e-mail?
Can you send and receive attachments?
Can you send/receive .exe or .bat files?
Does the system have a virus scanner? Is it active?
Can you update your DAT files (the virus scanner's updates)? Are you supposed to do this?
Try these things from a different PC on the LAN.
Can you log onto another PC? Is there any restriction? Do you need a password?
How often is the password changed? Are there any restrictions on the type or length of password?
Does the PC have a backup system (tapes, CDs, and so on)?
Who makes the backup copies of the data? How often? Where are the tapes stored?

4. Ask others to log onto the network PCs from their own PCs and see what they can access.

5. Keep track of who can gain the various unrestricted levels of access.

6. Are you and others supposed to have all of these privileges?

Step 3: Make a Physical Inspection of the Wiring.

1. Take a walk around the building. Look for the obvious problems:

Are the wall plates attached to the wall firmly?
Are multiplug wall plates in use? Can you move a phone plug to the data port? Can you move the data plug to the phone port? Will that cause some problems in the future?
Are the station cables extending from the wall to the terminal (or phone) on the floor? Are people rolling over the cables with their chairs?
Are the jacks all labeled using some form of standard (closet, cable, or jack)?
Who is allowed to plug in a device?
Are any rules set allowing or denying people access to these?
Could a user plug a laptop PC into a spare port and access the LAN?
Do you know what protocols are used on the LAN? (NETBUI?)
Are people abusing their phones or terminals in fits of rage?
Are any maintenance logs around? Are they up to date?
Do people know who to call for problems with phones or PCs?

2. Step into a telephone closet and see the condition of the wiring and the neatness.

3. Was the closet locked or secured in any way? Is there more than one closet?

4. If the closet(s) is locked, who has access and keys? Is there a list of authorized key holders?

5. Is there a wiring book showing all the connections? Who maintains it?

6. Are drawings and labels on all the devices? Are these kept secure?

7. If you had to conduct a major renovation, see if the installed wires have wiring logs by office, building, floor, closet, and so on. If you need to move a department around, how easy would it be to connect them differently?

8. Do this for voice and data connections. Do separate wiring racks and frames for both voice and LAN connections.

9. Are critical data circuits labeled and tagged? Are the circuit IDs in place?

10. Are all the telco circuits inventoried?

11. Are they listed in the site book?

12. Are they accurate and up to date?

13. Do you have a number to call in the event new work is needed? Are you using outside contractors for this part of the job?

Step 4: Make a List of Features and Functions Added to the Phone and Data Network.

1. Are any peripheral boxes (voice mail, ACDs, and so on) installed?

2. Who has a list of these?

3. Who maintains the peripheral boxes?

4. Who is financially responsible (using department, facilities, telecommunications, IS)?

5. Who is operationally responsible?

6. Is there a list of these boxes on the (financial) books? How old are they?

7. What revision levels are you running? What is the current revision level of hardware and software that the vendor is offering? Are you more than two revisions behind?

8. What about the data connection? Does the network have a router or a bridge?

9. What type of connection are you using to the Internet? Do you have an xDSL, a CATV connection, or a dedicated T1 link?

10. If a router is installed, do you have a firewall (hardware and software)?

11. Do you have the circuit IDs on all the data circuits?

Step 5: Talk to the Users.

1. Meet with the department managers to determine what their needs are.

2. What needs are critical? Can you isolate the needs assessment into three categories (must have, should have, and nice to have)?

3. Are you meeting these needs in a reasonable manner?

4. What needs do you not satisfy? Are they critical to the performance of the department's role?

5. What is the perception of your department's ability to meet the needs of the operational groups?

6. Are any seasonal issues coming soon? (For example, Christmas is a very busy time for retailers. Summer is a big time for travel departments.)

7. Are you prepared to satisfy these seasonal demands?

8. Meet with some of the actual users in the managers' departments and see if their issues are the same or different from the managers' perception.

9. Find out who the power users are in each department if possible.

10. Try to determine if in the past the telecommunications department has not met the needs successfully. This will have an impact on your future application and support issues. Are you trying to overcome the past ills of others?

Step 6: Meet with the Appropriate Departments.

(These departments will have some impact on your ability to get your job done. You can meet with these people in any order you feel appropriate. However, the author prefers to meet with the finance department first.)

1. Finance department

What is the allotted budget for the department?
What percentage of revenues is the budget?
What percentage of profits is the budget?
What is the company hurdle rate? (What rate of return do you need to achieve to get projects approved?)

What is the contribution factor considered in sales and production? (Your services help the user departments do their job, whether they sell or produce widgets. Is a portion of the credit applied to your contribution to their mission?)

What has been the historical value of the department budget (increases/decreases per year at what percent)?

Did the department come in under budget, over budget, or within budget within the last year or last 5 years?

Does finance have one person allotted to telecommunications projects who is familiar with terms and products?

What is the depreciation schedule used for the department equipment (3, 5, or 7 years)?

2. Purchasing

Are there special provisions for acquiring needed telecommunications equipment? Does purchasing have a person who deals with the telecommunications equipment?

Are any national contracts in place?

Has purchasing been actively involved in the selection process of telecommunications equipment in the past?

Would they be willing to assign a team member to the future selection and acquisition process?

Does purchasing conduct vendor evaluations? Do they conduct the acid ratio tests on the vendor viability?

Is a process in place to buy equipment (3 to 6 months or 6 to 12 months)?

3. Facilities

Who is responsible for controlling the facilities allocation for telecommunications equipment?

Does facilities have a process to notify telecommunications whenever a department (or person) is scheduled for interoffice moves and reconstruction?

Has facilities kept pace with the power, air conditioning, and space requirements for the operational equipment as well as future needs?
Does facilities control the keys to janitorial and telephone closets?
Is a process in place for expansion needs in the event of a major acquisition?

4. Operational personnel in telecommunications

What are the skill sets of the people working in the telecommunications department?
What problems (if any) do they have in delivering the services they are responsible for?
Who installs the terminal equipment and the telephony equipment? Is the installation by contract or are the installers internal?
What do they perceive as their role in meeting the company's objectives? Do they feel like they are a part of the company?
Do morale problems need addressing?
Does the staff have the appropriate management tools to address the systems and procedures?
Do policies and procedures exist for the procurement of equipment, the installation of equipment, and the use of services?
Who has the signature authority (and at what dollar level) for normal operational needs?

5. Meet with other departments such as security, human resources, advertising, and marketing.

6. Meet with your vendors and establish the rapport necessary to facilitate the plan and implement changes as necessary. Do not be afraid to ask the vendor to brief you with their service offerings and current usage figures.

Wrap up What You Learned

Assuming that you have met with the appropriate departments, management, users, and internal operational personnel, you should be armed to produce a report to management. This report should highlight your assessment of the current state of the technology used within the organization, the degree of sophistication in use, and any shortcomings that can be highlighted. This report should project the current expenditures, a plan for new expenditures, and the projected reduction in cost or increase in productivity if the plan is implemented. Further, a look at new technologies that can be installed should include the targeted audiences (departments) and the contribution effect that will result.

Examples of contribution will be (numbers are generic for exemplary purposes):

- A reduction of expenses by 10 to 15 percent
- Reduced travel costs by telecommuting resulting in a savings of $4,000 monthly
- Reduced turnover (20 percent) of key personnel due to implementation of telecommuting programs
- Increased security through the implementation of VPN technologies
- Increased sales in a specific department of 10 to 20 percent
- Increased marketing penetration in a new area of the country or a new market (at 5 to 10 percent)
- Decreased turnaround time to get the marketing brochures or literature to the market (by 2 weeks)
- Quicker time to market for new production through faster design in the production department (by 1 month)

None of these are extraordinary challenges, but they represent significant turnaround times, reduced cost of sales, or improved customer services. Each of these improvements may be unquantifiable; therefore, you will need to recruit the management in the appropriate departments to lend credibility to your numbers. The real point is that if you recruit others as your allies and champions, the approval process for your plan will be easier and quicker.

Plan the Plan

Create a 5-year implementation plan, including the applications and technologies that you may want to introduce. Include the application with the technology so that management can see what the goal is and what the expected result is that accompanies the new services. An example may be the reduced Federal Express costs ($5,000 net savings per month) by implementing a high-speed remote printer at a division office. Note the operative word is the net savings per month. If I offer to reduce your shipping cost by $20,000 monthly, but have to increase your communications cost by $30,000 monthly, you have a negative savings. You must show the total costs and the resultant differences.

In many cases, the application may not be a reduced telecommunications cost but an increased cost. However, the increase in telecommunications costs of $5,000 per month will produce an increase in the sales through telemarketing techniques of $50,000 monthly, which is a great justification. However, this is where the added telemarketing costs must be tracked against the increased sales in another budget area. The risk is that the department does not pass along the credit to the telecommunications department, but claims the increased sales due to some other procedure that they implement. This happens, so you need to be careful whom you recruit and that they will spread the glory and rewards across the departmental lines. After all, we do work for the same company!

Give numbers and percentages wherever possible in a quantitative mode rather than a qualitative measure. An example is to improve customer support by 10 percent; this is tough to quantify. On the other hand, improvement in customer support that generates 10 percent more business or $10,000 new sales monthly can be quantified.

Improving internal staff satisfaction with the telecommunications is very difficult to track. However, reducing customer complaints by 20 percent can be tracked so long as you have a good benchmark.

Use the technologies for the purpose that they were designed. The telecommunications function moves information across a medium, over a distance in a usable and understandable way. This includes

- Voice
- Data

- Fax
- Video
- Multimedia

Implement the Plan

If we install technologies such as LANs, then we expect to increase connectivity to other in dynamic workgroups and move the data internally at speeds of megabits per second instead of kilobits per second. Moreover, by using the LAN on a dedicated cabling system, we improve the overall quality of the cable and therefore have a resultant increase in the reliability and integrity of the data.

If we add some communications devices, such as a router,, we extend the LAN boundary to the WAN. Now we can add connectivity across a frame relay or ATM network and get faster, better, and cheaper data transfers across the WAN (across the state, country, or world).

By adding an Internet connection, we can stream our audio or video files and save the cost of transmission on a packet-networking basis or dial-up connection. However, by increasing our exposure to the Internet, we increase the risk of interception. Therefore, by including some shim software at the user device and renting the necessary hardware, we can include a VPN connection and reduce the exposure. Using the Internet reduces transmission costs.

Track the Results

By converging the voice- and data-networking strategies, we can introduce a voice over data technology, run the voice and data on a fixed-cost data network, and achieve a significant reduction of voice dial-up costs through packet-switching voice over IP. Cost per minute can be dropped from $.10 to as little as $.03. If you are conducting 1,000,000 minutes per month, the costs will be reduced by $.07 per minute ($70,000 monthly) or whatever proportionate rate that you have.

Add to the voice savings, the possibility of transferring data at a rate of $.01 per packet of 512 bytes. Comparing that to a dial-up connection, savings of $.03 per 512 bytes can be achieved from dial-up connections. That mounts up quickly!

Video can be streamed across the same converged network eliminating as much as $.45 per minute per location conferenced. This could save us up to $.42 per minute per site. Assuming a 30-minute conference, three times per month among five sites, the results are a savings of $190 per month. Yet, if you add five sites and couple the math, the savings are $380 per month. This can go on for many more sites and many more conferences of longer duration. Some organizations have amassed savings of upwards of $10,000 by integrating their voice and video on their data networks.

Using the access to the Internet, a DSL line operating at a 960 Kbps download and 768 Kbps upload may cost as little as $80 per month, compared to renting a fractional T1 (or a full T1) at similar speeds for $2,800 per month. This saves a $2,720 access fee per month.

Report the Results

One can see that the savings can be amassed in many ways for many applications. These savings mount quickly. However, an infrastructure installation is still required first. An organized plan of what pieces need to be installed first and what services will move over is important.

Do not be afraid to tell it like it is. Oftentimes things do not go exactly as planned. Sometimes, the savings are not as dramatic as we originally thought because of a change in philosophy, a change in carrier charges, or a shift in business plans. Do not hide this variation. If you play the game honestly, you will succeed.

INDEX

Symbols

1's density rule, T1, 332
100Base-T Ethernet, 595, 598–599
100VGAnyLAN, 599–600
10Base-F Ethernet, 589–590
10Base-T Ethernet, 587–588
10Base2 Ethernet, 582–586
10Base5 Ethernet, 577–578
10Broad36 Ethernet, 590–592
1XRTT, 943
3G wireless, 937–938
   applications, 947–948
   data transmission, 939–941, 945
   spectrum selection, 944
   UTRA, 946
56Kbps modems, 307
800 services, 111–112, 124
900 services, 125
911 calls, 875–876

A

A links, SS7, 848
A/D converters (analog to digital), 84–85
AAL (ATM Adaptation Layer), 782–783
absorption, light systems, 958
acceptance rates, cellular systems, 892
access
   Internet, 405, 422–423
   Intranets, 465, 469, 481
   MANs, 701–702
ACDs, 222–225
   ANI feature, 227
   collections, 246
   CPI interfaces, 230
   customer calls, screen pops, 245
   database queries, 244
   scripting, 227
ACKs, TCP datagrams, 393
acoustic couplers, 7
ad hoc networks, IEEE 802.11 standard, 604
add-on costs, telecommunications system
     financing, 1010
address signaling, 148
address translation tables, 469
addresses, Ethernet, 573
addressing mechanism, telephones, 64
administration, LNP services, 868
ADSL (Asymmetric DSL), 806
   data rates, 801
   distances, 801
   service deployment, 813
   telco development, 13
ADSL Lite, 13, 810
advantages
   Frame Relay, 743
   infrared systems, 970
   packet networks, 509
adverse unit mounting conditions, light systems,
     961–962
advertising on the Internet, 411
AH (Authentication Header), IPSec, 453
air interface, WAPindependence, 930
AM (Amplitude Modulation), 303
AMI (Alternate Mark Inversion), T1, 326
amplifiers
   analog communications, 82
   analog transmission, 315–316
amplitude, 21 -22
analog cellular systems
   drawbacks, 894
analog communications, 77
   amplifiers, 82
   attenuation, 82
   band-limited channels, 82

compression, 79
noise, 83
rarefaction, 79
signal translation, 78
sinusoidal waves, 79
analog PBXs, 181
analog signaling, broadband LANs, 664
analog transfer, voice signals, 21
analog transmission systems, 314
amplifiers, 315–316
signal loss, 315
analog-to-digital conversion, 320–322
ANI feature (Automatic Number Identification), 227
anonymous access, Telnet, 418
AOL (America Online), 405
Application layer, OSI model, 366
application servers, LANs, 535
application services, ISDN, 763
applications
3G wireless, 947–948
cable modems, 831
communications, 1037
FDDI LANs, 683–684
fiber optic cabling, 1031
full service Intranets, 477–478
SS7, 854–855
WAP, 925
architecture
data communications, 273
DQDB, 704–705
ISDN, 756
networks, 381–383, 389
SONET, 978
SS7, 843
area codes, telephone networks, 42
ARPANET (Advanced Research Projects Agency Network), 390
ASCII code sets, 299
associated signaling links, SS7, 846
asynchronous communications, 274–275
asynchronous connections, packet networks, 511
AT&T
acquisition of small companies, 6
cable TV acquisitions, 13–14
divestiture of Bell System, 8–10
formation, 4
tariffs, 11

telephone network development, 6
TSAPI, 257
Western Electric divestiture, 7
ATM (Asynchronous Transfer Mode), 775
AAL, 782–783
access rates, 787
bandwidth, 780
broadband, 777
C plane, 786
cell relay, 776–779
convergence sublayer, 783
encapsulating the traffic, 792
Frame Relay comparisons, 792
LAN-to-LAN connections, 791
local switches, 790
M plane, 786
PDUs, 783
PMD sublayer, 788
protocols, 785
public switches, 790
SAR, 783
switches, 789
TC sublayer, 788
tunneling through the network, 792
U plane, 786
UNIs, 776
ATM Forum, 789
atmospheric conditions, light systems, 957
attenuation
analog communications, 82
CATV, 660
AUIs (Attachment Unit Interfaces), 577
authentication, VPNs, 454
automated attendants, 216–220
CTI, 262
integrated PBXs, 250
suggestions for system, 221–222
automatic call distributors, 222

B

backbone
FDDI LANs, 683
Internet, 404
LANs, 555
backhoe fade, 33–35, 705

backup servers, LANs, 535
band-limited channels, 23, 82
bands, WATS, 107
bandwidth, 24–25
   ATM, 780
   CATV, 660
   Ethernet, 572
   Intranets, 481
   light systems, 963
banner ads, 411
barrel connectors, 10Base5 Ethernet, 578
base of telephone, 58
baseband cable
   CSMA/CD, 822
   local nets, 646–647
baseband LANs, 654–655
   cheaper cost than broadband, 656
   efficiency, 657
   issues for selection, 666
   scalability, 656
   waveform degradation, 654
basic data flow, Frame Relay, 737–738
baud rate, data communications, 304
Bc (committed burst rate), 729
Be (burst excess rate), 729
bearer independence, WAP, 930
bearer services, ISDN, 770
Bell System
   AT&T divestiture, 8–10
   regulated monopoly, 7
Bell Telephone Company, 5
Bell, Alexander Graham, invention of
      telephone, 1–2
bipolar format, T1, 326, 331
bit robbing, T1, 338
bit synchronization, T1, 3400
bit times, 86
BOCs (Bell Operating Companies), 9, 93
   high-speed communications, 13
   tariffs, 11
   telephone networks, 36
boundaries, LANs, 527
branch exchanges, telephone networks, 37
break-even analysis, telecommunications system
      financing, 1001
BRI ISDN, 756–758, 769
bridges
   FDDI LANs, 686

   LANs, 552
broadband
   ATM, 777
   cable, 823
   local nets, 646–647
broadband LANs, 658–659, 825
   analog signaling, 664
   cabling, 661
   channels, 661
   FAMs, 664
   FDM, 661
   forward direction, 663
   issues for selection, 666
   reverse direction, 662
   TDM, 661
   TDMA, 661
browsers, Web. *See* Web browsers.
burstable Frame Relay, 729
buses
   Ethernet, 568–569
   LAN nodes, 542
business needs, CTI, 251–252
business services, 99
busy calls, LNP, 878
busy studies, traffic engineering, 155–157
byte synchronous transmissions, T1, 326, 332

C

C links, SS7, 848
C plane, ATM, 786
cable modems, 825–833
cable TV
   AT&T acquisition, 13–14
   data-centric applications, 12
cabling, 1013–1014
   10Base-F Ethernet, 590
   10Base-T Ethernet, 587
   10Base5 Ethernet, 578
   10Broad36 Ethernet, 590–592
   broadband LANs, 661
   coax, 1025
   Fast Ethernet, 595
   fiber optic, 1027–1029
   interbuilding, 1017

jacks, 1014–1015
key telephone systems, 196
structured systems, 1016
Token Ring LANs, 624
twisted pair, 1018–1022
UTP, 1023–1024
calculating savings, telecommunications system
financing, 998
call forwarding, LNP, 879
call hold, 73
call lengths, traffic engineering, 159
call processing times, traffic engineering, 157, 160
call setup
SS7, 852
telephones, 70
call transfer, 73
caller displays, 75
calling card services, 119–121
CAP (Carrierless Amplitude Phase), 812
CAPs (Competitive Access Providers), 129
carbon particles, handsets, 61
carriers
800 services, 111–112
business services, 99
CAPs, 129
Centrex, 98
CLECs, 115–116
direct inward dial, 99
direct outward dial, 99
directory services, 112
DLECs, 117
Equal Access, 115
FX service, 105–106
IECs, 118
ILECs, 93–94
intrastate WATS, 110
local calling services, 101
local dial tone, 96
OPXs, 113–114
party lines, 97
pay phones, 101–102
private lines, 103–105, 149–150
residential services, 99
WATS, 107
Carter Electronics of Texas, mobile radio-to-
telephone network connections, 8
CATV (Communicationsunity Antenna
Television), 824

attenuation, 660
bandwidth, 660
broadband cable, 823
cable modems, 825–828
channels, 27
FAMs, 824
FDM, 661
fiber optic upgrades, 826
head ends, 659
Internet, 826
remote office connections, 831
security, 832
TDM, 661
traffic engineering, 827
CCS (Communications Channel Signaling), 339
CDMA
IS-95 air interface, 942–943
PCS, 907
Cdma2000 1X, 943
CdmaOne, 943
CDSL (Consumer DSL), 807
cell relay, ATM, 776–779
cell splitting, cellular systems, 893
cellular systems, 883, 886
acceptance rates, 892
cell splitting, 893
data transmission, 902
demand, 890
drawbacks, 894
fax, 900–901
increasing revenue, 893
LNP, 861
mobile sets, 891
MSAs, 886
MTSOs, 886
network honeycombing, 889
PCS, 905
RSAs, 886
SS7, 889
transmitter placement, 888
voice applications, 898–899
Centrex, 98, 187
components, 188
lines, 136
peripherals, 190
providers, 188
channel works, 10Broad36 Ethernet, 592
channelized service, T1, 326, 334

channels, 25, 661
CHAP (Challenge Handshake Authentication
    Protocol), 451
character code sets, data communications, 299
characteristics of voice. *See* voice characteristics.
CIR (Communicationsitted Information Rate),
    Frame Relay, 729
circuit mode services, ISDN, 760
circuit switching
    TDM, 724
    X.25, 725–727
circuits, 135
CIT (computer-integrated telephony), 238
class-4 offices. *See* toll centers.
clear channels, ISDN, 752
clear line of sight, light systems, 960
CLECs (Competitive Local Exchange Carriers),
    115–116
    Centrex, 98
    DSL, 800
    loss leaders, 15
    return on LNP investment, 865
    small communications unity providers, 15
client/server
    Ethernet networks, 604
    LANs, 537
clients
    VPNs, 442
    WAP, 923
clocking
    data communications, 275–277
    T1, 339
clouds, packet networks, 499
CLP (Cell Loss Priority), ATM cells, 782
coax cabling, 1025
coin phones, 103
collision avoidance, LANs, 558
combined linksets, SS7, 849
communications
    analog, 77
    digital, 77, 89
communications application planning, 1037, 1047
    assessing current system, 1038
    contribution effects, 1046
    data connections, 1039
    department meetings, 1043–1045
    implementation, 1048
    peripherals, 1042

physical wiring inspection, 1041
    talking to users, 1042
communications servers, LANs, 535
communications speeds, LANs, 525
communications systems, linking to computers,
    253–254
compatibility issues, LANs, 651
components
    Ethernet LANs, 576
    LNP, 867
    PBXs, 178
components of telephone, 54
    addressing mechanism, 64
    bases, 58
    call setup, 70
    carbon particles, 61
    dial pad, 66–68
    diaphragm, 61
    handset cords, 63
    handsets, 59
    receivers, 62
    ringer, 64, 70
    rotary phone, 67
    side tone, 63
    switch hooks, 56
    switchhook, 65–66
    tip and ring, 71
    touch tone phone, 68
    transmitters, 61
compression, 21
    analog communications, 79
    data communications, 289–293
computers, linking to communications systems,
    253–254
concentrators, 10Base-T, 588
conference calls, 73
configuring
    DID, 140
    DOD, 141
    FDDI LANs, 674
    FX, 142
    Intranets, 479–480
    OPX, 143
    TIE lines, 144
    Token Ring LANs, 636–640
connection topologies, telephone networks, 32
connections
    ATM LANs, 791

Internet, 405, 423
light systems, 964
packet networks, 501, 504
telephone network, 48
VPNs, 442
connectors
handsets, 63
key telephone systems, 196
consumer WAP applications, 925
contribution effects, communications application
planning, 1046
control signaling, Frame Relay interfaces, 739
Convergence sublayer, ATM, 783
cookies, 420
cords, handsets, 63
corporate data access, Intranets, 471–472
corporate WAP applications, 925
COs (Central Offices), telephone networks, 33
cost-and-benefit analysis, telecommunications
system financing, 1000
cost issues
FDDI LANs, 671–673
key telephone systems, 199
LANs, 651–652
telecommunications system financing, 1000
Web sites, 414
CPI interfaces (Computer to PBX), 230
crank phones, 57
CRC (Cyclic Redundancy Checking), 284–286
Ethernet, 575
packet switching, 498
CRC-6, T1, 350
credit card calls, 101, 119
criteria for light systems implementation, 954
cross-platform compatibility, 362–366
CRTC (Canadian Regulatory Telecommunications
Committee), 16
CSD (Circuit Switched Data), 921
CSMA/CD, Ethernet, 569–571
CTI (computer-to-telephony integration), 238, 243
advantages, 250
automated attendants, 262
business needs, 251–252
fax-back, 263–264
integrated PBXs, 247
IVR, 263
linking computers and communications,
253–254

OCR, 265
PBX interfaces, 260
selectivity, 258
speech to text, 264
technology enhancements, 259–260
text to speech, 264
third-party call control, 257
unified messaging, 255
voice messaging, 261–262
customer pairs, telephone networks, 35
customer Web servers, 466

D

D links, SS7, 848
D3 frames, T1, 343
D4 frames, T1, 343
D4 superframes, T1, 329
daisy chains, 10Base 2 Ethernet, 585
DARPANET (Defense Advanced Research
Projects Agency), 400
DASs (Dual Attached Stations), FDDI LANs, 675
data access, Intranets, 472
data communications, 89, 269–270, 755
architecture, 273
baud rate, 304
cellular systems, 902
channel directions, 286
character code sets, 299
clocking, 275–277
compression, 289–293
DCE devices, 308
DTE devices, 308–309
duplex, 288
error detection, 279–280
FDM, 295
half duplex, 287
iterative teaching, 271
modulation, 303
multiplexing, 293
packet switching, 490–495
protocols, 274
SDM, 294
simplex, 286
standards, 271–272
STDM, 298

TDM, 295–296
transmission problems, 488–489
transmission protocols, 274
V.90 modems, 307
Data connections, communications application
  planning, 1039
data frames, Token Ring LANs, 632–635
data link layer
  FDDI LANs, 678
  OSI model, 368
data-modeling tools, traffic engineering, 163
data payload, Ethernet, 575
data rates
  3G wireless, 939–941
  ADSL, 801
  LANs, 648
  MANs, 696, 709
data units, SMDS
database queries, ACDs, 244
database servers, LANs, 535
datagrams, IP, 391
DCE devices, data communications, 308
DDD (Direct Distance Dialing), 101, 118
de facto standards, data communications,
  271–272
de jure standards, data communications, 271–272
DEC, 360–361
decision-making process, telecommunications
  system financing, 1005
DECNet, 389
dedicated links, packet networks, 507
demarc, 32, 48
department meetings, communications
  application planning, 1043–1045
Dept. of Justice, AT&T Western Electric
  divestiture, 7
destination addresses, Ethernet, 573
device independence, WAP, 930
DHCP (Dynamic Host Control Protocol), 422, 470
dial pads, telephones, 66
diaphragm of telephone, 61
DID (Direct Inward Dialing), 140
digital cellular, 897, 904
digital coding, ISDN, 754
digital communications, 77
  bit times, 86
  repeaters, 87–88

unipolar signals, 86
digital connections, ISDN, 89, 753
digital PBXs, 178, 182–186
digital switching, 319
digital telephones, 57, 72
  call hold, 73
  call transfer, 73
  caller displays, 75
  conference calls, 73
  hands free dialing, 74
  redial, 74
  speakerphones, 74
  speed dialing, 72
digital transmission systems, end users, 324
direct inward dial, 99
direct outward dial, 99
directory assistance, IECs, 128
directory services, 112
discard eligibility rate, Frame Relay, 730
distances, ADSL, 801
distributed processing, LANs, 536
distribution patterns, traffic engineering, 161
diverse routing, 424
divestiture of Bell System, 8–10
DLECs (Data Local Exchange Carriers), 117
DMS, 319
DMT (Discrete Multitone) Modulation, 810
DNA (Digital Network Architecture), 361, 389
DNS, IP address translation, 421
DOCSIS (Data Over Cable Service Interface
  Specification), 829
DQDB (Distributed Queue on a Dual Bus), 699
  MAN access units, 707–708
  SMDS, 699
DS-x (Digital Signal level), 85, 335–336
DSL (Digital Subscriber Line), 799
  ADSL, 801, 806
  ADSL-lite, 810
  CAP, 812
  CDSL, 807
  DMT, 810
  HDSL, 803–804
  IDSL, 802
  RADSL, 806
  SDSL, 806
  SHDSL, 808
  VDSL, 807

VoATM, 815–817
VoDSL, 813–814
DTE devices, data communications, 308–309
duplex data communications, 288
DWDM (Dense Wave Division Multiplexing), 990, 1030
dynamic bandwidth allocation, Frame Relay, 732

E

E links, SS7, 848
E&M
   T1 signaling, 338
   TIElines, 146–147
EBCDIC code sets, 301
EDGE, 941
EDI (Electronic Document Interchange), 255, 466
Edison, Thomas, telephone transmitter, 5
efficiency, baseband LANs, 657
e-mail, 402
   MIME, 419
   PPP, 463
   SMTP, 402, 418, 463
encapsulation
   bridges, FDD ILANs, 686
   SMDS data units, 711
   VPNs, 440
encryption, 450
end offices, telephone networks, 37
end users, digital transmission systems, 324
engineering traffic. *See* traffic engineering.
enterprise management, VPNs, 455
Equal Access, 115
Erlang distribution, traffic engineering, 167–172
error checking, Frame Relay, 731
error detection
   data communications, 279–280
   T1, 345
Error rates, LANs, 526
ESF (Extended Superframe Format), T1, 343, 347, 351
ESP (Encapsulating Security Payload), IPSec, 453
ESSs (electronic switching systems), 319
Ethernet, 272, 567–568, 825
   bandwidth, 572
   bus, 568–569
   components, 576
   CSMA/CD, 569–571
   destination addresses, 573
   Fast Ethernet, 593–599
   full duplex, 558
   Gigabit, 600–601
   half duplex, 571
   naming standards, 576–592
   source addresses, 573
even parity error checking, 280
exchange carrier networks, ISDN, 764–765
exchange codes, telephone networks, 43
Extended ASCII, 301, 403
extended offices, VPNs, 443
external routers, 468

F

F links, SS7, 849
facilities-based environment, WANs, 14
facility data links, T1, 351
FAMs (Frequency Agile Modems), 824
   10Broad36 Ethernet, 592
   broadband LANs, 664
Fast Ethernet, 561, 593–599
fast select
   packet switching, 496
   X.25, 517
fax
   cellular systems, 900–901
   CTI processing, 263–264
fax-backs, 263–264
FCC (Federal Communications Commission)
   MFJ, 10
   mobile radio-to-telephone connections, 8
   Part 68 registration, 8
   regulations on recording conversations, 7
   tariffs, 11
FCS (Frame Check Sequence), 284
FDDI LANs (Fiber Distributed Data Interface), 670
   applications, 683–684
   backbone, 683
   bridges, 686
   configuring, 674
   costs, 671–673

DASs, 675
data link layer, 678
design goals, 670–671
frames, 681
increased throughput, 673
LLC, 678
MAC layer, 679
nodes, 677
NRZI, 679
physical layer, 678
random arrival traffic, 680
recovery, 688
SASs, 675
stations, 676
synchronization, 683
token passing, 680
users, 676
FDDI MANs, 687
FDDI-II, 689
FDM (Frequency Division Multiplexing)
CATV, 661
data communications, 295
female voice characteristics, 27
fiber optic cabling, 1027–1029
applications, 1031
CATV upgrades, 826
DWDM, 1030
Fast Ethernet, 596
indexes of refraction, 1032
financial life cycles, telecommunications system
financing, 1001
financing telecommunications systems, 993–995
add-on costs, 1010
calculating savings, 998
cost-and-benefit analysis, 1000
decision making process, 1005
financial life cycles, 1001
hard benefits, 996
initial costs, 1008
justifying costs, 1005–1006
life cycles, 1000
maintenance issues, 1006–1007
objectives of new system, 1007
payback analysis, 1001
pricing issues, 1004
ROI, 1003
soft benefits, 997–998
finger, 404

firewalls, 450, 466, 469
flat-rate pricing
Frame Relay, 742
residential service, 100
flip telephones, 896
FM (Frequency Modulation), 304
focused Internet advertising, 411
fog, scattering-in-light systems, 958
forward direction, broadband LANs, 663
four wire circuits, T1, 325
Frame Relay, 719–720
advantages, 743
ATM comparisons, 792
basic data flow, 737–738
burstable, 729
CIR, 729
data interfaces, 735
development, 721
discard eligibility rate, 730
dynamic bandwidth allocation, 732
ease of reconfiguration, 733
error checking, 731
flat rate pricing, 742
guaranteed delivery, 730
improved response time, 733
inproved uptime, 732
interfaces, 734
internal networking, 740
IPX/SPX services, 734
LAN-to-LAN communications, 736
limitations, 743
network consolidation, 732
PLLs, 723
simplicity of network design, 722
speeds, 728
standards, 733, 737
TCP/IP services, 734
UNI, 740
usage sensitive rates, 742
voice services, 740–741
X.400 fax, 734
frames
Ethernet, 574
FDDI LANs, 681
SDH, 987–989
SONET, 980–981
T1, 326, 329, 341
telephone networks, 33

Token Ring LANs, 628–629
free space systems, 972
frequencies, 21–22, 27
frequency spectrum, TV channels, 27
front-end processors, mainframe systems, 529
FTP, 403, 417
full duplex
  channels, 49
  data communications, 288
  Ethernet LANs, 558
  T1, 325
full service Intranets, 474–478
full time WATS, 109
functions
  OSI model, 370–380
  telephone, 55–56
  traffic engineering, 157
FX (Foreign Exchange) service, 105–106, 127, 142

G

G.lite, 13
gateways
  LANs, 553
  WAP, 923–924
gathering data, traffic engineering, 159
geographic boundaries, LANs, 527
geometry, light systems, 955–956
GFC (General Flow Control Identifier), ATM
    cells, 780
Gigabit Ethernet, 600–601
gopher, 404
GOSIP (Government Open Systems Interconnect
    Profile), 369
GPRS (General Packet Radio Service), 922, 941
grade of service, traffic engineering, 164–166
Graham-Willis Act, telephone natural monopoly, 6
Gray, Elisha, invention of telephone, 2
growth of Internet, 425–426
GSM, 938
guaranteed delivery, Frame Relay, 730
GUIs, Intranets, 466

H

hackers, VPN security, 448
half duplex
  channels, 48
  data communications, 287
  Ethernet, 571
hand-held phones, 895
handholes, telephone networks, 35
hands free dialing, 74
handsets, 59
  cellular systems, 891
  cords, 63
HDSL (High Bit-Rate DSL), 803
head ends, CATV, 659
headers
  IPdatagrams, 391–392
  TCP datagrams, 393
HEC (Header Error Control), 782
Hertz, Heinrich, 22
high speed data transfers, SMDS, 699
history of Internet, 400
hits, Web sites, 415
HLRs (Home Location Registers), LNP, 877
home offices, VPNs, 444
homologated servers, Frame Relay, 734
horizontal cabling, 1017
horizontal runs, key telephone systems, 196
hourly distribution, traffic engineering, 160
HSCSD (High-Speed Circuit-Switched Data), 940
HTML (HyperText Markup Language), 413
HTTP (HyperText Transfer Protocol), 419
hub-and-spoke connections, SONET, 984
hubs, 10Base-T Ethernet, 588
Hush-a-Phone, 7
hybrid telephone networks, 45
Hz, 22

I

I/O request signals, analog PBXs, 181
IBM
  SNA, 382
  Token Ring LANs, 616
IDDD (International DDD), IECs, 125

IDSL (ISDN DSL), 802
IECs (InterExchange Carriers), 10, 118
    800 services, 124
    900 services, 125
    calling card services, 119–121
    data-centric applications, 12
    DDD, 118
    directory assistance, 128
    Equal Access, 115
    FX service, 106, 127
    IDDD, 125
    operator assistance, 128
    OPXs, 127
    RCF, 129
    WATS, 121–122
IEEE 802.11 standard
    BSSs, 603
    client/server networks, 604
    wireless LANs, 603
IEEE 802.6 standard, SMDS, 703
ILECs, 93–94
    800 services, 111–112
    business services, 99
    Centrex, 98
    direct inward dial, 99
    direct outward dial, 99
    directory services, 112
    DSL, 800
    Equal Access, 115
    FX service, 105–106
    intrastate WATS, 110
    local calling services, 101
    local dial tone, 96
    OPXs, 113–114
    party lines, 97
    pay phones, 101–102
    private lines, 103–105
    residential services, 99
    return on LNP investment, 865
    telephone networks, 39
    WATS, 107
implementing
    communications application planning, 1048
    Intranets, 479–480
IMTS (Improved Mobile Telephone Services), 884
in-band signaling, T1, 338

incoming calls
    LNP, 877–878
    VLR, 878
indexes of refraction, fiber optic, 1032
information superhighway, 12
informational signaling, 148
infrared light systems, 965–967
    absorption, 958
    advantages, 970
    adverse unit mounting conditions, 961–962
    atmospheric conditions, 957
    bandwidth, 963
    clear line of sight, 960
    connections, 964–967
    disadvantages, 971
    LAN traffic, 969
    licensing, 963
    limitations, 954
    microwave connections, 965
    scattering, 958
    shimmer, 959
    site selection, 960
    system geometry, 955–956
initial costs, telecommunications system
        financing, 1008
integrated PBXs, 247
    automated attendants, 250
    LANs, 653
    multimedia applications, 249
    voice messaging, 250
    voice servers, 247–249
integrated resources, LANs, 649
integrated services, 755
interbuilding cabling, 1017
intercom cards, key telephone systems, 195
intercoms, key telephone systems, 201
interconnections
    LANs, 648
    SS7, 844
interexchange carrier networks, ISDN, 765
interfaces
    Frame Relay, 734–735
    key telephone systems, 203–204
    mobile
internal networking, Frame Relay, 740
internal Web sites, 465

Internet, 462
  access fees, 405
  access options, 422–423
  backbone, 404
  banner ads, 411
  CATV access, 826
  connections, 405, 423
  DHCP, 422
  diverse routing, 424
  DNS, 421
  e-mail, 402
  Extended ASCII, 403
  external connections, 464
  focused advertising, 411
  FTP, 403
  growth, 425–426
  IP address translation, 469–470
  ISPs, 404
  origins, 400
  protocols, 390
  publishing services, 408
  SMTP, 463
  spam, 410
  TCP/IP, 462
  Telnet access, 418
  URLs, 420
  voice transmission, 426–428
  VoIP, 428–430
  Web sites, 412–415
internetworking LANs, 551
interoffice trunks, telephone networks, 34
interoperability, WAP, 931
interrupts, mainframe systems, 529
interstate calling, 108
Intranets, 462
  access, 469
  bandwidth, 481
  corporate data access, 471–472
  customer Web servers, 466
  data access, 472
  DHCP, 470
  external routers, 468
  firewalls, 466
  full service, 474–475
  GUIs, 466
  implementing, 479–480
  internal Web sites, 465

IP address translation, 469–470
  mail servers, 466
  marketing servers, 466
  modem servers, 468
  off-site access, 465
  online forms, 477–478
  remote access servers, 468
  servers, 466
  transmitting data to Internet, 464
  user access, 481
  virtual offices, 473–474
  Web browsers, 464
Intraprises, 472
intrastate WATS, 110
invention of telephone, 1–2
IOTs (InterOffice Trunks), 318
IP (Internet Protocol)
  addresses, DNS translation, 421, 469–470
  datagrams, 391
  routing loops, 392
  telephones, 204, 207, 429
IPSec
  AH, 453
  ESP, 453
  VPN encryption, 450
  VPNs, 454–455
IPX/SPX services, Frame Relay, 734
IS-95 air interface, 942–943
ISAKMP (Internet Security Association and Key
      Management), 454
ISDN (Integrated Services Digital Network),
      90, 747, 756
  application services, 763
  BRI, 756–758, 769
  circuit mode services, 760
  clear channel capacity, 752
  digital connections, 753
  exchange carrier networks, 764–765
  interexchange carrier networks, 765
  need for, 751
  nodes, 759
  operations, 769
  packet mode services, 762
  premises networks, 767–768
  PRI, 756, 759, 770
  services, 748–749
  standards, 750

ISO (International Organization for Standards),
    OSI model, 366
ISPs (Internet Service Providers), 404
    DHCP, 422
    Internet access, 422–423
ISUP (ISDN User Part), SS7 call setup, 852–854
iterative teaching, data communications, 271
IVR (Interactive Voice Response), 237–238, 263
IWF (Interworking Function), ATM, 794
IXCs. *See* IECs.

J–K

jacks, cabling, 1014–1015
jitter, 987
justifying costs, telecommunications system
    financing, 1005–1006
key telephone systems
    cabling, 196
    connectors, 196
    cost issues, 199
    features, 202
    horizontal runs, 196
    intercom cards, 195
    intercoms, 201
    interface features, 203–204
    IP telephones, 204, 207
    KSUs, 194
    line cards, 194
    logic cards, 195
    monthly costs, 200
    power supplies, 195
    reasons for use, 197–198
    station cards, 194
    telephone sets, 195
    vendor proposals, 207–208
    wiring infrastructure, 195
KHz (Kilohertz), 22
KSUs (key service units), 194

L

L2TP, VPN security, 451–452
lack of connections, Token Ring LANs, 618

lack of power, Token Ring LANs, 618
LAN-to-LAN communications, Frame Relay, 736
LANs (Local Area Networks)
    100VGAnyLAN, 599–600
    application servers, 535
    ATM LAN connections, 791
    backbones, 555
    backup servers, 535
    baseband, 654–655
    broadband, 658–659, 825
    cabling, 1014
    carrying traffic over light systems, 969
    client/server, 537
    communications servers, 535
    compatibility issues, 651
    cost issues, 651–652
    data rates, 648
    database servers, 535
    distributed processing, 536
    error rates, 526
    Ethernet, 567–568
    Fast Ethernet, 593–599
    FDDI, 670
    geographic boundaries, 527
    Gigabit Ethernet, 600–601
    high communications speeds, 525
    infrared connections, 966
    integrated PBXs, 653
    integrated resources, 649
    interconnections, 648
    internetworking, 551
    Intranets, 466
    issues for selection, 666
    logical topologies, 547–548
    logins, 528
    mixed topologies, 549–550
    nodes, 539
    NOSs, 528
    passwords, 528
    peer to peer, 550
    performance, 529
    physical topologies, 544–545
    resource sharing, 524, 534
    scalability, 537
    servers, 528, 551
    single cable system, 527
    SMDS, 714
    switching, 553–557

Token Ring, 615–619
topologies, 543
twisted-pair cabling, 1023
wiring, 530
LATAs (Local Access and Transport Areas), 10, 46–47
lateral distributions, telephone networks, 35
layers, OSI model, 366–368
leased lines, SMDS MANs, 694
LECs (Local Exchange Carriers), 9
Centrex, 187
SMDS MANs, 697
telephone networks, 39
length of calls, traffic engineering, 159
licensing light systems, 963
life cycles, telecommunications system financing, 1000
light systems, 953
absorption, 958
adverse unit mounting conditions, 961–962
atmospheric conditions, 957
bandwidth, 963
clear line of sight, 960
connections, 964
implementation criteria, 954
infrared connections, 965–967
LAN traffic, 969
licensing, 963
microwave connections, 965
scattering, 958
shimmer, 959
site selection, 960
system geometry, 955–956
limitations
Frame Relay, 743
infrared light systems, 954
WAP devices, 934
line cards, key telephone systems, 194
line layer, SONET, 978
line of sight, light systems, 960
line part, SONET, 978
line rates, SONET, 977
lines, 136–138
links
SS7, 845
Web sites, 411
linksets, SS7, 849

LLC, FDDI LANs, 678
LMI, Frame Relay, 736
LNP (Local Number Portability), 859
911 calls, 875
busy calls, 878
call forwarding, 879
cellular providers, 861
components, 867
demand, 870
differences between wireline and wireless carriers, 863
incoming calls, 877–878
message waiting, 879
operations, 871
over-the-air provisioning, 872
PCS, 862
phases, 860
rate issues, 870
roaming capabilities, 877
routing impact, 870
services administration, 868
SMR, 862
wireless carrier issues, 864
wireless/wireline provisioning examples, 873–874
local calling services, 101
local dial tone, 9, 96
local loop, 32, 90
improving cable infrastructure, 13
telephone networks, 34
local nets, 645–647
local switches, ATM, 790
logic cards, key telephone systems, 195
logical topologies, LANs, 547–548
logins, LANs, 528
loops, routing, 392
loss leaders, 15
lossless compression, 293
lossy compression, 293
loudness, 21
LRC (Longitudinal Redundancy Checking), 282–284
LRN (Location Routing Number), 868–869
LUs (Logical Units), 386

M

M plane, ATM, 786
MAC layer
 FDDI LANs, 679
 LAN switching, 556
 Token Ring LANs, 627
mail servers, Intranets, 466
mainframe systems, 529
maintenance
 T1, 344
 telecommunications system financing,
 1006–1007
male voice characteristics, 27
MAN access units, DQDB, 707–708
manholes, telephone networks, 35
MANs (Metropolitan Area Networks)
 data transfers, 709
 FDDI, 687
 SMDS, 694
market differentiation, WAP, 932–933
marketing servers, 466
MAUs (Multistation Access Units), Token Ring
 LANs, 620–623
MCI, 8
MDF (Main Distribution Frame), 181
measured rate WATS, 109
media filters, Token Ring LANs, 625
media for transmission, 20
messages, SS7
messge waiting, LNP, 879
metadata, error detection, 279
MFJ (Modified Final Judgment), 10, 9
MHz (mega hertz), 26
Microsoft
 MSN (Microsoft Network), 405
 TAPI, 257
microwave connections, light systems, 965
MIME (Multipurpose Internet Mail
 Extensions), 419
mixed topologies, LANs, 549–550
mobile interfaces, WAP, 916
mobile radios, telephone network connections, 8
mobile telephones, 883–885
modem servers, 468

modems
 56 K, 307
 cable, 825
 V.90, 802
modulation, data communications, 303–306
monopolies, Bell System, 7
monthly costs, key telephone systems, 200
MPRs (Multi-Part Repeaters), 10Base 2
 Ethernet, 584
MTSOs (Mobile Telephone Switching Offices), 886
multimedia applications, integrated PBXs, 249
multimode fiber optic cabling, 1029
multiplexing data communications, 293

N

N-carrier system, 313
NAKs, TCP datagrams, 393
naming standards
 Ethernet, 576–592
 Internet, 420
NAPs (national access providers), 405
NAUs (Network Addressable Units), 383
network architectures, 381
 DNA, 389
 SNA, 382–383
network interface drivers, LAN nodes, 540
network layer, OSI model, 367
network-centric environment, full service
 Intranets, 476
networks
 AT&T devel, 6
 hybrid telephone, 45
 private telephone, 44
 telephone, 31
 VLANS, 603
 VPNs, 442
New England Telephone Company, 5
newbies, 410
NICs (Network Interface Cards)
 10Base 2 Ethernet, 583
 LAN nodes, 540–542
NIUs (Network Interface Units), 94

nodes
10Base 2 Ethernet, 586
FDDI LANs, 677
ISDN, 759
LANs, 539
noise, analog communications, 83
non-facilities-based environment, leasing
facilities, 14
nonchannelized service, T1, 327, 334
nonconforming end offices, telephone
networks, 40
NOSs (Network Operating Systems)
LAN nodes, 540–541
peer to peer, 550
Novell TSAPI, 257
NRZI (Nonreturn to Zero Inverted), FDDI
LANs, 679
numbering plan, X.25, 514
Nyquist theorem, 84, 320

O

objectives of new system, telecommunications
system financing, 1007
obtaining data, traffic engineering, 156
OCR (Optical Character Recognition), 265
odd parity checking, 281
off-site access, Intranets, 465
omission errors, T1, 346
One Plus WATS, 110
one way channels, 48
online forms, Intranets, 477–478
operations
ISDN, 769
LNP, 871
SS7, 845
operator assistance, IECs, 128
OPXs (Off Premises Extensions), 113–114,
127, 143
origins of Internet, 400
OSI model (Open Systems Interconnect),
357–360, 366–369
out-of-band signaling, SS7, 841
outlets, 1015
outside dial tones, analog PBXs, 182
outside plants, telephone networks, 35

over-the-air provisioning, LNP, 872
overhead
ATM cells, 780
packetswitching, 496

P

packet filtering, VPNs, 453
packet information, packet switching, 497
packet mode services, ISDN, 762
packet networks
advantages, 509
asynchronous connections, 511
cloud, 499
dedicated links, 507
PSEs, 499
statmux, 509
user connections, 501, 504
packet switching, 487–495, 755
CRC, 498
fast select, 496
overhead, 496
packet data, 497
PADs, 496
PTI, 498
X.25, 496, 720–722
packet types, X.25, 498
PADs (Packet Assembler/Disassemblers), 496
PAP (Password Authentication Protocol), 451
parity checking, 281
part 68 registration, FCC, 8
party lines, telephone networks, 35
passwords, LANs, 528
path layer, SONET, 978
path part, SONET, 978
pay phones, 101–102
payback analysis, telecommunications system
financing, 1001
payload, Ethernet, 575
PBXs (private branch exchanges), 98, 175–176
components, 178
CTI interfaces, 260
digital, 182, 186
digital transmission connections, 967
integrated, 247
integrating into LANs, 653

lines, 136
MDF, 181
peripherals, 190
single line sets, 176–177
stations, 178
TIE lines, 103–105
trunks, 137–138
PCM (Pulse Code Modulation), 322, 326
PCS (Personal Communications Services), 905
CDMA, 907
LNP, 861–862
system setup, 908–909
TDMA, 907
technology deployments, 907
PDAs (Personal Digital Assistants), increasing
Web access speed, 945
PDUs (Protocol Data Units), ATM, 783
peer-to-peer NOSs, 550
peg counts, traffic engineering, 157
performance
100Base-T Ethernet, 598–599
LANs, 529
T1, 342
peripherals
Centrex, 190
communications app planning, 1042
PBXs, 190
phases of LNP, 860
Photonic layer, SONET, 977
physical layer
FDDI LANs, 678
OSI model, 368
physical topologies, LANs, 544–545
physical wiring inspection, communications
application planning, 1041
PICs (Presubscribed Interexchange Carriers), 115
PINs (Personal Identification Numbers), IVR
systems, 238
pitches, 21
PKI (Public Key Infrastructure), VPNs, 454
planning communications applications,
1037, 1047
assessing current system, 1038
contribution effects, 1046
data connections, 1039
department meetings, 1043–1045
implementation, 1048
peripherals, 1042

physical wiring inspection, 1041
talking to users, 1042
planning technology implementations, 252
plesiochronous communications, 987
PLLs (Permanent Logical Links), Frame
Relay, 723
PM (Phase Modulation), 305
PMD (Physical Media Dependent) sublayer,
ATM, 788
point-to-multipoint connections, SONET, 983
point-to-point connections, SONET, 982
POIs (Points of Interface), telephone networks, 41
Poisson distribution, traffic engineering, 163
portable phones, 895
power supplies, key telephone systems, 195
PPP (Point-to-Point Protocol), 463
premises networks, ISDN, 767–768
presentation layer, OSI model, 367
PRI ISDN, 756, 759, 770
primary centers, telephone networks, 38
private lines, 103–105, 149–150
private telephone networks, 44
processing faxes, CTI, 263–264
protocol converters, 363–366
protocol stack
SS7, 851
WAP, 918
protocols. See also specific protocol.
data communications, 274
Internet, 390
security, 451
providers, Centrex service, 188
PSEs (Packet Switching Exchanges), packet
networks, 499
PT (Payload Type), ATM cells, 781
PTI (Packet Type Identifier), packet
switching, 498
PTS (Per-Trunk Signaling), 838
PTTs (Post Telephone and Telegraph
organizations), 11
public switches, ATM, 790
Public Utilities Commission, tariffs, 11
public-switched network, 41
publishing services, Internet, 408
PUs (Physical Units), SCCP, 385
PVCs (Permanent Virtual Circuits), Frame
Relay, 723

Q

QAM (Quadrature Amplitude Modulation), 306
QoS (Quality of Service), IP telephony, 430
Qwest International, high-speed
        communications, 14

R

RADSL (Rate Adaptive DSL), 806
rain, scattering in light systems, 958
random arrival traffic, FDDI LANs, 680
rarefaction, 21, 79
rate issues, LNP, 870
RBHCs (Regional Bell Holding Companies), 39
RBOCs (Regional Bell Operating Companies), 39
RCF (Remote Call Forwarding), IECs, 129
receivers, 62
recovery, FDDI LANs, 688
redialing last number, 74
reduced rate residential service, 100
regulated monopolies, Bell System, 7
remote access, VPNs, 443–447
remote access servers, 468
remote database lookups, SS7, 840
remote office connections, CATV, 831
repeaters, 85–88, 552
residential services, 99
resource sharing, LANs, 524, 534
return path, cable modems, 830
reverse direction, broadband LANs, 662
RFC1597, IPaddress translation, 469
ring architecture, SONET, 984
ring configurations, telephone networks, 33
ring LAN topology, 545
ringer, telephones, 64, 70
roaming, LNP users, 877
robust networks, 576
ROI (Return on Investment), telecommunications
        system financing, 1003
rotary phones, 67
routers, LANs, 553
routes, SS7, 850
routesets, SS7, 850
routing, LNP, 870

routing loops, IP, 392
routing messages, SS7, 850
RTSP (Real Time Streaming Protocol), 432

S

sampling, 84–85
SAP (Session Announcement Protocol), 432
SAR (Segmentation and Reassembly)
    ATM, 783
    SMDS, 709
SASs (Single Attached Stations), FDDI LANs, 675
satellite offices, VPNs, 444
scalability
    baseband LANs, 656
    LANs, 537
scattering, light systems, 958
SCCP (Systems Services Control Part), 384
screen pops, ACDs, 245
scripting ACDs, 227
SDH (synchronous digital hierarchy), 975, 985
    frames, 987–989
    synchronous communications, 986
SDM (Space Division Multiplexing), 294
SDMS, 701–702
SDSL (Symmetric DSL), 806
search engines, 416
section layer, SONET, 977–978
sectional centers, telephone networks, 38
security
    CATV, 832
    protocols, 451
    VPNs, 439, 448
servers
    application, 535
    backup, 535
    communications, 535
    email, 466
    Intranets, 466, 479
    LANs, 528, 551
    marketing, 466
    modem, 468
    remote access, 468
    sdatabases, 535
    VPNs, 441
    WAP, 924
    Web, 463

services
   ISDN, 748–749
   T1, 338
   telephone network, 28
   X.25, 514, 517
session layer, OSI model, 367
SF (Superframe Format), T1, 343
sharing resources, LANs, 534
SHDSL (Single Pair High Speed DSL), 808
shimmer, light systems, 959
shirt pocket phones, 896
side tone, 63
signal loss, analog transmission, 315
signal translation, analog communications, 78
signaling, 148, 338
signaling links, SS7, 842–848
SIM Application Toolkit, 924
simplex channels, 48
simplex data communications, 286
single cable LAN systems, 527
single line services, 96
single line sets, PBXs, 176–177
single mode fiber optic, 1029
sinusoidal waves
   analog communications, 79
   analog transfer, 22
SIR (Sustained Information Rates), 715
site selection, light systems, 960
SKIP (Simple Key management for IP), 454
SMDS (Switched Multimegabit Data
     Services), 693
   access rates, 700
   backhoe fade, 705
   DQDB, 699
   encapsulating data units, 711
   high speed data transfers, 699
   IEEE 802.6 standard, 703
   MANs, 694–697
   LAN environments, 714
smog, scattering in light systems, 958
SMS (Simple Messaging System), 921
SMTP (Simple Mail Transfer Protocol), 402,
     417–418, 463
SNA (Systems Network Architecture), 360,
     382–383
   LUs, 386
   NAUs, 383

SCCP, 384
SNMP (Simple Network Management Protocol),
     417–419
snow, scattering in light systems, 959
soft benefits, telecommunications system
     financing, 997–998
software, LAN nodes, 540
SONET (Synchronous Optical Network), 975
   architecture, 978
   development, 976
   DWDM, 990
   hub-and-spoke connections, 984
   line layer, 978
   line part, 978
   line rates, 977
   path layer, 978
   path part, 978
   photonic layer, 977
   point-to-multipoint connections, 983
   point-to-point connections, 982
   ring architecture, 984
   section layer, 977
   section part, 978
   STS-1, 977
   topologies, 982
   WDM, 990
sound, 20
   amplitude, 22
   analog transfer, 21
   band-limited channels, 23
   bandwidth, 24–25
   channels, 25
   compression, 21
   frequencies, 22
   rarefaction, 21
   sinusoidal waves, 22
   telephone transfer process, 23
spam, 410
speakerphones, 74
spectrum, 3G wireless, 944
speech to text, 264
speed dialing, 72
speeds
   Frame Relay, 728
   LANs, 525
   Token Ring LANs, 626
SS6 (Signaling System 6), 839
SS7 (Signaling System 7), 837

applications, 854–855
architecture, 843
cellular systems, 889
combined linksets, 849
interconnections, 844
links, 845
linksets, 849
operations, 845
out-of-band signaling, 841
protocol stack, 851
remote database lookups, 840
routes, 850
routesets, 850
routing messages, 850
signaling links, 842, 845
standards
  cable modems, 829
  data communications, 271–272
  Ethernet, 568
  Frame Relay, 737
  ISDN, 750
  WAP, 926–929
  X.25, 511
star configurations, telephone networks, 33
star LAN topology, 546
station cards, key telephone systems, 194
station drops, telephone networks, 35
stations
  FDDI LANs, 676
  PBXs, 178
statmux, packet networks, 509
STDM (Statistical Time Division Multiplexing)
  data communications, 298
  X.25, 725
structured cabling systems
  horizontal wiring, 1017
  vertical wiring, 1016
STS-1, SONET, 977
subcompact phones, 896
subscriber extensions, telephone networks, 43–44
superframes, D4, 329
supervisory signaling, 148
switch hooks, 56
switched Ethernet, 594
switches
  ATM, 789
  telephone networks, 33
switchhooks, telephones, 65–66

switching LANs, 553–557
synchronization
  FDDI LANs, 683
  T1, 340–341, 350
synchronous communications, 274–275, 986
system geometry, light systems, 955–956
system setup, PCS, 908–909

T

T connectors, 10Base 2 Ethernet, 583
T-Carrier system, 313, 317–319
T1 lines
  1's density rule, 332
  AMI, 326
  bipolar format, 326, 331
  bit robbing, 338
  bit synchronization, 340
  byte synchronous transmissions, 326, 332
  CCS, 339
  channelized service, 326, 334
  clocking, 339
  communicationsission errors, 346
  CRC-6, 350
  D4 superframes, 329
  DS channels, 335–336
  E&M signaling, 338
  error detection, 345
  ESF, 343, 347, 351
  facility data links, 351
  four-wire circuits, 325
  frame synchronization, 341
  frames, 326, 329
  full duplex, 325
  in-band signaling, 338
  infrared connections, 968
  local-loop failures, 342
  maintenance, 344
  nonchannelized service, 327, 334
  omission errors, 346
  PCM, 326
  performance characteristics, 342
  services, 338
  SF, 343
  synchronization problems, 341
  TDM, 325–327

termination, 327
time slot synchronization, 340
transparent signaling mode, 339
troubleshooting, 344
tags, HTML, 413
talk off, 69
talking to users, communications application
planning, 1042
tandem offices, telephone networks, 38
TAPI (Telephony Application Program
Interface), 257
tariffs, 11, 100
TC (Transmission Convergence) sublayer,
ATM, 788
TCP/IP, 390, 417, 462, 734
TDM (Time Division Multiplexing)
CATV, 661
circuit switching, 724
data communications, 295–296
T1, 325–327
TDMA
broadband LANs, 661
digital cellular, 904
PCS, 907
telcos, 13–14
Telecommunications Act of 1996, information
superhighway, 12
telecommunications system financing, 993–995
add-on costs, 1010
calculating savings, 998
cost-and-benefit analysis, 1000
costs, 1000
decision-making process, 1005
financial life cycles, 1001
hard benefits, 996
initial costs, 1008
justifying costs, 1005–1006
life cycles, 1000
maintenance issues, 1006–1007
objectives of new system, 1007
payback analysis, 1001
pricing issues, 1004
ROI, 1003
soft benefits, 997–998
telegraph, digital coding, 754
telephone, 53

amplitude, 22
analog transfer, 21
band-limited channels, 23
bandwidth, 24–25
channels, 25
components, 54
digital, 72
frequencies, 22
functions, 55–56
invention of, 1–2
side tone, 63
sinusoidal waves, 22
sound transfer process, 23
transmission media, 20
transmitter development, 5
voice characteristics, 19
telephone companies, initial development, 5–6
telephone network, 31
area codes, 42
BOCs, 36
branch exchanges, 37
circuits, 135
connections, 32, 48
COs, 33
customer pairs, 35
demarc, 32, 48
DID, 140
DOD, 141
E&M TIE lines, 146–147
end offices, 37
exchange codes, 43
frames, 33
full duplex channels, 49
FX, 142
handholes, 35
ILECs, 39
interconnect business, 8
interoffice trunks, 34
key telephone systems
LATAs, 46–47
lateral distributions, 35
LECs, 39
lines, 136–138
local loop, 32–34
manholes, 35
mobile phone connections, 8

nonconforming end offices, 40
North American numbering plans, 41
one way channels, 48
OPX, 143
outside plants, 35
party lines, 35
PBXs, 175–176
POIs, 41
primary centers, 38
ring configurations, 33
sectional centers, 38
services, 28
signaling, 148
star configurations, 33
station drops, 35
subscriber extensions, 43–44
switches, 33
tandem offices, 38
TIE lines, 144
toll centers, 37
trunks, 36, 137–139
two way channels, 48
wire centers, 33
telephone sets, key telephone systems, 195
Telex, 754
Telnet, 417–418
terminators
   10Base5 Ethernet, 578
   T1, 327
text to speech, 264
Thick wire Ethernet, 577
third-party call control, 257
throughput
   FDDI LANs, 673
   SMDS, 715
TIE (terminal interface equipment), 103–105, 144
time slot synchronization, T1, 340
tip and ring, telephones, 71
token passing, FDDI LANs, 680
Token Ring LANs, 615–619
   abort sequence, 632
   cabling, 624
   data frames, 632–635
   example configuration, 636–640
   frames, 628–629
   lack of connections, 618
   lack of power, 618
   MAC layer, 627

MAUs, 620–623
   media filters, 625
   speeds, 626
   tokens, 629–632
toll centers, telephone networks, 37
topologies
   LANs, 543
   SONET, 982
   telephone connections, 32
   Token Ring LANs, 615–617
touch tone
   phones, 57, 68
   voice processing, 214–215
traffic engineering, 153
   busy hour, 155
   busy studies, 157
   call processing times, 157, 160
   CATV, 827
   data modeling tools, 163
   distribution patterns, 161
   functional steps, 157
   gathering data, 159
   grade of service, 164–166
   hourly distribution, 160
   length of calls, 159
   line and trunk installs, 154
   obtaining data, 156
   obtaining open lines, 154
   peg counts, 157
transceivers, 10Base5 Ethernet, 577
translating bridges, FDDILANs, 686
translating IP addresses, 421, 469–470
translating signals, analog communications, 78
transmission media, 20
transmission modes, VPNs, 456
transmission protocols, 274
transmitter placement, cellular systems, 888
transmitters, 61
transparent signaling mode, T1, 339
transport layer, OSI model, 367
transportable phones, 895
troubleshooting T1, 341–344
trunks, 36, 137–139
TSAPI (Telephony Services Application
      Programmers Interface), 257
TTLs (Time to Live), IPdatagrams, 393
tunnels, VPNs, 442
twisted-pair cabling, 1018–1022

two repeater rule, 580
two way channels, 48
two way simultaneous channels, 49
two-factor authentication, VPNs, 456

U

U plane, ATM, 786
UCDs (Uniform Call Distributors), 223
UMTS, 941–942
unanswered calls, LNP, 878
Unicode code sets, 303
unified messaging, 255
unipolar signals, 86
UNIs (User to Network Interfaces)
    ATM, 776
    Frame Relay, 740
updating Web sites, 415
upgrades, fiber optic
URLs (Uniform Resource Locators), 420
usage sensitive rates, Frame Relay, 742
user IDs, LANs, 528
users
    authentication, VPNs, 456
    connections, packet networks, 501, 504
    FDDI LANs, 676
    Intranet access, 481
USSD (Unstructured Supplementary Services
        Data), 921
UTP (Unshielded Twisted Pair), 1023
UTRA, 3G wireless, 946

V

V.90 modems, 307, 802
vampire taps, 10Base5 Ethernet, 577
VCI (Virtual Channel Identifier), ATM cells, 781
VDSL (Very High Speed DSL), 13, 807
vertical cabling, 1016
virtual offices, 443, 473–474
VLANs (Virtual LANs), 603
VLR (Visitor Location Register), incoming
        calls, 878
VoATM, 815–817

VoDSL, 813–814
voice applications, cellular phones, 898–899
voice characteristics, 19
    amplitude, 22, 27
    analog transfer, 21
    band-limited channels, 23
    bandwidth, 24–25
    channels, 25
    frequencies, 22, 27
    telephone transfer process, 23
voice dialing, 216
voice mail, 231–236
voice messaging, 213, 261–262
    integrated PBXs, 250
Voice over Frame Relay, 740–741
Voice over the Internet, 426–428
voice processing, 214
    automated attendants, 216–220
    automatic call distributors, 222–225
    IVR, 237–238
    Touch-Tone™, 214–215
    voice dialing, 216
    voice mail, 231–236
voice recognition, 215
voice servers, integrated PBXs, 247–249
voice transcription systems, 215
VoIP, 428–430
VPI (Virtual Path Identifier), ATM cells, 781
VPNs (Virtual Private Networks), 437–439
    authentication, 454
    clients, 442
    connections, 442
    encapsulation, 440
    encryption, 450
    enterprise management, 455
    extended offices, 443
    firewalls, 450
    home offices, 444
    Internet security, 439
    IPSec, 450, 454–455
    networks, 442
    packet filtering, 453
    PKI, 454
    protocols, 442
    remote access, 443–447
    satellite offices, 444

security, 448
servers, 441
transmission modes, 456
tunnels, 442
two-factor authentication, 456
user authentication, 456
virtual offices, 443
VRC (Vertical Redundancy Checking), 280–281

W

WAE (Wireless Application Environment), 918
WANs (Wide Area Networks)
facilities-based environment, 14
fiber optic cabling, 1027
WAP (Wireless Access Protocol), 915
applications, 925
bearer independence, 930
clients, 923
configuration difficulty, 917
device independence, 930
gateways, 923–924
interoperability, 931
limitations of devices, 934
market differentiation, 932–933
mobile interface, 916
network differences from wired networks, 933
protocol stack, 918
servers, 924
WDP, 920
WTLS, 920
WAP Forum, 927–929
WATS (Wide Area Telecommunications Services),
107, 149
bands, 107
full-time, 109
IECs, 121–122
intrastate, 110
measured rate, 109
One Plus, 110
waveform degradation, baseband LANs, 654
WDM, SONET, 990
WDP (Wireless Datagram Protocol), 920
Web browsers, 464
Web servers, 463
Web sites, 412–414

cookies, 420
diverse routing, 424
hits, 415
links, 411
searchers, 416
updating, 415
Western Electric, AT&T divestiture, 7
wire centers, telephone networks, 33
wireless LANs, IEEE 802.11 standard, 603
wireless systems
911 calls, 875
LNP issues, 863–864, 873–874
wireline systems
911 calls, 875
LNP issues, 863, 873–874
wiring
key telephone systems, 195
LANs, 530
WML (Wireless Markup Language), 918
WMLScript, 918–919
workgroups, LANs, 559
WSP (Wireless Session Protocol), 919
WTA (Wireless Telephony Application), 918
WTLS (Wireless Transport Layer Security), 920
WTP (Wireless Transaction Protocol), 919
WWW (World Wide Web), 461
WYSIWYG (what-you-see-is-what-you-get), 413

X

X.121 worldwide network numbering plan, 514
X.25
changing standards, 511
circuit switching, 725–727
fast select, 517
Frame Relay interfaces, 734
numbering plan, 514
packet switching, 496, 720–722
packet types, 498
services, 514, 517
STDM, 725
X.29, 511
X.400 fax, Frame Relay, 734
X.75, 514

INTERNATIONAL CONTACT INFORMATION

AUSTRALIA
McGraw-Hill Book Company Australia Pty. Ltd.
TEL +61-2-9417-9899
FAX +61-2-9417-5687
http://www.mcgraw-hill.com.au
books-it_sydney@mcgraw-hill.com

CANADA
McGraw-Hill Ryerson Ltd.
TEL +905-430-5000
FAX +905-430-5020
http://www.mcgrawhill.ca

**GREECE, MIDDLE EAST,
NORTHERN AFRICA**
McGraw-Hill Hellas
TEL +30-1-656-0990-3-4
FAX +30-1-654-5525

MEXICO (Also serving Latin America)
McGraw-Hill Interamericana Editores S.A. de C.V.
TEL +525-117-1583
FAX +525-117-1589
http://www.mcgraw-hill.com.mx
fernando_castellanos@mcgraw-hill.com

SINGAPORE (Serving Asia)
McGraw-Hill Book Company
TEL +65-863-1580
FAX +65-862-3354
http://www.mcgraw-hill.com.sg
mghasia@mcgraw-hill.com

SOUTH AFRICA
McGraw-Hill South Africa
TEL +27-11-622-7512
FAX +27-11-622-9045
robyn_swanepoel@mcgraw-hill.com

**UNITED KINGDOM & EUROPE
(Excluding Southern Europe)**
McGraw-Hill Publishing Company
TEL +44-1-628-502500
FAX +44-1-628-770224
http://www.mcgraw-hill.co.uk
computing_neurope@mcgraw-hill.com

ALL OTHER INQUIRIES Contact:
Osborne/McGraw-Hill
TEL +1-510-549-6600
FAX +1-510-883-7600
http://www.osborne.com
omg_international@mcgraw-hill.com

ABOUT THE AUTHOR

Regis J. (Bud) Bates Jr., President
TC International Consulting, Inc.
PO Box 51108
Phoenix, AZ 85076-1108
Tel. (800) 322-2202, Fax (800) 260-6440
http://www.tcic.com

Mr. Bates has more than 35 years of experience in telecommunications and information systems. He oversees the overall operation of TCIC, a full-service management consulting organization that specializes in designing and integrating information technologies. Bud's experience has served in major network designs from *local area networks* (LANs) to *wide area networks* (WANs) using high-quality, all-digital transmission services. His studies and recommendations have resulted in significant financial savings. One project included the design and implementation of a Frame Relay network that spanned over 14 countries and 80 locations.

He has authored numerous books published by McGraw-Hill and Artech House. His recent published books Voice and Data Communications, Third Edition and the Broadband Telecommunications Handbook are on McGraw-Hill's 2000 bestseller list. Bud also develops and conducts various public seminars throughout the world, ranging from managerial overviews to very technical instructions on voice, data, and LAN communications. He spends much of his time working with the major telecommunications manufacturers in training their staff members on the innovations of technology and the convergence of voice and data networks for the future. Many of his materials are used throughout the higher education institutions in certification and graduate-level classes in telecommunications management.

WWW.TCIC.COM

1-800-322-2202
info@tcic.com